AIA

Professional 2 Level

DEVELOPMENTS IN ASSURANCE AND ACCOUNTABILITY

LEARNING & PRACTICE WORKBOOK

In this 2025 edition

- A **user-friendly format** for easy navigation
- **Exam-centred topic coverage**, directly linked to AIA's syllabus
- **Exam focus points** showing you what the examiner will want you to do
- Regular **fast forward** summaries emphasising the key points in each chapter
- **Questions** and **quick quizzes** to test your understanding
- **Practice question bank** containing exam-standard questions with answers
- **Exam question bank** containing recent questions with answers
- **Mock exam** for real exam practice
- A full index

FOR EXAMS FROM MAY 2025

Second edition 2024
ISBN 9781 0355 2581 2
eISBN 9781 0355 2609 3

British Library Cataloguing-in-Publication Data
A catalogue record for this book
is available from the British Library

Published by
BPP Learning Media Ltd
BPP House, Aldine Place
142-144 Uxbridge Road
London W12 8AA

learningmedia.bpp.com

Printed in the United Kingdom

> Your learning materials, published by BPP Learning Media Ltd, are printed on paper obtained from traceable sustainable sources.

All rights reserved. No part of this publication may be reproduced, stored in a retrieval system or transmitted in any form or by any means, electronic, mechanical, photocopying, recording or otherwise, without the prior written permission of BPP Learning Media.

Contains public sector information licensed under the Open Government Licence v3.0.

The contents of this book are intended as a guide and not professional advice. Although every effort has been made to ensure that the contents of this book are correct at the time of going to press, BPP Learning Media makes no warranty that the information in this book is accurate or complete and accept no liability for any loss or damage suffered by any person acting or refraining from acting as a result of the material in this book.

We are grateful to the Association of International Accountants for permission to reproduce past examination questions. The suggested solutions in the exam answer bank have been prepared by BPP Learning Media Ltd.

BPP Learning Media is grateful to the IASB for permission to reproduce extracts from IFRS® Accounting Standards, IAS® Standards, SIC and IFRIC. This publication contains copyright © material and trademarks of the IFRS Foundation®. All rights reserved. Used under license from the IFRS Foundation®. Reproduction and use rights are strictly limited. For more information about the IFRS Foundation and rights to use its material please visit www.IFRS.org.

Disclaimer: To the extent permitted by applicable law the Board and the IFRS Foundation expressly disclaims all liability howsoever arising from this publication or any translation thereof whether in contract, tort or otherwise (including, but not limited to, liability for any negligent act or omission) to any person in respect of any claims or losses of any nature including direct, indirect, incidental or consequential loss, punitive damages, penalties or costs. Information contained in this publication does not constitute advice and should not be substituted for the services of an appropriately qualified professional.

©
BPP Learning Media Ltd
2024

A note about copyright

Dear Customer

What does the little © mean and why does it matter?

Your market-leading BPP books, course materials and e-learning materials do not write and update themselves. People write them on their own behalf or as employees of an organisation that invests in this activity. Copyright law protects their livelihoods. It does so by creating rights over the use of the content.

Breach of copyright is a form of theft – as well as being a criminal offence in some jurisdictions, it is potentially a serious breach of professional ethics.

With current technology, things might seem a bit hazy but, basically, without the express permission of BPP Learning Media:

- Photocopying our materials is a breach of copyright
- Scanning, ripcasting or conversion of our digital materials into different file formats, uploading them to Facebook or e-mailing them to your friends is a breach of copyright

You can, of course, sell your books, in the form in which you have bought them – once you have finished with them. (Is this fair to your fellow students? We update for a reason.) Please note the e-products are sold on a single user licence basis: we do not supply 'unlock' codes to people who have bought them secondhand.

And what about outside the UK? BPP Learning Media strives to make our materials available at prices students can afford by local printing arrangements, pricing policies and partnerships which are clearly listed on our website. A tiny minority ignore this and indulge in criminal activity by illegally photocopying our material or supporting organisations that do. If they act illegally and unethically in one area, can you really trust them?

NO AI TRAINING. Unless otherwise agreed in writing, the use of BPP material for the purpose of AI training is not permitted. Any use of this material to "train" generative artificial intelligence (AI) technologies is prohibited, as is providing archived or cached data sets containing such material to another person or entity.

Copyright © IFRS Foundation

All rights reserved. Reproduction and use rights are strictly limited. No part of this publication may be translated, reprinted or reproduced or utilised in any form either in whole or in part or by any electronic, mechanical or other means, now known or hereafter invented, including photocopying and recording, or in any information storage and retrieval system, without prior permission in writing from the IFRS Foundation. Contact the IFRS Foundation for further details.

The Foundation has trade marks registered around the world (Trade Marks) including 'IAS®', 'IASB®', 'IFRIC®', 'IFRS®', the IFRS® logo, 'IFRS for SMEs®', IFRS for SMEs® logo, the 'Hexagon Device', 'International Financial Reporting Standards®', NIIF® and 'SIC®'.

Further details of the Foundation's Trade Marks are available from the Licensor on request.

Contents

Page

Introduction

The introduction pages contain lots of valuable advice and information. They include tips on studying for and passing the exam, also the content of the syllabus and what has been examined.

How the BPP Learning Media Learning & Practice Workbook can help you pass – Help yourself study for your AIA exams – Syllabus – Command words and learning outcomes – The exam paper

Part A Regulatory issues and professional practices

1	Introduction to assurance	3
2	Corporate governance	13
3	Other reporting requirements	33
4	Rules of professional conduct	61
5	The public interest	93
6	Professional responsibility and liability	107
7	Changes in professional appointment	135

Part B Statutory audit and other evaluation

8	Practice management	153
9	Company audits – special considerations	169
10	Not-for-profit organisations	191
11	Management responsibilities including internal audit	209

Part C Audit strategy, process and reporting

12	Audit planning	233
13	Risk	255
14	Quality management	279
15	Fraud and non compliance with regulations	305
16	Using the work of others	327
17	Audit evidence I	339
18	Audit evidence II	373
19	Information technology	425
20	Reporting	451

Appendix	493
Answers to end of chapter questions	511
Practice question bank	539
Practice answer bank	579
Exam Question Bank	625
Exam Answer Bank	667
Mock exam	711
Index	729

How the BPP Learning Media Learning & Practice Workbook can help you pass

> It provides you with the knowledge and understanding, skills and application techniques that you need to be successful in your exams

This Learning & Practice Workbook has been targeted at the **Developments in Assurance and Accountability** syllabus.

- It is **comprehensive**. It covers the syllabus content. No more, no less.
- It is written at the **right level**. Each Chapter is written with AIA's syllabus in mind.
- It is aimed at the **exam**. We have taken account of recent exams, guidance the examiner has given and the assessment methodology.

> It allows you to study in the way that best suits your learning style and the time you have available, by following your personal Study Plan (see page vii)

You may be studying at home on your own or you may be attending a course. You may like to read every word, or you may prefer to do a fast read through and learn through doing practice questions the rest of the time. However you study, you will find the BPP Learning Media Learning & Practice Workbook meets your needs in designing and following your personal Study Plan.

Help yourself study for your AIA exams

Exams for professional bodies such as AIA are very different from those you have taken at college or university. You will be under **greater time pressure before** the exam – as you may be combining your study with work. Here are some hints and tips.

The right approach

1 **Develop the right attitude**

Believe in yourself	Yes, there is a lot to learn. But thousands have succeeded before and you can too.
Remember why you're doing it	You are studying for a good reason: to advance your career.

2 **Focus on the exam**

Read through the Syllabus	This tells you what you are expected to know and is supplemented by **Exam focus points** in the text.
Study the Exam paper section	Past modules are likely to be good guides to what you should expect in the exam.

3 **The right method**

See the whole picture	Keeping in mind how all the detail you need to know fits into the whole picture will help you understand it better. • The **introduction** of each chapter puts the material in context. • The **Syllabus content** and **Exam focus points** show you what you need to **grasp**.
Use your own words	To absorb the information (and to practise your written communication skills), you need to **put it into your own words**. • Take **notes**. • Answer the **questions** in each chapter. • Draw **mind maps**. • Try **'teaching' a subject** to a colleague or friend.
Give yourself cues to jog your memory	The Learning & Practice Workbook uses **bold** to **highlight key points**. • Try **colour coding** with a highlighter pen. • Write **key points** on cards.

4 **The right recap**

Review, review, review	Regularly reviewing a topic in summary form can **fix it in your memory**. The Learning & Practice Workbook helps you review in many ways. • **Chapter roundups** summarise the 'Fast forward' key points in each chapter. Use them to recap each study session. • The **quick quiz** actively tests your grasp of the essentials. • Go through the **examples** in each chapter a second or third time.

Developing your personal Study Plan

BPP recommends that you follow a study plan. Planning and sticking to the plan are key elements of learning successfully.

Step 1   **How do you learn?**

What types of intelligence do you display when learning? You might be advised to brush up on certain study skills before launching into this Learning & Practice Workbook but refer to the 'tackling your studies' section below which will help.

Step 2   **What do you prefer to do first?**

If you prefer to get to grips with a theory before seeing how it is applied, we suggest you concentrate first on the explanations we give in each chapter before looking at the examples and case studies. If you prefer to see first how things work in practice, read through the detail in each chapter, and concentrate on the examples and case studies, before supplementing your understanding by reading the detail.

Step 3   **How much time do you have?**

Work out the time you have available per week, given the following:

- The standard you have set yourself
- The other exam(s) you are sitting
- Practical matters such as work, travel, exercise, sleep and social life

		Hours
Note your time available in box A.	A	

Step 4   **Allocate your time**

- Take the time you have available per week for this Learning & Practice Workbook shown in box A, multiply it by the number of weeks available and insert the result in box B.   B ☐
- Divide the figure in box B by the number of chapters in this text and insert the result in box C.   C ☐

Remember that this is only a rough guide. Some of the chapters in this book are longer and more complicated than others, and you will find some subjects easier to understand than others.

Step 5   **Implement**

Set about studying each chapter in the time shown in box C, following the key study steps in the order suggested by your particular learning style.

This is your personal **Study Plan**. You should try to combine it with the study sequence outlined below. You may want to modify the sequence to adapt it to your **personal style**.

Tackling your studies

The best way to approach this Learning & Practice Workbook is to tackle the chapters in order. Taking into account your individual learning style, you could follow this sequence for each chapter.

Key study steps	Activity
Step 1 **Topic list**	This topic list helps you navigate each chapter; each numbered topic is a numbered section in the chapter.
Step 2 **Introduction**	This sets your objectives for study by giving you the big picture in terms of the context of the chapter. The content is referenced to the syllabus, and exam guidance shows how the topic is likely to be examined. The introduction tells you **why** the topics covered in the chapter need to be studied.
Step 3 **Fast forward**	Fast forward boxes give you a quick summary of the content of each of the main chapter sections. They are listed together in the roundup at the end of each chapter to help you review each chapter quickly.
Step 4 **Explanations**	Proceed methodically through each chapter, particularly focusing on areas highlighted as significant in the chapter introduction, or areas that are frequently examined.
Step 5 **Key terms and exam focus points**	• Key terms are definitions of important concepts that you really need to know and understand before the exam. • Exam focus points highlight areas or topics that may be examined.
Step 6 **Note taking**	Take brief notes, if you wish. Don't copy out too much. Remember that being able to record something yourself is a sign of being able to understand it. Your notes can be in whatever format you find most helpful; lists, diagrams, mind maps.
Step 7 **Examples**	Work through the examples very carefully as they illustrate key knowledge and techniques.
Step 8 **Case studies**	Study each one and try to add flesh to them from your own experience. They are designed to show how the topics you are studying come alive in the real world.
Step 9 **Questions**	Attempt each one, as they will illustrate how well you've understood what you've read.
Step 10 **Answers**	Check yours against ours, and make sure you understand any discrepancies.
Step 11 **Chapter roundup**	Review it carefully, to make sure you have grasped the significance of all the important points in the chapter.
Step 12 **Quick quiz**	Use the quick quiz to check how much you have remembered of the topics covered and to practise questions in a variety of formats.
Step 13 **Question practice**	Attempt the quick quiz suggested at the very end of each chapter. These are designed for you to confirm some of the key concepts set out in each chapter. Some of these questions are designed to cover more than one topic area to develop your ability to apply syllabus learning. You are then ready to attempt the questions related to this chapter which are contained in the question bank at the end of this Learning & Practice Workbook.

INTRODUCTION

AIA Achieve Academy

AIA provides an interactive course of study, AIA Achieve Academy, which offers students the tools, resources and learning environment to study for the exams. The study tools include a course of study e-book, marked practice questions, marked mock exam paper and feedback and technical advice via an e-Tutor. Contact the Study Support team at: Achieve@aiaworldwide.com

Moving on...

When you are ready to start revising, you should still refer back to this Learning & Practice Workbook.

- As a source of **reference** (you should find the index particularly helpful for this)
- As a way to review (the Fast forwards, Exam focus points, Chapter roundups and Quick quizzes help you here)

PQ Qualification Syllabus

The assessment requirements in the AIA exams at the Foundation, Professional 1 and 2 stages reflect a progression of cognitive levels which successful students are expected to demonstrate in satisfying each stage of the qualification. The levels progress from an emphasis on 'knowledge and comprehension' at the Foundation stage, to a predominance of 'application and analysis' at the subsequent Professional 1 and 2 stages and incorporate 'synthesis and evaluation' at the Professional 2 stage.

Indicative weightings for the cognitive levels at each stage of the qualification are defined in the following table.

Stage of qualification	Cognitive levels of learning*			Associated learning outcomes
	Knowledge and comprehension	Application and analysis	Synthesis and evaluation	
Foundation Level	90%	10%	0%	Outcomes consistent with the International Education Standards Board (IAESB) standards
Professional 1 Level	50%	50%	0%	
Professional 2 Level	10%	70%	20%	

*The cognitive levels of learning are associated with the following:

'Knowledge and comprehension' refer to

The acquisition of concepts, ideas, terms, facts, practices and techniques in accounting and related disciplines and understanding of how they relate to the conduct, management, reporting and assessment of the activities of business and other organisations.

'Application and analysis' refer to

The ability to apply knowledge and comprehension to actual circumstances and situations and to identify constituent components involved (concepts, ideas, terms, facts, practices, and techniques) and the relationship between these elements.

'Synthesis and evaluation' refer to

The ability to bring together a variety of components in order to form a coherent whole, and to form judgements about the application of and value of those components in a particular context or for a particular purpose.

Professional 2 Level Syllabus

Developments in Assurance and Accountability

In designing the syllabus and the related examination papers AIA has employed 'intended learning outcomes' as the means to communicate expectations to potential students and stakeholders and to inform the specification requirements to be tested in the assessment of students.

The use of learning outcomes:

- Is consistent with what is commonly acknowledged as good practice in the higher education sector; and
- Is consistent with the approach embodied in International Accounting Education Standards

At the Professional 2 Levels students are expected to demonstrate that they are able to achieve the following:

Intended Learning Outcomes[1] – Description of expectations	
Professional 2 level	At the Professional 2 level students are expected to demonstrate that they: • Can critically evaluate current issues and developments relevant to accounting and related practices. • Are able to integrate knowledge, understanding and technical ability from different areas of accounting and related practices to analyse situations, make judgements and recommend actions. • Understand fundamental principles and concepts underpinning accounting and related practices in organisations and can discuss the conceptual rationale that provides the basis for those practices. • Understand the role of accounting and related practices within the financial and governance context of organisations. • Are able to apply relevant regulations and standards in accounting, auditing, law and taxation. • Know and can execute basic recording and measurement techniques relevant to accounting, management and assurance. • Are able to analyse financial information and interpret it for the purpose of supporting decision making.

---

[1] The description of the levels of proficiency supports the IAESBs use of learning outcomes in its International Education Standards (IESs) 2, 3, and 4.

Relationship to Qualification Structure

Aims

The aim of this paper is to develop and examine the candidate's ability to:

- Present, discuss and critique advanced auditing approaches and techniques;
- Demonstrate how these can be applied in different situations mainly (but not only) in relation to financial statement audits; and
- Discuss and critique developments in auditing and accountability.

Wider aspects of accountability are also covered within this paper.

Developments in Assurance and Accountability Learning Outcomes

In order to successfully complete this paper, candidates will demonstrate (in addition to the learning outcomes in Principles of Governance and Audit) they are able to:

1. Appraise and critique the implications of current professional issues and developments involving the modern-day audit, the accounting profession and corporate governance;
2. Develop and justify appropriate audit and assurance responses to complex or technical corporate and other reporting needs;
3. Critically appraise the importance of appropriate practice management in maintaining professional standards; and
4. Evaluate issues involving a wider degree of accountability reporting to a more extended stakeholder group (eg provide assurance for CSR, sustainability, or environmental reports).

Structure of the Paper

Assessment is by a three-hour 15-minute examination (including 15 minutes reading time) consisting of three compulsory questions.

Question 1 is a compulsory case study question worth 50 marks. Questions 2 and 3, which are also compulsory, will be discussion questions involving shorter case scenarios and will count for 25 marks each.

All of these questions could assess any of the learning outcomes but the requirements in Question 1 will be more integrative and may draw from any aspect of the syllabus.

Relationship to Qualification Structure

This paper is supported by the Foundation Unit component 'Corporate Governance & Audit' and the Professional 1 'Principles of Governance and Audit' paper which provide the technical underpinning for much of the paper and the Financial Accounting and Reporting papers (Professional 1 and 2) which provide the technical accounting know how in relation to this paper.

Ethics

Ethical issues are covered in this and the previous paper and it is anticipated that each paper will have at least a part of a question which raises some ethical issue and the coverage of the paper is consistent with the relevant learning outcomes in IES 4 Professional Values, Ethics and Attitudes. Ethical issues will also appear in other papers and the 'Ethics and Professional Practice' paper.

Recommended reading

This reading list is recommended and not essential for your studies.

You can purchase any of the books listed quickly and easily on the AIA website www.aiaworldwide.com/books

AIA International Accountant Magazine

ISSN: 1465-5144

AIA Learning and Practice Workbooks

Developments in Assurance and Accountability

Publisher: BPP Learning Media
ISBN: 9781035525812

FRC publications and transcripts/online coverage of meetings such as:

- Developments in Corporate Governance and Stewardship and developments in audit
- Current research and professional body reports relating to auditing skills
- Corporate Governance Review

Principles of External Auditing (4th Edition) (e-book)

Author: Porter, B, Simon, J, Hatherly, D
Publisher: John Wiley & Sons Ltd
ISBN: 9780470974452

Auditing: Assurance and Risk (4th Edition)

Authors: Knechel, W, R, Salerio, S, E
Publisher: Routledge NY/London
ISBN: 9781138692794

Relevant journal articles

Extant accounting and auditing standards, as stated in Sections 3.4 and 3.5; may be tested in this paper subject to the rule for New Legislation.

Command words

The following list contains active command words appropriate for use at the Professional 2 Level of the AIA qualification. Reference to the command words is essential to understanding how the assessment is applied in AIA exams.

Cognitive Levels of Learning	Command Words	Definitions
Professional 2 Synthesis and Evaluation 20% Application and Analysis 70% Knowledge and Comprehension 10%	Appraise	Assess the worth, value, or quality of
	Assess	Determine the strength, weakness and significance
	Calculate/Compute	Select the appropriate method and techniques and apply your knowledge and understandings to work out and show how figures were arrived at
	Critically analyse	Examine in detail using arguments for and against, and develop a view
	Develop	Elaborate or expand in detail
	Evaluate	Determine the value in light of arguments for and against
	Integrate	Combine information and/or standards and theory from different accounting disciplines or different parts of the case study to provide holistic professional recommendations or conclusions
	Justify	Demonstrate the correctness of an action, claim or conduct
	Prepare	To make or get ready for use
	Recommend	Advise the appropriate action in terms the recipient will understand
	Report	Give an account of the results of the investigation

Regulatory issues and professional practices

Introduction to assurance

Topic list	Syllabus reference
1 The nature of assurance services	LO1
2 Revision: Single company audit	LO1
3 Revision: Chronology of an audit	LO1

Introduction

The auditing environment has been subject to changes in recent years. Growth in information available in all aspects of business has led to a **need for assurance** as to the **quality** and **reliability** of that information.

Traditionally, the auditor has been involved in **giving assurance** on the **assertions made** by management **in the financial statements**. This has been an **assurance service** offered to the **shareholders of a company**.

The **profession** has therefore been at the **forefront of the answer** to the global need for assurance services, and has taken, and is continuing to take, steps to **use its business skills and acumen** to **provide a wider range of assurance services** to meet the increasing requirement for such assurance.

PART A REGULATORY ISSUES AND PROFESSIONAL PRACTICES

1 The nature of assurance services

1.1 Assurance services

FAST FORWARD

There are many different types of assurance service, providing different levels of assurance. The external audit is an example of an assurance service which provides a reasonable (high) level of assurance.

Key term

An **assurance engagement** is an engagement in which a practitioner aims to obtain sufficient appropriate evidence in order to express a conclusion designed to enhance the degree of confidence of the intended users other than the responsible party about the outcome of the measurement or evaluation of an underlying subject matter against criteria.

As you commence your studies for Developments in Assurance and Accountability, it is **vital** that **you have a good understanding** of **what an assurance service is**. The definition given above is from the IAASB's *International Framework for Assurance Engagements*. It can be **illustrated** by an assurance service with which you should be very familiar.

Case Study

Assurance service: statutory audit

Practitioner	=	Auditor
Subject matter	=	Financial statements
Responsible parties	=	Management
Intended users	=	Shareholders
Criteria	=	Accounting standards/law
Conclusion	=	Truth and fairness
Level of assurance	=	High (rendered as 'reasonable assurance')

The framework states that an assurance engagement will display all the following elements:

(a) A three party relationship involving:

- Practitioner
- Responsible party
- Intended users

(b) An appropriate underlying subject matter
(c) Suitable criteria
(d) Sufficient appropriate evidence
(e) Written assurance report in appropriate form

There are **two general types** of assurance engagement:

(a) An **attestation** engagement where a party other than the practitioner measures or evaluates the underlying subject matter against the criteria.

(b) A **direct** engagement, where the practitioner measures or evaluates the underlying subject matter against the criteria. In addition, the practitioner applies assurance skills and techniques to obtain sufficient appropriate evidence about the outcome of the measurement or evaluation of the underlying subject matter against the criteria.

Continuing with the example used above, the **statutory audit** is an **attestation engagement**. This is because the auditors' opinion is given in relation to the attestations made by the directors in the financial statements, that is, the **financial statement assertions**. You should be familiar with these.

1.2 Why is it important to have assurance?

As stated in the introduction, the basic reason for the growth in assurance services is the **growth in availability of information** available to users in the modern world. The basis for this availability of information is two-fold.

First, information is **physically** more easily available, given the **growth in international communication methods**, most recently the use of the World Wide Web and the increase of reporting on the **Internet**.

Second, information is required in more extensive areas than merely financial assertions. There is an increasing public requirement for **corporate accountability** and for **social and environmental awareness**, there is a rapidly increasing use and reliance on **information technology systems**.

Businesses have gone **global** and information has to be communicated further and further afield. This sometimes leads to the **need for information to be interpreted**, or **converted** to a familiar form, and in the long run leads to the **growing desire for international harmony in reporting, particularly on financial issues**.

1.3 Levels of assurance

Various levels of assurance may be given in engagements as have been described above. You should already be aware that a level of **absolute assurance** cannot be given in such engagements due to the limitations inherent in the process.

The level of assurance will vary depending on the engagement itself, the criteria and the subject matter. However, **two levels of assurance** are identified by the Framework:

(a) A **reasonable** level of assurance (where the professional accountant would conclude that the subject matter materially conforms with the criteria)

(b) A **limited** level of assurance (where the professional accountant has no reason to believe that the subject matter does not conform with the criteria, that is, it is plausible that it does so)

A **statutory audit** therefore gives a **reasonable (high) level of assurance**.

1.4 Types of engagement

The two general types of assurance engagement (attestation and direct) were outlined above. There is potential for assurance engagements to be many and varied, depending on the subject matter, which is likely to fall into one of three categories:

- **Data** (for example, financial statements or projections)
- **Systems and processes** (for example, internal control systems or computer systems)
- **Behaviour** (for example, social and environmental or corporate governance)

In order for an assurance service to be provided on the underlying **subject matter**, however, it must have several **characteristics**. It must be **identifiable**. It must be capable of **consistent evaluation and measurement**. It must also be capable of being **subject to procedures and evidence gathering**.

> **Exam focus point**
>
> Through the rest of this Learning & Practice Workbook we are going to focus on statutory and non statutory external audit and internal audits.

You learnt most of the basics of auditing practice in your earlier studies. Apart from one or two higher level issues which you will be introduced to in this Learning & Practice Workbook, you have the knowledge of what is required to carry out a company audit. Questions at this level require significantly more judgement from you about higher level audit issues, particularly in terms of ethical requirements, the requirements of clients and the more complex auditing areas. It is vital that you practise answering questions and compare your answer to the specimen answers in this Workbook.

1.5 Implications of assurance services for the accountancy profession

The implications for accountants of providing a range of assurance services are wide-ranging.

Implications of assurance provision	
On audit	The increase in fee income from assurance services may **replace fee income** lost due to a dwindling audit requirement. It may also cause **existing audit fees to fall** due to less audit work being required in the light of assurance work already undertaken. There is also a significant independence issue for auditors if they carry out other work other than audit for audit clients, and although the standard setters have made provision for this in recent years, it remains a contentious issue.
On skills	The accountancy profession will increasingly require its members to have a **broad skills base** and to be all-round business professionals, expert both in finance and other areas.
On liability	Assurance services other than audit are often based in areas of risk to a business (which is why they require assurance services in relation to them). This will lead to an **increase in the potential liability** of accountants. The accountants will also need to ensure they have **limited their liability in respect of users**, and that they have identified very clearly in contract **to whom they extend liability**.
On public perception	Two issues are raised here. The first is that in extending the range of services that audit firms provide, there is potential for increasing the **expectations gap** which exists between what **auditors** are required to do (in respect of the statutory audit) and what the public thinks that they do. The second is an issue relating to the image of the profession. There is a danger that if assurance services are misunderstood, the public might see them simply as **audit, repackaged**. This could lead to assurance services suffering the same **distrust** in terms of **value for money** and **necessity** as is sometimes the case with the statutory audit.

2 Revision: Single company audit

An audit is an exercise to give an independent opinion on the truth and fairness of financial statements.

2.1 Audit

Key term

The purpose of an **audit** is to enhance the degree of confidence of intended users in the financial statements. This is achieved by the expression of an opinion by the auditor on whether the financial statements are prepared, in all material respects, in accordance with an applicable financial reporting framework.

ISA 200

The auditor's report reassures readers of the accounts that the accounts have been examined by a **knowledgeable, impartial** professional.

The assurance auditors give is governed by the fact that they use **judgement** in deciding what audit procedures to use and what conclusions to draw, and also by the limitations of every audit.

Auditors can only express an opinion; they cannot certify whether accounts are completely correct.

Material misstatements may exist in financial statements and auditors will plan their work on this basis, that is with **professional scepticism**.

Even where auditors assess the risk of litigation or adverse publicity as very low, they must still perform sufficient procedures according to auditing standards, that is, there can never be a reason for carrying out an audit of a lower **quality** than that demanded by the auditing standards.

In most countries, audits are required under national statute in the case of a large number of undertakings, including limited liability companies. Other organisations and entities requiring a statutory audit may include charities, investment businesses, trade unions and so on. 'Small' companies are often exempt from the requirement to have an audit.

2.2 Responsibility for the financial statements

ISA 200 *Overall objectives of the independent auditor and the conduct of an audit in accordance with international standards on auditing* makes the very important point, which many non-auditors and members of the public fail to appreciate – that an audit is conducted on the premise that **management and those charged with governance have fundamental responsibilities to prepare financial statements in accordance with an applicable financial reporting framework and present them fairly**. ISA 200 states that 'the audit of the financial statements does not relieve management or those charged with governance of their responsibilities'.

Another key fact about responsibility which is often perceived incorrectly is that the **auditor does not have responsibility with regard to the prevention of fraud** which is the responsibility of **management**. However, he should plan and perform the audit conscious that fraud could lead to material misstatements in the financial statements, and be alert for risk indicators of fraud.

2.3 Benefits of an audit

The key benefit of audit has been mentioned above. It is the fact that through an audit, the owners of the company (**members**) are given an **independent opinion** as to the **truth and fairness of the accounts** which have been prepared for them by the directors, giving them an impression of how their investment has performed in the period.

There are also a number of subsidiary benefits. Examples include:

(a) The financial statements can be used by **third parties such as banks**, to make decisions about the company. An audit will give them more **confidence in the financial statements**.

(b) The auditors can use their experience as business advisors to **help the directors improve the business** as a by-product of audit. This can be achieved by:

- Reporting control deficiencies and other audit matters to management
- Discussions during the audit

(c) Specifically, the existence of the auditor can help to **mitigate against risks, such as fraud,** as the fact that the company will be audited acts as a deterrent.

2.4 Non-statutory audit

Non-statutory audits are performed by independent auditors because the owners, proprietors, members, trustees, professional and governing bodies or other interested parties want them, rather than because the law requires them.

Auditors may also give an **audit opinion** on **statements other than annual accounts**, including:

- Summaries of sales in support of a statement of royalties
- Statements of expenditure in support of applications for regional development grants
- The circulation figures of a newspaper or magazine

In all such audits the auditors must take into account any **regulations** contained in the internal rules or constitution of the undertaking. Examples of the regulations which the auditors would need to refer to in such assignments would include:

- The rules of clubs, societies and charities
- Partnership agreements

3 Revision: Chronology of an audit

FAST FORWARD

A company audit conducted in accordance with auditing standards will tend to follow the same chronology.

3.1 Determine audit approach

Stage 1 Determine the **scope** of the audit and the auditors' approach. For statutory audits the scope is laid down by legislation and expanded by International Standards on Auditing. The auditor should carry out risk assessment procedures.

The auditors must prepare an overall **audit strategy,** which should be placed on file. Audit strategy (approach) will be considered in Part C of this Workbook.

3.2 Ascertain the system and controls

Stage 2 Determine the **flow of documents** and **extent of controls** in existence in the client's system.

This is a fact-finding exercise which is achieved by discussing the accounting system and document flow with all the relevant departments (for example, sales, purchases, cash, inventory and accounts personnel).

It is good practice to make a rough record of the system during this fact finding stage which will be converted to a formal record at Stage 3.

Stage 3 Prepare a **comprehensive record** of the **system to facilitate evaluation** of the systems. The records may be in various formats (for example, charts, narrative notes, internal control questionnaires and flowcharts).

Stage 4 Confirm that the **system recorded** is the same as that **in operation**.

This is achieved by performing walk-through tests. These involve tracing a handful of transactions through the system and observing the operation of controls over them.

This test is useful because sometimes client staff will tell the auditors what they **should be doing** rather than **what is actually done**.

3.3 Assess the system and internal controls

Stage 5 **Evaluate the systems** to gauge their reliability and formulate a basis for testing their effectiveness in practice.

Auditors will be able to identify any deficiencies and communicate them to those charged with governance, but also crucially, determine the nature and extent of further tests at Stages 6 and 8 below.

3.4 Test the system and internal controls

Stage 6 *(This should only be carried out if the controls are evaluated as effective at Stage 5. If not, Steps 6 and 7 should be omitted and a fully substantive approach taken.)*

If controls are effective, tests designed to establish compliance with the system should be selected and performed.

Tests of controls, which cover a larger number of items than walkthrough tests and cover a more representative sample of transactions through the period, should be carried out.

If **controls are strong**, the records should be reliable and the amount of detailed testing can be reduced. If **controls are ineffective** in practice, more extensive substantive procedures will be required.

Stage 7 After evaluating the systems and testing controls, auditors may send an interim **report to management** identifying deficiencies and recommending improvements.

3.5 Test the financial statements

Stages 8 and 9 These tests are concerned with **substantiating the figures** given **in the final financial statements**.

Substantive procedures also serve to assess the effect of misstatements, should they exist.

Before designing a substantive procedure it is essential to consider whether any misstatements produced could be significant. If the answer is no, there is no point in performing a test.

3.6 Review the financial statements

Stage 10 The financial statements should be reviewed to determine the overall reliability of the account by making a **critical analysis of content and disclosures**.

3.7 Express an opinion

Stage 11 The auditors evaluate the evidence that they have obtained and they **express their opinion** to members in the form of an **auditor's report.**

Stage 12 The **final report to management** is an important **non-statutory end-product** of the audit to make further **suggestions for improvements** in the systems and to **place on record specific matters** in connection with the audit and the financial statements.

Chapter Roundup

- There are many different types of assurance service, providing different levels of assurance. The external audit is an example of an assurance service which provides a reasonable (high) level of assurance.
- An audit is an exercise to give an independent opinion on the truth and fairness of financial statements.
- A company audit conducted in accordance with auditing standards will tend to follow the same chronology.

Quick Quiz

1. Assurance services are required by statute.

    True ☐
    False ☐

2. What five elements are required for an engagement to be an assurance engagement?

    (1) ....
    (2) ....
    (3) ....
    (4) ....
    (5) ....

3. Name four limitations of an audit.

    (1) ....
    (2) ....
    (3) ....
    (4) ....

4. There is a debate about the value of audit to smaller companies. Fill in the arguments for and against the audit.

	For	Against
Shareholders		
Banks		
Management		

5. Name three key benefits of an audit.

    (1) ....
    (2) ....
    (3) ....

6. A statutory audit gives a .... level of assurance.

PART A   REGULATORY ISSUES AND PROFESSIONAL PRACTICES

Answers to Quick Quiz

1   False

2   A three party relationship, an underlying subject matter, suitable criteria, sufficient appropriate evidence and a written assurance report in appropriate format.

3   Any four from:
   (1)   Not an objective exercise
   (2)   Not every item checked
   (3)   Limitations of accounting and internal control systems
   (4)   Possibility of collusion in fraud
   (5)   Evidence indicates what is probable, not certain
   (6)   Auditors report after the year end
   (7)   Limitations of the auditor's report

4

	For	Against
Shareholders	Shareholders who are not management need the assurance given by an audit. Audited financial statements can be used to obtain the fair value of shares.	Where shareholders are directors the benefit gained from an audit may not be worth its cost.
Banks	Banks rely on the accounts for the purpose of making loans.	An audit need not be a pre-condition of a loan.
Management	Audit can be a useful independent check on accounting systems.	Specialist systems review might be more helpful at little extra cost.

5   Opinion on truth and fairness given to members and (subsidiary benefits): added confidence to third parties, improvements to business, audit may mitigate other risks.

6   Reasonable (high)

End of Chapter Question

At the end of each chapter in this book you will find an exam standard question relating to the content of the chapter. However, since this chapter consists largely of revision of previous auditing studies, we have not included one here.

Corporate governance

Topic list	Syllabus reference
1 Corporate governance	LO2, 3
2 Codes of best practice	LO2, 3
3 Audit committees	LO2, 3
4 Internal control effectiveness	LO2, 3
5 Auditor's review of the Corporate Governance Statement	LO2, 3

Introduction

In this chapter we will look at the **frameworks that have been developed to ensure that companies deal fairly with their members**, and the auditor's role in respect of that framework, given their pivotal position between the company and its members. This will lead to an understanding of the relationship between the auditor, the directors and more specifically the audit committee, which is required to oversee the role of the company auditor, and assess its independence.

PART A   REGULATORY ISSUES AND PROFESSIONAL PRACTICES

1 Corporate governance

FAST FORWARD   It is important that company management deals fairly with the investment of the shareholders.

1.1 Importance of good corporate governance

Key term   The UK's Cadbury Report defined **corporate governance** as 'the system by which companies are directed and controlled'.

The roles of those concerned with the financial statements were described in the Cadbury Report which was commissioned by the UK government in 1991.

- The **directors** are responsible for the corporate governance of the company.
- The **shareholders** are linked to the directors via the financial reporting system.
- The **auditors** provide the shareholders with an external objective check on the directors' financial statements.
- Other concerned **users**, particularly employees, are indirectly addressed by the financial statements.

Before looking at the codes that have been issued to support good corporate governance, it is important to understand **why good corporate governance is considered to be important**.

The ideas which are central to the importance of good corporate governance are illustrated in the two diagrams below.

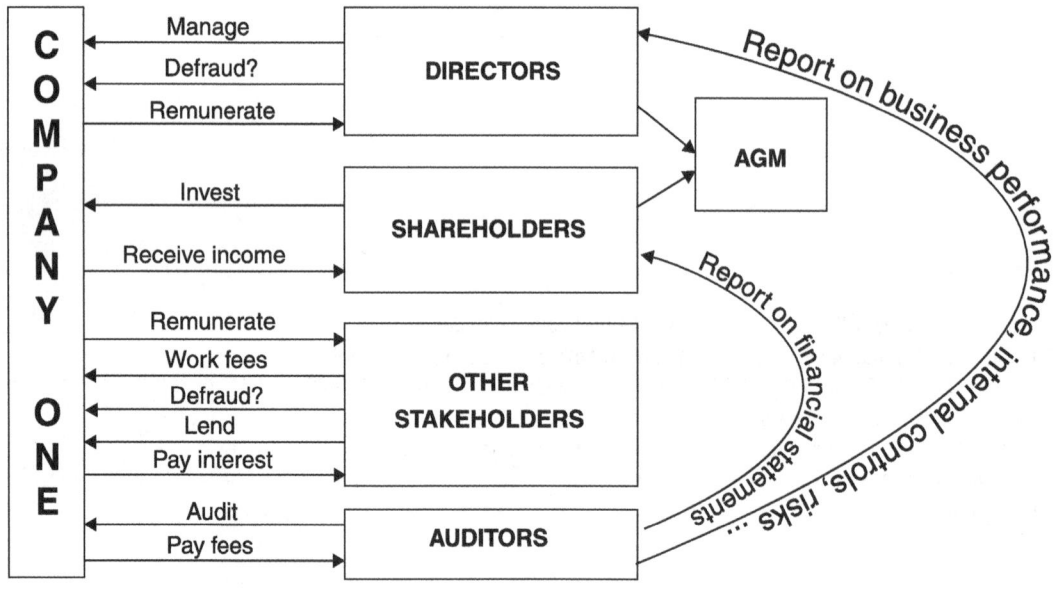

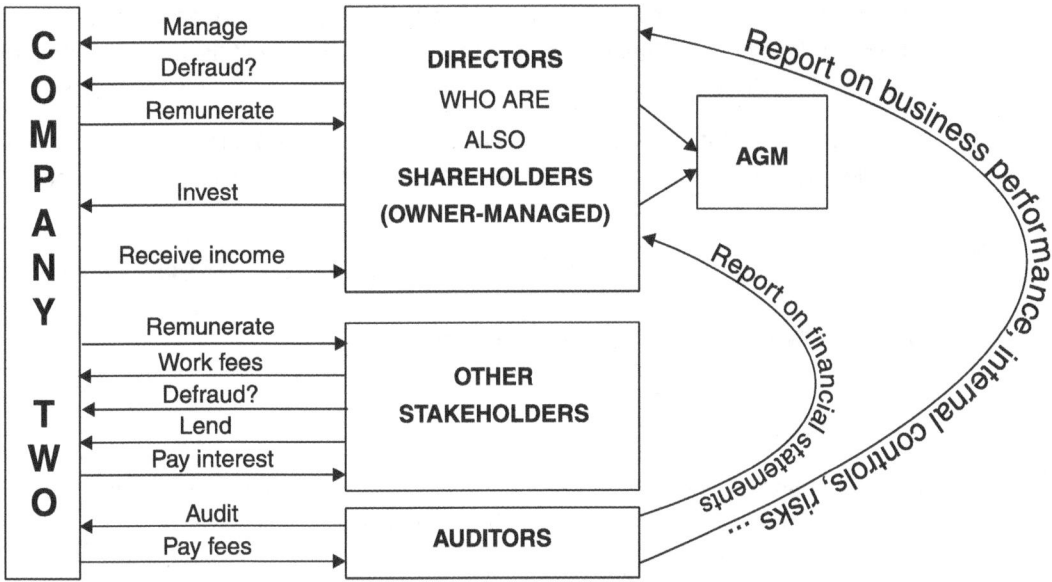

The diagrams show two companies and their relationships with the key people associated with corporate governance.

The key difference between the diagrams is that while in **company two**, the **shareholders** are **fully informed about** the **management** of the business, being directors themselves, in **company one**, the **shareholders** only have an opportunity to find out about the management of the company at the **Annual General Meeting (AGM)**.

The **day to day running of a company is the responsibility of the directors** and other management staff to whom they delegate, and although the company's results are submitted for shareholders' approval at the AGM, there is often apathy and acquiescence in director's recommendations.

AGMs are often very poorly attended. For these reasons, there is the **potential** for **conflicts of interest** between management and shareholders.

1.2 Role of the company auditors

FAST FORWARD

Auditors report on the truth and fairness of the financial statements **only**, in their statutory role.

An **audit** is an exercise carried out on behalf of the shareholders and it seeks to give assurance that the financial statements issued by the directors are true and fair. Vitally for some investors, it **does not report on** two aspects of their investment which are of paramount importance to them:

- How their investment is being managed
- Whether their investment is subject to fraud

This is not necessarily a problem in owner-managed businesses, but many companies are not managed by their owners. Investors, particularly **institutional investors** were **concerned at the knowledge gap** that they were left with.

The UK government took up these concerns in the wake of **some high profile scandals and frauds** in the 1980s and early 1990s.

Having established that it is important that companies are managed well (that there is good corporate governance), the questions that had to be addressed were:

- **How to enforce good practice** by directors, and what that 'good practice' should be
- **How to communicate the adherence to good practice** by management to the shareholders

These issues, which include **directors** by virtue of their being the **management** of the companies, and **auditors** by virtue of their **already communicating information** about the company to the shareholders are addressed in the codes which we shall look at now.

As codes of practice for directors have developed, so has the role of the auditor, who in some cases (listed companies) is required to give some assurance about a company's compliance with codes of practice.

Question — Good corporate governance

Explain why good corporate governance is important.

Answer

Shareholders and managers are usually separate in a company and it is important that the management of a company deals fairly with the investment made by the owners.

2 Codes of best practice

> **FAST FORWARD**
> The UK government has set up voluntary codes of best practice.

2.1 The Cadbury Report

Financial aspects of corporate governance in the UK were addressed in the 1992 report of the Cadbury Committee.

The **Code of Best Practice** included in the Cadbury Report was aimed at the directors of all UK public companies, but the directors of all companies were encouraged to use it for guidance.

2.2 The UK Corporate Governance Code

> **FAST FORWARD**
> UK listed companies are required to conform to the requirements of the UK Corporate Governance Code.

Since the Cadbury Report, there have been several other committees, which all produced recommendations about various issues such as directors' remuneration. In 1998, the key guidance from all the reports was re-issued in the form of the Combined Code, which has subsequently been reissued to take account of more recent additions and comments. In its most recent form, it is known as the **UK Corporate Governance Code**.

The UK Corporate Governance Code is issued by the Financial Reporting Council (FRC) and applies to all companies with a premium listing of equity shares in the UK. However, it is generally considered to be good practice for other companies also, both in the UK and globally.

The current UK Corporate Governance Code, on which this book is based, is the UK Corporate Governance Code 2024 which was published in January 2024. The 2024 Code applies to financial years beginning on or after 1 January 2025, other than provision 29 which will apply to financial years beginning on or after 1 January 2026.

2.2.1 'Comply or explain'

The UK Corporate Governance Code is structured into a set of **broad principles** and more **specific provisions**, which seek to apply those principles. Companies are only required to apply the principles and are permitted to depart from the specific provisions. However, if they do depart from the specific provisions they must explain why they have done this. This is known as the '**comply or explain**' basis, according to which a board must either comply with the specific provisions, or explain why they have not. The board can only choose not to comply with a provision if they believe that doing so would have failed to apply the broad principle, ie if not complying results in a better application of the principle.

The reasons for not complying with a specific provision should be clearly and fully explained to the shareholders. Any explanation must include details of how actual practices are consistent with the overall principle to which a provision is related.

2.2.2 Principles of the UK Corporate Governance Code

The UK Corporate Governance Code sets out standards of good practice that cover a number of different areas: board leadership and company purpose; the division of responsibilities; composition, succession and evaluation; audit, risk and internal control, and remuneration.

The broad principles of the Code are as follows:

Principles of the UK Corporate Governance Code (for listed UK companies)

Board Leadership and Company Purpose

A A successful company is led by an effective and entrepreneurial board, whose role is to promote the long-term sustainable success of the company, generating value for shareholders and contributing to wider society.

B The board should establish the company's purpose, values and strategy, and satisfy itself that these and its culture are aligned. All directors must act with integrity, lead by example and promote the desired culture.

C Governance reporting should focus on board decisions and their outcomes in the context of the company's strategy and objectives. Where the board reports on departures from the Code's provisions, it should provide a clear explanation.

D In order for the company to meet its responsibilities to shareholders and stakeholders, the board should ensure effective engagement with, and encourage participation from, these parties.

E The board should ensure that workforce policies and practices are consistent with the company's values and support its long-term sustainable success. The workforce should be able to raise any matters of concern.

(FRC *UK Corporate Governance Code*: Section 1)

Principles of the UK Corporate Governance Code (for listed UK companies)

Division of Responsibilities

F   The chair leads the board and is responsible for its overall effectiveness in directing the company. They should demonstrate objective judgement throughout their tenure and promote a culture of openness and debate. In addition, the chair facilitates constructive board relations and the effective contribution of all non-executive directors, and ensures that directors receive accurate, timely and clear information.

G   The board should include an appropriate combination of executive and non-executive (and, in particular, independent non-executive) directors, such that no one individual or small group of individuals dominates the board's decision-making. There should be a clear division of responsibilities between the leadership of the board and the executive leadership of the company's business.

H   Non-executive directors should have sufficient time to meet their board responsibilities. They should provide constructive challenge, strategic guidance, offer specialist advice and hold management to account.

I   The board, supported by the company secretary, should ensure that it has the policies, processes, information, time and resources it needs in order to function effectively and efficiently.

(FRC *UK Corporate Governance Code*: Section 2)

Composition, Succession and Evaluation

J   Appointments to the board should be subject to a formal, rigorous and transparent procedure, and an effective succession plan for the board and senior management should be maintained. Both appointments and succession plans should be based on merit and objective criteria. They should promote diversity, inclusion and equal opportunity.

K   The board and its committees should have a combination of skills, experience and knowledge. Consideration should be given to the length of service of the board as a whole and membership regularly refreshed.

L   Annual evaluation of the board should consider its composition, diversity and how effectively members work together to achieve objectives. Individual evaluation should demonstrate whether each director continues to contribute effectively.

(FRC *UK Corporate Governance Code*: Section 3)

Audit, Risk and Internal Control

M   The board should establish formal and transparent policies and procedures to ensure the independence and effectiveness of internal and external audit functions and satisfy itself on the integrity of financial and narrative statements.

N   The board should present a fair, balanced and understandable assessment of the company's position and prospects.

O   The board should establish and maintain an effective risk management and internal control framework, and determine the nature and extent of the principal risks the company is willing to take in order to achieve its long-term strategic objectives.

(FRC *UK Corporate Governance Code*: Section 4)

> **Principles of the UK Corporate Governance Code (for listed UK companies)**
>
> **Remuneration**
>
> P Remuneration policies and practices should be designed to support strategy and promote long-term sustainable success. Executive remuneration should be aligned to company purpose and values, and be clearly linked to the successful delivery of the company's long-term strategy.
>
> Q A formal and transparent procedure for developing policy on executive remuneration and determining director and senior management remuneration should be established. No director should be involved in deciding their own remuneration outcome.
>
> R Directors should exercise independent judgement and discretion when authorising remuneration outcomes, taking account of company and individual performance, and wider circumstances.
>
> (FRC *UK Corporate Governance Code*: Section 5)

Exam focus point

The May 2022 exam had a question asking candidates to critically appraise the quality of corporate governance reporting at an audit client. The November 2023 exam also had a 25 mark question on corporate governance.

2.3 Non-executive directors

The principles of the UK Corporate Governance Code assume that some directors on the board will be non-executives. Remember, non-executive directors are directors who do not have a day to day or executive function in the company and so this will improve the board's ability to exercise objective judgement. The more detailed code provisions state that except in the case of small companies, at least half the board, excluding the chair should be independent non-executives (FRC *UK Corporate Governance Code*: Principle G, provision 11). A smaller company should have at least two independent non-executive directors. The Code sets out criteria for independence. Such independent non-executives must be identified in the annual report.

2.4 Audit committees

The Code provisions in relation to 'audit, risk and internal control' state that the company should set up an audit committee. We shall look at provisions relating to audit committees in more detail in the next section.

2.5 Risk management and internal control effectiveness

The Code requires that the directors confirm in the annual report that they have made a robust assessment of the risks facing the company, which should include a description of its principal risks, and an outline of how they are being managed and mitigated. In relation to this, they should explain how they have assessed the prospects of the company and whether they have reasonable expectation that it will continue in operation (FRC *UK Corporate Governance Code*: Principle O, provision 28 and Principle N, provision 31).

The Code states that the board should monitor the company's risk management and internal control framework and, at least annually, conduct a review of their effectiveness The review should cover all material controls, including financial, operational, reporting and compliance controls. The annual report should include a description of how the board has monitored and reviewed the effectiveness of the framework and a declaration of effectiveness of the material controls at year end. It should also include a description of any material controls which have not operated effectively, the action taken, or proposed, to improve them and any action taken to address previously reported issues (FRC *UK Corporate Governance Code*: Principle O, provision 29). We shall look in more detail at internal control effectiveness in Section 4.

2.6 Corporate governance statement

Note. This refers only to UK listed companies.

The UK Stock Exchange rules require that, as part of the **annual report**, a company must **include** a narrative **statement of how it has applied the principles set out in the UK Corporate Governance Code**. This statement must include an explanation which allows the shareholders to evaluate how the company has applied the principles. The directors must state that they have complied with the Code or explain why they have not. This is because, as the Code observes:

It is recognised that an alternative to following a provision may be justified in particular circumstances if good governance can be achieved by other means. A condition of doing so is that the reasons for it should be explained clearly and carefully to shareholders, who may wish to discuss the position with the company and whose voting intentions may be influenced as a result. In providing an explanation, the company should aim to illustrate how its actual practices are both consistent with the principle to which the particular provision relates and contribute to good governance and promote delivery of business objectives.

Exam focus point

> The directors must also provide a statement showing how they have applied the principles relating to directors' remuneration (not examined in detail here).

The auditors must review the corporate governance statement before it is published. We shall look at their specific duties in respect of this statement in Section 5.

2.7 Benefits of a voluntary code

The UK Corporate Governance Code is a **voluntary code**. The UK Stock Exchange requires that disclosures be made as to whether it has been complied with, but there are **no statutory requirements to comply** with it.

The main benefit in having a voluntary code is that the code can be **applied flexibly**, where management believe that it is relevant. The **disclosure** requirements ensure that **shareholders** are **aware** of the position and they can make any points they want to about compliance with the code at general meetings.

It has been argued that making such a code obligatory would have **punitive effects** on some companies, due to their size or investor make up and that legislation would create a **burden of requirement** which **could be excessive in many cases**.

Critics of the view would argue:

- Disclosure of non-compliance is insufficient as the AGM is still not sufficient protection for shareholders.
- Having a voluntary code allows some companies not to comply freely, to the detriment of their shareholders.
- The requirement to disclose is only a Stock Exchange requirement, and there are many unlisted companies who should be encouraged more strongly to apply the Code.

The government has shown concern for this area in the past and it is believed that it **might take action in the future to regulate this area** more heavily.

However, at the moment, having a **voluntary code is a compromise** based on the points made above.

Question — Voluntary codes

Explain the benefits of corporate governance codes being voluntary.

Answer

- Code can be applied flexibly, as is best for the company.
- The burden of statutory requirement is not created.

3 Audit committees

FAST FORWARD

Audit committees are made up of non-executive directors and are perceived to increase confidence in financial reports.

3.1 UK Corporate Governance Code provisions

Audit committees were the subject of the Smith Report in 2003. The Smith Report contained a summary of recommendations which have been included in the UK Corporate Governance Code.

One of the principles of the UK Corporate Governance Code is that:

> The board should establish formal and transparent policies and procedures to ensure the independence and effectiveness of internal and external audit functions and satisfy itself on the integrity of financial and narrative statements.

(FRC *UK Corporate Governance Code*: Principle M)

The provisions relating to this principle are set out in the following table:

Extract of UK Corporate Governance Code provisions relating to the audit committee
The board should establish an **audit committee of independent non-executive directors**, with a minimum membership of three, or in the case of smaller companies, two.
The chair of the board should **not** be a member.
The board should satisfy itself that at least one member has recent and relevant **financial experience**.
The committee as a whole shall have competence relevant to the sector in which the company operates.
The main role and responsibilities should be set out in **written terms of reference** and should include: • **Monitoring the integrity of the financial statements** of the company and any formal announcements relating to the company's financial performance, and reviewing significant financial reporting judgements contained in them.   • **Providing advice** (where requested by the board) on whether the **annual report and accounts**, taken as a whole, are fair, balanced and understandable, and provide the information necessary for shareholders to assess the company's position and performance, business model and strategy.   • Following the *Audit Committees and the External Audit: Minimum Standard* (a document published by the FRC setting out clear expectations and guidelines to audit committees in their role on external audits).   • **Reviewing the company's risk management and internal control framework**, unless expressly addressed by a separate board risk committee composed of independent non-executive directors, or by the board itself.

> - Monitoring and reviewing the effectiveness of the company's **internal audit function** or, where there is not one, considering annually whether there is a need for one and making a recommendation to the board.
> - Reporting to the board on how it has discharged its responsibilities.
>
> The directors should explain in the annual report their responsibility for preparing the annual report and accounts.
>
> (FRC *UK Corporate Governance Code*: Provisions 24, 25, 27)

The above provisions highlight the specific responsibilities of the audit committee relating to advising the company on its relationship with the external auditor. Although the shareholders are legally responsible for appointing and removing the external auditor, the audit committee should guide them in the right direction.

3.2 Advantages and disadvantages of audit committees

The key advantage **to an external auditor** of having an audit committee is that a committee of independent non-executive directors provides the auditor with an independent point of reference other than the executive directors of the company, in the event of disagreement arising.

Other more general **advantages** that are claimed to arise from the existence of an audit committee include:

(a) It will lead to **increased confidence** in the credibility and objectivity of financial reports.

(b) By specialising in the problems of financial reporting and thus, to some extent, fulfilling the directors' responsibility in this area, it will allow the **executive** directors to **devote their attention to management**.

(c) In cases where the interests of the company, the executive directors and the employees conflict, the audit committee might provide an **impartial body** for the auditors to consult.

(d) Internal audit will be able to report to the audit committee.

Opponents of audit committees argue that:

(a) There may be **difficulty selecting** sufficient non-executive directors with the necessary competence in auditing matters for the committee to be really effective.

(b) The establishment of such a **formalised reporting procedure** may **dissuade** the **auditors** from raising matters of judgement and limit them to reporting only on matters of fact.

(c) **Costs** may be **increased**.

3.3 Role and function of audit committees

In an appendix to the Cadbury Report, the Cadbury Committee expanded on the role and function of the audit committee.

> 'If they operate effectively, audit committees can bring significant benefits. In particular, they have the potential to:
>
> (a) Improve the quality of financial reporting, by reviewing the financial statements on behalf of the board;
>
> (b) Create a climate of discipline and control which will reduce the opportunity for fraud;
>
> (c) Enable the non-executive directors to contribute an independent judgement and play a positive role;

(d) Help the finance director, by providing a forum in which he can raise issues of concern, and which he can use to get things done which might otherwise be difficult;

(e) Strengthen the position of the external auditor, by providing a channel of communication and forum for issues of concern;

(f) Provide a framework within which the external auditor can assert his independence in the event of a dispute with management;

(g) Strengthen the position of the internal audit function, by providing a greater degree of independence from management;

(h) Increase public confidence in the credibility and objectivity of financial statements.'

Question — Audit committees

Since 1978, all public companies in the United States of America have been required to have an audit committee as a condition of listing on the New York Stock Exchange.

(a) Explain what you understand by the term 'audit committee'.
(b) List and briefly describe the duties and responsibilities of audit committees.
(c) Discuss the advantages and disadvantages of audit committees.

Answer

(a) An **audit committee** reviews financial information and liaises between the auditors and the company. It normally consists of the non-executive directors of the company, though there is no reason why other senior personnel should not also be involved.

(b) (i) To monitor the integrity of the financial statements of the company, reviewing significant financial reporting issues and judgements contained in them

   (ii) To provide advice (where requested by the board) on whether the annual report and accounts, taken as a whole, are fair, balanced and understandable, and provide the information necessary for shareholders to assess the company's position and performance, business model and strategy

   (iii) To follow the *Audit Committees and the External Audit: Minimum Standard*

   (iv) To review the company's risk management and internal control framework, unless expressly addressed by a separate risk committee or by the board itself

   (v) To monitor and review the effectiveness of the company's internal audit function

   (vi) To report to the board on how it has discharged its responsibilities.

In addition to these responsibilities, any responsible audit committee is likely to want:

   (i) To **ensure that the review procedures** for interim statements, rights documents and similar information are **adequate**

   (ii) To **review both the management accounts** used internally and the **statutory accounts** issued to shareholders for reasonableness

   (iii) To make **appropriate recommendations for improvements in management control**

(c) There are a number of advantages and disadvantages.

Disadvantages

(i) Since the findings of audit committees are rarely made public, it is **not** always **clear what they do** or how effective they have been in doing it.

(ii) It is possible that the audit committee's **approach** may prove somewhat **pedestrian,** resolving little of consequence but acting as a drag on the drive and entrepreneurial flair of the company's senior executives.

(iii) Unless the requirement for such a body were made compulsory, as in the US, it is likely that those **firms most in need** of an audit committee would nevertheless **choose not to have one**. (Note that the Cadbury Report now requires listed companies to have an audit committee.)

Advantages

(i) By its very existence, the audit committee should make the **executive directors more aware of their duties and responsibilities**.

(ii) It could act as a **deterrent to the commission of illegal acts** by the executive directors and may discourage them from behaving in ways which could be prejudicial to the interests of the shareholders.

(iii) Where **illegal or prejudicial acts** have been carried out by the executive directors, the **audit committee** provides an **independent body** to which the auditor can turn. In this way, the problem may be resolved without the auditor having to reveal the matter to the shareholders, either in his report or at the AGM.

4 Internal control effectiveness

> **FAST FORWARD**
>
> Internal control is a key part of good corporate governance. **Directors** are **responsible** for maintaining a system of control that will safeguard the company's assets.

4.1 Importance of internal control and risk management

Internal controls are essential to management, as they contribute to:

- Safeguarding the company's assets
- Helping to prevent and detect fraud
- Therefore, safeguarding the shareholders' investment

Good internal control helps the business to run efficiently. A system of internal control reduces identified risks to the business. It also helps to ensure reliability of reporting, and compliance with laws.

4.2 Directors' responsibilities

The **ultimate responsibility** for a company's system of internal controls lies with the board of directors. It should set procedures of internal control and regularly monitor that the system operates as it should.

Part of setting up a system of internal control will involve **assessing the risks** facing the business, so that the **system** can be **designed** to ensure those **risks are avoided**. This is a process you should be familiar with, as external auditors are required to evaluate the effectiveness of internal controls relevant to financial reporting. Remember that the directors will be setting up a system of controls that is considerably wider than the controls the auditors are specifically interested in, including controls to ensure satisfactory operations as well as correct reporting.

As you know from your earlier studies, the system of internal control in a company will reflect the **control environment**, which includes the attitude of the directors towards risk, and their awareness of it.

Systems of internal control will always have **inherent limitations**, the most important being that a system of internal control cannot eliminate the possibility of **human error**, or the chance that staff will **collude in fraud**.

The directors should explain in the annual report their responsibility for preparing the annual report and accounts, and state that they consider the annual report and accounts as a whole to be **fair, balanced and understandable** and provides the information necessary for shareholders to assess the entity's performance, business model and strategy (FRC *UK Corporate Governance Code*: Principle N, provision 27).

Directors are required to state in annual and half-yearly financial statements whether they considered it appropriate to adopt the **going concern basis of accounting**, and identify any material uncertainties in relation to going concern over a period of at least 12 months from the date of approval of the financial statements (FRC *UK Corporate Governance Code*: Principle M, provision 30). The 2018 revision of the *Code* goes further, requiring the board to explain how it has assessed the company's prospects, and the time period on which this assessment is based. It should then state whether it reasonably expects the company to be able to continue in operation and meet its liabilities in this period (FRC *UK Corporate Governance Code*: Principle N, provision 31).

Once the directors have set up a system of internal control, they are responsible for **reviewing** it regularly, to ensure that it **still meets its objectives**.

The board is required to carry out a 'robust' **risk assessment** for the company, covering both the principal and the emerging risks. The board then states in the annual report that it has carried out this assessment, and describes the principal risks and how they are being managed (FRC *UK Corporate Governance Code*: Principle O, provision 28).

The board may decide that in order to carry out their review function properly they have to employ an **internal audit function** to undertake this task. The role of internal audit is discussed in more detail in Chapter 8, but you should be aware that this is potentially part of its function.

If the board does not see the need for an internal audit function, the UK Corporate Governance Code requires companies to consider the need for one at least annually, so that the **need for internal audit is regularly reviewed** (FRC *UK Corporate Governance Code*: Principle M, provision 25).

The UK Corporate Governance Code states that the board of directors should **report** on their review of the company's risk management and internal control framework as part of their annual report (FRC *UK Corporate Governance Code*: Principle O, provision 29). The statement should cover all material controls including, financial, operational, reporting and compliance controls.

The auditor is not required to report specifically on this report (other than as part of their general reporting duties in relation to other information per ISA 720), but reading this section of the report will be an important aspect of their risk assessment procedures and controls' evaluation.

5 Auditor's review of the Corporate Governance Statement

> **FAST FORWARD**
>
> Auditors are required by listing rules to review the Corporate Governance Statement published in the Annual Report of listed companies.

The duty of auditors to review the Corporate Governance Statement in the Annual Report of listed companies extends to the following items:

- Directors should explain in their annual report their responsibility for preparing the financial statements and there should be statement by the auditors about their reporting responsibilities.

- The board should, at least annually, conduct a review of the group's system of internal controls and should report to shareholders that they have done so. The review should cover all material controls, including financial, operational and compliance controls and risk management systems.

- The board should establish an audit committee of at least three, or in the case of smaller companies, two independent non-executive directors. The board should satisfy itself that at least one member of the audit committee has recent and relevant financial experience.

- The main role and responsibilities of the audit committee should be set out in written terms of reference and should include:

    - To monitor the integrity of the financial statements of a company, and any formal announcements relating to the company's performance, reviewing significant financial reporting judgements contained in them

    - To review the company's internal financial controls and, unless expressly addressed by a separate board risk committee composed of independent directors or by the board itself, to review the company's internal control and risk management systems

    - To monitor and review the effectiveness of the company's internal audit function

    - To make recommendations to the board, for it to put to shareholders for their approval in general meeting, in relation to the appointment, re-appointment and removal of the external auditor and to approve the remuneration and terms of engagement of the external auditor

    - To review and monitor the external auditor's independence and objectivity and the effectiveness of the audit process, taking into consideration relevant UK professional and regulatory requirements

    - To develop and implement policy on the engagement of the external auditor to supply non audit services, taking into account relevant ethical guidance regarding the provision of non-audit services by the external audit firm; and to report to the board, identifying any matters in respect of which it considers that action and improvement is needed and making recommendations as to the steps to be taken

- The terms of reference of the audit committee, including its role and the authority delegated to it by the board, should be made available. A separate section of the annual report should describe the work of the committee in discharging those responsibilities.

- The audit committee should review arrangements by which staff of the company may, in confidence, raise concerns about possible improprieties in matters of financial reporting or other matters. The audit committee's objective should be to ensure that arrangements are in place for the proportion and independent investigation of such matters and for appropriate follow up action.

- The audit committee should monitor and review the effectiveness of internal control activities. Where there is no internal audit function, the audit committee should review annually whether there is a need for an internal audit function and make a recommendation to the board, and the reasons for the absence of such a function should be explained in the relevant section of the report.

- The audit committee should have primary responsibility for making a recommendation on the appointment, reappointment or removal of the external auditors. If the board does not accept the audit committee's recommendation, it should include in the annual report, and in any papers recommending appointment or re-appointment, a statement from the audit committee explaining the recommendation and should set out the reasons why the board has taken a different position.

- The annual report should explain to shareholders how, if the auditor provides non audit services, auditor objectivity and independence is safeguarded.

Guidance for auditors on carrying out this review is given in a bulletin which means is not directly examinable material.

Under ISA 720 (Revised) *The auditor's responsibilities relating to other information* (which is examinable), the auditors have a requirement to read all other information included in the annual report, in order to make sure that there are no material inconsistencies with the financial statements, so the auditor does not simply ignore the other aspects of the report.

For RPQ students, in the UK, ISA 720 (UK) requires the auditor to perform procedures necessary in the auditor's professional judgement to identify:

(a) Any material inconsistencies between the Corporate Governance Statement and the financial statements;

(b) Any material inconsistencies between the Corporate Governance Statement and the auditor's knowledge obtained in the audit, in the context of audit evidence obtained and conclusions reached in the audit; and

(c) Whether the Corporate Governance Statement appears to be materially misstated in the context of the auditor's understanding of the legal and regulatory requirements applicable to the statutory other information.

ISA 720 (UK) sets out specific reporting requirements where the auditors are required to report on whether the Corporate Governance Statement is consistent with the financial statements and the auditor's knowledge obtained in the audit.

In the UK, the *Companies Act* 2006 also requires the auditor to report on whether or not the company has prepared a Corporate Governance Statement. The auditor is required to report by exception, in a 'Matters on which we are required to report by exception' paragraph in the auditor's report. This would not affect the overall opinion given in the auditors' report (that is, an unqualified audit opinion can still be given, if appropriate).

5.1 Auditor procedures

In order to carry out the review of the corporate governance statement parts of the annual report, the auditor may carry out the following general types of procedure:

- Reviewing the minutes of board meetings, and other sub-committee meetings
- Reviewing supporting documentation prepared for the board
- Making enquiries of relevant persons charged with governance
- Attending relevant meetings of the audit committee
- Reviewing the audit committee's terms of reference and ensuring they are publicly available
- Reviewing documentation relating to staff raising concerns

Chapter Roundup

- It is important that company management deals fairly with the investment of shareholders.
- Auditors report on the truth and fairness of the financial statements **only,** in their statutory role.
- The UK government has set up voluntary codes of best practice.
- UK listed companies are required to conform to the requirements of the UK Corporate Governance Code.
- Audit committees are made up of non-executive directors and are perceived to increase confidence in financial reports.
- Internal control is a key part of good corporate governance. **Directors** are **responsible** for maintaining a system of control that will safeguard the company's assets.
- Auditors are required by listing rules to review the Corporate Governance Statement published in the Annual Report of listed companies.

Quick Quiz

1. Complete the statement.

   The .... Report defines .... as 'the system by which companies are directed and controlled'.

2. All companies must include a corporate governance statement in their annual report.

   True ☐
   False ☐

3. Name four potential duties of the audit committee.

   (1) ....
   (2) ....
   (3) ....
   (4) ....

4. Auditors are responsible for a company's system of internal control.

   True ☐
   False ☐

5. Auditors are required to carry out a review of the Corporate Governance Statement and include the results of this review in their auditor's report.

   True ☐
   False ☐

6. Name four procedures auditors might perform when reviewing a company's corporate governance statement.

   (1) ....
   (2) ....
   (3) ....
   (4) ....

Answers to Quick Quiz

1. Cadbury, corporate governance
2. False – only listed companies are required to.
3. (1) Review of financial statements
   (2) Liaison with external auditors/following the *Audit Committees and the External Audit Minimum Standard*
   (3) Review of internal audit
   (4) Review of company's risk management and internal control framework
4. False – this is the directors' duty.
5. False – auditors of **listed companies** are required to carry out the review as this is a listing rules requirement, but the listing rules do not require that the auditor reports as a result of this review.
6. Any three from:
   - Reviewing the minutes of board meetings, and other sub-committee meetings
   - Reviewing supporting documentation prepared for the board
   - Making enquiries of relevant persons charged with governance
   - Attending relevant meetings of the audit committee
   - Reviewing the audit committee's terms of reference and ensuring they are publicly available
   - Reviewing documentation relating to staff raising concerns

End of Chapter Question

Megafirm (AIA November 04, amended)

Megafirm is a major quoted company. The directors have prepared a Corporate Governance Statement to be published in the company's Annual Report.

The auditor is, however, concerned that the Corporate Governance Statement does not reveal a particularly accurate impression of the company's management at board level. Essentially, the company has a very dominant chief executive and a weak board. Even the chair and the non-executive directors are afraid to challenge him over anything. One example of this was with respect to the audit committee meeting prior to the finalisation of the financial statements. This was attended by the chief executive, even though he was not formally a member of the committee. During the meeting he overruled the arguments put forward by the external auditor for changes to the accounting policies.

After careful consideration, the external auditor is satisfied that the financial statements do give a true and fair view.

Required

(a) Identify the audit implications of the inaccurate impression given in the Corporate Governance Statement.
(10 marks)

(b) Explain whether the auditor should disclose the disagreement over the accounting policies in the auditor's report. **(5 marks)**

(c) Explain whether you agree that recent developments in corporate governance disclosures have led to a focus on the appearance of sound governance rather than the fact. **(5 marks)**

(Total 20 marks)

PART A REGULATORY ISSUES AND PROFESSIONAL PRACTICES

Other reporting requirements

Topic list	Syllabus reference
1 Other Reported Information	LO4
2 Sustainability Reporting and Assurance	LO4
3 Integrated Reporting	LO4
4 Future of Audit	LO4

Introduction

Annual reports are required to include a large amount of information in addition to the company's financial statements. The different types of information and the requirements in relation to it are covered in section 1.

In particular, increasing importance is being placed on social and environmental issues in business. Recent years have seen a substantial weight of environmental and sustainability legislation passed, which puts a significant burden of compliance on companies. Section 2 explores the latest developments in this area and the impact on assurance.

Section 3 turns to integrated reporting, which developed relatively recently as a way of understanding an organisation's ability to create medium and long term value.

Finally we look at the future of audit, an area that is shrouded in as much mystery as it has ever been, and which raises fundamental questions about what the audit profession should be doing.

1 Other reported information

> **FAST FORWARD**
> Companies report a large amount of information beyond just the financial numbers alone.

The starting point of this chapter is the idea that there may be more to what a company does than the information that is presented in its financial statements. Thus a full understanding of its past performance and future prospects – not to mention its interaction with the wider social and natural environment – would be facilitated by the reporting of information beyond just the financial.

Companies do in fact report a wide variety of 'other information', both in their annual reports and in other reports that they may issue. The annual reports of UK listed companies are required to include an extensive Corporate Governance Statement, in addition to the company's Strategic Report.

1.1 Corporate governance statement

> **FAST FORWARD**
> Annual reports must **convey** a **fair and balanced view** of the organisation. They should state whether the organisation has complied with governance regulations and codes. It is considered best practice to give specific disclosures about the board, internal control reviews, going concern status and relations with stakeholders.

The Singapore Code of Corporate Governance summed up the importance of reporting and communication rules:

> Companies should engage in regular, effective and fair communication with shareholders ... In disclosing information, companies should be as descriptive, detailed and forthcoming as possible, and avoid boilerplate disclosures.

Good disclosure helps reduce the gap between the information available to directors and the information available to shareholders, and addresses one of the key difficulties of the agency relationship between directors and shareholders.

1.1.1 Principles vs compulsory

The emphasis in principles-based corporate governance regimes is on **complying or explaining**. Companies either act in accordance with the principles and guidelines laid down in the code or explain why and specifically how or in what regard they have not done so.

The London Stock Exchange requires the following general disclosures.

(a) A **narrative statement** of how companies have **applied the principles** set out in the UK Corporate Governance Code, providing explanations which enable their shareholders to assess how the principles have been applied.

(b) A **statement** as to whether they **complied** throughout the accounting period with the **provisions** set out in the UK Corporate Governance Code. Listed companies that did not comply throughout the accounting period with all the provisions must specify the provisions with which they did not comply, and give reasons for non-compliance.

Case Study

The Catlin Group disclosed examples of non-compliance in a couple of areas.

The Company complies with the UK Corporate Governance Code other than in respect of the following.

(a) Until 30 June, one member of the Compensation Committee (Michael Eisenson) was not 'independent' due to his affiliation with a shareholder. Since 30 June, all members of the Compensation Committee are independent, so membership is now compliant with the Code.

(b) Certain directors' appointment letters, originally issued some years ago, do not specify a minimum time commitment. The affected individuals have been directors for at least five years, and over that time each has demonstrably devoted sufficient time and attention to their responsibilities.

Beyond these basic requirements disclosure guidelines in principles-based regimes tend to be based on the ideas of **providing balanced and detailed information** that enables shareholders to assess the company's potential. They acknowledge that **judgement** is important in deciding what to disclose.

1.1.2 UK Corporate Governance Code disclosure requirements

We looked at the detailed requirements of the UK Corporate Governance Code in Chapter 2. Companies applying the Code are required to report on how they have applied the Code's principles, but some of the particular provisions of the Code contain reporting requirements. These may be summarised as follows (divided according to the sections of the Code).

Board leadership and company purpose

The opportunities and risks that the company faces, the corresponding sustainability of the current business model and how the current system of governance adopted by the company helps to achieve each of these (Provision 1).

An overview of the company culture and how this has been embedded and how the company manages the workforce (Provision 2).

Details of any significant disagreements between the board and shareholders when voting on a resolution (Provision 4).

An overview of how the company has engaged with the company's key stakeholders (Provision 5).

Division of responsibilities

The independence of non-executive directors and the company's rationale for reaching this assessment (Provision 10).

The number of meetings of the board and its committees and individual attendance by all directors (Provision 14).

Composition, succession and evaluation

Transparency over the identity and independence of any external recruiters used as part of any board recruitment and any external evaluators used when assessing board performance (Provisions 20 and 21).

An overview of the work of the nomination committee, including processes, policies and its initiative on diversity and inclusion (Provision 23).

Audit, risk and internal control

There should be disclosure of the work of the audit committee including:

- reasons for the absence of an internal audit function where there is none; and
- the matters set out in the Audit Committees and the External Audit: Minimum Standard (Provision 26).

An explanation from the directors of their responsibility for preparing the financial statements and how they believe these statements support shareholders in holding them to account (Provision 27).

The processes used by directors for identifying and managing the company's principal risks (Provision 28).

A report on the board's review of the effectiveness of the company's risk management and internal control framework (Provision 29).

Confirmation that the company will continue to be a viable going concern and any material uncertainties that might place this under some form of jeopardy (Provision 30).

An assessment of the company's future prospects and ability to meet future liabilities (Provision 31).

Remuneration

Where remuneration consultants have been appointed, whether they have any other connection with the company (Provision 35).

A description of the work of the remuneration committee, including the rationale behind the processes used and how the company has engaged with the shareholders and the workforce (Provision 41).

1.2 Strategic report

The Companies Act 2006 requires all UK companies (other than small companies) to prepare a strategic report. The purpose of the strategic report is to provide information for shareholders and help them to assess how the directors have performed their duty to promote the success of the company. The strategic report should reflect the board's view of the company and provide context for the related financial statements.

The strategic report should include a description of the entity's strategy, objectives, and business model, as well as an explanation of the main trends and factors affecting the entity, a description of its principal risks and uncertainties, and an analysis of the development and performance of the business, including key performance indicators. Companies must disclose information about the environment, employees, social, community, human rights, and anti-corruption and anti-bribery matters when material. There is also a requirement to include disclosures on gender diversity.

The strategic report may therefore disclose **performance information** regarding the company. Much of this is likely to be financial in nature, but it will also include measures of the company's performance against non-financial criteria, such as selected **Key Performance Indicators (KPIs)**.

Case Study

The 2023 annual report of Centrica plc was 57 pages long, and included four main sections:

- Strategic Report
- Governance
- Financial statements
- Other information

3: OTHER REPORTING REQUIREMENTS

The strategic report begins with the following statement:

Source: https://www.centrica.com/media/f0balevh/strategic-report-ar-2023.pdf

1.2.1 Section 172 statements

The Companies (Miscellaneous Reporting) Regulations 2018 introduced the requirement for all large companies (including subsidiary companies within a group) to include a **Section 172 statement** (also known as a s172 statement) within their strategic report. This statement requires the directors to describe how they have regard to the matters set out in section 172(1) of the **Companies Act 2006**.

> A director of a company must act in the way he considers, in good faith, would be most likely to promote the success of the company for the benefit of its members as a whole, and in doing so have regard (amongst other matters) to—
>
> (a) the likely consequences of any decision in the long term,
>
> (b) the interests of the company's employees,
>
> (c) the need to foster the company's business relationships with suppliers, customers and others,
>
> (d) the impact of the company's operations on the community and the environment,
>
> (e) the desirability of the company maintaining a reputation for high standards of business conduct, and
>
> (f) the need to act fairly as between members of the company.
>
> *Companies Act 2006 s172(1)*

The FRC published *Guidance on the Strategic Report* in July 2018 which explained that 'the section 172 duty is consistent with the principle of enlightened shareholder value; recognising that companies are run for the benefit of shareholders, but that the long-term success of a business is dependent on maintaining relationships with stakeholders and considering the external impact of the company's activities. The section 172(1) statement should explain how the board has had regard to the broader matters in their actions, behaviours and decisions.'

1.3 Risk reporting

The FRC *Guidance on risk management, internal control and related financial and business reporting* ('Risk Guidance') in the UK encourages companies to adopt a **risk-based approach** to establishing a system of internal control, ie to manage and control risk appropriately rather than eliminate it. The principal role of internal auditors is to assist management in **monitoring** risks.

The Risk Guidance emphasises the importance of an embedded and ongoing process of identifying and responding to risks. Thus **a company** must:

- Establish business objectives
- Identify the **principal risks** associated with these
- Agree the **controls** to address the risks
- Set up a **system to implement the decision**, including regular feedback

Responsibilities of directors, management and employees

The directors, employees and management are then responsible for implementing this guidance.

Directors are responsible for **designing and implementing** systems of internal control and risk management. They determine the risks and how these are to be managed (in line with the organisation's risk appetite). Directors establish an appropriate organisational culture, and ensure adequate internal and external communications.

Management implements board policies on internal control, provides timely information to the board, and establishes responsibilities within the organisation. **Employees** acquire the knowledge and skill to establish and monitor the system of internal controls.

Review of internal financial control

The Risk Guidance defines risk management and internal control systems as 'the policies, culture, organisation, behaviours, processes, systems and other aspects of a company that:

- Facilitate its effective and efficient operation by enabling it to assess current and emerging risks, respond appropriately to risks and significant control failures and to safeguard its assets;
- Help to reduce the likelihood and impact of poor judgement in decision-making; risk-taking that exceeds the levels agreed by the board; human error; or control processes being deliberately circumvented;

- Help ensure the quality of internal and external reporting; and
- Help ensure compliance with applicable laws and regulations, and also with internal policies with respect to the conduct of business.'

A risk management and internal control system is likely to include:

(a) **Risk assessment** – process to identify major risks and assess their impact

(b) **Management and monitoring of risks** – including controls processes (segregation of duties, authorisation, etc)

(c) **Information and communication systems** – include monthly reporting, comparison with budgets etc as well as non-financial performance indicators

(d) **Monitoring** – procedures designed to ensure risks are monitored and the internal controls continue to be effective (audit committees, internal audit, etc)

Risk Disclosures

The Risk Guidance recommends that the assessments and processes used to manage and monitor risk should inform disclosures in the annual reports and financial statements. The disclosures comprise the following:

- The principal risks facing the company and how they are managed or mitigated
- Whether the directors have a reasonable expectation that the company will be able to continue in operation and meet its liabilities as they fall due
- The going concern basis of accounting
- Reporting on the review of the risk management and internal control system, and the main features of the company's risk management and internal control system in relation to the financial reporting process

There is an expectation that the period used by the company in assessing whether the going concern basis of accounting is appropriate will be significantly longer than 12 months.

2 Sustainability reporting and assurance

> **FAST FORWARD**
>
> Sustainability reporting is a rapidly evolving area. As sustainability reporting standards have developed, this has resulted in a need for assurance over the information reported using these standards.

Sustainability reporting is of growing importance to investors and other stakeholders as they use it to help inform their decisions. Investors are driving the pressure for more consistent and comparable reporting in this area as they need reassurance about the resilience of their investments. This has resulted in the development of a number of sustainability reporting standards internationally.

2.1 IFRS Sustainability Disclosure Standards

The Trustees of the IFRS® Foundation announced the formation of the **International Sustainability Standards Board™ (ISSB)** on 3 November 2021 at COP26 in Glasgow, following strong market demand for its establishment. The ISSB has four key objectives:

(a) To develop standards for a global baseline of sustainability disclosures

(b) To meet the information needs of investors

(c) To enable companies to provide comprehensive sustainability information to global capital markets

(d) To facilitate interoperability with disclosures that are jurisdiction-specific and/or aimed at broader stakeholder groups

In June 2023, the International Sustainability Standards Board (ISSB) issued its first two **IFRS Sustainability Disclosure Standards** designed to highlight the risks and opportunities faced by organisations in relation to ESG issues:

- IFRS S1 *General Requirements for Disclosure of Sustainability-related Financial Information*
- IFRS S2 *Climate-related Disclosures*

These two standards require commentaries to be included in directors commentary section of the annual report for organisations with accounting period starting after 1 January 2024.

2.1.1 IFRS S1 *General Requirements for Disclosure of Sustainability-related Financial Information*

IFRS S1 requires a company to disclose information about all sustainability-related risks and opportunities that could reasonably be expected to affect its cash flows, its access to finance or cost of capital over the short, medium, or long term.

It prescribes how a company should prepare and report its sustainability-related financial disclosures. It sets out general requirements for the content and presentation of those disclosures so that the information disclosed is useful to users in making decisions relating to providing resources to the company.

IFRS S1 sets out the requirements for disclosing information about a company's sustainability-related risks and opportunities. In particular, a company is required to provide disclosures about its sustainability related governance, strategy, processes, and performance, as follows:

- The **governance** processes, controls and procedures the entity uses to monitor, manage and oversee sustainability-related risks and opportunities
- The company's **strategy** for managing sustainability-related risks and opportunities
- The **processes** the company uses to identify, assess, prioritise and monitor sustainability-related risks and opportunities
- The company's **performance** in relation to sustainability-related risks and opportunities, including progress towards any targets the company has set or is required to meet by law or regulation

By adhering to IFRS S1, organisations can establish a solid foundation for comprehensive and credible sustainability reporting, promoting consistency and comparability across various entities.

2.1.2 IFRS S2 Climate-related Disclosures

The objective of IFRS S2 is to require an entity to disclose information about its climate-related risks and opportunities that is useful to users of financial reports in making decisions relating to providing resources to the entity.

> **Key term**
>
> **Climate-related risks** refer to the potential negative effects of climate change on an entity.

IFRS S2 requires an entity to disclose information about climate-related risks and opportunities that could reasonably be expected to affect the entity's cash flows, its access to finance or cost of capital over the short, medium, or long term (collectively referred to as 'climate-related risks and opportunities that could reasonably be expected to affect the entity's prospects').

IFRS S2 applies to:

- Climate-related risks to which the entity is exposed, which are:
    (1) Climate-related physical risks
    (2) Climate-related transition risks
- Climate-related opportunities available to the entity

Key terms

> **Climate-related physical risks** are risks resulting from climate change that can be event-driven or from longer-term shifts in climatic patterns (such as storms, drought, long term changes in temperature that result in sea level rise).
>
> **Climate-related transition risks** are the risks associated with the switch to a low carbon economy (such as the increased operating costs or asset impairment due to new or amended climate-related regulations).

IFRS S2 sets out the requirements for disclosing information about an entity's climate-related risks and opportunities. In particular, IFRS S2 requires an entity to disclose information that enables users of general-purpose financial reports to understand:

- The governance processes, controls, and procedures the entity uses to monitor, manage, and oversee climate-related risks and opportunities
- The entity's strategy for managing climate-related risks and opportunities
- The processes the entity uses to identify, assess, prioritise, and monitor climate-related risks and opportunities, including whether and how those processes are integrated into and inform the entity's overall risk management process
- The entity's performance in relation to its climate-related risks and opportunities, including progress towards any climate-related targets it has set, and any targets it is required to meet by law or regulation

2.2 EU Disclosures

The European Union (EU) **Corporate Sustainability Reporting Directive (CSRD)** was launched in January 2023 and requires all large and listed EU companies to disclose certain information on social and environmental matters. The CRSD also applies to certain non-EU companies (ones that generate over EUR 150 million in the EU). The first companies will have to apply the new rules for the first time in the 2024 financial year, for reports published in 2025.

In order to support this directive, on 31 July 2023, the EU published the **European Sustainability Reporting Standards (ESRS)** which will be used to disclose sustainability information under the CSRD. The EFRS have been developed so that they effectively incorporate and are compatible with IFRS S1 and S2. The published ESRS are as follows.

ESRS 1	General requirements
ESRS 2	General disclosures
ESRS E1	Climate change
ESRS E2	Pollution
ESRS E3	Water and marine resources
ESRS E4	Biodiversity and ecosystems
ESRS E5	Resource use and circular economy
ESRS S1	Own workforce
ESRS S2	Workers in the value chain
ESRS S3	Affected communities
ESRS S4	Consumers and end-users
ESRS G1	Business conduct

2.3 UK Disclosure Standards

In the UK, the Department for Business and Trade plans to create **UK Sustainability Disclosure Standards** (UK SDS) by July 2024. These standards will be based on IFRS S1 and S2 only divert from these standards if absolutely necessary for UK specific matters.

2.4 US Disclosure Standards

In March 2024, the United States (US) Securities and Exchange Commission (SEC) announced rules requiring registrants to provide comprehensive climate disclosures in their annual reports and registration statements. Disclosures required include the following.

- Description of any climate-related risks that have materially impacted or are reasonably likely to have a material impact on the registrant, including on its strategy, results of operations, and financial condition, as well as the actual or potential material impacts of those same risks on its strategy, business model, and outlook
- Specified disclosures, regarding a registrant's activities, if any, to mitigate or adapt to a material climate-related risk or use of transition plans, scenario analysis or internal carbon prices to manage a material climate-related risk
- Disclosure about any oversight by the registrant's board of directors of climate-related risks and any role by management in assessing and managing material climate-related risks
- Description of processes the registrant uses to assess or manage material climate-related risks
- Disclosure about any targets or goals that have materially affected or are reasonably likely to materially affect the registrant's business, results of operations, or financial condition
- Disclosure of emissions by certain larger registrants when those emissions are material
- Disclosure of the financial statement effects of severe weather events and other natural conditions including costs and losses

2.5 Current UK reporting requirements for listed companies

In the UK, the Companies Act 2006 requires that where a company has more than 500 employees and is a PIE, AIM listed company or company with revenue greater than £500 million, the directors must make '**climate-related financial disclosures**' in their strategic report. The following disclosures are required.

- A description of the company's governance arrangements in relation to assessing and managing climate-related risks and opportunities
- A description of how the company identifies, assesses, and manages climate-related risks and opportunities
- A description of how processes for identifying, assessing, and managing climate-related risks are integrated into the company's overall risk management process
- A description of:
  - The principal climate-related risks and opportunities arising in connection with the company's operations; and
  - The time periods by reference to which those risks and opportunities are assessed
- A description of the actual and potential impacts of the principal climate-related risks and opportunities on the company's business model and strategy
- An analysis of the resilience of the company's business model and strategy, taking into consideration different climate-related scenarios
- A description of the targets used by the company to manage climate-related risks and to realise climate-related opportunities and of performance against those target

- A description of the key performance indicators used to assess progress against targets used to manage climate-related risks and realise climate-related opportunities and of the calculations on which those key performance indicators are based

2.6 Sustainability assurance

As sustainability reporting standards have developed, this has resulted in a need for assurance over the information reported using these standards.

Exam focus point

> Climate-related disclosures were examined in a 25-mark question in November 2021. Students were required to explain the benefits of assurance on climate disclosures and justify whether an audit firm could provide such assurance for an audit client.

2.6.1 Current practice in sustainability assurance

Currently, there is no standard assurance standard specifically for sustainability. Practitioners will use ISAE 3000 (Revised) *Assurance Engagements other than Audits or Reviews of Historical Financial Information* to provide assurance on sustainability information. Clearly, there is a demand for a standard to guide practitioners specifically on sustainability assurance following the expansion of compulsory sustainability reporting. The IAASB has responded swiftly and issued an exposure draft of its first International Standard on Sustainability Assurance (ISSA).

2.6.2 ED ISSA 5000 *General Requirements for Sustainability Assurance Engagements*

In June 2023, the IAASB prepared an exposure draft of its proposed International Standard on Sustainability Assurance 5000 *General Requirements for Sustainability Assurance Engagements*. The reason for this proposed ISSA is to address the need for high-quality assurance engagements that enhance the degree of confidence of intended users about sustainability reporting. The documentation published by the IAASB refers to the proposed standard as both ED-5000 and ISSA 5000 so be aware of both of these terms.

Developing ED-5000

Taking existing best practice from existing ISAs, ISAE 3000, ISAE 3410 and the guidance on Extended External Reporting (EER), ISSA 5000 will be the primary standard for assurance engagements on sustainability information, except when a separate conclusion on a GHG statement is required, when ISAE 3410 will continue to be the appropriate standard for such engagements.

ED-5000 will relate to attestation engagements only, not direct reporting engagements, meaning that assurance providers will use it to evaluate disclosures that are the responsibility of the reporting entity.

At the time of writing, the IESBA is also considering the ethics and independence standards necessary for practitioners conducting sustainability assurance engagements.

The IAASB expects that other ISSAs will be developed over time and has developed ED-5000 to be principles-based to accommodate the following:

- A broad range of sustainability topics that could be reported by any organisation in any location
- Variety in the way such topics are disclosed (such as integrated reports, part of the annual report, as a stand-alone report)
- The ability to use different criteria and methodologies (for example, the ISSB standards or the EU's CSRD)
- Intended users with different requirements (investors, policy makers and other stakeholders: it is noted that ED-5000 recognises the term 'double materiality')
- The availability of accurate and complete evidence may vary, meaning that sufficiency and appropriateness of evidence may be subjective

- The ability to issue a conclusion which delivers both limited and reasonable assurance to suit the jurisdiction (the IAASB concluded that assurance might also be affected by the extent to which practitioners could obtain an understanding of the reporting entity's system of internal control)
- A range of assurance providers with different skills and resources (ED-5000 suggests that unlike audits, sustainability engagements could be conducted by non-accountants, although the need for relevant ethical and quality standards would remain)

(IAASB, 2023)

Terminology used in ED-5000

To accommodate the range of different assurance providers (some of whom may not be accountants and therefore not familiar with other forms of assurance engagements) ED-5000 has considered some of the terminology it wants to include as follows:

- **Sustainability information** (the equivalent of subject matter information in other assurance standards) is defined as information about sustainability matters.
- **Sustainability matters** (the equivalent of underlying subject matter in other assurance standards) includes environmental, social, economic and cultural matters (the IAASB has deliberately broadened the definition of sustainability matters beyond ESG to accommodate the evolving nature of this area).
- The term **engagement leader** will be used instead of engagement partner.
- There is a distinction between the criteria used by the assurance provider to measure or evaluate sustainability matters depending on the applicable reporting framework:
    - **Compliance criteria** are used when the framework explicitly requires something to be disclosed; and
    - **Fair presentation criteria** are used when a departure from the strict requirements of the framework is necessary in order to achieve fair presentation.
- **Materiality** needs to be understood if the conclusions reached under ED-5000 are to be meaningful for users of sustainability information, but the variety of topics covered makes materiality levels difficult to set. ED-5000 therefore requires practitioners to do the following:
    - Consider materiality for qualitative disclosures; and
    - Determine materiality for quantitative disclosures.
- Given the underlying subject matter may be complex and technical, and reporting entities may be more geographically spread, the need for **additional expertise or resource** is recognised by ED 5000 and could be one of the following:
    - Practitioner's internal expert (who is a member of the engagement team);
    - Practitioner's external expert (from outside of the firm); or
    - Other practitioners (including network firms and non-network firms whose work is not subject to directions, supervision and review by the practitioner).

(IAASB, 2023)

Other relevant information about ED-5000

The IAASB acknowledges that there is a risk of fraud being present in sustainability disclosures (including use of the term 'greenwashing' where sustainability disclosures are made to distract the reader from other unsustainable practices) especially if the reporting entity has created an expectation that it will be perceived in a certain way but the underlying facts will not support that perception. Heightened levels of professional scepticism (like for all engagements) should therefore be deployed.

In order to align the approach of the practitioner more closely with that of the auditor, the IAASB decided to present the required order of the assurance report under ED-5000 to mirror the auditor's report as follows:

- Title
- Addressee
- The practitioner's conclusion
- The basis for that conclusion
- Other information
- Responsibilities for the sustainability information
- Inherent limitations in preparing the sustainability information
- Practitioner's responsibilities
- Summary of work completed
- Practitioner's signature, jurisdiction and the date of the report

Note. The IAASB did consider whether there was a need to provide detail equivalent to key audit matters (KAMs) in the ED-5000 report but concluded that as KAMs are not required for all audited entities, they would not be included in this report (but their use would at least be considered for future ISSAs) (IAASB, 2023).

3 Integrated reporting

FAST FORWARD

Integrated reporting draws together the many different types of capital which an organisation has, and aims to paint a broad picture of an organisation's ability to create value into the medium to long term.

Integrated reporting is topical, and is in line with the recent focus across the profession on non-financial forms of reporting. The idea is to produce a single report that integrates the various strands of information reported into a coherent whole – ie financial, management commentary, governance and remuneration, and sustainability reporting.

By reporting on more than just financial capital, users are to be provided with information on how an organisations creates **value over time**. This entails a more **forward-looking focus** than historical financial statements, which is more meaningful to determining business value. It is hoped that the integrated report will help prepare the foundation for the next generation of annual reports.

3.1 International IR Framework

The International Integrated Reporting Council (IIRC) issued its '**International IR Framework**' in 2013, which aims to encourage the adoption of integrated reporting across the world. The *Framework* is **aimed primarily at private sector companies**, but it could also be adapted for public sector or not for profit organisations.

The *Framework* is **principles-based**, acting as a platform to explain what creates value in a business. It is envisaged that reports will draw on material that is already available to management from a variety of different sources.

The *Framework* refers to an organisation's resources as 'capitals'. Capitals are used to assess value creation. Increases or decreases in these capitals indicate the level of value created or lost over a period. Capitals cover various types of resources found in a standard organisation. These may include financial capitals, such as the entity's financial reserves through to its intellectual capital which is concerned with intellectual property and staff knowledge.

The broader landscape containing the various ESG and sustainability reporting frameworks is constantly evolving – for example, back in 2021, the International Integrated Reporting Council (IIRC) and the Sustainability Accounting Standards Board (SASB) merged to form an organisation called the Value

Reporting Foundation (VRF), although the methodology for integrated reporting has not changed. During 2022, the VRF and another organisation (the Climate Disclosure Standards Board or CDSB) were absorbed into the IFRS Foundation.

3.1.1 Key elements

The key elements of an integrated report are as follows.

- **Overview** of organisation and its environment
- **Governance structure** and how this supports value
- **Business model**
- **Risks and opportunities**
- **Strategy** and resource allocation
- **Performance** and **achievement of objectives**
- **Future outlook** and challenges
- **Basis of preparation and presentation** for the integrated report

(IR Framework (2013): p5)

3.1.2 Capital types

The integrated reporting framework classifies the capitals as follows (IR Framework (2013): pp11–12).

Capital	Comment
Financial	The pool of funds that is: • Available for use in the production of goods/the provision of services • Obtained through financing, or generated through operations/investments
Manufactured	Manufactured physical objects, including: • Buildings • Equipment • Infrastructure (eg roads, ports, bridges and waste and water treatment plants) Manufactured capital is often created by other organisations, but includes assets manufactured by the reporting organisation for sale or when they are retained for its own use.
Intellectual	Organisational knowledge-based intangibles, including: • Intellectual property, eg patents, copyrights, software, rights and licences • 'Organisational capital' eg tacit knowledge, systems, procedures and protocols
Human	People's competencies, capabilities and experience, and their motivations to innovate, including their: • Alignment with and support for an organisation's governance framework, risk management approach and ethical values • Ability to understand, develop and implement an organisation's strategy • Loyalties and motivations for improving processes, goods and services, including their ability to lead, manage and collaborate
Natural	All environmental resources and processes that support the prosperity of an organisation, including: • Water, land, minerals and forests • Biodiversity and ecosystem health

Capital	Comment
Social and relationship	The institutions and the relationships within and between communities, groups of stakeholders and other networks, and the ability to share information to enhance individual and collective wellbeing. Social and relationship capital includes: • Shared norms and common values and behaviours • Key stakeholder relationships and the trust and willingness to engage that an organisation has developed and strives to build and protect with external stakeholders • Intangibles associated with the brand and reputation that an organisation has developed • An organisation's social licence to operate

3.1.3 Interaction of capitals

Capitals continually interact with one another, and an increase in one may result in a decrease in another. For example, a decision to purchase a new IT system would improve an entity's 'manufactured' capital while decreasing its financial capital in the form of its cash reserves.

At present, adopting integrated reporting is voluntary, and as a result organisations are free to report only on those 'capitals' felt to be most relevant in communicating performance.

3.1.4 Short term vs long term

Integrated reporting forces management to balance the organisation's short-term objectives against its longer-term plans. Business decisions which are solely dedicated to the pursuit of increasing profit (financial capital) at the expense of building good relations with key stakeholders such as customers (social capital) are likely to hinder value creation in the longer term. It is thought that by producing a holistic view of organisational performance that this will lead to improved management decision making, ensuring that decisions are not taken in isolation.

3.1.5 Monetary values

Integrated reporting is **not aimed at attaching a monetary value** to every aspect of the organisation's operations. It is fundamentally concerned with evaluating value creation through the communication of qualitative and quantitative performance measures. KPIs are effective in communicating performance. Fundamentally, the *Framework* takes the view that **assessments of value should be left to users**, with most of the information in the report being **qualitative** in nature.

For example, when providing detail on customer satisfaction this can be communicated as the number of customers retained compared with the previous year. Best practice in integrated reporting requires organisations to report on both positive and negative movements in 'capital' to avoid only providing half the story.

3.1.6 Materiality

When preparing an integrated report, management should disclose matters which are likely to impact on an organisations ability to create value. Both internal and external risks, opportunities and outcomes regarded as being materially important are evaluated and quantified.

Importantly, while the financial reporting model determines financial reporting entities based on concepts of control or significant influence, the integrated reporting standard encourages organisations to look further – to evaluate what might be the source of the main risks, opportunities and outcomes affecting the organisation. For example, if an organisation considers that its ability to create value is dependent upon its suppliers' labour practices (ie ensuring that its suppliers do not engage in illegal child labour), then it will decide to disclose information about this in its integrated report.

3.2 Global Reporting Initiative (GR)

The **Global Reporting Initiative (GR)** (2016) is a reporting framework and arose from the need to address the failure of the current governance structures to respond to changes in the global economy. The GR aims to develop transparency, accountability, reporting and sustainable development. Its vision is that reporting on **economic**, **environmental** and **social** importance should become as routine and comparable as financial reporting.

The GR guidance consists of a set of general Reporting Principles, together with guidance for a number of sectoral issues.

The GR Reporting Principles are divided into principles for defining report content, and principles for defining report quality. They are as follows.

Reporting Principles for defining report content	Reporting Principles for defining report quality
Stakeholder Inclusiveness	Accuracy
Sustainability Context	Balance
Materiality	Clarity
Completeness	Comparability
	Reliability
	Timeliness

GRI 101: Foundation 2016: p7

It is striking that the Principles for defining quality bear from relationship to any list of qualitative characteristics that might be drawn up for financial information, and which would be relevant to an audit of financial statements. The Principles for defining report content, by contrast, are unique to the kind of reporting that is required for stakeholders, where the matters covered by a report will be different in the case of each company.

3.3 Implications of introducing integrated reporting

Implications	Comment
IT costs	The introduction of integrated reporting will most likely require significant upgrades to be made to the organisation's IT and information system infrastructure. Such developments will be needed to capture KPI data. Due to the broad range of business activities reported on using integrated reporting (customer, supplier relations, finance and human resources) it is highly likely the costs of improving the infrastructure will be significant.
Time/staff costs	The process of gathering and collating the data for inclusion in the report is likely to require a significant amount of staff time. This may affect staff morale if they are expected to undertake this work in addition to existing duties. Additional staff may need to be employed.
Consultancy costs	Organisations producing their first integrated report may seek external guidance from an organisation which provides specialist consultancy on integrated reporting. Consultancy fees are likely to be significant.
Disclosure	There is a danger that organisations may volunteer more information about their operational performance than intended. Disclosure of planned strategies and key performance measures are likely to be picked up by competitors.

3.4 IAASB Discussion Paper on integrated reporting

In August 2016, the IAASB released the succinctly-titled discussion paper, *Supporting Credibility and Trust in Emerging Forms of External Reporting: Ten Key Challenges for Assurance Engagements*.

The Paper introduces a new piece of jargon: EER, **E**merging forms of **E**xternal **R**eporting.

The key points were as follows.

The issue is **credibility and trust**, and how best to achieve this. EER is part of the picture. There is a strong overlap with existing assurance services, but flexibility is required to meet the needs of stakeholders.

Four factors influence credibility and trust:

- Sound reporting framework
- Strong governance
- Consistent wider information
- External professional services and other reports

The external audit does **not** include a separate assurance engagement on EER (see ISA 720). Instead, other types of engagement are needed. Determining exactly what type of engagement is not straightforward – hence the core of the paper: the 'Ten Key Assurance Challenges':

Ten key assurance challenges (IAASB, 2016: pp34–39)
Determining the scope of an EER assurance engagement can be **complex**
Evaluating the **suitability of criteria** in a consistent manner
Addressing **materiality** for diverse information with little guidance in EER frameworks
Building assertions for subject matter information of a diverse nature
Lack of maturity in governance and internal control over EER reporting processes
Obtaining assurance with respect to **narrative information**
Obtaining assurance with respect to **future-oriented information**
Exercising **professional scepticism** and **professional judgement**
Obtaining the **competence** necessary to perform the engagement
Communicating effectively in the assurance report

Following a period of consultation with many different stakeholders, IAASB issued a Feedback Statement in January 2018 which delivered the following messages:

- There should be greater awareness of the limitations of ISA 720 among stakeholders so they can decide on the best way of providing assurance on EER alongside the audit opinion.

- While the use of a specific standard to provide assurance consistently on EER is favoured (probably ISAE 3000) it should still reflect the fluid nature of such reporting and should therefore not be too specific or rigid.

- Respondents felt that the top three assurance challenges from the original list of ten were suitable criteria, materiality and the form of reporting that should be used.

- While this is still an evolving area of reporting, EER will inevitably grow in significance as more stakeholders get on board and this growth will drive the way that EER should be both created and reviewed.

(IAASB, 2018: pp 5–14)

3.5 Non-authoritative guidance on applying ISAE 3000 (Revised) to Extended External Reporting (EER) assurance engagements

In April 2021, the IAASB published this non-authoritative guidance to support practitioners that perform assurance engagements using ISAE 3000 (Revised) for entities that publish financial and non-financial information that fits the category of Extended External Reporting (EER – while the name is slightly different, this is effectively the same EER as mentioned above). In issuing this guidance, the IAASB aimed to support the credibility of any assurance provided on EER which would in turn lead to enhanced credibility and trust in the underlying EER information in the eyes of its intended users.

Examples of EER information given in the guidance includes:

- An integrated report
- A UK strategic report
- Other specific quantitative or qualitative, financial or non-financial information on matters ranging from greenhouse gases, value for money or corporate social responsibility

The need for guidance stems from the varied and diverse nature of the EER – it could be voluntarily produced or part of a legal or regulatory framework. It could be based on criteria specified by external organisations or regimes or could use criteria developed by the reporting entity. The EER information may be published or presented as a video and subject to the internal controls in place at the reporting entity. As a result of the broad spectrum of work that such an engagement might entail, the guidance complements the existing advice in ISAE 3000 (Revised) to allow it to be applied successfully in the following areas:

(a) Applying appropriate competence and capabilities
(b) Exercising professional scepticism and professional judgement
(c) Determining preconditions and agreeing the scope of an EER engagement
(d) Considering the entity's process to identify reporting topics
(e) Determining the suitability and availability of criteria
(f) Consideration of process used to prepare the EER information
(g) Using assertions
(h) Obtaining evidence
(i) Considering the materiality of misstatements
(j) Addressing qualitative EER information
(k) Addressing future-oriented EER information
(l) Communicating effectively in the Assurance report

(IAASB, 2021: contents pages, paras. 1–20)

Note how familiar the process is by comparison to other engagements that you are familiar with.

However, remember that while the concept of providing assurance to any kind of subject matter might be fairly universal, the specific nature of the process of designing suitable procedures to obtain sufficient and appropriate evidence for this EER is what makes this guidance necessary.

3.6 Auditing integrated reports

Auditors may be engaged to produce an independent verification statement on an integrated report. This is an assurance report and would therefore need to be performed in line with the guidance contained in ISAE 3000 *Assurance engagements other than audits or reviews of historical financial information*.

This could be either a direct or an attestation engagement, with the practitioner presenting the integrated report themselves (direct), or providing a report on information presented by the entity.

Practitioners in this area face many of the difficulties outlined above in relation to the audit of public sector performance information. The measurement of financial or even physical capital is relatively unproblematic because these areas may be readily subject to quantification. But intellectual, human and social capital are much more difficult to present objectively; their measurement involves a good deal of judgement. It is therefore difficult to see how an assurance engagement on an integrated report could offer much more than **limited assurance**, sticking as much as possible to the factual assertions made by the report and wording its conclusion negatively.

4 Future of audit

> **FAST FORWARD**
>
> The audit profession is going through a period of change, both as a result of technological developments and regulatory reviews.

4.1 Technological advances

Audit procedures can be performed using a number of tools or techniques, which can be manual or automated (and often involving a combination of both). The use of automated tools and techniques (ATTs) by audit firms has grown as technology has evolved. As technology evolves and new approaches to auditing develop, the relevance of a particular ATT and its relative advantages may change. ATTs include:

- Audit software
- Test data
- Embedded audit facilities
- Data analytics
- Robotic process automation (RPA)
- Artificial Intelligence (AI)
- Blockchain

Of these, the most immediately relevant to audit is the use of data analytics and data visualisations, which have brought about many changes in the last several years. These data analytics procedures are the result of the application of 'big data' to the audit process, and can be seen as representing a major challenge to existing ways of auditing. Big data technology allows the auditor to monitor very large or complete sets of data, rather than samples, on a more frequent (possibly continuous) basis, and to mine unstructured sets of data, such as email, to identify anomalies for further investigation.

Big data is a prominent current issue at the moment.

Key terms

> **Big data:** A broad term for the larger, more complex datasets that can be held by modern computers. The term refers to a qualitative shift in the amount of data that is available in comparison with the past.
>
> **Data analytics:** The examination of data to try to identify patterns, trends or correlations. As the quantity of data has increased, it has become increasingly necessary to evolve ways of processing and making sense of it.

The general idea is that having so much more data around allows a surprising number of new things to be done. One **example** of this is **Google Maps**, which uses 'big data' to help predict traffic flows. Google is able to process speed data obtained from smartphones to work out where traffic is moving more slowly than usual. This is then indicated on the Maps app. The whole process, then, is dependent on the collection of enormous quantities of data from smartphones; something that would not have been possible 20 years ago, before the expansion of computing and data collection.

4.1.1 Revolutionising audit?

Big data also has implications for auditors. Recent advances in IT make it increasingly possible for auditors to examine a complete data set – **100% of the transactions** – and to represent trends graphically, almost instantly. Some have claimed that these techniques may bring about a **long-term revolution** in audit approaches, since they enable auditors to focus on 100% of the transactions, rather than just a sample (as auditing standards assume).

This raises a question not only about sampling, but about the whole approach of placing reliance on an entity's internal controls. It is a basic assumption of the concept of an audit contained in ISAs that it is impractical to test 100% of transactions. It is because of this that the audit is conceived as a risk management exercise, in which the auditor obtains evidence of the effectiveness of the entity's own internal controls, as a way of assessing the risk of there being a material misstatement. But if the auditor can now test 100% of the transactions, why worry about controls at all?

Even if nothing else, the auditor relying on data analytics would still have to understand the system which produced the data being analysed. The auditor would also need to understand and test how data got into the system in the first place: for example, a data set might show that a certain amount of cash has been received by an entity, but the only way you can really tell whether this is reliable is by testing the actual cash receipts. Data analytics is unlikely to help here.

It appears likely that, even if they do not eliminate controls testing *in toto*, data analytics will lead to a reconsideration of how controls are tested, particularly controls in an IT environment. Data analytics are also likely to lead to an **improvement in audit quality**, although this is, of course, dependent on data analytics processes being implemented intelligently.

We will consider how the auditor uses automated tools and techniques, including data analytics, in Chapter 19.

4.2 Reviews of the audit profession

The audit profession in the UK has been the subject of three major connected reviews in the last few years, all of which have now reported their findings:

- The Kingman review (2018), into the Financial Reporting Council (FRC)
- A study by the Competition and Markets Authority (2019)
- The Brydon report (2019), into the quality and effectiveness of audit

These reviews took place against the background of a profession in crisis, struggling first with the legacy of the financial crisis of 2007-8 and then with a string of high-profile corporate failures in the UK. Most prominent among these was Carillion in 2018, the largest-ever trading liquidation in UK history, of a company whose auditors had considered it to be a going concern just four months beforehand. That such an important audit could so manifestly fail to warn of the company's problems prompted many to ask searching questions of the audit profession and its regulator.

4.2.1 Kingman

The most important outcome of the Kingman review was its recommendation that the FRC be abolished, and replaced with a successor organisation to be called the **Audit, Reporting and Governance Authority (ARGA)**.

In its fundaments, the ARGA is to have more teeth than the FRC did. It is to be able to:

- Directly regulate the biggest audit firms
- Impose greater sanctions in cases of corporate failure
- Require rapid explanations from companies
- Publish reports about a company's conduct and management

4.2.2 Competitions and Market Authority (CMA)

The CMA has reviewed the audit market and made a number of proposals. The key recommendations were:

- Robust regulatory oversight of the committees that run the selection process for audited companies, and oversee the audit, to make them more accountable and ensure that they prioritise quality

- **Mandatory joint audit**, to increase the capacity of challenger firms, to increase choice in the market and thereby drive up audit quality
- An **operational split between the Big Four's audit and non-audit businesses**, to ensure maximum focus on audit quality
- A five-year review of progress by the regulator

The most radical changes are the mandatory joint audit and the 'operational split' between the Big Four's audit and non-audit businesses. It remains to be seen, of course, whether and to what extent these recommendations result in changes.

4.2.3 Brydon

Lord Brydon's report called for a total reconfiguration of the audit profession, with the aim of trying to restore some of the public's trust in audit. The reconfiguration in question is the separation of audit from the accountancy profession, a point on which the Brydon report echoed the CMA review.

The key recommendations included (*Independent review into the quality and effectiveness of audit*: para. 2.0.6):

- A redefinition of audit and its purpose;
- The creation of a corporate auditing profession governed by principles;
- The introduction of suspicion into the qualities of auditing;
- The extension of the concept of auditing to areas beyond financial statements;
- Mechanisms to encourage greater engagement of shareholders with audit and auditors;
- A change to the language of the opinion given by auditors;
- The introduction of a corporate Audit and Assurance Policy, a Resilience Statement and a Public Interest Statement;
- Suggestions to inform the work of BEIS on internal controls and improve clarity on capital maintenance;
- Greater clarity around the role of the audit committee;
- A package of measures around fraud detection and prevention;
- Improved auditor communication and transparency;
- Obligations to acknowledge external signals of concern;
- Extension of audit to new areas including Alternative Performance Measures; and
- The increased use of technology.

Exam focus point

> The May 2022 exam contained a question where students were asked to evaluate whether the suggestions in the Brydon report might help improve audit quality.

4.2.4 Restoring trust in audit and corporate governance

In order to draw together the outputs from various reviews that have been conducted in recent years, the UK government started to identify the next steps that should be taken regarding corporate reporting, auditing and regulation. In March 2021, the department for Business, Energy and Industrial Strategy (BEIS) published a white paper called '*Restoring trust in audit and corporate governance*' in which it stated the objectives of the reform process as it stood:

PART A REGULATORY ISSUES AND PROFESSIONAL PRACTICES

- Restore public trust in the way that the UK's largest companies are run and scrutinised
- Ensure that the UK's most significant corporate entities are governed responsibly
- Empower investors, creditors, workers, and other stakeholders by giving them access to reliable and meaningful information on a company's performance
- Keep the UK's legal frameworks for major businesses at the forefront of international best practice

Consultation with stakeholders was sought between March and July 2021, after which the UK government analysed the feedback and then unveiled its proposals in May 2022 which are summarised below:

- Greater numbers of companies (including large unlisted entities with at least 750 employees and an annual turnover of at least £750 million – referred to as the 750:750 test) will be subject to the same scrutiny as public interest entities.
- The FRC will be replaced by the more powerful ARGA (it is anticipated that ARGA will fulfil this role in the UK from 2025).
- Regulatory reforms will allow financial statements to be restated and also allow directors, accountants and auditors to be investigated and sanctioned for reporting and auditing issues.
- There will be consultation on governance controls to allow bonuses to be clawed back.
- There will be greater transparency over risks, fraud, internal controls and amounts of distributable reserves and greater scrutiny of items reported outside of the audited financial statements (including climate, risk and internal control).
- FTSE 350 companies will be required to have joint audits or have a proportion of their audit conducted by a firm from outside the 'Big Four'.

Case Study — Joint audit in practice

The need for audits of the top 350 UK listed companies to be conducted using 'challenger' firms from outside of the 'Big Four' of Deloitte, EY, KPMG and PwC is an attempt to remove some of these firms' dominance and thus improve audit quality. It has also been observed that with so little competition in this field, should one of the Big Four no longer be able to provide audit services to clients, the entry barriers for firms outside of the Big Four are considered detrimental to increasing quality through competition.

The UK government refers to this approach as 'managed shared audits' but this is an example of how joint audits could be seen in practice, where the Big Four firm takes the lead and the smaller challenger firm can be allocated subsidiaries more appropriate to their size.

Since committing to this new approach, the proposals have not received the response the UK government was after. Some critics suggest that these arrangements would lead to duplicated work and higher fees, with estimates of the additional audit fees for this approach topping £1 billion over the next ten years, raising questions over what benefit this additional cost will bring to the people being asked to pay for them. Big Four firms appear sceptical that the approach will work in practice, while some challenger firms have expressed a preference for completing smaller audits on their own as opposed to helping out on larger engagements.

Note. BEIS was split up by the UK government in 2023 and replaced by the following:

- Department for Business and Trade (DBT)
- Department for Energy Security and Net Zero (DESNZ)
- Department for Science, Innovation and Technology (DSIT)

4.2.5 EU audit reform

The EU as a whole also agreed to implement a framework for audit market reform. The following reforms came into force in June 2016:

- Public interest entities must rotate their auditors every 10 years (or sooner), although this can be extended to 20 years if the audit is put out to tender
- Prohibition of certain non-audit services, including stringent limits on tax advice and services linked to the financial and investment strategy of the audit client
- A fee cap of 70% on fees from non-audit services (based on a three-year average)

Chapter Roundup

- Companies report a large amount of information beyond just the financial numbers alone.

- Annual reports must **convey** a **fair and balanced view** of the organisation. They should state whether the organisation has complied with governance regulations and codes. It is considered best practice to give specific disclosures about the board, internal control reviews, going concern status and relations with stakeholders.

- Sustainability reporting is a rapidly evolving area. As sustainability reporting standards have developed, this has resulted in a need for assurance over the information reported using these standards.

- Integrated reporting draws together the many different types of capital which an organisation has, and aims to paint a broad picture of an organisation's ability to create value into the medium to long term.

- The audit profession is going through a period of change, both as a result of technological developments and regulatory reviews.

Quick Quiz

1. Is the following statement true or false?

   "Companies listed on the London Stock Exchange only need to explain how they have applied the UK Corporate Governance Code where they have not complied with its detailed provisions."

2. What is the responsibility of management (as distinct from the Directors) in relation to a company's system of internal control?

3. What are the six capitals mentioned by the Integrated Reporting framework?

4. Is the following statement true or false?

   "The statutory auditor is concerned only with the financial statements, and has no responsibilities in relation to the other information included in the annual report."

5. Is the following statement true or false?

   "Audit data analytics is the application of blockchain to the audit process."

6. Of which term is this the definition?

   "The examination of data to try to identify patterns, trends or correlations."

Answers to Quick Quiz

1. False. Although it is true in general terms that the UK Corporate Governance Code operates on a 'comply or explain' basis as described in the quotation, companies listed on the London Stock Exchange are also required to explain how they have applied the Code, so that shareholders may assess whether they have complied with it.

2. The responsibility of management is to implement board policies on internal control, to provide timely information to the board, and to establish responsibilities within the organisation.

3. Financial, Manufactured, Intellectual, Human, Natural, Social and relationship.

4. False. The auditor has certain responsibilities as set out by ISA 720 *The auditor's responsibilities in relation to other information*. These include disclosing, in the auditor's report, any identified but uncorrected misstatements of the information in the annual report.

5. False. Audit data analytics has to do with big data, and is not related to blockchain.

6. This is the definition of data analytics.

End of Chapter Question

Integrated Reporting

Required

(a) What are the perceived benefits from an entity's point of view of paying for assurance on its integrated report?

(b) What would you expect to be the key contents of the practitioner's conclusion on an integrated report?

PART A REGULATORY ISSUES AND PROFESSIONAL PRACTICES

Rules of professional conduct

Topic list	Syllabus reference
1 Fundamental principles and professional guidance	LO1, 3
2 Independence	LO1, 3
3 Threats to independence	LO1, 3
4 Confidentiality	LO1, 3
5 Conflicts of interest	LO1, 3
6 Professional scepticism	LO3

Introduction

You have learnt about rules of professional conduct for auditors in your earlier studies. In *Developments in Assurance and Accountability* we will examine the issues in more detail and consider some of the complex ethical issues that auditors may face. We have already noted in Chapter 2 that it is an important aspect of corporate governance that the external auditors are independent, and the audit committee of a company is charged with ensuring that these independence requirements are met.

The onus is very much on auditors to ensure that they meet ethical requirements themselves. Ethical rules are imposed by professional bodies, such as AIA, but also, in the UK, by the Financial Reporting Council.

Throughout this chapter we will refer to the ethical guidance of the International Federation of Accountants issued by IESBA which many professional bodies have adopted. You should be aware of the FRC's Ethical Standard from your studies at Professional Level 1. Ethics is approached in a conceptual manner but there are a number of rules that auditors are required to follow as well.

Some of this chapter is likely to be revision, but that does not mean you should ignore it. Professional issues are a key syllabus area. Complex ethical issues are introduced in this chapter. You particularly need to work through the questions given so that you practise **applying** ethical guidelines in given scenarios.

PART A REGULATORY ISSUES AND PROFESSIONAL PRACTICES

1 Fundamental principles and professional guidance

FAST FORWARD Accountants require an ethical code because they hold positions of trust, and people rely on them.

1.1 The public interest

The Code of Ethics for Professional Accountants issued by the International Ethics Standards Board for Accountants (the IESBA Code) gives the key reason why accountancy bodies produce ethical guidance: the public interest.

> 'A distinguishing mark of the accountancy profession is its acceptance of the responsibility to act in the public interest. By acting in the public interest, a professional accountant considers not only the preferences or requirements of an individual client or employing organisation, but also the interests of other stakeholders when performing professional activities.'
>
> (IESBA *Code of Ethics*: paras. 100.1 and 100.6 A4)

The term 'public interest' is not defined by the *Code of Ethics*, but it can be considered to be the collective well-being of the community of people and institutions the professional accountant serves, including clients, lenders, governments, employers, employees, investors, the business and financial community, and others who rely on the work of professional accountants.

The **key reason** for which **accountants need** to have an **ethical code** is that **people rely on them and their expertise**.

Accountants deal with a range of issues on behalf of clients. They often have access to confidential and sensitive information. Auditors claim to give an independent view. It is therefore critical that accountants, and particularly auditors, are, and are seen to be, independent.

As the auditor is required to be, and seen to be, ethical in their dealings with clients, AIA publishes guidance for its members. This guidance is given in the form of fundamental principles, specific guidance and explanatory notes.

1.2 The fundamental principles

• **Integrity**: To be **straightforward** and **honest** in all professional and business relationships.
• **Objectivity**: To exercise professional or business judgement without being compromised by: – Bias – Conflict of interest; or – Undue influence of, or undue reliance on, individuals, organisations, technology or other factors.
• **Professional competence and due care**: – To attain and maintain professional knowledge and skill at a level required to ensure that a client or employing organisation receives competent professional service based on current technical and professional standards and relevant legislation; and – To act diligently and in accordance with applicable technical and professional standards.
• **Confidentiality**: To respect the confidentiality of information acquired as a result of professional or business relationships.
• **Professional behaviour**: To: – Comply with relevant laws and regulations – Behave in a manner consistent with the profession's responsibility to act in the public interest in all professional activities and business relationships; and – Avoid any action that the professional accountant knows or should know might discredit the profession.

1.3 Ethical framework

The ethical guidance discussed above is in the form of a **framework**. It contains some rules, for example, AIA prohibits making loans to clients, but in the main it is flexible guidance. It can be seen as being a **framework rather than a set of rules**. There are a number of advantages of a framework over a system of ethical rules. These are outlined in the table below.

Advantages of an ethical framework over a rules-based system
A framework of guidance places the onus on the auditor to **actively consider** independence for every given situation, rather than just agreeing a checklist of forbidden items. It also requires them to **demonstrate** that a responsible conclusion has been reached about ethical issues.
The framework **prevents auditors interpreting legalistic requirements narrowly** to get around the ethical requirements. There is an extent to which rules engender deception, whereas principles encourage compliance.
A framework **allows for** the variations that are found in every **individual situation**. Each situation is likely to be different.
A framework can accommodate a **rapidly changing environment**, such as the one that auditors are constantly in.
However, a **framework can contain prohibitions** (as noted above) where these are necessary as safeguards are not feasible.

2 Independence

FAST FORWARD Professional accountants must maintain independence.

2.1 Conceptual framework

You should be familiar with the concept of independence from your earlier studies. AIA has adopted the *Code of Ethics for Professional Accountants*, produced by the International Ethics Standards Board for Accountants (IESBA) of IFAC.

The conceptual framework in the IESBA Code specifies a series of steps.

Step 1   **Identify threats** to compliance with the fundamental principles

Step 2   **Evaluate** the threats identified

Step 3   **Address** the threats by **eliminating** or **reducing** them to an acceptable level (by applying safeguards where available)

It also recognises that there may be occasions **where no safeguard is available**. In such a situation, it is only appropriate to

- **Eliminate the interest,** relationship or activities causing the threat
- **Decline the engagement**, or discontinue it

Exam focus point   You should apply these three steps when approaching questions of independence, and show the examiner that you have done so in your answer. Remember, if there appears to be no safeguard, you must consider the fallback option of not continuing with the professional relationship.

Factors that are relevant in responding appropriately include reviews of significant judgements made or conclusions reached and the use of 'the **reasonable and informed third party test**' (asking if the conclusion reached by the professional accountant would also have been reached by an independent and informed third party if faced with the same set of circumstances).

The use of professional scepticism (see Section 6) is also reinforced as being 'inter-related' with the fundamental ethical principles.

2.2 What is independence?

A provider of assurance services must 'be, and be seen to be, independent'. What is required for this to be the case?

> **Independence of mind:** The state of mind that permits the expression of a conclusion without being affected by influences that compromise professional judgement, thereby allowing an individual to act with integrity, and exercise objectivity and professional scepticism.
>
> **Independence in appearance:** The avoidance of facts and circumstances that are so significant that a reasonable and informed third party would be likely to conclude that a firm's or an audit or assurance team member's integrity, objectivity, or professional scepticism has been compromised.

2.3 Threats to independence

There are five general types of threat:

- **Self-interest** threat (for example, having a financial interest in a client)
- **Self-review** threat (for example, auditing financial statements prepared by the firm)
- **Advocacy** threat (for example, advocating for the client in a lawsuit)
- **Familiarity** threat (for example, an audit team member having a close relationship with the client)
- **Intimidation** threat (for example, threats of replacement due to disagreement)

> **RPQ students**
> The FRC's *Ethical Standard* also refers to the concept of **management threat**, where there is a threat of the auditor taking management decisions on behalf of a client, which will impair their objectivity.

2.4 When must the assurance provider be independent?

The team and the firm should be independent '**during the engagement period and the period covered by the financial statements**'.

The period of the engagement is from the commencement of work until the signing of the final report being produced. For a **recurring audit**, independence may only cease on **termination of the contract** between the parties.

2.5 Public interest entities

The IESBA Code distinguishes between 'public interest entities' and other entities because the ethical requirements applicable to public interest entities are frequently stricter than for other entities. Stakeholders have heightened expectations about the independence of firms performing audits of public interest entities. At this level of your studies, you must be able to recognise a public interest entity in a question and adapt your answer accordingly.

Key term

> A **public interest entity** is:
>
> (a) A publicly traded entity, ie one that issues financial instruments that are transferrable and traded through a publicly accessible market mechanism, including through listing on a stock exchange (in other words, a listed entity);
>
> (b) An entity one of whose main functions is to take deposits from the public (clearly this means banks, but there may be other financial institutions that do not fall into the above category, such as pension funds or other investment companies);
>
> (c) An entity one of whose main functions is to provide insurance to the public; or
>
> (d) An entity specified as a public interest entity by law, regulation or professional standards due to the significance of the public interest in its financial condition and which consequently will mean stakeholders have higher expectations regarding the independence of any firm performing its audit.
>
> (IESBA Code: Section 400 and Glossary)

3 Threats to independence

FAST FORWARD

The IESBA *Code of Ethics* gives examples of a number of situations where independence might be threatened and suggests safeguards to independence.

3.1 Revision of threats to independence

The area of threats to independence should not be new to you. You should be aware of many of the threats to independence from your earlier studies. To refresh your memory about independence issues, try the following question.

Question   Revision of audit independence

Using your brought forward knowledge, and any practical experience of auditing you may have, write down as many potential ethical risk areas as you can in the table below. (Some issues may be relevant in more than one column.)

Personal interests	Review of your own work	Disputes	Intimidation

PART A REGULATORY ISSUES AND PROFESSIONAL PRACTICES

Answer

Personal interests	Review of your own work	Disputes	Intimidation
Undue dependence on an audit client due to fee levels	Auditor prepares the accounts	Actual litigation with a client	Any threat of litigation by the client
Overdue fees becoming similar to a loan	Auditor participates in management decisions	Threatened litigation with a client	Personal relationships with the client
An actual loan being made to a client	Provision of any other services to the client	Client refuses to pay fees and they become long overdue	Hospitality
Contingency fees being offered			Threat of other services provided to the client being put out to tender
Accepting commissions from clients			Threat of audit services being put out to tender
Provision of lucrative other services to clients			
Relationships with persons in associated practices			
Relationships with the client			
Long association with clients			
Beneficial interest in shares or other investments			
Gifts and hospitality			

The IESBA *Code of Ethics* lists examples of threats to independence and applicable safeguards. In the rest of this section, these threats, and relevant factors and potential safeguards will be outlined. Definite rules are shown in bold. You should learn these.

Exam focus point

It is important that you read through this section and think about the issues raised in each example, rather than just trying to learn rules for each situation. In this exam, it is important that you can apply the spirit of the guidance to a given situation, using the three steps given in Section 2.

3.2 Self-interest threat

The IESBA *Code of Ethics* highlights a great number of areas in which a self-interest threat might arise.

3.2.1 Financial interests

Key term

A **financial interest** exists where an audit firm has a financial interest in a client's affairs, for example, the audit firm owns shares in the client, or is a trustee of a trust that holds shares in the client.

A financial interest in a client constitutes a substantial self-interest threat. The **parties listed below are not allowed to own either a direct financial interest, or a material indirect financial interest, in an audit client**:

- The firm
- A member of the audit team (or their immediate family)
- Any other partner is the same office (or their immediate family)
- Other partners who provide non-audit services to the audit client

For members of the audit team, if the interest is not direct (eg is held by an employee's pension scheme) or is not material (so the client cannot exercise significant influence over the auditor), then the following safeguards may be relevant:

- Disposing of the interest
- Removing the individual from the team if required
- Using an independent partner to review work carried out if necessary

Such matters will involve judgement on the part of the partners making decisions about such matters. For example, what constitutes a material interest? A small percentage stake in a company might be material to its owner. How does the firm judge the closeness of a relationship between staff and their families, in other words, what does immediate mean in this context?

Audit firms should have quality management policies or procedures requiring staff to disclose relevant financial interests for themselves and close family members. They should also foster a culture of voluntary disclosure on an ongoing basis so that any potential problems are identified on a timely basis.

PART A REGULATORY ISSUES AND PROFESSIONAL PRACTICES

Question — Financial interests

You are the Ethics Partner at Stewart Brice, a firm of accountants. The following situations exist.

(1) Teresa is the audit manager assigned to the audit of Recreate, a large publicly traded company. The audit has been ongoing for one week. Yesterday, Teresa's husband inherited 1,000 shares in Recreate. Teresa's husband wants to hold on to the shares as an investment.

(2) The Stewart Brice pension scheme, which is administered by Friends Benevolent, an unconnected company, owns shares in Tadpole Group, a publicly traded company with a number of subsidiaries. Stewart Brice has recently been invited to tender for the audit of one of the subsidiary companies, Kermit Co.

(3) Stewart Brice has been the auditor of Kripps Bros, a limited liability company, for a number of years. It is a requirement of Kripps Bros' constitution that the auditor owns a token $1 share in the company.

Required

Comment on the ethical and other professional issues raised by the above matters.

Answer

(1) Teresa is at present a member of the audit team and a member of her immediate family owns a direct financial interest in the audit client. This is unacceptable.

In order to mitigate the risk to independence that this poses on the audit, Stewart Brice needs to apply one of two safeguards:

- Ensure that the connected person divests the shares
- Remove Teresa from the engagement team

Teresa should be appraised that these are the options and removed from the team while a decision is taken whether to divest the shares. Teresa's husband appears to want to keep the shares, in which case, Teresa should be removed from the team immediately.

The firm should appraise the audit committee of Recreate of what has happened and the actions they have taken. The partners should consider whether it is necessary to bring in an independent partner to review audit work. However, given that Teresa's involvement is subject to the review of the existing engagement partner and she was not connected with the shares while she was carrying out the work, a second partner review is likely to be unnecessary in this case.

(2) The audit firm has an indirect interest in the parent company of a company it has been invited to tender for by virtue of its pension scheme having invested in Tadpole Group.

This is no barrier to the audit firm tendering for the audit of Kermit Co.

Should the audit firm win the tender and become the auditors of Kermit Co they should consider whether it is necessary to apply safeguards to mitigate against the risk to independence on the audit as a result of the indirect financial interest.

The factors that the partners will need to consider are the materiality of the interest to either party and the degree of control that the firm actually has over the financial interest.

In this case, the audit firm has no control over the financial interest. An independent pension scheme administrator is in control of the financial interest. In addition, the interest is unlikely to be substantial and is therefore immaterial to both parties. The IESBA *Code of Ethics* states that only if the threat is significant should the interest be divested.

It is likely that this risk is already sufficiently minimal as to not require safeguards. However, if the audit firm felt that it was necessary to apply safeguards, they could consider the following.

- Notifying the audit committee of the interest
- Requiring Friends Benevolent to dispose of the shares in Tadpole Group

(3) In this case, Stewart Brice has a direct financial interest in the audit client, which is technically forbidden by AIA rules. However, it is a requirement of any firm auditing the company that the share be owned by the auditors.

The interest is not material. The audit firm should safeguard against the risk by not voting on its own re-election as auditor. The firm should also strongly recommend to the company that it removes this requirement from its constitution as it is at odds with ethical requirements for auditors.

3.2.2 Business relationships

Examples of when an audit firm and an audit client have an inappropriately close business relationship include:

- Having a financial interest in a joint venture with the client, or a controlling owner, director, officer or other individual who performs senior managerial activities for that client.
- Arrangements to combine one or more services or products of the firm with one or more services or products of the client and to market the package with reference to both parties.
- Distribution or marketing arrangements under which the firm acts as distributor or marketer of the client's products or services or vice versa.

Again, it will be necessary for the partners to judge the materiality of the interest and therefore its significance. However, **unless the financial interest is clearly immaterial or the business relationship insignificant, an audit provider shall not participate in such a venture with an audit client**. Appropriate safeguards are therefore to end the audit provision or to terminate the (other) business relationship.

If an individual member of an audit team has such an interest, they should be removed from the assurance team.

However, if the firm or a member (and immediate family of the member) of the audit team has an interest in an entity when the client or its officers also has an interest in that entity, the threat might not be so great.

Generally speaking, **purchasing goods and services from an audit client on an arm's length basis does not constitute a threat to independence**. If there are a substantial number of such transactions, there may be a threat to independence and safeguards may be necessary.

3.2.3 Employment with an audit client

It is possible that staff might transfer between an audit firm and a client, or that negotiations or interviews to facilitate such movement might take place. Both situations are a threat to independence.

- An audit staff member might be motivated by a desire to impress a future possible employer (objectivity is therefore affected).
- A former partner turned Finance Director has too much knowledge of the audit firm's systems and procedures.

The extent of the threat to independence depends on various factors, such as the role the individual has taken up at the client, the involvement the individual will have with the audit team, the length of time since the individual was an audit team member and the former position of the individual within the audit team or firm.

Examples of actions that might be safeguards to address such familiarity or intimidation threats include:

- Modifying the audit plan.
- Assigning to the audit team individuals who have sufficient experience relative to the individual who has joined the client.
- Having an appropriate reviewer review the work of the former audit team member.

The firm shall ensure that no **significant connection** remains between the firm and a former partner or audit team member who has joined the audit client as a director, officer or an employee in a position to exert significant influence over the preparation of the accounting records or the financial statements on which the firm will express an opinion.

However, independence is not compromised if:

- The individual is not entitled to any benefits or payments from the firm, unless made in accordance with fixed pre-determined arrangements, and any amount owed to the individual is not material to the firm; and
- The individual does not continue to participate or appear to participate in the firm's business or professional activities.

A firm shall have quality management policies or procedures setting out that an individual involved in **employment negotiations** with an audit client must notify the firm. Safeguards to address the self-interest threat created include removing the individual from the engagement team and reviewing their work for any indication of bias.

For **public interest entities**, the rules are stricter and 'cooling off' periods are required. The IESBA Code states that when a key audit partner joins such a client, either as a director or as an employee with significant influence on the financial statements, the client must have issued audited financial statements covering at least 12 months before the employment can begin. The partner in question must also not have been a member of the audit team in relation to those audited financial statements.

In the case of a senior or managing partner joining an audit client, 12 months must have passed (ie there is no requirement for audited financial statements to have been issued).

3.2.4 Serving as a director or officer of an audit client

A partner or employee of the firm shall not serve as a director or officer an audit client.

It may be acceptable for a partner or an employee of an audit firm to perform the role of company secretary for an audit client, if:

- The role is essentially administrative, with no managerial decision making; and
- This practice is specifically permitted under local law and professional rules.

3.2.5 Family and personal relationships

Key terms

> **Immediate family** is a spouse (or equivalent) or dependent.
> **Close family** is a parent, child or sibling who is not an immediate family member.

Family or close personal relationships between audit firm staff and client staff could seriously threaten independence. Each situation has to be evaluated individually. Factors to consider are:

- The individual's responsibilities on the assurance engagement
- The closeness of the relationship
- The role of the other party at the assurance client

When an immediate family member of a member of the audit team is a director, an officer or an employee of the audit client in a position to exert significant influence over the financial statements, the individual shall be removed from the assurance team.

The audit firm should also consider whether there is any threat to independence if an employee who is not a member of the assurance team has a close family or personal relationship with a director, an officer or an employee of an assurance client. Safeguards might need to be applied such as removing the individual from the audit team or structuring the responsibilities of the audit team so that the audit team member does not deal with matters that are within the responsibility of the close family member.

A firm should have quality management policies and procedures under which staff should disclose if a close family member employed by the client is promoted within the client.

If a firm inadvertently violates the rules concerning family and personal relationships they should apply additional safeguards, such as undertaking a quality review of the audit and discussing the matter with the audit committee of the client, if there is one.

3.2.6 Gifts and hospitality

Accepting gifts or hospitality from a client may give rise to self-interest, intimidation or familiarity threats. Unless the value of the gift/hospitality is **trivial and inconsequential**, a firm or a member of an audit team should not accept it.

Exam focus point

> The May 2023 exam contained a question about whether auditors should accept hospitality offered by an audit client.

3.2.7 Loans and guarantees

The advice on loans and guarantees falls into two categories:

- The client is a bank or other similar institution
- Other situations

If a lending institution client lends an immaterial amount to an audit firm or member of assurance team on normal commercial terms, there is no threat to independence. If the loan were material it would be necessary to apply safeguards to bring the risk to an acceptable level. A suitable safeguard is likely to be an independent review (by a partner from another office in the firm).

Loans to members of the audit team from a bank or other lending institution client are likely to be material to the individual, but provided that they are on normal commercial terms, these do not constitute a threat to independence.

An audit firm or individual on the assurance engagement or a member of that individual's immediate family must not enter into any loan or guarantee arrangement with a client that is not a bank or similar institution.

3.2.8 Overdue fees

In a situation where there are overdue fees, the auditor runs the risk of, in effect, making a loan to a client, whereupon the guidance above becomes relevant.

Audit firms should guard against fees building up and being significant by discussing the issues with those charged with governance, and, if necessary, the possibility of resigning if overdue fees are not paid.

3.2.9 Contingent fees

Key term

> **Contingent fees** are fees calculated on a predetermined basis relating to the outcome or result of a transaction or the result of the services performed by the firm.

A firm shall not charge a contingent fee for an audit.

A firm shall not enter into any fee arrangement for an assurance engagement under which the amount of the fee is contingent on the result of the assurance work or on items that are the subject matter of the assurance engagement, because the self-interest threat created is too great to be mitigated by appropriate safeguards.

It would also usually be inappropriate to accept a contingent fee for non-assurance work from an assurance client. The self-interest threat is considered too significant if:

- The **fee** charged by the firm expressing an opinion on the financial statements of the client **is material** (/expected to be material) **to the firm**
- The **fee** is charged by a network firm which is involved in a significant part of the audit and the fee **is material** (/expected to be material) **to the network firm**
- The **outcome of the** non-assurance **service**, and therefore the amount of the fee, is dependent on a future **judgement related to the audit** of a material amount in the financial statements

For other contingent fee arrangements, factors to consider in deciding whether a contingent fee is acceptable or not include:

- The range of possible fee outcomes
- Whether an appropriate authority determines the outcome of the matter upon which the fee will be determined
- The nature of the service
- The effect on the event or transaction on the financial statements

In other circumstances **it may be appropriate** to accept a contingent fee for non assurance work if suitable safeguards are in place to address the self-interest threat. Examples include:

- Having an independent professional accountant review the work
- Obtaining an advance written agreement with the client on the basis of renumeration

3.2.10 Fee dependency

When a firm receives a high proportion of its fee income from just one audit client, there is a risk of a self-interest or intimidation threat, as the firm will be concerned about losing the client. A high percentage fee income does not by itself create an insurmountable threat. This depends on the following:

- The operating structure of the firm
- Whether the firm can diversify its operations so that fee dependency is reduced

Possible safeguards include reducing the dependence on the client (eg by increasing the client base), reducing the amount of any non-audit work undertaken for that client, extending the amount of work undertaken for other clients or review the work by an independent reviewer.

It is not just a matter of the audit firm actually being independent in terms of fees, but also of it being seen to be independent by the public. It is as much about public perception as reality.

The IESBA Code also states that a threat may be created where an individual partner or office's percentage fees from one client is high. The safeguards include reducing dependence on the client and, in addition, having an internal quality review.

For audit clients that are not public interest entities, the IESBA Code now states that if total fees from the client (for the audit and any non-audit services) represent more than 30% of the firm's total fees for five consecutive years, the firm should evaluate whether there are any threats to independence by either pre- or post-issuance reviews of the fifth year's audit work.

For public-interest entity clients, when total fees from one client represent more than 15% of the firm's fees for two consecutive years, prior to issuing the auditor's report on the second year's financial statements, the equivalent of an engagement quality review should be performed.

> **Key terms**
>
> A **pre-issuance review** also known as a hot review) is a review carried out by an accountant who was not part of the engagement team, **before** the auditor's report is signed.
>
> A **post-issuance review** (also known as a cold review) is a review carried out by an accountant who was not part of the engagement team, **after** the auditor's report is signed.

> **RPQ students**
>
> The FRC's *Ethical Standard* has a more stringent rule in the UK, where audit firms may not retain client when fees are regularly expected to exceed the following limits:
>
> - Publicly traded/listed entity: 10% (with reviews between 5% and 10%)
> - Any other entity: 15% (with reviews between 10% and 15%)

3.2.11 Lowballing

It is not unethical for a firm to charge a lower fee for a service than another firm. However, doing so may create a self-interest threat to professional competence and due care, as it may not be possible to carry out the engagement in accordance with ISAs at such a low price. In this case, if the firm's tender is successful, the firm must apply safeguards such as:

- Making the client aware of the terms of the engagement, including the basis on which fees are charged and which services are covered by the quoted fee
- Maintaining records such that the firm is able to demonstrate that appropriate staff and time are spent on the engagement
- Complying with all applicable assurance standards, guidelines and quality management policies and procedures

3.2.12 Recruitment

Recruiting senior management for an audit client, particularly those able to affect the financial statements might create a self-interest, familiarity or intimidation threat to independence. Audit firms must not make management decisions for the client. Their involvement could be limited to reviewing the professional qualifications of a number of applicants and providing advice on their suitability for the position.

Audit firms are prohibited from providing recruiting services to audit clients that relate to:

- Searching for or seeking out candidates
- Undertaking reference checks of prospective candidates
- Recommending the person to be appointed
- Advising on the terms of employment, remuneration or related benefits of a particular candidate.

3.3 Self-review threat

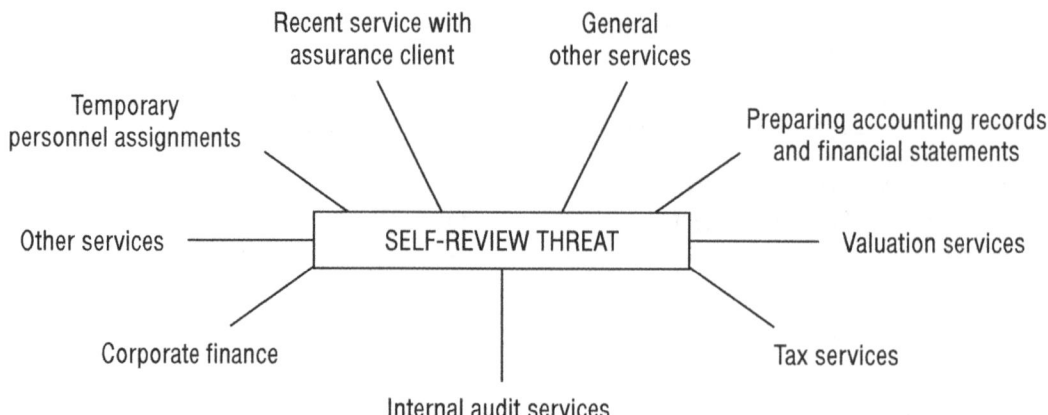

The key area in which there is likely to be a self-review threat is where an assurance firm provides services other than assurance services to an assurance client. There is a great deal of guidance in the IESBA *Code* about various other services accountancy firms might provide to their clients, and these are dealt with below.

3.3.1 Assuming a management responsibility

In general, **firms cannot accept any management responsibilities for an audit client** and must always actively consider risk factors such as the nature of the engagement, the nature of the client and the perception of a reasonable and informed third party in determining the extent of any ethical threats. Examples of activities that would be considered a management responsibility include:

- Setting policies and strategic direction
- Hiring or dismissing employees
- Directing and taking responsibility for the actions of the entity's employees
- Authorising transactions
- Determining which recommendations of the company should be implemented
- Taking responsibility for the preparation and fair presentation of the financial statements
- Taking responsibility for designing, implementing, monitoring or maintaining internal control

3.3.2 Accounting and bookkeeping services

There is clearly a significant risk of a self-review threat if a firm prepares accounting records and financial statements and then audits them.

On the other hand auditors routinely assist management with the preparation of financial statements and give advice about accounting treatments and journal entries.

Therefore, assurance firms must analyse the risks arising and put safeguards in place to ensure that the risk is at an acceptable level. If this can be done, these services may be provided.

Examples of the kinds of 'routine or mechanical' services which may be provided include:

- Preparing payroll calculations or reports for approval and payment by the client
- Recording recurring transactions for which amounts are easily determinable from source documents or originating data
- Calculating depreciation on non-current assets (property, plant and equipment) when the client determines the accounting policy and estimates of useful life and residual values
- Posting transactions coded by the client to the general ledger or client-approved entries to the trial balance
- Preparing the financial statements based on information in the client-approved trial balance and preparing the related notes based on client-approved records

For audit clients that are **not public interest entities**, assurance firms are only allowed to provide services of a **routine or mechanical nature**, avoiding any management responsibilities, and must consider any threats arising from these services, applying safeguards such as using staff members other than audit team members to carry out the work and an independent review.

The rules are more stringent when the client is a public interest entity. **Firms cannot prepare accounts or financial statements for public interest clients**. There is a minor exception to this: the auditor can provide accounting and bookkeeping services to a division of a public interest entity, provided that the matters that the services relate to are immaterial to both the division and the overall entity, and the work is not carried out by audit team

3.3.3 Valuation services

Key term

> A **valuation** comprises the making of assumptions with regard to future developments, the application of appropriate methodologies and techniques, and the combination of both to compute a certain value, or range of values, for an asset, a liability or for the whole or part of an entity.

If an audit firm performs a valuation for which will be included in financial statements audited by the firm, a self-review threat arises. Advocacy threats may also arise.

Audit firms shall not carry out valuations for public interest entities if the work creates a self-review threat. Advocacy threats for public interest entity clients could be managed by the use of separate teams.

If the client is not a public interest entity, then the firm cannot provide a valuation service if the valuation would have a material effect on the financial statements and it involves a significant degree of subjectivity.

If the valuation is for an immaterial matter which is not subjective in nature, the audit firm should apply safeguards to ensure that the risk is reduced to an acceptable level. Safeguards include:

- Second partner review
- Using separate personnel for the valuation and the audit

3.3.4 Taxation services

The IESBA Code divides taxation services into six categories.

(a) Tax return preparation
(b) Tax calculations for the purpose of preparing the accounting entries
(c) Tax advisory services
(d) Tax planning services
(e) Tax services involving valuations
(f) Assistance in the resolution of tax disputes

The revisions to the Code in 2021 added in a prohibition that firms shall not provide tax services that support tax avoidance or any other course of action that is not supported by current tax laws or regulations.

Tax work could lead to self-review and advocacy threats. Guidance in respect of each of these categories is as follows:

(a) **Tax return preparation** does not generally threaten independence, as long as management takes responsibility for the returns.

(b) **Tax calculations for the purpose of preparing accounting entries** may not be prepared for public interest entities due to the associated potential self-review threats. For non-public interest entities, the materiality of the accounting entries is considered when determining whether it is acceptable. If agreed, safeguards such as independent reviews and the use of separate teams are then applied.

(c) **Tax planning and tax advisory services** may be acceptable in certain circumstances, eg where the advice is clearly supported by tax authority or other precedent. However, if the effectiveness of the tax advice depends on a particular accounting treatment or presentation in the financial statements, the audit team has reasonable doubt about the accounting treatment, and the consequences of the tax advice would be material, then the service should not be provided. Should the work apply to a public interest entity and create a self-review threat, the firm is prohibited from acting. Advocacy threats could be managed by the use of separate teams.

(d) **Tax services involving valuations** may be acceptable if the effect on the financial statements is not material and only affects tax amounts, but can still provide self-review threats that might not be managed by safeguards. Where appropriate, such engagements can be carried out for all clients with safeguards such as independent review, separate teams and obtaining pre-clearance from the local tax authority. Valuation work for tax purposes may not be carried out for public interest entity clients if it creates a self-review threat. Advocacy threats could be managed by the use of separate teams.

(e) **Assistance in the resolution of tax disputes** may be provided, depending on whether the firm itself provided the service, which is the subject of the dispute, and whether the effect is material to the financial statements. Safeguards include using professionals who are not members of the audit team to perform the service, and obtaining advice on the service from an external tax professional. As with other tax work, the creation of any self-review threats will lead to a prohibition but advocacy threats could be managed by the use of separate teams.

(f) **Acting as advocate in the resolution of tax matters** before a tribunal or court in most instances is prohibited for all audit clients.

3.3.5 Internal audit services

The FRC *Ethical Standard* expressly prohibits a firm from providing internal audit services to an audit client.

This is a point of difference from the IESBA *Code*, which states that, for audit clients who are **not public interest entities**, an audit firm must consider any self-review threats identified by evaluating the materiality of the work to the financial statements, any associated risk of misstatement and the extent that the firm would rely on the internal work concerned. If these threats can be managed by safeguards (such as the use of separate teams), the work can be carried out.

The IESBA Code also states that if the client is a **public interest entity**, then internal audit services must not be provided if they create a self-review threat.

3.3.6 Corporate finance

Providing corporate finance services to audit clients might create self-review or advocacy threats that cannot be reduced to an acceptable level by safeguards. Therefore, **firms are not allowed to promote, deal in, underwrite or provide advice on investment in an audit client's shares, debt or other financial instruments**.

Other corporate finance services, such as assisting a client in defining corporate strategies, assisting in identifying possible sources of capital and providing structuring advice may be acceptable, providing that safeguards, such as using different teams of staff, and an independent review of the work undertaken to ensure no management decisions are taken on behalf of the client.

A firm shall not provide corporate finance advice where:

(a) The effectiveness of such advice depends on a particular accounting treatment or presentation in the financial statements on which the firm will express an opinion; and

(b) The audit team has doubt as to the appropriateness of the related accounting treatment or presentation under the relevant financial reporting framework.

Corporate finance work for **public interest entity** audit clients that might create a self-review threat is prohibited. Advocacy threats at PIEs could be managed by the use of separate teams.

3.3.7 Temporary personnel assignments

Personnel may be loaned to an audit client, but only for a short period of time. Personnel must not assume management responsibilities or undertake any non-assurance work that is prohibited elsewhere in the Code.

The audit client must be responsible for directing and supervising the activities of the loaned personnel.

Possible safeguards include:

- Conducting an additional review of the work performed by the loaned personnel;
- Not giving the loaned personnel audit responsibility for any function or activity on the audit, that they performed during the temporary staff assignment; or
- Not including the loaned personnel in the audit team.

3.3.8 Other services

The audit firm might sell a variety of other services to audit clients, such as:

- IT services
- Litigation support
- Legal services

The assurance firm should consider whether there are any threats to independence, such as if the firm were asked to design internal control IT systems, which it would then review as part of its audit. The firm should consider whether the threat to independence could be reduced by appropriate safeguards.

In the case of an audit client that is a public interest entity, a firm shall not provide IT system services, litigation support or legal services if the provision of such services might create a self-review threat.

3.4 Advocacy threat

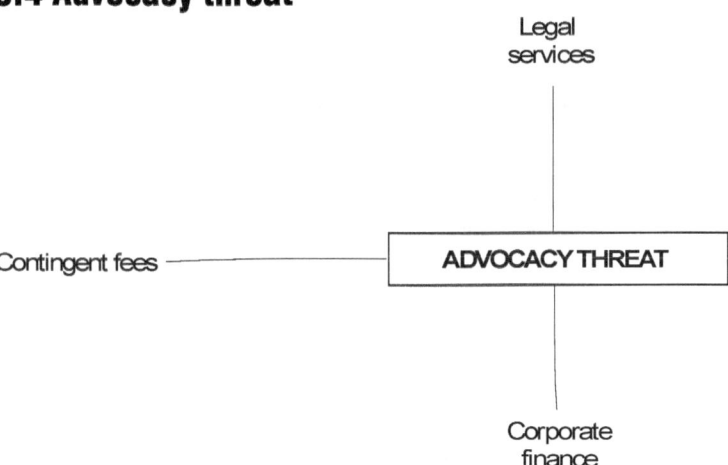

An advocacy threat arises in certain situations where the assurance firm is in a position of taking the client's part in a dispute or somehow acting as their advocate. The most obvious instances of this would be when a firm offered legal services to a client and, say, defended them in a legal case or provided evidence on their behalf as an expert witness.

Advocacy threat might also arise if the firm carried out corporate finance work for the client, for example, if the audit firm was involved in advice on debt reconstruction and negotiated with the bank on the client's behalf, and as suggested above, could result from tax services.

As with the other threats above, the firm has to appraise the risk and apply safeguards as necessary. Relevant safeguards might be using different departments in the firm to carry out the work and making disclosures to the audit committee. Remember, the ultimate option is always to withdraw from an engagement if the threat to independence is too high.

The IESBA Code includes the following requirements where an advocacy threat might be present.

- A partner or employee of the firm shall not serve as General Counsel of an audit client.
- A firm shall not act in an advocacy role for an audit client that is not a public interest entity in resolving a dispute or litigation before a tribunal or court when the amounts involved are material to the financial statements on which the firm will express an opinion.
- A firm shall not act in an advocacy role for an audit client that is a public interest entity in resolving a dispute or litigation before a tribunal or court.

3.5 Familiarity threat

A familiarity threat is where independence is jeopardised by the audit firm and its staff becoming over familiar with the client and its staff. There is a substantial risk of loss of professional scepticism in such circumstances.

We have already discussed some examples of when this risk arises, because very often a familiarity threat arises in conjunction with a self-interest threat.

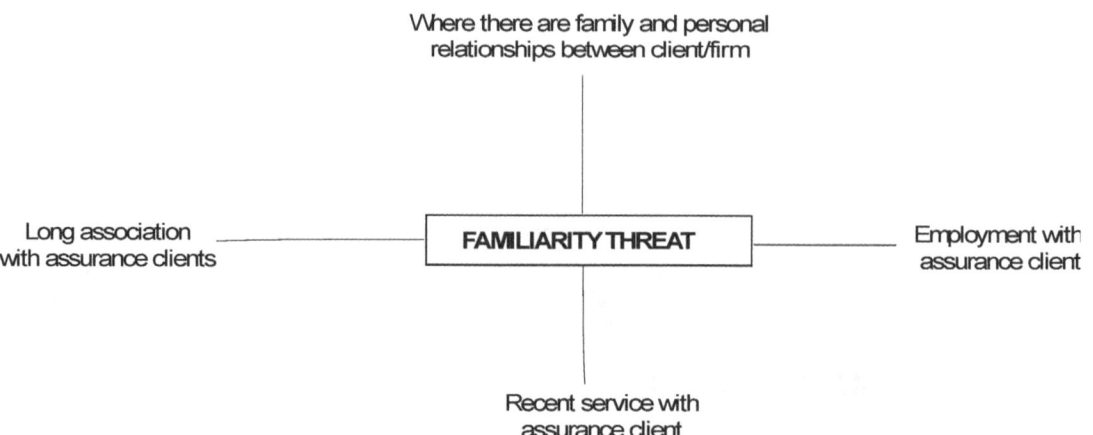

3.5.1 Long association of senior personnel with audit clients

A familiarity and self-interest threat to independence may be created if individuals at an audit firm have a long association with a client. All firms should therefore monitor the relationship between staff and established clients and use safeguards to address the threat to independence such as rotating senior staff off the assurance team, involving second partners to carry out reviews and obtaining independent internal or external quality reviews.

In addition, the IESBA *Code* sets out specific rules for public interest entities which are stricter. These state that for the audit of **public interest entities:**

- **An individual shall not act as engagement partner, engagement quality reviewer or key audit partner (or a combination of these roles) for more than seven years.**

After this, they must be rotated off the audit and serve a '**cooling off**' period, the length of which depends upon the role they have vacated.

Role	Cooling off period
Engagement partner	5 years
Engagement quality reviewer	3 years
Key audit partner	2 years

During this cooling off period, the individual cannot be on the engagement team, perform an engagement quality review or consult with the engagement team.

The Code does allow some flexibility here: if key partner continuity is particularly beneficial to audit quality, and there is some unforeseen circumstance (such as the intended engagement partner becoming seriously ill), then the key audit partner can remain on the audit for an additional year, making eight years in total.

Key term

The **key audit partner** is the engagement partner, the individual responsible for the engagement quality review, and other audit partners, if any, on the engagement team who make key decisions or judgements on significant matters with respect to the audit of the financial statements on which the firm will express an opinion. Depending upon the circumstances and the role of the individuals on the audit 'other audit partners' may include, for example, audit partners responsible for significant subsidiaries or divisions.

When an entity becomes a public interest entity, the seven year limit still applies. However, the key audit partner may continue in this position for another two years if those charged with governance agree.

These rules should be followed, but there may be circumstances in which it is necessary to be flexible, such as when the firm is so small as to make rotation impracticable and when the person involved is particularly important to the audit. In this situation, an independent regulator must give permission for the exemption and alternative safeguards must be applied, such as regular external review.

RPQ Students

FRC's *Ethical Standard* states that for public interest entities, the audit engagement partner and key audit partner shall not be in position for more than five years. A cooling off period of five year then applies.

3.5.2 Recent service with an audit client

Individuals who have been a director or officer of the client, or an employee in a position to exert significant influence over the accounting records or financial statements on which the firm shall express an opinion shall not be assigned to the audit team.

The level of self-interest, self-review and familiarity threat created will depend on factors such as the position the individual held at the client, the length of time since the individual left the client, and role of the individual on the audit team. Appropriate safeguards include obtaining a quality review of the individual's work on the assignment.

3.6 Intimidation threat

An intimidation threat arises when members of the assurance team have reason to be intimidated by client staff.

These are also examples of self-interest threats, largely because intimidation may only arise significantly when the assurance firm has something to lose.

3.6.1 Actual and threatened litigation

The most obvious example of an intimidation threat is when the client threatens to sue, or indeed sues, the audit firm for work that has been done previously. The firm is then faced with the risk of losing the client, bad publicity and the possibility that they will be found to have been negligent, which will lead to further problems. This could lead to the firm being under pressure to produce an unqualified auditor's report when they have been qualified in the past, for example.

Generally, audit firms should seek to avoid such situations arising. If they do arise, factors to consider are:

- The materiality of the litigation
- Whether the litigation relates to a prior audit engagement

The following safeguards could be considered:

- Removing specific affected individuals from the engagement team
- Involving an additional professional accountant to review work

However, if the litigation is at all serious, it may be necessary to resign from the engagement, as the threat to independence is so great.

3.6.2 Second opinions

Another way that auditors can suffer an intimidation threat is when the audit client is unhappy with a proposed audit opinion, and seeks a **second opinion** from a different firm of auditors.

In such a circumstance, the second audit firm will not be able to give a formal audit opinion on the financial statements – only an appointed auditor can do that. However, the problem is that if a different firm of auditors indicates to someone else's audit client that a different audit opinion might be acceptable, the appointed auditor may feel under pressure to change the audit opinion. In effect, a self-interest threat arises, as the existing auditor may feel that he will lose next year's audit if he does not change this year's opinion.

There is nothing to stop a company director talking to a second firm of auditors about treatments of matters in the financial statements. However, the firm being asked for a second opinion should be very careful, because it is very possible that the opinion they form could be incorrect anyway if the director has not given them all the relevant information. For that reason, firms giving a second opinion should ensure that they seek permission to communicate with the existing auditor and they are appraised of all the facts. If permission is not given, the second auditors should decline to comment on the audit opinion.

Given that second opinions can cause independence issues for the existing auditors, audit firms should generally take great care if asked to provide one anyway.

Increasingly, new standards do not give a choice of accounting treatments, meaning that second opinions might be less called for.

Question — Threats to independence

You are a partner in a firm of international accountants. The following issues have emerged in relation to three of your clients.

(1) Easter is a major client. It is listed on a stock exchange. The audit team consists of eight members, of whom Paul is the most junior. Paul has just invested in a personal pension plan that invests in all the publicly traded companies on the Exchange.

(2) You are at the head of a team carrying out due diligence work at Electra, a limited company which your client, Powerful, is considering taking over. Your second in command on the team, Peter, has confided in you that in the course of his work he has met the daughter of the managing director of Electra, and he is keen to invite her on a date.

4: RULES OF PROFESSIONAL CONDUCT

(3) Your longest standing audit client is Teddies, which you have been involved in for ten years, four as engagement partner. You recently went on an extended cruise with the managing director on his yacht.

Required

Comment on the ethical and other professional issues raised by the above matters.

(**Note.** Your answer should outline the threat arising, the significance of the threat, any factors you have taken into account, and, if relevant, any safeguards you could apply to eliminate or mitigate against the threat.)

Answer

(1) In relation to Easter, there is a threat of self-interest arising, as a member of the audit team has an indirect financial interest in the client.

The **relevant factors** are as follows.

- The interest is unlikely to be **material** to the client or Paul, as the investment is recent and Paul's interest is in a pool of general investments made in the Exchange on his behalf.
- Paul is the **audit junior** and **does not have a significant role** on the audit in terms of drawing audit conclusions or audit risk areas.

The risk that arises to the independence of the audit here is **not significant**. It would be inappropriate to require Paul to divest his interest in the audit client. If I wanted to eliminate all elements of risk in this situation, I could simply change the junior assigned to my team, but such a step is not vital in this situation.

(2) In relation to Powerful, two issues arise. The first is that the firm appears to be providing multiple services to Powerful, which could raise a **self-interest threat**. The second is that the manager assigned to the due diligence assignment wants to engage in a personal relationship with a person connected to the subject of the assignment, which could create a **familiarity or intimidation threat**.

With regard to the issue of multiple services, **insufficient information** is given to draw a conclusion as to the significance of the threat. **Relevant factors** would be matters such as the nature of the services, the fee income and the team members assigned to each. **Safeguards** could include using different staff for the two assignments. The risk is likely to be significant only if one of the services provided is **audit**, which is not indicated in the question.

In relation to the second issue, the **relevant factors** are these:

- The assurance team member has a significant role on the team as second in command.
- The other party is closely connected to a key staff member at the company being reviewed.
- Timing

In this situation, the firm is carrying out a one off review of the company, and **timing is a key issue**. Presently Peter does not have a personal relationship which would significantly threaten the independence of the assignment. In this situation, the **safeguard is to request that Peter does not take any action in that direction until the assignment is completed**. If he refuses, then I may have to consider rotating my staff on this assignment, and removing him from the team.

(3) In relation to Teddies, there is a risk that my long association and personal relationship with the client will result in a **familiarity** threat. This is compounded by my acceptance of significant hospitality on a personal level which may result in a self-interest or intimidation threat.

The **relevant factors** are:

- I have been involved with the client for ten years and have a personal relationship with client staff.
- The company is not a publicly traded or public interest company.
- It is an audit assignment.

The risk arising here is **significant**, but as the client is not publicly traded, it is not insurmountable. However, it would be a good idea to implement some safeguards to mitigate against the risk. I could invite a second partner to provide a **review** of the audit of Teddies, or even consider requesting that I am **rotated** off the audit of Teddies for a period, so that the engagement partner is another partner in my firm.

In addition, I must cease accepting hospitality from the directors of Teddies since the value is not trivial and inconsequential. The cruise on the managing director's personal yacht might be seen as an inducement with the intent to improperly influence my opinion expressed in the auditor's report.

The timing of the cruise relative to the signing of the auditor's opinion, the seniority of our roles and the degree of transparency with which it was offered will be important in determining whether there was any actual intent to improperly influence my behaviour. Since the cruise has already happened, it is too late to decline the hospitality for this year's audit. Actions that might be appropriate at this stage will include:

- Informing those charged with governance of the acceptance of the hospitality
- Registering the acceptance of the cruise in a log monitored by senior management of the firm responsible for ethics compliance
- Having an independent reviewer review the audit prior to the auditor's report being signed
- Reimbursing the cost of the cruise to the managing director

---

There are other practical safeguards individual members and firms can use. Some of these have been suggested in the guidance outlined above. They are discussed in more detail in the rest of this section.

3.7 Quality management

The IAASB's quality management standard for firms, ISQM 1 *Quality management for firms that perform audits or reviews of financial statements, or other assurance or related services engagements* and ISA 220 (Revised) *Quality management for an audit of financial statements*, which we shall look at in detail in Chapter 14, contains a section looking at the firm's procedures with regard to ethics and, in particular, independence.

> **ISQM 1.29**
>
> The firm shall establish the following quality objectives that address the fulfilment of responsibilities in accordance with relevant ethical requirements, including those related to independence:
>
> (a) The firm and its personnel:
>
>   (i) Understand the relevant ethical requirements to which the firm and the firm's engagements are subject; and
>
>   (ii) Fulfil their responsibilities in relation to the relevant ethical requirements to which the firm and the firm's engagements are subject.
>
> (b) Others, including the network, network firms, individuals in the network or network firms, or service providers, who are subject to the relevant ethical requirements to which the firm and the firm's engagements are subject:
>
>   (i) Understand the relevant ethical requirements that apply to them; and
>
>   (ii) Fulfil their responsibilities in relation to the relevant ethical requirements that apply to them.

At least annually, firms are required to obtain a documented confirmation of compliance with independence requirements from all personnel required by relevant ethical requirements to be independent.

Engagement partners have responsibilities relating to ethical requirements on individual engagements designated by ISA 220. This states engagement partners shall have an understanding of the relevant ethical requirements, including those related to independence, that are applicable given the nature and circumstances of the audit engagement.

> **ISA 220.17**
>
> The engagement partner shall take responsibility for other members of the engagement team having been made aware of relevant ethical requirements that are applicable given the nature and circumstances of the audit engagement, and the firm's related policies or procedures, including those that address:
>
> (a) Identifying, evaluating and addressing threats to compliance with relevant ethical requirements, including those related to independence;
>
> (b) Circumstances that may cause a breach of relevant ethical requirements, including those related to independence, and the responsibilities of members of the engagement team when they become aware of breaches; and
>
> (c) The responsibilities of members of the engagement team when they become aware of an instance of non-compliance with laws and regulations by the entity.

If there is an indication that a threat to compliance with relevant ethical requirements exists, the engagement partner shall evaluate the threat and take appropriate action.

The engagement partner shall remain alert throughout the audit engagement, through observation and making inquiries as necessary, for breaches of relevant ethical requirements or the firm's related policies or procedures by members of the engagement team. If there is an indication that relevant ethical requirements have not been fulfilled, the engagement partner, in consultation with others in the firm, shall take appropriate action. Appropriate actions may include:

- Following the firm's policies or procedures regarding breaches of relevant ethical requirements, including communicating to or consulting with the appropriate individuals so that appropriate action can be taken, including as applicable, disciplinary action(s)
- Communicating with those charged with governance
- Communicating with regulatory authorities or professional bodies. In some circumstances, communication with regulatory authorities may be required by law or regulation.
- Seeking legal advice.
- Withdrawing from the audit engagement when withdrawal is possible under applicable law or regulation.

Prior to dating the auditor's report, the engagement partner shall take responsibility for determining whether relevant ethical requirements, including those related to independence, have been fulfilled.

3.8 Procedures to resolve ethical problems

Safeguards required should be assessed by an independent partner. They might include:

- Rotation of the senior engagement partner
- Rotation of the audit staff

The IESBA *Code of Ethics* states that firms should have established policies to resolve conflict and should follow those established policies.

Professional accountants should consider:

- The facts
- The ethical issues involved
- Related fundamental principles
- Established internal (firm) procedures
- Alternative courses of action

If professional accountants cannot resolve the matter, they should no longer be associated with the matter.

4 Confidentiality

> **FAST FORWARD**
>
> A professional accountant shall comply with the principle of confidentiality, which requires an accountant to respect the confidentiality of information acquired in the course of professional and business relationships.

Confidential information is any information, data or other material in whatever for or medium (including written, electronic, visual or oral) that is not publicly available. An accountant shall:

- Be alert to the possibility of inadvertent disclosure, including in a social environment, and particularly to a close business associate or an immediate or a close family member.
- Maintain confidentiality of information within the firm or employing organisation.
- Maintain confidentiality of information disclosed by a prospective client or employing organisation.

- Not disclose confidential information acquired as a result of professional and business relationships outside the firm or employing organisation without proper and specific authority unless there is a legal or professional duty or right to disclose.
- Not use confidential information acquired as a result of professional and business relationships for the personal advantage of the accountant or for the advantage of a third party.
- Not use or disclose any confidential information, either acquired or received as a result of a professional or business relationship, after that relationship has ended.
- Take reasonable steps to ensure that personnel under the accountant's control, and individuals from whom advice and assistance are obtained, comply with the accountant's duty of confidentiality.

Accountants must take action to protect the confidentiality of information in the course of its collection, use transfer, storage, retention, dissemination and lawful destruction.

In exchange for this duty of confidence owed by the auditor to the client, the client must agree to disclose in full all information relevant to the engagement. The professional accountant must make the client aware of the duty of confidentiality, and of the fact that it can be overridden where there is a right or duty to disclose.

4.1 Exceptions to the rule of confidentiality

Binding though the duty of confidence is, there are nevertheless exceptions to it. The Code identifies two general circumstances where disclosure may be appropriate.

- Disclosure is required by law or regulation (eg for legal proceedings).
- There is a professional duty or right to disclose or use, when not prohibited by law or regulation (eg to comply with a quality review by a professional body such as AIA; to respond to an investigation by a regulatory body; to protect the professional accountant's interests in legal proceedings; to comply with technical and professional standards, including ethics requirements).

In deciding whether to disclose, some general factors to consider include:

- Whether it would harm the interests of all parties (including third parties)
- Whether all relevant information is known and substantiated
- The type of communication that is expected
- Whether the parties to whom the communication is addressed are appropriate recipients

> **RPQ students**
>
> Under ISA 250A *Consideration of laws and regulations in an audit of financial statements*, if auditors become aware of an identified or suspected non-compliance with law and regulation this may give rise to a duty to report to an appropriate authority outside the entity under law, regulation or relevant ethical requirements. The auditor may need to seek legal advice or consider withdrawal from the engagement.

4.2 Insider dealing

Key term

> **Insider dealing** can be described as dealing in securities while in possession of insider information as an insider, the securities being price-affected by the information.
>
> There are various anti-avoidance measures in legislation, including those relating to the disclosure of information to other parties. *(UK Criminal Justice Act 1993)*

Auditors can be seen as insiders in the context of insider dealing as they are privy to sensitive information which might price-affect the securities.

For auditors, the duty not to deal as an insider is an extension of their professional duty of confidentiality which they owe to clients. This duty of confidentiality does not just cover information passed to third parties but information used for personal gain.

Audit firms must take care that the insider dealing regulations are not breached for two reasons: the law and their professional duties. Many firms insist that their staff sign forms each year which state that neither they nor any of their 'connected persons' have dealt in any client company shares.

4.2.1 Staff disclosure procedures

If such confirmations reveal that relationships do exist, the firm should lay down clear procedures for ensuring that the member of staff concerned is not involved in undertaking work for that client on behalf of the firm and that controls exist from preventing that member of staff from having access to the files on the client if considered prudent. Such restrictions can easily be set up in computer systems.

5 Conflicts of interest

> Auditors should identify potential conflicts of interest as they could result in the ethical codes being breached.

There are two kinds of conflict of interest:

- Conflicts between the interests of different clients
- Conflicts between members' and clients' interests

Audit firms should take reasonable steps to identify circumstances that could pose a conflict of interest. Examples of conflicts of interest include:

- Using confidential information obtained during an audit to help another client to acquire the audit client
- Advising two clients at the same time who are competing to acquire the same company
- Providing services to both a vendor and a purchaser in relation to the same transaction
- Representing two clients who are in a legal dispute with each other (eg during divorce proceedings)

The Code emphasises the importance of considering potential conflicts of interest **before accepting** a new client. An issue here is first identifying that there is a conflict – it may be that, for example, the engagement partner for a new client is not aware that there is a conflict because they do not know all of the firm's other clients. It is therefore necessary to have an effective conflict identification process.

As with all threats, safeguards should be applied if necessary. If safeguards would not be enough, then the engagement should be declined or discontinued. This is because a conflict of interest could result in the ethical code being breached (for example, if it results in a self-interest threat arising). Possible safeguards include:

- Disclosure of the nature of the conflict of interest (and related safeguards) to clients affected, to obtain their consent to the professional accountant performing the services

- Mechanisms to prevent unauthorised disclosure of confidential information, such as:
    - Separate engagement teams
    - Creating separate areas of practice for specialty functions within the firm
    - Establishing policies and procedures to limit access to client files (such as passwords)

- Review of safeguards by a senior individual not involved with the engagement(s)

- External review by a professional accountant

- Consulting with third parties, such as a professional body, legal counsel or another professional accountant

- Clear guidelines for the respective teams on issues of security and confidentiality

- The use of confidentiality agreements signed by the partners and staff

Disclosure is the key safeguard here. If the client refuses to give consent, then the engagement giving rise to the conflict should be discontinued.

6 Professional scepticism

> **FAST FORWARD**
>
> All professional accountants (including auditors) are required to exercise professional scepticism when planning and performing audits, reviews and other assurance engagements in order to scrutinise and challenge what is placed before them.

The IESBA Code cites three categories where professional scepticism can be applied:

Integrity	'For example, the accountant complies with the principle of integrity by: • Being straightforward and honest when raising concerns about a position taken by a client. • Pursuing inquiries about inconsistent information and seeking further audit evidence to address concerns about statements that might be materially false or misleading in order to make informed decisions about the appropriate course of action in the circumstances. • Having the strength of character to act appropriately, even when facing pressure to do otherwise or when doing so might create potential adverse personal or organisational consequences. Acting appropriately involves: (a) Standing one's ground when confronted by dilemmas and difficult situations (b) Challenging others as and when circumstances warrant, in a manner appropriate to the circumstances.'
Objectivity	'For example, the accountant complies with the principle of objectivity by: • Recognising circumstances or relationships such as familiarity with the client, that might compromise the accountant's professional or business judgement. • Considering the impact of such circumstances and relationships on the accountant's judgement when evaluating the sufficiency and appropriateness of audit evidence related to a matter material to the client's financial statements.'
Professional competence and due care	'For example, the accountant complies with the principle of professional competence and due care by: • Applying knowledge that is relevant to a particular client's industry and business activities in order to properly identify risks of material misstatement. • Designing and performing appropriate audit procedures. • Applying relevant knowledge when critically assessing whether audit evidence is sufficient and appropriate in the circumstances'

(IESBA Code: para 120.16 A2)

The IESBA Code requires all professional accountants to have an **inquiring mind** when identifying, evaluating and addressing threats to the fundamental principles. Having an inquiring mind involves:

- Considering the source, relevance and sufficiency of information obtained, taking into account the nature, scope and outputs of the professional activity being undertaken.
- Being open and alert to a need for further investigation or other action.

The Code also highlights the importance of being aware of conscious and unconscious **bias**.

Chapter Roundup

- Accountants require an ethical code because they hold positions of trust, and people rely on them.
- Professional accountants must maintain independence.
- The IESBA *Code of Ethics* gives examples of a number of situations where independence might be threatened and suggests safeguards to independence.
- A professional accountant shall comply with the principle of confidentiality, which requires an accountant to respect the confidentiality of information acquired as a result of professional and business relationships
- Auditors should identify potential conflicts of interest as they could result in the ethical codes being breached.
- All professional accountants (including auditors) are required to exercise professional scepticism when planning and performing audits, reviews and other assurance engagements in order to scrutinise and challenge what is placed before them.

Quick Quiz

1. Match the fundamental ethical principle to the characteristic.

    (a) Integrity

    (b) Objectivity

        (i) To be straightforward and honest in all professional and business relationships.

        (ii) To exercise professional or business judgement without being compromised by bias, conflict of interest, or undue influence of, or undue reliance on, individuals, organisations, technology and other factors.

2. Name five general threats to independence.

    (1) ....

    (2) ....

    (3) ....

    (4) ....

    (5) ....

3. Name three relevant safeguards against a financial interest in a client.

    (1) ....

    (2) ....

    (3) ....

4. Complete the definition.

    .... are fees calculated on a pre-determined basis relating to the outcome or result of a transaction of the result of the work performed.

5. What is a specialist valuation?

6. Complete the following definition.

    Insider dealing can be described as .... in .... while in possession of .... as an insider, the securities being .... - .... by the information.

PART A REGULATORY ISSUES AND PROFESSIONAL PRACTICES

Answers to Quick Quiz

1. (a)(i), (b)(ii)

2. (1) Self-review
   (2) Self-interest
   (3) Familiarity
   (4) Intimidation
   (5) Advocacy

3. (1) Disposing of the interest
   (2) Removing the relevant individual from the audit team
   (3) Review of work undertaken by team member with the financial interest

4. Contingent fees

5. They include:

   Actuarial valuation, valuation of intellectual property and brands, other intangible assets, property and unquoted investments

6. Dealing, securities, insider information, price-affected

End of Chapter Question

Flatbuilder plc (AIA November 2006 amended)

The engagement partner in charge of the external audit of Flatbuilder plc has recently purchased a flat from the company. He paid the full market price for the flat. In the interests of full disclosure, he notified the other partners in his office of the purchase and showed them all of the correspondence. His colleagues were most concerned by the following.

- The partner arranged the transaction by dealing directly with the company's finance director and had no direct contact with the sales staff.

- Flatbuilder plc has agreed to have the flat professionally decorated and carpeted at no extra cost. The company normally sells flats undecorated and uncarpeted.

- Flatbuilder plc has asked a bank to give the partner a mortgage on preferential terms. The bank is an independent third party, but has had substantial business dealings with Flatbuilder plc. The bank has offered the partner a mortgage at a substantially reduced rate of interest.

Required

(a) Explain whether the above transaction is acceptable. **(6 marks)**

(b) Explain how the audit firm should deal with this issue in terms of both its treatment of the partner and the ongoing audit relationship with the audit problems arising from the above concerns. **(7 marks)**

(c) Explain why an audit firm might have a formal system for reporting and discussing ethical concerns affecting partners and staff. **(7 marks)**

(Total 20 marks)

PART A REGULATORY ISSUES AND PROFESSIONAL PRACTICES

The public interest

Topic list	Syllabus reference
1 Safeguarding independence	LO3
2 Implementing professional ethics	LO3
3 Public Expectations	LO3
4 Developments in Audit Reporting	LO3

Introduction

The public interest is a key consideration for the audit profession. It is to this end that auditors work together with the already existing governance structures of their clients, particularly where those clients are large. This is the subject of section 1.

In section 2 we consider the difficulties involved in implementing professional ethics, covering the balancing act that must be performed between proximity to, and independence from, clients. The issue of the gap between public expectations of audit and the reality arises, which is covered in more detail in section 3.

Finally in section 4 we look at recent developments in auditor reporting, which have aimed to make the audit more relevant to the needs of the public.

1 Safeguarding independence

> **FAST FORWARD**
> The auditor works alongside the company's audit committee and corporate governance mechanisms in order to provide a high quality audit.

1.1 Audit committee

The FRC's *Guidance on Audit Committees* provides useful information on what audit committees do and how they should work. The audit committee's role is varied, but it includes the following elements.

Annual reports. The audit committee reviews **significant issues and judgements** in financial reporting. Management is responsible for preparing the financial statements – the audit committee then reviews them, taking into account the external auditor's point of view.

Internal controls and risk management systems. These systems are **management's responsibility**, but the audit committee reviews them and approves statements made about them in the annual report.

Internal audit. The audit committee reviews the effectiveness of the internal audit function, including assessing whether one is needed (if it is not already present).

External audit. The audit committee is responsible for overseeing the company's relations with the external auditor:

Role and responsibilities of audit committee towards external auditor	
Appointment and tendering	The audit committee **makes a recommendation on the appointment**, reappointment and removal of the external auditors. If this is not accepted, then the **annual report** must contain a statement explaining the differing opinions of the audit committee and the board.
	The committee **assesses the auditor's qualifications, expertise, resources, and independence annually**.
	Public interest entities put the audit out to **tender** at least every **ten years**.
Terms and remuneration	The audit committee **approves the terms of engagement and the remuneration** of the **external auditor**.
	The audit committee reviews: • The engagement letter (each year) • The scope of the audit
Annual audit cycle	At the start of each annual audit cycle, the audit committee ensures appropriate plans exist for the audit.
	The committee considers whether the **auditor's overall work** plan, including planned levels of **materiality**, and proposed **resources are appropriate**.
	The committee **discusses with auditor**: • Major issues found • Key judgements • Levels of errors, including uncorrected misstatements
	The committee reviews: • Written representations from management • Auditor's management letter

Role and responsibilities of audit committee towards external auditor	
	The committee reviews the effectiveness of the audit process annually, and reports to the board on its findings.
Independence	The committee **assess auditor's independence annually**.
	The committee recommends and develops **company's policy on the provision of non-audit services** by the auditor.

1.2 Working with the audit committee

From the point of view of the external auditor, the audit committee would be included within what auditing standards (ISAs) call 'Those charged with governance' (TCWG). The following definition comes from ISA 260 *Communication With Those Charged With Governance*:

Key terms

> **Those charged with governance** The person(s) or organisation(s) (eg a corporate trustee) with responsibility for overseeing the strategic direction of the entity and obligations related to the accountability of the entity. This includes overseeing the financial reporting process. For some entities in some jurisdictions, those charged with governance may include management personnel – for example, executive members of a governance board of a private or public sector entity, or an owner-manager.
>
> In the UK, those charged with governance include the directors (executive and non-executive) of a company and the members of an audit committee where one exists. For other types of entity it usually includes equivalent persons such as the partners, proprietors, committee of management, or trustees.

In addition to reporting to shareholders, the external auditor is expected to communicate matters of **audit importance** to TCWG. This should be an ongoing, two-way dialogue and is initiated at the engagement stage to avoid any omissions, as well as **how** (in writing) and **when** (described in the ISA as 'timely').

The **items to be communicated** relate to the **auditor's responsibilities** as part of the audit and information relevant to the audit from TCWG, as well as any **issues arising** from the audit. This is sometimes referred to as a **report to management** and includes **significant findings** from the audit, such as views about the chosen **accounting policies**, **difficulties** encountered **during the audit** and any other matters relevant to the **oversight of the financial reporting purpose**.

ISA 260 advocates a process of communication that is both **ongoing** and **two-way**. The auditor must do more than simply send a management letter at the end of the audit.

The auditor may communicate with the whole board, the supervisory board or the audit committee depending on the governance structure of the organisation. To avoid misunderstandings, the **engagement letter** should explain that auditors will only communicate matters that come to their attention as a **result** of the **performance** of the audit. It should state that the auditors are **not required** to **perform procedures** for the purpose of identifying matters of governance interest; however, if the auditors have agreed any specific matters of governance interest to be communicated, it will set these out.

1.2.1 Communication process

The **communication process will vary with the circumstances**, including:

- The size and governance structure of the entity
- How those charged with governance operate
- The auditor's view of the significance of the matters to be communicated

For example, reports of relatively minor matters to a small client may be best handled orally via a meeting or telephone conversation.

Before communicating matters with those charged with governance, the auditor may discuss them with management, unless that is inappropriate. For example, it would not be appropriate to discuss questions of management's competence or integrity with management.

> **Exam focus point**
>
> The May 2022 exam contained a 25 mark scenario question on audit committees. Candidates were asked to assess ethical issues following an ongoing issue with the audit committee.

1.2.2 Matters to be communicated

Matters would include the following.

Matters to be communicated (ISA 260)	
The **auditor's responsibilities** in relation to the financial statements	Including that: • The auditor is responsible for forming and expressing an opinion on the financial statements • The audit does not relieve management or those charged with governance of their responsibilities
Planned **scope and timing** of the audit	Including: • How the audit proposes to address the significant risks of material misstatement from fraud or error • How the auditor plans to address areas of higher assessed risks of material misstatement • The auditor's approach to internal control • Application of materiality • The extent to which the auditor will use an auditor's expert • When ISA 701 applies, the auditor's preliminary views about matters that may be areas of significant auditor attention in the audit and therefore may be key audit matters • The auditor's planned approach to significant changes in the applicable reporting framework, environment financial condition or activities When ISA 701 applies, ISA 260 requires the auditor to communicate the most significant risks of material misstatement.
Significant findings from the audit	Including: • The auditor's views about accounting policies, accounting estimates and financial statement disclosures • Significant difficulties, if any, encountered during the audit (eg delays in provision of required information, brief time in which to complete audit, unavailability of expected information)

Matters to be communicated (ISA 260)	
	• Significant matters arising during the audit that were discussed or subject to correspondence with management • Written representations the auditor is requesting • Circumstances that affect the form and content of the auditor's report • Other significant matters including material misstatements or inconsistencies in other information that have been corrected Entities reporting on the application of the UK Corporate Governance Code must communicate to the audit committee any information relevant to the board and the audit committee in fulfilling their responsibilities under the Code. For audits of public interest entities, the auditor submits an additional report to the audit committee explaining the results of the audit, and giving the following information: • A declaration of independence • Identity of key audit partners • A description of the scope and timing of the audit • A description of the methodology used • The quantitative level of materiality applied • Events or conditions that may cast significant doubt on the entity's ability to continue as a going concern • Significant deficiencies in the system of internal control • Report significant difficulties encountered and significant matters arising from the audit
Auditor independence	In the case of public interest entities matters, include: • A statement that relevant ethical requirements regarding independence have been complied with • All relationships (including total fees for audit and non-audit services) which may reasonably be thought to bear on independence • The related safeguards that have been applied to eliminate/reduce identified threats to independence The auditor must: • Confirm to the audit committee annually that the firm and partners, senior managers and managers conducting the audit are independent • Discuss with the audit committee the threats to the auditor's independence and the safeguards applied

2 Implementing professional ethics

> **FAST FORWARD**
>
> Implementing professional ethics involves the auditor acting with an independent mindset that includes professional scepticism and professional judgement.

It is one thing to say that auditors ought simply to behave ethically, and that they should be independent of their clients; but it is quite another thing entirely to implement this in reality, since the auditor needs not only to be independent of their clients but also to rely on them. It is fundamental to the theory and practice of modern auditing that the auditor seeks to place reliance on the work done by the client's management, and that is not merely critical or dismissive of that management. Further, as we have seen above, modern corporations involve an element of independence in their governance structures; the auditor therefore does best when they work alongside these elements within the client, instead of simply pushing back against them. It is an aspect of what is sometimes called the '**expectations gap**' that this aspect of auditing is often not well understood by a public that expects auditors to be more separate from their clients than they should be – from the standpoint of the audit profession.

This approach to auditing foregrounds the auditor's **mindset**, which can be considered from the point of view of independence of mind, professional scepticism, and the exercise of professional judgement.

Key terms

> **Independence of mind**. The state of mind that permits the expression of a conclusion without being affected by influences that compromise professional judgement, thereby allowing an individual to act with integrity, and exercise objectivity and professional scepticism. (IESBA *Code of ethics*: para. 120.15 A1)
>
> **Professional judgement**. The application of relevant training, knowledge and experience, within the context provided by auditing, accounting and ethical standards, in making informed decisions about the courses of action that are appropriate in the circumstances of the audit engagement.
>
> **Professional scepticism**. An attitude that includes a questioning mind, being alert to conditions which may indicate possible misstatement due to error or fraud, and a critical assessment of evidence.
>
> (FRC *Glossary of terms - Auditing and Ethics*)

Where an auditor's mindset includes these characteristics, they would be expected to apply the fundamental principles of professional ethics (which were discussed in chapter 4).

2.1 Independence vs effectiveness

Auditor independence is rarely a matter of clear questions with black and white answers. It is not just an issue of whether the 'rules' say that an audit engagement should be accepted or declined ('yes or no'), but rather of the auditor exercising proper judgement in the complex circumstances of an actual audit.

The basic dilemma is this. The auditor must be independent of the client in order to express their own opinion on whether the client's financial statements give a true and fair view. However, the auditor must also place some trust in the client if the audit is to be conducted effectively, as they will need to rely on anything from the accounting systems and controls to explanations provided by management.

It is between the two extremes of this dilemma that the concept of 'professional scepticism' attempts to place itself:

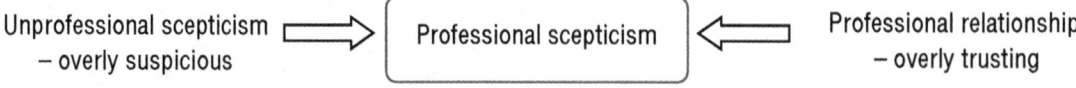

Unprofessional scepticism ⟹ Professional scepticism ⟸ Professional relationship
– overly suspicious   – overly trusting

If the auditor is **too** sceptical about everything the client does or says, then it will be impossible for them to conduct the audit effectively. At the extreme, this would mean checking every transaction in the financial statements, without accepting any internal records or documents at all as genuine. More practically, a breakdown in trust would mean that the audit would be conducted less efficiently: if the auditor must assume that management is not at all competent to prepare the financial statements, then much more audit work will need to be done than if management could be trusted. This would take more time and would make the audit more costly. Some degree of trust is therefore essential to the effective and professional running of the audit process.

On the other hand, if the auditor is not sceptical enough then the quality of the audit is likely to suffer. The auditor may easily be deceived in the case of fraud, or may mistakenly place too much trust in the validity of evidence and explanations provided by the client.

2.2 Expectations gap

The 'expectations gap' is a term used within the audit profession to refer to the gap between the expectations of the public regarding auditors, and the expectations of the audit profession itself. The auditor's responsibilities in relation to **fraud** are a key component of this gap.

The issue of the expectations gap is consistently in and out of the financial press. In recent years, there has been a focus on the role of auditors in evaluating whether a company is a going concern, as for example in the case of the collapse of Carillion in the UK. In the USA, the collapse of Lehman Brothers brought with it accusations from some quarters that its auditor, Ernst & Young, had failed to discharge its responsibilities as auditor.

A good example of such coverage relates to auditors Ernst & Young (EY) and its audit client, the Olympus Corporation. A scandal was precipitated when Olympus's recently-appointed chief executive was ousted from his position after having exposed what was described as a loss-hiding arrangement of fraudulent financial reporting. A succession of auditors had issued unmodified reports throughout this period. An internal Olympus inquiry into the fraud concluded that the scheme had been too well-concealed for the auditors to detect it:

> The masterminds of this case were hiding the illegal acts by artfully manipulating experts' opinions...

High profile cases such as these have brought up the question of the extent to which auditors should be responsible for detecting fraud, and how this differs from the way that the responsibilities of the auditor are perceived.

2.2.1 Narrowing the expectations gap

Logically, the expectations gap could be narrowed in two ways.

(1) **Educating users** – The auditor's report as outlined in ISA 700 *Forming an opinion and reporting on financial statements* includes an explanation of the auditor's responsibilities, but also quite extensive discussions of the key matters arising from the audit.

(2) **Extending the auditor's responsibilities** – Research indicates that extra work by auditors with the inevitable extra costs is **likely to make little difference to the detection of fraud** because:

- Most material frauds involve management
- More than half of frauds involve misstated financial reporting but do not include diversion of funds from the company
- Management fraud is unlikely to be found in a financial statement audit
- Far more is spent on investigating and prosecuting fraud in a company than on its audit

Suggestions for expanding the auditor's role have included:

- Requiring auditors to report to boards and audit committees on the adequacy of controls to prevent and detect fraud
- Encouraging the use of targeted forensic fraud reviews
- Increasing the requirement to report suspected frauds

3 Public expectations

> **FAST FORWARD**
>
> There is frequently a conflict between what the public wants auditors to do, and what auditors themselves are willing and able to do.

As we have seen, audit takes place within a broader regulatory and economic context. The audit profession is a vital function of economic activity; it may be claimed that in order for the economy to flourish then there must be trust, which is where audit comes in. There are a whole range of **stakeholder groups** who have an interest in what companies are doing, and who need to be able to place trust in those companies. In an ideal world, perhaps, audit would be able to guarantee transparent and trustworthy information for all of the stakeholders who have an interest in the company. But in the real world, auditors are unable to do this because there is often **conflict** between different groups about the kinds of information that is needed.

Part of the difficulty, then, is in **defining the scope of an audit**: a **broad scope** would try to meet the needs of all stakeholders, but the work required to do this would seem to expand almost infinitely - not to mention the enormous risks to which auditors would be exposed. Alternatively, a **very narrowly scoped audit** – for instance, a non-assurance engagement simply to check the financial statements on the behalf of shareholders – would be of little benefit, either to the shareholders or to anyone else in the economy. It is possible to view the modern audit as taking place between these extremes of scope.

It could be said that significant **conflict** exists between what auditors are willing and able to do, and what the public would like them to do. Auditors are sometimes seen as part of an accountancy profession that is primarily interested in earning fees from clients, with the exercise of scrutiny over those clients being only of secondary interest to them. It has been claimed that public trust in audit is so low that without fundamental reform, auditors' claims about the expectations gap are likely to continue to fall on deaf ears.

A further element of the problem has to do with the **historical origins** of the audit as a simple report to shareholders, which arose in the course of the separation between ownership and management. These include the development of limited liability companies with the Joint Stock Companies Act 1844, and the introduction of mandatory audits in the Companies Act 1900. In more recent history, an **expectation** has arisen that the audit will seek to answer questions that go beyond the purpose that was originally envisaged for the audit, and for which it was designed. For example, the public may want answers to questions such as whether a company will continue trading, or if it is a good investment, but the auditor may not be in a position to offer information about these matters, not least because they may go beyond the requirements of the accounting frameworks in terms of which they are conducting their audit.

Changes to the auditor's report in recent years have tried to make the audit more meaningful to the public (such as the inclusion of details of key audit matters), but the continuing trend of corporate casualties such as Carillion has only served to make the public sceptical of the auditor's work, and the expectation gap remains as wide as ever. Indeed, as we saw in chapter 3, there is considerable uncertainty about the future of audit in the UK, with it being claimed in many quarters that audit is simply unfit for purpose.

4 Developments in Audit Reporting

> **FAST FORWARD**
>
> Changes to the auditor's report in recent years have sought to improve communication with users and deliver greater value to the public.

As has been said above, public trust in audit is low and has been for some years. The audit market in the UK is in the midst of a process of change, with the planned replacement of the FRC by the Audit, Reporting and Governance Authority (ARGA), and the Brydon Report's proposal to uncouple the auditing profession from the accountancy profession.

But standard-setters have also sought to respond to the problem by overhauling auditing standards (ISAs) in recent years, placing a particular focus on the visible outcome of the audit: the auditor's report. If one considers the auditor's report to be an **act of communication**, then it makes sense that it is a platform for auditors to try to **regain trust**. The idea is that by providing further information to users, auditors can play a valuable role in the economy. The changes to ISAs were part of the global trend within the profession towards non-financial and integrated reporting, representing an effort to make the auditor's report more than just a 'yes/no' opinion on the financial statements, in this case by including more qualitative information about the audit.

In the UK, the FRC for some time required auditors to provide an extended discussion of the audit process, one respect in which the requirements made of UK listed company auditors were for a while ahead of the game internationally. The IAASB caught up in 2015 when it completed its project on auditor reporting, issuing a raft of new standards in the area.

The IAASB did two key things: it changed the format of the auditor's report in ISA *700 Forming an Opinion and Reporting on Financial Statements*, and introduced ISA 701 *Communicating Key Audit Matters in the Independent Auditor's Report*. The intended benefits of these changes were:

- Enhanced communication between auditors and investors, as well as those charged with corporate governance;
- Increased user confidence in audit reports and financial statements;
- Increased transparency, audit quality, and enhanced information value;
- Increased attention by management and financial statement preparers to disclosures referencing the auditor's report;
- Renewed auditor focus on matters to be reported that could result in an increase in professional scepticism; and
- Enhanced financial reporting in the public interest.

The revised auditor's report required by ISA 700 represented a **radical change** from what went before it. The main purpose of these changes was to make the auditor's report more **informative**, providing users with more relevant information based on the audit that was performed. The intention was not to create significant additional work for auditors, but to make better use of the work that auditors already do. The aim was to improve **transparency**, by helping users to understand the most significant issues the auditor faced. This should enhance the **communicative value** of the auditor's report.

ISA 701 introduced the requirement to report Key Audit Matters (KAMs) in the auditor's reports of listed companies, but they can be included by auditors of non-listed entities if so required. KAMs are those matters that, in the auditor's professional judgement, were of most significance in the audit. The disclosure of KAMs in the auditor's report effectively enables the auditor to speak to **stakeholders** and to provide further information to users of the financial statements, but without the auditor having to do much additional work, since these are matters that the auditor will have considered in any case, as part of their audit.

Chapter Roundup

- The auditor works alongside the company's audit committee and corporate governance mechanisms in order to provide a high quality audit.

- Implementing professional ethics involves the auditor acting with an independent mindset that includes professional scepticism and professional judgement.

- There is frequently a conflict between what the public wants auditors to do, and what auditors themselves are willing and able to do.

- Changes to the auditor's report in recent years have sought to improve communication with users and deliver greater value to the public.

Quick Quiz

1. Indicate whether the following statement is true or false.

    "The external audit is the sole check on the significant issues and judgements made in a company's financial reporting."

2. For companies applying the UK Corporate Governance Code, who is responsible to recommending which audit firm to appoint?

3. List the four general matters which the auditor must communicate with those charged with governance.

4. Match the term to its definition below:

    (i) Professional judgement
    (ii) Professional scepticism
    (iii) Independence of mind

    (a) An attitude that includes a questioning mind, being alert to conditions which may indicate possible misstatement due to error or fraud, and a critical assessment of evidence

    (b) The application of relevant training, knowledge and experience, within the context provided by auditing, accounting and ethical standards, in making informed decisions about the courses of action that are appropriate in the circumstances of the audit engagement

    (c) The state of mind that permits the expression of a conclusion without being affected by influences that compromise professional judgement, thereby allowing an individual to act with integrity, and exercise objectivity and professional scepticism

5. Between whom does the audit profession consider there to be an 'expectations gap'?

6. Indicate whether the following statement is true or false.

    "The inclusion of KAMs in the auditor's report means extra work for auditors."

PART A   REGULATORY ISSUES AND PROFESSIONAL PRACTICES

Answers to Quick Quiz

1. False. The audit committee is also required to review these matters.
2. This is the responsibility of the audit committee.
3. The auditor's responsibilities in relation to the financial statements, the planned scope and timing of the audit, significant findings from the audit, and auditor independence.
4. (i) b; (ii) a; (iii) c
5. The expectations gap is said to exist between the audit profession and the public.
6. False. The inclusion of KAMs in the report is intended to increase the usefulness of the auditor's report to users but without entailing significant additional work.

End of Chapter Question

Horrow (AIA May 2015 amended)

Elaine is the partner in charge of the external audit of Horrow, a chemical manufacturer. The audit for the year ended 31 March 2017 has recently been completed and Elaine is finalising the auditor's report.

Elaine's firm has audited Horrow for the past seven years and she has been the audit partner for the past two years. It has never been necessary for the firm to issue Horrow with a qualified auditor's report.

Elaine has been interested in the impact of the publication of ISA 701 *Communicating key audit matters in the independent auditor's report*. Elaine believes that this new standard is an improvement because she sees how detailed her firm's audit working papers are and how much useful information they contain and yet the shareholders to whom she reports never get to see any of that material.

Required

Draft a report to Elaine that:

(a) Critically evaluates the potential benefit to the shareholders of the external auditor adding a commentary including information about the materiality threshold and any discussion of difficult accounting issues resolved during the audit. **(10 marks)**

(b) Critically evaluates the potential implications for the external auditor of publishing Key Audit Matters. **(13 marks)**

Marks will be awarded for a professional and well-structured report and clarity of writing. **(4 marks)**

(Total 27 marks)

PART A REGULATORY ISSUES AND PROFESSIONAL PRACTICES

Professional responsibility and liability

Topic list	Syllabus reference
1 Misconduct	LO2
2 Professional liability under statute	LO2
3 Professional liability in the tort of negligence	LO2
4 Auditor accountability	LO2
5 Limitation of liability	LO2
6 Money laundering and bribery	LO2

Introduction

Auditors have responsibilities to several parties. This chapter explores the various **responsibilities** and the **liability that can arise** in respect of them. It also looks at safeguards against the liabilities, particularly the issue of insurance, covered in Section 5.

The auditor's responsibility to members and other readers of the accounts in tort and contract can give rise to **liability**, particularly in the event of **negligence**. Case law on this matter is complex and not wholly satisfactory. It results in auditors being liable to some readers and not others. However, **auditor's liability** is a dynamic issue in that it **evolves as cases are brought to court**.

There are some interesting **current developments** for auditors with regard to liability, for example the **negotiations** that auditors are now entitled to have with their clients over liability limitation.

The legal issues arising in connection with money laundering and suspicion of money laundering are a practical, important issue for auditors.

PART A REGULATORY ISSUES AND PROFESSIONAL PRACTICES

1 Misconduct

FAST FORWARD Misconduct includes (but is not confined to) any act or default likely to bring discredit to the member, relevant firm or registered student in question.

1.1 Prohibition of misconduct

The AIA's by-laws state that members, relevant firms and registered students shall be liable to disciplinary action if he or it, in the course of carrying out his or its professional duties or otherwise, has been guilty of misconduct.

They go on to say that the following are **conclusive proof** of misconduct:

- Pleading or being found guilty of any offence discreditable to him, the Association or the profession before a competent court; or
- Being found to have acted fraudulently or dishonestly by a competent court.

Any code of practice, ethical or technical, adopted by the AIA Council and any regulation affecting members, relevant firms or registered students laid down or approved by the Council' may be considered when determining whether misconduct had taken place.

1.2 Types of misconduct

The AIA gives examples of misconduct; these include convictions relating to personal life, for example:

- Obtaining money/goods by false pretences
- Forgery
- Theft
- Other offences involving dishonesty

However, the disciplinary committee judges each case on its merits. The investigations committee **might** take a more lenient view if the conviction had arisen over a petty issue, such as a student prank, or isolated instances of disorderliness due to intoxication.

Honesty is considered to be a key virtue of accountants. This is because they are people in a **position of trust**. Therefore incidents involving dishonesty will be taken seriously.

1.3 Penalties

The penalties for misconduct are at the discretion of the Investigations, Disciplinary and Appeals Committees.

Question Misconduct

Elizabeth is a student member of AIA. She has worked for the firm Kendall Watts for two years, and has nearly completed her final exams.

On Saturday, Elizabeth threw a hen weekend for her best friend Annie. During that weekend, and under the influence of alcohol, Elizabeth was dared to steal a bottle of champagne from a shop. Elizabeth took the dare and was caught by the shopkeeper. The shop is going to prosecute, and the whole incident was caught on the shop's security cameras.

Comment on the issues arising from this situation.

Answer

The AIA's by-laws state that a member is likely to be subject to disciplinary action if they, in the course of carrying out professional duties, or otherwise, have been guilty of misconduct.

Misconduct is described as any act or default likely to bring discredit to the member or registered student in question.

It is important to note that the rules in regard of misconduct do relate to students as well as members of AIA, so that despite the fact that Elizabeth is not a full member, AIA will potentially be interested in this matter.

Misconduct?

It is important to assess whether the act of shoplifting in this scenario would constitute misconduct. It does not matter that it did not occur in business life, as AIA is concerned with any matters which discredit the person involved.

AIA gives 'theft' as an example of misconduct. The AIA by-laws state that being found guilty of an offence discreditable to the member is **conclusive proof** of misconduct. Hence if Elizabeth is found guilty of the offence by the court, which is likely given the evidence against her, she will have been guilty of misconduct.

Mitigation?

The disciplinary committee considers each case on its merits. It may take a more lenient view if the conviction has arisen as a result of a prank and is a petty issue. While Elizabeth's conviction has arisen in the course of a prank, it arguable whether it is merely a petty issue, and this does not really seem to fall into the category of 'harmless student prank'.

Action by AIA

As stated above, the disciplinary committee will handle each case on its merits, so it is impossible to predict the level of punishment that AIA would consider necessary in this case. Elizabeth could be suspended from student membership for a period, or have to wait a period before she can apply for full membership. She might be fined. Alternatively, a more serious view might be taken, and she might be excluded from membership for longer, or permanently.

2 Professional liability under statute

> **FAST FORWARD** Auditors may have professional liability under statutory law.

Under certain legislation, notably **insolvency** legislation, auditors may be found to be officers of the company and could be charged with criminal offences or found liable for civil offences in connection with the winding up of the company.

Auditors may also be found guilty of the offence of **insider dealing**, which is a criminal offence, as they are privy to inside information. We considered insider dealing in Chapter 4.

Auditors could be found guilty of a criminal offence if they knew or suspected a person was carrying out **money laundering** offences and they failed to report their suspicions to the proper authority. We shall look at these laws, and their impact on auditors, in Section 6 of this chapter.

PART A   REGULATORY ISSUES AND PROFESSIONAL PRACTICES

3 Professional liability in the tort of negligence

FAST FORWARD Auditors may have professional liability in the tort of negligence.

Negligence is a common law concept. It seeks to provide compensation to a person who has suffered loss due to another person's wrongful neglect. To succeed in an action for negligence, an injured party must prove three things:

(a) A **duty of care** which is enforceable at law existed.

(b) This duty of care was **breached**.

(c) The breach caused the injured party **loss**. In the case of negligence in relation to financial advisers/auditors, this loss must be pecuniary (ie financial) loss.

3.1 Who might bring an action for negligence?

The parties likely to want to bring an action in negligence against the auditors, for example, if they have given the wrong audit opinion through lack of care, are parties such as:

- The company
- Shareholders
- The bank
- Other lenders
- Other interested third parties

A key differences between the various potential claimants is the **nature** of the **duty of care** owed to them.

3.2 The audit client

FAST FORWARD The auditor owes a duty of care to the audit client automatically under law.

The audit client is the **company**. It is a basic maxim of company law that the company is all the shareholders acting as a body. In other words, the company in this respect, cannot be represented by a single shareholder.

| COMPANY | = | SHAREHOLDERS AS A BODY |

| COMPANY | ≠ | SHAREHOLDER | + | SHAREHOLDER |

The **company** has a **contract** with the audit firm. In the law of many countries, a contract for the supply of a service such as an audit has a duty or reasonable care implied into it by statute.

In other words, whatever the express terms of any written contract between the company and the audit firm, the law always implies a duty of care into it. Therefore, if the company (all the shareholders acting as a body) want to bring a case for negligence, the situation would be as follows.

CLIENT	
Duty of care exists?	AUTOMATIC
Breached?	MUST BE PROVED
Loss arising?	MUST BE PROVED

In order to prove whether a duty of care had been breached, the court has to give further consideration to what the duty of 'reasonable' care means in practice.

3.2.1 The auditor's duty of care

The standard of work of auditors is generally as defined by legislation. A number of judgements made in law cases show how the auditor's duty of care has been gauged at various points in time because legislation often does not clearly state the manner in which the auditors should discharge their duty of care. It is also not likely that this would be clearly spelt out in any contract setting out the terms of an auditor's appointment.

Case Study

Re Kingston Cotton Mill

When Lopes L J considered the degree of skill and care required of an auditor he declared:

'... it is the duty of an auditor to bring to bear on the work he has to perform that skill, care and caution which a reasonably competent, careful and cautious auditor would use. What is reasonable skill, care and caution, must depend on the particular circumstances of each case.'

Lopes was careful to point out that what constitutes reasonable care depends very much upon the **facts** of a particular case. Another criterion by which the courts will determine the adequacy of the auditors' work is by assessing it in relation to the generally accepted auditing standards of the day.

Case Study

The courts will be very much concerned with accepted advances in auditing techniques, demonstrated by Pennycuick J in *Re Thomas Gerrard & Son Ltd 1967* where he observed:

'... the real ground on which *Re Kingston Cotton Mill* ... is, I think, capable of being distinguished is that the standards of reasonable care and skill are, upon the expert evidence, more exacting today than those which prevailed in 1896.'

Case Study

Lord Denning in the case of *Fomento (Sterling Area) Ltd v Selsdon Fountain Pen Co Ltd 1958* sought to define the auditor's proper approach to their work by saying:

'... they must come to it with an inquiring mind – not suspicious of dishonesty .... – but suspecting that someone may have made a mistake somewhere and that a check must be made to ensure that there has been none.'

The auditors have a responsibility to keep themselves abreast of professional developments. Auditing standards are likely to be taken into account when the adequacy of the work of auditors is being considered in a court of law or in other contested situations.

When the auditors are exercising judgement they must act both honestly and carefully. Obviously, if auditors are to be 'careful' in forming an opinion, they must give due consideration to all relevant matters. Provided they do this and can be seen to have done so, then their opinion should be above criticism.

However, if the opinion reached by the auditors is one that no reasonably competent auditor would have been likely to reach then they would still possibly be held negligent. This is because however carefully the auditors may appear to have approached their work, it clearly could not have been careful enough, if it enabled them to reach a conclusion which would be generally regarded as unacceptable.

If the auditor's suspicions are aroused, they must conduct further investigations until such suspicions are either confirmed or allayed. Over the years, there have been many occasions where the courts have had to consider cases in which it has been held, on the facts of those cases, that the auditors ought to have been put upon enquiry.

3.3 Third parties

FAST FORWARD

The auditor only owes a duty of care to parties other than the audit client if one has been established.

'Third parties' in this context means anyone other than the company (audit client) who wished to make a claim for negligence. It therefore includes any individual shareholders in the company and any potential investors. It also includes, importantly, the bank, who is very often a key financier of the company.

The key difference between third parties and the company is that third parties have no contract with the audit firm. There is therefore no implied duty of care. The situation is therefore as follows.

THIRD PARTIES	
Duty of care exists?	MUST BE PROVED
Breached?	MUST BE PROVED
Loss arising?	MUST BE PROVED

Traditionally the courts have been **averse** to **attributing a duty of care to third parties** to the auditor. We can see this by looking at some past cases that have gone to court. Some of this law may appear UK-based only, but it tends to be applicable world-wide.

A **very important case** is *Caparo Industries plc v Dickman and Others 1990*, which is described here.

Case Study

The **facts as pleaded** were that in 1984 Caparo Industries purchased 100,000 Fidelity shares in the open market. On June 12, 1984, the date on which the accounts (audited by Touche Ross) were published, they purchased a further 50,000 shares. Relying on information in the accounts, further shares were acquired. On September 4, Caparo made a bid for the remainder and by October had acquired control of Fidelity. Caparo alleged that the accounts on which they had relied were misleading in that an apparent pre-tax profit of some £1.3 million should in fact have been shown as a loss of over £400,000. The plaintiffs argued that Touche owed a duty of care to investors and potential investors.

The conclusion of the **House of Lords** hearing of the case in February 1990 was that the auditors of a public company's accounts owed **no duty of care** to members of the public at large who relied upon the accounts in deciding to buy shares in the company. And as a purchaser of further shares, while relying upon the auditor's report, a shareholder stood in the same position as any other investing member of the public to whom the auditor owed no duty. The purpose of the audit was simply that of fulfilling the statutory requirements of the Companies Act 1985. There was nothing in the statutory duties of company auditors to suggest that they were intended to protect the interests of investors in the market. And in particular, there was no reason why any special relationship should be held to arise simply from the fact that the affairs of the company rendered it susceptible to a takeover bid.

The Cadbury Report on Corporate Governance in the UK (in 1992) gave an opinion on the situation as reflected in the *Caparo* ruling. It felt that *Caparo* did not lessen the auditor's duty to use skill and care because auditors are **still fully liable in negligence** to the companies they audit and their shareholders collectively. Given the number of different users of accounts, it was impossible for the House of Lords to have broadened the boundaries of the auditor's legal duty of care.

The decision in *Caparo v Dickman* considerably **narrowed the auditor's potential liability to third parties**. The judgement appears to imply that members of various such user groups, which could include creditors, potential investors or others, will not be able to sue the auditors for negligence by virtue of their placing reliance on audited annual accounts.

Case Study

In *James McNaughton Paper Group Ltd v Hicks Anderson & Co 1990,* Lord Justice Neill set out the following position in the light of *Caparo* and earlier cases:

(a) In England a restrictive approach was now adopted to any extension of the scope of the duty of care beyond the person directly intended by the maker of the statement to act upon it.

(b) In deciding whether a duty of care existed in any particular case it was necessary to take all the circumstances into account.

(c) Notwithstanding (b), it was possible to identify certain matters which were likely to be of importance in most cases in reaching a decision as to whether or not a duty existed.

Another court case produced a **development** in the subject of audit liability. In December 1995, a High Court judge awarded electronic security group ADT £65 million plus interest and costs (£40m) in damages for negligence against the former BDO Binder Hamlyn (BBH) partnership.

Case Study

The firm had jointly audited the 1988/89 financial statements of Britannia Security Group (BSG), which ADT acquired in 1990 for £105 million, but later found to be worth only £40 million. Although, under *Caparo*, auditors do not owe a duty of care in general to third parties, the judge found that BBH audit partner Martyn Bishop, who confirmed that the firm stood by BSG's accounts at a meeting with ADT in the run-up to the acquisition, had thereby **taken on a contractual relationship** with ADT. This development has occurred, apparently, because (post-*Caparo*) solicitors and bankers are advising clients intent on acquisitions to get direct assurances from the target's auditors on the truth and fairness of the financial statements.

BBH appealed this decision; the liable partners, because of a shortfall in insurance cover, were left facing the prospect of coming up with £34 million. An out of court settlement was reached with ADT.

A case in 1997 appeared to take a slightly different line, although this case related to some management accounts on which no written report had been issued.

Case Study

In *Peach Publishing Ltd v Slater & Co 1997* the Court of Appeal ruled that accountants are not automatically liable if they give oral assurances on accounts to the purchaser of a business. The case involved management accounts, which the accountant stated the accounts were right subject to the qualification that they had not been audited. The Court held that the purpose of giving the assurance was not to take on responsibility to the purchaser for the accuracy of the accounts. The purchaser's true objective in this case was to obtain a warranty from the accountant's client, the target. Therefore the accountant was not assuming responsibility to the purchaser but giving his client information on which it could decide whether or not to give the warranty. The Court of Appeal also observed that the purchaser should not have relied on the management accounts without having them checked by its advisers.

# Case Study

In a further case the Court of Appeal gave guidance on the effect of a disclaimer which stated that the report had been prepared for the client only and no-one else should rely on it. In *Omega Trust Co Ltd v Wright Son & Pepper 1997* (which related to surveyors but the facts of which can be applied to accountants) the Court held that the surveyor was entitled to know who his client was and to whom his duty was held. He was entitled to refuse liability to an unknown lender or any known lender with whom he had not agreed.

All this case law raised some **problems**. In spite of the judgement in *Caparo*, the commercial reality is that creditors and investors (especially institutional ones) do use audited accounts. The UK Companies Act requires most companies to file accounts with the Registrar. Why is this a statutory requirement? It is surely because the public, including creditors and potential investors, have a need for a credible and independent view of the company's performance and position.

It would be unjust if auditors, who have **secondary responsibility** for financial statements being prepared negligently, bore the full responsibility for losses arising from such negligence just because they are insured. It would also be unjust if the auditors could be sued by all and sundry. While the profession has generally welcomed *Caparo*, two obvious problems are raised by decision.

- Is a restricted view of the usefulness of audited financial statements in the profession's long-term interests?
- For private companies there will probably be an increase in the incidence of personal guarantees and warranties given by the directors to banks and suppliers.

Recent developments in the US appear to try and redress the **balance of liability** by highlighting the responsibilities of management with regard to published financial statements. The UK has also seen some recent developments. The UK Companies Act 2006 requires the Directors' Report to contain a statement to the effect that in the case of each director:

(a) So far as the director is aware, there is no relevant audit information of which the auditor is unaware.

(b) He has taken all the steps that he ought to have taken, as a director, in order to make himself aware of any relevant audit information and to establish that the auditor is aware of that information.

If the statement in the Directors' Report is false, every director who knew it was false or who was reckless as to whether it was false, and failed to take reasonable steps to prevent the report from being approved, commits an offence. In addition, the requirements of the UK Corporate Governance Code set out the responsibilities of those charged with governance in companies to manage risk properly on behalf of shareholders and to report to them on management and financial issues.

3.3.1 Banks and other major lenders

Banks and other major lenders have generally been excluded from the extent of negligent auditor's liability by the decision in *Caparo*.

Banks often include clauses in loan agreements referring to audited accounts and requesting that they have access to audited accounts on a regular basis or when reviewing the loan facility. In other words, banks may **document a 'relationship'** with the auditors to establish that a duty of care exists.

A Scottish case involved a situation similar to this and may suggest that judicial thinking on the matter is developing.

Case Study

In a *Royal Bank of Scotland v Bannerman Johnstone Maclay and Others 2002* the bank, who provided an overdraft facility to the company being audited, claimed the company had misstated its position due to a fraud and that the auditors were negligent in not discovering the fraud. The auditors claimed that they had no duty of care to the bank. However, the judge determined that the auditors would have known that the bank required audited accounts as part of the overdraft arrangement and could have issued a disclaimer to the bank. The fact that they had not issued a disclaimer was an important factor in deciding that the auditors did owe a duty of care to the bank.

3.4 Settlements out of court

Many liability claims are settled out of court. The advantages of doing so are claimed to be a **saving** in **time** and **cost**, and also perhaps a **lower settlement**. An out of court settlement also avoids a high profile court case which **potentially damages** a firm's **reputation**.

Arguments against an out of court settlement include the allegations that they often arise through the **unwillingness** of an auditor's **insurance company** to risk a settlement in court. An out of court settlement also **leaves** the **question** of the audit **firm's responsibility unsettled**, but nevertheless the firm's **insurance premiums** may **rise**.

Exam focus point

Read the financial and accountancy press on a regular basis between now and your examination and note any new cases or developments in the question of auditor liability.

 Question — Negligence claims

Although auditors can incur civil liability under various statutes it is far more likely that they will incur liability for negligence under the common law, as the majority of cases against auditors have been in this area. Auditors must be fully aware of the extent of their responsibilities, together with steps they must take to minimise the danger of professional negligence claims.

Required

(a) Discuss the extent of an auditor's responsibilities to shareholders and others during the course of their normal professional engagement.

(b) List six steps which auditors should take to minimise the danger of claims against them for negligent work.

Answer

(a) *Responsibility under statute*

An auditor of a limited company has a responsibility, imposed upon him by statute, to form and express a professional opinion on the financial statements presented by the directors to the shareholders. He must report upon the truth and fairness of such statements and the fact that they comply with the law. In so doing, the auditor owes a duty of care to the company imposed by statute. But such duty also arises under contract and may also arise under the common law (law of tort).

Responsibility under contract

The Companies Act does not state expressly the manner in which the auditor should discharge his duty of care; neither is it likely that this would be clearly spelt out in any contract setting out the terms of an auditor's appointment (eg the engagement letter). Although the articles of a company may extend the auditor's responsibilities beyond those envisaged by the Companies Act, they cannot be used so as to restrict the auditor's statutory duties, neither may they place any restriction upon the auditor's statutory rights which are designed to assist him in the discharge of those duties.

The comments of Lopes when considering the degree of skill and care required of an auditor in *Re Kingston Cotton Mill* are still relevant.

> ... it is the duty of an auditor to bring to bear on the work he has to perform the skill, care and caution which a reasonably competent, careful and cautious auditor would use. What is reasonable skill, care and caution must depend on the particular circumstances of each case.

Clearly, with the advent of auditing standards, a measure of good practice is now available for the courts to take into account when considering the adequacy of the work of the auditor.

Responsibility in tort

The law of tort has established that a person owes a duty of care and skill to 'our neighbours' (common and well-known examples of this neighbour principle can be seen in the law of trespass, slander, libel and so on). In the context of the professional auditor the wider implications, however, concern the extent to which the auditor owes a duty of care and skill to third parties who rely on financial statements upon which he has reported but with whom he has no direct contractual or fiduciary relationship.

Liability to third parties

In *Caparo Industries plc v Dickman & Others 1990*, it was held that the auditors of a public company's accounts owed no duty of care to members of the general public who relied upon the accounts in deciding to buy shares in the company. And as a purchaser of more shares, a shareholder placing reliance on the auditor's report stood in the same position as any other investing member of the public to whom the auditor owed no duty. This decision appeared to radically reverse the tide of cases concerning the auditor's duty of care. The purpose of the audit was simply that of meeting the statutory requirements of the Companies Act 1985. There was nothing in the statutory duties of a company auditor to suggest that they were intended to protect the interests of investors in the market. In particular, there was no reason why any special relationship should be held to arise simply from the fact that the affairs of the company rendered it susceptible to a take-over bid.

A case between BDO Binder Hamlyn and ADT seems to have moved the argument on. In this case it was argued that proximity between a prospective investor and the auditors of a company could be created if the investor asked the auditors whether they stood by their last audit. An appeal is likely in this case as the auditors involved face a large shortfall in insurance proceeds. The *Bannerman* case suggests that judges may be more likely to impute a duty of care to the auditors if they were aware that the bank made use of audited accounts and did not disclaim liability to them.

(b) In order to provide a means of protection for the auditor arising from the comments in (a) above, the following steps should be taken.

    (i) Agreements concerning the duties of the auditor should be:

        (1) Clear and precise
        (2) In writing
        (3) Confirmed by a level of engagement, including matters specifically excluded

    (ii) Audit work should be:

        (1) Relevant to the system of internal control, which must be ascertained, evaluated and tested. Controls cannot be entirely ignored: for the auditor to have any confidence in an accounting system there must be present and evident the existence of minimum controls to ensure completeness and accuracy of the records.

(2) Adequately planned before the audit commences.

(3) Reviewed by a senior member of the firm to ensure qualify control of the audit and to enable a decision to be made on the form of audit report.

(iii) Any queries arising during the audit should be:
(1) Recorded on the current working papers.
(2) Cleared and filed.

(iv) A management letter should be:
(1) Submitted to the client or the board of directors in writing immediately following an audit.
(2) Seen to be acted upon by the client.

(v) All members of an auditing firm should be familiar with:
(1) The standards expected throughout the firm.
(2) The standards of the profession as a whole by means of adequate training, which should cover the implementation of the firm's audit manual and the recommendations of the professional accountancy bodies.

(vi) Insurance should be taken out to cover the firm against possible claims.

4 Auditor accountability

FAST FORWARD

Corporate collapses, such as Carillion, and accounting irregularities, such as at Patisserie Valerie, once again raise the issue of auditor accountability.

4.1 The concern

Over recent decades there has been an ever increasing number of high profile corporate collapses despite such companies issuing financial statements which contain an unmodified auditor's report just months before their collapse.

There have also been instances where material financial irregularities have not been identified during financial statement audits.

These issues raise genuine concern as to whether auditors are sufficiently robust in their work and mindful to challenge directors where corporate governance is weak or whether they are too focussed on their own profits.

Case Study

Let us consider Carillion as an example.

In January 2018, the UK's second-largest construction company, Carillion, **collapsed with liabilities of almost £7 billion** as well as one of the largest deficits on its pension scheme of any of the FTSE 350 companies.

July 2017:

Carillion issued a profit warning stating that its profits would suffer a charge of £845 million. However it appears that although this profit warning marked the beginning of the end for Carillion, it was in fact many **poor decisions** in the years leading up to this date that caused the company serious problems.

September 2017:

Carillion's half-year financial statements revealed a total hit to the company's worth of £1.2 billion, an amount greater than the profits from the previous eight years put together.

Corporate governance at Carillion **was poor** and the board of directors failed in its responsibilities to run Carillion appropriately, with the **directors preferring to pursue their own personal incentives** rather than those of the shareholders.

During the eight years from 2009 to 2016, Carillion paid out £554 million in dividends, three quarters of the cash generated from operations. In the period from January 2012 to June 2017, Carillion paid out £333 million **more** in dividends than it generated in cash from its operations but no action was taken by the directors to attempt to reduce the pension deficit.

Carillion had been audited by KPMG since its incorporation in 1999 and its latest financial statements were prepared using the going concern basis of accounting and contained an unmodified auditor's report.

Carillion also used Deloitte as their internal auditors and had also engaged the services of Ernst & Young in an attempt to turn the company around. PricewaterhouseCoopers was advising Carillion on pensions and the Government on Carillion contracts.

This chain of events raises questions as to whether these Big Four auditors should have raised an alarm before Carillion collapsed.

Similarly, there is the example of Patisserie Valerie.

Case Study

Grant Thornton's audits of **Patisserie Valerie** over three years, from 2015 to 2017, failed to uncover significant and potentially fraudulent accounting irregularities at the café chain.

Christopher Marsh, Patisserie Valerie's Chief Financial Officer, was arrested and later released but is facing a criminal investigation by the **Serious Fraud Office** after the board discovered £10 million of secret overdrafts. The Chief Executive, Paul May, also stepped down having faced heavy criticism from shareholders over the company's handling of the crisis.

The café chain came close to collapse in the wake of the scandal but was **saved with the help of a loan** from chair, Luke Johnson.

Auditors, Grant Thornton, are to be investigated by the Financial Reporting Council.

4.2 Are the auditors at fault?

Sadly, the Carillion case is not the first time that a Big Four auditor has given a 'clean bill of health' to a company that has subsequently collapsed and the Patisserie Valerie case will not be the first or last time an auditor has failed to uncover material irregularities in the financial statements.

The Big Four audit almost all (97%) of the FTSE 350 companies in the UK and enjoy significant fees for both audit and non-audit services. Furthermore, Grant Thornton, the fifth largest audit firm, has recently said it will no longer pitch for the audits of FTSE 350 companies as the costs involved in the tender are too high to be awarded second place. This suggests there is a real lack of competition and therefore accountability in the industry.

Following the collapse of Carillion, the UK's Financial Reporting Council (FRC) asked the Competition and Markets Authority (CMA) to launch a review of the audit sector and to consider banning the Big Four from acting as consultants for the firms they audit.

The Competition Commission (the CMA's predecessor) introduced measures to try to improve competition in 2012/13. At that point the Big Four audited 95% of the FTSE 350 companies and so these measures do not appear to have improved competition.

This is clearly an area which will involve much future discussion but possible solutions include:

- **'Audit only' firms** where auditors could be forced to break their audit and consulting arms into separate businesses; and
- Placing a **cap** on the number of FTSE 350 companies that an audit firm can audit.

Case Study

In 2021, EY announced a proposed a split of its audit and consulting businesses in a plan named Project Everest. Under the proposed plan, audit partners and staff would remain as an EY partnership and the consulting partners and staff would be moved into a new publicly listed corporation. Audit partners were to receive large cash payouts on the split and partners in the new consulting business would receive equity in the newly proposed corporation.

However, a large number of internal disagreements arose following the announcement. Some country's partners announced they did not agree with the plan and refused to participate with the split. A key sticking point was the difficulty in splitting the tax partners and staff between the audit and consulting businesses.

In April 2023, EY announced that it was abandoning Project Everest.

5 Limitation of liability

FAST FORWARD

There are various ways that auditors can limit their firm's and their personal exposure to liability.

5.1 Litigation avoidance

Firms may try to avoid litigation. This strategy has various aspects.

- **Client acceptance procedures** are very important, particularly the screening of new clients which helps auditors avoid high risk clients, and the use of engagement letters which ensure that all parties understand their responsibilities. We shall look at these in more detail in Chapter 8.
- **Performance of audit work**. Firms should make sure that all audits are carried out in accordance with professional standards and best practice.
- **Quality management**. This includes not just controls over individual audits but also stricter 'whole-firm' procedures. This is considered in more detail in Chapter 14.
- **Issue of appropriate disclaimers**. We shall look at disclaimers below. It is not possible for auditors to disclaim liability for the audit opinion.

5.2 Professional indemnity insurance

Key terms

Professional indemnity insurance is insurance against civil claims made by clients and third parties arising from work undertaken by the firm.

Fidelity guarantee insurance is insurance against liability arising through any acts of fraud or dishonesty by any partner, director or employee in respect of money or goods held in trust by the firm.

It is important that accountants have insurance so that if negligence occurs, the client can be **compensated** for the error by the accountant. The appropriate compensation could be far greater than the resources of the accountancy firm.

Remember that accountants usually trade as **partnerships,** so all the partners are jointly and severally liable to claims made against individual partners.

AIA requires that firms holding practising certificates and auditing certificates have professional indemnity insurance with a reputable insurance company. If the firm has employees, it must also have fidelity guarantee insurance.

The insurance must cover 'all civil liability incurred in connection with the conduct of the firm's business by the partners, directors or employees'.

The cover must continue to exist for **six years** after a member ceases to engage in public practice.

5.2.1 Advantages

The key advantage of such insurance is that it provides funds for an innocent party to be compensated in the event of a wrong having been done to them.

An advantage to the auditor is that it provides some protection against bankruptcy in the event of successful litigation against the firm. This is particularly important for a partnership, as partners may be sued personally for the negligence of their fellow partners.

5.2.2 Disadvantages

A key disadvantage is that the existence of insurance against the cost of negligence might encourage auditors to take less care than

- Would otherwise be the case
- Their professional duty requires

Another **problem** associated with such insurances are that there are limits of cover (linked with the cost of buying the insurance) and any compensation arising from a claim could be higher than those limits. This could lead to partners being bankrupted despite having insurance.

A simple disadvantage associated with the above is the regular cost of the insurance to the partnership.

5.3 Structures for accountancy practices

5.3.1 Incorporation

The major accountancy firms have been interested in methods of reducing personal liability for partners in the event of negligence for some time. For example, some years ago KPMG (one of the Big Four of accountancy firms) incorporated its UK audit practice. This was allowed under Companies Act 1989.

The new arrangement created 'a firm within a firm'. KPMG Audit plc is a limited company wholly owned by the partnership, KPMG. The reason behind this is to protect the partners from the crushing effects of litigation. The other side of incorporation means that KPMG Audit plc are subject to the statutory disclosure requirements of companies.

5.3.2 Limited liability partnerships

An alternative to incorporation as a company is incorporation as a limited liability partnership.

Limited liability partnership can be operated in some countries, for example, some of the states in the US and the UK.

The Limited Liability Partnership Act 2000 enables UK firms to establish limited liability partnerships as separate legal entities. These combine the flexibility and tax status of a partnership with limited liability for members.

The effect of this is that the partnership, **but not its members**, will be liable to third parties; however the personal assets of **negligent** partners will still be at risk.

Limited liability partnerships are set up by similar procedures to those for incorporating a company. An incorporation document is sent to the Registrar of Companies. The Registrar will issue a certificate of incorporation to confirm that all statutory requirements have been fulfilled.

In a similar way to traditional partnerships, relations between partners will be governed by internal partner agreements, or by future statutory regulations.

Each member of the partnership will still be an agent of the partnership unless he has no authority to act and an outside party is aware of this lack of authority.

5.3.3 Advantages and disadvantages of different structures

	Advantages	Disadvantages
Partnership	• Less regulation than for companies • Financial statements not on public record	• Joint and several liability • Personal assets at risk
Incorporation	• Limited liability	• Public filing of audited financial statements • Management must comply with Companies Act
LLP	• Protection of personal assets • Limited liability of members • Similar tax effect of partnership • Flexible management structures	• Public filing of audited financial statements

5.4 Disclaimers

The cases discussed above suggest that a duty of care to a third party may arise when an accountant does not know that his work will be relied upon by a third party, but only knows that it is work of a kind which is liable in the ordinary course of events to be relied upon by a third party.

Conversely, an accountant may sometimes be informed or be aware, before he carries out certain work, that a third party will rely upon the results. An example is a report upon the business of a client which the accountant has been instructed to prepare for the purpose of being shown to a potential purchaser or potential creditor of that business. In such a case an accountant should assume that he will be held to owe the same duty to the third party as to his client. The *Bannerman* case suggests this is also necessary for **audit work**. Since the *Bannerman* case, many audit firms have included a disclaimer in their audit report.

However, there are areas of professional work (for example, when acting as an auditor under the Companies Act on behalf of shareholders), where it is not possible for liability to be limited or excluded. There are other areas of professional work (for example, when preparing reports on a business for the purpose of being submitted to a potential purchaser) where although such a limitation or exclusion may be included, its effectiveness will depend on the view which a court may subsequently form of its reasonableness.

5.5 Proportionate liability

Even with PII and other means of restricting liability there has been great concern throughout the audit profession globally at the remaining risks to firms' survival in the face of claims which might exceed their insurance cover.

The profession has lobbied for further protection in the form of **proportionate liability** or **capping liability**.

> **Key terms**
>
> **Proportionate liability** would allow claims arising from successful negligence claims to be split between the auditors and the directors of the client company, the split being determined by a judge on the basis of where the fault was seen to lie. This would require the approval of shareholders.
>
> **Capping liability** would set a maximum limit on the amount that the auditor would have to pay out under any claim.

5.5.1 UK Companies Act 2006

Chapter 6 of the Companies Act 2006 makes it possible for auditors to limit their liability by agreement with a company. It does this by defining a **liability limitation agreement**, which is a contractual limitation of the auditor's liability to a company, requiring shareholder agreement by resolution and only effective if it is **fair and reasonable**.

The agreement can cover liability for negligence, default, breach of duty or breach of trust by the auditor in relation to the audit of accounts for a particular year.

It is currently open to negotiation between auditors and their client companies as to what form the agreement will take, for example, a liability cap, or proportionate liability.

5.5.2 Ongoing debate

There have been concerns that the new regulations may distort competition in the audit market. If the biggest firms set caps at very high levels, mid-tier firms could be disadvantaged. In the UK the government has left a provision for the relevant government ministers to issue specific rules specifying what can and cannot be included in agreements in case competition problems arise.

There are also arguments that capping liability will reduce the value of the audit to investors and may bring pressure on firms to reduce fees.

Overall the profession has reacted positively to the new rules. The reaction has been less positive to the other major effect of the new bill, introducing a criminal offence of 'knowingly or recklessly' including in the auditor's report any matter that is misleading, false or deceptive in a material particular.

The government saw this as being a necessary change in order to maintain audit quality.

6 Money laundering and bribery

> **FAST FORWARD**
>
> Money laundering and bribery are significant issues for accountants and auditors.

6.1 Accountants and money laundering

> **Key term**
>
> **Money laundering** is the process by which criminals attempt to conceal the true origin and ownership of the proceeds of their criminal activity, often with the unwitting assistance of professionals such as accountants and lawyers. It is a global phenomenon that affects all countries to varying degrees.

As money laundering is an important global topic, an international body, the Financial Action Task Force on Money Laundering (FATF) has set out a number of recommendations to governments relating to money laundering. Examples are:

- Money laundering should be made a criminal offence.
- Business should take certain measures to prevent money laundering.
- Measures relating to international cooperation to prevent money laundering.

In response to the recommendations, many countries have now made money laundering a criminal offence. In some countries, notably the UK, Australia, Singapore, Ireland and the US, the criminal offences include criminal offences directed at persons such as accountants. Under the Proceeds of Crime Act 2002, UK law makes it illegal to:

- Possess, deal with or conceal the proceeds of any crime
- Attempt, assist or incite others to commit money laundering
- Fail to report a knowledge or suspicion of money laundering if you are a person in a regulated sector (such as accountancy)
- Tip off (which means to disclose to the party under investigation of money laundering that such an investigation is taking place)

All these criminal offences, and particularly the last two, could affect accountants acting intentionally or unintentionally in the course of their work. All the crimes listed above carry significant penalties. Money laundering is therefore a significant issue for accountants and one they must take extremely seriously.

There are legal defences against money laundering which accountants may be able to use, such as:

- Having made an appropriate report
- Having a reasonable excuse (such as fear of physical violence or other menaces) for not having done so
- Acquiring or using property for adequate consideration in good faith

6.2 Money Laundering Regulations

The basic requirements of the UK Money Laundering Regulations are for accountants to keep records of clients' identity and to report suspicions of money laundering to the UK's National Crime Agency (NCA).

A firm must establish an **anti money laundering programme** such as that set out below, which includes appointing a **Money Laundering Compliance Principal (MLCP)** who is responsible for the firm's compliance with anti-money laundering regulations. A **nominated officer** (the 'Money Laundering Reporting Officer (MLRO)' under the old Money Laundering Regulations 2007) must also be appointed, who is responsible for reporting suspicions to the NCA. Individuals within the firm are then legally required to report any offences to the nominated officer, who can be the same person as the MLCP.

Elements of a money laundering programme:

Procedures	Explanations
• Appoint a **Money Laundering Compliance Principal (MLCP)**	• The MLCP must be either on the board of directors, or be a member of senior management.
• Appoint a **nominated officer** and implement internal reporting procedures	• Individuals should make internal reports of money laundering to the nominated officer. • The nominated officer must consider whether to report to the NCA, and document the process.

Procedures	Explanations
• Screen relevant **employees**	• Firms must assess relevant employees' skills, knowledge, conduct and integrity. • Relevant employees are those who are involved in identifying, mitigating, preventing or detecting money laundering and terrorist financing in the course of business.
• Train **individuals** to ensure that they are aware of the relevant legislation, know how to recognise and deal with potential **money laundering**, how to report suspicions to the **nominated officer**, and how to identify **clients**	• Individuals should be trained in the firm's obligations under law, and their personal obligations. • Staff should be **assessed for competence, conduct and integrity**, including in relation to money laundering. • They must be made aware of the firm's identification, record-keeping and reporting procedures.
• Establish an independent **audit function**	• This function should assess the adequacy and effectiveness of the firm's anti-money laundering policies, controls and procedures.

• Establish internal procedures appropriate to forestall and prevent **money laundering**, and make relevant **individuals** aware of the procedures	• Procedures should cover
	  – Client acceptance
	  – Gathering 'know your client' (KYC) information (see Section 6.2.1 below)
	  – Controls over client money and transactions through the client account
	  – Advice and services to clients that could be of use to a money launderer
	  – Internal reporting lines
	  – The role of the nominated officer

• Verify the identity of new and existing **clients** and maintain evidence of identification (ie customer due diligence (CDD) measures)	• The firm must be able to establish that new clients are who they claim to be. • Typically, this will include taking copies of evidence such as passports, driving licences and utility bills. • For a company this will include identities of directors and certificates of incorporation.
• Maintain records of **client** identification, and any transactions undertaken for or with the **client**	• Special care needs to be taken when handling clients' money to avoid participation in a transaction involving money laundering.
• **Report** suspicions of **money laundering** to the NCA	• NCA has standard disclosure forms.

6.2.1 'Know your client' information

The firm must gather 'know your client' (KYC) information to assist in spotting suspicious transactions. This includes:

- Who the client is
- Who controls it
- The purpose and intended nature of the business relationship
- The nature of the client

6: PROFESSIONAL RESPONSIBILITY AND LIABILITY

- The client's source of funds
- The client's business and economic purpose

KYC enables the audit firm to understand their clients' business well enough to spot any unusual business activity. This assists the firm in identifying suspicions of money laundering.

Customer due diligence (CDD) requirements have increased significantly since the introduction of money laundering regulations in the UK. The Money Laundering Regulations 2017 extended the circumstances under which CDD must be carried out from new to existing clients.

6.3 Risk-based approach

On any assignment, the auditor should assess the risk of money laundering activities. Clearly, every circumstance is different, but the following diagram illustrates some key risk factors.

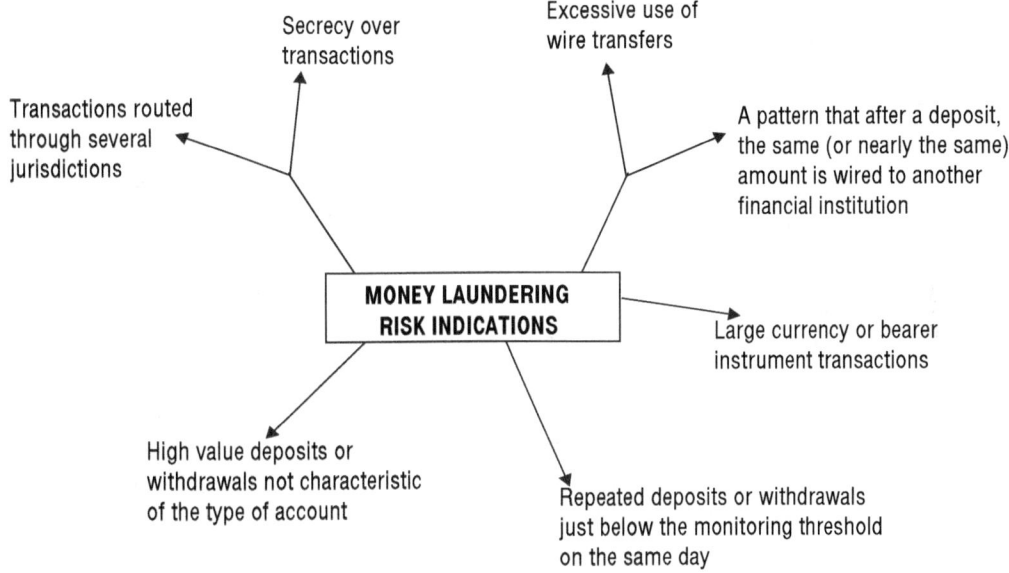

6.4 The Bribery Act 2010

The Bribery Act 2010 is a piece of UK legislation which came into force in 2011. The legislation has been dubbed 'the toughest anti-corruption legislation in the world' and various concerns have been raised, particularly concerning its impact on UK companies that trade overseas.

6.4.1 Bribery offences

The Bribery Act 2010 introduced four kinds of offences into UK law:

- Bribing another person
- Being bribed
- Bribing a foreign public official
- Failure by a commercial organisation to prevent bribery

Key terms

> **Bribery** occurs when a person offers, promises or gives a financial or other advantage to another person with the intent of inducing them to perform improperly a relevant function or activity. The offence of **being bribed** is defined as requesting, agreeing to receive or accepting such an advantage, in exchange for improperly performing such a function or activity.

The Bribery Act 2010 does not explain what 'financial or other advantage' means, but it could include contracts, non-monetary gifts or offers of employment. 'Relevant function or activity' is explained in the legislation as covering 'any function of a public nature; any activity connected with a business, trade or profession; any activity performed in the course of a person's employment; or any activity performed on

6.4.2 Impact of the Bribery Act 2010 on companies and auditors

The UK Secretary of State for Justice published guidance about the legislation three months before it came into force. This guidance identified six principles that all business should follow, which cover the following areas:

- Proportionate procedures
- Top-level commitment
- Risk assessment
- Due diligence
- Communication
- Monitoring and review

Companies will need to demonstrate that there are controls in place in each of these areas to mitigate the risk of bribery, should they or an employee be accused of bribery.

The penalties imposed if individuals or companies are found guilty of bribery are severe. Individuals may be imprisoned for up to ten years and face an unlimited fine. Companies may face an unlimited fine. In addition to this, there will be the associated bad publicity and loss of reputation.

Although the legislation has not added any additional requirements to the statutory audit, under ISA 250 *Consideration of Laws and Regulations in an Audit of Financial Statements* auditors do have a duty to have an understanding of the legal and regulatory framework under which the client operates. If auditors consider that there is a risk that they may be affected under the Bribery Act 2010, they must discuss with management what steps they have put in place to reduce the risk. There are also ethical considerations, which we looked at in Chapter 4. The IESBA *Code of Ethics* covers issues such as gifts and hospitality and inducements. The Bribery Act 2010 clearly has an impact on auditors where these issues could lead to the offence of being bribed being committed.

Question — Money laundering

You are the audit manager of Loft, a chain of nightclubs across the north-west of England. During the course of the audit Mr Roy, an employee of the company, informed you that a substantial cash deposit was paid into the company's bank account and a month later, the same amount was paid by direct transfer into a bank account in the name of Evissa, a company based overseas. The employee also informed you that Mr Fox, the managing director of Loft had instructed him not to record the transaction in the accounting records as it had nothing to do with Loft's business.

Required

Comment on the situation outlined above.

Answer

The transaction described in the scenario raises suspicion of money laundering for several reasons.

(a) It has been alleged by Mr Roy that the purpose of the transaction has nothing to do with the nightclub business. This could be a sign that Mr Fox is attempting to legitimise the proceeds of a crime through Loft by concealing the illegal source of the cash.

(b) The amount of the transaction is substantial for Loft. An unusually large transaction should alert the auditor to the possibility of money laundering, especially as it does not seem to relate to the business of Loft.

(c) The cash amount paid into Loft's bank account is the same as the amount paid to Evissa. This could be an attempt by Mr Fox to make the cash appear legitimate by moving it through several companies and jurisdictions.

(d) Mr Roy was instructed not to record the transaction in the accounting records of Loft. Increased secrecy over transactions is another indicator of money laundering.

Loft's bank statement should be checked to confirm Mr Roy's assertion. The suspicious transaction should be reported to the firm's MLRO or the NCA as soon as possible and any tipping off must be avoided. It is a criminal offence to not report suspicions of money laundering.

Question

Complex ethical question

Exam focus point

This is a past exam question. The question contains an 'approaching the answer section' which has been annotated to try and illustrate the thought processes a candidate might go through when reading through and attempting this question. You may find it helpful to read the requirements to such a question first, to focus your thoughts on the information given in the question.
It is important to understand the requirement properly and to answer each part of it separately.

Dayson is an audit firm with 6 offices and a total of 27 partners and 180 professional staff. The firm specialises in the audit of large unquoted companies.

Dayson has a detailed 'ethics policy' in place for all partners and staff. This complements the IESBA *Code of Ethics* by laying down detailed guidance for staff to follow within the context of Dayson's business.

The following extracts appear in Dayson's ethics policy:

- No partner or member of staff will, under any circumstances, communicate any information relating to a client company to any third party unless so authorised by the firm's managing partner.

- Any concerns about the legality or morality of any action should be brought to the attention of the partner in charge of the assignment. In the event that this does not resolve matters, a written statement should be submitted to Dayson's ethics committee, whose membership will comprise senior professional staff.

During the course of the audit of a client company's pension scheme the audit manager discovered that the pension scheme director was insisting on having three days' warning before the scheme bought any shares on the stock market. There were no internal control or management reasons for such a warning. The audit manager suspected that the director was abusing this information. Large purchases of shares, such as those made by pension schemes, often make share prices rise. The director could make a personal investment immediately before the pension fund invested and then resell the shares at a profit immediately afterwards. Abusing such 'inside knowledge' is a criminal offence and also creates the risk of the markets anticipating the pension fund's next investment and so making the fund's investments more expensive.

The audit manager brought this to the attention of the audit partner and the company's audit committee was consulted on these suspicions. Immediately afterwards the pension scheme director resigned and took up a post with another pension fund that is not linked to the client company in any way.

The audit manager wished to report these suspicions to the police, but both the audit partner and Dayson's ethics committee refused to permit this, on the grounds that the director was no longer a threat to the company's pensioners and that the firm would be open to criticism for breaching professional confidence if a report was made. Furthermore, the pension fund director would simply deny the accusation and then seek damages from Dayson.

PART A   REGULATORY ISSUES AND PROFESSIONAL PRACTICES

Required

[Margin note: Consider both 'good' implications and 'bad' implications.]

(a) Discuss the implications of requiring professional audit staff to communicate any ethical concerns exclusively to partners and a firm's ethics committee.

(6 marks)

[Margin note: Outline:
(1) The wrongdoing
(2) The public interest question
(3) Confidentiality conflict]

(b) Discuss the ethical implications of permitting the director of the pension fund to resign in this way.

[Margin note: Make comments specific to this scenario.]

(8 marks)

(c) Discuss the problems associated with bringing the audit manager's concerns in this case to the attention of the appropriate authorities.

[Margin note: Lack of proof, conflict with confidence, audit firm liability for partner actions, bad publicity.]

(6 marks)

(Total 20 marks)

Approaching the answer

Dayson is an audit firm with 6 offices and a total of 27 partners and 180 professional staff. The firm specialises in the audit of large unquoted companies.

Dayson has a detailed 'ethics policy' in place for all partners and staff. This complements the IESBA *Code of Ethics for Professional Accountants* by laying down detailed guidance for staff to follow within the context of Dayson's business.

The following extracts appear in Dayson's ethics policy:

[Margin note: Codes of conduct deal with individual conscience so could override duty to employer?]

- No partner or member of staff will, under any circumstances, communicate any information relating to a client company to any third party unless so authorised by the firm's managing partner.

[Margin note: What about money laundering? Is complex system instead of just MRLO
Risk of delay in reporting and personal liability...]

- Any concerns about the legality or morality of any action should be brought to the attention of the partner in charge of the assignment. In the event that this does not resolve matters, a written statement should be submitted to Dayson's ethics committee, whose membership will comprise senior professional staff.

[Margin note: Public interest? Pensioners have no direct say...]

[Margin note: Possible insider trading.]

[Margin note: Individual ethical requirements v firm's requirements. No whistleblowing protection. Could consult professional body in confidence. Could seek legal advice as individual.]

During the course of the audit of a client company's pension scheme the audit manager discovered that the pension scheme director was insisting on having three days' warning before the scheme bought any shares on the stock market. There were no internal control or management reasons for such a warning. The audit manager suspected that the director was abusing this information. Large purchases of shares, such as those made by pension schemes, often make share prices rise. The director could make a personal investment immediately before the pension fund invested and then resell the shares at a profit immediately afterwards. Abusing such 'inside knowledge' is a criminal offence and also creates the risk of the markets anticipating the pension fund's next investment and so making the fund's investments more expensive.

The audit manager brought this to the attention of the audit partner and the company's audit committee was consulted on these suspicions. Immediately afterwards the pension scheme director resigned and took up a post with another pension fund that is not linked to the client company in any way.

The audit manager wished to report these suspicions to the police, but both the audit partner and Dayson's ethics committee refused to permit this, on the grounds that the director was no longer a threat to the company's pensioners and that the firm would be open to criticism for breaching professional confidence if a report was made. Furthermore, the pension fund director would simply deny the accusation and then seek damages from Dayson.

Answer

This question tests candidates' understanding of the issues associated with the auditor's responsibilities with regard to fraud and illegal acts by management and the associated duties of confidence.

(a) All professional accountants have a host of duties and responsibilities that can come into conflict in certain circumstances. For example, an accountant could discover something about a client company that ought to be communicated to the authorities in the public interest. Doing so would, however, be a breach of the formal duty of confidence owed to clients.

It is desirable for accounting firms to establish a system for ensuring that all ethical dilemmas are discussed and considered by senior and experienced members of the firm. That way, the firm can ensure that the public interest is adequately protected without compromising the duties to clients unless there is a compelling reason to do so.

It may be that a report to the firm does not achieve the desired result. This may be because the partners on the ethics committee disagree with the staff member's analysis of the facts, but it could be due to the fact that the firm wishes to avoid losing a lucrative appointment. It would be difficult for an audit firm to remain in post working for a client whom it had to report to the authorities and it is quite unlikely that the client would wish to retain the firm in any case.

The IESBA *Code of Ethics* imposes a duty on individual accountants. This means that the accountant may feel an obligation to take matters into his or her own hands and go to the authorities in defiance of a decision by the ethics committee not to do so.

In addition, some ethical issues may raise issues of reporting money laundering suspicions, in which case a shorter reporting route will be vital to ensure that individuals are not exposed to liability due to delay. The firm should appoint a Money Laundering Reporting Officer to whom ethical dilemmas involving the suspicion of money laundering can be reported to without delay.

(b) Stock market participants have a huge incentive to gather and make use of all information that can help them to identify movements in the stock market. It is quite likely that the broker who places orders on the director's behalf knows that the director manages a pension fund and will have access to information that is not generally known by the markets as a whole. The pattern of large trades and price rises following the director's purchases will be a clear signal of the fund's intentions to the stock market. That will mean that the pension fund will pay more for its investments than it really should and that the returns obtained on behalf of pensioners will be lower.

The audit manager has strong suspicions that the director has been breaking the law. The act itself has been harming a large number of people, who are effectively being abused without their knowledge and so they are unable to protect themselves.

The fact that the suspicions have been dealt with by encouraging the director to slip away and carry on committing this crime is a serious matter for concern. The company's pensioners are unable to seek compensation from him. They are no longer subject to his misbehaviour, but a different group of pensioners are now going to be affected.

(c) Technically, the director is innocent until proved guilty by a criminal court. The auditor does not have any more than a collection of suspicions based upon an observation prior to the director's resignation and the fact that he resigned to move to another post. If the auditor makes a formal accusation against the director then the director may deny all guilt and seek compensation from the audit firm. The director may even be able to seek damages from the auditor through the civil courts.

The facts themselves do not seem sufficient to support a serious allegation. It is not particularly difficult for the director of a pension scheme to argue that he or she should be informed of any major investment decisions. Nor is it particularly surprising that a manager might wish to move to a position with a different organisation.

If the auditor does take the matter to the authorities then there will definitely be a breach of professional confidence. This is an inescapable result of the report. There is no guarantee that it will have a positive impact on the public interest. The authorities may decide not to pursue the matter or they may investigate and find the allegation very difficult to pursue. Alternatively, there are mechanisms in place to monitor share transactions and there is no guarantee that it will require a report from the auditor to bring about the detection of the director's misbehaviour.

Chapter Roundup

- **Misconduct** includes (but is not confined to) any act or default likely to bring discredit to the member, relevant firm or registered student in question.
- Auditors may have professional liability under statutory law.
- Auditors may have professional liability in the tort of negligence.
- The auditor owes a duty of care to the audit client automatically under law.
- The auditor only owes a duty of care to parties other than the audit client if one has been established.
- Corporate collapses, such as Carillion, and accounting irregularities, such as at Patisserie Valerie, once again raise the issue of auditor accountability.
- There are various ways that auditors can limit their firm's and their personal exposure to liability.
- Money laundering and bribery are significant issues for accountants and auditors.

PART A REGULATORY ISSUES AND PROFESSIONAL PRACTICES

Quick Quiz

1 Complete the definition.

   .... includes (but is not confined to) any act or .... likely to bring discredit to ...., relevant .... or registered .... in question.

2 AIA has set penalties for misconduct.

   True   ☐
   False ☐

3 What three matters must a plaintiff satisfy the court in an action for negligence?

   (1) ....
   (2) ....
   (3) ....

4 Name four aspects of litigation avoidance.

   (1) ....
   (2) ....
   (3) ....
   (4) ....

5 Professional indemnity insurance is insurance against liability arising through any acts of fraud or dishonesty by partners in respect of money held in trust by the firm.

   True   ☐
   False ☐

6 Name six elements of an anti-money laundering programme.

Answers to Quick Quiz

1. Misconduct, default, the member, firm, student

2. False

3. (1) A duty of care existed
   (2) Negligence occurred
   (3) The client suffered pecuniary loss as a result

4. (1) Client acceptance procedures
   (2) Performance of audit work in line with ISAs
   (3) Quality management
   (4) Disclaimers

5. False. That is fidelity guarantee insurance

6. Dedicated resources, written policies and procedures, comprehensive coverage, timely escalation and resolution of matters, explicit management support, regular review.

End of Chapter Question

Suspect (AIA May 2009)

You are partner in charge of the external auditor of Suspect, a local company that owns several large shops that sell expensive electronic equipment. Your firm operates in a country which imposes a legal duty upon auditors and other professionals to report any suspicions of money laundering to the authorities.

In your country, money laundering is defined as: 'The process by which criminals attempt to conceal the true origin and ownership of the proceeds of their criminal activity, allowing them to maintain control over the proceeds and, ultimately, providing a legitimate cover for their sources of income'.

Suspect's chief accountant resigned recently after three years with the company. His resignation letter stated that he was leaving in order to take up an alternative post with a larger company and that he wished Suspect every success in the future. After his resignation he visited you in your office to tell you that he had been concerned that Suspect may have been engaged in money laundering. He claimed that he had not seen any positive proof of such activity and that he had left as quickly and as quietly as he could in order to avoid coming into possession of evidence that a crime was being committed. He refused to put his allegations in writing or to give you any further information in support of his allegation.

You have audited the financial statements of Suspect for several years and have never had to express a qualified audit opinion. The only things that are remarkable about the company is the fact that it has a very high gross profit percentage compared to its rivals and that it offers a 4% discount to customers who pay by cash rather than by credit card. The sales director has always claimed that the company is skilled at buying inventory for much less than the competition and that cash payments should be encouraged because they speed up cash flow, avoid the need to pay a commission to credit card companies and even speed up transactions at the tills.

Required

(a) Explain why a criminal might wish to launder the proceeds of criminal activity, given that it will involve paying tax on those proceeds. **(4 marks)**

(b) Explain why it would be difficult for an external auditor to detect money laundering activity. **(6 marks)**

(c) Describe the work that you would undertake to check that the cash sales recorded by Suspect were, in fact, legitimate receipts from customers and not deposits made by a criminal who wished to launder cash through the company. **(10 marks)**

(Total 20 marks)

Changes in professional appointment

Topic list	Syllabus reference
1 Change in auditors	LO2
2 Advertising and fees	LO2
3 Agreeing terms	LO2
4 Books and documents	LO2

Introduction

It is a commercial fact that companies change their auditors. To thrive, firms of auditors need to understand the answer to the question: **why do companies change their auditors?** We shall examine some of the common reasons here.

Related to entities changing their auditors is the fact that **many auditing firms advertise their services**. The AIA has set out rules for members who advertise their services. We shall examine these rules and the reasons behind them in Section 2.

As we will discover in Section 1, the **audit fee** can be a very key item for an entity when it makes decisions about its auditors. Determining the price to offer to potential clients can be a difficult process

The general issues surrounding agreeing audit terms and transferring **books and documents** are discussed in Section 4.

PART A REGULATORY ISSUES AND PROFESSIONAL PRACTICES

1 Change in auditors

FAST FORWARD

Common reasons behind companies changing the auditor include audit fee, auditor not seeking re-election and size of company.

1.1 Why do companies change their auditors?

It is a fact of life that companies change their auditors sometimes. Not all new clients of a firm are new businesses, some have decided to change from their previous auditors. Obviously, it is often not in the interests of audit firms to lose clients. Therefore a key issue in practice management for auditors is to understand why companies change their auditors, so that, as far as they are able, they can seek to prevent it. We will look in more detail at aspects of practice management in Chapter 8.

Question — Change of auditors

Before you read the rest of this chapter, spend a minute thinking about the reasons that companies might change their auditors. You might want to shut the Learning & Practice Workbook and write them down and then compare them with the reasons that we give in the rest of this section.

Answer

Read through the rest of Section 1 and compare your answer to the commentary given.

The following diagram shows some of the more common reasons that companies might change their auditors.

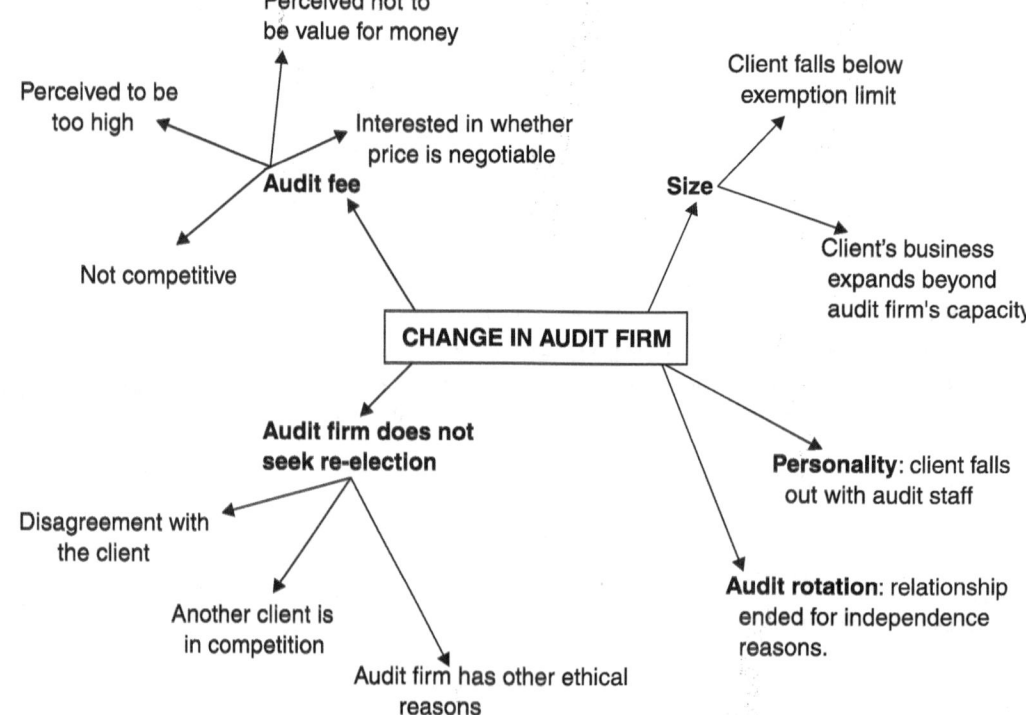

1.2 Audit fee

The audit fee can be a very **sensitive issue**. Audit is required by statute. Some people perceive that it has very little intrinsic value. Therefore, when setting audit fees, auditors must take account of the fact that clients may hold this opinion. Setting fees will be discussed later in the chapter. Here, we shall explore some of the fee related reasons that companies change their auditors.

1.2.1 Perceived to be too high

This is a common reason for auditors being changed. It is strongly linked to people's perception that audit has no intrinsic value. If directors of a company believe that audit is a necessary evil, they will seek to obtain it for as little money as they can.

Much of the 'value', in cost terms, of an audit is carried out away from a client's premises. This is because the most expensive audit staff (managers and partners) often do not carry out their audit work on site. If the client does not understand this, the following sort of situation may arise.

Case Study

Bob is the owner-manager of Fixings Co, a small business which manufactures metal fixings. It has revenue of $4.5 million and the auditors come in for the second week of October every year. Every year a different senior is in charge and they ask similar questions to the ones asked the previous year, because the business rarely changes and the audit is low risk. The partner and manager rarely attend the audit itself because it is not considered cost effective or necessary to do so.

Bob's audit fee was set at $4,500 five years ago when the business was incorporated for tax and inheritance reasons, and has gone up at 3% a year ever since. It now stands at $5,200. During that time, he has paid the same firm $1,200 a year to organise his tax return and deal with the tax authorities on his behalf. He considers this service far more valuable as he has no understanding of tax issues and is exceedingly nervous of a taxation inspection.

Bob cannot understand how the audit fee is four times the size of the tax fee when the auditors attend for a week and do the same work every year. He is also irritated that it continues to steadily rise while the service does not change.

The case example given above is a little exaggerated and generalisations have been made. However, there is some truth in it. An auditor understands the costs that go in to making up the audit fee. It is essential that the client does too.

1.2.2 Perceived not to be value for money

This often goes hand in hand with the audit fee being seen to be too high. In the above example of Bob and Fixings Co, this was certainly the case. However, it is possible that a company could be paying their audit firm a fee that they consider reasonable for an audit, they just believe that another firm could give them a better audit for a similar fee.

1.2.3 Not competitive

Again, this issue can be linked with the value for money perception. It is true to say that in some cases, audit firms will offer audit services at low prices. This is on the grounds that they then sell other services to the same clients at profitable prices. It is through practices like this that the problem of lowballing can arise. In such conditions, a well-set audit fee may not be competitive even if it is a reasonable fee for the service provided.

1.2.4 Interest in whether price is negotiable

This reason may be linked to all of the above fee-related issues, or it may just arise out of interest on the client's part. It costs the client very little except some time on his part to put his audit out to tender. He might even do this with every intention of keeping the present auditor.

Putting the audit out to tender would give him more insight into how competitive his audit fee is and keep his auditor 'honest', in that he will have to justify his fee and risk it being higher than competitors in the tender.

The by-product might be that he receives a competitive tender which offers him far more than he receives from his current auditor and he changes his auditor anyway. It could also mean that, when forced to justify his position, the current auditor reassesses his service and comes up with a far more competitive deal.

1.3 The auditor does not seek re-election

Another key reason for the auditor changing is that the auditor chooses not to stand for election for another year. You should be familiar with many of the reasons behind this:

- There could be ethical reasons behind the auditor choosing not to stand.
- The auditor might have to resign for reasons of competition between clients.
- The auditor might disagree with the client over accounting policies.
- The auditor might not want to reduce his audit fee.

Question — Ethical reasons

Name three ethical reasons why an auditor might not seek re-election or might resign, explaining the nature of the problem and the reasoning behind the resignation.

Answer

As you know from your earlier studies and from studying Chapter 4, there are countless ethical issues that could have arisen. Here are some common ones. Refer to Chapter 4 if you have included one that does not appear here.

(a) **Fee level**

The audit fee which is necessary to carry out the audit at a profit may have reached a level which is inappropriate according to the AIA's guidance on fee levels causing an independence problem. This is because the audit opinion might be influenced by a fear of losing the client.

In such a situation, or if the practice had a large client below the limits but whose forecast suggested future growth, it might be necessary for the auditor to end the relationship to ensure that he did not become dependent on the client.

(b) **Integrity of management**

The auditor might feel that they have reason to doubt the integrity of management. There are many reasons why this could be the case. It could be as a result of a breakdown in relationship, or an unproven suspected fraud.

However, if the auditor does not feel that the client is trustworthy they should not continue their relationship with them.

(c) **Other services**

The auditor may offer a number of services to the client. They may be offered some lucrative consultancy work by the client which they want to undertake, but they feel that the independence of the audit will be severely affected by the provision of the consultancy work because of the heavy involvement that means they will have in the client's business.

As the audit fee is substantially lower than the fees associated with the consultancy work and the auditor is trying to develop their business advice department, they may decide to resign from the audit to take on the consultancy.

1.4 Size of the company

This can be a major reason for a change in auditors. There are two key reasons, one of which has been touched on already.

- Client experiences rapid growth to the point where the audit is no longer practicable for the audit firm.
- Client retrenches or restructures in such a way that it no longer needs a statutory audit.

In the first instance, the auditor may no longer be able to provide the audit for several reasons:

- Insufficient resources
- Staff
- Time
- Fee level issue

In the second instance, the client has chosen no longer to take advantage of the audit.

In either situation, there is little that the auditor can do to prevent losing the work.

1.5 Personality

For many small owner-managed companies, audit is almost a personal service. The relationship between such a client and auditor may be strongly based on personality, and if relationships break down, it may be necessary for the audit relationship to discontinue.

Personality may not be such an issue for bigger entities and audit firms where the audit engagement partner could be transferred if required, while the audit stayed within the firm.

1.6 Audit rotation

Rotation of audit staff was discussed in Chapter 4 as a safeguard to audit independence. However, the partners in a firm may sometimes conclude that the firm as a whole has been associated too long with a client and divest the audit.

Exam focus point

From the nature of the issues raised above, it is clear that some of them will affect small firms and not larger ones and some will more pre-dominantly affect larger ones. You should bear that in mind when approaching exam questions, and as usual, apply common sense.

PART A   REGULATORY ISSUES AND PROFESSIONAL PRACTICES

Question   Control over re-appointment

(a) Of the reasons for a change in auditors given above, which do you feel that an auditor may have control over and which they can therefore guard against? Ignore the cases when the auditor does not seek re-election or resigns.

(b) What should the auditor do to guard against the issues you have identified in part (a)?

Answer

(a) **Issues auditor may have control over**

There are two key issues identified above that an auditor may have some control over:

(i) **Fees**

(1) Perception
(2) Competitiveness

(ii) **Personality**

(b) **Actions to guard against issues arising**

(i) With regard to fees, the auditor can ensure that the audit is conducted in such a way as to foster the perception that the audit is good value for the fee. This can be done by encouraging the attitude of audit staff and ensuring that a professional manner is always maintained. It also requires a constant awareness by staff of the need to add value, and to ensure that the audit provides more of a service than fulfilling a statutory requirement. This can be achieved by offering relevant advice to the client as a by-product of the audit, predominantly through the report to management, but also as an integral part of the culture of the audit.

(ii) Also with regard to fees, the auditors can ensure they are competitive in the first instance, by setting reasonable fees and in the second instance by conducting research into what their competitors charge. As companies have to file accounts and the audit fee must be disclosed, this is readily available information.

(iii) Personality is obviously not an issue that an auditor can legislate against. However, part of an auditor's professionalism is to ensure that if personality problems arise, they are handled sensitively and they arise only due to issues on the side of the client.

If serious conflict arise, firms should have a procedure for rotating audits between audit partners.

2 Advertising and fees

> **FAST FORWARD**
> The guidance in the IESBA's *Code of Ethics* on advertising is that the method of advertising used should not reflect adversely on the accountancy profession as a whole.

2.1 AIA guidance

Auditors are in business, and in business it is necessary to advertise. However, accountants are professional people and people rely on their work. It is important therefore that their advertisements do not project an image that is inconsistent with that fact.

AIA has adopted the IESBA *Code of Ethics*, which provides guidance about marketing professional services. It states the following:

> **IESBA *Code of Ethics*: para. R115.2**
>
> When undertaking marketing or promotional activities, a professional accountant shall not bring the profession into disrepute. A professional accountant shall be honest and truthful and shall not make:
>
> (a) Exaggerated claims for the services offered by, or the qualifications or experience of, the accountant; or
>
> (b) Disparaging references or unsubstantiated comparisons to the work of others.
>
> If the professional accountant in public practice is in doubt about whether a proposed form of advertising or marketing is appropriate, the professional accountant in public practice shall consider consulting with the relevant professional body.

2.2 Fees

> **FAST FORWARD**
> It is generally inappropriate to advertise fees.

Three issues arise with regard to fees:

- Referring to fees in promotional material
- Commissions
- Setting and negotiating fees

The last two issues are inter-related and are also closely connected with tendering, which is discussed in Chapter 8.

2.2.1 Advertising fees

The fact that it is difficult to explain the service represented by a single fee in the context of an advertisement and that **confusion might arise as to what a potential client might expect to receive in return for that fee** means that it is **seldom appropriate** to include information about fees in short advertisements.

In longer advertisements, where reference is made to fees in promotional material, the **basis** on which those fees are calculated, hourly and other charging rates etc, **should be clearly stated**.

The key issue to remember with regard to advertising fees is that the **greatest care should be taken to not mislead potential clients**. It is appropriate to advertise free consultations to discuss fee issues. This free consultation will allow fees to be explained, thus avoiding the risk of confusion. It is inappropriate to advertise discounts on existing fees.

2.2.2 Commissions

> **FAST FORWARD** Members may accept or pay referral fees if appropriate safeguards exist.

AIA members may offer commission (and by implication receive commission) for introducing clients. However, they should only do so if there are appropriate safeguards such as:

- Disclosing to the client any arrangements to pay or receive a referral fee.
- Obtaining agreement in advance from the client for commission arrangements, in connection with the sale by a third party of goods or services to the client.

2.3 Use of the AIA logo

Members of the AIA may be either associates or fellows, in which case they are allowed to use the designatory letters AIA or FAIA behind their name.

A firm may describe itself as a firm of 'Accountants' where:

- At least half of the partners are AIA members, and
- Those partners hold at least 51% of voting rights under the partnership agreement.

A firm in which all the partners are International Accountants may use the description 'Members of the Association of International Accountants'.

A firm which holds a firm's auditing certificate from AIA may describe itself as Registered Auditors.

Question — Advertising and fees

Felicity Carr and Frank Harrison both qualified with the AIA five years ago. They have now decided to set up in practice together. Their new firm holds an auditing certificate from AIA and they intend to undertake small audits and some tax work. They will charge themselves out at $200 per hour initially. They will operate from Frank's home. They are a little rusty on the rules concerning advertising and obtaining professional work and so have asked you to advise them.

They have decided to call their practice Harrison Carr and to advertise in the local paper. As they are launching themselves, they have decided to take out a full page advertisement one week and then run a series of smaller adverts in the future. They have also decided to advertise in a local business newspaper.

Required

(a) Explain the ethical guidance on advertising, including advertising fees.
(b) Advise Harrison Carr how they should proceed in relation to:

  (i) How they may describe the firm
  (ii) The adverts in the paper

Answer

(a) **General guidance on advertising**

Generally members may not advertise in a manner that reflects adversely on themselves and their profession. This means that they should consider the quality of the paper in which they intend to advertise. The local paper is appropriate. They should also ensure that they do not discredit the services offered by others in their advert.

Advertising fees

The key issue of importance when advertising fees is to ensure that the reference to fees is not misleading. Generally, it is seldom appropriate to mention fees on a small advert.

7: CHANGES IN PROFESSIONAL APPOINTMENT

(b) (i) **Description of firm**

As both partners are qualified accountants it is acceptable to advertise the firm as being a member of the Association of International Accountants. They may also describe themselves as registered auditors.

(ii) **The proposed advertisements**

While they are planning a larger advert followed by several smaller ones, it may still not be appropriate to mention fees. This is because while they could refer to charge out rates, it would be impossible in the paper to describe how much each service would cost without estimating the time jobs would take. It is impossible to generalise such matters and the reference to fees could therefore be misleading.

It would be more appropriate to advertise that they will give free consultations to discuss fees. They may include all the details given above, their name, the membership of the AIA and their registered auditor status.

3 Agreeing terms

FAST FORWARD Certain issues must be agreed in writing when an audit is accepted.

3.1 Clarifying the agreement

It is important when entering into a contract to provide services to ensure that both parties fully understand what the agreed services are. Misunderstanding could lead to a break down in the relationship, and eventually result in legal action being undertaken.

3.2 Audit engagement letter

An auditor will outline the basis for the audit agreement in his tender to provide services. However, once he has accepted nomination, it is vital that the basis of his relationship is discussed with the new client and laid out in contractual form. This is the role of the **audit engagement letter**, which you should be familiar with from your earlier studies.

Matters which should be clarified in the audit engagement letter

- **Responsibilities of both parties**
  - The auditor is responsible for reporting on the financial statements to members.
  - Directors have a statutory duty to maintain records and take responsibility for the financial statements.
  - Directors are responsible for the detection and prevention of fraud.
- **Fees**
  - Level
  - Billing and credit terms
  - Potential increases
- **Timing**
  - Audit timing

PART A   REGULATORY ISSUES AND PROFESSIONAL PRACTICES

You should already be familiar with the concept and contents of an audit engagement letter. You should also be familiar with ISA 210 *Agreeing the terms of audit engagements* which sets out best practice concerning audit engagement letters.

In practice, the auditor and the new client will meet to negotiate the terms of the audit agreement, which the auditor will later clarify in the audit engagement letter. The first audit should not take place until the client has returned the audit engagement letter with an indication that he agrees to its terms.

4 Books and documents

FAST FORWARD

Audit working papers belong to the auditor.

4.1 Ownership

As you know, **audit working papers are owned by the auditor**. In the event of auditors taking over an audit from another firm, they are **not entitled** to take over all the audit files that that firm has put together on the client.

The AIA rules state that in order to ensure continuity of a client's affairs, the previous auditors must provide the new auditors will all the **reasonable carry-over information** they request, and they should do this **promptly**. The previous auditor should ensure that he transfers all the books and documents belonging to the client to the new auditors without delay. He is only allowed to keep the books where he is entitled to exercise a **lien**.

4.2 The right of lien

Key term

A **lien** is a creditor's right to retain possession of a debtor's property until the debtor pays what is owed to the creditor.

If the previous auditor is still owed fees by the client, he may have a right to exercise a lien over some of the client's books. General liens over property can rarely be established. However, it may be possible for an auditor to have a particular lien when a debtor owes a debt specifically in respect of that property.

A right of particular lien will only exist where the following conditions are fulfilled.

- The documents must be the property of the client itself (not a closely related third party).
- The documents must have come into the member's possession by proper means.
- The work must have been done and a fee note rendered in respect of it.
- The fee must relate to the retained documents.

4.3 Third party rights to information

As discussed in Chapter 4, the auditor owes a duty of confidentiality to the client. This means that documents containing information about the client should not be given to third parties unless:

- The client agrees to the disclosure before it is made.
- Disclosure is required by statute or court order.
- Disclosure is otherwise in accordance with the rules of professional conduct.

4.4 Client rights to information

Audit working papers are the property of the auditor and as such, the **client has no right of access to them**. The member may allow the client access to the working papers if he so chooses.

However, the position is more complicated when the work undertaken is something other than audit. For example, if the accountant puts together the **financial statements** on behalf of the client, those financial statements will belong to the client.

With tax work, documents created in carrying out **tax compliance work** will belong to the client.

Chapter Roundup

- Common reasons behind companies changing the auditors include audit fee, auditor not seeking re-election and size of company.
- The guidance in the IESBA's *Code of Ethics* on advertising is that the method of advertising used should not reflect adversely on the accountancy profession as a whole.
- It is generally inappropriate to advertise fees.
- Members may accept or pay referral fees if appropriate safeguards exist.
- Certain issues must be agreed in writing when an audit is accepted.
- Audit working papers belong to the auditor.

Quick Quiz

1 Name three reasons why an auditor might not seek re-election.

    (1) ....

    (2) ....

    (3) ....

2 Why should accountants not usually advertise fees?

3 List five matters which may be referred to in an audit engagement letter.

    (1) ....

    (2) ....

    (3) ....

    (4) ....

    (5) ....

4 Accountants are permitted to receive a referral fee, provided adequate safeguards are in place.

    True ☐   False ☐

5 Explain the ethical guidance regarding the advertisement of professional services by Chartered Accountants.

6 Audit working papers are the property of the .... and as such, the client has .... to them.

PART A REGULATORY ISSUES AND PROFESSIONAL PRACTICES

Answers to Quick Quiz

1   (1)   Ethical reasons (eg fees)
    (2)   Another client in competition
    (3)   Disagreement over accounting policy

2   The advert is unlikely to be detailed, and facts given about fees could mislead potential clients.

3   Five from:

    - The objective of the audit of financial statements
    - Management's responsibility for the financial statements
    - The applicable reporting framework
    - The scope of the audit, including reference to applicable legislation, regulations, or pronouncements of professional bodies to which the auditor adheres
    - The form of any reports or other communication of results of the engagement
    - The fact that because of the test nature and other inherent limitations of an audit, together with the inherent limitations of any accounting system and system of internal control, there is an unavoidable risk that even some material misstatement may remain undiscovered
    - Unrestricted access to whatever records, documentation and other information requested in connection with the audit
    - Arrangements regarding the planning of the audit
    - Expectations of receiving from management written confirmation concerning representations made in connection with the audit
    - Request for the client to confirm the terms of engagement by acknowledging receipt of the audit engagement letter
    - Description of any other letters or reports the auditor expects to issue to the client
    - Basis on which fees are computed and any billing arrangements
    - Arrangements concerning the involvement of other auditors and experts in some aspects of the audit
    - Arrangements concerning the involvement of internal auditors and other client staff
    - Arrangements to be made with the predecessor auditor, if any, in the case of an initial audit
    - Any restriction of the auditor's liability when such possibility exists
    - A reference to any further agreements between the auditor and the client

4   True

5   A professional accountant shall not bring the profession into disrepute. A professional accountant shall be honest and truthful and shall not make exaggerated claims for the services offered by, or the qualifications or experience of, the accountant or disparaging references or unsubstantiated comparisons to the work of others.

6   auditor, no right of access

End of Chapter Question

Partner (AIA November 2006)

The managing partner of a firm of accountants was asked to appear on a radio programme to discuss recent criticisms of external auditors in the business press. He was introduced by name and the name of his firm was referred to on two occasions during the interview. In the course of the discussion, the managing partner made the following statement:

> Most of the criticisms of audit firms voiced in the press are the result of incompetent management of the audit process. My firm is one of the very few in the country that is managed in a competent and professional manner.

At the conclusion of the interview, the radio presenter offered the managing partner an opportunity to summarise his advice to concerned listeners. The managing partner's response was:

> Any shareholders or finance directors who are concerned about their present auditors should telephone me tomorrow. My firm will be happy to take the place of any incompetent audit firm that is presently in place.

Required

(a) Explain whether it is appropriate for a partner in a firm of accountants to make such comments in a radio broadcast. **(10 marks)**

(b) Explain why audit is frequently the subject of public concern and discussion, despite the many ways in which professional bodies have striven to regulate the audit process. **(10 marks)**

(Total 20 marks)

PART A REGULATORY ISSUES AND PROFESSIONAL PRACTICES

PART B

Statutory audit and other evaluation

Practice management

Topic list	Syllabus reference
1 Risks to which firms are exposed	LO2
2 The client acceptance/retention decision	LO2
3 Managing and developing professional staff	LO2
4 Maintaining and developing the firm's audit approach	LO2
5 Tendering	LO2

Introduction

Some **practice management** issues were considered in Chapter 7, for example, consideration of why clients change auditors and how an auditor should go about obtaining professional work. We continue our consideration of practice management issues in this chapter.

Two of the **key risks** to a firm have been touched on in previous chapters, namely

- The risk of **losing clients**, and consequently the business failing
- The risk of **litigation**, and consequently the business failing

We shall review these, and other risks faced by the audit firm, in Section 1, as well as some general safeguards that a firm can put in place against these risks.

It is also important for firm's quality management practices and continued business that its staff are managed and developed well, so that audit engagement teams work effectively. The firm will need to ensure that its firm wide approach to audit is suitable and competitive, as well as maintaining a high quality so that it can compete in the difficult audit market.

Lastly, we shall look at the issue of tendering, by which firms usually obtain audit work.

1 Risks to which firms are exposed

FAST FORWARD A key risk facing audit firms is that the business will fail.

1.1 Overall business risk

An audit firm is a business. It faces risks as any business does, and, as with any other business, the **key risk is that the business will fail**. In this section we will consider the risks specific to audit firms which may result in business failure. The risks are outlined in the diagram below.

The diagram shows the links which can exist between some of the risks. These should be self explanatory links. The risks shall be considered individually below.

1.2 Litigation

In Chapter 6 we discussed the responsibilities that auditors have in tort and contract law. The auditor also has professional duties of care to his clients. Should the auditor fail to uphold those responsibilities, the result can be litigation against the auditor. As the claim would be made under civil law, the redress to the claimant would be **compensation** should the claim be upheld.

This could result in business failure for several reasons:

- The loss of the client itself may impact so heavily on the business that it cannot continue.

    (Under the ethical fee guidance, loss of the litigious client only should not cause business failure.)

- There might be bad publicity arising from the litigation which could cause
    - Loss of existing clients
    - Inability to grow or replace client base over time

1.3 Client loss

The firm might lose clients for reasons other than litigation. Possible reasons for this have been discussed already in Chapter 7.

1.4 Disciplinary action by AIA

A situation might arise where AIA felt it necessary to discipline the firm for **misconduct** under its byelaws. This could result in the partners being **excluded from membership of AIA**, which would result in them not being able to practise as auditors.

1.5 Key personnel

This is a particular risk to small firms. As with all small businesses, the risk might exist that the **firm relies** too heavily on **particular personnel**, to the extent that the firm cannot continue in existence in their absence.

1.6 Competition

The audit market is competitive, and audit firms face the risk of competition in a similar way to other businesses. The exception in the case of auditors is that there are **strict qualification requirements** to be an auditor, so **competition is restricted** in that way. We shall look at managing overall audit approach in Section 4. It is vital that the firm keeps up with trends and audits in the most effective way or it will be priced out of the market.

There are other issues associated with competition or actually the lack of it, in the audit market in current times. Questions have been raised recently as to whether the concentration in the audit market, with the Big Four firms supplying audit services to most large companies, creates any risks in the market.

The situation is unlikely to change in the short term as there are significant barriers to entry to the market for auditors of large companies. It may not be economical for other firms to break into this market given the need to demonstrate:

- A credible reputation with large companies, their investors and other stakeholders
- Appropriate resources and expertise in place to carry out large company audits, including relevant sector-specific skills
- An effective capability to secure timely and reliable audit opinions on overseas subsidiaries for audits of companies with significant international operations

In other words, a risk some smaller mid-tier firms might face is not being able to break into the market serving the largest companies, or overextending themselves trying to do so.

Following a decade of reviews into the audit market, the Competition and Markets Authority (CMA) published a study in 2018 which found that:

- Companies choose their own auditors, and as a result we have seen too much evidence of them picking those with whom they have the best 'cultural fit' or 'chemistry' rather than those who offer the toughest scrutiny;
- Choice is too limited, with the Big Four audit firms conducting 97% of the audits of the biggest companies; and
- Auditors' focus on quality appears diluted by the fact that at least 75% of the revenue of the Big Four comes from other services like consulting.

As a result of this, the CMA proposed to:

- Separate audit from consulting services;
- Introduce measures to substantially increase the accountability of those chairing audit committees in firms, and
- Impose a 'joint audit' regime giving firms outside the Big Four a role in auditing the UK's biggest companies.

The extent to which these recommendations will be implemented remains to be seen.

PART B STATUTORY AUDIT AND OTHER EVALUATION

1.7 Risk management

> **FAST FORWARD**
> Risk of business failure can be mitigated by observing regulatory or professional requirements.

Auditors have to manage their business effectively and so should have a risk management system in place. For example, in Chapter 7 we briefly discussed the client loss situations which a firm can seek to avoid.

The firm can take steps to mitigate general business risks, for example, by taking out **key man insurance**, or instigating **client care procedures**.

1.7.1 Professional standards

As you know, the International Auditing and Assurance Standards Board (IAASB), a standing committee of IFAC, issues international standards. We have already seen how the ethical and quality management standards operate together to ensure that auditors maintain independence. Adhering to auditing standards can reduce some of the risks outlined above, by ensuring quality audits are carried out.

Exam focus point

> You should be aware of the ISAs from your earlier studies. You should check up to date examination guidance for your exam on the AIA website.

The ISAs give a **framework** for all auditors to follow. This **ensures a level of quality and consistency** between audit firms. It means that a **client can have assurance** of that level of quality being used.

For this reason, if auditors do not follow the statements of auditing standards, they face disciplinary action, and in negligence litigation, the courts will take into account if the auditor followed the appropriate guidance when conducting the audit.

2 The client acceptance/retention decision

> **FAST FORWARD**
> ISQM 1 sets out what a firm must consider and document in relation to accepting or continuing engagement, which is, the nature and circumstances of the engagement, the integrity and ethical values of the client and the firm's ability to perform the engagement.

2.1 Ethical requirements

There are a number of ethical procedures associated with accepting engagements which you have studied previously.

Knowledge brought forward from earlier studies

Procedures before accepting nomination

(a) Ensure that there are **no ethical issues** which are a **barrier** to accepting nomination.

(b) Ensure that the auditor is **professionally qualified** to act and that there are no legal or technical barriers.

(c) Ensure that the existing **resources** are **adequate** in terms of staff, expertise and time.

(d) Obtain **references for the directors** if they are not known personally to the audit firm.

(e) **Consult the previous auditors** to ensure that there are not any reasons behind the vacancy which the new auditors ought to know. This is also a courtesy to the previous auditors.

8: PRACTICE MANAGEMENT

Procedures after accepting nomination

(a) **Ensure** that the **outgoing auditors' removal** or **resignation** has been **properly conducted** in accordance with the law.

The new auditors should see a valid notice of the outgoing auditors' resignation, or confirm that the outgoing auditors were properly removed.

(b) **Ensure** that the **new auditors' appointment is valid**. The new auditors should obtain a copy of the resolution passed at the general meeting appointing them as the company's auditors.

(c) Set up and **submit a letter of engagement** to the directors of the company.

Exam focus point

The November 2021 exam included a question on whether an audit firm should accept an audit client in a given scenario.

2.2 Requirements of ISQM 1 and ISA 220

We touched on some of the ethical requirements of ISQM 1 *Quality management for firms that perform audits or reviews of financial statements, or other assurance or related services engagements* and ISA 220 (Revised) *Quality management for an audit of financial statements* earlier in this workbook. As it sets out standards and guidance in connection with the acceptance and continuance of client relationships and specific engagements we shall consider it further here. ISQM 1 and SSA 220 will also be covered in Chapter 14 of this workbook.

ISQM 1: para.30

The firm shall establish the following quality objectives that address the acceptance and continuance of client relationships and specific engagements:

(a) Judgements by the firm about whether to accept or continue a client relationship or specific engagement are appropriate based on:

  (i) Information obtained about the **nature and circumstances** of the engagement and the **integrity** and **ethical** values of the client (including management, and, when appropriate, those charged with governance) that is sufficient to support such judgements; and

  (ii) The firm's **ability to perform the engagement** in accordance with professional standards and applicable legal and regulatory requirements.

(b) The **financial and operational priorities** of the firm do not lead to inappropriate judgements about whether to accept or continue a client relationship or specific engagement.

2.2.1 Obtain information

Audit firms may obtain information from internal and external sources including the following.

- Information from current or previous engagements (for existing clients)
- The communications auditors must make with the previous auditors
- Other relevant communications, for example with other parties in the audit firm, bankers or legal counsel
- Searches on relevant databases

2.2.2 Identify issues

Here are some matters that the auditors might consider in relation to the acceptance decision.

Matters to consider	
Nature and circumstances of the engagement	The industry of the entity and relevant regulatory factors
	The nature of the entity, for example, its operations, organisational structure, ownership and governance, its business model and how it is financed
	The nature of the underlying subject matter and the applicable criteria
Integrity and ethical values of the client	Nature of the entity for which the engagement is being performed, including the complexity of its ownership and management structure
	Nature of the client's operations, including its business practices
	Information concerning the attitude of the client's principal owners, key management, those charged with governance towards matters such as aggressive interpretation of accounting standards/internal control environment
	Whether the client is aggressively concerned with maintaining the firm's fees as low as possible
	Indications of an inappropriate limitation in the scope of work
	Indications that the client might be involved in money laundering or other criminal activities
	The reasons for the proposed appointment of the audit firm and non-reappointment of the previous firm
	The identity and business reputation of related parties
Firm's ability to perform the engagement	The circumstances of the engagement and the reporting deadline
	Availability of individuals with the necessary competence and capabilities, including sufficient time to perform the engagement including: • Individuals to take overall responsibility for directing and supervising the engagement • Individuals with knowledge of the relevant industry or the underlying subject matter and experience with relevant regulatory or reporting requirements • Individuals to perform audit procedures on the financial information of a component for purposes of an audit of group financial statements
	Are experts available, if needed?
	Are individuals meeting the eligibility requirements to perform the engagement quality review available where applicable?
	The need for technological resources, for example, IT applications that enable the engagement team to perform procedures on the entity's data
	The need for intellectual resources, for example, a methodology, industry or subject matter specific guides, or access to information sources

In addition, the audit firm needs to ensure its **financial and operational priorities** do not lead to inappropriate judgements about whether to accept or continue a client relationship or specific engagement. Financial priorities may focus on the profitability of the firm, and fees obtained for the performance of engagements have an effect on the firm's financial resources. Operational priorities may include strategic focus areas, such as growth of the firm's market share, industry specialisation or new service offerings.

There may be circumstances when the firm is satisfied with the fee quoted for an engagement but it is not appropriate for the firm to accept or continue the engagement or client relationship (eg when the client lacks integrity and ethical values). There may be other circumstances when the fee quoted for an engagement is

not sufficient given the nature and circumstances of the engagement, and it may diminish the firm's ability to perform the engagement in accordance with professional standards and applicable legal and regulatory requirements.

> **ISA 220.23–24**
>
> The engagement partner shall take into account information obtained in the acceptance and continuance process in planning and performing the audit engagement in accordance with the ISAs and complying with the requirements of this ISA.
>
> If the engagement team becomes aware of information that may have caused the firm to decline the audit engagement had that information been known by the firm prior to accepting or continuing the client relationship or specific engagement, the engagement partner shall communicate that information promptly to the firm, so that the firm and the engagement partner can take the necessary action.

Such action might include assigning more staff or staff with specific expertise.

Question — Accepting nomination

You are a partner in Hamlyn, Jones and Co, a firm of International Accountants. You have just successfully tendered for the audit of Lunch Co, a chain of sandwich shops across west London. The tender opportunity was received cold, that is, the company and its officers are not known to the firm. The company has just been incorporated and has not previously had an audit. You are about ready to accept nomination.

Required

(a) Explain the procedures should you carry out prior to accepting nomination.

In the course of your acceptance procedures you received a reference from a business contact of yours concerning one of the five directors of Lunch Co, Mr V Loud. It stated that your business contact had done some personal tax work for Mr Loud ten years previously, when he had found Mr Loud to be difficult to keep in contact with, slow to provide information and he had suspected Mr Loud of being economical with the truth when it came to his tax affairs. As a result of this distrust, he had ceased to carry out work for him.

Required

(b) Comment on the effect this reference would have on accepting nomination.

Answer

(a) The following procedures should be carried out.

   (i) Ensure that I and my audit team are professionally qualified to act and consider whether there are ethical barriers to my accepting nomination

   (ii) Review the firm's overall work programme to ensure that there are sufficient resources to enable my firm to carry out the audit

   (iii) Obtain references about the directors as they are not known personally by me or anyone else in my firm

(b) The auditor must use their professional judgement when considering the responses they gets to references concerning new clients. The guidance cannot legislate for all situations so it does not attempt to do so. In the circumstance given above there is no correct answer therefore, as in practice, an auditor would have to make a justified decision backed up with documentation.

   Matters to be considered

   The reference raises three issues for the auditor considering accepting nomination.

- The issue that the director has been difficult to maintain a relationship with in the past
- The issue that the director was slow to provide information in the past
- The suspicion of a lack of integrity in relation to his tax affairs

The auditor must **consider** these **in the light of several factors**:

- The length of time that has passed since the events
- What the references which refer to the interim time say
- The difference between accepting a role of auditing a company and personal tax work
- The director's role in the company and therefore, the audit
- The amount of control exercised by the director
    - Relationships with other directors
    - Influence

At this stage the auditors **should not be considering** how highly they **values** the **opinion** of the referee. That should have been considered before they sent the reference request. At this stage they should only be considering the implications of the reference for their current decision.

Auditing a company is different from auditing personal affairs in terms of obtaining information and contacting personnel. In this case, the **key issue** is the question over the **integrity** of the director.

As we do not have information about interim references and details of the business arrangements it is difficult to give a definite answer to this issue. However, Mr Loud is likely to only have **limited control over decisions** of the entity being one of five directors, which might lead to the auditor deciding that the reference was insufficient to prevent him accepting nomination. If Mr Loud were the **finance director**, the auditor would be more inclined not to take the nomination.

2.3 Money laundering

As we discussed in Chapter 6, accountants are now required to carry out specific client identification procedures when accepting new clients.

'**Know your client**' (KYC) is an important part of being in a position to comply with the law on money laundering, because as we mentioned in Chapter 6, knowledge of the client is at the bottom of 'suspicion' in the context of making reports about money laundering.

It is important from the outset of a relationship with a new client to obtain KYC information, such as:

- Expected patterns of business
- The business model of the client
- The source of the client's funds

When the client's money is to be handled by the professional, there is a higher than normal risk to the professional, so even more detailed KYC procedures will be required.

2.3.1 Politically exposed persons (PEPs)

Being involved with PEPs may be particularly risky for firms, particularly in terms of reputation risks if things go wrong. The FATF Guidance on PEPs distinguishes foreign from domestic PEPs, but auditors must consider both.

Key term

> **Foreign PEPs** are individuals who are, or have been, entrusted with prominent public functions in a foreign country, for example, heads of state or of government, senior politicians, senior government, judicial or military officials, senior executives of state-owned corporations, important political party officials.
> **Domestic PEPs** are individuals who are or have been entrusted domestically with prominent public functions, for example, heads of state or of government, senior politicians, senior government, judicial or military officials, senior executives of state-owned corporations, important political party officials.
>
> (FATF *Politically exposed persons (recommendations 12 and 22)*: p4–5)

Firms and institutions should have risk management systems set up to determine whether an individual is a PEP when client identification procedures are being carried out. When a person has been identified as a PEP, a member of senior management should approve establishing a business relationship with that person.

The firm should then take reasonable measures to establish the source of that individual's wealth and funds and conduct enhanced ongoing monitoring of the firm's relationship with that individual.

2.4 Client acceptance checklist

Many audit firms use a client acceptance checklist to assist them in making the decision to accept a client and ensuring that ISQM 1 requirements are met.

2.5 Commercial considerations

Those in leadership in a firm will need to reflect on how the firm approaches audits regularly to ensure that quality management requirements are met, but also to ensure that the firm's approach is commercially viable, otherwise, as we shall see below, a firm will not win tenders and will price itself out of the audit market.

For example, if a firm has not embraced the risk and controls approach to audit and still takes a more historic, fully substantive approach to audit, then there is a risk that the time they will budget for an audit will be far greater than firms they are competing against in a tender, resulting in a much higher audit price. This is unlikely to be competitive. Clearly a firm must follow auditing standards, but it is important to consider audit approach in such a commercial fashion as well.

2.5.1 Nature of the audit firm

The nature of the audit firm will impact on how it approaches an audit as well. For instance, one trend in the market is for firms to be affiliated under an international brand name. Once consideration for a firm when affiliating with other firms in this fashion is the control over matters such as audit approach the firm will retain, or whether there will be an 'affiliation approach'.

Similarly, there has been a trend in the audit market for firms to merge. When considering a merger, partners will have to consider if they are comfortable with the other firm's general approach to audits, and whether they can agree on the way forward for the combined firm.

A small, unaffiliated, independent audit firm may have greater flexibility in the way it can approach different audit clients as it is a smaller operation and the partners will be able to be more flexible in their approach. On the other hand, smaller firms do not have the staff and resources to meet some of the demands of quality control requirements, and with the increasing requirement to divest other services to audit clients to ensure independence from the audit, are being pushed out of the audit market.

PART B STATUTORY AUDIT AND OTHER EVALUATION

3 Tendering

When approaching a tender, it is important to consider both fees and practical issues.

3.1 Approach

A firm puts together a tender if:

- It has been approached by a prospective client; and
- The partners have decided that they are capable of doing the work for a reasonable fee.

When approached to tender, the auditor has to consider whether he wants to do the work. You should be aware of all the ethical considerations that would go into this decision. The auditor will also have to consider:

- Fees
- Practical issues

3.1.1 Fees

Determining whether the job can be done for a reasonable price will involve a substantial number of estimates. The key estimate will be how long the partner thinks it will take to do the work. This will involve meeting with the prospective client to discuss their business and systems and making the estimate from there.

The first stage of setting the fee is therefore to ascertain **what the job will involve**. The job should be broken down into its respective parts, for example, audit and tax, or if it is a complex and/or pure audit, what aspects of the job would be undertaken by what level staff.

The second stage is closely linked with the first, therefore. It involves **ascertaining which staff**, or which level of staff, **will be involved** and in what proportions they will be involved.

Once estimates have been made of how long the work will take and what level of expertise is needed in each area, **the firm's standard charge out rates can be applied** to that information, and a **fee estimated**.

Clearly, it is **commercially vital** that the estimates of time and costs are **reasonable**, or the audit firm will be seeking to undertake the work at a loss or not tender at a competitive price. However, it is also ethically important that the fee estimate is reasonable, or the result will be that the client is being misled about the sustainable fee level.

3.1.2 Lowballing

Problems can arise when auditing firms appear to be charging less than this, or at least less than the 'market rate' for the audit. The practice of undercutting, usually at tender for the audit of large companies, has been called **lowballing**. In other cases, the audit fee has been reduced even though the auditors have remained the same. The problem here is that, if the audit is being performed for less than it is actually worth, then the auditors' independence is called into question.

This is always going to be a topical debate, but in terms of negotiating the audit fee the following factors need to be taken into account.

(a) The audit is perceived to have a fluctuating 'market price' as any other commodity or service. In a recession, prices would be expected to fall as companies aim to cut costs everywhere, and as auditors chase less work (supply falls). Audit firms are also reducing staffing levels and their own overhead costs should be lower.

(b) Companies can **reduce external audit costs** through various legitimate measures:

    (i) Extending the size and function of internal audit
    (ii) Reducing the number of different audit firms used world-wide

(iii) Selling off subsidiary companies leaving a simplified group structure to audit
(iv) The tender process itself simply makes auditors more competitive
(v) Exchange rate fluctuations in audit fees

(c) Auditing firms have increased productivity, partly through the use of more sophisticated information technology techniques in auditing.

The AIA's guidance on quotations states that it is **not improper** to secure work by **quoting a lower fee** so long as the **client has not been misled** about the level of work that the fee represents, and a self-interest threat does not arise.

In the event of investigations into allegations of unsatisfactory work, the level of fees would be considered with regard to member's conduct with reference to the ethical guidelines.

3.1.3 Practical issues

The firm will have to consider the practical points arising from the approach. Common considerations include:

- Does the proposed timetable for the work fit with the current work plan?
- Does the firm have suitable personnel available?
- Where will the work be performed and is it accessible/cost effective?
- Are (non-accounting) specialist skills necessary?
- Will staff need further training to do the work?
- If so, what is the cost of that further training?

Certain information will be required to put together a proposal document. This has already been touched on briefly, when discussing the audit fee. It is likely that audit staff would have to have a meeting with the prospective client to discuss the following issues:

- What the client requires from the audit firm, for example:
  - Audit
  - Number of visits (interim and final)
  - Tax work
- What the future plans of the entity are, for example:
  - Is it planning to float its shares on an exchange in the near future?
  - Is growth, or diversification anticipated?
- Whether the entity is seeking its first auditors and needs an explanation of audit
- Whether the entity is seeking to change its auditors
- If the entity is changing its auditors, the reason behind this

3.2 Content of an audit proposal

An audit proposal, or tender, does not have a set format. The prospective client will indicate the format that he wants the tender to take. This may be merely in document form, or could be a presentation by members of the audit firm.

Although each tender will be tailored to the individual circumstances, there are some matters which are likely to be covered in every one. These are set out below.

Matters to be included in audit proposal
• The fee, and how it has been calculated
• An assessment of the needs of the prospective client
• An outline of how the firm intends to meet those needs

Matters to be included in audit proposal
• The assumptions made to support that proposal
• The proposed approach to the engagement
• A brief outline of the firm
• An outline of the key staff involved

If the tender is being submitted to an **existing client**, some of those details will be unnecessary. However, if it is a competitive tender, the firm should ensure they submit a comparable tender, even if some of the details are already known to the client. This is because the tender must be **comparable** to competitors and must appear professional.

3.3 Evaluation of a tender

Each company will have its own criteria for what it wants from a firm of auditors. This means that there are no hard and fast rules about how a tender will be evaluated. However, there are some general points to bear in mind when putting together a proposal.

Evaluation factors	
Fee	The fee, as discussed earlier, **can be the most important factor** for people assessing tenders. It is possible that a reader might look at the fee and decide not to continue reading the tender, despite the rest of the content.
Professionalism	Auditors provide a **professional service** and the first impressions a prospective client may have of the firm are the staff involved with the proposal and the tender document itself. It is therefore vital that the professionalism which should mark the audit relationship is clear.
Proposed approach	An audit can cause a disruption to the ordinary course of a business, particularly in the finance department. The client might be seeking the **least disruptive approach**. This might mean they look for an audit with the shortest number of proposed days on site.
Personal service	It is important that the relationship between the auditors and the management of the entity is good and the client perceives that they are getting value for money. It is important to highlight key staff and to **foster relationships** with management from the outset of a relationship, and this means during the tender process.

Chapter Roundup

- A key risk facing audit firms is that the business will fail.
- ISQM 1 sets out what a firm must consider and document in relation to accepting or continuing engagement, which is, the nature and circumstances of the engagement, the integrity and ethical values of the client and the firm's ability to perform the engagement.
- When approaching a tender, it is important to consider both fees and practical issues.

PART B STATUTORY AUDIT AND OTHER EVALUATION

Quick Quiz

1 Name two reasons an audit may be lost due to size.

   (1) ....
   (2) ....

2 ISAs are prescriptive.

   True ☐   False ☐

3 The objective of ISQM 1 is that:

   'The firm is to design, implement and operate a system of ……………. ……………… for audits or reviews of financial statements, or other assurance or related services engagements performed by the firm, that provides the firm with …………. assurance that: (a) The firm and its personnel fulfil their responsibilities in accordance with ……………. standards and applicable ……………. ………… …………… requirements, and conduct engagements in accordance with such standards and requirements; and (b) …………… issued by the firm or engagement partners are ………….. in the circumstances.'

4 List three sources of information about a new client which can be used when making a decision whether to accept the engagement.

   (1) ....
   (2) ....
   (3) ....

5 According to the IESBA Code, when considering whether to accept an engagement with a new or existing client, the auditors must consider whether a ……………………………. ……….. …………………………. arises.

6 List five practical issues that an auditor should consider when approaching a tender.

   (1) ....
   (2) ....
   (3) ....
   (4) ....
   (5) ....

7 Draw a diagram showing the key stages in a tender, explaining what happens at each stage.

8: PRACTICE MANAGEMENT

Answers to Quick Quiz

1. (1) Client becomes too large for audit firm's capacity.
   (2) Client becomes too small to require an audit by statute.

2. True

3. Quality management, reasonable, professional, legal and regulatory, engagement reports, appropriate

4. (1) Communications with existing/previous auditors
   (2) Communications with other third parties (eg bankers/legal counsel)
   (3) Relevant databases

5. Conflict of interest

6. (1) Does the timetable fit with current work plan?
   (2) Are suitable personnel available
   (3) Where will work be performed? Is it cost effective?
   (4) Are specialist skills needed?
   (5) Will staff need further training? If so, what is the cost?

7.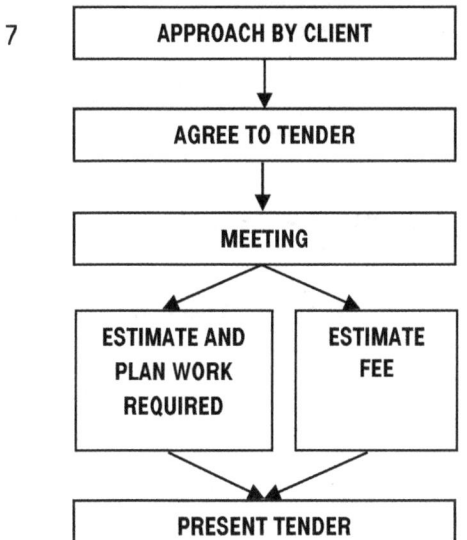

   Auditor considers if it is possible to undertake work at a reasonable fee

   Arrange meeting to obtain information prior to tender

   Obtain knowledge of the business and the service required

   Allocate potential staff to work plan and calculate fee by reference to standard charge out rates

   This could be in the form of:
   – Letter
   – Report
   – Presentation

PART B STATUTORY AUDIT AND OTHER EVALUATION

End of Chapter Question

Audit firm approach (AIA May 2009 amended)

An audit firm has 15 partners and 150 professional staff. The managing partner is keen to ensure that the firm has a consistent approach to the evaluation of inherent audit risk. This matter was discussed at a partnership meeting and it was agreed that the firm should do something to encourage a consistent approach.

An initial attempt was made to compare a sample of the audit working papers prepared by teams working for each audit partner, but this proved to be remarkably difficult to do properly. The members of the review team did not feel that they were able to compare different audit working papers in a meaningful way. For example, the planning section of two different audit files would clearly explain why a particular evaluation of inherent risk had been arrived at, but that did not necessarily mean that every partner or manager in the firm would have reached exactly the same conclusion.

The partners have decided that they will invest some additional time and resources in this matter because they regard it as an important one for the overall quality management of their firm. They have agreed that further work will be undertaken on the question of whether there is consistency in the work being undertaken and also on working towards managing consistency in all future evaluations of inherent risk.

Required

(a) Explain how a team of reviewers comprising partners and managers from within the firm might evaluate the consistency of past judgements on inherent risk. **(8 marks)**

(b) Explain why an audit firm might be keen to ensure that judgements concerning inherent risk are being made consistently. **(4 marks)**

(c) Explain how a firm might ensure that future decisions on inherent risk are being made in a consistent way. **(8 marks)**

(Total 20 marks)

Company audits – special considerations

Topic list	Syllabus reference
1 Single company audit	LO1
2 Audit of group financial statements	LO1
3 Auditing components located abroad	LO1
4 Joint audits	LO1

Introduction

You should be familiar with the basic audit of a single company from your earlier studies. There are some more advanced aspects which we shall look at in the course of this book, but in principle, the concept should be familiar to you.

The audit of a group of financial statements is a new auditing topic for you, one which is concerned with practical difficulties of communication between auditors and the problems of geography.

Group audits fall into two categories.

(1) Where the same firm of auditors audits the whole group

(2) Where one firm of auditors has responsibility for the opinion on the consolidated accounts and a different firm audits part of the group

Even where the audit of each individual company in the group is carried out by the same firm, there may be administrative complications where some audits are carried out by different branches, perhaps overseas, with different practices and procedures. ISA 600 (Revised) *Special considerations – audit of group financial statements (including the work of component auditors)* sets out guidance for the group auditor.

Lastly we consider particular issues associated with auditing foreign subsidiaries and carrying out joint audits.

1 Single company audit

> **FAST FORWARD**
>
> You should be familiar with the concept of a single company audit from your earlier studies.

You have covered the basics of a company audit in your studies at earlier. As you were reminded in Chapter 1, you should be aware of the basic chronology of an audit, the stages that auditors go through in carrying out an audit in accordance with auditing standards and in providing a basis for an appropriate audit opinion.

Later in this Learning & Practice Workbook some more complicated aspects of single company auditing will be introduced, for example, the audit of related parties, and some complex and important areas such as the audit of fraud and quality management on individual audits will be revisited.

We shall go on in this Chapter and the next to look at audits where the auditor has other things to consider as well as all the matters required for a normal company audit, namely when he is both auditing a company's single financial statements and its group financial statements, and in Chapter 10, when the focus of the company or entity is non-profit making.

2 Audit of group financial statements

> **FAST FORWARD**
>
> A group audit is the audit of the group financial statements.

Key terms

A **group** is a reporting entity for which group financial statements are prepared. This can include legal or other entities (such as parents, subsidiaries, joint ventures and associates) as well as business units, functions, activities, branches or divisions.

Group financial statements are financial statements that include the financial information of more than one entity or business unit through a consolidation process.

A **group audit** is the audit of the group financial statements.

A **group auditor** is the group engagement partner and members of the engagement team other than component auditors. The group auditor is responsible for establishing the overall group audit strategy and plan, directing and supervising any component auditors and forming an opinion on the group financial statements.

A **group engagement partner** is the engagement partner who is ultimately responsible for the group audit. In order to fulfil the requirements of ISA 220 (Revised), the group engagement partner is responsible for managing quality on the group audit engagement, including the audit of any components undertaken by either the group auditor or a component auditor.

A **component** is an entity, business unit, function or business activity that is identified as such by the group auditor for the purposes of planning and performing the group audit.

A **component auditor** is an auditor who performs audit work related to a component for the purposes of the group audit. A component auditor is a part of the engagement team for a group audit.

ISA 600 (Revised): Paras 4, 11, 14, 16

You should be familiar with concept of groups of companies. We are now looking at the considerations of the auditors that are auditing the group financial statements. All the ISAs that you are currently aware of apply to an audit of group financial statements, and the normal audit considerations apply to such an audit.

However, due to the fact that financial information relating to several components is included in group financial statements, an auditor of group financial statements has additional considerations and requirements to fulfil, and we shall look at those in this chapter.

The following is an example of a group of companies and their auditors, to try and illustrate the relationships that are created in a group audit. You may well be asked to deal with this type of question in the exam.

Example

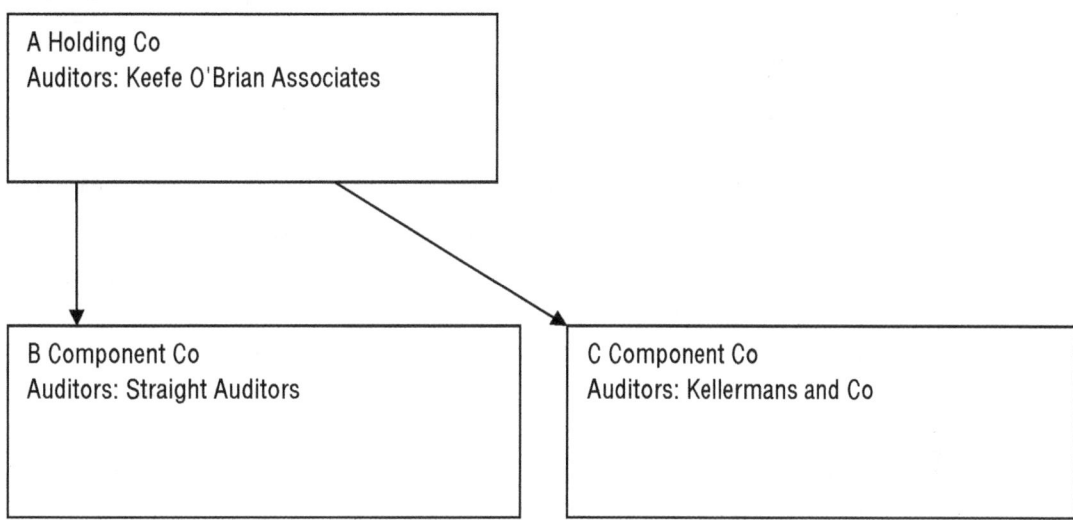

This is the ABC group of companies. A Holding Co is the parent of two subsidiaries, B Component Co and C Component Co. A Holding Co produces group financial statements which are audited by Keefe O'Brian Associates. In relation to the group financial statements, Keefe O'Brian Associates are required to obtain sufficient appropriate audit evidence to express an opinion on the financial statements, which include information about the component companies.

They could obtain this information by carrying out audit work at all three companies in the group. However, both the component companies require audits of their own financial statements and hence a large amount of audit information and evidence will be gathered in respect of those companies anyway. A Holding Co may not want to pay for full audits by their auditors of their component companies, particularly as company audits have been carried out.

On the other hand, Keefe O'Brian cannot simply rely on the audits that have already been carried out on the component companies because:

- Keefe O'Brian is solely responsible for the opinion on the group financial statements and need to ensure that it is true and fair and they are not giving an opinion negligently.

- Risks and materiality levels for the group may be different from those considered/applied in the individual audits.

Therefore, Keefe O'Brian needs to obtain sufficient appropriate information from the component auditors in order to express an opinion on the group financial statements.

2.1 ISA 600 (Revised) Special Considerations – Audits of Group Financial Statements (Including the Work of Component Auditors)

FAST FORWARD

Group auditing requirements and guidance is found in ISA 600 (Revised) *Special considerations – audits of group financial statements (including the work of component auditors)*.

The objectives of ISA 600 (Revised) are as follows:

(a) With respect to the acceptance and continuance of the group audit engagement, determine whether sufficient appropriate audit evidence can reasonably be expected to be obtained to provide a basis for forming an opinion on the group financial statements

(b) Identify and assess the risks of material misstatement of the group financial statements, whether due to fraud or error, and plan and perform further audit procedures to appropriately respond to those assessed risks

(c) Be sufficiently and appropriately involved in the work of component auditors throughout the group audit, including communicating clearly about the scope and timing of their work, and evaluating the results of that work

(d) Evaluate whether sufficient appropriate audit evidence has been obtained from the audit procedures performed, including with respect to the work performed by component auditors, as a basis for forming an opinion on the group financial statements. (ISA 600 (Revised): para. 13)

ISA 600 (Revised) reiterates the importance of the auditor displaying both professional judgement and professional scepticism, which needs to be displayed by all members of the group engagement team. Examples of areas where there may be impediments to professional scepticism:

- Any unconscious bias (such as those that might be caused by cultural differences in foreign components) that could occur when designing and performing audit procedures and evaluating audit evidence

- Auditors are unable to identify risks of material misstatement due to fraud or error from groups with complex organisational structures

- Intra-group trading and other activity across the group may be so complex as to make the identification of fraud risk factors more challenging

- Tight reporting deadlines imposed by group management may put pressure on engagement team members to rush their work, affecting quality and increasing audit risk

- Remaining alert to inconsistent information from components, their auditors and group management may present a challenge to auditors (ISA 600 (Revised): paras. 9, A14–18)

ISA 600 (Revised) has been written to support all group audits regardless of their size or complexity. There will be engagements where the group auditor does not require the services of a component auditor, meaning some of the requirements in the standard will not necessarily be relevant. This supports the idea that ISAs are scalable to the context of the engagement. (ISA 600 (Revised): para.10)

2.2 Leadership responsibility for quality

The overall responsibility for quality rests with the group engagement partner.

As laid down in the quality management standards, the overall responsibility for quality rests with the group engagement partner who needs to be actively involved in the group audit and who will decide on who performs the work on the group audit. The management of quality may require certain cultural and even practical solutions to be adopted (for example, if there are large numbers of component auditors to be managed simultaneously across multiple locations, some degree of delegation may be inevitable) but the group engagement partner still maintains overall responsibility for quality across the group audit. (ISA 600 (Revised): paras. 16, A29–31)

In order to support this leadership responsibility for quality, the group engagement partner needs to make sure the group audit has the right resources, including the involvement (if required) of the component auditor.

2.3 Acceptance and continuance

> **FAST FORWARD**
>
> The group engagement partner needs to ensure that sufficient appropriate evidence can reasonably be expected to be obtained to provide a basis for forming an opinion in order to accept or continue with the engagement.

2.3.1 Determining the availability of sufficient appropriate audit evidence

Just like any other audit engagement, the group engagement partner determines whether or not the group auditor is able to obtain sufficient appropriate audit evidence to form an opinion on the group financial statements.

ISA 600 (Revised) provides more detail of the sources of information that may be used by the group engagement partner when deciding on the availability of sufficient and appropriate audit evidence:

- The group's structure, activities and any other relevant factors (such as the complexity of the industry in which the group operates)
- The use of support services and other organisations by the group
- The consolidation process used by the group
- Access to information, management and those charged with governance (TCWG) throughout the group and its components

For initial group audits, the availability of information from management and TCWG will be a crucial part of the acceptance decision. For recurring engagements, there may be additional factors that become relevant to the continuance decision as the group auditor considers the changes that have occurred since the previous engagement. These include changes to:

- Group structure
- Component significance
- The composition of management and TCWG throughout the group and its components
- The display of integrity and competence of group or component management
- The applicable financial reporting framework
- Social, economic, cultural or other factors (such as the outbreak of war or disease)

Note. On a practical level, the materiality of the portion of the group financial statements which the group auditor audits (and therefore, by implication, the proportion that they do not audit) will also be relevant to this decision.

2.3.2 Terms of the engagement

Assuming the group engagement partner is satisfied that such evidence will be made available by the group and its management, the group audit terms of engagement are agreed for the coming year, including confirmation of the various communication protocols necessary for the successful completion of the engagement and that all relevant group and component information will be made available as required by the group auditor.

2.3.3 Restrictions imposed by management

Should there be any doubt about the availability of sufficient appropriate audit evidence due to some form of limitation imposed by management, the group engagement partner will need to consider the possible effects on the group audit when deciding whether or not to accept or continue the engagement. If the only option available would be to disclaim the audit opinion, the engagement should not be accepted or continued. In situations when the group engagement partner is unable to decline or withdraw from the engagement for legal or regulatory reasons, the group audit will require a disclaimer of opinion. (ISA 600 (Revised): paras. 17-21, A32-36, A45-46)

2.4 Risk assessment and planning

FAST FORWARD | The group auditor shall formulate an overall audit strategy and audit plan.

2.4.1 Group audit strategy and group audit plan

Once engagement-related acceptance and continuance issues have been settled, the group auditor will establish the overall group audit strategy and group audit plan which will confirm the group's components that will be subject to audit work and the necessary resources required for the satisfactory completion of the group audit. As part of this process, the involvement (if any) of any component auditors will also be decided. (ISA 600 (Revised): para.22)

2.4.2 Performance materiality and aggregation risk

It is the responsibility of the group auditor to set materiality and performance materiality levels for the group audit. However, due to the nature of the way that group financial statements are created using consolidation techniques that include some form of aggregation, the group auditor needs to set materiality and performance materiality levels for the group audit that take the risk associated with this consolidation (in other words, aggregation risk) into consideration.

Key term | **Aggregation risk** is the probability that the aggregate of uncorrected and undetected misstatements exceeds materiality for the financial statements as a whole. (ISA 600 (Revised): para.14(a))

The group auditor will determine which components require attention as part of the group audit. As the amount, size and complexity of components increase across the group, the level of aggregation risk presented by these components will also increase. It therefore seems logical that in order to manage this aggregation risk down to an acceptable level, the group auditor must determine the amount of audit work required on transactions, account balances and disclosures at each component (and who will perform that work). This requires the creation of what is referred to as component performance materiality.

Key term | **Component performance materiality** is an amount set by the group auditor to reduce aggregation risk to an appropriately low level for purposes of planning and performing audit procedures in relation to a component. (ISA 600 (Revised): para. 14(e))

The group auditor will use professional judgement in determining an appropriate level of component performance materiality for each component, although it is possible that through ongoing dialogue with the group auditors, the component auditors may be involved in this process too. The amounts set will be lower than overall group performance materiality and may be different for different components. The sum of all the various amounts of component performance materiality will not necessarily reconcile back to the group performance materiality level.

The group auditor may also choose to determine other, lower levels of component performance materiality for certain classes of transactions, account balances or disclosures if considered appropriate in the context of the group audit. The group auditor may also treat certain transactions or balances across all components as a single population and apply group performance materiality to these items instead.

It is most likely that as aggregation risk increases, component performance materiality amounts will fall, meaning more items will get tested to address this heightened risk of material misstatement in the group financial statements. However, should the group consist of larger components that lead to less aggregation in the compilation of the group financial statements (because of the diminished amounts made up by other components) component and group performance materiality levels may be closer together. (ISA 600 (Revised): paras.35, A117-123)

2.4.3 Determining the components at which to perform audit work

In the context of ISA 600 (Revised), the core issue is deciding which components require audit work to be performed as part of the group audit, whether a separate component auditor exists and if their involvement in the group audit is required.

Factors that are relevant to the determination of those components that are subject to audit include events or conditions which may lead to risk of material misstatement at the assertion level within the group financial statements that are associated with certain components, such as:

- Newly formed or acquired components
- Components where significant change has occurred
- Significant transactions either with related parties or that are unusual
- Inconsistencies identified through analytical procedures

There will also need to be a judgement made by the group auditor about which components to audit based on aggregation risk and materiality levels.

Once the scope of the group audit has been determined, the group auditor uses professional judgement to confirm the resources that should be involved in the group audit engagement and whether a component auditor's involvement would be advantageous. Factors that may get taken into account when making this judgement include:

- The group auditor's level of understanding of the group
- The knowledge and experience of the group auditor compared with that of the component auditor
- The relative importance of having local knowledge and experience of laws, language and culture that a component auditor may be able to bring
- Complexity, geography and the ease of gaining physical access to each component
- The degree of decentralisation in the group's system of internal control and whether a component auditor may be better positioned to evaluate component-level controls
- Any previous experience with a component auditor

The group auditor again uses professional judgement to determine the extent and the stages within the audit that any component auditors will be involved. This involvement may include participation in planning decisions for the group audit engagement. The revised ISA also reminds auditors that despite the fact that there may be fee constraints which might limit the number of components subject to audit and dictate those fees (if any) that can be allocated to component auditors, the group engagement partner is still responsible for fulfilling the necessary quality objectives when delivering their audit opinion on the group. (ISA (UK) 600 (Revised): paras. 22, A51-56)

2.4.4 Additional considerations when component auditors are involved

At various points throughout ISA 600 (Revised), there are sections titled '**Considerations when component auditors are involved**' which explain the additional responsibilities that the group auditor needs to address if the group engagement team is expected to include component auditors.

Exam focus point

The November 2023 exam contained a question on component auditors.

2.4.5 Understanding the group and the risk of material misstatement

In exactly the same way as an auditor undertaking a standalone engagement, the group auditor has a responsibility under ISA 315 to obtain the following:

Core ISA 315 elements	Specific ISA 600 (Revised) matters
An understanding of the group and its environment	This would include the group's structure, the nature of the business and its locations, the group's reliance on IT, relevant legal and regulatory matters, and any financial performance measures used across the group
The applicable financial reporting framework	Accounting policies and practices in use across the group
The group's system of internal control	Centralised or decentralised, financial reporting controls including consolidation methods and the process of managing the preparation of the group financial statements

Key term

Common controls are controls designed by group management that are intended to operate in a common manner across multiple entities or business units (for example, a common inventory management system in use across all parts of the group). These may be either direct or indirect controls.

When component auditors are involved, there is a requirement for **timely communication** between group auditor and component auditor.

Matters that the group auditor communicates to component auditors	Matters that the component auditors must communicate to the group auditor
Anything that is considered relevant to the component auditor's design or performance of risk assessment procedures	Financial information about a component that is relevant to the assessment of risk of material misstatement in the group financial statements whether due to fraud or error
Information about related party relationships or transactions that is relevant to the component auditor's work	Any additional related party information relevant to the group audit that the group auditor is not aware of
Information about the group's going concern status that is relevant to the component auditor's work	Any information identified by the component auditor that may cast doubt on the group's ability to continue as a going concern

As with all engagements, risk assessment is expected to be **iterative** and **dynamic** and should consider **inherent risk factors** that may indicate material misstatement within the group financial statements, whether due to fraud or error. Examples of inherent risk factors at the assertion level could include the following:

Complexity	Variations in regulatory regimes across the group or inconsistent application of accounting policies across the group
Subjectivity	Decisions surrounding the existence of special-purpose entities and how they are to be incorporated within the group financial statements
Change	Frequent acquisitions, disposals or reorganisations across the group
Uncertainty	The risk that entities or business units in the group may be subject to external influences (such as changes in government policy that restrict the treatment of currency and dividends)
Management bias or fraud	The risk of manipulating the group financial statements via creative tax planning across business units or entities and unusual transfers or adjustments across the group

Regular dialogue across all parties within the group audit engagement team (including component auditors) is necessary to ensure all relevant information is captured and acted upon. It is worth reiterating that although there may be significant involvement with component auditors at this stage of the group audit, the **overall responsibility** for identifying and assessing risk of material misstatement in the group financial statements remains solely with the group auditor. (ISA 600 (Revised): paras. 30-33, A88-112, Appendix 3)

2.4.6 Responding to assessed risks of material misstatement, including evaluating the work of the component auditor

Once risk has been assessed, the group auditor decides on the most suitable responses as per ISA 330. This will include the **nature, timing and extent** of any further audit procedures and the **components where such procedures will be performed**. This will also include any necessary audit work on the consolidation process (covered in more detail in a later section) and any associated adjustments to consider the risk of material misstatement as a result of either fraud or error.

The work of the component auditor (including any testing performed on the consolidation process) will need to be **communicated** to the group auditor. Matters that are expected to be communicated are as follows:

- The work allocated to the component auditor by the group auditor and whether it has been performed
- Whether the component auditor has complied with all relevant ethical requirements
- Any non-compliance with laws or regulations identified by the component auditor
- Any corrected and uncorrected misstatements identified by the component auditor that exceed the materiality levels set by the group auditor
- Evidence of any fraud (or suspected fraud), management bias or deficiencies in the system of internal control
- Significant matters that need to be reported to component management or TCWG by the component auditor
- Any other matters that the component auditor determines the group auditor needs to be aware of
- The overall findings or conclusions of the component auditor

The group auditor will discuss the findings of the component auditor with group and component management and the component auditor if necessary and will evaluate whether the evidence communicated is **adequate**. Should the information communicated by the component auditor be considered inadequate for the purposes of the group audit, the group auditor can request additional audit procedures to be performed and will decide on the extent, if any, of the component auditor's involvement and the level of direction, supervision and review if the component auditor is to be involved in performing those additional procedures. (ISA 600 (Revised): paras.37-48)

As with regular audits, there are **audit completion activities** that will be necessary before the group audit opinion can be communicated:

- **Subsequent events procedures** in line with ISA 560 will be conducted by the group auditor but component auditors will be required to notify the group auditor of any subsequent events they are aware of that may require adjustment or disclosure in the group financial statements.
- The group auditor needs to conclude they have **sufficient appropriate audit evidence**, including that which has been obtained from component auditors, for their audit opinion (this includes an evaluation by the group engagement partner of **uncorrected misstatements** and any **inability to obtain sufficient appropriate audit evidence**).
- Unless specified in the reporting jurisdiction by law or regulation, **the group auditor's report will not mention the use of component auditors** (ISA 600 (Revised): paras.45-53).

2.5 Communication

> **FAST FORWARD**
>
> ISA 600 (Revised) requires some specific types of communication with group management and those charged with governance.

Ultimately, an audit is all about communication and group audits are no different – they are just more complicated, as there are likely to be more players involved and the findings from across the group audit team (including the component auditor) need to be reflected in the group auditor's communication via the auditor's report. There are also some specific types of communication that ISA 600 (Revised) requires as follows.

2.5.1 Communication with group management

At the acceptance or continuation stage of the group audit, the **planned scope and timing** of the audit, including the **work to be performed** across the group, should be communicated by the group auditor to group management.

At any point throughout the group audit, should **fraud** be identified anywhere within the group, the group auditor shall **communicate this in a timely manner** to group management. (However, you should remember that in cases when management are suspected of being involved in such fraud, to **avoid tipping off**, these concerns should be raised with TCWG instead).

It is possible that there may be matters identified during the group audit process (such as potential litigation involving the group or significant changes to the group's business) that may affect a component but due to the need to keep such **sensitive information confidential**, the component's own management are unaware of such matters and group management are reluctant to communicate them at that time to the management of that component.

While there may be a responsibility for the component auditor to inform the component of matters identified during the group audit via the component auditor's report, the group auditor may conclude that after communication with group management, the publication of the component auditor's report should be **delayed** until the matter is resolved. (ISA 600 (Revised): paras. 54–56, A160)

2.5.2 Communication with TCWG

ISAs (UK) 260 (Revised) and 265 describe the responsibilities of the auditor when communicating matters to TCWG. In the context of a group audit engagement, the following information also needs to be communicated by the group auditor:

- Audit work that is to be performed at components and the extent of any involvement that the group auditor will have in the work undertaken by component auditors

- Concerns that the group auditor may have about the quality of the work of the component auditor and how these concerns were addressed

- Any limitations on the scope of the group audit, such as restrictions on access to people or information

- Any fraud that leads to material misstatement in the group financial statements

- Deficiencies in the group's system of internal control that have been identified by component auditors (ISA 600 (Revised): paras. 57–58)

2.6 Implications for the auditor's report where a component's report has been modified

FAST FORWARD

Where a component auditor's report is modified, the group auditor's report is not necessarily modified as a result.

In a group situation, materiality and risk must be assessed in the context of the group as a whole. The group auditor must consider the materiality of any modifications to a component's auditor's report in relation to the whole of the consolidated financial statements.

This can lead to situations where a component may have a material qualification that has no impact on the group opinion which would then remain unmodified. Similarly, a pervasive modification in a component's auditor's report may only have a material impact on the group opinion.

Ultimately the decision as to the impact of a modification to a component's auditor's report on the consolidated opinion is a matter of judgement for the group auditor. Where the group auditor concludes that adequate evidence about the work of the component auditor cannot be obtained and has been unable to perform sufficient additional procedures with respect to that component, they should consider the implications for the auditor's report. A subsequent modification in these circumstances would be on the grounds of insufficient inappropriate audit evidence.

2.7 Documentation

FAST FORWARD

ISA 600 (Revised) proscribes certain matters which must be documented for a group audit.

Audit documentation exists to allow an unconnected but experienced auditor to understand the audit work performed and the rationale for any conclusions reached. For a group audit, the documentation shall also contain the following:

- Any access restrictions during the group audit and how they were addressed
- The group auditor's determination of components for the purposes of planning and performing the group audit
- The determination of component performance materiality
- The group auditor's evaluation of any component auditor(s) used on the group audit
- Details of the group's system of internal control
- The direction, supervision and review of the work of the component auditor(s) and their work, including the retention of any key information obtained from the component auditor's own documentation
- All communication with the component auditor(s)
- The group auditor's responses to the component auditor's findings

(ISA 600 (revised): paras. 59, A176)

2.8 The consolidation

FAST FORWARD

Consolidation procedures include:

- Checking **consolidation adjustments** have been correctly made
- Checking **treatment of additions and disposals** has been done correctly
- **Arithmetical** checks

ISA 600 requires the auditor to identify and assess the risks of material misstatement through obtaining an understanding of the entity and its environment. Part of that process involves obtaining an understanding of the consolidation process, including instructions issued by group management to components.

To achieve uniformity and comparability of financial information, the group management will normally issue instructions to components. The instructions ordinarily cover:

- The accounting policies to be applied
- Statutory and other disclosure requirements, including:
    - The identification and reporting of segments
    - Related party relationships and reporting of segments
    - Intra-group transactions and unrealised profits
    - Intra-group account balances
- A reporting timetable

The group auditor will consider:

- The clarity and practicality of the instructions for completing the reporting package
- Whether the instructions:
    - Adequately describe the applicable financial reporting framework
    - Provide for adequate disclosures
    - Adequately provide for the identification of consolidation adjustments
    - Provide for the approval of the financial information by component management

The group auditor is also responsible for the audit of the consolidation process itself.

After receiving and reviewing all the subsidiaries' (and associates') accounts, the principal auditors will be in a position to audit the consolidated accounts. An important part of the work on the consolidation will be checking the consolidation adjustments. Consolidation adjustments generally fall into two categories:

- **Permanent consolidation adjustments**
- **Consolidation adjustments for the current year**

The audit steps involved in the consolidation process may be summarised as follows.

Step 1 Compare the audited accounts of each subsidiary/associate to the consolidation schedules to ensure figures have been transposed correctly and that all components have been included.

Step 2 Review the adjustments made on consolidation to ensure they are appropriate and comparable with the previous year. This will involve:

- **Recording** the **dates** and **costs** of **acquisitions** of subsidiaries and the assets acquired
- **Calculating goodwill** and **pre-acquisition reserves** arising on consolidation
- **Preparing** an overall **reconciliation** of movements on reserves and minority interests
- Reconciling any **inter-company** balances, and eliminating **intra-group** items from profit or loss

Step 3 For business combinations determine:

- Whether combination has been **appropriately** treated as an acquisition or uniting of interests
- The **appropriateness** of the **date** used as the date of combination

9: COMPANY AUDITS – SPECIAL CONSIDERATIONS

- The **treatment** of the **results** of **investments** acquired during the year
- If acquisition accounting has been used, that the **fair value** or acquired **assets** and **liabilities** is reasonable (to ascertainable market value by use of an expert)
- **Goodwill** has been **calculated correctly**

Step 4 For disposals:
- Agree the **date** used as the date for disposal to sales documentation
- Review management accounts to ascertain whether the **results** of the **investment** have been **included** up to the date of disposal, and whether figures used are reasonable

Step 5 **Consider** whether **previous treatment** of **existing subsidiaries** or **associates** is still **correct** (consider level of influence, degree of support)

Step 6 Verify the **arithmetical accuracy** of the consolidation workings by recalculating them

Step 7 **Review** the **consolidated accounts** for **compliance** with the legislation, accounting standards and other relevant regulations. Care will need to be taken where:
- Group companies do not have coterminous accounting periods
- Accounting policies of group members differ because foreign subsidiaries operate under different rules

Other important areas include:
- Treatment of participating interests and associates
- Treatment of goodwill and intangible assets
- Foreign currency translation
- Treatment of loss-making subsidiaries
- Treatment of restrictions on distribution of profits of a subsidiary

Step 8 **Review** the **consolidated accounts** to confirm that they give a true and fair view in the circumstances

Remember that when auditing a consolidation, the relevant related parties are those related to the **consolidated group.** Transactions with consolidated subsidiaries need **not** be disclosed, as they are incorporated in the financial statements.

The principal auditors are often requested to carry out the consolidation work even where the accounts of the subsidiaries have been prepared by the client. In these circumstances the auditors are of course acting as **accountants and auditors** and care must be taken to ensure that the **audit function** is carried out and evidenced.

Question — Inter-company balances/profits

Your firm is the auditor of Beeston Industries, a limited liability company, which has a number of subsidiaries in your country (and no overseas subsidiaries), some of which are audited by other firms of professional accountants. You have been asked to consider the work which should be carried out to ensure that inter-company transactions and balances are correctly treated in the group financial statements.

Required

(a) Describe the audit procedures you would perform to check that inter-company balances agree, and to state why inter-company balances should agree, and the consequences of them not agreeing.

PART B STATUTORY AUDIT AND OTHER EVALUATION

(b) Describe the audit procedures you would perform to verify that inter-company profit in inventory has been correctly accounted for in the group financial statements.

Answer

(a) Inter-company balances should agree because, in the preparation of consolidated financial statements, it is necessary to cancel them out. If they do not cancel out then the group financial statements will be displaying an item which has no value outside of the group and profits may be correspondingly under- or over-stated. The audit work required to check that inter-company balances agree would be as follows.

  (i) Obtain and review a copy of the holding company's instructions to all group members relating to the procedures for reconciliation and agreement of year-end inter-company balances. Particular attention should be paid to the treatment of 'in-transit' items to ensure that there is a proper cut-off.

  (ii) Obtain a schedule of inter-company balances from all group companies and check the details therein to the summary prepared by the holding company. The details on these schedules should also be independently confirmed in writing by the component auditors.

  (iii) Nil balances should also be confirmed by both the group companies concerned and the component auditors.

  (iv) The details on the schedules in (iii) above should also be agreed to the details in the financial statements of the individual group companies which are submitted to the holding company for consolidation purposes.

(b) Where one company in a group supplies goods to another company at cost plus a percentage, and such goods remain in inventory at the year end, then the group inventories will contain an element of unrealised profit. In the preparation of the group financial statements, best accounting practice requires that a provision should be made for this unrealised profit.

In order to verify that inter-company profit in inventory has been correctly accounted for in the group financial statements, the audit work required would be as follows.

  (i) Confirm the group's procedures for identification of such inventories and their notification to the parent company who will be responsible for making the required provision.

  (ii) Obtain and review schedules of inter-group inventories from group companies and confirm that the same categories of inventory have been included as in previous years.

  (iii) Select a sample of invoices for goods purchased from group companies and check to see that as necessary these have been included in year end inter-group inventories and obtain confirmation from component auditors that they have satisfactorily completed a similar exercise.

  (iv) Check the calculation of the provision for unrealised profit and confirm that this has been arrived at on a consistent basis with that used in earlier years, after making due allowance for any known changes in the profit margins operated by various group companies.

  (v) Check the schedules of inter-group inventory against the various inventory sheets and consider whether the level of inter-group inventories appears to be reasonable in comparison with previous years, ensuring that satisfactory explanations are obtained for any material differences.

3 Auditing components located abroad

FAST FORWARD
Auditing a **component located abroad** can pose practical problems for auditors. An appreciation of the features of doing business and auditing in the country concerned is vital.

3.1 Circumstances

When an auditing firm has a client which owns components located abroad, the client may:

- Choose to have the component located abroad audited by local firms
- Request that its own auditors undertake the audit of the components located abroad

Even when the auditors are a large firm, and local offices audit the components located abroad, the principal auditors at the client's head office often undertake an audit visit to a major component located abroad each year. This is particularly the case with world-wide clients, such as major airlines. Audit firms may also have an international network and may be able to use an affiliated partnership to audit the component located abroad.

3.2 Problems

A summary of the difficulties and possible solutions involved in auditing components located abroad would include the following.

Language difficulties might be overcome by finding a member of the office who speaks the relevant language, or a translator.
Cultural differences should be tackled by the auditors learning as much as possible about the country.
Differences in local accounting and auditing conventions, as well as legislation, can again be tackled by study before the audit begins (as discussed in Section 2).
Some countries may have very **specific problems**, including civil unrest, high inflation or hyper inflation, currency restrictions and so on. The auditors will need to consider how such issues should be tackled in the audit (as well as the eventual consolidation).
The auditors may face difficulties obtaining the necessary **permit to work** or even enter the country in question. The client company should help the auditors as much as possible in this respect.
The auditors must ensure that they have **sufficient support** in their base office to help them if any difficulty arises.

3.3 Globalisation of audit firms

Globalisation is an issue which affects the larger of the medium-sized firms and the Big Four. There are two approaches to globalisation.

(a) **Affiliation.** This method allows an international brand name to develop and is commonly used by Big Four firms which have international coverage by a firm using the same name.

(b) **Co-operation.** Medium-sized firms often attach themselves to an international co-operative of firms operating under a title which can be incorporated into the firm's name (for example, BDO Stoy Hayward) so that a UK firm has an international network of 'sister firms'.

The key benefit of internationalisation is that many clients are companies which are international, so the audit firm can meet their needs around the world. However, as was the case with Andersens and Enron, collapse of the firm in one part of the world can have substantial 'knock-on' effects elsewhere.

3.4 Transnational audits

3.4.1 The Forum of Firms

In response to the trend towards globalisation and the associated issues, an international grouping, the Forum of Firms (FoF) was founded by the following networks: BDO, Deloitte Touche Tohmatsu, Ernst & Young Global, Grant Thornton, KPMG International Cooperative and PricewaterhouseCoopers International.

Membership is open to firms and networks that have transnational audit appointments or are interested in accepting such appointments.

These firms have a voluntary agreement to meet certain requirements that are set out in their constitution. These relate mainly to:

- Promoting the use of high quality audit practices worldwide, including the use of ISAs.
- Maintaining quality management standards in accordance with International Standards on Quality Management issued by the IAASB, and conducting globally co-ordinated internal quality assurance reviews.

3.4.2 The Transnational Auditors Committee

The IAASB has set up the **Transnational Auditors Committee** (TAC) to provide guidance to the members of the FoF.

The TAC has issued the following definition of transnational audit.

Key terms

> **Transnational audit** means an audit of financial statements which are or may be relied upon outside the audited entity's home jurisdiction for purposes of significant lending, investment or regulatory decisions; this will include audits of all financial statements of companies with listed equity or debt and other public interest entities which attract particular public attention because of their size, products or services provided.
>
> **Other public interest entities** shall include those entities in either the public or the private sectors which have **significant transactions across national borders**, whether or not having either listed equity or debt. These would include, for example, large charitable organisations or trusts, major monopolies or duopolies, providers of financial or other borrowing facilities to commercial or private customers, deposit-taking organisations and those holding funds belonging to third parties in connection with investment or savings activities.
>
> **Significant transactions across national borders** shall include transactions such that there is a reasonable expectation that the financial statements of the entity may be relied upon by a user outside the entity's home jurisdiction for purposes of significant lending, investment or regulatory decisions. Significant in this context does not include use of financial statements to establish normal trade terms with vendors or to open accounts with financial institutions (ie accounts for purposes of collecting customer receipts or making vendor payments). For the avoidance of doubt, an office required solely for the purpose of legal formation and continuing legal existence in a particular jurisdiction does not constitute a significant transaction across national borders.
>
> In principle, the definition of transnational audit should be applied to the consolidated entity as a whole including the individual entities comprising the consolidated entity.

Example	Explanation
Private company in US raising debt finance in Canada	This would qualify as a transnational audit as it is reasonable to expect that the financial statements of the company would be used across national borders in obtaining the debt financing.
Private Savings and Loans operating entirely in the US (ie only US depositors and US investments)	Although it could be considered a public interest entity, this would not qualify as a transnational audit assuming it can be demonstrated that there are no transnational users. In applying the definition of transnational audit, there should be a rebuttable presumption that all banks and financial institutions are included, unless it can be clearly demonstrated that there is no transnational element from the perspective of a financial statement user and that there are no operations across national borders. Potential transnational users would include investors, lenders, governments, customers, regulators, etc.
International charity taking donations through various national branches and making grants around the world	This entity can clearly be considered a public interest entity and operating across borders. Further, the international structure would create a reasonable expectation that the financial statements could be used across national borders by donors in other countries if not by others for purposes of significant lending, investment or regulatory decisions.
Private Internet betting company registered in BVI, which operates from Costa Rica and takes wagers by credit card on a worldwide basis via internet	Assuming there is no restriction on gamblers then it would be public interest and operate across borders and therefore classified as a transnational audit.

3.4.3 Features of transnational audits

In the globalised business and financial environment, many audits are clearly transnational, and this produces a number of specific problems which can limit the reliability of the audited financial statements:

- Regulation and oversight of auditors differs from country to country
- Differences in auditing standards from country to country
- Variability in audit quality in different countries

3.4.4 Role of the international audit firm networks

The 'Big Four' and other international networks of firms can be seen as being ahead of governments and institutions in terms of their global influence. They are in a position to establish consistent practices worldwide in areas such as:

- Training and education
- Audit procedures
- Quality management

These firms may as a result be in a better position than national regulators to ensure consistent implementation of high quality auditing standards.

Membership of the Forum of Firms imposes commitments and responsibilities, namely:

- To perform transnational audits in accordance with ISAs
- To comply with the IESBA *Code of Ethics*
- Be subject to a programme of quality assurance

4 Joint audits

FAST FORWARD | In joint audits, more than one auditor is responsible for the audit opinion and it is made jointly.

The relationship between group and component auditors discussed in the previous sections is **not** the same as that between the auditors involved in a joint audit.

Key term | A **joint audit** is one 'where two or more auditors are responsible for an audit engagement and jointly produce an auditor's report to the client'.

4.1 Reasons for joint audits

Two or more firms of accountants could act as joint auditors for a number of reasons.

(a) **Takeover**. The holding company may insist that their auditors act jointly with those of the new subsidiary.

(b) **Locational problems**. A company operating from widely dispersed locations may find it convenient to have joint auditors.

(c) **Political problems**. Overseas subsidiaries may need to employ local auditors to satisfy the laws of the country in which they operate. It is sometimes found that these local auditors act jointly with those of the holding company.

(d) Companies preferring to use **local accountants**, while at the same time enjoying the wider range of services provided by a large national firm.

4.2 Accepting a joint audit

There are several practical points that must be borne in mind before accepting a joint audit. In particular it will be necessary to assess the **experience** and **standards** of the other firm by looking at the audit techniques used, by scrutinising their working papers and establishing whether they have had experience in similar jobs.

Where there are joint auditors, the audit engagement should be explained in similar terms by each set of auditors. The auditors should agree whether joint or separate letters should be sent to the client. Separate letters would normally need to be sent where other services are provided.

Once a joint position has been accepted the **programme** to be adopted and the **split** of the **detailed work** will have to be discussed.

4.3 Problems with joint audits

One of the major criticisms of joint audits is that they may be expensive. This is probably true, but if the two firms have organised the work between them properly the difference should be minimal. Furthermore, an increase in the fees may be justified by improved services not least because the two firms of accountants are likely to work as efficiently as possible from a sense of professional pride.

Both firms must sign the auditor's report and both are responsible for the whole audit whether or not they carried out a particular area of the audit programme. It follows that both firms will be **jointly liable** in the event of litigation.

Chapter Roundup

- You should be familiar with the concept of a single company audit from your earlier studies.
- A group audit is the audit of the group financial statements
- Group auditing requirements and guidance is found in ISA 600 (Revised) *Special considerations – audits of group financial statements (including the work of component auditors)*.
- The overall responsibility for quality rests with the group engagement partner.
- The group engagement partner needs to ensure that sufficient appropriate evidence can reasonably be expected to be obtained to provide a basis for forming an opinion in order to accept or continue with the engagement.
- The group auditor shall formulate an overall audit strategy and audit plan.
- ISA 600 (Revised) requires some specific types of communication with group management and those charged with governance.
- Where a component auditor's report is modified, the group auditor's report is not necessarily modified as a result.
- ISA 600 (Revised) proscribes certain matters which must be documented for a group audit.
- Consolidation procedures include:
    - Checking **consolidation adjustments** have been correctly made
    - Checking **treatment of additions and disposals** has been done correctly
    - **Arithmetical** checks
- Auditing a **foreign subsidiary** can pose practical problems for auditors. An appreciation of the features of doing business and auditing in the country concerned is vital.
- In joint audits, more than one auditor is responsible for the audit opinion and it is made jointly.

PART B   STATUTORY AUDIT AND OTHER EVALUATION

Quick Quiz

1   The group engagement partner is responsible for the group audit opinion, covering information audited by component auditors.

    True   ☐

    False   ☐

2   Which of the following might influence the group auditor's decision about whether to perform audit work at a specific component?

    A   The group auditor does not have an office or network firm in the country in which the component is located
    B   The group has a complex structure
    C   In the previous year, the component was audited by a component auditor whose work was found to be inadequate for the purposes of the group audit
    D   The component has been newly acquired in the year

3   Name two matters that the group auditors must communicate to the component auditors when gaining an understanding of the group and its environment.

    (1) ....
    (2) ....

4   List the eight steps involved in auditing a consolidation.

    (1) ....
    (2) ....
    (3) ....
    (4) ....
    (5) ....
    (6) ....
    (7) ....
    (8) ....

5   If two firms undertake a joint audit, they shall be jointly liable in the event of litigation.

    True   ☐

    False   ☐

6   Name four difficulties which might arise from the audit of a foreign subsidiary.

    (1) ....
    (2) ....
    (3) ....
    (4) ....

Answers to Quick Quiz

1. True

2. D

3. From:

    (1) Matters the group auditor determines to be relevant to the component auditor's design and performance of risk assessment procedures for purposes of the group audit

    (2) Related party relationships or transactions relevant to the component auditor's work

    (3) Any events or conditions casting significant doubt on the group's ability to continue as a going concern that are relevant to the component auditor's work

4.

STEP ONE	Check the transposition from individual audited accounts to the consolidation workings
STEP TWO	Check consolidation adjustments are correct and comparable with prior years
STEP THREE	Check for, and audit, business combinations
STEP FOUR	Check for, and audit, disposals
STEP FIVE	Consider whether previous treatment of subsidiaries and associates is still correct
STEP SIX	Verify the arithmetical accuracy of the workings
STEP SEVEN	Review the consolidated financial statements for compliance with law and standards
STEP EIGHT	Review the consolidated financial statements to ensure they give a true and fair view

5. True

6. From:

    (1) Language difficulties
    (2) Cultural difficulties
    (3) Differences in auditing/accounting conventions
    (4) Specific problems such as high inflation or civil unrest
    (5) Requirement to obtain a permit to work

End of Chapter Question

Startfund (AIA November 2009 amended)

Startfund is a company that exists to provide equity funding to small and expanding companies in the Northern region of its home country. The company focuses on a specific geographical region because it takes a very active interest in each of the businesses that it funds.

Typically, Startfund invests in 'disruptive technologies'. These are business opportunities created by inventions that are new and are typically developed by individuals with interests in areas such as engineering and electronics. Very few of the people who approach Startfund for funding have any real understanding of business.

Startfund never lends money. It always invests in a substantial block of equity. Applicants must be incorporated as companies. Startfund buys an agreed proportion of the issued share capital on the understanding that it will sell its shares once the company has grown to a reasonable size, which usually takes five to ten years. Depending on the nature of the product and the amount of funding required, Startfund will buy anything from 40% to 60% of the applicant's share capital. Regardless of the size of the investment, Startfund insists on a contract that grants it the right to appoint two board members. For the first two years after investing and in certain other circumstances, such as where the funded company is in financial difficulty, Startfund's directors have the right to exercise total control over all board decisions. Applicants are prepared to agree to such demands because Startfund takes a substantial risk with every investment that it makes. Furthermore, the directors who are appointed to manage the company offer an understanding and experience of business that the applicants often lack.

Startfund has asked you to consider taking over the external audit of the company's financial statements. The directors are unhappy with their present external auditor because the partner of the current audit firm insists that Startfund should be obliged to consolidate the results of many of the companies that the company has invested in. Startfund's directors do not wish to do so because they believe that their interest in these companies is temporary and so consolidated statements will create the impression that the company's performance is volatile. They have decided to seek a replacement auditor. The offer of this appointment is conditional upon your agreement that you will not seek to force a consolidation of these businesses.

Required

(a) Explain how you would determine whether any of these companies ought to be treated as subsidiaries of Startfund. **(8 marks)**

(b) Explain whether it would be acceptable for an audit firm to take an appointment that is conditional upon agreement over a contested accounting policy. **(6 marks)**

(c) Assuming that the directors of Startfund agreed to prepare consolidated financial statements that included all relevant subsidiaries, discuss the extent to which the external auditors of the various companies that are to be included in the Startfund Group would be responsible for the fair presentation of the group financial statements. **(6 marks)**

(Total 20 marks)

Not-for-profit organisations

Topic list	Syllabus reference
1 Objectives	LO1
2 Planning	LO1
3 Evidence	LO1
4 Reporting	LO1
5 Public sector	LO1

Introduction

This chapter looks at the audit of not-for-profit organisations. Remember, that such entities may or may not be required to have a **statutory audit** under legislation. They may choose to have a **non statutory audit** under the terms of a charitable deed, or as part of good practice.

Once thing an auditor should do when conducting a non statutory audit is confirm that a statutory opinion is not required.

The points made in this chapter about the issues inherent in these entities are **relevant for any kind of assurance work in not-for-profit organisations**, that is, internal auditors and external auditors undertaking audits or reviews. These entities will have inherent features, the most obvious being the difference in **objective** of the entity, which will **affect the way the work is carried out**.

PART B   STATUTORY AUDIT AND OTHER EVALUATION

1 Objectives

FAST FORWARD

There are various types of organisation which do not exist for the purpose of maximising shareholder wealth, which may require an audit.

A key objective of directors of companies is to manage well the shareholders' investments. In a large majority of cases, 'manage the shareholders' investment' means 'create a profit', as this will create returns to the shareholders in the terms of dividends or growth in the capital value of the share.

Some companies and other entities who do not operate for the purpose of making profit will require an audit, either statutory or otherwise.

1.1 Not-for-profit organisations

Before considering what a not-for-profit organisation's audit will entail, it will be helpful to consider what sort of entities might exist with objectives other than to make a profit and what their objectives are, as these will impact on the way that they report and the audit that is carried out.

Question   Not-for-profit organisations

List as many types of not-for-profit organisations as you can.

Answer

The following diagram shows a number of organisations you might have come up with in your answer to the question.

You may be thinking that some of the associations above might aim to operate at a profit, and you are correct, not-for-profit organisations may (conversely it may seem) operate at a profit, however, this may not be their key aim.

1.2 Example: Not-for-profit

A hospital could operate at a profit by not spending all the money it receives in its budget. However, the key objective of a hospital is to provide health services to the public, not to make a profit. As its income is wholly fixed, it is more likely to focus on **cost-saving** so that it can operate within its budget.

Question: Objectives

Identify the key objectives and focus of the types of association listed above.

Answer

Charities and friendly societies	To meet the *raison d'être* of the charity, that is, to carry out the charitable purpose. May involve fund-raising, receiving donations, managing invested funds, controlling costs.
Schools	To provide education. Likely to involve managing a tight budget (either from fees or government funds).
Clubs, associations, societies, unions	To further the aims of the club, provide a service to members. May include managing subscriptions paid and keeping costs of running the club down.
Housing association	Managing the related houses and providing facilities for residents. May involve rent collection and maintenance costs or even building costs of future developments.
Local councils, public services	To provide local services to a budget based on public money. Likely to be focused on value for money as they are in the public eye.

1.3 Reporting

Many of these organisations are subject to legislation which may specify how they are to report their results.

Many of the organisations mentioned above are companies (often companies limited by guarantee) and so are required to prepare financial statements and have them audited under companies legislation.

Some of the entities will have Statements Of Recommended accounting Practice (SORP). For example, in the UK, there is a charities' SORP outlining what a charity's accounts should comprise, as listed below.

(a) A **statement of financial activities** (SOFA) that shows all resources made available to the charity and all expenditure incurred and reconciles all changes in its funds

(b) Where the charity is required to prepare accounts in accordance with the Companies Act 2006, or similar legislation, or where the governing instrument so requires, a **summary income and expenditure account** (in addition to the SOFA) in certain circumstances

(c) A **statement of financial position** that shows the assets, liabilities and funds of the charity. The statement of financial position (or its notes, see (e) below) should also explain, in general terms, how the funds may or, because of restrictions imposed by donors, must be utilised

(d) A **statement of cash flows**, where required by accounting standards

(e) **Notes**

1.4 Audit

Where a statutory audit is required, the auditors will be required to produce the statutory audit opinion concerning the truth and fairness of financial statements.

Where a statutory audit is not required, it is possible that the organisation might have one anyway for the benefit of interested stakeholders, such as the public or people who give to a charity.

It is also possible that such entities will have special, additional requirements of an audit. These may be required by a regulator, or by the constitution of the organisation. For example, a charity's constitution may require an audit of whether the charity is operating in accordance with its charitable purpose.

1.5 Conclusion

An audit of a not-for-profit organisation may vary from a 'for profit audit' owing to:

- Its objectives and the impact on operations and reporting
- The purpose an audit is required

When carrying out an audit of a not-for-profit organisation, it is vital that the auditor establishes:

- Whether a statutory audit is required
- If not, what the objectives of the engagement are
- What the engagement is to report on
- To whom the report should be addressed
- What form the report should take

As we have seen, there are many types of not-for-profit organisation and their audits could all be different depending on the purpose the audit is required and correspondingly, the objectives of the organisation.

Exam focus point

You should think around the issues raised for the audit in relation to all the following entities, and be able to apply similar facts and reasoning to any not-for-profit organisation which comes up in the exam.

Case Study

Small charity scenario

Headington Hospice Co is a small, local charity which operates a small children's hospice and two charity shops which raise money for the ongoing work of the hospice. The hospice receives grants from the health authority, sponsorship from some local businesses, receives income from the charity shop which is entirely voluntarily operated and receives donations from individuals. It employs three nurses, a part-time hospice manager and an accountant donates his time to keep the books and produce the annual accounts. As the company's turnover falls below the exemption limit, it is not required to have an audit by law, but the terms of its constitution require that an audit of the accounts is required for the benefit of the trustees that gives an opinion as to whether the financial statements give a true and fair view and to whether the charity is meeting its objects, as set out in the constitutional document.

Case Study

Small association scenario

The Midvale League is a small association. It runs several local football leagues for various ages and stages. It employs a general administrator and some casual bar staff. Any player who appears in more than 30% of a team's games for the season is required to pay a subscription to the association. The subs pay for the administrator's wages, the referee's fees, team coaches' expenses and a lease on a sport's club comprising a clubhouse and changing facilities and three football pitches. The administrator also acts as groundsman. There is a bar in the clubhouse which is run for the benefit of members at a profit which covers bar staff wages and contributes to other expenses of the club. The association pays a local firm of accountants to prepare management accounts every quarter and to produce annual financial statements which it then audits for the benefit of members of the club.

2 Planning

> **FAST FORWARD**
> The audit risks associated with not-for-profit organisations may well be different from those of other entities.

2.1 Small charity

When planning the audit of a charity, the auditors should particularly consider the following:

- The **scope** of the audit
- Recent **recommendations** of the **Charity Commissioners** or the other regulatory bodies
- The **acceptability of accounting policies** adopted
- **Changes in circumstances** in the sector in which the charity operates
- **Past experience** of the effectiveness of the charity's accounting system
- **Key audit areas**
- The **amount of detail included** in the financial statements on which the auditors are required to report

In the case of Headington Hospice, the scope of the audit is twofold. The auditors are to report on the truth and fairness of the financial statement for the benefit of the trustees and also on whether the charity is meeting its objectives. The auditors should therefore establish what the objectives are, and consider how they are to identify whether the objectives are being met.

The auditors should consider whether any recommendations of the Charity Commissioners apply to Headington Hospice. It is unlikely that there have been any substantial changes in the sector in which it works.

In order to identify the key audit areas, the auditors will have to consider audit risk.

2.2 Audit risk

> **FAST FORWARD**
> Cash may be significant in small not-for-profit organisations and controls are likely to be limited. Income may well be a risk area, particularly where money is donated or raised informally.

There are certain risks applicable to charities that might not necessarily be applicable to other small companies. The auditors should consider the following.

Problem	Key factors
Inherent risk	- The complexity and extent of regulation - The significance of donations and cash receipts - Difficulties of the charity in establishing ownership and timing of voluntary income where funds are raised by non-controlled bodies - Lack of predictable income or precisely identifiable relationship between expenditure and income - Uncertainty of future income - Restrictions imposed by the objectives and powers given by charities' governing documents - The importance of restricted funds - The extent and nature of trading activities must be compatible with the entity's charitable status

Problem	Key factors
	• The complexity of tax rules (whether income, capital, sales or local rates) relating to charities
	• The sensitivity of certain key statistics, such as the proportion of resources used in administration
	• The need to maintain adequate resources for future expenditure while avoiding the build up of reserves which could appear excessive
Control risk	• The amount of time committed by trustees to the charity's affairs
	• The skills and qualifications of individual trustees
	• The frequency and regularity of trustee meetings
	• The form and content of trustee meetings
	• The independence of trustees from each other
	• The division of duties between trustees
	• The degree of involvement in, or supervision of, the charity's transactions on the part of individual trustees

Key elements in control environment	
Control environment	• A recognised plan of the charity's structure showing clearly the areas of responsibility and lines of authority and reporting
	• Segregation of duties
	• Supervision by trustees of activities of staff where segregation of duties is not practical
	• Competence, training and qualification of paid staff and any volunteers appropriate to the tasks they have to perform
	• Involvement of the trustees in the recruitment, appointment and supervision of senior executives
	• Access of trustees to independent professional advice where necessary
	• Budgetary controls in the form of estimates of income and expenditure for each financial year and comparison of actual results with the estimates on a regular basis
	• Communication of results of such reviews to the trustees on a regular basis

In the case of Headington Hospice, the auditor will need to devote attention to cash receipts and income, as the Hospice receives donations from the public and also receives cash income from the charity shop.

It will also be necessary to consider non current assets, to determine whether the premises the hospice and the charity shop should be included on the statement of financial position of the charity. The auditor will also need to assess the nature of the grants received from the health authority to determine how they should be accounted for. These things should all be considered as part of the accounting policy review. The auditor should also be aware of issues such as depreciation during this review, as the hospice may own specialised medical equipment which makes such issues complex.

Another matter which the auditor must consider is the issue of going concern. This will include an assessment of the sponsorship deals which the charity has in place and any consideration of future sponsorship. The grant position must also be considered, as must the likelihood of future donations. The auditors should also consider matters such as personnel, for example, whether any existing arrangements with doctors' practices will continue in existence.

2.3 Internal controls

Small charities will generally suffer from internal control weaknesses common to small enterprises, such as **lack of segregation of duties** and use of **unqualified staff**. Shortcomings may arise from the staff's lack of training and also, if they are volunteers, from their attitude, in that they may resent formal procedures.

The auditors will have to consider particularly carefully whether they will be able to obtain adequate assurance that the accounting records do reflect all the transactions of the enterprise and bear in mind whether there are any related statutory reporting requirements.

The following sorts of internal control might be typical of a number of charities.

Cash donations	
Source	**Examples of controls**
Collecting boxes and tins	Numerical control over boxes and tins
	Satisfactory sealing of boxes and tins so that any opening prior to recording cash is apparent
	Regular collection and recording of proceeds from collecting boxes
	Dual control over counting and recording of proceeds
Postal receipts	Unopened mail kept securely
	Dual control over the opening of mail
	Immediate recording of donations on opening of mail or receipt
	Agreement of bank paying-in slips to record of receipts by an independent person

Other donations	
Source	**Examples of controls**
Deeds of covenant	Regular checks and follow-up procedures to ensure due amounts are received
	Regular checks to ensure all tax repayments have been obtained
Legacies	Comprehensive correspondence files maintained in respect of each legacy,
	Regular reports and follow-up procedures undertaken in respect of outstanding legacies
Donations in kind	In case of charity shops, separation of recording, storage and sale of stock

Other income	
Source	**Examples of controls**
Fund-raising activities	Records maintained for each fund raising event
	Other appropriate controls maintained over receipts
	Controls maintained over expenses as for administrative expenses
Central and local government grants and loans	Regular checks that all sources of income or funds are fully utilised and appropriate claims made
	Ensuring income or funds are correctly applied

Use of resources	
Resource	**Examples of controls**
Restricted funds	Separate records maintained of relevant revenue, expenditure and assets Terms controlling application of fund Oversight of application of fund money's by independent personnel or trustees
Grants to beneficiaries	Records maintained, as appropriate, of requests for material grants received and their treatment
	Appropriate checks made on applications and applicants for grants, and that amounts paid are *intra vires*
	Records maintained of all grant decisions, checking that proper authority exists, that adequate documentation is presented to decision-making meetings, and that any conflicts of interest are recorded
	Control to ensure grants made are properly spent by the recipient for the specified purpose, for example requirements for returns with supporting documentation or auditors' reports concerning expenditure, or monitoring visits

For Headington Hospice, the issues relating to cash donations and grants will be particularly relevant.

2.4 Small association

The Midvale League (ML) requires an audit for the benefit of its members. This makes the audit of ML similar to any small company audit such as those which we have considered throughout this Learning & Practice Workbook.

However, the nature of the association may give rise to some particular audit risks and control issues.

Question   Audit risks

Identify any audit risks arising from The Midvale League.

Answer

Inherent risks

The classification of the sport's club **lease** may be problematic. It is certainly likely to be their biggest financial commitment. The auditor will need to determine whether the terms of the lease mean that it should be included on the statement of financial position as an asset, showing the corresponding liability or whether it does not so qualify (this would only be the case if the lease were a short-term lease (less than 12 months duration) which is unlikely).

Note. Leases will be discussed in more detail in Chapter 18.

The auditors should also consider the affordability of the lease in order to determine whether this has implications for the **going concern** of the association, as if it cannot afford the lease payments, it might be faced with the situation where it has nowhere to operate in the foreseeable future, in which case, the purpose of the association is gone.

The auditors will also have to consider the role of the general administrator, who fulfils a number of roles. He is clearly a **key person** to the association, and it might find that it had difficulties if he was incapacitated, not least perhaps in affording a replacement and any sickness benefit they were required to pay by law.

It is unclear what degree of financial record keeping the administrator takes on. The audit firm are hired to produce quarterly management **accounts**. They will gain some assurance from the fact that they prepare the accounts themselves, but there is also a risk that day to day transactions are not **properly recorded**, as there appears to be no one with financial expertise 'at the coal face'. Given that the administrator will record or maintain the relevant records to be passed on to the accountancy firm, there is also an issue of **segregation of duties** here.

The auditors should also be aware of any legal issues relating to the bearing of a license for the bar, particularly perhaps the danger that the license might be jeopardised by the sale of liquor to underage drinkers. The loss of the license to serve alcohol could severely diminish the income of the club to the point where it could no longer function.

The auditors will also need to pay attention to the membership of the association from the point of view of completeness of income.

3 Evidence

FAST FORWARD

Obtaining audit evidence may be a problem, particularly where associations have informal arrangements and there might be limitations on the scope of the audit.

3.1 Small charity

When designing substantive procedures for charities the auditors should give special attention to the possibility of:

- **Understatement or incompleteness** of the **recording of all income** including gifts in kind, cash donations, and legacies
- **Overstatement of cash grants or expenses**
- **Misanalysis** or misuse in the application of funds
- **Misstatement** or omission of **assets** including donated properties and investments
- The existence of **restricted or uncontrollable funds** in foreign or independent branches

Completeness of income can be a particularly problematic area. Areas auditors may check:

- Loss of income through fraud
- Recognition of income from professional fundraisers
- Recognition of income from branches, associates or subsidiaries
- Income from informal fundraising groups
- Income from grants

Particular matters which might be an issue at Headington Hospice are:

- Completeness of cash income from various sources
- Accounting for the grants from the local authority

3.1.1 Overall review of financial statements

FAST FORWARD

It will be necessary to ensure accounting policies used are appropriate.

The auditors must consider carefully whether the **accounting policies** adopted are **appropriate** to the activities, constitution and objectives of the charity, and are consistently applied, and whether the financial statements adequately disclose these policies and fairly present the state of affairs and the results for the accounting period.

In particular the auditors should consider the basis of disclosing income from fundraising activities (for example, net or gross), accounting for income and expenses (accruals or cash), the capitalising of expenditure on non-current assets, apportioning administrative expenditure, and recognising income from donations and legacies.

Charities without significant endowments or accumulated funds will often be dependent upon future income from voluntary sources. In these circumstances auditors may question whether a going concern basis of accounting is appropriate.

3.2 Small association

In the case of the Midvale League, establishing the **number of members** might prove to be difficult. Once the number of members has been established, there should be good analytical evidence available about the income from subscriptions. It would also be sensible for the auditor to encourage the association to foster subscription by bank transfer, as this would reduce the problems associated with any subscriptions which are made by cash and would provide a record of subscriptions being made (the bank records).

The problem of the **maintenance** and **retention of relevant accounting records** for the association has already been mentioned. It is possible that the auditors might find that their audit suffers a **limitation in scope** if sufficient records have not been kept.

In the absence of the association employing qualified accountancy staff, the audit firm will also need to consider whether the association has accounted correctly for **income tax** on wages, as it is possible that significant **tax liabilities** could ensue if they have not.

3.2.1 Accounting policies

As has already been mentioned in connection with risk, the lease is likely to pose an issue for the auditor in terms of accounting policies.

4 Reporting

> **FAST FORWARD**
>
> The nature of the report will depend on statutory and entity requirements, but it should conform to ISA 700 criteria.

On not-for-profit audits where a statutory auditor's report is required, the auditors should issue the same report. They should also consider whether any additional statutory requirements fall on the auditor's report.

Where an association or charity is having an audit for the benefit of its members or trustees, the standard auditor's report may not be required or appropriate. The auditor should bear in mind the objectives of the audit and make suitable references in the auditor's report. However, the ISA 700 *Forming an opinion and reporting on financial statements* format will still be relevant. The auditor should ensure that he makes the following matters clear:

- The addressees of the report
- What the report relates to
- The scope of the engagement
- The respective responsibilities of auditors and management/trustees/directors
- The work done
- The opinion drawn

> **Exam focus point**
>
> The points made above are general points, the remember that not all clubs and charities will be the same. If you have a question in the exam relating to a charity, apply this general knowledge to the specifics given in the question and be **logical** when formulating your answer.

Question — Charity audit

You have recently been appointed auditor of Links Famine Relief, a small registered charity which receives donations from individuals to provide food in famine areas in the world.

The charity is run by a voluntary management committee, which has monthly meetings, and it employs the following full-time staff:

(a) A director, Mr Roberts, who suggests fundraising activities and payments for relief of famine, and implements the policies adopted by the management committee; and

(b) A secretary (and bookkeeper), Mrs Beech, who deals with correspondence and keeps the accounting records.

You are planning the audit of income of the charity for the year ended 5 April 20X7 and are considering the controls which should be exercised over income.

The previous year's accounts, to 5 April 20X6 (which have been audited by another firm) show the following income.

	$	$
Gifts under non-taxing arrangements		14,745
Tax reclaimed on gifts under non-taxing arrangements		4,915
		19,660
Donations through the post		63,452
Autumn Fair		2,671
Other income		
Legacies	7,538	
Bank deposit account interest	2,774	
		10,312
		96,095

Notes

1 Income from gifts under non-taxing arrangements is stated net. Each person who pays by deed of covenant has filled in a special tax form, which is kept by the secretary, Mrs Beech.

2 All gifts under non-taxing arrangements are paid by banker's order – they are credited directly to the charity's bank account from the donor's bank. Donors make their payments by deed of covenant either monthly or annually.

3 The tax reclaimed on these gifts is 1/3 of the net value of the gifts, and relates to income received during the year – as the tax is received after the year end, an appropriate amount recoverable is included in the balance sheet. The treasurer, who is a voluntary (unpaid) member of the management committee, completes the form for reclaiming the income tax, using the special tax forms (in 1 above) and checks to the full-time secretary's records that each donor has made the full payment in the year required by the arrangement.

4 Donations received through the post are dealt with by Mrs Beech, the full-time secretary. These donations are either cheques or cash (bank notes and coins). Mrs Beech prepares a daily list of donations received, which lists the cheques received and total cash (divided between the different denominations of bank note and coin). The total on this form is recorded in the cash book. She then prepares a paying-in slip and banks these donations daily. When there is a special fund-raising campaign, Mrs Beech receives help in dealing with these donations from voluntary members of the management committee.

5 The Autumn Fair takes place every year on a Saturday in October – members of the management committee and other supporters of the charity give items to sell (for example, food, garden plants, clothing) – a charge is made for entrance to the fair and coffee and biscuits are available at a small charge. At the end of the fair, Mrs Beech collects the takings from each of the stalls, and she banks them the following Monday.

6 Legacies are received irregularly, and are usually sent direct to the director of the charity, who gives them to Mrs Beech for banking – they are stated separately on the daily bankings form (in 4 above).

7 Bank deposit account interest is paid gross of income tax by the bank, as the Links Famine Relief is a charity.

Required

List and briefly describe the work you would carry out on the audit of income of the charity, the controls you would expect to see in operation and the problems you may experience for the following sources of income, as detailed in the income statement above.

(a) Gifts under non-taxing arrangements
(b) Tax reclaimed on gifts made under non-taxing arrangements
(c) Donations received through the post
(d) Autumn Fair

Answer

The audit considerations in relation to the various sources of income of the Links Famine Relief charity would be as follows.

(a) **Gifts made under non-taxing arrangements**

This type of income should not present any particular audit problem as the donations are made by banker's order direct to the charity's bank account and so it would be difficult for such income to be 'intercepted' and misappropriated.

Specific tests required would be as follows:

(i) Check a sample of receipts from the bank statements to the cash book to ensure that the income has been properly recorded.

(ii) Check a sample of the receipts to the special tax forms to ensure that the full amount due has been received.

Any discrepancies revealed by either of the above tests should be followed up with Mrs Beech.

(b) **Tax reclaimed on gifts made under non-taxing arrangements**

Once again this income should not pose any particular audit problems. The auditors should check the claim form submitted to the tax authorities and ensure that the amount of the claim represents $1/3$ of the net value of the covenants recorded as having been received.

(c) **Donations received through the post**

There is a serious problem here as the nature of this income is not predictable and also because of the lack of internal check with Mrs Beech being almost entirely responsible for the receipt of these monies, the recording of the income and the banking of the cash and cheques received. The auditors may ultimately have to express a qualified opinion relating to the uncertainty surrounding the completeness of income of this type.

Notwithstanding the above reservations, specific audit tests required would be as follows:

(i) Check the details on the daily listings of donations received to the cash book, bank statements and paying-in slips, ensuring that the details agree in all respects and that there is no evidence of any delay in the banking of this income.

(ii) Check the donations received by reference to any correspondence which may have been received with the cheques or cash.

(iii) Consider whether the level of income appears reasonable in comparison with previous years and in the light of any special appeals that the charity is known to have made during the course of the year.

(iv) Carry out, with permission of the management committee, surprise checks to vouch the completeness and accuracy of the procedures relating to this source of income.

(d) **Autumn Fair**

Once again there is a potential problem here because of the level of responsibility vested in one person, namely Mrs Beech.

Specific work required would be as follows.

(i) Attend the event to observe the proper application of laid down procedures and count the cash at the end of the day.

(ii) Check any records maintained by individual stallholders to the summary prepared by Mrs Beech.

(iii) Check the vouchers supporting any expenditure deducted from the proceeds in order to arrive at the net bankings.

(iv) Agree the summary prepared by Mrs Beech to the entry in the cash book and on the bank statement.

5 Public sector

FAST FORWARD The public sector comprises a large number of different not-for-profit organisations.

The public sector in most countries comprises a great variety of organisations. They all must have their accounts audited by an independent external auditor, in order to provide external accountability to the community at large.

In the public sector there is a tendency for an external audit to cover a much wider scope than in the private sector. The scope of public sector audit includes not only auditing of financial records and auditing to check compliance with regulations but also auditing the achievement of economy, efficiency and effectiveness.

The audit is an important part of public accountability and it provides an independent check on how public funds have been raised and spent. More specifically audit is needed to ensure that:

(a) **Public funds** have been **spent on proper, authorised purposes** and **legally within statutory powers.**

(b) **Organisations install and operate controls** to limit the possibility of corrupt practice, fraud and poor administration.

(c) Arrangements are in place to secure **economy, efficiency and effectiveness** in the use of resources.

5.1 The regulatory framework

The public sector is often subject to a high degree of regulation. For most public sector audits, the scope and objectives of the audit are affected by the interests and requirements of certain third party organisations such as audit supervisory bodies and government sponsoring departments which have specific regulatory responsibilities.

The manner in which the auditors conduct their work is affected by auditing standards and other regulatory influences including:

- Specific statutory requirements
- Requirements of an audit supervisory body or sponsoring department
- Contractual requirements contained in terms of engagement

The nature of regulation affecting public sector bodies ranges from statutory to detailed administrative requirements.

The auditors of a public body are expected to take reasonable steps to consider compliance by the audited body with regulations relevant to its activities and operations, and to ensure that expenditure made is not *ultra vires* (ie outside the scope of the body's legal powers).

Chapter Roundup

- There are various types of organisation which do not exist for the purpose of maximising shareholder wealth, which may require an audit.
- The audit risks associated with not-for-profit organisations may well be different from those of other entities.
- Cash may be significant in small not-for-profit organisations and controls are likely to be limited. Income may well be a risk area, particularly where money is donated or raised informally.
- Obtaining audit evidence may be a problem, particularly where associations have informal arrangements and there might be limitations on the scope of the audit.
- It will be necessary to ensure accounting policies used are appropriate.
- The nature of the report will depend on statutory and entity requirements, but it should conform to ISA 700 criteria.
- The public sector comprises a large number of different not-for-profit organisations.

Quick Quiz

1. Explain why income can be a problem when auditing charities.

2. Draw up the table below, giving two examples of controls in each area.

Cash donations	Other donations	Other income

3. All limited companies must have a statutory audit.

   True ☐
   False ☐

4. Which of the following would be included in a statutory auditor's report for a not-for-profit entity?

   (i) Statement that the audit was conducted in accordance with ISAs
   (ii) Basis for Conclusion section
   (iii) Addressee
   (iv) Responsibilities of the trustees

5. Which of the following must a UK charity produce, in line with the Charities' SORP?

   (i) Statement of financial activities
   (ii) Statement of financial position
   (iii) Statement of profit or loss and other comprehensive income

6. Explain three areas that public sector auditing will address in addition to the audit of financial statements.

   (1) ....
   (2) ....
   (3) ....

Answers to Quick Quiz

1.
   - Loss of income through fraud
   - Recognition of income from professional fundraisers
   - Recognition of income from branches, associates or subsidiaries
   - Income from informal fundraising groups
   - Income from grants

2. Note: only two examples were required by the question.

Cash donations	Other donations	Other income
Numerical control over boxes and tins	Regular checks and follow up procedures to ensure due amounts are received	Records maintained for each fund raising event
Satisfactory sealing of boxes and tins so that any opening prior to recording cash is apparent	Regular checks to ensure all tax repayments have been obtained	Other appropriate controls maintained over receipts
Regular collection and recording of proceeds from collecting boxes	Comprehensive correspondence files maintained in respect of each legacy	Controls maintained over expenses as for administrative expenses
Dual control over counting and recording of proceeds	Regular reports and follow-up procedures undertaken in respect of outstanding legacies	Regular checks that all sources of income or funds are fully utilised and appropriate claims made
Unopened mail kept securely	In case of charity shops, separation of recording, storage and sale of inventory	Ensuring income or funds are correctly applied
Dual control over the opening of mail		
Immediate recording of donations on opening of mail or receipt		
Agreement of bank paying-in slips to record of receipts by an independent person		

3. False

4. (i), (iii), (iv)

5. (i), (ii)

6. (1) Public funds have been spent on proper, authorised purposes and legally within statutory powers.

   (2) Organisations install and operate controls to limit the possibility of corrupt practice, fraud and poor administration.

   (3) Arrangements are in place to secure economy, efficiency and effectiveness in the use of resources.

PART B   STATUTORY AUDIT AND OTHER EVALUATION

End of Chapter Question

Tap!

You are an audit assistant in the firm Rogers and Smith. You have been asked to plan the audit of 'Tap!' for the year ended 30 June 20X4. It is the first time your audit firm has audited the charity, which has not been audited previously. The trustees have expressed interest in receiving a 'value added' audit and are particularly interested in business advice, especially in the area of systems controls.

'Tap!' is a registered charity that raises money for projects building wells in Africa through musical entertainment. The group consists of volunteers who travel around the country, putting on variety shows of music and dance, the proceeds of which are put towards building the wells. The main show is a tap dance production, acting out the difficulties many people face when they are not near a clean water supply.

The administrative offices of 'Tap!' are located in a large provincial town. It owns a house, donated by legacy in the past, where the administration is carried out and where the volunteers stay during off periods.

A large proportion of 'Tap!'s income comes from box office receipts which are taken by the theatre at which they are performing. The theatres usually waive their standard terms for use of the premises and merely take a 10% commission on ticket receipts to cover light and heat and other such expenses. Income usually comes in after every booking in the form of a lump sum cheque from the theatre, together with a break down of takings and commission.

Tap also receives donations towards the work. These come from a variety of sources:

- Cash donations from buckets passed around at the interval of each performance
- Cash donations on the (rare) occasion that the team do street performances
- Cash donations made over the phone or by post by interested donors

The troupe consists largely of volunteers so they are only paid expenses for their work. The cost of housing the group while they are on the road is borne by the charity. The charity employs an administrator who organises bookings, handles publicity and co-ordinates all the finances.

Required

(a)   Discuss the risks arising for the audit of the year ending 30 June 20X4.   **(8 marks)**

(b)   Outline the audit procedures you would undertake in respect of cash income in the financial statements.
   (6 marks)

(c)   Outline some controls over cash which the charity should implement.   **(6 marks)**

(Total 20 marks)

Management responsibilities including internal audit

Topic list	Syllabus reference
1 Management responsibilities	LO1
2 Internal audit	LO1
3 Outsourcing	LO1
4 Impact of outsourcing on auditors	LO1

Introduction

You should be familiar with the responsibilities of management which have been set out in Chapter 2. A key responsibility is to establish a system of internal control and to report to shareholders on its effectiveness.

An aspect of management responsibility is establishing an internal audit function if required, and in this chapter we **revise internal audit** which you studied in some detail in your earlier studies. It may be possible for the external auditor to make use of the work of internal audit, in line with the provisions of ISA 610 *Using the work of internal auditors*.

In the second half of the chapter, we look at outsourcing. **Outsourcing is an important factor in business today**. The key issues for management are **cost and control**.

Lastly we look at the impact on external auditors when management outsources part of its function, particularly control issues. ISA 402 *Audit considerations relating to an entity using a service organisation* is relevant here.

1 Management responsibilities

> **FAST FORWARD**
>
> Management is responsible for creating a system of internal control in a company to safeguard assets, allow efficient operations and compliance with regulation. They are also required to report on various issues to shareholders.

1.1 The control environment and internal control

You learnt a great deal about the control environment and internal control in your earlier studies. The UK Corporate Governance Code's requirements relating to monitoring and reporting on internal control take for granted that the board should maintain a sound system of internal control to safeguard shareholders' investment and the company's assets.

You may find that you are asked questions about the directors and the internal control systems they set up in the exam, so if you are not sure about what internal controls are or how they work, you should find your paper and Learning & Practice Workbook and revise this area.

Of course, a key part of internal control, specifically the monitoring of internal control, is sometimes delegated to an internal audit function. As we saw in Chapter 2, directors are responsible for considering if an internal audit function is needed in a company. We shall look in more detail at the role of internal audit in the next section.

1.2 Reporting

We also outlined the reporting requirements on management in Chapter 2. The most notable requirement, as far as external auditors are concerned, is that management is required to report on the financial activity of the company in the form of the financial statements, but the Code also refers to other financial reporting, such as interim financial statements and other price-sensitive reports.

The Code also contains other important reporting requirements, for example, the requirement to produce a statement of Corporate Governance, which the auditor reviews. Remember, this statement is required for **listed** companies, but is considered good practice for all companies.

The audit committee of a company has a critical role in the company's financial and other reporting. Remember that the members of the audit committee should be non executive directors, so they do not have an executive role in the business, and will be liaising closely with the financial director and the internal audit team.

2 Internal audit

> **FAST FORWARD**
>
> Internal audit has a key role in corporate governance, providing objective assurance on control and risk management.

2.1 Revision

The internal audit function was considered in detail in your earlier studies. Work through the following question to ensure that you remember the basic principles of internal auditing.

Question

Revision: Internal audit

(a) Describe the principal differences between internal and external auditors, considering the following factors.

    (i)   Eligibility
    (ii) Security of appointment
    (iii) Main objectives and limitations on the scope of their work

(b) Explain how external auditors would evaluate specific work carried out by internal auditors.

Answer

(a) **Eligibility**

Under the Companies Act 2006, a person is ineligible to act as external auditor if he is an officer or employee of the company, a partner or employee of such a person or a partnership in which such a person is a partner. An internal auditor is an employee of the company.

The Companies Act also requires external auditors to belong to a recognised supervisory body, and this means they must hold an appropriate qualification, follow technical standards and maintain competence.

By contrast anyone can act as an internal auditor even if they do not have a formal accounting qualification. It is up to the company's management who they appoint.

Security

Under the Companies Act, the external auditors of a private company are appointed, in effect, indefinitely. They can be dismissed by an ordinary resolution of shareholders with special notice in general meeting, and have the right to make representations.

External auditors cannot be dismissed by individual directors or by a vote of the board. The only influence directors can have on the removal of external auditors is through their votes as shareholders. The rules on security of tenure are there because of the need for external auditors to protect the interests of shareholders by reporting on directors' stewardship of the business.

By contrast, as internal auditors are employees of the company, they can be dismissed by the directors or lower level of management, subject only to their normal employment rights.

Objectives and limitations on the scope of the audit work

The primary objective of external auditors is laid down by statute, to report on whether the company's accounts show a true and fair view of the state of the company's affairs at the period-end, and of its profit or loss for the period. External auditors are also required to report if certain other criteria have not been met, for example the company fails to keep proper accounting records or fails to make proper disclosure of transactions with directors.

Internal auditors' objectives are whatever the company's management decide they should be. Some of the objectives may be similar to those of external audit, for example to confirm the quality of accounting systems. Other objectives might be in areas which have little or no significance to the external auditor, for example recommending improvements in economy, efficiency and effectiveness.

Statutory rules mean that management cannot limit the scope of external auditors' work. External auditors have the right of access to all a company's books and records, and can demand all the information and explanations they deem necessary. As the objectives of internal audit's work are decided by management, management can also decide to place limitations on the scope of that work.

(b) External auditors should consider whether:

- The work is performed by persons having adequate technical training and proficiency as internal auditors.
- The work of assistants is properly supervised, reviewed and documented.
- Sufficient appropriate audit evidence is obtained to afford a reasonable basis for the conclusions reached.
- The conclusions reached are appropriate in the circumstances.
- Any reports prepared by internal audit are consistent with the results of the work performed.
- Any exceptions or unusual matters disclosed by internal audit are properly resolved.
- Amendments to the external audit programme are required as a result of matters identified by internal audit work.
- To what extent the external auditors need to test the work of internal audit to confirm its adequacy.

Hopefully you could answer that question. If you struggled, you might want to refer back to your notes from your earlier studies, but here is a summary of the key revision points on internal audit in this syllabus.

Knowledge brought forward from earlier studies

Role of internal audit in corporate governance

All companies face risks arising from their operational activities. Risks arise in different areas.

- Risk the company will go bankrupt
- Risks arising from regulations and law
- Risks arising from publicity

This risk must be managed. This gives rise to another role for the internal audit function, **risk management**.

Risk awareness and management should be the role of everyone in the organisation. The extended role of internal audit with regard to risk is the monitoring of integrated risk management within a company, and the reporting of results to the board to enable them to report to shareholders.

Internal auditor relationships

Internal auditors have relationships with the following people:

- **Management**: by whom they are employed and may report to
- **Audit committee**: to whom they report
- **External auditors**: who may make use of their work

Using the work of internal auditors by external auditors

The external auditors may make use of the work of internal audit. The guidance over when this appropriate is given to them in ISA 610 *Using the work of internal auditors*.

The ISA states that the external auditors must give consideration to whether the work of internal audit is likely to be adequate for audit purposes, by evaluating the scope and organisation of the internal audit function, its professional competence, and whether work is systematic and directed (and whether the function has quality management measures).

> In respect of the specific audit work they are interested in, the following factors must be considered.
> - Proficiency and training of the people who have undertaken the work
> - Level of supervision, review and documentation of the work of assistants
> - Sufficiency and appropriateness of evidence to draw conclusions
> - Appropriateness of conclusions drawn
> - Consistency of any reports prepared with the work performed
> - Whether the work necessitates amendment to the external audit programme
>
> The auditors may also consider using internal auditors to provide direct assistance to the audit, and gives requirements relating to how that would take place.

2.2 Internal auditors and risk management

Directors need to ensure three steps are taken in their business:

- Identify risks
- Control risks
- Monitor risks

It is not internal audit's primary role to manage risk in a company. It is the responsibility of the directors, usually delegated to individual managers in various departments.

The risks are identified and assessed, and a policy is taken in respect of each of them. To recap, this policy is usually one of four:

- Accept risk (if it is low impact and likelihood)
- Reduce risk (by setting up a system of internal control)
- Avoid risk (by not entering market, accepting contract etc)
- Transfer risk (by taking out insurance)

With their skills in business systems, internal auditors are ideally placed to **monitor** this process and add value to it. They can:

- Give advice on the best design of systems and monitor their operation
- Be involved in a process that continually improves internal control systems
- Provide assurance on systems set up on each department

The involvement of internal audit as a monitoring unit will help to ensure that the process of risk identification and management in a business is a **continual process** rather than a one-off exercise.

2.3 Operational and compliance audits

Key terms

> **Operational audits** are audits of the operational processes of the organisation and check not only compliance with controls but also the effectiveness of controls as part of the risk management process.
>
> **Compliance audits** are audit checks intended to determine whether the actions of employees are in accordance with company policy or laws and regulations.

Compliance audits are the traditional realm of internal auditors. They involve having a knowledge of the company policy and carrying out tests to ensure that company policy is being followed in practice.

Operational audits are different to compliance audits in that the scope is more extensive. As part of an operational audit, the internal audit function might undertake a compliance audit, but the scope **also includes an assessment of the effectiveness** of the procedures that are being audited.

2.4 Multi-site operations

Some organisations have several outlets which all operate the same systems. A good example of this would be a retail chain, which would have a number of shops where systems relating to inventory and cash, for example, would be the same.

The objective of audits of multi-site operations is the same as the objective of single site operations. However, as results might vary across the different location, the internal auditor has to take a different approach. Some possible approached to multi-site operations audits are set out below.

(a) **Compliance based audit approach**

With a compliance based audit approach, a master audit programme is drawn up which is used to check the compliance of the branches with the set procedures, after which the results from the branches are compared. There are two possible ways of undertaking the compliance based approach:

(i) **Cyclical**: This approach is based on visiting all of the sites within a given timeframe.

(ii) **Risk based approach**: This alternative determines which branches are to be visited based on the risk attached to them.

(b) **Process based audit approach**

With a process based audit approach, the audit is planned so that specific key processes are audited. In a retail operation, for example, this could involve the important process of cash handling being audited. This approach can also be undertaken in two ways:

(i) **Cyclical**: Aims to audit all processes in a business within a set timeframe.

(ii) **Risk-based**: The processes to be audited are determined with reference to the risk attached to them.

2.4.1 Practical considerations

The practical issues to consider in relation to multi-site operations are:

- Which sites to visit
- How often to visit various sites
- Whether to conduct routine or surprise visits and what mix of these types of visit

Remember that the considerations behind which sites to visit will **not** be the same as for external auditors. Internal auditors may consider issues (among others) such as:

- Size of operation
- History of systems compliance
- Quality/experience of staff on site
- Past results of testing
- Management interest in particular sites

Question

Audit risk

You are the Chief Internal Auditor of Adam Co, which owns and operates three large departmental stores in Wandon, Thuringham and Tonchester. Each store has more than 22 departments.

You are at present preparing your audit plan and you are considering carrying out detailed audit tests on a rotational basis. You consider that all departments within the stores should be covered over a period of five years but that more frequent attention should be given to those where the 'audit risk' demands it.

Required

Describe the factors which you would consider in order to evaluate the audit risk attaching to each department.

Answer

Risk may be evaluated by considering:

(a) The probability of an event
(b) The potential size of the event

In the case of an audit the event concerned is undetected material error or fraud.

In evaluating risk in the context of the audit of a company owning and operating three large department stores the factors to be considered are as follows.

(a) Factors influencing probability

    (i) Strengths and weaknesses in the system of internal control, overall and for each individual store and department in respect of all types of internal control. It would be appropriate to consider such controls under the following headings.

        (1) Organisation of staff
        (2) Segregation of staff
        (3) Physical controls
        (4) Authorisation and approval
        (5) Arithmetic and accounting
        (6) Personnel
        (7) Supervision
        (8) Management

    (ii) Experience derived from previous audits and the conclusion of previous auditor's reports.

    (iii) Whether the prices of goods sold are fixed by head office or variable by local store or departmental managers.

    (iv) Extent of local purchasing for each store or department.

    (v) The nature of the inventory (for example high unit value, attractiveness).

    (vi) Effectiveness of cash-handling systems.

(b) Factors influencing size

    (i) Relative size of department in terms of:

        (1) Revenue
        (2) Number of transactions
        (3) Average value of inventory

    (ii) Internal statistics of losses through shoplifting and staff theft.

(c) Other general factors

    (i) Comparison among stores and among like departments in the three stores, using ratio analysis.

    (ii) Risk of deterioration or obsolescence of inventories.

    (iii) Rate of turnover of store staff.

3 Outsourcing

FAST FORWARD

Outsourcing is the contracting out of certain functions. A business can outsource a small part of the function, or the entire function, or practically all its functions!

3.1 Why outsource?

Key terms

Outsourcing is the process of purchasing key functions from an outside supplier. In other words, it is **contracting-out** certain functions, for example, internal audit or information technology.

Insourcing is when an organisation decides to retain a centralised department for the key function, but brings experts in from an external market on a short-term basis to account for 'peak' and 'trough' periods.

There are three general reasons for outsourcing:

- Financial efficiency
- Change management
- Strategy

3.1.1 Financial efficiency

It is often argued that outsourcing **reduces cost**. This **may not necessarily be the case**, but businesses often find that it is worth investigating. If outsourcing is never considered, it is often the case that the cost of maintaining the function in-house is never calculated, and therefore not considered either.

This fact links into the next point about financial efficiency. Outsourcing a function can lead to **greater cost control** over that function. This is as a result of the function now being subject to a contractual fee rather than a previously not completely identified, cost of maintaining the function in-house. This aspect of outsourcing might substantially **improve budgeting and cost control**.

Outsourcing may considerably **reduce the number of employees** for whom the business is responsible. The logistics of shedding staff may make outsourcing a difficult legal and human issue, but the **cost savings** in this area (salary, tax, pension, for example) could be substantial.

Outsourcing can have a fundamental effect on the **shape of an entity's financial statements**, particularly if a function with a high capital investment (for example, information technology) is being outsourced. In some cases, it might be possible to sell the company's assets to the service provider, producing a cash injection, or reduced initial fees.

3.1.2 Change management

Outsourcing can be a way of managing change in a company. For example, if the company decides to change its software, outsourcing the software provision might mean that all **staff training** on the new system is incorporated into the service.

Outsourcing a function such as finance might facilitate the smooth running of a **merger** of two firms who have different accounting systems. This may also be true when a business is **restructured**.

3.1.3 Strategy

Outsourcing can also be part of a strategy to **refocus on the core competencies** of a business, or a thrust to **improve technical services**. It can be a way of **entering a market in the most low risk way**. For example, a previously low-tech business wanting to engage in e-commerce could outsource its website development and maintenance.

3.2 Outsource what?

Generally, if a company chooses to outsource, it will outsource functions which are not perceived to be key competencies. The different approaches which can be taken to outsourcing depend on the extent to which a company contracts out non-core functions. This can be seen by way of an example.

Case Study

The Toy Company

The Toy Company is a small company, owned and run by Edward T. Bear. It was left to him by his father, T. Bear, who was a skilled toy maker. The business began as a one-man operation in the garage and it now has 250 employees and technical computerised processes and is run from its own factory complex.

Edward joined the company on leaving school. He worked alongside his father for ten years. Last year his father died and left the shares in the company to Edward and his sister Victoria. Victoria has never had any role in the company and has no wish to become involved.

The company employed an accountant twenty years ago, who remains an employee of the firm. In the intervening years, the accounts department has grown to now incorporate five other employees, with one having specific payroll duties. The accounts department has a computer system which is separate from the computer system used in operations.

In operations, there are several divisions: design, manufacture, packaging, sales and marketing.

The company also employs a part-time human resources manager who deals with staff matters and recruitment. The office cleaner is the longest serving member of staff. She has worked for Mr Bear since he set up in his first workshop forty years ago.

There are several areas where management could consider outsourcing. We will consider the advantages and disadvantages of this below. At this stage we are only looking to see where the potential lies.

The core competency of the company is the manufacture of toys. This means that there are several functions which do not fall within this competency:

- Accounting
- Human Resources
- Cleaning

Of the above areas, cleaning would be the least risky to outsource because the cleaning does not directly impact on the operation of the business. Cleaning is a commonly outsourced function in the private sector.

However, as accountants we are more interested in the accounting function. The accounts department is not part of the core competency, so potentially, it could be outsourced. Within this decision, there are several others to be made.

The company could outsource:

- Pension functions
- Tax related functions
- The entire payroll function
- Invoicing
- Credit control
- The entire accounting function

When considering **the extent to which the company wants to adopt outsourcing**, it must consider the risk involved and the control which management want to maintain over the function. There is less risk involved in outsourcing a part of the payroll function (for example, pensions) than in outsourcing the whole finance function.

Similar subdivisions can be seen when considering the outsourcing of other functions:

Human Resources	Welfare
	Health and safety
	Recruitment
	The entire department
Information Technology	Maintenance
	Project management
	Network management
	The entire IT function

Just to extend the point about outsourcing to its furthest extremes, it is possible to consider outsourcing more of the business than has been discussed above.

Case Study continued

In the first instance, Edward could critically appraise the core competency of his business (the manufacture of toys) and subdivide it further. He might decide that the production processes are the core competency and that functions such as design and sales and marketing should be outsourced.

In an extreme case, it is possible to create a **virtual organisation**. For example, Edward could decide that he has no particular personal interest in toy manufacture, but that he does wish to retain the business. In which case, he could outsource all the different functions of the business, but maintain control of the contracts and therefore ultimately the business.

An example of an industry where this could be the case is the airline industry, where it is possible to contract out the aircraft and their maintenance and the crew to fly them.

3.3 Advantages and disadvantages of outsourcing

We will look in detail at the advantages and disadvantages of outsourcing some specific functions below. For now, however, we shall consider some general advantages and disadvantages of outsourcing that apply to them all.

Advantages of outsourcing
Cost. A key advantage of outsourcing is that it is often cheaper to contract a service out than it is to conduct it in house. It may also significantly improve cost control.
Specialist service. Outsourcing results in specialist being used to provide the service when that would not have been the case if the function was performed in house.
Indemnity. The service organisation may provide indemnity in the event of problems arising. If problems arise in house, there is no such comfort zone.
Cash flow. Obtaining the service through a contract may assist with cash flow, as the contract will represent a flat fee, whereas the cost of providing the service in house might have led to fluctuating costs (for example, if temporary staff are required in a busy period).

Disadvantages of outsourcing
The single biggest disadvantage of outsourcing, is the extent to which the company loses **control** over the function itself, although not over cost control.
The **initial cost** of outsourcing may be **substantial if** an aspect of the decision is to close a current department of the business. The question of **potential redundancies** may dissuade companies from considering outsourcing.
The contract has to be **managed** to ensure that the service being provided is appropriate and in accordance with the contract. This may take a disproportionate amount of **time**.
The contract might limit the **liability** of the contractor, leading to problems if the contract is not performed well. This might even result in **court action** being required.
Should these disadvantages be realised, the **cost** of outsourcing could outweigh the benefit, even though in theory outsourcing should reduce cost.

3.4 Outsourcing internal audit

Internal audit is rarely a core competency of a company. However, it is a valuable service to management. Management are required to assess annually whether their company needs one.

There are **problems associated with setting up an internal audit function**, however. These are:

- Cost of recruiting staff
- Difficulty of recruiting staff of sufficient skill and qualification for the company's preference or need
- The fact that management are not accounting specialist and therefore might struggle to direct the new function in their duties
- The time frame between setting up the function and seeing the results of having the function
- The fact that the work required may not be enough to justify engaging full time staff
- The fact that a variety of skills and seniority levels are required, but only one member of full time staff can be justified

3.4.1 Advantages

The advantage of outsourcing internal audit is that outsourcing can overcome all these problems:

- Staff need not be recruited, as the service provider has good quality staff
- The service provider has specialist skill and can assess what management require them to do. As they are external to the operation, this will not cause operational problems
- Outsourcing can provide an immediate internal audit function
- The service contract can be for the appropriate time scale (a two week project, a month, etc)
- Because the time scale is flexible, a team of staff can be provided if required
- The service provider could also provide less than at team, but, for example, could provide one member of staff on a full-time basis for a short period, as a secondment

A key advantage of outsourcing internal audit is that **outsourcing can be used on a short term basis**, to:

- Provide immediate services
- Lay the basis of a permanent function, by setting policies and functions
- Prepare the directors for the implications of having an internal audit function
- Assist the directors in recruiting the permanent function

Outsourced internal audit services are provided by many audit firms, particularly the Big Four. This can range from a team of staff for a short-term project, or a single staff member on a long-term project.

3.4.2 Disadvantages

However, the fact that internal audit services are typically provided by external auditors can raise problems as well.

- The company might wish to **use the same firm** for internal and external audit services, but this may lead to **complications for the external auditors**.
- The **cost** of sourcing the internal audit function might be high enough to make the directors choose not to have an internal audit function at all.

3.5 Outsourcing finance and accounting functions

Various functions will be considered in the table below. Remember, however, the key advantages and disadvantages set out above as they are all likely to be true of the functions discussed more specifically below.

Function	
Data processing	
Disadvantages	There may be logistical difficulties in outsourcing data processing, due to the high level of paper involved (invoices, goods received notes etc). This information will have to be given to the service organisation.
	A secondary, and more important, effect is that the company might not always have control of their key accounting documentation and records. It is a legal requirement that the directors maintain this information. While they may delegate the practicalities, they are still responsible for maintaining the records.
Pensions	
Advantages	Pensions are a specialist area and there is merit in getting a specialist to operate the company's pension provision.
Disadvantages	Pensions are closely related to the payroll and the company will share sensitive information with the pension provider, which may complicate the situation.
Information technology	
Advantages	A key advantage of outsourcing all, or elements of, the IT function is that this will enable the company to keep pace with **rapid technological advances**.
	It also allows the company to take advantage of the work of specialist in a field that many people still find difficult but which they use regularly to carry out their business.
	Outsourcing can provide a useful **safety net** of a technical helpline or indemnity in the event of computer disaster.
	It is also possible that through outsourcing, the company will be able to obtain **added-value**, such as new ways of doing business identified (for example, e-commerce).

Function	
Due diligence	
Advantages	A key advantage in relation to outsourcing due diligence is the high level of **expertise** that can be brought in.
	The company can expect **quality** from its service contractor, and can seek **legal compensation** from them in the event of negligence.
Taxes	
Advantages	In relation to taxes, the key advantage is also the buying in of **expertise**.
Disadvantages	The disadvantage of outsourcing tax work is that while the work can be outsourced, the **responsibility** cannot. The tax authorities will deal with the responsible person, not the agent, so the loss of control is particularly risky in this case.

4 Impact of outsourcing on auditors

FAST FORWARD

When a company uses a service organisation, there are special considerations for the auditors.

Exam focus point

There are both **ethical** and **practical audit implications** of outsourcing on an audit – either could be examined.

4.1 Use of service organisations

The impact of outsourcing on an external audit is considered in ISA 402 *Audit considerations relating to an entity using a service organisation*.

Key terms

A **service organisation** is a third party organisation (or segment of a third party organisation) that provides services to user entities that are part of those entities' information systems relevant to financial reporting.

A **service auditor** is an auditor who, at the request of the service organisation, provides an assurance report on the controls of a service organisation.

A **user auditor** is an auditor who audits and reports on the financial statements of a user entity.

A **user entity** is an entity that uses a service organisation and whose financial statements are being audited.

As we have discussed above, some companies choose to outsource activities necessary to the running of their business to **service organisations**. Examples of such activities that may be outsourced are:

- Information processing
- Maintenance of accounting records
- Facilities management
- Asset management (for example, investments)
- Initiation or execution of transactions on behalf of the other entity

Some outsourced activities may be directly relevant to the audit. The most obvious example above is the maintenance of accounting records, but most of them actually could impact on the audit.

Auditors need to obtain sufficient, appropriate audit evidence to express an opinion on financial statements. they therefore need to consider an approach towards the parts of the audit affected by the service organisation.

4.2 Considerations of the client auditor

A service organisation may establish and execute policies and procedures that affect a client organisation's accounting and internal control systems. These policies and procedures are physically and operationally separate from the client organisation.

(a) When the services provided by the service organisation are **limited to recording** and **processing client transactions** and the client retains authorisation and maintenance of accountability, the client may be able to implement effective policies and procedures within its organisation.

(b) When the service organisation **executes** the client's **transactions** and **maintains accountability**, the client may deem it necessary to rely on policies and procedures at the service organisation.

> **ISA 402.9**
>
> In obtaining an understanding of the user entity in accordance with ISA 315 (Revised 2019) the auditor shall obtain an understanding of how a user entity uses the services of a service organisation in the user entity's operations...

In doing so, the client auditor would need to consider the following, as appropriate:

- The **nature of the services** provided by the service organisation
- The nature of materiality of the transactions processed or accounts or financial reporting processes affected by the service organisation
- The degree of interaction between the activities of the service organisation and those of the user entity
- The nature of the relationship between the user entity and the service organisation, including the relevant contractual terms for the activities

The auditor can obtain information about these matters by reading the contract between the parties and making enquiries of management. The client auditor should also consider the existence of **third-party reports** from service **organisation** auditors, internal auditors, or regulatory agencies as a means of providing information about the accounting and internal control systems of the service organisation and about its operation and effectiveness.

> **ISA 402.10**
>
> When obtaining an understanding of internal control relevant to the audit in accordance with ISA 315 (Revised 2019), the user auditor shall evaluate the design and implementation of relevant controls at the user entity that relate to the services provided by the service organisation, including those that are applied to the transactions processed by the service organisation.

The auditor should then consider whether sufficient information has been obtained to identify and assess risks of material misstatement. If so, then the auditor should assess risks and design audit procedures to respond to those risks.

If the information is insufficient, the client auditor should obtain that information by obtaining a report from the service organisation (see below), by contacting the service organisation through the user, or visiting the service organisation, or by having another auditor visit the service organisation. In practice, service organisations are likely to provide reports, which we shall consider now.

4.3 Service organisation auditor's reports

The ISA refers to two types of service organisation reports.

Key terms

> A **type 1 report** is a report on the description and design of controls at a service organisation.
>
> A **type 2 report** is a report on the description, design and operating effectiveness of controls at a service organisation.

A type 1 report comprises:

(a) A description, prepared by management of the service organisation, of the service organisation's system, control objectives and related controls that have been designed and implemented as at a specified date; and

(b) A report by the service auditor with the objective of conveying reasonable assurance that includes the service auditor's opinion on the description of the service organisation's system, control objectives and related controls and the suitability of the design of the controls to achieve the specified control objectives.

A type 2 report comprises:

(a) A description, prepared by management of the service organisation, of the service organisation's system, control objectives and related controls, their design and implementation as at a specified date or throughout a specified period and, in some cases, their operating effectiveness throughout a specified period; and

(b) A report by the service auditor with the objective of conveying reasonable assurance that includes:

   (i) The service auditor's opinion on the description of the service organisation's system, control objectives and related controls, the suitability of the design of the controls to achieve the specified control objectives, and the operating effectiveness of the controls; and

   (ii) A description of the service auditor's tests of the controls and the results thereof.

While reports on design may be useful to a client auditor in gaining the required understanding of the accounting and internal control systems, an auditor would not use such reports as a basis for reducing the assessment of control risk.

By contrast a report on operating effectiveness may provide such a basis since tests of control have been performed. If this type of report is maybe to be used as evidence to support a lower control risk assessment, a client auditor would have to consider whether the controls tested by the service organisation auditor are relevant to the client's transactions (significant assertions in the client's financial statements) and whether the service organisation auditor's tests of control and the results are adequate.

4.4 Reporting

When the auditor uses a report from the auditor of a service organisation, no references should be made in the statutory auditor's report to the type 1 or 2 report on the service organisation which the auditors have used as audit evidence.

4.5 Impact on internal audit

External auditors will be affected when outsourced functions impact on the financial statements. Internal audit will be interested in outsourced functions which affect the business (that is, any outsourced function).

Internal audit will be interested in the contractual arrangements made with the service organisation. They may want to pay a visit to the organisation and undertake a review of its systems to ensure that they are sufficient for the business's needs.

Question: Outsourcing

(a) Explain the meaning of the word 'outsourcing' and distinguish it from 'insourcing'.

(b) Discuss the risks and benefits of outsourcing the payroll function of a small business, employing a management accountant and an accounts clerk.

(c) You are planning the audit of a company that has just outsourced its credit control function. Describe the planning issues that arise as a result of this action.

Answer

(a) **Outsourcing** is the practice of purchasing a specific function from an outside service provider. In other words, it is the practice of contracting-out functions of the business to an expert.

Insourcing, by contrast, is the practice of maintaining a specialist function in house, but buying in external expertise on a short-term basis to balance peaks and troughs in demand for that expertise.

(b) Payroll is a complicated accounting area, particularly due to the issues of taxation arising. It is also susceptible to fraud in the absence of strong controls.

In a small company, such as the one described, there is **little scope for segregation of duties** in relation to payroll. It is likely that payroll would be managed by the accountant, as it the clerk is likely to have a full time job in relation to sales and purchases, and the accountant has greater expertise. However, it is possible that an accountant in such a position, even in a small business, might **not have time to manage payroll** in addition to other accounting duties. In order for there to be **adequate authorisation** and segregation in relation to payroll, **another senior figure should be involved** in authorising the payroll.

In this situation, it might be **cost effective to outsource** the payroll function to an **expert**. This might also **reduce the control problems** inherent in the small department. However, there are some disadvantages related to outsourcing the function. The key issue is one of **confidentiality**, as payroll records contain sensitive data about personnel (for example, their bank details). **Personnel might object** to this information being given to an outside provider. The company would also have to **institute controls over the transfer of data** (such as weekly hours worked) to the service provider.

(c) The auditors should determine whether the outsourced function is **relevant to the audit**. In the case of the credit control function, this is clearly **relevant to receivables** reported in the statement of financial position and to **sales and irrecoverable receivables**.

The auditor must ensure that he **understands the terms of the contract** between the client and the service provider. As part of planning the audit, therefore, he **must obtain a copy** of the contract and **become familiar with its terms**.

The auditor must **ascertain whether he will have access to the records** that he will require as part of his audit evidence. As part of planning he must **make arrangements to enable this access**.

As part of the risk assessment at the planning stage, the auditor must consider whether the outsourcing arrangements affect the risk of material misstatement in the financial statements. In doing so he will consider factors such as the contract (referred to above), the reputation of the service provider and the effectiveness of past controls when the function was maintained in house and present controls over the outsourcing arrangements.

Chapter Roundup

- Management is responsible for creating a system of internal control in a company to safeguard asset, allow efficient operations and compliance with regulation. They are also required to report on various issues to shareholders.
- Internal audit has a key role in corporate governance, providing objective assurance on control and risk management.
- Outsourcing is the contracting out of certain functions. A business can outsource a small part of the function, or the entire function, or practically all its functions!
- When a company uses a service organisation, there are special considerations for the auditors.

PART B STATUTORY AUDIT AND OTHER EVALUATION

Quick Quiz

1. List six factors which the external auditors should consider in relation to the work of internal audit.

    (1) ....

    (2) ....

    (3) ....

    (4) ....

    (5) ....

    (6) ....

2. Complete the definitions.

    .... audits are audits of the ....
    .... of the organisation and check not only compliance with controls but also the
    .... of controls as part of the risk management process.

    .... audits are audit checks intended to determine whether the actions of
    employees are in .... with company .... or
    .... and ....

3. Outsourcing is another term that means staff recruitment.

    True ☐

    False ☐

4. Name five elements of the accounts function which could be outsourced.

    (1) ....

    (2) ....

    (3) ....

    (4) ....

    (5) ....

5. Complete the table, putting the advantages made under the right headings and naming the specific function, if relevant.

General advantages	Function-specific advantages

   - Cost
   - Keeping pace with technological advance
   - Liability/indemnity
   - Cashflow
   - Specialist service
   - Immediacy
   - Flexibility (particularly with regard to time scale)

6   The auditor may refer to the responsibility of the service organisation when giving his opinion on the financial statements.

    True   ☐

    False   ☐

PART B STATUTORY AUDIT AND OTHER EVALUATION

Answers to Quick Quiz

1. (1) Proficiency and training of staff
   (2) Level of supervision, documentation and review of the work
   (3) Sufficiency and appropriateness of evidence
   (4) Appropriateness of conclusion
   (5) Consistency of reports with work performed
   (6) Whether work necessitates amendment to original audit plan

2. Operational, operational processes, effectiveness

   Compliance, accordance, policy, law, regulations

3. False. It is contracting-out functions.

4. (1) Pension
   (2) Tax
   (3) Payroll
   (4) Invoicing
   (5) Credit control

5.

General advantages	Function-specific advantages
• Cost	• Technological advance (IT)
• Liability/indemnity	• Liability/indemnity (IT/due diligence)
• Cashflow	• Immediacy (IA)
• Specialist service	• Flexibility/time scale (IA)
• Flexibility	

6. False

   - Responsibility for accounting records still lies with directors
   - Responsibility for auditing them still lies with auditors

End of Chapter Question

City Trading (AIA November 2007)

City Trading is a large company which owns several shops which sell a range of goods including clothing and electrical goods. The company has recently opened a new shop in the centre of a major city. The directors of City Trading have asked their internal audit function to investigate and report on two issues:

- The new shop has several thousand customers every day. City Trading is conscious that it might be prosecuted if its operating practices are unsafe. In addition, customers might seek compensation if they are injured while in the store, for example if they trip or fall while on the premises or if they are hurt in the event of a fire. The directors of City Trading wish a risk assessment to be carried out on customer safety in the new shop.

- The directors are unsure whether the new shop is selling the correct range of goods. They wish you to investigate the way in which floor space has been allocated to different departments (eg ladies' clothes, mens' clothes, furniture, electrical goods). They wish to use this report to reallocate space so that profit is maximised.

Required

(a) Explain how the internal audit function should conduct its risk assessment of customer safety.

(10 marks)

(b) Explain how the internal audit function could investigate the performance of different departments. Your answer should assume that the shop's accounting system makes it possible to analyse revenues and expenses by department and also that it would be possible to conduct some investigation and analysis specifically for the purpose of this exercise.

(10 marks)

(Total 20 marks)

PART B STATUTORY AUDIT AND OTHER EVALUATION

Audit strategy, process and reporting

Audit planning

Topic list	Syllabus reference
1 Overview of audit planning	15.3
2 Understanding the entity	
3 Materiality	15.3
4 General planning matters	15.3

Introduction

The issue of audit planning should not be new to you. You learnt how to plan an audit in your previous auditing studies. Why then is this chapter here? There are two answers:

- To **revise** the details that should be included in an **audit strategy and plan** and the general considerations included in planning
- To **consider** some of the **finer points of planning** from the point of view of the engagement partner, specifically to consider the issue of the **risk associated with the assignment** (which is a personal risk to the partner in the event of litigation arising)

Materiality considerations are also important at the planning stage. The calculation of materiality should be based on experience and judgement and will assist the auditor in determining the nature, timing and extent of audit procedures to include in the audit plan.

Risk is a key issue in an audit, and the most common approach to audits incorporates a recognition of those risks in the approach taken. It is called the **risk-based approach**.

PART C AUDIT STRATEGY, PROCESS AND REPORTING

1 Overview of audit planning

FAST FORWARD

Auditors must plan their work so that it is undertaken in an effective manner.

1.1 ISA 200 Overall objectives of the audit

ISA 200 *Overall Objectives of the Independent Auditor and the Conduct of an Audit in Accordance with International Standards on Auditing* states that in conducting an audit of financial statements, the overall objectives of the auditor are:

(a) To obtain reasonable assurance about whether the financial statements as a whole are free from material misstatement, whether due to fraud or error, thereby enabling the auditor to express an opinion on whether the financial statements are prepared, in all material respects, in accordance with an applicable financial reporting framework; and

(b) To report on the financial statements, and communicate as required by the ISAs, in accordance with the auditor's findings (ISA 200: para. 11)

ISA 200 states that the key requirements for the auditor to obtain reasonable assurance and to express an opinion are:

- **Ethics**: Comply with relevant ethical requirements (para. 14)

- **Professional scepticism**: Plan and perform an audit with professional scepticism, recognising that circumstances may exist that cause the financial statements to be materially misstated (para. 15)

- **Professional judgement**: Exercise professional judgement in planning and performing an audit (para. 16)

- **Sufficient appropriate audit evidence and audit risk**: Obtain sufficient appropriate audit evidence to reduce audit risk to an acceptably low level thereby enabling reasonable conclusions to be drawn by the auditor for their audit opinion (para. 17)

Managing audit risk allows the auditor to express an audit opinion and is therefore central to audit planning and risk assessment.

1.2 Professional scepticism

The ability to exercise professional scepticism is one of the key attributes of the auditor.

Key term

> **Professional scepticism** is an attitude that includes a questioning mind, being alert to conditions which may indicate possible misstatement due to error or fraud and a critical assessment of audit evidence. (ISA 220: para. 13)

Professional scepticism is necessary to the critical assessment of audit evidence. Adopting an attitude of professional scepticism includes being alert to the following:

- Audit evidence that contradicts other audit evidence obtained

- Information that brings into question the reliability of documents and responses to inquiries to be used as audit evidence

- Conditions that may indicate possible fraud

- Circumstances that suggest the need for audit procedures in addition to those required by the ISAs (ISA 220: paras. A20–21)

Maintaining professional scepticism throughout the audit reduces the risk of overlooking unusual circumstances, over-generalising when drawing conclusions and using inappropriate assumptions in determining the nature, timing and extent of audit procedures and evaluating results.

Whilst the auditor is not expected to disregard past experience of the honesty and integrity of the entity's management and those charged with governance, a belief that they are honest and have integrity does not relieve the auditor of the need to maintain professional scepticism or allow the auditor to be satisfied with less than persuasive audit evidence. (ISA 220: para. A24)

1.3 Professional judgement

The ability to apply professional judgement is another key skill that an auditor must develop.

> **Key term**
>
> **Professional judgement** is the application of relevant training, knowledge and experience, within the context provided by auditing, accounting and ethical standards, in making informed decisions about courses of action that are appropriate in the circumstances of the audit engagement. (ISA 220: para. 13)

Professional judgement is essential to the proper conduct of an audit as interpretation of the relevant ethical requirements and the ISAs and the informed decisions required throughout the audit cannot be made without the application of relevant knowledge and experience of the facts and circumstances. It is particularly necessary when making decisions about:

- Materiality and audit risk
- The nature, timing and extent of audit procedures
- Evaluating whether sufficient appropriate audit evidence has been obtained
- The evaluation of management's judgements in applying the entity's applicable financial reporting framework
- The drawing of conclusions based on the audit evidence obtained (ISA 200: para. A25)

1.4 ISA 300 Planning an audit

ISA 300 *Planning an audit of financial statements* requires auditors to plan the audit to ensure that the work is carried out in an effective manner (ISA 300: para. 4).

The ISA refers to two documents, the **overall audit strategy**, setting out in general terms how the audit is to be carried out, and the **audit plan**, which details specific procedures to be carried out to implement the strategy and complete the audit.

The specific reasons for planning are to:

- Ensure that appropriate attention is devoted to important areas of the audit
- Ensure that potential problems are identified and resolved on a timely basis
- Ensure that the engagement is properly organised and managed in order to be performed in an effective and efficient manner
- Assist in the proper assignment of work to engagement team members
- Facilitate the direction, supervision and review of engagement team members
- Assist in co-ordination of work done by auditors of components and experts

The nature of the audit might change during the term of the engagement for a variety of reasons so all such changes and reasons shall be documented. The auditor shall also address as part of planning those ethical issues under ISA 220 (Revised) *Quality management for an audit of financial statements* for initial audit engagements such as acceptance and communication with previous auditors.

Planning shall not be a one-off process only carried out at the start of the engagement – it is iterative and so the need for any additional procedures should be constantly reviewed.

PART C AUDIT STRATEGY, PROCESS AND REPORTING

2 Understanding the entity

> **FAST FORWARD**
>
> Auditors must obtain an understanding of the entity and its environment in order to be able to assess the risks of material misstatement.

The objective of the auditor from ISA 315 (Revised 2019) *Identifying and assessing the risks of material misstatement* is to identify and assess the risks of material misstatement, whether due to fraud or error, at the financial statement and assertion levels, thereby providing a basis for designing and implementing responses to the assessed risks of material misstatement (ISA 315 (Revised 2019): para. 11).

ISA 315 (Revised 2019) emphasises gaining an understanding of the entity first, and then using this knowledge and insight to work out where the highest risks of material misstatement might be.

Understand the entity, in order to:

| Identify and assess risks of material misstatement | Design and perform audit procedures | Provide a frame of reference for judgements |

2.1 What do we need to get an understanding of?

The ISA sets out a number of areas of the entity and its environment that the auditor should gain an understanding of.

Areas to gain an understanding of	
The entity and its environment	The entity's organisational structure, ownership and governance, and its business model, including the extent to which the business model integrates the use of IT
	Industry, regulatory and other external factors
	The measures used, internally and externally, to assess the entity's financial performance
	The applicable financial reporting framework
	Selection, application and reasons for changes of accounting policies (ISA 315 (Revised 2019): para. 19)
The entity's system of internal control	Control environment
	Risk assessment process
	Process to monitor the system of internal control
	Information system and communication
	Control activities (ISA 315 (Revised 2019) paras.21–26)

2.1.1 The applicable financial reporting framework

The auditor needs to obtain an understanding of the applicable financial reporting framework (including an assessment of the suitability of the client's chosen accounting policies) to ensure their assessment of risk of material misstatement within the financial statements addresses all appropriate classes of transactions, account balances and disclosures.

The auditor may also need to consider the accounting implications for certain higher-risk areas, for example:

- Revenue recognition (eg for online retailers and resellers)
- Industry-specific accounting principles and practices (eg loans held by for banks or research and development in the pharmaceutical industry)
- Accounting for assets, liabilities and transactions in a foreign currency
- Accounting for unusual or emerging issues (eg cryptocurrency)

(ISA 315 (Revised 2019): para. A82)

2.1.2 The entity's system of internal control

Control environment

This encompasses an assessment of the following:

- How management discharge their oversight responsibilities (including culture, integrity and ethics)
- Where appropriate, the oversight of those changed with governance (TCWG) over management
- How the entity assigns responsibility and authority and how it holds individuals accountable for their responsibilities in pursuit of the achievement of objectives
- The attraction, development and retention of competent individuals
- Whether a culture of honesty and ethical behaviour exists
- Whether the control environment supports the other components of internal control
- The impact of control deficiencies on other components of internal control

(ISA 315 (Revised 2019): para. 21)

The entity's risk assessment process

The entity should have a process for identifying risks that may affect its financial reporting, assessing these risks and then responding to them.

Examples of business risks that might be included in this category:

- Inappropriate objectives or strategies
- Failure to recognise the need to change, such as new markets, products or services, or in response to changes in the regulatory, economic and operating environment
- Incentives or pressures on management that may lead to some kind of bias in the way the financial statements are produced
- Others include new technology, new business models, corporate restructurings, expanded foreign operations and new accounting pronouncements.

(ISA 315 (Revised 2019): paras. 22–23, A62–64, Appendix 3)

Monitoring of controls

The auditor needs to assess how management monitors the systems of internal control in place within an entity that are relevant to the preparation of the financial statements. This is undertaken by performing risk assessment procedures to understand the following:

- Ongoing and separate evaluations of monitoring the effectiveness of controls and the identification and remediation of any control deficiencies identified
- The entity's internal audit function and whether they are effective in their work (for example, should they fail to regularly review bank reconciliations, staff may no longer prepare them)

- The information used for this monitoring process and the rationale for management considering its reliability
- Whether the monitoring process used by management is appropriate for the entity

(ISA 315 (Revised 2019): para. 24, Appendix 3)

Information system and communication

The auditor needs to understand the information system relevant to the preparation of the financial statements and will therefore perform risk assessment procedures on activities related to significant classes of transactions, account balances and disclosures. These will include the following:

- How information flows through the entity's information system (including how transactions are initiated and how all relevant data gets processed and reported and whether any form of manual override exists)
- The various forms of accounting records within the information system (and how they are operated, such as suspense accounts and how they are managed)
- The process used for preparing the financial statements (including the entity's IT and other resources)
- How important information is shared among key stakeholders (such as staff, management, those charged with governance and external parties) and how it supports good decision-making across the entity
- Whether the information system supports the preparation of the financial statements in accordance with the applicable financial reporting framework (and allows events and conditions other than transactions, such as depreciation, amortisation and the recoverability of assets, to be adequately reflected)
- Confirmation of how information is communicated across all relevant parts of the entity to allow effective reporting to take place

(ISA 315 (Revised 2019): para. 25, Appendix 3)

Control activities

The auditor performs risk assessment procedures to understand the control activities component. This includes identifying controls that address risks of material misstatements at the assertion level, evaluating whether the control has been designed effectively and then determining its successful implementation.

Relevant controls include those that relate to the following:

- Controls that address significant risks
- Controls relevant to the determination of the nature, timing and extent of any substantive testing
- Any other controls that, in the auditor's professional judgement, would be relevant in assessing risks of material misstatement
- Any form of IT that will support controls
- Control activities can consist of authorisation and approvals, reconciliations, verifications, physical controls and segregation of duties
- Certain limitations will always exist in control activities, such as human error, collusion or management override and cost vs benefit decisions on how controls are designed and implemented

(ISA 315 (Revised 2019): para. 26, Appendix 3)

2.1.3 Considerations for understanding IT and general IT controls

Systems of internal control contain a combination of both manual and automated systems so the auditor must understand the extent of any IT that is used during the preparation and presentation of the financial statements as part of the assessment of the risk of material misstatement.

The process of obtaining an understanding of the role played by IT in an entity's internal controls will consider following factors:

- The size and complexity of any software and hardware used
- The extent of any automation to the input, processing and output of data (such as the extent of paperless processing)
- The use of different storage solutions (such as switching from local sites to cloud-based solutions and the extent of databases and other automated forms of storage)
- Whether systems used are 'off the shelf' or more bespoke (the use of emerging technologies to produce financial and other information will clearly add to risk)
- The extent of any third parties operating within the entity's IT infrastructure and processes
- How the entity approaches issues such as cybersecurity (and the resultant need for cyber controls to counter any cyberthreats) plus change management (including new systems and the risks of migrating data) alongside the potential risks associated with personnel
- Consideration of general IT controls, such as applications, databases, operating systems and networks and those in relation to access and change (such as segregation of duties or passwords)
- The risks associated with change management, data conversion, back-up controls and intrusion detection
- The ongoing development of emerging technologies creates opportunities but also threats, which auditors must always be alert to (for example, the shift to more end-user computing can have an impact on the quality of an entity's controls)

(ISA 315 (Revised 2019): Appendix 5 and 6)

2.2 How do we get this understanding?

The ISA sets out ways of getting this understanding:

Methods of obtaining an understanding of the entity	Examples
Inquiries of management and appropriate individuals within the entity including individuals within the internal audit function (if this exists)	Inquiry of IT staff about IT system changes or failures Inquiry of in-house legal counsel about any ongoing litigation Inquiry of the internal audit function of any identified control deficiencies or risks
Analytical procedures (on both financial and non-financial data)	Calculating ratios for example the relationship between sales and square metres of selling space
Observation and inspection	Reading internal control manuals, business plans and strategies
Other sources	Information gained in the acceptance or continuance process Other engagements performed by the engagement partner for the entity

Methods of obtaining an understanding of the entity	Examples
Audit team discussion of the susceptibility of the financial statements to material misstatement	More experienced members of the audit team passing on knowledge to new team members
Prior period knowledge (but should check that it is still relevant and reliable)	Whether past misstatements have been corrected on a timely basis
	Deficiencies in controls documented in prior period audit files

After the auditor has documented their understanding of a system or process, they may confirm their understanding is correct by tracing a transaction or item through the system, known as a 'walkthrough'.

The auditors shall design and perform risk assessment procedures in a manner that is not biased towards obtaining evidence that may be corroborative or towards excluding evidence that may be contradictory (ISA 315 (Revised 2019): para. 13).

The engagement partner and other key engagement team members should discuss the susceptibility of the entity's financial statements to material misstatement, and the application of the applicable financial reporting framework to the entity's facts and circumstances. Obtaining an understanding of the entity is a continuous dynamic process of gathering, updating and analysing information throughout the audit. The auditor may use information obtained from the auditor's previous experience from the entity and previous audits, but must make inquiries and perform procedures to evaluate whether this information remains relevant and reliable as audit evidence for the current audit (ISA 315 (Revised 2019): para. 16–17).

Understanding the entity enables the auditor to identify areas of the business which might impact upon the audit. The auditor needs to understand who the client is, what they do and how they do it, any specific laws or regulations surrounding their business and the integrity and competence of client personnel. Once the auditor can understand this, they will be able to perform an effective risk assessment.

For example, for a client owning a chain of restaurants, understanding the entity will include the auditor gaining some basic knowledge of food hygiene regulations. This knowledge and understanding allows the auditor to identify the risk that if the client fails to comply with the regulations, they may be shut down by the authorities.

ISA 315 (Revised 2019) requires the auditor to:

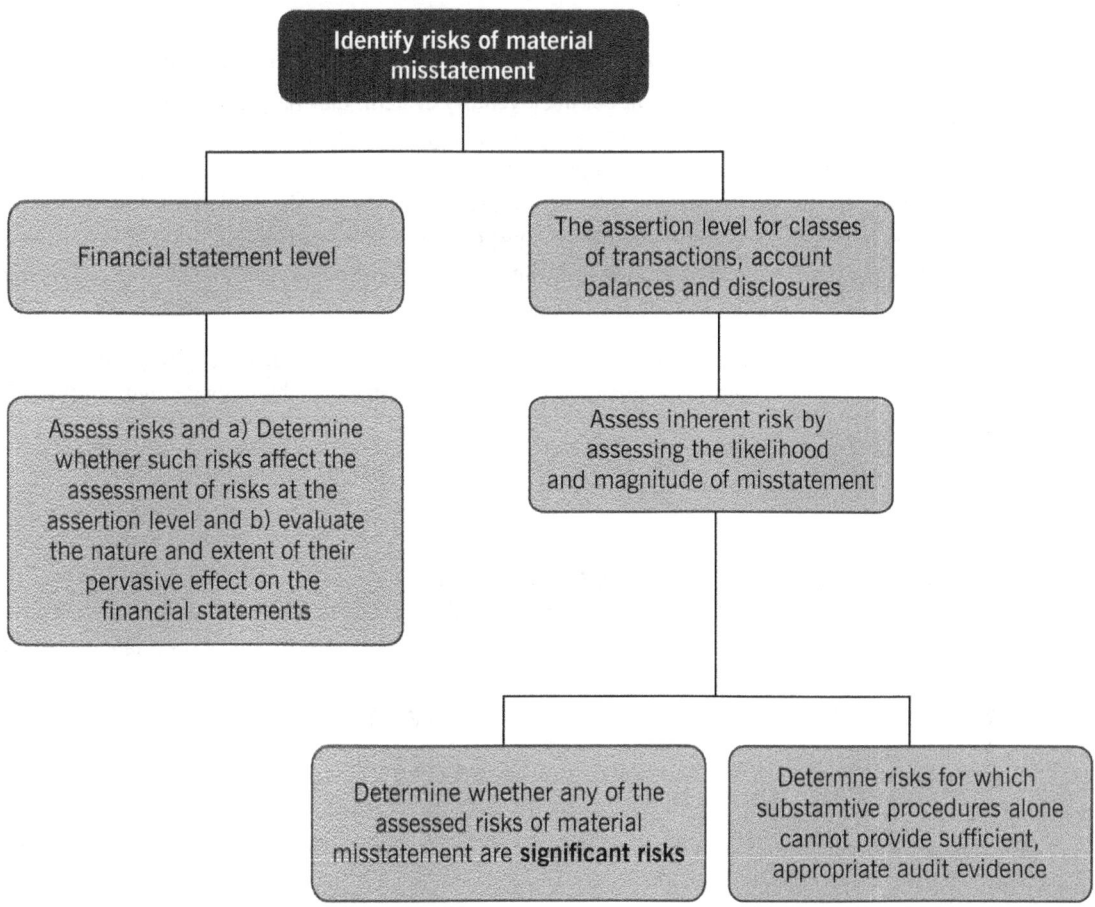

Throughout this process the size of the entity being audited must be considered. For example, in a small entity there is likely to be limited segregation of duties. This may be compensated for by increased management oversight, however this in turn increases the risk of override of controls by management.

> ### Simple example
>
> The audit team at Ockey Co has been carrying out procedures to obtain an understanding of the entity. In the course of making enquiries about the inventory system, they have discovered that Ockey Co designs and produces tableware to order for a number of high street stores. It also makes a number of standard lines of tableware, which it sells to a number of wholesalers. By the terms of its contracts with the high street stores, it is not entitled to sell uncalled inventories designed for them to wholesalers. Ockey Co regularly produces 10% more than the high street stores have ordered, in order to ensure that they meet requirements when the stores do their quality control check. Certain stores have more stringent control requirements than others and regularly reject some of the inventories.
>
> The knowledge above suggests two risks, one that the company may have obsolescent inventory, and another that if their production quality standards are insufficiently high, they could run the risk of losing custom.
>
> We shall look at each of these risks in turn and relate them to the assertion level.
>
> **Inventories**
>
> If certain of the inventories are obsolescent due to the fact that it has been produced in excess of the customer's requirement and there is no other available market for the inventory, then there is a risk that inventory as a whole in the financial statements will not be carried at the appropriate value. Given that inventory is likely to be a material balance in the statement of financial position of a manufacturing company, and the value could be up to 10% of the total value, this has the capacity to be a material misstatement.
>
> The factors that will contribute to the likelihood of these risks causing a misstatement are matters such as:
>
> - Whether management regularly review inventory levels and scrap items that are obsolescent
> - Whether such items are identified and scrapped at the inventory count
> - Whether such items can be put back into production and changed so that they are saleable
>
> **Losing custom**
>
> The long-term risk of losing custom is a risk that in the future the company will not be able to operate (a going concern risk, which we shall revise in Chapter 17). It could have an impact on the financial statements, if sales were attributed to them that they dispute, sales and receivables could be overstated, that is, not carried at the correct value. However, it appears less likely that this would be a material problem in either area, as the problem is likely to be restricted to a few number of customers, and only a few number of sales to those customers.
>
> Again, review of the company's controls over the recording of sales and the debt collection procedures of the company would indicate how likely these risks to the financial statements are to materialise.

2.3 Significant risks

Some risks identified may be significant risks.

Key term

> A **significant risk is** an identified risk of material misstatement:
>
> (i) For which the assessment of inherent risk is close to the upper end of the spectrum of inherent risk due to the degree to which inherent risk factors affect the combination of the likelihood of a misstatement occurring and the magnitude of the potential misstatement should that misstatement occur; or
> (ii) That is to be treated as a significant risk in accordance with the requirements of other ISAs.
>
> (ISA 315 (Revised 2019): para. 12)

Significance can be described as the relative importance of a matter, and is judged by the auditor in the context in which the matter is being considered. The following factors indicate that a risk might be significant:

- Transactions for which there are multiple acceptable accounting treatments such that subjectivity is involved
- Accounting estimates that have high estimation uncertainty or complex models
- Complexity in data collection and processing to support account balances
- Account balances or quantitative disclosures that involve complex calculations
- Accounting principles that may be subject to differing interpretation
- Changes in the entity's business that involve changes in accounting, for example, mergers and acquisitions (ISA 315 (Revised 2019): para. A10 and A221)

The determination of significant risks is a matter of professional judgement, unless the risk is required to be treated as a significant risk in line with another ISA. Significant risks will vary from entity to entity and may vary for the same entity over different periods. Determining significant risks allows the auditor to focus more attention on riskier areas through the performance of certain required responses. For example, ISA 330 *The Auditor's Response to Assessed Risks* requires controls that address significant risks to be tested in the current period (when the auditor intends to rely on the operating effectiveness of such controls) and substantive procedures to be planned and performed that are specifically responsive to the identified significant risk.

When the auditor identifies a significant risk, he/she should evaluate the design and implementation of the entity's controls addressing that risk. Failure by management to implement controls over a significant risk is an indicator of a significant deficiency in internal control.

2.4 Documentation requirements

The auditor shall include in the audit documentation:

- The discussion among the engagement team and the significant decisions reached
- Key elements of the auditor's understanding gained of the entity including the elements of the entity and its control specified in the ISA as mandatory, the sources of the information from which the auditor's understanding was obtained and the risk assessment procedures performed
- The evaluation of the design of identified controls, and determination whether such controls have been implemented, in accordance with the requirements in ISA 315 (Revised 2019)
- The identified and assessed risks of material misstatement at the financial statement level and at the assertion level, including significant risks and risks for which substantive procedures alone cannot provide sufficient appropriate audit evidence, and the rationale for the significant judgements made (ISA 315 (Revised 2019): para. 38)

3 Materiality

FAST FORWARD

An item might be material due to its nature, value or impact on readers of the financial statements.

3.1 Materiality in planning and performing an audit

ISA 320 *Materiality in planning and performing an audit* provides guidance to auditors in this area.

> **Key term**
>
> Misstatements, including omissions, are considered to be **material** if they, individually or in the aggregate, could reasonably be expected to influence the economic decisions of users taken on the basis of the financial statements. (ISA 320: para. 2)

An item might be deemed material due to its:

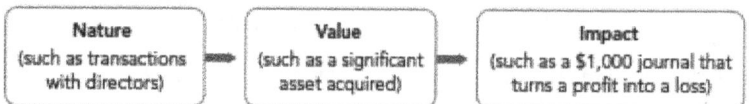

The level of materiality set at planning will always be a matter of **professional judgement**. Most audit firms set criteria for which benchmark figure to use depending on what is most appropriate.

For example:

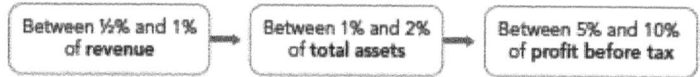

The percentage guidelines of assets, revenues and profits that are commonly used for materiality must be handled with care. The auditor must bear in mind the focus of the company being audited: for example, profit before tax might be more appropriate for a manufacturer judged on its performance, but revenues may be a more appropriate for a not-for-profit entity (ISA 320: para. A8).

The materiality level adopted will have an impact on three key areas:

- How many and what items to examine
- Whether to use sampling techniques
- What level of error is likely to lead to a modified audit opinion

Materiality levels will be determined when planning the audit and may need to be revised if new information becomes available during the audit that affects the materiality for the financial statements as a whole.

> **Exam focus point**
>
> The November 2021 exam contained a question asking students to justify and explain any adjustments to the materiality level in a given scenario.

3.2 Performance materiality

ISA 320 also requires the calculation of performance materiality.

> **Performance materiality** is the amount or amounts set by the auditor at less than materiality for the financial statements as a whole to reduce to an appropriately low level the probability that the aggregate of uncorrected and undetected misstatements exceeds materiality for the financial statements as a whole. If applicable, performance materiality also refers to the amount or amounts set by the auditor at less than the materiality level or levels for particular classes of transactions, account balances or disclosures. (ISA 320: para. 9)

The concept of performance materiality allows an auditor to set different materiality levels for different areas of the financial statements, according to their judgement of the audit risk that is particular to that area. The idea is that overall materiality needs to be adjusted for the actual 'performance' of the audit in particular areas, and cannot just be applied blindly. A better word for the concept might have been **'applied materiality'**, since it is mainly about how overall materiality is applied to particular areas.

The concept of performance materiality focuses in on the difference between the level of tolerable misstatement and the level of actual misstatements detected. For example, if a misstatement were detected that was just below overall materiality, then there is a difficulty for the auditor: the financial statements are not materially misstated, but there is a risk that there may be undetected misstatements which would push over the materiality threshold. The auditor should not just compare the amount of detected misstatements with materiality as a whole, but should take into account the fact that only some specific items have been tested (eg because sampling is used).

Consideration of materiality needs to take into account the possible undetected misstatements which might be lurking. Thinking in terms of performance materiality means thinking of what the effect of individual misstatements might be on audit risk for the financial statements as a whole.

This provides the auditor with a margin of safety in relation to any undetected misstatements, which are then less likely to exceed materiality as a whole.

Performance materiality therefore entails a prudent approach to materiality, and to determining the procedures that are needed to conclude on whether or not the financial statements are materially misstated. The higher the assessed risk, the lower the performance materiality must be set. This means that the auditor will perform more audit work than if the concept of performance materiality did not exist. As with overall materiality, setting performance materiality involves the use of professional judgement. This judgement must take into account qualitative aspects, such as the level of risk attached to a particular balance in the financial statements.

Case Study

The auditor judged Tamworth Ltd's non-current assets to be a high-risk area. If non-current assets were $20 million and total assets $50 million, then overall materiality might be set at 2% of total assets, ie $1 million.

Performance materiality for non-current assets could then be set as a simple proportion of materiality, eg $400,000 (= $20m/$50m × $1m).

Taking into account the auditor's judgement that non-current assets are higher risk, this could thus be decreased to $300,000 in order to provide a greater margin of safety. Any misstatements above this level would be judged material.

3.3 Qualitative materiality

Most of the discussion on materiality focuses on quantitative materiality, but materiality must also be applied to **qualitative disclosures** in the financial statements. Essentially the same concept of materiality applies, ie a misstatement must be viewed in terms of its effect on the economic decisions of users.

Examples of disclosures to which misstatements might be material include:

- Liquidity/debt covenants
- Events leading to recognition of impairment losses
- Changes in accounting policies, eg because of a new IFRS Accounting Standards, where this has a significant impact
- Share-based payments
- Related parties (and transactions with related parties)

3.4 Problems with materiality

As discussed above, materiality is a matter of judgement for the auditor. Therefore, prescriptive rules will not always be helpful when assessing materiality. A **significant risk** of prescriptive rules is that a **significant matter, which falls outside the boundaries of the rules**, could be overlooked, leading to a **material misstatement in the financial statements.**

The percentage guidelines of assets and profits that are commonly used for materiality must be handled with care. The auditor must bear in mind the **focus** of the company being audited. For example, in some companies, **post-tax profit** is the key figure in the financial statements, as the level of dividend is the most important factor in the accounts.

In **owner managed businesses**, if owners are paid salary and are indifferent to dividends, the key profit figure stands higher in the statement of profit and loss, say at **gross profit** level. Alternatively in this situation, the auditor should consider a figure that does not appear on the statement of profit and loss : **profit before directors' salaries and benefits**.

Some companies are **driven by assets** rather than the need for profits. In such examples, higher materiality might need to be applied to assets. In some companies, say charities, **costs** are the driving factor, and materiality might be considered in relation to these.

While rules or guidelines are helpful to auditors when assessing materiality, they must always keep in mind the **nature** of the business they are dealing with. Materiality must be **tailored to the business and the anticipated user** of financial statements, or it is not truly materiality.

3.5 Documentation

The auditor must document:

- Materiality for the financial statements as a whole
- Materiality for particular balances, classes of transactions or disclosures
- Performance materiality
- Any revisions to the above

(ISA 320: para. 14)

Question — Materiality

You are the manager responsible for the audit of Albreda Co. The draft consolidated financial statements for the year-ended 30 September 20X6 show revenue of $42.2 million (20X5 $41.8 million), profit before taxation of $1.8 million (20X5 $2.2 million) and total assets of $30.7 million (20X5 $23.4 million). In September 20X6, the management board announced plans to cease offering 'home delivery' services from the end of the month. These sales amounted to $0.6 million for the year to 30 September 20X6 (20X5 $0.8 million). A provision of $0.2 million has been made at 30 September 20X6 for the compensation of redundant employees (mainly drivers).

Required

Comment upon the materiality of these two issues.

Answer

Home delivery sales

The appropriate indicator of materiality with regard to the home delivery sales is revenue, as the home delivery sales from part of the total revenue of the company.

$0.6 million is 1.4% of the total revenue for 20X6 (see Working 1 below).

An item is generally considered to be material if it is the region of 1% of revenue, so **the home delivery services are material**.

Provision

The appropriate indicators of materiality with regard to the provision are total assets and profit, as the provision impacts both the statement of financial position (it is a liability) and the statement of profit and loss (it is a charge against profit).

$0.2 million is 0.65% of total assets in 20X6 (see Working 2 below). As an item is generally considered to be material if it is the region of 2–5% of total assets, **the provision is not material to the statement of financial position**.

However, **$0.2 million is 11% of profit before tax for 20X6 (see Working 3 below).** An item is considered material to profit before tax if it is in the region of 5%. **Therefore, the provision is material to the statement of profit and loss.**

Working 1

$$\frac{\$0.6m}{\$42.2m} \times 100\% = 1.4\%$$

Working 2

$$\frac{\$0.2m}{\$30.7m} \times 100 = 0.65\%$$

Working 3

$$\frac{\$0.2m}{\$1.8m} \times 100 = 11\%$$

4 General planning matters

> **FAST FORWARD**
>
> There are various administrative matters which auditors must also consider as part of their overall audit strategy.

4.1 Logistics

When planning an audit, the audit engagement partner or manager has to consider many practical things. We shall consider a few of them here:

- Staff
- Client management
- Locations of the audit
- Deadlines

4.1.1 Staff

There are several considerations with regard to audit staff, and these are shown in the diagram below.

> **Exam focus point**
>
> Bear in mind that not all will be relevant to all audits, and when answering questions, you should concentrate on the facts given in the question rather than listing all these factors regardless of information given in the question.

Case Study

Skills in an e-commerce environment

Specialist skills will be required to plan and carry out an audit is where the company engages in e-commerce.

Specialist knowledge is required to carry out various key aspects of the audit:	
Inherent risk evaluation	A degree of specialist understanding of the inherent nature of the IT environment will be required to understand the inherent risk arising from the business being involved in e-commerce.
Control environment assessment	Similarly, to be able to make intelligent queries about the control environment, and to be able to understand the answers given, a degree of knowledge is required.
Determining procedures	In a heavily IT environment, it is going to be impossible to ascertain what procedures are required, and what the extent and timing of those procedures is going to be, without a specialist knowledge.
Evaluating going concern	An understanding of the technological environment will be required in order to properly assess the impact of that environment on the going concern basis of accounting, the risks that exist and the potential impact of those risks on the business and its ability to continue.

4.1.2 Client management

The management of the client company may have preferences regarding audit staff, for example, a finance director may be keen that there is continuity of audit staff on the assignment, so that last year's semi senior is this year's senior, or that the same staff are used from year to year.

This may not always be possible, but the person planning the audit will try and bear in mind the needs of the client in such matters. Consistency of audit staff may help audit efficiency in terms of knowledge of the business and its staff.

4.1.3 Locations

The person planning the audit will have to give consideration to the location of the audit. There are several issues that could arise.

Factor	Consideration
Location	Distance for audit staff to travel
	Mobility of audit staff
	Location of audit review by manager/engagement partner
Multiple locations	All the above considerations
	Determination of which locations to visit
	Allocation of audit staff to each site
	Liaising with client staff to ensure each site visit is convenient

4.1.4 Deadlines

It is of vital importance that the audit team know the deadlines involved in the audit. The key dates that the team will need to know are likely to be:

- Date of inventory count
- Date the financial statements are due to have been drafted by
- Dates of main audit visit
- Date of manager review
- Date of engagement partner review
- Date of engagement partner's post audit meeting with client management
- Date on which the auditor's report is due to be signed
- Date of AGM

It is important that the audit team is aware of these dates and that the audit is planned so that the work can be achieved in relation to these dates. It is vitally important, for instance, that the audit is completed by the date on which the auditor's report is to be signed. It would also be foolish to try and start detailed substantive testing before the financial statements had been drafted.

4.2 Use of IT

The use of IT is increasingly common in auditing. There are several factors which may need to be considered.

- Whether the client has a computerised system.
- If so, whether the auditors will make use of automated tools and techniques (ATTs).
- Assuming the members of the audit team are equipped with laptops, what security procedures are put in place over those laptops.
- What the engagement partner requires to be done on the computer and how and when audit work will be made available to the partner and manager, for example, by emailing work or sharing it via cloud based systems.
- When work will be reviewed, and resulting quality management issues arising from the need to indicate whether a working paper is complete or only partially finished.

The use of IT by auditors is covered in further detail in Chapter 19.

4.3 Time budgets

We discussed the importance of time estimation when we discussed setting the fee in Chapter 7. It is important to the engagement partner that the audit is completed in a cost effective manner. Therefore, the time taken to conduct each part of the audit will have been estimated and the fee set accordingly.

It follows these time budgets are an important part of planning.

- It is important that the time is estimated accurately.
- It is important that the audit team is aware of the time budget.
- It is important that the audit team records variances from the time budget.

The time budget will be based on issues such as:

- Prior year time records
- Risk assessments
- Materiality considerations

In other words, if inventory is the most material and risky item on the statement of financial position, it will have a large estimate of time attached to it, especially if it took a long time last year. In contrast an item such as long-term bank loans could be material, but it is low risk due to the existence of good third party evidence and use can be made of procedures such as analytical review. It may therefore have less time budgeted to it.

4.4 Subsidiary objectives of the assignment

The key purpose of the audit, as you know, is to obtain sufficient, appropriate evidence to express an opinion on the financial statements.

However, there may be subsidiary (non-statutory) objectives of the audit assignment. An example would be the report to management. The audit plan should set out these subsidiary objectives and also set deadlines and any specific requirements for these.

Question — Donaldson

You are the audit manager planning the audit of Donaldson, a listed multinational food and drinks manufacturer. Donaldson has plants all over the world and its head office is based in London.

Required

What general matters would you consider when planning the engagement?

Answer

- **Logistics** – Assignment of staff to the audit: consider the client's locations and arrange visits where appropriate or consider using staff from other offices/countries if possible; also Donaldson is listed, so it is important to consider what reporting deadlines the client is working towards.

- **Time budgets** – The audit of a large multinational will generate a significant fee but is at risk of going over budget; it is therefore important at the planning stage to prepare and communicate a time budget to the audit team and monitor this throughout the engagement.

- **Reporting** – The audit manager should consider what other reports the client may require over and above the statutory auditor's report. A large manufacturer such as Donaldson is likely to produce a social and environmental report as part of the annual report; the audit manager should ascertain whether they require assurance on these issues on this report.

- **Client interface** – Consideration should be given to the method and timing of communication with the client management and/or audit committee at certain stages of the audit.

- **Preliminary materiality** – Materiality should be assessed and calculated at the planning stage (although it is likely to be based on draft figures).

- **Risk assessment** – The key aspect of the planning stage of an audit is the performance of a risk assessment. This will ensure that the work performed is focused on the important areas of the accounts.

Chapter Roundup

- Auditors must plan their work so that it is undertaken in an effective manner.
- Auditors must obtain an understanding of the entity and its environment in order to be able to assess the risks of material misstatement.
- An item might be material due to its nature, value or impact on readers of the financial statements.
- There are various administrative matters which auditors must also consider as part of their overall audit strategy.

PART C   AUDIT STRATEGY, PROCESS AND REPORTING

Quick Quiz

1. What is the purpose of an audit strategy document?
2. Which of the following procedures might an auditor use in gaining an understanding of the entity?

   (a) Inquiry

   (b) Recalculation

   (c) Analytical procedures

   (d) Automated tools and techniques

   (e) Observation and inspection

3. Name three factors which might indicate a significant risk.

   (1) ....

   (2) ....

   (3) ....

4. Name four considerations relating to audit staff an audit plan should cover.

   (1) ....

   (2) ....

   (3) ....

   (4) ....

5. What is performance materiality?
6. Name the five elements of an entity's system of internal control as per ISA 315 (Revised 2019).

Answers to Quick Quiz

1. The audit strategy document sets out in general terms how the audit is to be carried out.

2. (a), (c), (d), (e)

3. Any three from the following:
   - Transactions for which there are multiple acceptable accounting treatments such that subjectivity is involved
   - Accounting estimates that have high estimation uncertainty or complex models
   - Complexity in data collection and processing to support account balances
   - Account balances or quantitative disclosures that involve complex calculations
   - Accounting principles that may be subject to differing interpretation
   - Changes in the entity's business that involve changes in accounting, for example, mergers and acquisitions

4. From:
   (1) Correct level of qualification
   (2) Availability
   (3) Correct level of experience
   (4) Relationship with client staff
   (5) Special skills
   (6) Travel logistics
   (7) Relationship with client staff

5. Performance materiality means the amount or amounts set by the auditor at less than materiality for the financial statements as a whole to reduce to an appropriately low level the probability that the aggregate of uncorrected and undetected misstatements exceeds materiality for the financial statements as a whole.

6. Control environment
   Risk assessment process
   Process to monitor the system of internal control
   Information system and communication
   Control activities

PART C   AUDIT STRATEGY, PROCESS AND REPORTING

End of Chapter Question

Kilo plc (AIA May 2004) (Amended)

The partner in charge of the external audit of Kilo plc is concerned about the audit of the financial statements for the year-ended 31 December 20X4. The partner has highlighted the following two issues during the review of the information obtained during the interim stages of the audit and gathered from regular meetings with the company's directors:

- Recent changes to the bookkeeping system, introduced in March 20X4, have weakened segregation of duties in the wages system. The directors have made two members of clerical staff redundant, a wages clerk from the payroll department and the supervisor from the personnel department, and have amalgamated the payroll and personnel departments under the overall supervision of the head of payroll.

- The company is losing sales to a competitor. Most of Kilo plc's sales are made over the Internet. The company's web page has not been redesigned for some time. This means that potential customers do not always find the company's Internet site when they search on-line for this type of business. Those customers who do find the site cannot always find important information, such as the availability of inventory.

It is now June 20X4. The audit partner is unsure whether to react to these risks by revising the audit plan or whether to resolve the risks by offering specific advice about remedying the deficiencies in the wages system and by offering to have one of the audit firm's IT consultants to redesign Kilo plc's web page.

Required

(a) Explain how each of the two issues highlighted above would affect the auditor's assessment of the risk of material misstatement and explain how each would affect the audit if it was left unresolved.

(10 marks)

(b) Explain how resolving the risks in the manner identified by the partner would affect the auditor's independence.

(5 marks)

(c) Modern audit techniques frequently involve heavy use of audit manager and audit partner time to review inherent and control risks in great detail in order to minimise the amount of substantive testing required. Discuss the advantages of this approach.

(5 marks)

(Total 20 marks)

Risk

Topic list	Syllabus reference
1 Audit risk	
2 Business risk	
3 Analytical procedures	
4 Response to risk	

Introduction

Risk is an important factor in the audit. It falls into two categories:

- Specific **assignment risk** (known as audit risk) which you have studied previously
- **Business risk** associated with the client which may form a part of inherent risk and therefore impacts on the audit

Risk is a key issue in an audit, and the most common approach to audits incorporates a recognition of those risks in the approach taken. It is called the **risk-based approach**. A risk-based audit approach directs the greatest audit effort at the areas in which the financial statements are most likely to be misstated.

Having assessed the risks of material misstatement, the auditor must then design and perform further audit procedures in response to those risks. The result must be audit work that will be sufficient and appropriate to support the audit opinion.

PART C AUDIT STRATEGY, PROCESS AND REPORTING

1 Audit risk

FAST FORWARD

Auditors must assess the risk of material misstatements arising in financial statements and carry out procedures in response to assessed risks.

Key terms

Audit risk is the risk that auditor expresses an inappropriate opinion when the financial statements are materially misstated. Audit risk is a function of the risk of material misstatement and detection risk.

Risk of material misstatement: The risk that the financial statements are materially misstated prior to audit. This consists of inherent risk and control risk. For the purposes of the ISAs, a risk of material misstatement exists when there is a reasonable possibility of a misstatement occurring (ie its likelihood) and being material if it were to occur (ie its magnitude).

Inherent risk is the susceptibility of an assertion about a class of transaction, account balance or disclosure to a misstatement that could be material, either individually or when aggregated with other misstatements, before consideration of any related controls.

Control risk is the risk that a misstatement:

- Could occur in an assertion about a class of transactions, account balance or disclosure;
- Could be material, either individually or when aggregated with other misstatements; and
- Will not be prevented, or detected and corrected on a timely basis, by the entity's controls.

Detection risk is the risk that the procedures performed by the auditor to reduce audit risk to an acceptably low level will not detect a misstatement that exists and that could be material, either individually or when aggregated with other misstatements.

Exam focus point

Identifying audit risk appeared in question 1 in exams from November 2021, May 2022, November 2022, May 2023 and November 2023. It is imperative that you read this chapter carefully and are able to identify audit risks in a given scenario.

1.1 Inherent risk

Inherent risk factors are characteristics of events or conditions that affect susceptibility of an assertion about a class of transactions, account balance or disclosure, to misstatement, whether due to fraud or error, and before consideration of controls. Such factors may be qualitative or quantitative. (ISA 315 (Revised 2019): para. 12(f))

Qualitative inherent risk factors that relate to the preparation of financial information need to be assessed to determine whether the financial statements comply with the applicable financial reporting framework. These qualitative risks could be influenced by matters such as **complexity**, **subjectivity**, **change**, **uncertainty** or any misstatement where either **fraud or management bias** could be involved.

Examples of inherent risk factors that may indicate risk of material misstatement at the assertion level	
Complexity	High degrees of complex industry regulation
	Complex corporate structures (such as alliances or joint ventures)
	Complex accounting measurements
	Transactions which have complex financing arrangements
Subjectivity	Accounting estimates where treatment is open to interpretation
	Valuation for assets (such as investment properties)

Examples of inherent risk factors that may indicate risk of material misstatement at the assertion level	
Change	Unstable economic factors (such as hyperinflation or limits on borrowing)
	Volatile markets (such as those used for derivatives)
	Conditions that lead to significant loss of customers
	Changes to an industry or the chosen business model of an entity
	Expansion of an entity into new geographical locations
	Business reorganisations that include structure, IT or staffing
	Changes to regulations or accounting standards
Uncertainty	Conditions that lead to significant measurement uncertainty
	Pending litigation or contingent liabilities
Management bias or fraud	Manipulation of the financial statements for personal gain
	Specific activity that may have ulterior motives (such as those between related parties and unusual or one-off transactions)

Other events or conditions that may indicate risks of material misstatement **at the financial statement level** include:

- A lack of personnel with appropriate accounting and financial reporting skills
- Control deficiencies, especially those not addressed by management
- Past misstatements, history of errors or a significant amount of adjustments at period end.

(ISA 315 (Revised 2019): Appendix 2)

1.1.1 Spectrum of inherent risk

The **susceptibility** of an assertion to any form of misstatement (both fraud and error) varies and will therefore sit on what is known as a **spectrum of inherent risk** which the auditor assesses in terms of **likelihood** and **magnitude** (supplemented by any financial statement level risks of material misstatement as appropriate).

Assessed risks of material misstatement that sit towards the higher end of the spectrum of inherent risk are considered to be **significant risks** and will therefore demand more of the auditor's attention and will therefore be prioritised. Unless specifically required by a separate ISA, the determination of significant risks will be a matter of the auditor's professional judgement.

Should assertion-level risks be considered to have a pervasive effect on the financial statements, they may be classed as financial statement level risks.

The assessment of inherent risk requires professional judgement by the auditor when determining both likelihood (how likely a misstatement is to occur) and magnitude (the misstatement itself, which could be expressed in either qualitative or quantitative terms) by reference to the nature, size and complexity of an audited entity. The resulting combination of likelihood and magnitude is then evaluated and the higher it gets, the higher the assessment of inherent risk. The ISA points out that for an assessment to be considered high, it does not necessarily require both likelihood and magnitude to be assessed as high (ISA 315 (Revised 2019): paras. A208–216).

1.1.2 Significant risks

Clearly, significant risks will require more of the auditor's attention and demand that responses are performed with greater urgency. Evidence to satisfy significant risks may need to be more persuasive than otherwise required. There may also need to be greater involvement with those charged with governance.

As a result, such significant risks may be considered key audit matters (KAMs). Some ISAs may automatically direct the auditor to consider certain inherent risks to be significant (such as frauds and ISA 240) but otherwise, it is a matter of professional judgement taking issues such as subjectivity and complexity into account (ISA 315 (Revised 2019): paras. A219–221).

1.2 Control risk

Control risk is the risk that a misstatement is not prevented, detected or corrected by internal controls.

The assessment of control risk is supported by the auditor testing the operating effectiveness of controls. However, if such testing is not undertaken, the overall risk of material misstatement is considered to be the same as the auditor's assessment of inherent risk.

When considering controls, the auditor will need to differentiate between:

- **Direct controls** (those that are precise enough to address the risks of material misstatement at the assertion level); and
- **Indirect controls** (those that support direct controls).

1.3 Detection risk

Detection risk is the risk that audit procedures will fail to detect material misstatements. Detection risk relates to the inability of the auditors to examine all evidence. Audit evidence is usually persuasive rather than conclusive so some detection risk is usually present, allowing the auditors to seek 'reasonable confidence'.

The auditors' **inherent and control risk assessments** influence the **nature, timing and extent of substantive procedures** required to reduce detection risk and thereby audit risk.

1.4 The audit risk model

> Audit Risk = (Inherent Risk × Control Risk) × Detection Risk

The model shows that audit risk has two major components. One is dependent on the entity, and is the risk of material misstatement arising in the financial statements (inherent risk and control risk). The other is dependent on the auditor, and is the risk that the auditor will not detect material misstatements in the financial statements (detection risk). Auditors will want their overall audit risk to be at an acceptable level, or it will be too risky to carry out the audit.

It is not in the auditors' power to affect inherent or control risk. These are risks integral to the client, and the auditor cannot change the level of these risks. The auditors therefore manage overall audit risk by managing detection risk, the only element of audit risk they have control over. The more audit work the auditors carry out, the lower detection risk becomes, although it can never be entirely eliminated due to the inherent limitations of audit. The auditors will decide what level of overall risk is acceptable and then determine a level of audit work so that detection risk is at such a level to achieve the required level of overall audit risk.

It is important to understand that there is not a standard level of audit risk which is generally considered by auditors to be acceptable. This is a matter of audit judgement and so will vary between firms and from audit to audit.

Exam focus point

> Try and learn to let key phrases trigger your thoughts about particular issues such as systems and going concern. Above all, think about the nature of the business in the scenario and the strengths and weaknesses likely to affect it.
>
> You should attempt the next question, which is a case study question focusing on risks. The answer to this question includes an 'approach' to answering such questions, which you can look at if you struggle to identify risks in the scenario.

Question — Audit risk

Forsythia is a small, limited liability company offering garden landscaping services. It is partly owned by three business associates, Mr Rose, Mr White and Mr Grass, who each hold 10% of the shares. The major shareholder is the parent company, Poppy. This company owns shares in 20 different companies, which operate in a variety of industries. One of them is a garden centre, and Forsythia regularly trades with it. Poppy is in turn owned by a parent, White Holdings.

The management structure at Forsythia is simple. Of the three non-corporate shareholders, only Mr Rose has any involvement in management. He runs the day to day operations of the company (marketing, sales, purchasing etc) although the company employs two landscape gardeners to actually carry out projects. The accounts department employs a purchase clerk and a sales clerk, who deal with all aspects of their function. The sales clerk is Mr Rose's daughter, Justine. Mr Rose authorises and produces the payroll. The company ledgers are kept on Mr Rose's personal computer. Two weeks after the year end, the receivables ledger records were severely damaged by a virus. Justine has a single print out of the balances as at year-end, which shows the total owed by each customer.

Forsythia owns the equipment which the gardeners use and they pay them a salary and a bonus based on performance. Mr Rose is remunerated entirely on a commission basis relating to sales and, as a shareholder he receives dividends annually, which are substantial.

Forsythia does not carry any inventory. When materials are required for a project, they are purchased on behalf of the client and charged directly to them. Most customers pay within the 60-day credit period, or take up the extended credit period which Forsythia offer. However, there are a number of accounts that appear to have been outstanding for a significant period.

Justine and her father do not appear to have a very good working relationship. She does not live at home and her salary is not significant. However, she appears to have recently purchased a sports car, which is not a company car.

The audit partner has recently accepted the audit of Forsythia. You have been assigned the task of planning the first audit.

Required

Identify and explain the audit and engagement risks arising from the above scenario.

Approaching the answer

Try and apply the points mentioned in the exam focus point above. Look for **key words** and **ask questions** of the information given to you. This is illustrated here:

Forsythia is a small, limited liability company offering garden landscaping services. It is partly owned by three business associates, Mr Rose, Mr White and Mr Grass, who each hold 10% of the shares. The major shareholder is the parent company, Poppy. This company owns shares in 20 different companies, which operate in a variety of industries. One of them is a garden centre, and Forsythia regularly trades with it. Poppy is in turn owned by a parent, White Holdings.

- Receivables likely to be significant
- Complicated corporate structure – why?
- Key man? Over-reliance?
- Is it slightly odd that a landscape gardening business isn't owned by landscape gardeners?
- Controlling party?
- Related party transaction

The management structure at Forsythia is simple. Of the three non-corporate shareholders, only Mr Rose has any involvement in management. He runs the day to day operations of the company (marketing, sales, purchasing etc) although the company employs two landscape gardeners to actually carry out projects. The accounts department employs a purchase clerk and a sales clerk, who deal with all aspects of their function. The sales clerk is Mr Rose's daughter, Justine. Mr Rose authorises and produces the payroll. The company ledgers are kept on Mr Rose's personal computer. Two weeks

- Independence?
- Poor controls
- No segregation of duties

PART C AUDIT STRATEGY, PROCESS AND REPORTING

after the year-end, the receivables ledger records were severely damaged by a virus. Justine has a single print out of the balances as at year-end, which shows the total owed by each customer.

Forsythia owns the equipment which the gardeners use and they pay them a salary and a bonus based on performance. Mr Rose is remunerated entirely on a commission basis relating to sales and, as a shareholder he receives dividends annually, which are substantial.

Forsythia does not carry any inventory. When materials are required for a project, they are purchased on behalf of the client and charged directly to them. Most customers pay within the 60-day credit period, or take up the extended credit period which Forsythia offer. However, there are a number of accounts that appear to have been outstanding for a significant period.

Justine and her father do not appear to have a very good working relationship. She does not live at home and her salary is not significant. However, she appears to have recently purchased a sports car, which is not a company car.

The audit partner has recently accepted the audit of Forsythia. You have been assigned the task of planning the first audit.

Annotations (left margin):
- Limitation? And given below, a suspicion of fraud? Teeming and lading?
- Very profit related focus – management bias?
- Any laws and regulations relevant?
- Detection risk. Opening balances. Comparatives – audited or not?

Annotations (right margin):
- How accounted?
- Problem with receivables. Fraud?
- Fraud?
- Any group planning issues?
- Why not all the other group companies? Why do they have different auditors?

Answer plan

Not all the points you notice will necessarily be **relevant** and you may also find that you do not have **time** to mention all the points in your answer. Now you should prioritise your points in a more formal answer plan and then write your answer:

Audit risks

Inherent

Related party transactions/group issues
Receivables
Fraud – possible indicators, professional scepticism
Profit driven management
Credit extended – accounting/law and regs

Control

Lack of segregation of duties
PC/virus
Suspicion of fraud?
Key man

Detection

First audit
Opening balances and comparatives – audited?

Engagement risks

Some questions raised which makes business look odd

- Group (complex/different auditors/who controls?)
- Nature of business – yet landscape gardeners hired

Indicators of potential fraud

Possible indicators of money laundering (complex structure/cash business)

These may be overstated, but auditor must

(a) Consider them
(b) Be prepared for consequences

Answer

The following matters are relevant to planning Forsythia's audit.

Audit risks – inherent

Related parties and group issues

Forsythia is part of a **complicated group structure**. This raises several issues for the audit:

- There is a risk of related party transactions existing and not being properly disclosed in the financial statements in accordance with IAS 24 *Related party disclosures*.
- Similarly, there is a risk that it will be difficult to ascertain the controlling party for disclosure.
- There is likely to be some group audit implications. My firm may be required to undertake procedures in line with the principal auditors' requirements if Forsythia is to be consolidated.

Receivables

Forsythia is a **service provider**, and it **extends credit** to customers. This is likely to mean that **trade receivables** will be a significant audit balance. However, there is **limited audit evidence** concerning trade receivables due to the effects of a computer virus. There are also indicators of a **possible fraud**.

Fraud?

There are various factors that may indicate a receivables ledger fraud has taken/is taking place:

- Lack of segregation of duties
- Extensive credit offered
- The virus only destroyed receivables ledger information – too specific?
- Poorly paid receivables ledger clerk – with expensive lifestyle
- Receivables ledger clerk is daughter of rich shareholder and they do not have a good relationship

None of these **factors** necessarily point to a fraud individually, but **added together raise significant concerns**.

Profit driven management

Mr Rose is motivated for the financial statements to show a profit for two reasons:

- He receives a commission (presumably sales driven, which impacts on profit).
- He receives dividends as shareholder, which will depend on profits.

There is a risk that the **financial statements** will be **affected by management bias**.

Credit extended

We should ensure that the credit extended to customers is standard business credit. There are unlikely to be any **complications**, for example, interest, but if there were, we should be aware of any **laws and regulations** which might become relevant, and any **accounting issues** which would be raised.

Audit risk – control

There are three significant control problems at Forsythia.

Segregation of duties

There appears to be a **complete lack of segregation of duties** on the three main ledgers. This may have led to a **fraud** on the receivables ledger. The fact that there is no segregation on payroll is also a concern as this is an area where frauds are carried out.

Lack of segregation of duties can also lead to **significant errors** arising and not being detected by the system. This problem means that **control risk** will have to be assessed as **high** and **substantial substantive testing** be undertaken.

Personal Computer

A PC is used for the accounting system. This may have **poor built-in controls** and further exacerbate the problems caused by the lack of segregation of duties. The **security** over PCs can be poor, as has been the case here, where a **virus** has destroyed evidence about the receivables ledger.

Key man

The fact that Mr Rose is dominant in management may also be a control problem, particularly if he were ever to be absent.

Audit risk – detection

The key detection risk is that this is the **first audit**, so we have no CAKE (cumulative audit knowledge and experience) of this client. We have not audited the **opening balances** and **comparatives**. We should have contacted any previous auditors and therefore be aware of whether these have been audited. If there were no previous auditors, these are unaudited. We must ensure that our auditor's report is clear on this issue. There is also significant detection risk in relation to **related parties**, as discussed above.

Engagement risk

There are several indicators that Forsythia may be an 'odd' company.

The first indicator is that it is part of a **complex and unexplained group**, and that the group is not audited by the same firm of auditors, although it is unclear how many firms of auditors are involved in the group audit. There may be good reasons for this audit policy, but we should **investigate those reasons**, in case any other reasons appear.

Another indicator that seems odd is a small company should exist to provide landscape gardening services, when it appears that the owners are not landscape gardeners, or at least, if they are, they do not work in the business. Again, there may be valid reasons for this, but we should **discover and document them**.

It is particularly important that these issues are cleared up. A complex group structure and a company dealing in cash transactions (Forsythia's potentially are) could indicate the possibility that the owners are trying to **launder money**. There are also indicators of **fraud**. If either of these issues exist, the auditor may have significant responsibility to report and co-operate with relevant authorities, and the professional relationship of client and auditor could be compromised. Therefore, the audit firm must ensure that it has suitable 'know your client' procedures in place and the appropriate systems for making suspicion reports should a suspicion arise. The partners must ensure that staff have appropriate training so that they are able to comply fully with legal requirements in relation to money laundering.

2 Business risk

FAST FORWARD

Business risk is the risk arising to companies through being in operation. In order to assess audit risks more effectively, auditors are required to understand the risks that a business faces.

Key term

Business risk is a risk resulting from significant conditions, events, circumstances, actions or inactions that could adversely affect an entity's ability to achieve its objectives and execute its strategies, or from the setting of inappropriate objectives and strategies (ISA 315 (Revised 2019): para. 12).

The business risk model is not a replacement for the traditional audit risk model but rather a vehicle, or mechanism, for the identification of audit risk, recognising that most business risks will eventually have financial consequences and, therefore, an effect on the financial statements.

The auditor identifies the risks that the business itself faces, which could threaten the business from meeting its goals, aims and objectives. Once identified, the auditor is then able to identify any corresponding audit risk. The approach allows the auditor to gain a greater understanding of the business and the overall risks it faces and therefore increases the likelihood of identifying the risks of material misstatement of the financial statements as well as being able to provide constructive business advice to aid the mitigation (through relevant controls) of such risks.

A key part of the process is therefore to **identify the business risks**. There are various tools used to do this that you may have come across before. They are listed below.

- SWOT analysis
- Porter's five forces model
- The PEST analysis
- Porter's value chain

Exam focus point

You should be able to identify business risks in a question. If you have previously used any of the above techniques, they may be useful to you, but in the exam, concentrate on developing a common sense response as you work through any given question, bearing in mind the three components of business risk given above.

Question — Business risk vs audit risk

(1) Football Planet operates a website selling football kits

(2) Mucha Pasta operates several Italian restaurants and is subject to comprehensive and stringent health and safety food hygiene legislation

(3) XYZ, based in the Eurozone, trades extensively in the US and invoices sales in US$

Required

For the above scenarios, identify the business risk and any corresponding audit risk.

Answer

Scenario	Business Risk	Audit risk
Football Planet operates a website selling football kits	• Overstocking of football kits resulting in inventories of previous season's kits • Excessive mark down and reductions in order to sell inventory of previous season's football kits • Impact on revenues, profits and cash flows	• Identification of obsolete inventories • Valuation of inventories (possibility of NRV < cost)
Mucha Pasta operates several Italian restaurants and is subject to comprehensive and stringent health and safety food hygiene legislation	• Breach of legislation could lead to fines, closure, bad press and costly improvement expenses • Potential impact on revenues due to impact on reputation/closure • Financial impact due to fines, legal actions and required improvements	• Provisions/contingent liability disclosure for legal action • Impact on going concern • Appropriateness of the capitalisation of improvements
XYZ, based in the Eurozone, trades extensively in the US and invoices sales in US$	• Company is exposed to exchange rate risk • Potential impact on profits and cash flows	• Correct retranslation of year-end receivables • Correct treatment of initial sale and receivable • Correct calculation, treatment and disclosure of exchange differences • Compliance with IAS 21

Business risk can be split into three categories to enable better identification.

2.1 Financial risks

Financial risks are the risks arising from the financial activities or financial consequences of an operation. Examples include the following.

- Cash flow issues
- Overtrading
- Business continuity problems (going concern)
- Credit risk
- Interest risk
- High cost of capital
- Unrecorded liabilities

2.2 Operational risk

Operational risks are the risks arising with regard to operations, for example, the risk that a major supplier will be lost and the company will be unable to operate.

2.3 Compliance risk

Compliance risk is the risk that arises from non-compliance with the laws and regulations that surround the business. Examples include the following.
- Breach of listing rules
- Breach of data protection legislation
- Litigation risk
- Sales tax (VAT) problems
- Tax penalties
- Health and safety risks
- Environmental issues (discussed in Chapter 11)

It is possible for some business risks to overlap into more than one category. For instance, exposure to foreign exchange movements is a financial risk, but it can also be an operational risk if the currency conversion moves against the entity and makes its products more expensive.

2.4 Business risks from climate change

The risks businesses will face due to climate change can be categorised into two areas:

(a) **Physical risks**, which arise from the physical effects of climate change such as storms, extreme temperatures, wildfires, flooding.

(b) **Transition risks**, which relate to social and economic shifts to a low-carbon economy such as changes to policy, regulation, technology and market.

As a result, business needs to consider potential impairment of assets which have become economically stranded as a result, having suffered from 'unanticipated or premature write-downs, devaluations or conversion to liabilities' (Smith School of Enterprise and the Environment, 2014).

These assets are referred to as **stranded assets**. Stranded assets can be caused by a range of environmental-related risks including:

- Climate change
- New Environmental, Social and Governance (ESG) related regulations
- Changing societal norms and stakeholders expectations
- Litigation from third parties.

Auditors must obtain an understanding of how climate change may significantly impact the financial statements and respond appropriately.

2.5 Business risk from current trends in IT

Increasing connectivity and the openness of computer networks in the global business environment exposes businesses to system and network failures and to cyberattack.

2.5.1 Audit considerations

Auditors must assess their clients' procedures for identifying and addressing these risks. Some main considerations are:

- Has management established an information and internet security policy?
- How does the entity identify critical information assets and the risk to these assets?
- Does the entity have cyber-insurance (many general policies now exclude cyber-events)?
- Is there a process for assuring security when linked to third-party systems (eg partners/contractors)?
- What controls are in place to ensure that employees only have access to files and applications that are required for their job?
- Are regular scans carried out to identify malicious activity?
- Are procedures in place to ensure that security is not compromised when the company's systems are accessed from home or on the road?
- What plans are in place for disaster recovery in case of an incident?

These issues will be built into the auditor's assessment of the control environment of the entity and in some cases, may influence the auditor's view as to whether there are any uncertainties relating to the going concern status of the entity.

If information about a security breach has been identified, the auditor ordinarily considers the extent to which such a breach had the potential to affect financial reporting. If financial reporting may be affected, the auditor may decide to understand, and test the related controls to determine the possible impact or scope of potential misstatements in the financial statements or may determine that the entity has provided adequate disclosures in relation to such security breach.

In addition, laws and regulations that may have a direct or indirect effect on the entity's financial statements may include data protection legislation. Considering an entity's compliance with such laws or regulations, in accordance with ISA 250 (Revised), may involve understanding the entity's IT processes and general IT controls that the entity has implemented to address the relevant laws or regulations.

Chapter 19 of this Workbook considers IT at audit clients in more detail.

2.5.2 E-commerce

Where an entity undertakes e-commerce, risk identification is crucial. E-commerce has become increasingly important in recent years, and to a large extent, early fears about security have proven to be unfounded. However, a number of recent high-profile security breaches in relation to e-commerce systems have underlined that this is an area that can carry significant operational risks, to which auditors must give specific consideration.

- Specific business risks include:
- Loss of transaction integrity
- Pervasive e-commerce security risks
- Improper accounting policies
- Non-compliance with tax, legal and regulatory requirements (eg local laws in relation to protection of customers' data)
- Overreliance on e-commerce
- Systems and infrastructure failures
- Damage to reputation if website fails or security is breached

Audit procedures regarding the integrity of the information in the accounting system relating to ecommerce transactions will be concerned with evaluating the reliability of the system for capturing and processing transactions.

Therefore, in contrast to audit procedures for traditional business activities which focus separately on control processes relating to each stage of transaction processing, audit procedures for sophisticated e-commerce often focus on automated controls.

Case Study

Risk in an e-commerce environment

Tripper is a travel agency operating in three adjacent towns. The directors have recently taken the decision that they should cease their High Street operations and convert into a dot.com. The new operation, Trippers.com, will benefit from enlarged markets and reduced overheads, as they will be able to operate from single, cheaper premises.

Such a business decision has opened Tripper up to significant new business risks.

Customers

Converting to a dot.com company in this way enforces a loss of 'personal touch' with customers. Trippers staff will no longer meet the customers face-to-face. In a business such as a travel agency, this could be a significant factor. Customers may have appreciated the service given in branches and may feel that this level of service has been lost if it is now redirected through computers and telephones. Trippers should be aware of the possibility of, and mitigate against, loss of customers due to perceived reduction in service.

Competition

By leaving the local area and entering a wider market, Trippers is opening itself up to much more substantial competition. Whereas previously, Trippers competed with other local travel agents, they will now be competing theoretically with travel agents everywhere that have internet facilities.

Technology issues

As Trippers has moved into a market that necessitates high technological capabilities, a number of business risks are raised in relation to technological issues:

Viruses

There is a threat of business being severely interrupted by computer viruses, particularly if the staff of Trippers are not very computer literate or the system the company invests in is not up to the standard required.

Viruses could cause interrupted sales and loss of customer goodwill, which could have a significant impact on the going concern status of the company.

Loss of existing custom

Technology could be another reason for loss of existing customers. Their existing customers might not have internet access or ability to use computers. We do not know what Trippers' demographic was prior to conversion.

However, if conversion means that Trippers lose their existing client base completely and have to rebuild sales, the potential cost in advertising could be excessive.

Cost of system upgrades

Technology is a fast-moving area and it will be vital that Trippers' website is kept up to current standards. The cost of upgrade, both in terms of money and business interruption, could be substantial.

PART C AUDIT STRATEGY, PROCESS AND REPORTING

New supply chain factors

Trippers may keep existing links with holiday companies and operators. However, they will have new suppliers, such as Internet service providers to contend with.

Personnel

Due to the conversion, Trippers.com will require technical staff and experts. They may not currently have these staff. If this is the case, they could be at risk of severe business interruption and customer dissatisfaction.

If the directors are not computer literate, they may find that they are relying on staff who are far more expert that they are to ensure that their business runs efficiently.

Legislation

There are a number of issues to consider here. The first is data protection and the necessity to comply with the law when personal details are given over the computer. It is important that the website is secure.

E-commerce is also likely to be an area where there is fast moving legislation as the law seeks to keep up with developments. Trippers must also keep up with developments in the law.

Lastly, trading over the internet may create complications as to what domain Trippers are trading in for the purposes of law and tax.

Fraud exposure

The company may find that it is increasingly exposed to fraud in the following ways.

- Credit card fraud relating from transactions not being face to face
- Hacking and fraud relating from the web site not being secure
- Over-reliance on computer expert personnel could lead to those people committing fraud

Trippers' auditors will be regarding the conversion with interest. The conversion will also severely affect audit risk.

Impact on audit risk

Inherent risk

Many of the business risks identified above could have significant impacts on going concern.

Control risk

The new operations will require new systems, many of which may be specialised computer systems.

Detection risk

The conversion may have the following effects.

- It may create a 'paper-less office' as all transactions are carried out online – this may make use of automated tools and techniques (AATs) essential.
- The auditors may have no experience in e-commerce which may increase detection risk.
- There are likely to be significant impacts on analytical review as results under the new operations are unlikely to be very comparable to the old.
- There may be a significant need to use the work of experts to obtain sufficient, appropriate audit evidence.

Exam focus point

In this case study, e-commerce was used to illustrate the issue of risks. E-commerce is a topical area, and you should be familiar with the issues arising for audit and assurance from e-commerce. However, you need to be able to recognise issues for any business scenario you are given.

2.6 Management's risk management process

Risk management is of vital importance in a business. The components of business risk are the risks that the company should seek to mitigate and manage.

Once risks are identified, management must decide whether it accepts the risk or what its control strategy will be to manage the risk.

Management needs to be satisfied that systems of risk management and internal controls are working properly. Internal audit can make a valuable contribution to the monitoring of risk management.

Question — Melon

Your firm has just been appointed auditor to the Melon Group, which operates a chain of fashion clothing shops for young women. The head office is based in Madrid. There are 280 shops spread across the Iberian peninsula and a further 65 shops across the European Union. The clothing is manufactured mainly in Spain and India by third-party manufacturers and fixed quantities are pre-ordered six months in advance of the season. Most of the shop buildings are held on long leases, although a small number are owned by the Group.

Approximately 40% of the shops outside the Iberian market are run on a franchise basis whereby shop fittings are supplied and installed by the Melon Group and paid for by the franchisee over five years, after which time they are replaced; the clothes are sold at a 40% discount on local retail price to the franchisees on a sale or return basis. Franchisees choose which lines of the full season's range of clothes they wish to hold, based on samples.

Required

Evaluate **FOUR** business risks and **FOUR** audit risks from the Melon Group scenario.

Answer

Business risks – any four from the following:

- **Foreign currency risk:** Many of Melon's supplies are from India and hence cost would depend on exchange rate with the Indian rupee. Also franchisees pay 60% of local retail price to Melon, which passes currency risk to Melon where the franchisees are located outside the Eurozone (eg in the UK).

- **Cash flow/financing risk:** The Group bears an ongoing cash flow risk with respect to the shop fittings provided to franchisees which are not paid for until later. Given that most shop fittings will be for new franchisees, this is coupled with the business risk that those franchisees may fail.

- **Leased vs owned properties:** Leased properties allows the Group the flexibility to open, close or move shops, but also subjects the Group to the risks of the rental market and the potential loss of prime retail sites when the rental agreements are up for renewal. Owned properties are more secure, but are less flexible when the retail centre of a town shifts location over time.

- **Fashion:** The market in which Melon operates is a fast-moving one. Success depends on being at the cutting edge of latest fashions. Given that the clothes are ordered six months in advance, it is essential that Melon's research and buying department calculations are based on accurate information. Miscalculations of the market could result in large amounts of unsaleable inventories to customers or indeed to franchisees. Further, goods unsold by the franchisees can be returned to Melon, increasing its risk.

- **Quality:** All clothing is manufactured by third parties. Controls are necessary to ensure that the quality of goods is adequate across suppliers and consistent between suppliers and over time.

- **Competitors:** There are many players in the fashion market which is becoming more globalised. What in the past may have been a stable national position could quickly turn sour if a new, but established, foreign player enters the market. This needs to be regularly monitored.

- **Supply issues**: Unexpected supply problems could occur for Melon, a foreign investor in India, as a result of local activists criticising the use of cheaper developing world workers.
- **Compliance risk**: Operations in various different markets pose risks due to different regulatory and reporting requirements which must be researched and complied with.

Audit risks – any four from the following:

- **New audit client**: The firm has no previous experience with this client, so the audit risk is high. This lack of familiarity could lead to potential misstatements being overlooked.
- **Overseas transactions**: The activities between Melon and its overseas suppliers and customers present possible risks of misstatement due to foreign currency fluctuations under IAS 21 in terms of statement of profit or loss items (such as revenues and purchases) and assets (such as inventory).
- **Shop fittings and franchises**: Depending on the recoverability of sums due from franchisees, there may be issues with the recognition and valuation of items in shops where a franchise may have ceased operating.
- **Owned vs leased PPE**: There may be a risk of misstatement in shop premises which are recorded as owned but are leased (and vice versa) meaning IAS 16 and/or IFRS 16 may not be adhered to.
- **Inventory**: This will be hard to value due to the volatile nature of fashion goods in general (establishing net realisable value under IAS 2, for example, may be difficult). Also, in cases where goods are returned, there may be a risk of misstatement where ownership of inventory is unclear and it is either carried incorrectly or omitted from Melon's financial statements (this could also affect revenue recognition under IFRS 15 if control of inventory is hard to establish).

3 Analytical procedures

FAST FORWARD

> ISA 315 (Revised 2019) states that analytical procedures must be performed as risk assessment procedures.

3.1 Revision of analytical procedures

Analytical procedures are covered by ISA 520 *Analytical procedures*. They include the following type of comparisons, using trend analysis and reasonableness tests:

- Prior periods
- Budgets and forecasts
- Industry information
- Predictive estimates
- Relationships between elements of financial information ie ratio analysis
- Relationships between financial and non-financial information eg payroll costs to the number of employees

The following ratios could be considered:

- Gross profit margin (gross profit divided by revenue × 100%)
- Net profit margin (net profit divided by revenue × 100%)
- Receivables collection period (receivables divided by revenue × 365)
- Inventory holding period (inventory divided by cost of sales × 365)
- Payables payment period (payables divided by cost of sales × 365)
- Current ratio (current assets to current liabilities)
- Quick or asset test ratio (liquid assets to current liabilities)
- Gearing ratio (debt capital to equity capital)
- Return on capital employed (profit before tax to total assets less current liabilities)

Ratios mean very little when used in isolation. They should be calculated for previous periods and for comparable companies. In addition to looking at the more usual ratios, the auditors should consider examining other ratios that may be relevant to the particular client's business, such as revenue per passenger mile for an airline operator client, or fees per partner for a professional office.

3.2 Analytical procedures as risk assessment procedures

The auditor's risk assessment procedures must include analytical procedures (ISA 315 (Revised 2019): para. 14). This enhances the auditor's understanding of the business. These procedures may:

- Help identify the existence of inconsistencies, unusual transactions or events
- Help identify amounts, ratios and trends that indicate matters have audit implications
- Assist the auditor in identifying risks of fraud and error (ISA 315 (Revised 2019): paras. a27–8)

Analytical procedures performed as risk assessment procedures may therefore assist in identifying and assessing the risks of material misstatement by identifying aspects of the entity of which the auditor was unaware or understanding how inherent risk factors, such as change, affect susceptibility of assertions to misstatement.

In other words analytical procedures at the planning stage help to identify risk and assists the auditor in planning the audit approach. Ratio analysis and identification of trends between one year and the next are particularly useful at this stage. However, at the planning stage of the audit, as compared to the rest of the audit, data forming the basis of analytical procedures is likely to be aggregated at a high level. The results therefore only provide a broad initial indication about whether a material misstatement may exist. Generally, analytical procedures are amongst the most efficient of audit procedures, as they cover most of the assertions, but substantive procedures are still required to audit significant accounts.

Data analytics can be an efficient and effective way of performing analytical procedures and are covered in more detail in Chapter 19 of this Workbook.

Note that analytical procedures may also be used as substantive procedures, but this is not compulsory.

Question — Analytical procedures: planning

You have been provided with the following draft accounts of Dress You Like Co for the year ended 30AC September 20X6:

EXTRACTS FROM THE DRAFT STATEMENT OF FINANCIAL POSITION AS ON 30 SEPTEMBER 20X6

	Draft 20X6 $'000	Actual 20X5 $'000
Inventory: Finished goods	13,800	4,900
Receivables: Trade (supermarket)	11,800	8,300
Trade (other)	700	600
Bank:	0	200
Payables: Trade	2,060	1,470
Other	500	450
Bank overdraft:	750	0

PART C AUDIT STRATEGY, PROCESS AND REPORTING

EXTRACTS FROM THE DRAFT STATEMENT OF PROFIT OR LOSS FOR THE YEAR ENDED 30 SEPTEMBER 20X6

	Draft 20X6 $'000	Actual 20X5 $'000
Revenue (supermarket)	53,500	49,000
Revenue (other)	8,200	6,700
Cost of sales (supermarket)	(51,895)	(45,080)
Cost of sales (other)	(7,380)	(5,900)
Gross profit	2,425	4,720
Other expenses	(1,400)	(2,450)
Profit before taxation	1,025	2,270

Required

Calculate three ratios for both years, which would assist the audit senior in planning the audit. Using the ratios calculated, describe the main audit risks at Dress You Like Co.

Answer

Any ratios from:

	20X6	20X5
Gross profit margin (supermarket)	1,650/53,500	3,920/49,000
	= 3%	= 8%
Gross profit margin (other)	820/8,200	800/6,700
	= 10%	= 12%
Receivables collection period (supermarket)	(11,800/53,500) × 365	(8,300/49,000) × 365
	= 81 days	= 62 days
Receivables collection period (other)	(700/8,200) × 365	(600/6,700) × 365
	= 31 days	= 33 days
Inventory holding period	(13,800/59,275) × 365	(4,900/50,980) × 365
	= 85 days	= 35 days

* 59,275 = 51,895 + 7,380
^ 50,980 = 45,080 + 5,900

- The draft financial statement extracts indicate that there may be cash flow problems leading to concern over going concern.

- Dress You Like Co has seen falling gross profit margins during the year. For the supermarket customer, these are from 8% in 20X5 to 3% in 20X6 and for other customers 12% (20X5) to 10% (20X6).

- The receivables collection period for the supermarket customer is 81 days in 20X6 compared to 62 days in 20X5. For other customers the receivables collection period is largely stable at 31 and 33 days.

- The inventory holding period has risen from 35 days in 20X5 to 85 days in 20X6.

- Overall, the fall in margins, lack of credit control and increased inventory holdings mean that the company has gone from a cash position of $200,000 in 20X5 to an overdraft of $750,000 in 20X6.
- This indicates concerns about cash flow and going concern and inventory may be overstated.

4 Response to risk

FAST FORWARD

The auditor must formulate an approach to assessed risks of material misstatement.

ISA 330 *The Auditor's Responses to Assessed Risks* states that the auditor must obtain sufficient, appropriate audit evidence regarding the assessed risks of material misstatement, through designing and implementing appropriate responses to those risks (ISA 330: para. 3).

4.1 Overall responses

Overall responses include the following.

- Emphasising to the audit team the need for professional scepticism
- Assigning additional/alternative staff to the audit
- Using experts
- Changing the nature, timing and extent of direction and supervision of members of the audit team and the review of work performed,
- Incorporating more unpredictability into the audit
- Changing the overall audit strategy or planned audit procedures (ISA 330: para. A1)

The auditors will need to determine whether they are going to take a substantive approach (focusing mainly on substantive procedures) or a combined approach (tests of control and substantive procedures).

4.2 Responses to the risks of material misstatement at the assertion level

The auditor are required to design and perform further audit procedures whose nature, timing, and extent are in response to the assessed risks of material misstatement at the assertion level (ISA 300: Para. 6).

When designing these further audit procedures, the auditors must consider the following:

- The **likelihood** and **magnitude** of misstatement due to the particular characteristics of the significant class of transactions, account balance, or disclosure (the inherent risk)
- Whether controls exist to address the identified risk of material misstatement? If so, the auditor may need to test whether controls are operating effectively before determining the nature, timing and extent of substantive procedures (ISA 330: para. 7).

The higher the auditor's assessment of risk, the more persuasive evidence is required. For significant risks the auditor must perform substantive procedures that are specifically responsive to that risk. Where the approach consists only of substantive procedures these must include tests of details.

High risk areas require evidence with a high level of reliability. For this reason the auditor should consider obtaining information from appropriate external parties (ISA 330: para 21).

Irrespective of the assessed risks of material misstatement the auditor shall design and perform substantive procedures for each material class of transactions, account balance and disclosure. The auditor must carry out substantive procedures on material items (ISA 330: para. 18).

4.3 Documentation

All conclusions reached using ISAs 300, 315 and 330 mist be fully documented to support the audit opinion.

Chapter Roundup

- Auditors must assess the risk of material misstatements arising in financial statements and carry out procedures in response to assessed risks.
- Business risk is the risk arising to companies through being in operation. In order to assess audit risks more effectively, auditors are required to understand the risks that a business faces.
- ISA 315 (Revised 2019) states that analytical procedures must be performed as risk assessment procedures.
- The auditor must formulate an approach to assessed risks of material misstatement.

PART C   AUDIT STRATEGY, PROCESS AND REPORTING

Quick Quiz

1   Complete the following definition:

……………….. risk is the risk that the auditor expresses an ………………..… audit opinion when the financial statements are ……………..………..……………

2   Identify whether the following matters, which represent potential business risks to the company are financial, operational or compliance risks.

Item	Potential business risk
Going concern	
Physical disasters	
Breakdown of accounting systems	
Loss of key personnel	
Credit risk	
Breach of legislation	
Sales tax problems	
Currency risk	
Poor brand management	
Environmental issues	

3   Analytical procedures are compulsory when the auditor is making their risk assessment.

   True ☐

   False ☐

4   Which one of the following would NOT be an appropriate response where the auditor has identified a risk that inventory has a lower net realisable value than cost, and is therefore overstated?

   (1)   Examine the instructions to identify slow moving inventory lines when attending the inventory count.

   (2)   Increase the emphasis on reviewing the year end aged inventory analysis for evidence of slow-moving inventory.

   (3)   Perform analytical procedures where monthly revenue is compared to expectations and budgeted revenue. Unexpected deviations should be investigated.

   (4)   Ascertain sales values for items sold post year end that were in inventory at the year end to ensure their NRV was higher than the cost recorded as part of the inventory value in the financial statements.

5   Business risks from climate change can be categorised into two categories. These are ……………….. risks and ……………….. risks.

6   Define 'spectrum of inherent risk'.

Answers to Quick Quiz

1. Audit, inappropriate, materially misstated

2.

Item	Potential business risk
Going concern	Financial
Physical disasters	Operational
Breakdown of accounting systems	Financial
Loss of key personnel	Operational
Credit risk	Financial
Breach of legislation	Compliance
Sales tax problems	Compliance
Currency risk	Financial
Poor brand management	Operational
Environmental issues	Compliance

3. True

4. (3) Perform analytical procedures where monthly revenue is compared to expectations and budgeted revenue. Unexpected deviations should be investigated.

    This would be an appropriate response where there is an increased risk of revenue being reported in the incorrect period.

5. physical, transition

6. The level of inherent risk varies on a scale that is referred to as the spectrum of inherent risk. The judgement about where on the scale inherent risk is assessed varies with the nature, size and complexity of the entity, and the assessed likelihood and magnitude of the misstatement and inherent risk factors.

End of Chapter Question

Netseller (AIA May 2009)

Netseller is an internet trading company that sells compact disks and DVD movies to consumers using its website. Netseller is considering diversifying slightly by acquiring 100% of the share capital of Renter. Renter is also an internet-based company, but its business model is based on renting out DVD movies rather than selling them.

Renter's customers sign up for the company's service over the internet. They enter their bank details and the company takes $20 per month from each customer's account. Each customer has a list of DVD movies that they wish to see and Renter's computer system selects four DVDs from the list for each customer. Every time a customer returns a DVD the system selects a replacement from the customer's list, so that every customer has four DVDs at any given time.

The system is highly automated. Customers can only update their selection of movies or their personal details, such as addresses or bank details, through the website. Each DVD has a unique barcode and this is used to log the return of disks electronically. Returned disks are even filed mechanically and are subsequently retrieved mechanically when they are reissued to other customers. The small team of staff who deal with receipts and despatches do little more than scan incoming disks and feed them into the filing system and take disks that have been picked for despatch from the output tray to the postbags.

Netseller has already fully considered the commercial aspects of this investment. They have asked you to prepare a detailed report on the one aspect of the acquisition that concerns them. Renter's business is totally dependent on its computer system and will remain so, even after Netseller takes them over. Renter uses very specialised hardware and software that is incompatible with Netseller's own systems.

Required

(a) Identify the areas where Renter would be vulnerable in the event of a problem with the computer system.

(8 marks)

(b) Explain what controls you would expect to see in place in order to counter the threats faced by Renter.

(12 marks)

(Total 20 marks)

Quality management

Topic list	Syllabus reference
1 Principles and purpose	LO2
2 Quality management at a firm level	LO2
3 Quality management on an individual audit	LO2
4 Engagement quality reviews	LO2
5 Revision: Documentation	LO2

Introduction

The role performed by auditors represents an activity of significant public interest. Quality independent audit is crucial, both to users and to the audit profession as a whole. Poor audit quality damages the reputation of the firm and may lead to loss of clients and thus fees, as well as an increased risk of litigation and concomitant professional insurance costs.

Although there are specific standards giving guidance on how auditors should perform their work with satisfactory quality, these can never cater for every situation. Quality at a general level is dealt with by ISQM 1 *Quality management for firms that perform audits or reviews of financial statements, or other assurance or related services engagements*.

Having examined quality management in general, we then turn to the auditing guidance in ISA 220 (Revised) *Quality management for an audit of financial statements*, and also the related guidance about what auditors should document during an audit of financial statements.

These topics are both revision at this level, but you should attempt higher level questions to practice the skills you will need at this level.

PART C   AUDIT STRATEGY, PROCESS AND REPORTING

1 Principles and purpose

> **FAST FORWARD**
>
> There is no simple definition of audit quality because there is no one 'correct' way to audit. It is often a matter of conducting an audit in line with the spirit as well as the letter of professional guidance.

Although each stakeholder in the audit will give a different meaning to audit quality, at its heart it is about delivering an **appropriate** professional **opinion** supported by the necessary **evidence** and **judgements**.

Many principles contribute to audit quality, including good leadership, experienced judgement, technical competence, ethical values and appropriate client relationships, proper working practices and effective quality management, and monitoring review processes.

The standards **ISQM 1** *Quality management for firms that perform audits or reviews of financial statements or other assurance or related services engagements* and **ISA 220 (Revised)** *Quality management for an audit of financial statements* provide guidance to audit firms on how to achieve these principles. These new standards were issued in December 2020 along with the new ISQM 2 *Engagement quality reviews*.

2 Quality management at a firm level

> **FAST FORWARD**
>
> The International Standard on Quality Management (ISQM 1) helps audit firms to establish quality standards for their business.

The fact that auditors follow international auditing standards provides a general quality management framework within which audits should be conducted. There are also specific quality management standards.

We touched on ISQM 1 earlier in this workbook (Chapters 4 and 8), and come to consider it in greater detail here.

2.1 Purpose of ISQM 1

> **ISQM 1.14**
>
> The objective of the firm is to design, implement and operate a system of quality management for audits or reviews of financial statements, or other assurance and related services engagements performed by the firm, which provides the firm with reasonable assurance that:
>
> (a) The firm and its personnel fulfil their responsibilities in accordance with professional standards and applicable legal and regulatory requirements, and conduct engagements in accordance with such standards and requirements; and
>
> (b) Engagement reports issued by the firm or engagement partners are appropriate in the circumstances.

Ultimate responsibility and accountability for the audit firm's system of quality management is assigned to the firm's CEO or managing partner (or equivalent), or, if appropriate, the firm's managing board of partners (or equivalent). This individual must **evaluate** the system of quality management at least **annually** and conclude whether it provides the firm with reasonable assurance that the objectives of the system of quality management are being achieved. The firm needs to take further action if this is not the case.

Firms shall assign **operational responsibility** for the system of quality management, including individual(s) with operational responsibility for two specific areas of the system of quality management:

- compliance with independence requirements
- monitoring and remediation

All individuals assigned to these roles must:

- Have appropriate experience, knowledge, influence and authority within the firm, and sufficient time, to fulfil their assigned responsibility
- Understand their assigned roles so that they are accountable for fulfilling them
- Have an understanding of the entire text of ISQM 1, including the application and other explanatory material, to understand the objective of ISQM 1 and to apply its requirements properly

We have already considered the sections of ISQM 1 relating to ethics in Chapter 4 and those relating to client acceptance are covered in Chapter 8 of this Study Text. We shall now consider the requirements of the rest of the standard, which fall into the following areas:

- The firm's risk assessment process
- Governance and leadership
- Engagement performance (see also, the requirements of ISA 220 (Revised) that follow in later sections)
- Resources
- Information and communication
- The monitoring and remediation process

2.2 The firm's risk assessment process

Firms apply a three step **risk-based approach** when designing, implementing and operating their system of quality management.

Step 1 Establish **quality objectives**.

Step 2 Identify and assess **quality risks** to the achievement of the quality objectives.

Step 3 Design and implement **responses** to address quality risks.

Key terms

A **quality objective** is the desired outcome in relation to the components of the system of quality management to be achieved by the firm.

A **quality risk** is a risk that has a reasonable possibility of:

(i) Occurring; and

(ii) Individually, or in combination with other risks, adversely affecting the achievement of one or more quality objectives.

Responses (in relation to a system of quality management) are policies or procedures designed and implemented by the firm to address one or more quality risk(s).

ISQM 1 specifies certain quality objectives which must be included in the system of quality management for all firms. These include obtaining, at least annually, a documented confirmation of compliance with independence requirements from all personnel required by relevant ethical requirements to be independent. Firms must also establish policies and procedures for the following matters.

- Identifying, evaluating and addressing threats to compliance with the relevant ethical requirements
- Identifying, communicating, evaluating and reporting of any breaches of the relevant ethical requirements and appropriately responding in a timely manner
- Receiving, investigating and resolving complaints and allegations about failures to perform work in accordance with professional standards and applicable legal and regulatory requirements, or non-compliance with the firm's policies or procedures established in accordance with ISQM 1

- Addressing circumstances when the firm becomes aware of information subsequent to accepting or continuing a client relationship or specific engagement that would have caused it to decline the client relationship or specific engagement had that information been known prior to accepting or continuing the client relationship or specific engagement
- Addressing circumstances where the firm is obligated by law or regulation to accept a client relationship or specific engagement
- Requiring communication with those charged with governance when performing an audit of financial statements of listed entities about how the system of quality management supports the consistent performance of quality audit engagements
- Addressing when it is appropriate to communicate with external parties about the firm's system of quality management and the information to be provided
- Addressing engagement quality reviews (detailed later in this chapter)

Firm's will also include any other quality objectives considered necessary to achieve the objectives of its system of quality management.

2.3 Governance and leadership

> **ISQM 1.28**
>
> The firm shall establish the following quality objectives that address the firm's governance and leadership, which establishes the environment that supports the system of quality management:
>
> (a) The firm demonstrates a commitment to quality through a culture that exists throughout the firm, which recognises and reinforces:
>
> (i) The firm's role in serving the public interest by consistently performing quality engagements;
>
> (ii) The importance of professional ethics, values and attitudes;
>
> (iii) The responsibility of all personnel for quality relating to the performance of engagements or activities within the system of quality management, and their expected behaviour; and
>
> (iv) The importance of quality in the firm's strategic decisions and actions, including the firm's financial and operational priorities.
>
> (b) Leadership is responsible and accountable for quality.
>
> (c) Leadership demonstrates a commitment to quality through their actions and behaviours.
>
> (d) The organisational structure and assignment of roles, responsibilities and authority is appropriate to enable the design, implementation and operation of the firm's system of quality management.
>
> (e) Resource needs, including financial resources, are planned for and resources are obtained, allocated or assigned in a manner that is consistent with the firm's commitment to quality.

2.4 Engagement performance

The firm should take steps to ensure that engagements are performed correctly, that is, in accordance with standards and guidance. Firms often produce a manual of standard engagement procedures to give to all staff so that they know the standards they are working towards. These may be in an electronic format.

Ensuring good engagement performance involves a number of issues:

- Direction
- Supervision
- Consultation
- Resolution of disputes

- Review
- Professional judgement
- Engagement documentation
- Professional scepticism

Many of these issues will be discussed in the context of an individual audit assignment (see Section 3 below).

2.5 Resources

Firms shall establish quality objectives that address appropriately obtaining, developing, using, maintaining, allocating and assigning resources in a timely manner to enable the design, implementation and operation of the system of quality management. These must cover the following areas:

Human resources

- Hiring, developing and retaining competent and capable personnel
- Personnel demonstrating a commitment to quality through their actions and behaviours and this being recognised through evaluations, compensation, promotion or other incentives
- Personnel developing and maintaining the appropriate competence for their roles, for example through continuing professional development
- Using external individuals to maintain quality where the firm does not have sufficient or appropriate personnel
- Assigning engagement team members with the appropriate competence and capabilities
- Personnel being given sufficient time to perform quality engagements or activities within the system of quality management

Technological resources

- Appropriate technological resources being obtained or developed, implemented, maintained and used
- Examples of technological resources include purchased IT applications, IT applications developed by the firm, IT infrastructure and IT processes

Intellectual resources

- Appropriate intellectual resources are obtained or developed, implemented, maintained and used

Intellectual resources include the information a firm uses to enable the operation of its system of quality management and promote consistency in the performance of engagements. Examples include written policies or procedures, methodologies, standardised documentation and subscriptions to websites providing in-depth information.

2.6 Information and communication

Firms shall establish the following quality objectives that address obtaining, generating or using information regarding the system of quality management, and communicating information within the firm and to external parties on a timely basis to enable the design, implementation and operation of the system of quality management.

- The information system identifies, captures, processes and maintains relevant and reliable information that supports the system of quality management, whether from internal or external sources
- Culture of the firm recognises and reinforces the responsibility of personnel to exchange information with the firm and with one another
- Relevant and reliable information is exchanged throughout the firm and with engagement teams
- Relevant and reliable information is communicated to external parties, for example service providers or regulatory authorities

2.7 Monitoring and remediation process

> **ISQM 1.35**
>
> The firm shall establish a monitoring and remediation process to:
>
> (a) Provide relevant, reliable and timely information about the design, implementation and operation of the system of quality management.
>
> (b) Take appropriate actions to respond to identified deficiencies such that deficiencies are remediated on a timely basis.

Step 1 Design and perform **monitoring** activities to identify deficiencies.

Step 2 Evaluate **findings** and identify and evaluate **deficiencies**.

Step 3 Design and implement **remedial actions** to address identified deficiencies.

2.7.1 Monitoring

Firms monitor their system of quality management as a whole. The nature, timing and extent of monitoring activities are risk-based and tailored to the individual firm, for example, they take into account the firm's quality risks, results of previous monitoring activities and complaints that work has not been performed in accordance with professional standards. There are two types of monitoring activity:

- **Ongoing** monitoring activities which might include such questions as, 'have we kept up to date with regulatory requirements?'.
- **Periodic** monitoring activities which are conducted at certain intervals by the firm. For example, ISQM 1 requires at least one completed engagement for each engagement partner to be selected for monitoring on a cyclical basis determined by the firm.

Individuals performing monitoring activities must have the competence, capability and sufficient time to perform the monitoring activity effectively. They must also be objective. Engagement team members or engagement quality reviewers are prohibited from performing a monitoring inspection of that engagement.

2.7.2 Evaluating findings and deficiencies

The firm shall evaluate findings to determine whether deficiencies exist, including in the monitoring and remediation process. Firms shall evaluate the **severity and pervasiveness** of identified deficiencies by:

- Investigating the **root cause**(s) of the identified deficiencies
- Evaluating the effect of the identified deficiencies, individually and in aggregate, on the system of quality management.

Identified deficiencies might be one-offs. The firm will be more concerned with systematic or repetitive deficiencies that require corrective action.

2.7.3 Responding to identified deficiencies

Firms shall design and implement **remedial actions** to address identified deficiencies that are responsive to the results of the root cause analysis. Examples of remedial action might include:

- Remedial action with an individual
- Communication of findings with the training department so they can ensure improvements are made to the firm's policies and procedures related to education and training
- Establishing new quality objectives, quality risks or responses
- Disciplinary action, if necessary, especially if an individual repeatedly fails to comply with the firm's policies and procedures

When evidence is gathered that an inappropriate report might have been issued, the firm must take appropriate action including considering the need to take legal advice.

The individual(s) assigned operational responsibility for the monitoring and remediation process shall evaluate whether remedial actions are:

- Appropriately designed to address the identified deficiencies and their related root cause(s) and determine that they have been implemented
- Effectively implemented to address previously identified deficiencies

3 Quality management on an individual audit

> **FAST FORWARD**
>
> ISA 220 deals with the responsibility of the auditor regarding quality management at the engagement level, for an audit of financial statements, and the related responsibilities of the engagement partner.

The requirements concerning quality management on individual audits are found in ISA 220 (Revised) *Quality Management for an audit of financial statements*. This ISA builds of the firm's system of quality management that we looked at in the previous section on ISQM 1.

> **ISA 220.11**
>
> The objective of the auditor is to manage quality at the engagement level to obtain reasonable assurance that quality has been achieved such that:
>
> (a) The auditor has fulfilled the auditor's responsibilities, and has conducted the audit, in accordance with professional standards and applicable legal and regulatory requirements; and
>
> (b) The auditor's report issued is appropriate in the circumstances.

The burden of this falls on the audit engagement partner, who is ultimately responsible, and therefore accountable, for compliance with the requirements of ISA 220 (Revised).

We have already considered the sections of ISA 220 (Revised) relating to ethics in Chapter 2 and those relating to client acceptance were covered in Chapter 8 of this Study Text. We shall now consider the requirements of the rest of the standard, which fall into the following areas:

- Leadership responsibilities for managing and achieving quality on audits
- Engagement resources
- Engagement performance
- Monitoring and remediation

3.1 Leadership responsibilities for managing and achieving quality on audits

The engagement partner is required to set an example with regard to the importance of quality.

> **ISA 220.13**
>
> The engagement partner shall take **overall responsibility for managing and achieving quality** on the audit engagement, including taking responsibility for creating an environment for the engagement that emphasises the firm's culture and expected behaviour of engagement team members.
>
> In doing so, the engagement partner shall be **sufficiently and appropriately involved throughout the audit** engagement such that the engagement partner has the basis for determining whether the significant judgements made, and the conclusions reached, are appropriate given the nature and circumstances of the engagement.

Engagement partners can delegate the design or performance of procedures or tasks or actions related to ISA 220 to other members of the engagement team. However, they are still responsible overall for managing and achieving quality on the audit through the direction and supervision of those team members and the review of their work.

The engagement partner shall take responsibility for clear, consistent and effective actions being taken that reflect the firm's commitment to quality and establish and communicate the expected behaviour of engagement team members, including emphasising:

- That all engagement team members are responsible for contributing to the management and achievement of quality at the engagement level
- The importance of professional ethics, values and attitudes to the members of the engagement team
- The importance of open and robust communication within the engagement team, and supporting the ability of engagement team members to raise concerns without fear of reprisal
- The importance of each engagement team member exercising professional scepticism throughout the audit engagement

The actions of the engagement partner and appropriate messages to the other members of the engagement team, in taking responsibility for the overall quality on each audit engagement emphasise the fact that quality is essential in performing audit engagements.

3.2 Engagement resources

> **ISA 220.25**
>
> The engagement partner shall determine that **sufficient and appropriate resources** to perform the engagement are assigned or made available to the engagement team in a timely manner, taking into account the nature and circumstances of the audit engagement, the firm's policies or procedures, and any changes that may arise during the engagement.

Resources include human resources, technological resources and intellectual resources. Human resources include members of the engagement team, any auditor's external experts and internal auditors who provide direct assistance. The engagement partner shall determine that all human resources collectively have the appropriate **competence** and **capabilities**, including **sufficient time**, to perform the audit engagement.

In determining whether the engagement team has the appropriate competence and capabilities, the engagement partner may take into consideration such matters as the team's:

- Understanding of, and practical experience with, audit engagements of a similar nature and complexity through appropriate training and participation
- Understanding of professional standards and applicable legal and regulatory requirements

- Expertise in specialised areas of accounting or auditing
- Expertise in IT used by the entity or automated tools or techniques that are to be used by the engagement team in planning and performing the audit engagement
- Knowledge of relevant industries in which the entity being audited operates
- Ability to exercise professional scepticism and professional judgement
- Understanding of the firm's policies or procedures

If the engagement partner determines that resources assigned or made available are insufficient or inappropriate in the circumstances of the audit engagement, the engagement partner shall take appropriate action, including communicating with appropriate individuals about the need to assign or make available additional or alternative resources to the engagement.

3.3 Engagement performance

> **ISA 220.29**
>
> The engagement partner shall take responsibility for the **direction** and **supervision** of the members of the engagement team and the **review** of their work.

The engagement partner shall determine that the nature, timing and extent of direction, supervision and review is:

- Planned and performed in accordance with the firm's policies or procedures, professional standards and applicable legal and regulatory requirements
- Responsive to the nature and circumstances of the audit engagement and the resources assigned or made available to the engagement team by the firm

3.3.1 Direction

The engagement partner directs the audit. This may involve informing the members of the engagement team of their responsibilities, such as:

- Contributing to the management and achievement of quality at the engagement level through their personal conduct, communication and actions
- Maintaining a questioning mind and being aware of unconscious or conscious auditor biases in exercising professional skepticism when gathering and evaluating audit evidence
- Fulfilling relevant ethical requirements
- The responsibilities of respective partners when more than one partner is involved in the conduct of an audit engagement
- The responsibilities of respective engagement team members to perform audit procedures and of more experienced engagement team members to direct, supervise and review the work of less experienced engagement team members
- Understanding the objectives of the work to be performed and the detailed instructions regarding the nature, timing and extent of planned audit procedures as set forth in the overall audit strategy and audit plan
- Addressing threats to the achievement of quality, and the engagement team's expected response. For example, budget constraints or resource constraints should not result in the engagement team members modifying planned audit procedures or failing to perform planned audit procedures.

3.3.2 Supervision

The audit is supervised overall by the engagement partner, but more practical supervision is given within the audit team by senior staff to more junior staff, as is also the case with audit engagement review (see Section 3.3.3 below). It includes:

- Tracking the progress of the audit engagement which includes monitoring:
    - The progress against the audit plan
    - Whether the objective of work performed has been achieved
    - The ongoing adequacy of assigned resources.

- Taking appropriate action to address issues arising during the engagement, including for example, reassigning planned audit procedures to more experienced engagement team members when issues are more complex than initially anticipated

- Identifying matters for consultation or consideration by more experienced engagement team members during the audit engagement

- Providing coaching and on-the-job training to help engagement team members develop skills or competencies

- Creating an environment where engagement team members raise concerns without fear of reprisals

3.3.3 Review

Audit engagement review includes consideration of whether:

- The work has been performed in accordance with the firm's policies and procedures, International Standards on Auditing and applicable regulatory and legal requirements

- Significant matters have been raised for further consideration

- Appropriate consultations have taken place and the resulting conclusions have been documented and implemented

- There is a need to revise the nature, timing and extent of work performed

- The work performed supports the conclusions reached and is appropriately documented

- The evidence obtained is sufficient and appropriate to provide a basis for the auditor's opinion

- The objectives of the audit procedures have been achieved

The engagement partner shall review audit documentation **at appropriate points in time** during the audit engagement, including audit documentation relating to:

- Significant matters

- Significant judgements, including those relating to difficult or contentious matters identified during the audit engagement, and the conclusions reached

- Other matters that, in the engagement partner's professional judgement, are relevant to the engagement partner's responsibilities

Timely review at appropriate stages throughout the audit enables significant matters to be resolved before the auditor's report is signed. The audit engagement partner need not review all audit documentation.

On or before the date of the auditor's report, the engagement partner must, through review of audit documentation and discussion with the audit team, ensure that sufficient and appropriate audit evidence has been obtained to support the conclusions reached and for the auditor's report to be issued. The engagement partner is also required to review the financial statements and the auditor's report to determine the report issued will be appropriate in the circumstances.

3.3.4 Consultation

The partner is also responsible for ensuring that if difficult or contentious matters arise the team takes appropriate consultation on the matter and that such matters and conclusions are properly implemented. Consultation may be taken inside or outside the firm, where appropriate.

> **ISA 220.35**
>
> The engagement partner shall:
>
> (a) Take responsibility for the engagement team undertaking consultation on:
>
>   (i) Difficult or contentious matters and matters on which the firm's policies or procedures require consultation; and
>
>   (ii) Other matters that, in the engagement partner's professional judgement, require consultation;
>
> (b) Determine that members of the engagement team have undertaken appropriate consultation during the audit engagement, both within the engagement team, and between the engagement team and others at the appropriate level within or outside the firm;
>
> (c) Determine that the nature and scope of, and conclusions resulting from, such consultations are agreed with the party consulted; and
>
> (d) Determine that conclusions agreed have been implemented.

3.3.5 Engagement quality review

The audit engagement partner has responsibilities where an engagement quality review is necessary. In this situation, they must:

- Determine that an engagement quality reviewer has been appointed
- Cooperate with the engagement quality reviewer and inform other members of the engagement team of their responsibility to do so
- Discuss significant matters and significant judgements arising during the audit engagement, including those identified during the engagement quality review, with the engagement quality reviewer
- Not date the auditor's report until the completion of the engagement quality review

We will look at the requirements for engagement quality reviewers in more detail in Section 4 of this Chapter.

3.3.6 Differences of opinion

If differences of opinion arise within the engagement team, or between the engagement team and the engagement quality reviewer or individuals performing activities within the firm's system of quality management, these differences shall be resolved according to the firm's policy for such differences of opinion. The engagement partner shall take responsibility for this and must also determine that conclusions reached are documented and implemented

When there are differences of opinion, the auditor's report shall not be dated until the matters have been resolved. This may involve consulting externally, for example with other firms, or the related professional body (eg AIA), particularly when the firm involved is small.

3.4 Monitoring and remediation

The engagement partner shall take responsibility for:

- Obtaining an understanding of the information from the firm's monitoring and remediation process, as communicated by the firm

- Determining the relevance and effect on the audit engagement of the information from the firm's monitoring and remediation process, as communicated by the firm, and take appropriate action
- Remaining alert throughout the audit engagement for information that may be relevant to the firm's monitoring and remediation process and communicate such information to those responsible for the process

3.5 Taking overall responsibility for managing and achieving quality

> **ISA 220.40**
>
> Prior to dating the auditor's report, the engagement partner shall determine that the engagement partner has taken overall responsibility for managing and achieving quality on the audit engagement. In doing so, the engagement partner shall determine that:
>
> (a) The engagement partner's involvement has been sufficient and appropriate throughout the audit engagement such that the engagement partner has the basis for determining that the significant judgements made and the conclusions reached are appropriate given the nature and circumstances of the engagement; and
>
> (b) The nature and circumstances of the audit engagement, any changes thereto, and the firm's related policies or procedures have been taken into account in complying with the requirements of this ISA.

3.6 Scalability

The regulation of audit is the same for all firms regardless of size. However, it is logical to see that it will impact on large and small firms differently. ISA 220 (Revised) *Quality Management for an Audit of Financial Statements* is scalable and can be applied to large firms who are likely to perform more complex audits, and small firms where audits are likely to be performed for less complex entities. It states that the requirements are intended to be applied in the context of the nature and circumstances of each audit.

For example, a large firm may have international quality management procedures. If not, it will certainly have national and regional ones. In order to meet some of the quality management requirements, small, single-partner firms may need to make use of external experts.

Question — Quality management issues

You are an audit senior working for the firm Addystone Fish. You are currently carrying out the audit of Wicker, a manufacturer of waste paper bins. You are unhappy with Wicker's inventory valuation policy and have raised the issue several times with the audit manager. He has dealt with the client for a number of years and does not see what you are making a fuss about. He has refused to meet you on site to discuss these issues.

The former engagement partner to Wicker retired two months ago. As the audit manager had dealt with Wicker for so many years, the other partners have decided to leave the audit of Wicker in his capable hands.

Required

Comment on the situation outlined above.

Answer

Several quality management issues are raised in the above scenario.

Engagement partner

An **engagement partner** is usually appointed to each audit engagement undertaken by the firm, to take responsibility for the engagement on behalf of the firm. Assigning the audit to the experienced audit manager is not sufficient.

The lack of audit engagement partner also means that several of the requirements of ISA 220 (Revised) are not in place. . For example, the engagement partner taking responsibility for the direction and supervision of the audit team and the review of their work.

Conflicting views

In this scenario the audit manager and senior have conflicting views about the valuation of inventory. This does not appear to have been handled well, with the manager refusing to discuss the issue with the senior.

ISA 220 (Revised) requires that the audit engagement partner takes responsibility for differences of opinion being addressed and resolved in accordance with the firm's policies and procedures. In this case, the lack of engagement partner may have contributed to this failure to resolve the difference of opinion. In any event, at best, the failure to resolve the difference of opinion is a breach of the firm's quality objectives under ISQM 1. At worst, it indicates that the firm does not have a suitable quality objective concerning such differences of opinion as required by ISQM 1.

4 Engagement quality reviews

> **FAST FORWARD**
>
> ISQM 2 *Engagement Quality Reviews* deals with the appointment and eligibility of the engagement quality reviewer, and the performance and documentation of the engagement quality review.

Key terms

> An **engagement quality review** is an objective evaluation of the significant judgements made by the engagement team and the conclusions reached thereon, performed by the engagement quality reviewer and completed on or before the date of the engagement report.
>
> An **engagement quality reviewer** is a partner, other individual in the firm, or an external individual, appointed by the firm to perform the engagement quality review.

An engagement quality review is a specified response designed and implemented by the firm under ISQM 1. ISQM 1 requires all firms to establish policies or procedures that address engagement quality reviews in accordance with ISQM 2, and requires an engagement quality review for:

- Audits of financial statements of listed entities

- Audits or other engagements for which an engagement quality review is required by law or regulation

- Audits or other engagements for which the firm determines that an engagement quality review is an appropriate response to address one or more quality risk(s)

4.1 Appointment and eligibility of engagement quality reviewers

The individual(s) in the firm assigned responsibility for appointing the engagement quality reviewer must have the competence, capability and appropriate authority within the firm to fulfil this responsibility. The engagement quality reviewer:

- Cannot be a member of the engagement team
- Must have the competence and capabilities, including sufficient time, and the appropriate authority to perform the engagement quality review
- Must comply with relevant ethical requirements, including in relation to threats to objectivity and independence of the engagement quality reviewer
- Must comply with provisions of law and regulation, if any, that are relevant to the eligibility of the engagement quality reviewer
- Cannot be an individual who has served as engagement partner in the previous two years, or a longer period if this is required by relevant ethical requirements

4.1.1 Using assistants

In certain circumstances, it may be appropriate for the engagement quality reviewer to be assisted by an individual or team of individuals with the relevant expertise. For example, highly specialised knowledge, skills or expertise may be useful for understanding certain transactions undertaken by the entity to help the engagement quality reviewer evaluate the significant judgements made by the engagement team related to those transactions. Individuals assisting the engagement quality reviewer:

- Cannot be a member of the engagement team
- Must have the competence and capabilities, including sufficient time, to perform the duties assigned
- Must comply with relevant ethical requirements, including in relation to threats to their objectivity and independence and, if applicable, the provisions of law and regulation

The engagement quality reviewer is required to take overall responsibility for the performance of the engagement quality review. Where individual(s) assist with the review, the engagement quality reviewer is responsibility for determining the nature, timing and extent of the direction, supervision and review of their work.

4.1.2 Impairment of eligibility to perform an engagement quality review

If the engagement quality reviewer becomes aware of circumstances that impair their eligibility to perform the engagement quality review, they must notify the appropriate individual(s) in the firm and then either decline or withdraw from the engagement quality review.

Firms shall establish policies or procedures that address circumstances in which the engagement quality reviewer's eligibility to perform the engagement quality review is impaired and the appropriate actions to be taken by the firm, including the process for identifying and appointing a replacement in such circumstances.

4.2 Performance of the engagement quality review

In performing the engagement quality review, the engagement quality reviewer shall:

- Read, and obtain an understanding of, information communicated by:
    - The engagement team regarding the nature and circumstances of the engagement and the entity
    - The firm related to the firm's monitoring and remediation process, in particular identified deficiencies that may relate to, or affect, the areas involving significant judgements made by the engagement team
- Discuss with the engagement partner and, if applicable, other members of the engagement team, significant matters and significant judgements made in planning, performing and reporting on the engagement
- Based on the information obtained, review selected engagement documentation relating to the significant judgements made by the engagement team and evaluate:

- – The basis for making those significant judgements, including, when applicable to the type of engagement, the exercise of professional skepticism by the engagement team
  - – Whether the engagement documentation supports the conclusions reached
  - – Whether the conclusions reached are appropriate
- For audits of financial statements, evaluate the basis for the engagement partner's determination that relevant ethical requirements relating to independence have been fulfilled
- Evaluate whether appropriate consultation has taken place on difficult or contentious matters or matters involving differences of opinion and the conclusions arising from those consultations
- For audits of financial statements, evaluate the basis for the engagement partner's determination that the engagement partner's involvement has been sufficient and appropriate throughout the audit engagement such that the engagement partner has the basis for determining that the significant judgements made and the conclusions reached are appropriate given the nature and circumstances of the engagement
- Review:
  - – For audits of financial statements, the financial statements and the auditor's report, including, if applicable, the description of the key audit matters
  - – For review engagements, the financial statements or financial information and the engagement report
  - – For other assurance and related services engagements, the engagement report, and when applicable, the subject matter information

The engagement quality reviewer must perform these procedures at **appropriate points in time** during the engagement. Conducting the review in a timely manner allows significant matters to be promptly resolved on or before the date of the auditor's report.

The engagement quality reviewer shall notify the engagement partner if the engagement quality reviewer has concerns that the significant judgements made by the engagement team, or the conclusions reached, are not appropriate. If such concerns are not resolved to the engagement quality reviewer's satisfaction, the engagement quality reviewer shall notify an appropriate individual(s) in the firm that the engagement quality review cannot be completed.

4.2.1 Completion of the engagement quality review

The engagement quality reviewer is required to 'stand-back' to determine whether the requirements in ISQM 2 have been fulfilled, and whether the engagement quality review is complete. If so, the engagement quality reviewer shall notify the engagement partner that the engagement quality review is complete. The engagement partner **cannot date the engagement report until notification of completion of the engagement quality review has been received** from the engagement quality reviewer.

4.2.2 Documentation

> **ISQM 2.30**
>
> The engagement quality reviewer shall determine that the documentation of the engagement quality review is sufficient to enable an experienced practitioner, having no previous connection with the engagement, to understand the nature, timing and extent of the procedures performed by the engagement quality reviewer and, when applicable, individuals who assisted the reviewer, and the conclusions reached in performing the review.

The engagement quality reviewer shall determine that documentation of the engagement quality review includes the following.

- The names of the engagement quality reviewer and individuals who assisted with the engagement quality review
- An identification of the engagement documentation reviewed
- The basis for the engagement quality reviewer's determination whether the requirements in ISQM 2 have been fulfilled, and whether the engagement quality review is complete
- The notification of completion of the engagement quality review sent to the engagement partner
- If applicable, notification that the engagement quality review cannot be completed due to unresolved concerns that the significant judgements made or conclusions reached are not appropriate
- The date of completion of the engagement quality review

5 Revision: Documentation

FAST FORWARD — The auditor should prepare documentation that provides a record of the basis of the audit opinion and evidence that the audit work was planned and performed properly.

5.1 Document what?

Audit work must be documented: the working papers are the **tangible evidence of all work done in support of the audit opinion**. ISA 230 *Audit documentation* provides guidance.

In your previous studies, you have learnt the practical issues surrounding how audit papers should be completed. The key general rule concerning what audit documentation should contain:

> What would be necessary to allow an experienced auditor, having no previous connection with the audit, to understand the nature, timing, and extent of the audit procedures performed to comply with the ISAs and applicable legal and regulatory requirements and the results of the audit procedures and the audit evidence obtained, and significant matters arising during the audit and the conclusions reached thereon and significant professional judgements, made in reaching those conclusions.

The key reason for having audit papers therefore is that they provide evidence of work done. They may be required in the event of litigation arising over the audit work and opinion given.

The ISA sets out certain requirements about what should be recorded, such as the identifying characteristics of the specific items being tested.

It also sets out what an auditor should record in relation to significant matters, such as discussions undertaken with directors and how the auditor addressed information that appeared to be inconsistent with his conclusions in relation to significant matters.

If an auditor felt it necessary to depart from customary audit work required by audit standards, he should document why, and how the different test achieved audit objectives.

The ISA also contains details about how the audit file should be put together and actions in the event of audit work being added after the date of the auditor's report (for example, if subsequent events result in additional work being carried out).

Exam focus point — We shall briefly revise here the review of working papers. Although we have dealt with this in your earlier studies, you need to know the documentation for this exam.

Review of working papers is important, as it allows a more senior auditor to **evaluate the evidence obtained** during the course of the audit for sufficiency and reliability, so that more evidence can be obtained to support the audit opinion, if required.

5.2 Review of audit working papers

FAST FORWARD

Working papers should be reviewed by a more senior audit staff member before an audit conclusion is drawn.

Work performed by each assistant should be reviewed by personnel of appropriate experience to consider whether:

- The work has been **performed** in **accordance with the audit plan**.
- The work performed and the results obtained have been **adequately documented**.
- Any **significant matters** have been **resolved** or are reflected in audit conclusions.
- The **objectives** of the audit procedures have been **achieved**.
- The **conclusions** expressed are **consistent** with the results of the work performed and support the audit opinion.

The following should be reviewed on a timely basis.

- The **overall audit strategy** and the **audit plan**
- The **assessments of inherent and control risks**
- The **results** of **control** and **substantive procedures** and the conclusions drawn therefrom including the results of consultations
- The **financial statements,** proposed audit adjustments and the proposed auditors' report

In some cases, particular in large complex audits, personnel not involved in the audit may be asked to review some or all of the audit work, the auditors' report etc. This is sometimes called a **pre-issuance review** or **hot review**.

5.3 Cloud-based audit working papers

Key term

Cloud based audit working papers are generated through the use of cloud-based software that enables collaboration between the audit team and efficient management of working papers.

Auditors are now more likely to keep electronic rather than paper working papers. Cloud-based software can be used by the auditor to manage the audit process and to generate audit working papers which are then stored safely and securely online. The cloud-based nature of the software means that the audit data is always accessible and is always backed up, thereby reducing the risk of loss of data.

reducing the risk of loss of data.

Real-time dashboards are available that enable audit managers to quickly assess the status of the audit and take corrective action where problems arise. The integration of up-to-date auditing standards and requirements means that compliance is made easier for the firm.

Cloud-based systems will often have state-of-the-art security and encryption which reduces the risk of storing data in comparison with storage on local hard drives. Security systems may then be updated more regularly in response to new threats.

The accessibility of the working papers is enhanced in a cloud-based system as it will be accessible in any location on any device and is usually supported by smartphones, laptop and tablets as well as desktop computers.

Other benefits of cloud based working papers include:

- Cloud-based systems will often integrate easily with a wide variety of other software used by the auditor and the client.
- There is often a large capacity for file storage which can be calibrated to the requirements of the firm.

- The nature of the software enables the audit team to collaborate more effectively with easy access from anywhere in the world.

As technology develops, paper-based audit files may become redundant as all evidence can be stored electronically, however, the electronic files must still meet the requirements of ISA 230 *Audit documentation*. Auditors might use computer packages such as a spreadsheet to assist in the calculation of materiality. If doing so, it will be important to ensure that audit judgement is still applied and that the calculation does not simply get done by the computer program, and that the requirements of ISA 230 are still followed.

Question — Working papers

Viewco is a manufacturer of TVs and DVD players. It carries out a full physical inventory count at its central warehouse every year on 31 December, its financial year end. Finished goods inventory are normally of the order of $3 million, with components and work in progress normally approximately $1 million.

You are the audit senior responsible for the audit of Viewco for the year ending 31 December 20X1. Together with a junior member of staff, you will be attending Viewco physical inventory count.

(a) Explain why it is necessary for an auditor to prepare working papers.

(b) State, giving reasons, what information the working papers relating to this inventory count attendance should contain.

Answer

(a) Working papers are necessary for the following reasons.

- So that the reporting partner can be satisfied that work delegated has been properly performed.
- To provide, for future reference, detail of problems encountered, evidence of work performed and conclusions drawn therefrom in arriving at the audit opinion.
- Their preparation encourages a methodical approach.
- To facilitate review.
- To provide evidence that International Standards on Auditing have been followed.

(b)

Information	Reasons
1. **Administration** Client name Year end Title Date prepared Initials of preparer Initials of senior to indicate review of junior's work	- Enables an organised file to be produced - Enables papers to be traced if lost - Any questions can be addressed top the appropriate person - Seniority of preparer is indicated - Evidence that guideline on planning, controlling and recording is being followed - Evidence of adherence to International Standards on Auditing

Information	Reasons
2. Planning	
(i) Summary of different models of TV and DVD player held and the approximate value of each	• Enables auditor to familiarise himself with different types of inventory line
Summary of different types of raw material held and method of counting small components	
Summary of different stages of WIP identified by client	
(ii) Time and place of count	• Audit team will not miss the count
(iii) Personnel involved	• Auditor aware who to address questions/ problems to
(iv) Copy of client's inventory count instructions and an assessment of them	• Enables an initial assessment of the likely reliability of Viewco's count
	• Assists in determining the amount of work audit team need to do
	• Enables compliance work to be carried out, that is, checking Viewco staff follow the instructions
(v) Plan of warehouse	• To ensure all areas covered at count
	• Clear where to find different models/components
	• Location of any third party/moving inventory clear
(vi) Details of any known old or slow moving lines	• Special attention can be given to these at count for example, include in test counts
(vii) Scope of tests counts to be performed that is, number/value of items to be counted and method of selection. For Viewco probably more counting of higher value finished goods	• Ensures appropriate amount of work done based on initial assessment
	• Clear plan for audit team
3. Objectives of attendance that is, to ensure that the quality of inventory to be reflected in the financial statements is materially accurate	• Reporting partner can confirm if appropriate/ adequate work done

Information	Reasons
4. Details of work done (a) Details of controls testing work performed – observing Viewco's counters and ensuring they are following the instructions and conducting the count effectively, for example,	• Provides evidence for future reference and documents adherence to International Standards on Auditing • Enables reporting partner to review the adequacy of the work and establish whether is meets the stated objective
(i) Note of whether the area was systematically tided	• Enable reassessment of likely reliability of Viewco's count
(ii) Note of whether or how counted goods are marked	• Enables assessment of chances of items being double counted or omitted
(iii) Note of how Viewco record and segregate any goods still moving on count day	
(iv) Note of adequacy of supervision and general impression of counters	• Enables assessment of overall of count and hence likely accuracy
(v) Note whether counters are in teams of two and whether any check counts are performed	• Evidence of independent checks may enhance reliability
(b) Details of substantive work performed	
(i) Details of items of raw materials or finished goods test counted:	
• From physical inventory to client's count sheet	• Evidence to support the accuracy and completeness of Viewco's count sheets
• From Viewco's count sheets to physical inventory	• Evidence to support the existence of inventory recorded by Viewco
For both of the above note inventory code, description, number of units and quality. Use a symbol to indicate agreement with Viewco's records	
(ii) Details of review for any old/ obsolete inventory for example, dusty/damaged boxes. Note code, description, number of units and problem	• Details can be followed up at final audit and the net realisable investigated
(iii) Details of review of WIP	
• Assessment of volume of part complete items of each stage	• Evidence in support of accuracy of quantity of WIP
• Assessment of appropriateness of degree of completion assigned to each stage by Viewco (could describe items at various stages)	• Details can be followed through at final audit to final inventory sheets • Basis for discussion of any description

Information	Reasons
(iv) Copies of: • Last few despatch notes • Last few goods received notes • Last few material requisitions • Last few receipts to finished goods. (v) Copies of client's inventory count sheets (where number makes this practical)	• Enables follow up at final audit to ensure cut-off is correct that is, goods despatched are reflected as sales, goods received as purchases and items in WIP are not also in raw materials and finished goods • Enables follow up at final audit to ensure that Viewco's final sheets are intact and no alterations have occurred
5. **Summary of results** In particular: (i) Details of any problems encountered. (ii) Details of any test count discrepancies and notes of investigation into their causes (iii) Details of any representations by the management of Viewco	• Senior/manager can assess any consequences for audit risk and strategy and decide any further work needed • Provides full documentation of issues that could require a judgemental decision and could ultimately be the basis for a qualified opinion
6. **Conclusion**	• Indicates whether or not the initial objective has been met and whether there are any implications for the audit opinion

Chapter Roundup

- There is no simple definition of audit quality because there is no one 'correct' way to audit. It is often a matter of conducting an audit in line with the spirit as well as the letter of professional guidance.

- The International Standard on Quality Management (ISQM 1) helps audit firms to establish quality standards for their business.

- ISA 220 deals with the responsibility of the auditor regarding quality management at the engagement level, for an audit of financial statements, and the related responsibilities of the engagement partner.

- ISQM 2 *Engagement Quality Reviews* deals with the appointment and eligibility of the engagement quality reviewer, and the performance and documentation of the engagement quality review.

- The auditor should prepare documentation that provides a record of the basis of the audit opinion and evidence that the audit work was planned and performed properly.

- Working papers should be reviewed by a more senior audit staff member before an audit conclusion is drawn.

Quick Quiz

1. The objective of a firm applying ISQM 1 is to:

    'Design, implement and operate a system of .... for audits or reviews of financial statements, or other assurance or related services engagements performed by the firm, that provides the firm with .... assurance that:

    (a) The firm and its personnel fulfil their responsibilities in accordance with .... and applicable .... and .... requirements; and

    (b) .... issued by the firm or engagement partners are .... in the circumstances.'

2. List five issues relating to good engagement performance that should be addressed in an audit of financial statements.

    (1)
    (2)
    (3)
    (4)
    (5)

3. Who reviews audit work in an audit of financial statements?

4. Who is responsible for the overall quality of an audit assignment?

    (a) Ethics partner
    (b) Pre-issuance reviewer
    (c) Engagement partner
    (d) Managing partner

5. ISQM 1 sets out requirements about the firm's governance and leadership.

    True ☐

    False ☐

6. What is a pre-issuance review?

Answers to Quick Quiz

1. Quality management, reasonable, professional standards, legal, regulatory, reports, appropriate

2. Any five from:
   (1) Direction
   (2) Supervision
   (3) Review
   (4) Consultation
   (5) Differences of opinion
   (6) Engagement quality review

3. Audit work is generally reviewed by the staff member who is more senior on the team than the person who did the work. The partner must carry out a review to ensure there is sufficient and appropriate evidence to support the audit opinion. It might also be necessary to obtain an engagement quality review by a suitable person outside the audit team. This will be necessary if the audit is of a listed entity, an engagement quality review is required by law or regulation and where the firm determines that this is an appropriate response to one or more quality risks.

4. (c) Engagement partner

5. True. ISQM 1 requires the firm to establish quality objectives that address the firm's governance and leadership.

6. A pre-issuance review is when a member of staff who has not been involved in the audit is asked to review all the working papers before the auditor's report is signed.

End of Chapter Question

Working papers and review (AIA November 2007 amended)

One fairly recent common criticism of audit firms has been that some firms were not recording sufficient detail concerning the audit tests conducted and results obtained.

Required

(a) Explain the problems that might be created by recording insufficient information concerning audit tests and work done in the audit working papers. **(10 marks)**

(b) Explain why it might be difficult for an external reviewer to form a judgement of the quality of work done by an audit firm on the basis of the review of a sample of files of audit working papers.

Your answer should assume that such reviews have not been hampered by inadequate recording of details of tests conducted and the results obtained. **(10 marks)**

(Total 20 marks)

PART C AUDIT STRATEGY, PROCESS AND REPORTING

Fraud and non compliance with regulations

15

Topic list	Syllabus reference
1 Fraud	LO1
2 Laws and regulations	LO1

Introduction

The responsibilities that auditors have with regard to discovering fraud causing a material misstatement in financial statements are outlined in Section 1. Auditors are required to follow the guidance of ISA 240 *The auditor's responsibilities relating fraud in an audit of financial statements*.

The auditors also have a responsibility ensure that the financial statements are not materially misstated as a result of material non compliance with regulations. Auditors are required to follow the guidance of ISA 250 (Revised) *Consideration of laws and regulations in an audit of financial statements*.

PART C   AUDIT STRATEGY, PROCESS AND REPORTING

1 Fraud

FAST FORWARD

Auditors **do not have a responsibility to prevent and detect fraud**, but must consider whether it has caused misstatements in the financial statements.

1.1 What is fraud?

Key term

Fraud is an intentional act by one or more individuals among management, those charged with governance (management fraud), employees (employee fraud) or third parties involving the use of deception to obtain an unjust or illegal advantage. Fraud may be perpetrated by an individual, or colluded in with people internal or external to the business.

Fraud is a wide legal concept, but the auditor's main concern is with fraud that causes a material misstatement in financial statements. It is distinguished from error, which is when a material misstatement is caused by mistake, for example, in the application of an accounting policy. Specifically, there are two types of fraud causing material misstatement in financial statements:

- Fraudulent financial reporting
- Misappropriation of assets

1.1.1 Fraudulent financial reporting

This may include:

- Manipulation, falsification or alteration of accounting records/supporting documents
- Misrepresentation (or omission) of events or transactions in the financial statements
- Intentional misapplication of accounting principles

Such fraud may be carried out by overriding controls that would otherwise appear to be operating effectively, for example, by recording fictitious journal entries or improperly adjusting assumptions or estimates used in financial reporting.

Aggressive earnings management is a topical issue and, at its most aggressive, may constitute fraudulent financial reporting. Auditors should consider issues such as unsuitable revenue recognition, accruals, liabilities, provisions and reserves accounting and large numbers of immaterial breaches of financial reporting requirements to see whether together, they constitute fraud.

1.1.2 Misappropriation of assets

This is the theft of the entity's assets (for example, cash, inventory). Employees may be involved in such fraud in small and immaterial amounts, however, it can also be carried out by management for larger items who may then conceal the misappropriation, for example by:

- Embezzling receipts (for example, diverting them to private bank accounts)
- Stealing physical assets or intellectual property (inventory, selling data)
- Causing an entity to pay for goods not received (payments to fictitious vendors)
- Using assets for personal use

1.2 Responsibilities with regard to fraud

Management and those charged with governance in an entity are primarily responsible for preventing and detecting fraud. It is up to them to put a strong emphasis within the company on fraud prevention.

Auditors are responsible for carrying out an audit in accordance with international auditing standards, one of which is ISA 240 *The auditor's responsibilities relating to fraud in an audit of financial statements*, the details of which we shall look at now.

1.3 The auditors' approach to the possibility of fraud

1.3.1 General

The key responsibility of an auditor is set out early in the ISA.

> **ISA 240.5**
>
> An auditor conducting an audit in accordance with ISAs is responsible for obtaining reasonable assurance that the financial statements taken as a whole are free from material misstatement whether caused by fraud or error. Owing to the inherent limitations of an audit, there is an unavoidable risk that some material misstatements of the financial statements may not be detected, even though the audit is properly planned and performed in accordance with the ISAs.
>
> **ISA 240.10**
>
> The objectives of the auditor are:
>
> (a) To identify and assess the risks of material misstatement due to fraud;
>
> (b) To obtain sufficient appropriate audit evidence regarding the assessed risks of material misstatement due to fraud, through designing and implementing appropriate responses; and
>
> (c) To respond appropriately to fraud or suspected fraud identified during the audit.

An overriding requirement of the ISA is that auditors are aware of the possibility of there being misstatements due to fraud.

> **ISA 240.12**
>
> In accordance with ISA 200 the auditor shall maintain professional scepticism throughout the audit, recognising the possibility that a material misstatement due to fraud could exist, notwithstanding the auditor's past experience of the honesty and integrity of the entity's management and those charged with governance.

The ISA also requires discussion by members of the engagement team of the susceptibility of the entity's financial statements to material misstatement due to fraud, including how fraud might occur.

The engagement partner must consider what matters discussed should be passed on to other members of the team who are not present at the discussion.

The discussion itself usually includes:

- An exchange of ideas between the engagement team about how fraud could be perpetrated
- A consideration of circumstances that might be indicative of aggressive earnings management
- A consideration of known factors that might give incentive to management to commit fraud
- A consideration of management's oversight of employees with access to cash/other assets
- A consideration of any unusual/unexplained changes in lifestyle of management/employees
- An emphasis on maintaining professional scepticism throughout the audit
- A consideration of the types of circumstance that might indicate fraud
- A consideration of how unpredictability will be incorporated into the audit
- A consideration of what audit procedures might be carried out to answer any suspicions of fraud
- A consideration of any allegations of fraud that have come to the auditors' attention
- A consideration of the risk of management override of controls

1.3.2 Risk assessment procedures

The auditor would undertake risk assessment procedures as set out in ISA 315 (Revised 2019) *Identifying and assessing the risks of material misstatement* which would include assessing the risk of fraud. These procedures will include:

- Inquiries of management and those charged with governance
- Consideration of when fraud risk factors are present
- Consideration of results of analytical procedures
- Consideration of any other relevant information

In identifying the risks of fraud, the auditor is required by ISA 240 to carry out some specific procedures.

ISA 240.17

The auditor shall make enquiries of management regarding:

(a) Management's assessment of the risk that the financial statements may be materially misstated due to fraud, including the nature, extent and frequency of such assessments;

(b) Management's process for identifying and responding to the risks of fraud in the entity, including any specific risks of fraud that management has identified or that have been brought to its attention, or classes of transactions, account balances or disclosures for which a risk of fraud is likely to exist;

(c) Management's communication, if any, to those charged with governance regarding its processes for identifying and responding to the risks of fraud in the entity; and

(d) Management's communication, if any, to employees regarding its views on business practices and ethical behaviour.

ISA 240.18

The auditor shall make enquiries of management and others within the entity as appropriate, to determine whether they have knowledge of any actual, suspected or alleged fraud affecting the entity.

ISA 240.19

For those entities that have an internal audit function, the auditor shall make enquiries of internal audit to determine whether it has knowledge of any actual, suspected or alleged fraud affecting the entity, and to obtain its views about the risks of fraud.

ISA 240.20

Unless all of those charged with governance are involved in managing the entity the auditor shall obtain an understanding of how those charged with governance exercise oversight of management's processes for identifying and responding to the risks of fraud in the entity and the internal control that management has established to mitigate these risks.

ISA 240.21

Unless all of those charged with governance are involved in managing the entity, the auditor shall make inquiries of those charged with governance to determine whether they have knowledge of any actual, suspected or alleged fraud affecting the entity. These inquiries are made in part to corroborate the responses to the inquiries of management.

ISA 240.24

The auditor shall evaluate whether the information obtained from the other risk assessment procedures and related activities performed indicates that one or more fraud risk factors are present.

The size, complexity and ownership characteristics of the entity have a significant influence on the consideration of relevant fraud risk factors. For example in the case of a large entity there may be factors that generally constrain improper conduct by management including effective oversight by those charged with governance, an effective internal audit function and a written code of conduct. These considerations are less likely in the case of a small entity.

1.3.3 Examples of fraud risk factors

ISA 240 does not attempt to provide a definitive list of risk factors but, in an appendix, identifies and gives examples of two types of fraud that are relevant to auditors:

- Fraudulent financial reporting
- Misstatements arising from misappropriation of assets

For each of these, the risk factors are classified according to three conditions that are generally present when misstatements due to fraud occur:

- Incentives/pressures
- Opportunities
- Attitudes/rationalisations

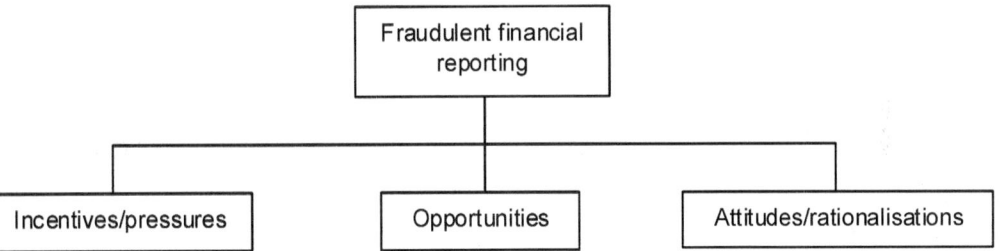

Incentives/pressures	Opportunities	Attitudes/rationalisations
• Financial stability/profitability is threatened	• Significant related party transactions	• Ineffective communication or enforcement of the entity's values or ethical standards by management
• Pressure for management to meet the expectations of third parties	• Assets, liabilities, revenues or expenses based on significant estimates	• Known history of violations of securities laws or other laws and regulations
• Personal financial situation of management threatened by the entity's financial performance	• Domination of management by a single person or small group	• A practice by management of committing to achieve aggressive or unrealistic forecasts
• Excessive pressure on management or operating personnel to meet financial targets	• Complex or unstable organisational structure	• Low morale among senior management
	• Internal control components are deficient	• Relationship between management and the current or predecessor auditor is strained

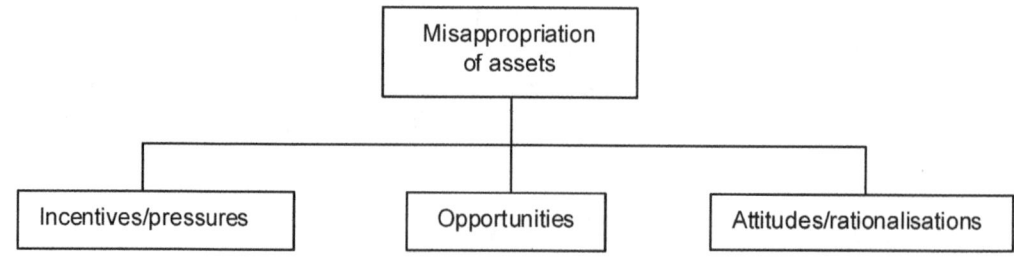

- Personal financial obligations
- Adverse relationships between the entity and employees with access to cash or other assets susceptible to theft

- Large amounts of cash on hand or processed
- Inventory items that are small in size, of high value, or in high demand
- Easily convertible assets, such as bearer bonds, diamonds, or computer chips
- Inadequate internal control over assets

- Overriding existing controls
- Failing to correct known internal control deficiencies
- Behaviour indicating displeasure or dissatisfaction with the entity
- Changes in behaviour or lifestyle

> **ISA 240.26**
>
> When identifying and assessing the risks of material misstatement due to fraud, the auditor shall, based on a presumption that there are risks of fraud in revenue recognition, evaluate which types of revenue, revenue transactions or assertions give rise to such risks.
>
> **ISA 240.27**
>
> The auditor shall treat those assessed risks of material misstatement due to fraud as significant risks and accordingly, to the extent not already done so, the auditor shall obtain an understanding of the entity's related controls, including control activities, relevant to such risks.

The auditor:

- Identifies fraud risks
- Relates this to what could go wrong at a financial statement level
- Considers the likely magnitude of potential misstatement

1.3.4 Responding to assessed risks

The auditor must then come up with responses to the assessed risks.

> **ISA 240.28**
>
> In accordance with ISA 330 the auditor shall determine overall responses to address the assessed risks of material misstatement due to fraud at the financial statement level.

In determining overall responses to address the risks of material misstatement due to fraud at the financial statement level the auditor should:

(a) Consider the assignment and supervision of personnel;

(b) Consider the accounting policies used by the entity; and

(c) Incorporate an element of unpredictability in the selection of the nature, timing and extent of audit procedures.

> **ISA 240.30**
>
> In accordance with ISA 330, the auditor shall design and perform further audit procedures whose nature, timing and extent are responsive to the assessed risks of material misstatement due to fraud at the assertion level.

The auditor may have to **amend** the **nature, timing or extent** of planned audit procedures to address assessed risks. The auditor should also consider the following:

- Audit procedures responsive to management override of controls
- Journal entries and other adjustments
- Accounting estimates
- Business rationale for significant transactions

1.3.5 Examples: specific audit procedures

The auditor might to choose to attend previously unvisited branches to carry out procedures on inventory or cash.

The auditor might perform detailed analytical procedures using disaggregated data, for example, comparing sales and costs of sales by location.

The auditor might use an expert to assess management estimates in a subjective area.

1.4 Evaluation of audit evidence

The auditor evaluates the audit evidence obtained to ensure it is consistent and that it achieves its aim of answering the risks of fraud. This will include a consideration of results of analytical procedures and other misstatements found. The auditor must also consider the reliability of management representations.

The auditor must obtain written representation that management accepts its responsibility for the prevention and detection of fraud and has made all relevant disclosures to the auditors.

1.5 Documentation

The auditor must document:

- The significant decisions as a result of the team's discussion of fraud
- The identified and assessed risks of material misstatement due to fraud
- The overall responses to assessed risks
- Results of specific audit tests
- Any communications with management
- Reasons for concluding that the presumption that there is a risk of fraud related to revenue recognition is not applicable

1.6 Reporting

There are various reporting requirements in ISA 240.

> **ISA 240.40**
>
> If the auditor has identified a fraud or has obtained information that indicates a fraud may exist, the auditor should communicate these matters, unless prohibited by law or regulation, on a timely basis with the appropriate level of management in order to inform those with primary responsibility for the prevention and detection of fraud of matters relevant to their responsibilities.

> **ISA 240.41**
>
> Unless all of those charged with governance are involved in managing the entity, if the auditor has identified fraud involving:
>
> (a) Management;
> (b) Employees who have significant roles in internal control; or
> (c) Others, where the fraud results in a material misstatement in the financial statements.
>
> the auditor should communicate these matters with **those charged with governance** on a timely basis.

The auditor should also make relevant parties within the entity aware of material weaknesses in the design or implementation of controls to prevent and detect fraud which has come to the auditor's attention, and consider whether there are any other relevant matters to bring to the attention of those charged with governance with regard to fraud.

The auditor may have a **duty** under law, regulation or ethical requirements to report fraudulent behaviour to **an appropriate authority** outside the entity. If no such duty arises, the auditor must consider whether reporting would breach their **professional duty of confidence**. In either event, the auditor should take **legal advice**.

Exam focus point

Remember your confidentiality checklist from Chapter 4. When you are considering whether to make a public interest disclosure, you should always bear it in mind.

1.7 Auditor unable to continue

The auditor should consider the need to withdraw from the engagement if he uncovers exceptional circumstances with regard to fraud.

> RPQ students should be aware that ISA (UK) 240 was revised in May 2021 and then updated again in May 2022. The 2021 updates address recent concerns that auditors are not doing enough to detect material fraud in financial statements following some high profile audit failures. They also respond to the recommendations of the Brydon Report which we covered in Chapter 3.
>
> ISA (UK) 240 provides additional clarification of certain matters and places a number of extra requirements on auditors in comparison to the version of ISA 240 issued by the IAASB. These include, but are not limited to, the following.
>
> - Assessing whether fraud is material needs to take into account qualitative as well as quantitative factors.
> - Clarifying and emphasising the objectives of the auditor.
> - Additional professional skepticism requirements including the need to be alert that documents may not be authentic.
> - Specifying particular matters to include in the discussion amongst the engagement team.
> - Risk assessment procedures must include obtaining a understanding of relevant fraud risk factors.
> - Auditors being required to make inquiries with the person at the audit client responsible for dealing with allegations of fraud.
> - Auditors must determine whether specialised skills or knowledge is required for risk assessment, performing audit procedures and evaluation of audit evidence.
> - Emphasising that the auditor needs to comply with ISA 540 with regards to possible management bias in accounting estimates.

- Prior to the conclusion of the audit, auditors must evaluate whether the assessments of the risks of material misstatement at the assertion level due to fraud remain appropriate.
- Prior to the conclusion of the audit, auditors must evaluate whether sufficient appropriate audit evidence has been obtained regarding the assessed risks of material misstatement due to fraud, and conclude whether, the financial statements are materially misstated as a result of fraud.
- Clarifying the auditor's report must contain an explanation of to what extent the audit was capable of detecting fraud (specific to that audit client).
- Extra documentation requirements relating to how auditors address any identified inconsistencies.

The 2022 update included conforming amendments from ISA (UK) 315 (Revised July 2020).

Question — Detection of fraud

Required

(a) Discuss what responsibility auditors have to detect fraud.
(b) Explain how the auditors might conduct their audit in response to an assessed risk of:
   (i) Misappropriation
   (ii) Fraudulent financial reporting

Answer

(a) The primary responsibility for the prevention and detection of fraud and irregularities rests with management and those charged with governance. This responsibility may be partly discharged by the institution of an adequate system of internal control including, for example, authorisation controls and controls covering segregation of duties.

The auditors should recognise the possibility of material irregularities or frauds which could, unless adequately disclosed, distort the results or state of affairs shown by the financial statements. ISA 240 states that the auditor is responsible for obtaining reasonable assurance that the financial statements taken as a whole are free from material misstatement whether caused by fraud or error. Auditors are required to carry out their audit with professional scepticism.

Auditors are required to carry out risk assessment procedures in respect of fraud. This will involve making enquiries of management, considering if any risk factors (such as the existence of pressure for management to meet certain targets) are present and to consider the results of analytical procedures if any method or unexpected relationships have been identified.

If these is an assessed risk of fraud, the auditor must make suitable responses. Overall responses include considering the personnel for the assignment (for example, using more experienced personnel), considering the accounting policies used by the entity (have they changed? are they reasonable?) and incorporating an element of unpredictability into the audit.

Specific responses to the risk of misstatement at the assertion level due to fraud will vary depending on the circumstances but could include:

(i) Changing the nature of audit tests (for example, introducing an automated tools and technique (ATT) such as data analytics, if more detail is required about a computerised system)

(ii) Changing the timing of audit tests (for example, testing throughout an audit period, instead of extending audit conclusions from an interim audit)

(iii) Changing the extent of audit tests (for example, increasing sample sizes)

(b) (i) **Misappropriation**

Employee frauds such as misappropriation are likely to take place when controls are weak. If controls are weak, auditors may not test controls and hence evidence of employee fraud might go undetected. However, if auditors have identified a risk of employee fraud, they might as a response test controls in the relevant area (such as purchases or sales) in order to identify any unexplained patterns in the company's procedures. For example, if a purchase fraud is suspected, auditors might scrutinise authorisation controls to see if a particular member of staff always authorises certain items/for certain people, where the system does not require that.

Many substantive procedures normally performed by the auditors may assist in isolating employee frauds if they are occurring. For example, tests performed on the receivables ledger may be aimed at revealing overstatement or irrecoverable receivables, but the design of such tests also assists with cash understatement objectives and may reveal irregularities such as 'teeming and lading'.

(ii) **Fraudulent financial reporting**

If the auditors conclude that there is a high risk of fraudulent financial reporting by management they will concentrate on techniques such as analytical procedures, scrutiny of unusual transactions and all journal entries, review of events after the reporting period (including going concern evaluation), and review of the financial statements and accounting policies for any changes or material distortions.

2 Laws and regulations

FAST FORWARD

Non-compliance with laws and regulations may have a direct effect on the financial statements or be fundamental to the operations of the business. Auditors must be aware whether laws, regulation or ethical requirements require the auditor to report identified or suspected non-compliance.

2.1 Legal requirements relating to the company

Companies are increasingly subject to laws and regulations with which they must comply. Some examples are given in the following diagram.

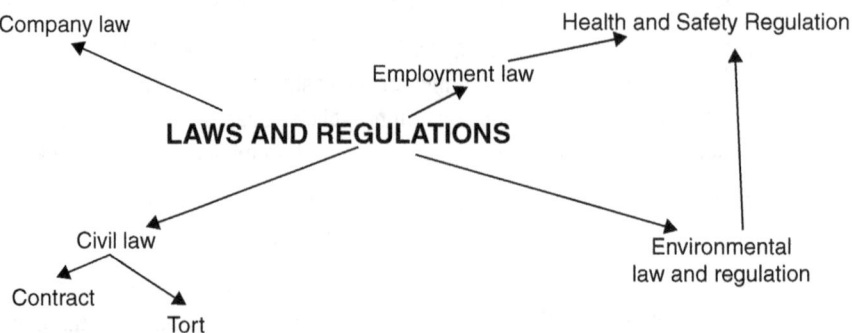

An auditor must be aware of the effect that non-compliance with the laws and regulations would have on the financial statements.

ISA 250 *Consideration of laws and regulations in an audit of financial statements* provides guidance on the auditor's responsibility to consider laws and regulations in an audit of financial statements.

2.2 Responsibility of management for compliance

It is the responsibility of management (with oversight from those charged with governance) to ensure a client's operations are conducted in accordance with laws and regulations.

The following policies and procedures, among others, may be implemented to assist management in the prevention and detection of non-compliance with laws and regulations.

- **Monitor legal requirements** and ensure that operating procedures are designed to meet these requirements.
- **Institute and operate** appropriate systems of **internal control** including internal audit and an audit committee.
- **Develop, publicise and follow a code of conduct**.
- Ensure **employees** are properly **trained** and **understand the code of conduct**.
- **Monitor compliance** with the code of conduct and act appropriately to **discipline** employees who fail to comply with it.
- **Engage legal advisors** to assist in monitoring legal requirements.
- **Maintain a register** of significant laws with which the entity has to comply within its particular industry and a record of complaints.

'**Non-compliance**' refers to acts of omission or commission, intentional or unintentional, committed by the entity, or by those charged with governance, by management or by other individuals working for or under the direction of the entity which are contrary to the prevailing laws or regulations. It does **not** include personal misconduct.

2.3 Responsibility of the auditor

As with fraud and error, the auditor is not, and cannot be held responsible for preventing non-compliance. There is an unavoidable risk that some material misstatements in the financial statements go undetected, even though the audit is properly planned and performed.

Certain factors will increase the risk of material misstatements due to non-compliance with laws and regulations not being detected by the auditor.

(a) There are many laws and regulations, relating principally to the operating aspects of an entity, that typically do **not affect the financial statements** and are not captured by the entity's information systems relevant to financial reporting.

(b) Non-compliance may involve conduct **designed to conceal** it, such as collusion, forgery, deliberate failure to record transactions, management override of controls or intentional misrepresentations being made to the auditor.

(c) Whether an act constitutes non-compliance is ultimately a matter to be determined by a court or other appropriate adjudicative body.

Laws and regulations governing a business entity can vary enormously (financial disclosure rules, health and safety, pollution, employment, etc). Whether an act constitutes non-compliance is a matter to be determined by a court or other appropriate adjudicative body which is ordinarily beyond the auditor's professional competence to determine. Nevertheless, the auditor may have a fair idea in many cases through his knowledge and training.

The further removed non-compliance is from the events and transactions normally reflected in the financial statements, the less likely the auditor is to become aware of it or recognise non-compliance.

> **ISA 250.11**
>
> The objectives of the auditor are:
>
> (a) To obtain sufficient appropriate audit evidence regarding compliance with the provisions of those laws and regulations generally recognised to have a direct effect on the determination of material amounts and disclosures in the financial statements;
>
> (b) To perform specified audit procedures to help identify instances of non-compliance with other laws and regulations that may have a material effect on the financial statements; and
>
> (c) To respond appropriately to identified or suspected non-compliance with laws and regulations identified during the audit.

2.4 The auditor's consideration of compliance

> **ISA 250.13**
>
> As part of obtaining an understanding of the entity and its environment in accordance with ISA 315 (Revised 2019), the auditor shall obtain a general understanding of:
>
> (a) The legal and regulatory framework applicable to the entity and the industry or sector in which the entity operates; and
>
> (b) How the entity is complying with that framework.

The auditor may obtain a general understanding of laws and regulations affecting the entity in the following ways.

- **Use the auditor's existing understanding** of the entity's industry, regulatory and other external factors.

- **Update the understanding** of those laws and regulations that **directly** determine the reported amounts and disclosures in the financial statements.

- **Enquire of management** as to other laws or regulations that may be expected to have a fundamental effect on the operations of the entity.

- **Enquire of management** concerning the entity's **policies and procedures** regarding compliance with laws and regulations.

- **Enquire of management** the **policies or procedures** adopted for identifying, evaluating and accounting for **litigation claims**.

The auditor should obtain sufficient appropriate audit evidence of compliance with those **laws and regulations which have a direct effect on the determination of material amounts** and disclosures in the financial statements. These laws and regulations will be well-established, known to the entity and within the entity's industry and be relevant to the entity's financial statements. They could relate to the following:

- The form and content of financial statements
- Industry specific financial reporting issues
- Accounting for transactions under government contracts
- The accrual or recognition of expenses for income tax or pension costs

Non-compliance with laws and regulations that have a **fundamental effect** on the operations of the entity, may cause the entity to cease operations or call into question the entity's continuance as a going concern. For example, non-compliance with the requirements of the entity's licence or other title to perform its operations could have such an impact (eg for a bank, non-compliance with capital or investment requirements).

15: FRAUD AND NON COMPLIANCE WITH REGULATIONS

> **ISA 250.15**
>
> The auditor shall perform the following audit procedures to help identify instances of non-compliance with **other laws and regulations that may have a material effect** on the financial statements:
>
> (a) Inquiring of management and, where appropriate, those charged with governance, as to whether the entity is in compliance with such laws and regulations; and
>
> (b) Inspecting correspondence, if any, with the relevant licensing or regulatory authorities.
>
> **ISA 250.16**
>
> During the audit, the auditor shall remain alert to the possibility that other audit procedures applied may bring instances of non-compliance or suspected non-compliance with laws and regulations to the auditor's attention.

Examples include the following.

- Reading minutes
- Enquiring of the entity's management and in-house legal counsel or external legal counsel concerning litigation, claims and assessments
- Performing substantive tests of details of classes of transactions, account balances or disclosures

> **ISA 250.17**
>
> The auditor shall request management and, where appropriate, those charged with governance to provide written representations that all known instances of non-compliance or suspected non-compliance with laws and regulations whose effects should be considered when preparing financial statements have been disclosed to the auditor.

In the absence of identified or suspected non-compliance, the auditor is not required to perform audit procedures other than those detailed above.

2.5 Audit procedures when non-compliance is identified or suspected

> **ISA 250.19**
>
> If the auditor becomes aware of information concerning an instance of non-compliance or suspected non-compliance with laws and regulations, the auditor shall obtain:
>
> (a) An understanding of the nature of the act and the circumstances in which it has occurred; and
> (b) Further information to evaluate the possible effect on the financial statements.

The ISA sets out examples of the type of information that might come to the auditor's attention that may indicate non-compliance.

- Investigation by a regulatory organisation or government department or payment of fines or penalties
- Payments for unspecified services or loans to consultants, related parties, employees or government employees
- Sales commissions or agents' fees that appear excessive in relation to those normally paid by the entity or in its industry or to the services actually received
- Purchasing at prices significantly above or below market price
- Unusual payments in cash, purchases in the form of cashiers' cheques payable to bearer or transfers to numbered bank accounts

- Unusual transactions with companies registered in tax havens
- Payments for goods or services made other than to the country from which the goods or services originated
- Payments without proper exchange control documentation
- Existence of an information system that fails, whether by design or by accident, to provide an adequate audit trail or sufficient evidence
- Unauthorised transactions or improperly recorded transactions
- Adverse media comment
- Information from a whistle blower

When evaluating the possible effect on the financial statements, the auditor should consider the following.

- The **potential financial consequences**, such as fines, penalties, damages, threat of expropriation of assets, enforced discontinuation of operations and litigation.
- Whether the **potential financial consequences** require **disclosure**.
- Whether the potential financial consequences are so serious as to call into question the **fair presentation** given by the financial statements, or otherwise make the financial statements misleading.

> **ISA 250.20**
>
> If the auditor suspects there may be non-compliance, the auditor shall discuss the matter, unless prohibited by law or regulation, with the appropriate level of management and, where appropriate, those charged with governance.

Such discussions are subject to the laws concerning 'tipping off'. In some jurisdictions, law or regulation may restrict the auditor's communication of certain matters with management and those charged with governance. In these circumstances, the issues considered by the auditor may be complex and the auditor may consider it appropriate to obtain legal advice.

If information provided by management is not sufficient, the auditor may find it appropriate to consult the entity's lawyer and, if necessary, his own lawyer on the application of the laws and regulations to the particular circumstances.

> **ISA 250.21/22**
>
> If sufficient information about suspected non-compliance cannot be obtained, the auditor shall evaluate the effect of the lack of sufficient appropriate audit evidence on the auditor's opinion
>
> The auditor shall evaluate the implications of identified or suspected non-compliance in relation to other aspects of the audit, including the auditor's risk assessment and the reliability of written representations, and take appropriate action.

On this last point, as with fraud and error, the auditor must evaluate the implication of identified or suspected non-compliance in relation to other aspects of the audit, including the auditor's risk assessment and the reliability of written representations. The implications of identified or suspected non-compliance will depend on the level of management or individuals involved and the relationship of the perpetration and concealment, if any, of the act to specific control activities.

Examples of circumstances that may cause the auditor to evaluate the implications of identified or suspected non-compliance on the reliability of written representations received from management and, where applicable, those charged with governance include the following.

- The auditor suspects or has evidence of the involvement or intended involvement of management and, where applicable, those charged with governance in any identified or suspected non-compliance.
- The auditor is aware that management and, where applicable, those charged with governance have knowledge of such non-compliance and, contrary to legal or regulatory requirements, have not reported, or authorised reporting of, the matter to an appropriate authority within a reasonable period.

In certain circumstances, the auditor may consider that withdrawing from the engagement is necessary (where permitted by law or regulation). It may be appropriate for the auditor to seek legal advice to determine if withdrawal is appropriate.

2.6 Communicating and reporting identified or suspected non-compliance

2.6.1 With those charged with governance

> **ISA 250.23/24/25**
>
> ...the auditor shall communicate, unless prohibited by law and regulation, with those charged with governance matters involving non-compliance with laws and regulations that come to the auditor's attention during the course of the audit, other than when the matters are clearly inconsequential.
>
> If, in the auditor's judgement, the non-compliance... is believed to be intentional and material, the auditor shall communicate the matter with those charged with governance as soon as practicable.
>
> If the auditor suspects that management or those charged with governance are involved in non-compliance, the auditor shall communicate the matter to the next higher level of authority at the entity, if it exists, such as an audit committee or supervisory board.

In relation to the last point, where no higher authority exists, or if the auditor believes that the communication may not be acted upon or is unsure as to the person to whom to report, the auditor shall consider seeking legal advice.

2.6.2 To the users of the auditor's report

> **ISA 250.26/27/28**
>
> If the auditor concludes that the identified or suspected non-compliance has a material effect on the financial statements and has not been adequately reflected in the financial statements, the auditor shall... express a qualified opinion or an adverse opinion on the financial statements.
>
> If the auditor is precluded by management or those charged with governance from obtaining sufficient appropriate audit evidence to evaluate whether non-compliance that may be material to the financial statements has, or is likely to have, occurred, the auditor shall express a qualified opinion or disclaim an opinion on the financial statements on the basis of a limitation on the scope of the audit...
>
> If the auditor is unable to determine whether non-compliance has occurred because of limitations imposed by the circumstances rather than by management or those charged with governance, the auditor shall evaluate the effect on the auditor's opinion...

2.6.3 To an appropriate authority outside the entity

Reporting identified or suspected non-compliance with laws and regulations to an appropriate authority outside the entity may be required or appropriate due to one of the following factors.

(a) Law, regulation or relevant ethical requirements require the auditor to report.
(b) The auditor has determined reporting is an appropriate action to respond to identified or suspected non-compliance in accordance with relevant ethical requirements.
(c) Law, regulation or relevant ethical requirements provide the auditor with the right to do so.

The determination of whether to report may involve complex considerations and professional judgements. Accordingly the auditor may consider consulting internally (eg within the firm or a network firm) or on a confidential basis with a regulator or professional body (unless doing so is prohibited by law or regulation or would breach the duty of confidentiality). The auditor may also consider obtaining legal advice to understand the auditor's options and the professional or legal implications of taking any particular course of action.

In other circumstances, the reporting of identified or suspected non-compliance with laws and regulations to an appropriate authority outside the entity may be precluded by the auditor's duty of confidentiality.

2.7 Documentation

The auditor must include the following in the audit documentation.

- Identified or suspected non-compliance with laws and regulations
- The audit procedures performed, the significant professional judgements made and the conclusions reached thereon
- The discussions of significant matters related to the non-compliance with management, those charged with governance and others, including how management and, where applicable, those charged with governance have responded to the matter

2.8 Practical problems with ISA 250

2.8.1 Distinction between types of law

The most difficult distinction in practice is between:

- Laws which have a **direct effect** on the determination of material amounts in the financial statements
- Other laws and regulations

In practice:

(a) For some business, certain laws and regulations have a direct effect on material amounts in the financial statements, for other businesses the **same** laws and regulations will not.

(b) For some businesses, laws and regulations which did not have a direct or material effect last year may have this year, (for example, where the maximum penalty for a first offence is a warning, but subsequent infringements may lead to closure of the business).

2.8.2 Procedures that should be performed

There is a distinction between checking systems of compliance and checking actual compliance. An example would be emissions from a chemical factory; auditors would review the company's systems for keeping these under control, and would also review correspondence with the environmental authority. However, the auditors would not be expected to check the actual emissions.

2.9 ISA (UK) 250 Section B

For RPQ students, UK auditors are required to comply with the requirements of an additional ISA: ISA (UK) 250B *The auditor's statutory right and duty to report to regulators of public interest entities and regulators of other entities in the financial sector.*

ISA (UK) 250B deals with the circumstances in which the auditor of an entity subject to statutory regulation (a regulated entity) is required to report directly to a regulator information which comes to the auditor's attention in the course of the work undertaken in the auditor's capacity as auditor of the regulated entity. Regulated entities are defined as entities carrying on business in the financial sector that are subject to statutory regulation or public interest entities (PIEs).

All staff involved in the audit of a regulated entity are required to have an understanding of the applicable statutory or regulatory requirements. If a breach of these requirements becomes apparent to the auditor, the auditors may have a **statutory duty** or **legal right** to report directly to the regulators.

Auditors have a statutory duty to report directly to the regulator	Auditors have a legal right to report directly to the regulator
Report to the regulator information concerning a PIE of which the auditor has become aware while carrying out the audit and which may bring about: • A material breach of the laws, regulations or administrative provisions which lay down, where appropriate, the conditions governing authorisation or which specifically govern pursuit of the activities of the PIE • A material threat or doubt concerning the continuous functioning of the PIE • A refusal to issue an audit opinion on the financial statements or the issuing of an adverse or qualified opinion	Where there is not a statutory duty to report, but the matter may be relevant to the regulator's exercise of its functions.
Do not inform those charged with governance of the report to the regulator if there is doubt about their integrity.	Consider whether the matter should be brought to the attention of the regulator under the terms of the appropriate legal provisions enabling the auditor to report direct to the regulator, and, if so advise those charged with governance that in the auditor's opinion the matter should be drawn to the regulators' attention.

The report to the regulator shall include the following.

- Name of the regulated entity concerned
- The statutory power under which the report is made
- A statement that the report has been prepared in accordance with ISA (UK) 250 Section B
- A description of the context in which the report is given
- A description of the matter giving rise to the report
- A request that the regulator confirms the report has been received
- The name of the auditor and the date of the written report
- If relevant, the date on which an oral report was made to the regulator and the name and title of the individual to whom the oral report was made

Chapter Roundup

- Auditors **do not have a responsibility to prevent and detect fraud**, but must consider whether it has caused misstatements in the financial statements.

- Non-compliance with laws and regulations may have a direct effect on the financial statements or be fundamental to the operations of the business. Auditors must be aware whether laws, regulation or ethical requirements require the auditor to report identified or suspected non-compliance.

Quick Quiz

1. Define fraud.

2. Draw a table showing the reporting requirements of ISA 240.

3. Name four areas of law which might affect a company.

    (1) ....

    (2) ....

    (3) ....

    (4) ....

4. It is the responsibility of the auditor to ensure a client's operations are conducted in accordance with laws and regulations.

    True ☐
    False ☐

5. Name three conditions generally present when misstatements due to fraud occur.

    (1) ....

    (2) ....

    (3) ....

6. Non-compliance with laws or regulations must always be reported to an authority outside the entity by the auditor.

    True ☐
    False ☐

Answers to Quick Quiz

1. Fraud is the use of deception to obtain unjust or illegal financial advantage and intentional misrepresentation by management, employees or third parties.

2. **Reporting Requirements of ISA 240**

    Management — If the auditors suspect or detect any fraud (even if immaterial) or if a material error is discovered, as soon as they can, they should tell management.

    Those charged with governance — If the auditor has identified fraud involving management, employees with significant roles in internal control, or others, if it results in a material misstatement, they must report it to those charged with governance.

    Third parties — Auditors may have a statutory duty to report to a regulator.

    Auditors should take legal advice if reporting externally to the company.

3. From:
    - (1) Company law
    - (2) Contract law
    - (3) Tort law
    - (4) Employment law
    - (5) Environmental law

4. False – it is the responsibility of management (with oversight from those charged with governance).

5. (1) Incentives/pressures
   (2) Opportunities
   (3) Attitudes/rationalisations

6. False.

End of Chapter Question

Bulldoze (AIA November 2007)

You are the external auditor of Bulldoze, a large construction company. You have received a letter from Bulldoze's legal advisers warning you that the company's board is considering taking legal action for the recovery of costs associated with an alleged fraud.

During the year ended 31 December 20X6, Bulldoze took delivery of eight very large and expensive earth-moving machines. These were standard models that had been manufactured by the world's largest manufacturer of such equipment. The manufacturer sells its equipment through a worldwide network of third party dealers. The dealer who supplied the equipment was selected by Bulldoze's production director. The production director signed the contract for the machines on behalf of Bulldoze.

The audit opinion for the year ended 31 December 20X6 was unmodified and the management letter did not refer to any serious problems with the systems of internal control. The auditor's report was signed in March 20X7 and your firm was reappointed for the year ended 31 December 20X7.

In June 20X7 Bulldoze received an anonymous letter from someone who claimed to be employed in the sales office of the dealer that had supplied the machines. The letter stated that the selling price of the eight machines had been overstated by 10%. Bulldoze's production director had asked the dealer's managing director to supply paperwork, including a sales invoice, which showed an inflated price. The dealer invoiced this overstated price and Bulldoze paid the invoice in full. The dealer's managing director then arranged for half of the additional 10% to be paid directly to Bulldoze's production director as a gift. The anonymous letter was supported by copies of the emails between the production director and the dealer's managing director.

Bulldoze's production director admitted the accusation when he was confronted with the evidence. He resigned immediately, but was unable to repay any of the overpayment for the machines. The dealer has refused to repay anything to Bulldoze.

Bulldoze's lawyers have asked that your audit firm repay the 10% overpayment on the grounds that the amount involved is material and that the financial statements did not give a fair presentation. They also allege that the overpayment should have been detected in the course of the audit and that the company should have been notified in the management letter.

According to the audit working papers, the acquisition of the equipment was checked as part of the audit of non-current assets. A member of the audit team agreed the debit to the equipment at cost account to the purchase invoice. This had been passed for payment by the production director. The details on the invoice agreed to a written purchase order which had been signed by the production director on behalf of the company. The decision to purchase the equipment had also been noted in the board minutes.

Required

(a) Explain whether the auditor was negligent in the above circumstances. **(12 marks)**

(b) Explain how a company might protect itself from a fraud of this type when buying large items of capital equipment. **(8 marks)**

(Total 20 marks)

PART C AUDIT STRATEGY, PROCESS AND REPORTING

Using the work of others

Topic list	Syllabus reference
1 Using the work of internal audit	LO1
2 Using the work of an auditor's expert	LO1

Introduction

In this Learning & Practice Workbook, we have already considered the use of the work of other auditors in a group situation, and when a company outsources aspects of its accounting function. Now we shall revise two topics you covered in your earlier studies, using the work of internal audit, and using an auditor's expert.

PART C AUDIT STRATEGY, PROCESS AND REPORTING

1 Using the work of internal audit

FAST FORWARD

External auditors may make use of internal audit work or the internal auditors themselves when carrying out external audit procedures.

ISA 610 *Using the work of internal auditors* applies when the external auditor expects to be able to use the work of internal audit as part of the external audit on the basis of their understanding of the internal audit function obtained as part of their procedures under ISA 315 (Revised 2019). It follows, of course, that where the company does not have an internal audit function, this ISA does not apply.

While the external auditor has sole responsibility for the opinion expressed, some internal auditor work may be helpful in obtaining audit evidence to form a decision on the truth and fairness of the financial statements. An effective internal audit (IA) function may reduce, modify or alter the timing of external audit procedures, but it can **never** eliminate them entirely. Even where the IA function is deemed ineffective, it may still be useful to be aware of the IA conclusions. The effectiveness of IA will have a great impact on how the external auditors assess the whole system of internal control and the assessment of audit risk.

> **ISA 610.13**
>
> 'The objectives of the auditor when he expects to be able to use the work of internal audit are:
>
> (a) To determine whether the work of the internal audit function or direct assistance from internal auditors can be used, and if so, in which areas and to what extent; and having made that determination:
>
> (b) If using the work of the internal audit function, to determine whether that work is adequate for purposes of the audit; and
>
> (c) If using internal auditors to provide direct assistance, to appropriately direct, supervise and review their work.'

1.1 Whether the work of internal audit can be used

1.1.1 Evaluating the internal audit function

The following will be evaluated by the external auditors in determining whether the work of internal audit can be used

Evaluation of internal audit	
Objectivity of the internal audit function	Consider **status** of internal audit function within the entity, **to whom** internal audit **reports** (should be the board), whether internal audit has any **conflicting responsibilities** and constraints or restrictions on it, extent to which **management acts** on recommendations.
Technical competence	Consider whether internal auditors have adequate **technical training** and proficiency, whether they are members of relevant **professional bodies**. Consider whether the function is **suitably resourced** and there are established policies for hiring, training and assigning internal auditors.
Systematic and disciplined approach	Consider whether internal audit is **properly planned**, **supervised**, **reviewed** and **documented**, existence and adequacy of **audit manuals**, **work programmes and documentation** and **quality management policies and procedures**.

The ISA states that if these determinations conclude that:

- IA's organisational status does not support the objectivity of the function
- IA is not sufficiently competent
- There is not a systematic and disciplined approach including quality management

Then the external auditor should not use the work of the internal audit function.

1.1.2 Nature and extent of work that can be used

The auditor should consider the nature and scope of specific work that has been or will be performed by IA. Examples of types of work that the external auditor might use are:

- Testing of the operating effectiveness of controls
- Substantive procedures involving limited judgement
- Observations of inventory counts
- Tracing transactions through the information system relevant to financial reporting
- Testing of compliance with regulatory requirements
- The auditor must also consider assessed audit risks of material misstatement for relevant classes of transaction/balances/disclosures (as the greater the risk, the less the external auditor should rely on IA work and the more directly involved in the audit work the external auditors should be)

If the external auditors are planning to use the work of the internal auditors, there are certain things that can be usefully agreed in advance, such as timing, extent of testing, materiality, sampling methods, documentation and reporting methods.

The external auditor needs to communicate with those charged with governance how the external auditor has planned to use the work of the internal audit function.

1.2 Using the work of the internal audit function

The auditor shall:

- Discuss the planned use of IA's with IA to coordinate their work (this will involve discussion of matters such as timing, materiality, sample sizes)
- Read IA reports relating to the work to be used to obtain an understanding of the nature and extent of procedures and the related findings
- Perform audit procedures on the work to assess its adequacy
- Evaluate the work carried out
- Evaluate whether the preliminary conclusions about whether the work of IA can be used are still valid

1.2.1 Audit procedures

The external auditor's audit procedures must include some reperformance of IA work. Examples of other audit tests might be:

- Examining other similar items for the purpose of comparison
- Observing internal audit carrying out their work

1.2.2 Evaluating internal audit work

Relevant questions for the external auditors to ask are:

- Is the work properly supervised, reviewed and documented?
- Has sufficient, appropriate audit evidence been obtained to afford a reasonable basis for the conclusions reached?
- Are the conclusions reached appropriate given the circumstances?

- Are the reports produce consistent with the result of work performed?
- Have any unusual matters or exceptions arising and disclosed by internal audit been resolved properly?

The auditors should consider whether the determinations made about the suitability of using internal audit work remain valid throughout the audit.

1.3 Using internal auditors for direct assistance

Key term

> **Direct assistance** is the use of internal auditors to perform audit procedures under the direction, supervision and review of the external auditor.

This is distinguished from using the work of the internal auditor, as that is using work already carried out in the course of the internal auditors' normal work. Direct assistance is co-opting internal auditors to do external audit work, as directed by the external auditors.

1.3.1 Whether internal auditors can be used in direct assistance

The three key issues are:

- Whether the external auditors are **legally entitled** to use internal auditors to directly assist the external audit
- Whether the internal auditors have sufficient **objectivity**
- Whether the internal auditors have sufficient **competence**

Objectivity would generally be determined by enquiry, and by knowledge of the systems in place at the client.

1.3.2 What work internal auditors can directly assist

> **ISA 610.29**
>
> 'The external auditor shall consider:
>
> (a) The amount of judgement involved in:
>
>   (i) Planning and performing relevant audit procedures; and
>   (ii) Evaluating the audit evidence gathered;
>
> (b) The assessed risk of material misstatement; and
>
> (c) The external auditor's evaluation of the existence and significance of threats to the objectivity and level of competence of the internal auditors who will be providing such assistance.'

Internal auditors should not assist with work that includes significant judgements or relates to higher assessed risk, or any work that would involve self-review.

1.3.3 Communication and quality management

The auditors will communicate with those charged with governance about direct assistance, in accordance with ISA 260, to ensure that all parties understand what is happening and are happy with the arrangement.

The external auditors will obtain written agreements from:

- Those charged with governance: that they will allow internal auditors to do this work for the external auditors and will not intervene in it.
- The internal auditors involved: that they will keep specific matters confidential as indicated by the external auditors and will advise the external auditors about any threats to objectivity.

The external auditors will direct, supervise and review the work of the internal auditors in direct assistance in accordance with the requirements of ISA 220. The review shall include the external auditor checking back to underlying audit evidence relating to some of the work done by the internal auditors.

1.4 Documentation

> **ISA 610.36**
>
> If the external auditor uses the work of the internal audit function, the external auditor shall include in the audit documentation:
>
> (a) The evaluation of:
>
>   (i) Whether the function's organizational status and relevant policies and procedures adequately support the objectivity of the internal auditors;
>
>   (ii) The level of competence of the function; and
>
>   (iii) Whether the function applies a systematic and disciplined approach, including quality management;
>
> (b) The nature and extent of the work used and the basis for that decision; and
>
> (c) The audit procedures performed by the external auditor to evaluate the adequacy of the work used.
>
> **ISA 610.37**
>
> If the external auditor uses internal auditors to provide direct assistance on the audit, the external auditor shall include in the audit documentation:
>
> (a) The evaluation of the existence and significance of threats to the objectivity of the internal auditors, and the level of competence of the internal auditors used to provide direct assistance;
>
> (b) The basis for the decision regarding the nature and extent of the work performed by the internal auditors;
>
> (c) Who reviewed the work performed and the date and extent of that review in accordance with ISA 230;
>
> (d) The written agreements obtained from an authorized representative of the entity and the internal auditors under paragraph 33 of this ISA; and
>
> (e) The working papers prepared by the internal auditors who provided direct assistance on the audit engagement.

Exam focus point

RPQ students should be aware that the UK has adopted this revised ISA, but that ISA 610 (UK) contains a paragraph (5.1) which clearly states that the use of internal auditors to provide direct assistance is prohibited in an audit conducted in accordance with ISAs (UK). Hence in the UK, the first bullet in Section 1.3.1 will never be met.

1.5 Impact on the auditor's report

If the external auditors feel that their own work and the work of the internal audit function gives them sufficient audit evidence to draw audit conclusions, they should draw those conclusions (if not, they should extend their tests). The auditors' responsibility for the audit opinion is their own, and they should not refer to the fact that they have used the work of the internal audit function in their report.

2 Using the work of an auditor's expert

> **FAST FORWARD**
> External auditors may make use of the work of an auditor's expert when carrying out audit procedures.

2.1 Experts

Key terms

> An **auditor's expert** is an individual or organisation possessing expertise in a field other than accounting and auditing, whose work in that field is used by the auditor to assist the auditor in obtaining sufficient appropriate audit evidence. An auditor's expert may be either an auditor's internal expert (who is a partner or staff, including temporary staff, of the auditor's firm or a network firm), or an auditor's external expert.
>
> A **management's expert** is an individual or organisation possessing expertise in a field other than accounting or auditing, whose work in that field is used by the entity to assist the entity in preparing the financial statements.

Professional audit staff are highly trained and educated, but their experience and training is limited to accountancy and audit matters. In certain situations it will therefore be necessary to employ someone else with different expert knowledge.

Auditors have **sole responsibility** for their opinion, but may use the work of an auditor's expert if they deem it necessary to obtain sufficient appropriate audit evidence.

ISA 620 *Using the work of an auditor's expert* does not deal with situations where the engagement team includes a member, or consults an individual or organisation, with expertise in a specialised area of accounting or auditing, (which are dealt with in ISA 220); or the auditor's use of the work of an individual or organisation possessing expertise in a field other than accounting or auditing, whose work in that field is used by the entity to assist the entity in preparing the financial statements (ie a **management's expert**, which is dealt with in ISA 500 *Audit evidence*).

ISA 620 states that the auditor needs to determine whether it is necessary to obtain the work of an auditor's expert to obtain sufficient appropriate audit evidence, and then to determine whether that auditor's expert's work is appropriate for audit purposes.

2.2 Determining the need to use the work of an auditor's expert

When considering whether to use the work of an auditor's expert, the auditors should review:

- Whether management has used a management's expert in preparing the financial statements
- The nature and significance of the matter, including its complexity
- The risks of material misstatement in the matter
- The expected nature of procedures to respond to identified risks, including: the auditor's knowledge of and experience with the work of experts in relation to such matters; and the availability of alternative sources of audit evidence

2.3 Nature, extent and timing of audit procedures

The auditor will use his audit judgement to determine the level of audit procedures required on the auditor's expert's work in order to draw audit conclusions. Relevant factors will be:

- The nature of the matter concerning which the auditor's expert is providing expertise
- The risk of material misstatement
- The significance of the auditor's expert's work in the context of the audit

- The auditor's knowledge of an experience with previous work by the auditor's expert
- Whether the auditor's expert is subject to the same quality management requirements as the audit team

The auditor has to assess the competence of the auditor's expert, understand his field of work, agree the scope of the work for the purposes of audit and evaluate the adequacy of that work when it has been completed.

2.3.1 Competence and objectivity of the auditor's expert

The auditor shall evaluate whether the auditor's expert has the necessary competence, capabilities and objectivity for the auditor's purposes. Information regarding the competence, capabilities and objectivity of an auditor's expert may come from a variety of sources, such as:

- Personal experience with previous work of that expert
- Discussions with that expert
- Discussions with other auditors or others who are familiar with that expert's work
- Knowledge of that expert's qualifications, membership of a professional body or industry association, licence to practice, or other forms of external recognition
- Published papers or books written by that expert
- The auditor's firm's quality management objectives, policies and procedures

The risk that an expert's objectivity is impaired increases when the expert is:

- **Employed** by the entity
- **Related** in some other manner to the entity, for example, by being financially dependent upon, or having an investment in, the entity

Exam focus point

> If the auditors have **reservations** about the competence or objectivity of the expert they may need to carry out other procedures or obtain evidence from another expert.

2.3.2 Understanding the field of work of the expert

The auditor needs to understand this enough to set the scope of the work he wants the expert to do for the purposes of the audit and to be able to evaluate whether the work is sufficient for audit purposes.

2.3.3 Agreement of terms

Written instructions usually cover the expert's terms of reference and such instructions may cover such matters as follows.

- Nature, scope and objectives of the auditor's expert's work
- The respective roles and responsibilities of the auditor and the auditor's expert
- Communications and reporting (eg nature and timing of expert's report)
- Confidentiality

2.3.4 Assessing the work of the expert

Auditors should assess the relevance and reasonableness of:

- The results of expert's work (including **consistency** with other audit evidence)
- The significant **assumptions** made
- The **source data**

2.3.5 Example

An expert valuation of a commercial building could be compared to the value of other, similar commercial building in estate agent's windows or on the web.

The auditors do **not** have the expertise to judge the assumptions and methods used; these are the responsibility of the expert. However, the auditors should seek to obtain an understanding of these assumptions etc, to consider their reasonableness based on other audit evidence, knowledge of the business and so on.

This may involve discussion with both the client and the expert. Additional procedures (including use of another expert) may be necessary.

2.4 Reporting

The auditor should not refer to the work of the expert in the auditor's report unless required to do so by law or regulation. The auditor must be clear that he retains responsibility for the audit opinion.

Chapter Roundup

- External auditors may make use of internal audit work or the internal auditors themselves when carrying out external audit procedures.
- External auditors may make use of the work of an auditor's expert when carrying out audit procedures.

PART C AUDIT STRATEGY, PROCESS AND REPORTING

Quick Quiz

1   An effective internal audit function may eliminate the need for external audit procedures.

    True   ☐
    False   ☐

2   Name **four** things the external audit function may consider when evaluating specific work of internal audit.

    (1) ……………………………………………
    (2) ……………………………………………
    (3) ……………………………………………
    (4) ……………………………………………

3   Complete the definitions using the words given below.

    An …………………………… …………………….. is a person or firm possessing …………………… ………………., knowledge and …………………… in a particular field other than accounting or auditing.

    > special, expert, experience, skills, auditor's

4   The auditor may not use the work of an expert employed by the organisation being audited.

    True   ☐
    False   ☐

5   If the auditor relies on the work of an expert, he may refer to that person in his report and share responsibility with him.

    True   ☐
    False   ☐

6   There are key criteria for assessing whether the work of the internal audit function may be suitable for audit purposes. Name two.

    (1) …………………………………………   (2) …………………………………………

Answers to Quick Quiz

1. False

2. From:

    (1) Have the internal auditors had sufficient and adequate technological training to carry out the work?
    (2) Are the internal auditors proficient?
    (3) Is the work of assistants properly supervised, reviewed and documented?
    (4) Has sufficient, appropriate audit evidence been obtained to afford a reasonable basis for the conclusions reached?
    (5) Are the conclusions reached appropriate, given the circumstances?
    (6) Are any reports produced by internal audit consistent with the result of the work performed?
    (7) Have any unusual matters or exceptions arising and disclosed by internal audit been resolved properly?
    (8) Are any amendments to the external audit programme required as a result of the matters identified by internal audit?
    (9) Has the work of internal audit been sufficiently tested by the external auditor to confirm its adequacy?

3. auditor's expert, special skill, experience

4. False

5. False

6. From:

    (1) Objectivity (including the effectiveness of communication)
    (2) Technical competence
    (3) Systematic and disciplined approach

End of Chapter Question

Powerplant (AIA May 2009 amended)

You are the partner in charge of the external audit of Powerplant, a company that generates electricity using nuclear power. The audit fieldwork has concluded for the year. The audit working papers carry the details of an impairment review on an important component of the reactor. This component has a carrying amount of $40 million, which is a material sum. The component is due to be inspected by a government inspection team within the next 12 months. This inspection is a major event, which requires shutting down the reactor for several days and draining a tank containing highly corrosive acid that has become radioactive because of its contact with that part of the reactor. This is not only an expensive process, it is also very dangerous and requires a team of highly trained inspectors. If the component in the centre of this tank is found to be contaminated then it will have to be replaced at a cost of $100 million before the tank can be refilled and the reactor started up again. If it is certified safe then the component will not be inspected again for at least 15 years.

You commissioned an independent expert in nuclear physics to report on whether this component is contaminated. The expert's report is inconclusive. He examined a small sample of the acid from the tank and used a remotely-controlled device to carry out a very distant observation of the component. This work indicated that there was nothing obviously wrong with the component, but the report stated that it could still be at quite an advanced stage of contamination without there being any obvious signs from these tests.

You have asked the directors to insert a note into the financial statements to the effect that there is a material inherent uncertainty with respect to the component's carrying amount. The directors have refused on the grounds that they have no specific reason to believe that the component is actually contaminated or that it is definitely impaired. The forthcoming government inspection is a routine one. They have suggested that you should rely on the fact that your independent expert conducted a review which did not identify any specific concern. Your auditor's report could then refer to relying upon expert assistance in gathering audit evidence.

You have confirmed that the potential replacement of the component could have a material impact on reported profits, but that the company will remain a going concern regardless. The legislation governing such businesses requires that the company has sufficient cash reserves to meet any major repair bills.

Required

(a) Explain the processes associated with employing an independent expert in the context of this audit.
(8 marks)

(b) Explain why it would not be appropriate to refer to the expert's assistance in the external auditor's report.
(4 marks)

(c) Explain the implications for the external auditor's report of the directors' refusal to insert the disclosures that you requested in the financial statements. Your explanation should include an explicit statement of the type of auditor's report that would be appropriate.
(8 marks)

(Total 20 marks)

Audit evidence I

Topic list	Syllabus reference
1 Revision: Audit evidence	LO1
2 Related parties	LO1
3 Written representations	LO1
4 Opening balances	LO1
5 Comparative information	LO1
6 Subsequent events	LO1
7 Going concern	LO1
8 Overall review of the financial statements	LO1

Introduction

Audit evidence is a vital part of any audit. The **basic issues** relating to **evidence** are that:

- **Auditors must obtain evidence** to support the financial statement assertions. This evidence must be **sufficient and appropriate**
- Audit evidence must be **documented** sufficiently

Related parties are a difficult area to obtain audit evidence on. The auditor must bear in mind, who evidence is from and how extensive it is. Obtaining evidence about related party transactions is considered in Section 2.

Often the auditors will have to rely on **written representations** from management about related parties and other issues. Written representations are **subjective evidence**, and the auditor must proceed with caution when dealing with them. This is discussed in Section 3.

Other matters that auditors must obtain evidence about are opening balances and comparative information. We look at the auditing guidance in relation to these issues.

Lastly, we revise the important reviews of subsequent events, going concern and an overall review of the financial statements.

1 Revision: Audit evidence

FAST FORWARD | Auditors need to obtain sufficient, appropriate audit evidence.

1.1 Obtaining evidence

You should be aware of the key points on audit evidence from your previous auditing studies. We shall revise them briefly here. Substantive procedures are designed to obtain evidence about the financial statement assertions.

Key term

> **Financial statement assertions** are the representations of the directors that are embodied in the financial statements. By approving the financial statements, the directors are making representations about the information therein. These representations or assertions may be described in general terms in a number of ways.

ISA 500 *Audit evidence* states that 'the auditor should use assertions for **classes of transactions**, **account balances**, and **presentation and disclosures** in sufficient detail to form the basis for the assessment of risks of material misstatement and the design and performance of further audit procedures'. You should be aware of examples of assertions.

Auditors obtain evidence by one or more of the following procedures which you should be equally familiar with.

1.2 Sufficient and appropriate audit evidence

'Sufficiency' and 'appropriateness' are interrelated and apply to both tests of controls and substantive procedures.

- **Sufficiency** is the measure of the **quantity** of audit evidence.
- **Appropriateness** is the measure of the **quality** or **reliability** of the audit evidence.

Auditors are essentially looking for enough reliable audit evidence. Audit **evidence usually indicates what is probable** rather than what is definite (is usually persuasive rather than conclusive) so different sources are examined by the auditors. However, auditors can only give **reasonable assurance** that the financial statements are free from misstatement, so **not all sources of evidence will be examined**. Auditors will use sampling, which you studied in detail in your earlier studies.

1.3 Audit sampling

ISA 530 *Audit Sampling* is based on the premise that auditors do not normally examine all the information available to them, as it would be impractical to do so and using audit sampling will produce valid conclusions.

Key terms

> **Audit sampling** involves the application of audit procedures to less than 100% of the items within a population of audit relevance such that all sampling units have an equal chance of selection in order to provide the auditor with a reasonable basis on which to draw conclusions about the entire population.
>
> **Statistical sampling** is any approach to sampling that involves random selection of a sample, and use of probability theory to evaluate sample results, including measurement of sampling risk.
>
> A **population** is the entire set of data from which a sample is selected and about which an auditor wishes to draw conclusions.
>
> **Sampling units** are the individual items constituting a population.

> **Stratification** is the process of dividing a population into sub-populations, each of which is a group of sampling units, which have similar characteristics (often monetary value).
>
> **Tolerable misstatement** is a monetary amount set by the auditor in respect of which the auditor seeks to obtain an appropriate level of assurance that the monetary amount set by the auditor is not exceeded by the actual misstatement in the population.
>
> The **tolerable rate of deviation** is a rate of deviation from prescribed internal control procedures set by the auditor in respect of which the auditor seeks to obtain an appropriate level of assurance that the rate of deviation set by the auditor is not exceeded by the actual rate of deviation in the population.
>
> An **anomaly** is a misstatement or deviation that is demonstrably not representative of misstatements or deviations in a population.
>
> **Sampling risk** arises from the possibility that the auditor's conclusion, based on a sample, may be different from the conclusion if the entire population were subjected to the same audit procedure.
>
> **Non-sampling risk** arises from factors that cause the auditor to reach an erroneous conclusion for any reason not related to the sampling risk. For example, most audit evidence is persuasive rather than conclusive, the auditor might use inappropriate procedures, or the auditor might misinterpret evidence and fail to recognise an error.
>
> (ISA 530: para. 5)

Some testing procedures do not involve sampling, such as:

- Testing 100% of items in a population
- Testing all items with a certain characteristic (for example, over a certain value) as the selection is not representative of the population

The ISA distinguishes between statistically-based sampling, which involves the use of random selection techniques from which mathematically constructed conclusions about the population can be drawn, and non-statistical methods, from which auditors draw a judgemental opinion about the population (ISA 530: para. A4). However, the principles of the ISA apply to both methods. You should be aware of the major methods of statistical and non-statistical sampling. The auditor's judgement as to what is sufficient appropriate audit evidence is influenced by a number of factors.

- Risk assessment
- The nature of the accounting and internal control systems
- The materiality of the item being examined
- The experience gained during previous audits
- The auditor's knowledge of the business and industry
- The results of audit procedures
- The source and reliability of information available

If they are unable to obtain sufficient, appropriate audit evidence, the auditors should consider the implications for their report.

1.4 External confirmations

The reliability of audit evidence is affected by its source. Audit evidence is more reliable when it is obtained from **independent** sources **outside the entity**.

Both ISA 330 *The auditor's responses to assessed risks* and ISA 505 *External confirmations* address the need for external confirmations in gathering sufficient and appropriate audit evidence.

> **ISA 330.19**
>
> The auditor shall consider whether external confirmation procedures are to be performed as substantive audit procedures.

ISA 330 Para. A48 identifies the following situations where external confirmations are appropriate.

- Bank balances and other information from bankers
- Accounts receivable balances
- Inventories held by third parties
- Property deeds held by lawyers
- Investments held for safekeeping by third parties or purchased from stockbrokers but not delivered at the end of the reporting period
- Loans from lenders
- Accounts payable balances

The auditor shall maintain control over external confirmation requests. So to take the example of a receivables circularisation, it is the auditor who should be in control of sending and receiving the requests and the responses from customers.

If management refuses to allow the auditor to send an external confirmation request, the auditor must consider whether this is reasonable and whether audit evidence can be obtained in another way. If evidence cannot be obtained from another source, the auditor should communicate this to those charged with governance, and consider the impact on the auditor's report (there is a possibility that the auditor's opinion will have to be modified (qualified) on the basis of an inability to obtain sufficient appropriate audit evidence, or that a disclaimer of opinion will be issued).

Exam focus point

RPQ students should note that ISA (UK) 505 *External confirmations* was revised in October 2023 and places additional obligations on UK auditors. When investigating exceptions that arise from an external confirmation request, auditors must consider:

- Whether the exception indicates fraud.
- Whether the exception indicates a deficiency in the entity's system of internal control.
- How additional procedures will allow the auditor to obtain sufficient appropriate audit evidence.

2 Related parties

FAST FORWARD

Related party transactions can be a difficult area to gain audit evidence about as evidence may be limited to representations by management.

2.1 Importance of related parties

Central to a number of government investigations in various countries have been companies trading with organisations or individuals **other than at arm's length**. Such transactions were made possible by a degree of control or influence exercised by directors over both parties to the transactions. ISA 550 *Related parties* covers auditing guidance in this area. The financial accounting treatment is covered by IAS 24 *Related party disclosures*.

Key terms

> A **related party** is a person or entity that is related to the entity that is preparing its financial statements (the reporting entity).
>
> A **related party transaction** is a transfer of resources, services or obligations between related parties, regardless of whether a price is charged.

The auditors' knowledge of the client must be sufficient to identify related party transactions for the following reasons:

(a) To recognise fraud risk factors, if any, arising from related party relationships and transactions that are relevant to the identification and assessment of the risks of material misstatement due to fraud

(b) To conclude whether financial statements reflecting such relationships and transactions are presented fairly

(c) To ensure the company has complied with IAS 24, if relevant

2.2 Inherent difficulties of detection

It may not be self-evident to management whether a party is related. Furthermore, many accounting systems are not designed to either distinguish or summarise related party transactions, so management will have to carry out additional analysis of accounting information.

An audit cannot be expected to detect all material related party transactions. The risk that undisclosed related party transactions will not be detected by the auditors is especially high when:

- **Related party transactions** have **taken place without charge**.
- **Related party transactions** are **not self-evident** to the auditors.
- Transactions are with a party that the auditors could **not reasonably** be expected to **know** is a **related party**.
- **Active steps** have been taken by **management** to **conceal** either the full terms of a transaction, or that a transaction is, in substance, with a related party.
- The **corporate structure** is **complex**.

2.3 Responsibilities of management

When the company is required to comply with IAS 24, management is responsible for the identification of related party transactions. Such transactions should be properly approved as they are frequently not at arm's length. Management is responsible for the relevant **disclosures** of related party transactions under IAS 24 in the financial statements.

2.4 Risk assessment procedures

The ISA sets out the following required procedures.

> - As part of the engagement team's discussion about fraud risk factors, specifically consider the susceptibility of the financial statements to material misstatement due to fraud or error that could result from the entity's related party relationships and transactions.
> - Enquire of management regarding:
>   - Identities of related parties and the nature of the relationship
>   - Whether any transactions took place between them and, if so, the type and purpose of the transactions

- What controls, if any, management has implemented to:
    (i) Identify, account for and disclose related parties and transactions
    (ii) Approve and authorise significant transactions with related parties/outside normal business
- Perform additional risk assessment procedures on these controls.

2.4.1 Company procedures

Auditors should enquire as to the company's procedures for ensuring that all disclosable transactions are properly identified and recorded. Such procedures are likely to include the following.

- **Advise** all **directors** and **officers** that they have a **responsibility** to disclose transactions in which they have an interest, either directly or through connected persons (such disclosure should take place at a meeting of the directors).
- **Record** all **transactions** notified in the minutes of directors' meetings.
- **Maintain** a **register** in which details of all transactions requiring disclosure are recorded.
- **Establish** some **method** of:
    - **Identifying proposed transactions** which will require the approval of the members in general meeting
    - **Ensuring** that the **company does not enter** into any **illegal transaction**
- **Monitor the system** by checking on a regular basis (as a minimum, once a year) that each director is in agreement with the company's record of his disclosable transactions and is satisfied that such records are both complete and accurate.
- **Obtain** from **each director** at the end of each financial year a **formal statement** indicating the disclosures necessary for the purposes of the statutory accounts.

With smaller organisations, auditors may well find that there may be no formalised procedures or that they are inadequate. Auditors should **advise each director** of his statutory responsibilities, and make a **written request** for **confirmation** of any disclosable transaction in which he has an interest.

In addition during the audit, the auditor should be alert for transactions which may indicate the existence of unidentified related parties.

Examples include:

- Transactions which have **abnormal terms of trade**, such as unusual prices, interest rates, guarantees and repayment terms
- Transactions which appear to **lack a logical business reason** for their occurrence
- Transactions in which **substance differs from form**
- Transactions **processed or approved in a non-routine manner** or by personnel who do not ordinarily deal with such transactions
- **Unusual transactions** which are entered into shortly before or after the end of the financial period
- **High volume** or **significant transactions** with certain customers or suppliers as compared with others
- **Unrecorded transactions** such as the receipt or provision of management services at no charge

The auditor **must** inspect the following for indications of unidentified related parties:

- Bank and legal confirmation obtained by the auditor in routine audit work
- Minutes of meetings of shareholders/those charged with governance
- Other relevant documents

2.4.2 Examining previously unidentified related party transactions and disclosures

If the auditor identifies information that suggest previously unidentified related parties exist, the auditor shall:

- Consider if other audit information suggests a related party exists.
- Tell the engagement team.
- Request management to identify transactions with that party.
- Enquire as to why company controls didn't pick up that related party.
- Perform relevant substantive procedures.
- Reconsider the risk that other related parties may exist.
- If non-disclosure appears intentional (indicative of fraud?), evaluate the implications for the audit.

2.5 Audit conclusions

The auditor should evaluate:

- Whether all related party relationships and transactions are appropriately accounted for and disclosed
- Whether related party relationships and transactions prevent the financial statements giving a true and fair view

2.6 Written representations regarding related parties

Where IAS 24 is relevant, auditors must obtain written representations that all related parties and transactions have been declared to the auditors and correctly accounted for and disclosed. We cover written representations in more detail in the next section.

Question — Related party transactions

You are the senior in charge of the audit of AB Milton for the year ended 31 May 20X1. Details of AB Milton and certain other companies are given below.

AB Milton

A building company formed by Alexander Milton and his brother, Brian.

AB Milton has issued share capital of 500 ordinary $1 shares, owned as shown below.

Name	Shares	%	Role
Alexander Milton	210	42%	Founder and director
Brian Milton	110	22%	Founder and director
Catherine Milton (Brian's wife)	100	20%	Company secretary
Diane Hardy	20	4%	
Edward Murray	60	12%	Director

Edward Murray is a local business man and a close friend of both Alexander and Brian Milton. He gave the brothers advice when they set up the company and remains involved through his position on the board of directors. His own company, Murray Design, supplies AB Milton with stationery and publicity materials.

Diane Hardy is Alexander Milton's ex-wife. She was given her shares as part of the divorce settlement and has no active involvement in the management of the company. Alexander's girlfriend, Fiona Dyson, is the company's solicitor. She is responsible for drawing up and reviewing all key building and other contracts, and frequently attends board meetings so that she can explain the terms of a particular contract to the directors. Her personal involvement with Alexander started in May 20X1 and, since that time, she has spent increasing amounts of time at the company's premises.

PART C AUDIT STRATEGY, PROCESS AND REPORTING

Cuts and Curls

A poodle parlour, of which 50% of the issued shares are owned by Diane Hardy and 50% by Gillian Milton, who is Alexander and Diane's daughter.

Cuts and Curls operated from premises owned by AB Milton for which rent is paid at the normal market rate.

Campbell Milton Roofing

A roofing company owned 60% by AB Milton and 40% by Ian Campbell, the managing director.

Campbell Milton Roofing carries out regular work for AB Milton and also does roofing work for local customers. Alexander Milton is a director of Campbell Milton Roofing and Catherine Milton is the company secretary. All legal work is performed by Fiona Dyson.

Required

(a) Based on the information given above, identify the potential related party transactions you expect to encounter during the audit of AB Milton and summarise, giving your reasons, what disclosure, if any, will be required in the full statutory accounts.

(b) Prepare notes for a training session for junior staff on how to identify related party transactions. Your notes should include:

   (i) A list of possible features which could lead you to investigate a particular transaction to determine whether it is in fact a related party transaction; and

   (ii) A summary of the general audit procedures you would perform to ensure that all material related party transactions have been identified.

Answer

(a)

Person/entity	Related party	Why	Transaction
Alex Milton	Yes	Director	
Brian Milton	Yes	Director	No transactions mentioned
Brian's wife	Yes	Wife of director	
Edward Murray	Yes	Director	Purchases of stationery
Murray Designs	Yes	Sub of Director	
Diane Hardy	No	No longer close family & ≥ 20%	
Fiona Dyson	Yes	Presumed close family & shadow director	Contracts drawn
Cuts & Curls	?	(see below)	Rental agreement
Campbell Milton Roofing	Yes	Sub of AB Milton	Work done for AB (see below)
Ian Campbell	Yes / No	Could be considered key management of group	

Cuts & Curls is not straightforward. For it to be a related party Gillian Milton would need to be in a position to control Cuts & Curls and then due to her relationship with Alex Milton her company would come under the related party umbrella. Gillian only holds 50% and therefore holds joint control with her mother.

Disclosure

Once a related party has been identified disclosure is required of any material transaction. Materiality is in most cases determined by considering both parties' perspective. For instance, the contracts drawn by Fiona Dyson may be material to her even if not for AB Milton.

Transactions with subsidiaries, that is, Campbell Milton Roofing:

Disclosure is not required of transactions which are cancelled on consolidation. However, if group accounts are not prepared due to a small/medium group exemption, material transactions between the two companies would need to be disclosed.

Disclosure should include:

(i) Names of the transacting related parties

(ii) A description of the relationship

(iii) A description of the transaction and the amounts included

(iv) The amounts due to or from the related party at the end of the year

(v) Any other element of the transaction necessary for an understanding of the financial statements

(b) Notes for staff training sessions:

(i) A logical place to start the audit of related party transactions would be to identify all possible related parties. This would always include:

- Directors and shadow directors
- Group companies
- Pension funds of the company
- Associates

It is likely that the other related parties would include:

- Key management (perhaps identified by which staff have key man cover)
- Shareholder owning > 20% of the shares
- Close relatives associates of any of the above

A related party transaction need to be reported if it is a material either to (i) the reporting entity or (ii) to the other party to the transaction.

Related party transactions do not necessarily have to be detrimental to the reporting entity, but those which will be easier to find. Features which may indicate a related party transaction may include:

- Unusually generous trade or settlement discounts
- Unusually generous payment terms
- Recorded in the nominal ledger code of any person previously identified as a related party (for example, director)
- Unusual size of transaction for customers (for example, if ABL were paying a suspiciously high legal bill for a building company)

(ii) Audit steps to find related party transactions may include:

- Identification of excessively generous credit terms by reference to aged trade accounts receivable analysis
- Identification of excessive discounts by reference to similar reports

- Scrutiny of cash book/cheque stubs for payments made to directors or officers of the company (probably more realistic for smaller entities)
- Review of board minutes for evidence of approval of related party transactions (directors are under a fiduciary duty to not make secret profits)
- Written representations from directors to give exhaustive list of all actual/potential related parties (that is, allow us to make the materiality assessment, not them)
- Review of accounting rewards for large transactions, especially near the year-end and with non-established customers/suppliers
- Identification of any persons holding > 20% of the shares in the entity by reference of the shareholders' register

They also **must** include:

- Inspection of bank and legal confirmations
- Inspection of minutes of shareholders' meetings
- Inspection of minutes of meetings of those charged with governance

3 Written representations

FAST FORWARD

> The auditor is required to obtain written representations from management about its responsibilities and to support other audit evidence where necessary.

3.1 Representations from management

The auditors receive many representations during the audit, both unsolicited and in response to specific questions. Some of these representations may be critical to obtaining sufficient appropriate audit evidence. Other representations are required about management meeting its responsibilities. ISA 580 *Written representations* covers this area.

Key terms

> A **written representation** is a written statement by management provided to the auditor to confirm certain matters or to support other audit evidence. Written representations in this context do not include financial statements, the assertions therein, or supporting books and records.
>
> **Management** comprises officers and those who also perform senior managerial functions.

The auditor's responsibilities are to:

- Obtain written representations from management that management believes that it has fulfilled the fundamental responsibilities that constitute the premise on which an audit is conducted.
- Support other audit evidence relevant to then financial statements if determined by the auditor or required by other ISAs.
- Respond appropriately to written representations or if management fails to provide written representations requested by the auditor.

Exam focus point

> Written representations were tested in the November 2022 exam. Candidates were asked to appraise the role of representations in providing audit evidence.

3.2 Written representations about management's responsibilities

Management should be asked to confirm in writing, in the manner in which those responsibilities are described in the terms of the audit engagement, that:

- It has fulfilled its responsibility for the **preparation and presentation of the financial statements**, in accordance with the applicable financial reporting framework.
- It has provided the auditor with all **relevant information** agreed in the terms of the audit engagement.
- **All transactions have been recorded and are reflected** in the financial statements.

3.3 Other written representations

In addition to representations relating to responsibility for the financial statements and those required by other ISAs, the auditors may wish to rely on written representations from management to **support** other audit evidence.

The following table includes examples of other written representations:

Written representations as audit evidence
Whether the selection and application of accounting policies are appropriate
Whether particular matters have been recognised, measured, presented or disclosed correctly, eg plans of intentions affecting asset value or legal issues that might affect the financial statements
Title to, or control over, assets, liens or encumbrances on assets and assets pledged as collateral
Aspects of laws, regulations and contractual agreements that may affect the financial statements, including non-compliance
All deficiencies in internal control that management is aware of and have been communicated to the auditor
Written representations about specific assertions in the financial statements
Significant assumptions used in making accounting estimates are reasonable
All subsequent events requiring adjustment or disclosure have been adjusted or disclosed
The effects of uncorrected misstatements are immaterial, both individually and in aggregate
Management has disclosed the results of its assessment of the risk that the financial statements may be materially misstated as a result of fraud
Management has disclosed all information in relation to fraud or suspected fraud involving management, employees with significant roles in internal control, and others where fraud could have a material effect on the financial statements
Management has disclosed all information in relation to allegations of fraud or suspected fraud communicated by employees, former employees, analysts, regulators or others
Management has disclosed all instances of non-compliance or suspected non-compliance with laws or regulations

It should be stressed that, in terms of the quality of audit evidence, although written representations are more reliable than oral representations, they are from an internal source and **on their own, they do not provide sufficient appropriate audit evidence** about the issues they relate to.

3.4 Documentation of representations by management

A written representation must be in the form of a **written representation letter** from management addressed to the auditor.

At the finalisation and review stage of the audit, the auditors will provide management with a draft representation letter containing the necessary representations. The auditors will then ask management to print the letter on the client's headed paper, review it and sign it. The date of the letter should be as near as practicable to, **but not after**, the date of the auditor's report on the financial statements. The letter must be for all the financial statements and period(s) referred to in the auditor's report.

The auditors may accept a published statement of management's responsibilities with regard to the financial statements if they are legally required to publish one.

A representation letter is usually signed by the members of management who have **primary responsibility** for the entity and its financial aspects (that is, the senior executive officer and the senior financial officer) based on the best of their knowledge and belief.

An example of a representation letter is provided in Appendix 2 to ISA 580. It is not a standard letter, and representations will vary from one period to the next and from one client to another.

3.5 Problems with written representations

3.5.1 Doubt as to reliability of written representations

If the auditor has doubt about management's integrity, he must consider how this will impact on the reliability of representations generally. Particularly this is the case if representations are inconsistent with other audit evidence.

If such inconsistencies arise, the auditor must resolve the matter. If the matter cannot be resolved, the auditor must reconsider the assessment of the competence, reliability, integrity and ethical values of management, and the effect this may have on the reliability of representations and audit evidence in general.

If the auditor concludes that written representations are not reliable, he should take appropriate action, including considering its impact on the auditor's report.

3.5.2 Written representations not provided

Where some or all of the written representations are not provided, the auditor must:

- Discuss this with management.
- Re-evaluate the integrity of management and its impact on the reliability of representations and audit evidence in general.
- Decide the implications for the auditor's report.

Question — Written representations

You are an audit manager reviewing the completed audit file of Leaf Oil.

(a) There have been no events subsequent to the period end requiring adjustment in the financial statements.

(b) The company has revalued two properties in the year. The directors believe that the property market is going to boom next year, so have decided to revalue the other two properties then.

(c) The directors confirm that the company owns 75% of the newly formed company, Subsidiary, at the year end.

(d) The directors confirmed that the 500 gallons of oil in Warehouse B belong to Flower Oil.

Required

Comment on whether you would expect to see these matters referred to in the representation letter.

Answer

(a) I would expect to see this referred to in a representation letter. ISA 580 gives this as an example of a matter to be included in the representation letter, as management should inform auditors of relevant subsequent events.

(b) This should not appear on a representation letter, even though management opinion is involved. This indicates an incorrect accounting treatment which the auditors should be in disagreement with the directors over.

(c) This should not appear on a representation letter as there should be sufficient alternative evidence for this matter. The auditor should be able to obtain registered information about Subsidiary from the companies' registrar.

(d) This should not appear on a representation letter. The auditors should be able to obtain evidence from Flower Oil that the inventory belongs to them.

4 Opening balances

FAST FORWARD

Specific procedures must be applied to **opening balances** in an initial audit engagement.

4.1 Audit procedures

Key terms

Opening balances are those account balances which exist at the beginning of the period. Opening balances are based upon the closing balances of the prior period and reflect the effects of:

- Transactions of prior periods
- Accounting policies applied to the prior period

An **initial audit engagement** is one in which either the financial statements for the prior period were not audited or one in which the financial statements for the prior period were audited by a predecessor auditor.

ISA 510 *Initial audit engagements – opening balances* provides guidance to auditors on the audit of opening balances when conducting an initial audit engagement.

The ISA states that for initial audit engagements the auditor's objective is to obtain sufficient appropriate audit evidence whether:

- Opening balances contain **misstatements** that **materially** affect the current period's financial statements

- **Appropriate accounting policies** are **consistently** applied or changes have been properly accounted for and adequately presented and disclosed

4.2 Audit evidence for opening balances

ISA 510 states that the auditor shall **read** the most recent financial statements and the predecessor auditor's report for information relevant to opening balances.

The auditor shall obtain sufficient appropriate audit evidence about whether opening balances contain misstatements that materially affect the current period's financial statements by:

- Determining whether the prior period's closing balances have been correctly brought forward or restated
- Determining whether the opening balances reflect the application of appropriate accounting policies
- Performing one or more of the following:
  - Where the prior period's financial statements were audited, reviewing the predecessor auditor's working papers
  - Evaluating whether audit procedures performed in the current period provide evidence relevant to opening balances
  - Performing specific audit procedures to obtain evidence regarding opening balances

4.3 Opening balances – audit conclusions and reporting

If the auditor cannot obtain **sufficient appropriate audit evidence** for opening balances, the auditor shall express a qualified opinion or a disclaimer of opinion.

If the opening balances contain misstatements that could **materially affect** the current year's financial statements, the auditor shall express a qualified opinion or an adverse opinion.

If the auditor concludes that the current period's **accounting policies** are not applied consistently in relation to opening balances, or that changes in accounting policies have not been properly accounted for and adequately presented and disclosed, the auditor shall express a qualified opinion or an adverse opinion.

If a prior period modification remains **relevant and material** to the current period's financial statements, the auditor shall modify the auditor's opinion on the current period's financial statements accordingly.

5 Comparative information

FAST FORWARD

> The auditor's responsibilities for **comparative information** vary depending on whether they are corresponding figures or comparative financial statements.

5.1 Comparative information

Key terms

> **Comparative information** is amounts and disclosures included in the financial statements in respect of one or more prior periods in accordance with the applicable financial reporting framework. There are two methods of presentation: corresponding figures or comparative financial statements.
>
> **Corresponding figures** are where amounts and other disclosures for the prior period are included as an integral part of the current period financial statements, and are intended to be read only in relation to the amounts and other disclosures relating to the current period.
>
> **Comparative financial statements** are where amounts and other disclosures for the prior period are included for comparison with the financial statements of the current period but, if audited, are referred to in the auditor's report.

An example of corresponding figures would be the figures for the prior year which appear in most sets of financial statements to the right of the current year figures. Comparative financial statements might be a separate set of financial statements for the prior year that are included within the same document as the current year's financial statements.

ISA 710 *Comparative information – corresponding figures and comparative financial statements* provides guidance to auditors on comparatives, both corresponding figures and comparative financial statements.

Whether corresponding figures or comparative financial statements are required is usually dictated by law or regulation but may also be specified in the terms of engagement.

In terms of audit reporting, for corresponding figures, the auditor's opinion refers to the current period only. For comparative financial statements, the auditor's opinion refers to each period for which financial statements are presented.

5.2 Auditor's responsibilities for comparative information

The ISA states that the auditor must determine whether the financial statements include the correct comparative information required by the applicable financial reporting framework, and whether it is appropriately classified. This includes an evaluation of whether:

- The **accounting policies** used for corresponding figures or comparative financial statements are consistent with the current period.
- The corresponding figures or comparative financial statements **agree** with the amounts and other disclosures presented in the prior period.

If the auditor becomes aware of a possible material misstatement regarding the comparative information, the auditor must perform additional audit procedures to obtain sufficient appropriate audit evidence to determine whether a material misstatement exists.

ISA 710 requires the auditor to obtain a **written representation** for all periods referred to in the auditor's opinion and a specific written representation regarding any restatements made to correct a material misstatement in prior period financial statements that affect the comparative information.

5.3 Corresponding figures – reporting

In terms of reporting, the auditor's report does not specifically refer to the corresponding figures because the opinion is on the current period's financial statements as a whole, and this includes the corresponding figures. The following table summarises the impact on the auditor's report in particular circumstances.

Scenario	Impact on auditor's report
Prior period report modified and matter unresolved and results in a material misstatement in the current period	Modified opinion regarding current period's financial statements
Prior period report unmodified but evidence of material misstatement and figures not restated	Modified (qualified or adverse) opinion regarding corresponding figures
Prior period financial statements audited by a predecessor auditor	Other matter paragraph stating that financial statements audited by predecessor auditor, type of opinion expressed, date of the report
Prior period financial statements not audited	Other matter paragraph stating that corresponding figures unaudited

5.4 Comparative financial statements – reporting

The auditor's opinion must refer to each period for which financial statements are presented and on which an audit opinion is expressed. The following table summarises the impact on the auditor's report in particular circumstances.

Scenario	Impact on auditor's report
Opinion on prior period financial statements different from opinion previously expressed	Other matter paragraph to explain different opinion
Prior period financial statements audited by a predecessor auditor	Other matter paragraph stating that prior period financial statements audited by a predecessor auditor, type of opinion expressed, date of the report

Scenario	Impact on auditor's report
Material misstatement affecting prior period financial statements on which predecessor auditor had expressed an unmodified opinion	If predecessor auditor is informed and financial statements are amended and new report issued, auditor reports only on current period
Prior period financial statements not audited	Other matter paragraph stating that comparative financial statements not audited

Question — Opening balances and comparative information

Auditing standards have been issued on opening balances for initial audit engagements and comparative information, and one of the matters considered is where one firm of auditors takes over from another firm. You have recently been appointed auditor of Lowdham Castings, a limited liability company which has been trading for about thirty years, and are carrying out the audit for the year ended 30 September 20X6. The company's revenue is about $500,000 and its normal profit before tax is about $30,000. Comparatives are shown as corresponding figures only.

Required

Explain your responsibilities in relation to the comparative information included in the accounts for the year ended 30 September 20X6. You should also outline the information you would require from the retiring auditors.

Answer

Consideration of the financial statements of the preceding period is necessary in the audit of the current period's financial statements in relation to three main aspects.

(a) Opening position: obtaining satisfaction that those amounts which have a direct effect on the current period's results or closing position have been properly brought forward.

(b) Accounting policies: determining whether the accounting policies adopted for the current period are consistent with those of the previous period.

(c) Comparative information: determining that comparative information is properly shown in the current period's financial statements.

The auditors' main concern will therefore be to satisfy themselves that there were no material misstatements in the previous year's financial statements which may have a bearing upon their work in the current year.

The new auditors do not have to 're-audit' the previous year's financial statements, but they will have to pay more attention to them than would normally be the case where they had themselves been the auditors in the earlier period. A useful source of audit evidence will clearly be the previous auditors, and, with the client's permission, they should be contacted to see if they are prepared to co-operate. Certainly, any known areas of weakness should be discussed with the previous auditors and it is also possible that they might be prepared to provide copies of their working papers (although there is no legal or ethical provision which requires the previous auditors to co-operate in this way).

6 Subsequent events

FAST FORWARD

Auditors should consider the effect of **subsequent events** on the financial statements.

6.1 Events after the reporting period

Key term

Subsequent events include:

- Events occurring between the period end and the date of the auditor's report
- Facts discovered after the date of the auditor's report

ISA 560 *Subsequent events* deals with this issue.

You should remember from your financial accounting studies that IAS 10 *Events after the reporting period* deals with the treatment in financial statement of events, both favourable and unfavourable, occurring after the period end. It identifies two types of event:

- Those that provide further evidence of conditions that existed at the period-end **(adjusting events)**
- Those that are indicative of conditions that arose subsequent to the period-end **(non-adjusting events)**

6.2 Events occurring up to the date of the auditor's report

ISA 560.6

The auditor shall perform procedures designed to obtain sufficient appropriate audit evidence that all events occurring between the date of the financial statements and the date of the auditor's report that require adjustment of, or disclosure in, the financial statements have been identified.

These procedures should be applied to any matters examined during the audit which may be susceptible to change after the year-end. They are in addition to tests on specific transactions after the period end, eg cut-off tests.

The ISA gives examples of procedures to be performed at the risk assessment stage and the substantive stage.

6.2.1 Risk assessment procedures

The auditor will have carried out risk assessment procedures about subsequent events, which must include:

(a) Obtaining an understanding of any procedures management has established to ensure that subsequent events are identified

(b) Enquiring of management and, where appropriate, those charged with governance as to whether any subsequent events have occurred which might affect the financial statements

(c) Reading minutes, if any, of the meetings, of the entity's owners, management and those charged with governance, that have been held after the date of the financial statements and inquiring about matters discussed at any such meetings for which minutes are not yet available

(d) Reading the entity's latest subsequent interim financial statements, if any

6.2.2 Other procedures

The ISA lists other tests which may be carried out to fulfil the requirements of paragraph 6.

- Read the entity's latest available budgets, cash flow forecasts and other related management reports for periods after the date of the financial statements;
- Enquire, or extend previous oral or written enquiries, of the entity's legal counsel concerning litigation and claims; or
- Consider whether written representations covering particular subsequent events may be necessary to support other audit evidence and thereby obtain sufficient appropriate audit evidence.

The auditors may also make certain inquiries of management and those charged with governance, for instance, relating to:

- Whether new commitments, borrowings or guarantees have been entered into
- Whether sales or acquisitions of assets have occurred or are planned
- Whether there have been increases in capital or issuance of debt instruments, such as the issue of new shares or debentures, or an agreement to merge or liquidate has been made or is planned
- Whether any assets have been appropriated by government or destroyed, for example, by fire or flood
- Whether there have been any developments regarding contingencies
- Whether any unusual accounting adjustments have been made or are contemplated
- Whether any events have occurred or are likely to occur that will bring into question the appropriateness of accounting policies used in the financial statements, as would be the case, for example, if such events call into question the validity of the going concern basis of accounting
- Whether any events have occurred that are relevant to the measurement of estimates or provisions made in the financial statements
- Whether any events have occurred that are relevant to the recoverability of assets

> **ISA 560.8**
>
> If ... the auditor identifies events that require adjustment of, or disclosure in, the financial statements, the auditor shall determine whether each such event is appropriately reflected in the financial statements.

6.3 Facts discovered after the date of the auditor's report but before the financial statements are issued

The financial statements are the management's responsibility. They should therefore inform the auditors of any material subsequent events between the date of the auditors' report and the date the financial statements are issued. The auditors do **not** have any obligation to perform procedures, or make enquires regarding the financial statements **after the** date of their report. However, if they become aware of an issue, they should discuss it with management and seek to have the financial statements amended.

When the financial statements are amended, the auditors should **extend the procedures** discussed above to the **date of their new report**, carry out any other appropriate procedures and issue a new auditor's report dated the day it is signed.

The situation may arise where the statements are not amended but the auditors feel that they should be.

If the auditors' report has already been issued to the entity then the auditors should notify those who are ultimately responsible for the entity (the management or possibly a holding company in a group), not to issue the financial statements or auditors' reports to third parties. If they have already been so issued, the auditors must take steps to prevent the reliance on the auditors' report. The action taken will depend on the auditors' legal rights and obligations and the advice of the auditors' lawyer.

6.4 Facts discovered after the financial statements have been issued

Auditors have no obligations to perform procedures or make enquiries regarding the financial statements after they have been issued. However, if an issue arises and management revises the financial statements. The auditors should:

(a) **Carry out the audit procedures** necessary in the circumstances

(b) **Review the steps taken by management** to ensure that anyone in receipt of the previously issued financial statements together with the auditors' report thereon is informed of the situation

(c) Extend the required audit procedures and **issue a new report** on the revised financial statements

The new auditor's report should include an **emphasis of matter** paragraph referring to a note to the financial statements that more extensively discusses the reason for the revision of the previously issued financial statements and to the earlier report issued by the auditor.

In our opinion, the revised financial statements give a true and fair view (or 'present fairly, in all material respects'), as at the date the original financial statements were approved, of the financial position of the company as of 31 December 20X1, and of the results of its operations and its cash flows for the year then ended in accordance with [relevant national legislation].

In our opinion the original financial statements for the year to 31 December 20X1, failed to comply with [relevant national standards or legislation].

Where local regulations allow the auditor to restrict the audit procedures on the financial statements to the effects of the subsequent event which caused the revision, the new auditor's report should contain a statement to that effect.

Where the management does **not** revise the financial statements but the auditors feel they should be revised, or if the management does not intend to take steps to ensure anyone in receipt of the previously issued financial statements is informed of the situation, then the auditors should consider steps to take, on a timely basis, to prevent reliance on their report. The actions taken will depend on the auditors' legal rights and obligations (for example, to contact the shareholders directly) and legal advice received.

Question — Subsequent events

You are auditing the financial statements of Hope Engineering, a limited liability company, for the year ending 31 March 20X8. The partner in charge of the audit instructs you to carry out a review of the company's activities since the financial year end. Mr Smith, the managing director of Hope Engineering, overhears the conversation with the partner and is surprised that you are examining accounting information which relates to the next accounting period.

Mr Smith had been appointed on 1 March 20X8 as a result of which the contract of the previous managing director, Mr Jones, was terminated. Compensation of $500,000 had been paid to Mr Jones on 2 March 20X8.

As a result of your investigations you find that the company is going to bring an action against Mr Jones for the recovery of the compensation paid to him, as it had come to light that two months prior to his dismissal, he had contractually agreed to join the board of directors of a rival company. The company's lawyer had informed Hope Engineering that Mr Jones' actions constituted a breach of his contract with them, and that an action could be brought against the former managing director for the recovery of the money paid to him.

PART C   AUDIT STRATEGY, PROCESS AND REPORTING

Required

(a) Explain the nature and purpose of a review of the period after the reporting date.

(b) Describe the audit procedures which would be carried out in order to identify any material subsequent events.

(c) Discuss the audit implications of the company's decision to sue Mr Jones for the recovery of the compensation paid to him.

Answer

(a) The auditors' active responsibility extends to the date on which they sign their auditor's report. As this date is inevitably after the year end, it follows that in order to discharge their responsibilities, the auditors must extend their audit work to cover the post reporting date period.

The objective of the audit of the post reporting date period is to ascertain whether management has dealt correctly with any events, both favourable and unfavourable, which occurred after the year end and which need to be reflected in the financial statements, if those statements are to show a true and fair view.

The general rule is that, in the preparation of year-end financial statements, no account should be taken of subsequent events unless to do so is required by statute or to give effect to retrospective legislation, or to take into account an event which provides information about a condition existing at the reporting date, for example realisable values of inventory, or indicates that the going concern concept is no longer applicable. Additionally, certain events may have such a material effect on the company's financial condition, for example a merger, that disclosure is essential to give a true and fair view.

(b) (i) Ask management if there have been any material subsequent events.

(ii) Identify and evaluate procedures implemented by management to ensure that all events after the reporting date have been identified, considered and properly evaluated as to their effect on the financial statements.

(iii) Review relevant accounting records to identify subsequent cash received in relation to accounts receivable, to check items uncleared at the year-end on the bank reconciliation, to check NRV of inventories from sales invoices.

(iv) Review budgets, profit forecasts, cash flow projections and management accounts for the new period to assess the company's trading position.

(v) Consider known 'risk' areas and contingencies, whether inherent in the nature of the business or revealed by previous audit experience, or by lawyers' letters.

(vi) Read minutes of shareholders' and management meetings, and correspondence and memoranda relating to items included in the minutes to identify any matters arising.

(vii) Consider relevant information which has come to the auditors' attention from sources outside the enterprise, including public knowledge of competitors, suppliers and customers.

(viii) Obtain written presentations concerning subsequent events from management.

(c) The compensation paid to Mr Smith would be disclosed as part of directors' remuneration for the year-ended 31 March 20X8. However, the question then arises as to whether or not the financial statements need to take any account of the possible recovery of the compensation payment.

The auditors should first ascertain from the board minutes that the directors intend to proceed with the lawsuit and should then attempt to assess the outcome by consulting the directors and the company's legal advisors. Only if it seems probable that the compensation will be recovered should a contingent gain be disclosed in the notes to the accounts (IAS 10), along with a summary of the facts of the case. A prudent estimate of legal costs should be deducted.

It could be argued that Mr Smith's breach of contract existed at the reporting date and that the compensation should therefore be treated as a current asset, net of recovery costs. However, this would not be prudent, given the uncertainties over the court case.

7 Going concern

FAST FORWARD

Auditors should consider whether the going concern basis of accounting is **appropriate**, and whether **disclosure** of any going concern problems is **sufficient**.

7.1 The going concern basis of accounting

Key term

Under the '**going concern basis of accounting**' an entity is ordinarily viewed as continuing in business for the foreseeable future with neither the intention nor the necessity of liquidation, ceasing trading or seeking protection from creditors pursuant to laws or regulations. Accordingly assets and liabilities are recorded on the basis that the entity will be able to realise its assets and discharge its liabilities in the normal course of business (ISA 570: para. 2).

ISA 570 (Revised) *Going concern* states that when preparing accounts, management should make an explicit **assessment** of the entity's ability to continue as a going concern. Most accounting frameworks, for example that provided by IAS 1 *Presentation of financial statements*, require management to do so (IAS 1: para. 26).

When management are making the assessment, the following factors should be considered.

- The **degree of uncertainty** about the events or conditions being assessed increases significantly the further into the future the assessment is made.
- Judgements are made on the basis of the **information available** at the time.
- Judgements are affected by the **size** and **complexity** of the entity, the **nature** and **condition** of the business and the **degree** to which it is **affected** by **external factors** (ISA 570: para. 5).

The following list gives examples of possible indicators of going concern problems IAS 570: para. A3).

(a) **Financial indications**

- Net liabilities or net current liability position
- Fixed-term borrowings approaching maturity without realistic prospects of renewal or repayment, or excessive reliance on short-term borrowings
- Indications of withdrawal of financial support by creditors
- Negative operating cash flows indicated by historical or prospective financial statements
- Adverse key financial ratios
- Substantial operating losses or significant deterioration in the value of assets used to generate cash flows
- Arrears or discontinuance of dividends
- Inability to pay creditors on due dates
- Inability to comply with terms of loan agreements

- Change from credit to cash on delivery transactions with suppliers
- Inability to obtain financing for essential new product development or other essential investments

(b) **Operating indications**
- Loss of key management without replacement
- Loss of a major market, franchises, licence, or principal supplier
- Labour difficulties or shortages of important supplies

(c) **Other indications**
- Non-compliance with capital or other statutory requirements
- Pending legal proceedings against the entity that may, if successful, result in judgements that could not be met
- Changes in legislation or government policy

The significance of such indications can often be **mitigated** by other factors.

(a) The effect of an entity being unable to make its normal debt repayments may be counterbalanced by management's plans to maintain **adequate cash flows** by alternative means, such as by disposal of assets, rescheduling of loan repayments, or obtaining additional capital.

(b) The loss of a principal supplier may be mitigated by the availability of a suitable alternative source of supply (ISA 570: para. A3).

7.2 Auditor's responsibilities

Auditors are responsible for considering:

- The appropriateness of the going concern basis of accounting
- The existence of **material uncertainties** about the going concern basis of accounting that need to be disclosed in the accounts
- The implications for the auditor's report (ISA 570: para. 9)

7.2.1 Risk assessment

Auditors will consider whether there are events or conditions which cast doubt on the entity's going concern status during risk assessment. During this process they will discover whether management has performed a preliminary assessment of going concern (ISA 570: para. 10).

7.2.2 Evaluating management's assessment

> **ISA 570.12**
> The auditor shall evaluate management's assessment of the entity's ability to continue as a going concern

The auditors will review potential problems management had identified, and management's plans to resolve them. If they have not, the auditors should discuss the basis for the intended use of the going concern basis of accounting.

The auditors should consider:

- The **process** management used
- The **assumptions** on which management's assessment is based
- Management's **plans** for future action

If management's assessment covers a period of **less than 12 months** from the date of the end of the last period covered by the financial statements, the auditor should ask management to extend its assessment period to 12 months from that date.

Management should not need to make a detailed assessment, and auditors carry out detailed procedures, if the entity has a **history of profitable operations** and **ready access** to **financial resources**.

The auditor should inquire of management as to its knowledge of events or conditions and related business risks beyond the period of assessment used by management that may cast significant doubt on the entity's ability to continue as a going concern.

Because the time period is some way into the future, the indications of potential going concern problems would have to be significant. Auditors do not have to carry out specific procedures to identify potential problems which may occur after the period covered by management's assessment. However, they should be alert during the course of the audit for any **indications** of future problems.

7.2.3 Additional audit procedures

> **ISA 570.16**
>
> If events or conditions have been identified that may cast significant doubt on the entity's ability to continue as a going concern, the auditor shall obtain sufficient appropriate audit evidence to determine whether or not a material uncertainty exists through performing additional audit procedures, including consideration of mitigating factors.

The ISA lists the following required procedures.

(a) When management has not yet performed an assessment of the entity's ability to continue as a going concern, requesting management to make its assessment.

(b) Evaluating management's plans for future actions in relation to its going concern assessment, whether the outcome of these plans is likely to improve the situation and whether management's plans are feasible in the circumstances.

(c) When the entity has prepared a cash flow forecast, and analysis of the forecast is a significant factor in considering the future outcome of events or conditions in the evaluation of management's plans for future action:

 (i) Evaluating the reliability of the underlying data generated to prepare the forecast; and
 (ii) Determining whether there is adequate support for the assumptions underlying the forecast.

(d) Considering whether any additional facts or information have become available since the date on which management made its assessment.

(e) Requesting written representations from management or, where appropriate, those charged with governance, regarding their plans for future action and the feasibility of these plans.

When questions arise on the appropriateness of the going concern basis of accounting, some of the normal audit procedures carried out by the auditors may take on an **additional significance**. Auditors may also have to carry out **additional procedures** or to update information obtained earlier. The ISA lists various additional procedures which the auditors could carry out in this context (ISA 570: para. A16).

> - **Analyse and discuss cash flow**, profit and other relevant forecasts with management.
> - **Analyse and discuss** the entity's latest available **interim financial statements**.
> - **Review the terms of debentures and loan agreements** and determine whether they have been breached.
> - **Read minutes** of the meetings of shareholders, the board of directors and important committees for reference to financing difficulties.
> - **Enquire** of the entity's lawyer regarding **litigation and claims**.
> - **Confirm the existence, legality and enforceability** of arrangements to provide or maintain financial support with related and third parties.
> - **Assess** the **financial ability** of such parties to **provide additional funds**.
> - **Consider the entity's position** concerning unfulfilled customer orders.
> - **Review events after the period-end** for items affecting the entity's ability to continue as a going concern.

The auditors should discuss with management its **plans** for **future action**, for example plans to liquidate assets, borrow money or restructure debt, reduce or delay expenditure or increase capital, and assess whether these are feasible and are likely to improve the situation.

When analysis of cash flow is a significant factor, auditors should consider:

- The **reliability** of the **system** for generating the information
- Whether there is **adequate support** for the assumptions underlying the forecast
- How **recent forecasts** have **differed** from **actual results**

7.3 Audit conclusions

> **ISA 570.18**
>
> Based on the audit evidence obtained, the auditor shall conclude whether, in the auditors' judgement, a material uncertainty exists related to events or conditions that individually or collectively, may cast significant doubt on the entity's ability to continue as a going concern.

An uncertainty will be material if it has so great a potential impact as to require clear disclosure of its nature and implications in the financial statements, which should:

- **Adequately describe** the **principal events or conditions** that give rise to the uncertainty about continuance as a going concern, and management's plans to deal with the situation
- **State clearly** that a **material uncertainty exists** and therefore the entity may be unable to realise its assets and discharge its liabilities in the normal course of business (ISA 570: para. 19)

The following table summarises the possible scenarios that could arise following the auditor's review of going concern. ISA 570 does provide example extracts in respect of these scenarios and these are presented after the following table.

Scenario	Impact on auditor's report
1 Going concern basis of accounting appropriate but material uncertainty which is adequately disclosed	Unmodified opinion and section on 'Material Uncertainty Related to Going Concern' which explains the uncertainty
2 Going concern basis of accounting appropriate but material uncertainty which is not adequately disclosed	Qualified or adverse opinion (ie modified opinion)
3 Use of going concern basis of accounting inappropriate	Adverse opinion (ie modified opinion)
4 Management unwilling to make or extend its assessment	Qualified opinion or disclaimer of opinion (ie modified opinion)

Scenario 1: Going concern basis of accounting appropriate but material uncertainty which is adequately disclosed

In this situation, the opinion on the financial statements will be **unmodified** but the auditor's report will include a section entitled 'Material Uncertainty Related to Going Concern'. This section is placed after the 'Basis for Opinion' section, and draws attention to the note in the financial statements which discloses information about the uncertainty. The auditor also points out that the auditor's opinion is not modified.

Material Uncertainty Related to Going Concern

We draw attention to Note 6 in the financial statements, which indicates that the Company incurred a net loss of ZZZ during the year ended 31 December 20X1 and, as of that date, the Company's current liabilities exceeded its total assets by YYY. As stated in Note 6, these events or conditions, along with other matters as set forth in Note 6, indicate that a material uncertainty exists that may cast significant doubt on the Company's ability to continue as a going concern. Our opinion is not modified in respect of this matter.

Scenario 2: Going concern basis of accounting appropriate but material uncertainty which is not adequately disclosed

In this situation, as inadequate disclosure has been made of the material uncertainty, the auditor's opinion will be modified – either a qualified or adverse opinion will be issued depending on the magnitude of the uncertainty. An extract from the auditor's report where a qualified opinion is issued is provided by the ISA follows.

Qualified Opinion

We have audited the financial statements of ABC Company (the Company), which comprise the statement of financial position as at 31 December 20X1, and the statement of comprehensive income, statement of changes in equity and statement of cash flows for the year then ended, and notes to the financial statements, including a summary of significant accounting policies.

In our opinion, except for the incomplete disclosure of the information referred to in the *Basis for Qualified Opinion* section of our report, the accompanying financial statements present fairly, in all material respects (or **give a true and fair view of**), the financial position of the Company as at 31 December 20X1, and (of) its financial performance and its cash flows for the year then ended in accordance with International Financial Reporting® Accounting Standards (IFRS® Accounting Standards).

Basis for Qualified Opinion

> As discussed in Note yy, the Company's financing arrangements expire and amounts outstanding are payable on 19 March 20X2. The Company has been unable to conclude re-negotiations or obtain replacement financing. This situation indicates that a material uncertainty exists that may cast significant doubt on the Company's ability to continue as a going concern. The financial statements do not adequately disclose this matter.
>
> We conducted our audit in accordance with International Standards on Auditing (ISAs). Our responsibilities under those standards are further described in the Auditor's Responsibilities for the Audit of the Financial Statements section of our report. We are independent of the Company in accordance with the ethical requirements that are relevant to our audit of the financial statements in [jurisdiction], and we have fulfilled our other ethical responsibilities in accordance with these requirements. We believe that the audit evidence we have obtained is sufficient and appropriate to provide a basis for our qualified opinion.

Scenario 3: Use of going concern basis of accounting inappropriate

When the going concern basis of accounting has been used but this is considered inappropriate by the auditor, an adverse opinion must be issued, regardless of whether or not the financial statements include disclosure of the inappropriateness of management's use of the going concern basis of accounting.

> *Adverse Opinion*
>
> We have audited the financial statements of ABC Company (the Company), which comprise the statement of financial position as at 31 December 20X1, and the statement of comprehensive income, statement of changes in equity and statement of cash flows for the year then ended, and notes to the financial statements, including a summary of significant accounting policies.
>
> In our opinion, because of the omission of the information mentioned in the *Basis for Adverse Opinion* section of our report, the accompanying financial statements do not present fairly (or **do not give a true and fair view of**), the financial position of the Company as at 31 December 20X1, and of its financial performance and its cash flows for the year then ended in accordance with International Financial Reporting Accounting Standards (IFRS Accounting Standards).
>
> *Basis for Adverse Opinion*
>
> The Company's financing arrangements expired and the amount outstanding was payable on 31 December 20X1. The Company has been unable to conclude re-negotiations or obtain replacement financing and is considering filing for bankruptcy. This situation indicates that a material uncertainty exists that may cast significant doubt on the Company's ability to continue as a going concern. The financial statements do not adequately disclose this fact.
>
> We conducted our audit in accordance with International Standards on Auditing (ISAs). Our responsibilities under those standards are further described in the Auditor's Responsibilities for the Audit of the Financial Statements section of our report. We are independent of the Company in accordance with the ethical requirements that are relevant to our audit of the financial statements in [jurisdiction], and we have fulfilled our ethical responsibilities in accordance with these requirements. We believe that the audit evidence we have obtained is sufficient and appropriate to provide a basis for our adverse opinion.

Scenario 4: Management unwilling to make or extend its assessment

In some circumstances, the auditor may ask management to make or extend its assessment. If management does not do this, a qualified opinion or a disclaimer of opinion in the auditor's report may be appropriate, because it may not be possible for the auditor to obtain **sufficient appropriate audit evidence** regarding the use of the going concern basis of accounting in the preparation of the financial statements.

7.4 Communicating to those charged with governance

The auditor shall **communicate with those charged with governance** events or conditions that may cast doubt on the entity's ability to continue as a going concern. This will include:

- Whether the events or conditions constitute a material uncertainty
- Whether the use of the going concern basis of accounting is appropriate in the preparation and presentation of the financial statements
- The adequacy of related disclosures

8 Overall review of the financial statements

> **FAST FORWARD**
>
> At the completion stage, the auditor performs an overall review of all work done to obtain reasonable assurance that the audit complies with professional standards and all applicable legal and regulatory requirements, and that the auditor's report issued is appropriate in the circumstances (ISA 220 (Revised): para. 11).

Under ISA 220 (Revised) the engagement partner has overall responsibility for managing and achieving quality within an audit engagement: in order to achieve this, the standard applies the firm-wide approach from ISQMs 1 and 2 to each audit engagement in the following areas:

- Leadership responsibilities for managing and achieving quality on audits
- Relevant ethical requirements, including those related to independence
- Acceptance and continuance of client relationships and audit engagements
- Engagement resources
- Engagement performance
- Monitoring and remediation
- Taking overall responsibility for managing and achieving quality
- Documentation

Engagements undertaken for listed entities and other entities that might either present certain quality risks to the firm or be subject to certain legal or regulatory requirements shall have an objective engagement quality review performed, which evaluates significant judgements and conclusions reached by the engagement team in the context of professional standards and the applicable legal and regulatory framework. This review should be conducted by an individual with suitable competence and capabilities, plus appropriate independence and authority, and is completed before the auditor's report is dated by the engagement partner. The guidance on engagement quality reviews from ISA 220 (Revised) is supported by ISQMs 1 and 2.

8.1 ISA 450 (Revised) *Evaluation of misstatements identified during the audit*

By the end of the audit, there may be a number of misstatements that have been identified as a result of the auditor's procedures (including disclosures where details could have been either omitted or misstated and which could indicate fraud). Those that are clearly trivial will be ignored, while those that the client has already agreed to amend will be reviewed to ensure this has occurred. What about any remaining misstatements though?

The auditor must consider the impact on the financial statements of uncorrected misstatements, especially those that are not individually material, because in aggregate, their cumulative effect may become material (ISA 450: para.11). The auditor needs to evaluate these misstatements and differentiate between those that are factual misstatements (those that are clearly misstated), judgemental misstatements (those relating to accounting policies or estimates) and projected misstatements (which cannot be quantified specifically) (ISA 450: para. A6).

Should the aggregate of uncorrected misstatements start to become material, then the auditor can either perform further procedures or request management to adjust the financial statements. Ultimately, this could lead to a modification of the audit opinion if corrections are not made, so it is essential to discuss this with those charged with governance.

During this stage of the audit, materiality may change due to adjustments made by management, so the auditor should be alert to the risk that some misstatements may now become material.

The summary of uncorrected misstatements will not only list misstatements from the current year, but also those from the previous year(s). This will allow misstatements to be highlighted which are reversals of misstatements in the previous year, such as in the valuation of closing/opening inventory. Cumulative misstatements may also be shown, which have increased from year to year. It is normal to show both the statement of financial position and the statement of profit or loss and other comprehensive income effect.

Chapter Roundup

- Auditors need to obtain sufficient, appropriate audit evidence.
- Related party transactions can be a difficult area to gain audit evidence about as evidence may be limited to representations by management.
- The auditor is required to obtain written representations from management about its responsibilities and to support other audit evidence where necessary.
- Specific procedures must be applied to **opening balances** in an initial audit engagement.
- The auditors' responsibilities for **comparative information** vary depending on whether they are corresponding figures or comparative financial statements.
- Auditors should consider the effect of **subsequent events** on the financial statements.
- Auditors should consider whether the going concern basis of accounting is **appropriate,** and whether **disclosure** of going concern problems is **sufficient**.
- At the completion stage, the auditor performs an **overall review of all work done** to obtain reasonable assurance that the audit complies with professional standards and all applicable legal and regulatory requirements, and that the auditor's report issued is appropriate in the circumstances (ISA 220 (Revised): para. 11).

PART C AUDIT STRATEGY, PROCESS AND REPORTING

Quick Quiz

1. Give five examples of financial statement assertions.

   (1) ....
   (2) ....
   (3) ....
   (4) ....
   (5) ....

2. Which of the following is not a procedure designed to obtain evidence?

   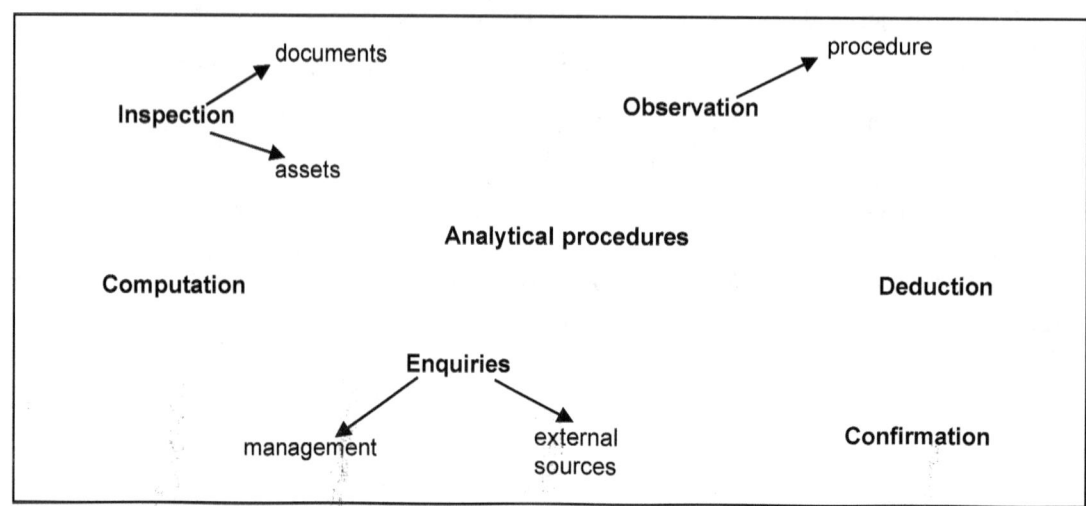

3. Give five instances where the risk of undisclosed related party transactions going undiscovered by the auditors is high.

   (1) ....
   (2) ....
   (3) ....
   (4) ....
   (5) ....

4. Where prior period financial statements were unaudited, the auditor should make no reference to the comparatives in their report.

   True ☐
   False ☐

5. Name two elements of 'subsequent events'.

   (1) ....
   (2) ....

6   List five enquiries which may be made of management in testing subsequent events.

    (1)   ....
    (2)   ....
    (3)   ....
    (4)   ....
    (5)   ....

7   Complete the definition.

    The .... basis of accounting: the enterprise will continue in business for the .... with neither the intention nor the necessity of liquidation.

8   The 'foreseeable future' is always a period of 12 months.

    True   ☐
    False ☐

Answers to Quick Quiz

1. From:
   (1) Existence
   (2) Rights and obligations
   (3) Occurrence
   (4) Completeness
   (5) Valuation
   (6) Cut-off
   (7) Classification
   (8) Valuation and allocation
   (9) Classification and understandability
   (10) Accuracy and valuation

2. Deduction

3. (1) There has been no charge.
   (2) Related parties are not evident to auditors.
   (3) Auditors could not reasonably know party was related.
   (4) Steps have been taken to conceal relationship.
   (5) Corporate structure is complex.

4. False

5. (1) Events occurring between the period end and the date of the auditors' report
   (2) Facts discovered after the date of the auditors' report

6. From:
   (1) Any new commitments
   (2) Sales of assets
   (3) Issues of shares or debentures
   (4) Assets destroyed
   (5) Developments in contingencies
   (6) Unusual accounting adjustments
   (7) Influences on accounting policies
   (8) Events affecting estimates
   (9) Events affecting recoverability of assets

7. Going concern, foreseeable future

8. False

End of Chapter Question

Sink plc (AIA May 2007)

The directors of Sink plc scheduled a special meeting between the audit committee and their external auditors. This meeting was attended by the company's chief executive and the finance director. During the meeting the directors presented a series of concerns that raised doubts about the company's ability to continue as a going concern. Essentially, the company is considered to be at risk because of cash flow problems. The directors believe that the company can survive in the following circumstances.

- The company has tendered for a large order. If the company wins this order then there will be sufficient work to ensure that the company is profitable for at least two years. The order will also create favourable publicity which will enable the company to win further orders more easily. Sink plc has invested a great deal of time and effort in this tender and the customer has indicated that Sink plc is one of the preferred bidders in terms of quality and price. The customer has, however, expressed some concern about Sink plc's financial position.

- The company requires a significant bank loan in order to meet its immediate cash flow commitments and also to meet the working capital needs that will be created by the large order if Sink plc's bid is successful. Sink plc's bank manager has referred the company's loan application for approval. The bank has given a provisional indication that it will grant the loan if Sink plc wins the order, but is unlikely to do so if Sink plc's tender is unsuccessful.

- The directors of Sink plc believe that both the order and the loan are vital to the survival of the company. They are keen to ensure that the external auditor does everything possible to assist.

Required

(a) Explain how the auditor can decide whether Sink plc is a going concern. Your answer should give specific suggestions as to the information that the auditor would seek from the company and its directors.

(10 marks)

(b) Explain the form of auditor's report that is most likely to be appropriate to Sink plc, assuming that the auditor is able to obtain satisfactory results from the work done in (a) above. Your answer should state any assumptions that you have made concerning the company's financial statements. **(5 marks)**

(c) Explain whether it is appropriate for an audit committee to meet with the external auditor in the manner described above and whether such meetings should include the chief executive and the finance director.

(5 marks)

(Total 20 marks)

PART C AUDIT STRATEGY, PROCESS AND REPORTING

Audit evidence II

Topic list	Syllabus reference
1 Assets	LO1
2 Income	LO1
3 Liabilities	LO1
4 Expenses	LO1
5 Disclosures	LO1

Introduction

You must be able to consider four key matters in relation to items appearing in financial statements: risk, materiality, relevant accounting standards and audit evidence. In this chapter, we shall focus on the last two of these, as the first two will depend more on the scenario presented in any given question.

You have studied the audit of a basic set of financial statements in your earlier studies. At this level, however, the issues you are presented with will be more complex, but remember that key basic points apply. Bear in mind the relevant **assertions** for the financial statement item.

You need a strong knowledge of all the accounting standards you have learned to apply in this paper. We suggest you keep the learning material from your previous studies as a reference point when working through this chapter and accounting issues questions.

PART C   AUDIT STRATEGY, PROCESS AND REPORTING

1 Assets

> **FAST FORWARD**
>
> Key assertions relating to assets are existence, completeness, valuation and rights and obligations.

1.1 Fair value

Exam focus point

Students should note that the accounting requirements for fair value have recently been developed. Below the definition of fair value according to IFRS 13 *Fair value measurement* is given. IFRS 13 applies going forward and students may need to refresh their technical knowledge.

Key term

Fair value is the price that would be received to sell an asset or paid to transfer a liability in an orderly transaction between market participants at the measurement date.   *(IFRS 13 definition)*

Fair value accounting is increasingly important and affects the audit of valuation for both assets and liabilities. Many standards allow valuation at fair value, for example, IAS 16 *Property, plant and equipment* and IFRS 5 *Non-current assets held for sale and discontinued operations*. These are both standards that have featured in recent exams.

For auditors, the determination of fair value will generally be more difficult than determining historical cost. It will be more difficult to establish whether fair value is reasonable for complex assets and liabilities than for more straightforward assets or liabilities which have a market and therefore a market value.

Generally speaking, the trend towards fair value accounting will increase audit work required, not only because determining fair values is more difficult, but because fair values fluctuate in a way that historical costs do not, and will need vouching each audit period.

Fair value estimates come within the more general topic of accounting estimates, which is the subject of ISA 540 (Revised) *Auditing accounting estimates and related disclosures*, which we shall look at now. This standard was revised in October 2018 and is effective for the audits of accounting periods beginning on or after 15 December 2019. The standard requires the auditor to obtain sufficient appropriate audit evidence about whether accounting estimates and related disclosures in the financial statements are reasonable in the context of the entity's applicable financial reporting framework. This means that the auditor must have a sound knowledge of the accounting requirements relevant to the entity and when accounting estimates are appropriate.

1.2 ISA 540 (Revised)

ISA 540 (Revised) emphasises that the auditor must be aware of the **inherent risks** present in their client's business that increase the risk of material misstatement due to the use of accounting estimates.

The auditor should also focus on identifying any **control risks** that may mean that misstatements made by management in calculating accounting estimates may be misstated.

Key terms

An **accounting estimate** is a monetary amount for which the measurement, in accordance with the requirements of the applicable financial reporting framework, is subject to estimation uncertainty.

Estimation uncertainty is the susceptibility of an accounting estimate to an inherent lack of precision in its measurement.

Management's point estimate is the amount selected by management for recognition or disclosure in the financial statements as an accounting estimate.

Management bias is a lack of neutrality by management in the preparation of information.

> **Auditor's point estimate** or **auditor's range** is the amount, or range of amounts, respectively, developed by the auditor (from audit evidence) for use in evaluating management's point estimate.
>
> **Outcome of an accounting estimate** is the actual monetary amount that results from the resolution of the transaction(s), event(s) or condition(s) addressed by an accounting estimate.
>
> (ISA 540 (Revised): para. 12).

ISA 540 (Revised) has the following requirements:

- The auditor shall obtain an understanding of the **entity and its environment**, including:
    - The entity's transactions and other events and conditions that may give rise to the need for, or changes in, accounting estimates and disclosures, including those subject to inherent risk factors
    - The requirements of the applicable financial reporting framework
    - Regulatory factors relevant to the entity's accounting estimates
    - The nature of expected accounting estimates and related disclosures
- The auditor shall obtain an understanding of the **entity's internal control and control activities**, including:
    - The oversight/governance in place over the financial reporting process relevant to accounting estimates
    - How management identifies the need for specialist skills relating to accounting estimates (including the use of a management's expert)
    - How the entity's risk assessment process identifies and addresses risks relating to accounting estimates
- For accounting estimates which give rise to significant risks the auditor should also evaluate how management:
    - Identifies and selects the relevant methods, assumptions and source data to be used for the estimate
    - Understands the degree of estimation uncertainty (including considering the range of possible measurement outcomes)
    - Addresses the estimation uncertainty (including selecting a point estimate and related disclosures for inclusion in the financial statements)
- The auditor should **review the outcome of previous accounting estimates** to help identify and assess the risks of material misstatements in the current period.
- The auditor should determine whether the audit engagement team has **sufficient skills and knowledge** in relation to accounting estimates and related disclosures.
- The auditor should consider the impact of accounting estimates and related disclosures on their **assessment of inherent risk and control risk**.
- Based on the assessed risks the auditor will determine whether the financial reporting framework has been properly applied and whether methods for making estimates are appropriate and have been applied consistently.
- The auditor will also:
    - Determine whether events occurring up to the date of the audit report provide evidence regarding the accounting estimate

- Test how management made the accounting estimate
- Test the operating effectiveness of controls together with appropriate substantive procedures
- Develop an auditor's point estimate or a range to evaluate the management's point estimate
- The possibility of management bias must be considered by the auditor.
- Written representations will be obtained from management as to whether management believes that significant assumptions used in making accounting estimates are reasonable.
- The auditor should also consider whether there are any matters to communicate with those charged with governance, management or other relevant parties in relation to accounting estimates and related disclosures.

1.3 Risk procedures: Fair value

The auditor is required to assess the entity's process for determining accounting estimates including fair value measurements and disclosures and the related control activities and to assess the arising risks of material misstatement.

Management's processes for determining fair values will vary considerably from organisation to organisation. Some companies will habitually value items at historical cost where possible, and may have very poor processes for determining fair value if required. Others may have complex systems for determining fair value if they have a large number of assets and liabilities which they account for at fair value, particularly where a high degree of estimation is involved in determining the fair value.

Once the auditors have assessed the risks associated with determining fair value, they should determine further procedures to address those risks.

1.4 Audit procedures: Fair value

Audit procedures will depend heavily on the complexity of the fair value measurement. Where the fair value equates to market value, the auditor should be able to verify this with reference to the market, for example, published price quotations for marketable securities, or by using the work of an expert, for example, an estate agent in the case of land and buildings.

However, in some cases, there may be a great deal of estimation and management assumption related to a fair value. Where this is the case, the auditor needs to consider matters such as the intent and ability of management to carry out certain actions stated in the assumptions. This includes:

- Considering management's past history of carrying out its stated intentions with respect to assets or liabilities
- Reviewing written plans and other documentation, including, where applicable, budgets, minutes etc
- Considering management's stated reasons for choosing a particular course of action
- Considering management's ability to carry out a particular course of action given the entity's economic circumstances, including the implications of its contractual commitments

IFRS Accounting Standards allows three valuation techniques for measuring fair value where fair value cannot be determined easily The auditor should consider whether the entity's method is appropriate, consistent with other fair value measurements in the financial statements and whether it is applied consistently.

The auditor should consider the following when considering fair value measurements:

- The length of time any assumptions cover (the longer, the more subjective the value is)
- The number of assumptions made in relation to the item
- The degree of subjectivity in the process
- The degree of uncertainty associated with the outcome of events
- Any lack of objective data
- The timings of any valuations used
- The reliability of third party evidence
- The impact of subsequent events on the fair value measurement

Where a fair value measurement is based on assumptions reflecting management's intent and ability to carry out certain actions, then the auditor should obtain **written representations** from management that these assumptions are reasonable and achievable.

1.5 Inventories

FAST FORWARD

When standard costing is used, the auditors must assess whether the valuation is reasonable.

IAS 2 *Inventories*

Inventories should be measured at the lower of cost and net realisable value. Costs include costs of purchase, conversion and others incurred in bringing inventories to present location and condition.

Exam focus point

You studied the audit of inventories in detail in your earlier studies. You should be able to design procedures to verify the existence and valuation of inventories. If you are in any doubt in this area go back to your previous auditing studies learning materials and revise.

An additional thing to consider in the audit of inventories is what **evidence** to obtain about **cost**, when there is a **standard costing system** in operation. Remember that IAS 2 allows standard costs to be used where prices are fluctuating.

Where standard costing is being used the auditor will have **two objectives**:

- Ensure that standard costing is an **appropriate basis** for valuing inventories.
- Ensure that the **calculation** of the standard cost is **reasonable.**

In evaluating whether standard costs are an appropriate basis, the auditor must:

- **Establish whether prices have fluctuated**. This can be done by reviewing purchase invoices, consulting a price index and enquiry of management.
- **Consider if the use of standard costing is the best accounting policy to use**. This should be discussed with the directors.
- If the accounting policy has changed from the previous year, the auditor must **consider the comparability of the accounts.**
- There should also be **disclosure** about any changes of accounting policy in the accounts, which the auditor should ensure is sufficient.

In ensuring that the calculation of the standard cost is reasonable, the auditor must:

- Obtain a copy of the calculation of standard cost.
- Check the additions and calculations.
- Consider whether the calculation is reasonable (for example, based on averages of costs over the year).

- Verify elements of the calculation to appropriate documentation, for example:
  - Purchase prices to invoices
  - Wages and salaries to personnel records
  - Overheads to expenses in the financial statements where possible
- Alternatively, the standard cost may be verifiable by analytical procedures by comparison to total expense figures in the statement of profit or loss and other comprehensive income, for example:
  - Wages should be based on the total wage cost divided by the production total for the year.

1.6 Assets arising from contracts with customers

The revenue aspects of IFRS 15 *Revenue from contracts with customers* are looked at in Section 2, but the aspects relating to any capitalised costs arising from revenue contracts will be considered briefly here. The auditor should ensure costs to fulfil a contract have been correctly capitalised in accordance with IFRS 15, which is when:

- They relate directly to a contract;
- They generate or enhance resources that will be used to satisfy performance obligations; and
- They are expected to be recovered.

Costs must be capitalised in a manner consistent with the pattern of transfer of the goods or services to which they relate. They must be amortised on a systematic basis that is also consistent with the pattern and transfer of the goods or services they relate to and tested for impairment.

Audit procedures

- Verify cost figures to invoices and ensure that they meet the standard criteria.
- Ensure that capitalised costs relating to future activity relate to future activity by reviewing invoices and work schedules.
- Review contract to ensure that capitalised costs are recoverable.
- Ensure assets are amortised and consider whether rate of amortisation is reasonable.
- Review impairment reviews for capitalised costs to fulfil a contract.

1.7 Tangible non-current assets

FAST FORWARD

> Auditors should ensure that both tangible and intangible assets have been subjected to an annual impairment review.

You covered all the key aspects relating to tangible non-current assets in your earlier studies. If you are in any doubt in this area, go back to your previous learning materials material and revise. IAS 16 *property, plant and equipment* sets out the accounting treatment for tangible non-current assets.

The issue of fair value discussed in Section 1.1 is likely to impact in an audit of non-current assets question.

1.7.1 Valuation of non-current assets

Non-current assets will be carried at cost or valuation (if an item has been revalued). Cost is straightforward to audit, it can be verified to original purchase documentation. Valuation may be straightforward to audit – it can be verified to the valuation certificate. The carrying value of non-current assets is therefore depreciated cost, or depreciated valuation.

Once a company has revalued assets, it is required to continue revaluing them on a regular basis so that the valuation is not materially different from the fair value at the reporting date. The auditors should therefore check that valuation is comparable to market value. They would do this by comparing the existing valuation to current market values (for example, in an estate agent's window).

Assets are depreciated, so their carrying value will not be original cost or valuation. Depreciation can be verified by reperforming the depreciation calculations. Often a 'proof-in-total' check will be sufficient, where auditors calculate the relevant depreciation percentage on the whole class of assets to see if it is comparable to the depreciation charged for that class of assets in the year.

The depreciation rate is determined by reference to the useful life of the asset. This is determined by management based on expectations of how long the asset is expected to be in use in the business. The auditors will audit this by scrutinising those expectations and verifying them where possible – for example, to the minutes of the meeting where management decided to buy the asset, to capital replacement budgets, to past practice in the business.

1.7.2 Impairment of non-current assets

An asset is impaired when its carrying amount (depreciated cost or depreciated valuation) exceeds its recoverable amount. You should be familiar with the following key terms from your accounting studies. Accounting treatment for impairment is provided by IAS 36 *Impairment of assets*.

Key terms

> An **impairment** occurs when the carrying amount of an asset exceeds its recoverable amount.
>
> The **carrying amount** is the amount at which an asset is recognised in the statement of financial position after deducting accumulated depreciation and accumulated impairment losses.
>
> The **recoverable amount** of an asset is the higher of its fair value less costs to sell (net selling price) and its value in use.
>
> **Fair value** is the amount obtainable from the sale of an asset in an arm's length transaction between knowledgeable, willing parties.
>
> **Value in use** is the discounted present value of the future cash flows expected to be derived from the continuing use of an asset and from its disposal at the end of its useful life.
>
> A **cash-generating unit** is the smallest identifiable group of assets that generates cash inflows that are largely independent of the cash flows from other assets or groups of assets. *(IAS 36)*

Management are required to determine if there is any indication that the assets are impaired.

The auditors will consider whether there are any indicators of impairment when carrying out risk assessment procedures. They will use the same impairment criteria laid out in IAS 36 as management do. If the auditors believe that impairment is indicated, they should request that management show them the impairment review that has been carried out. If no impairment review has been carried out, then the auditors should discuss the need for one with management, and if necessary, qualify their report on the grounds of a material misstatement if management refuse to carry out an impairment review.

If an impairment review has been carried out, then the auditors should audit that impairment review. Management will have estimated whether the recoverable amount of the asset or cash-generating unit is lower than the carrying amount.

For auditors, the key issue is that recoverable amount requires estimation. As estimation is subjective, this makes it a risky area for auditors.

Management have to determine if recoverable amount is higher than carrying amount. It may not have been necessary for them to estimate both fair value and value in use, because if one is higher than carrying amount, then the asset is not impaired. However, it may have been necessary to calculate both fair value and value in use.

The audit of **fair value** was set out in Section 1.1. Costs to sell such as taxes can be recalculated by applying the appropriate tax rate to the fair value itself. Delivery costs can be verified by asking delivery companies what their rates are.

If management have calculated the value in use of an asset or cash-generating unit, then the auditors will have to audit that calculation. The following procedures will be relevant.

Value in use

- Obtain management's calculations of value in use
- Reperform calculations to ensure that they are mathematically correct
- Compare the cash flow projection to recent budgets and projections approved by the board to ensure that they are realistic
- Calculate/obtain from analysts the average growth rate for the products over previous 20-year period and ensure that the growth rates assumed in the calculation of value in use do not exceed it
- Refer to competitors' published information to compare how much similar assets are valued at by companies trading in similar conditions
- Compare to previous calculations of value in use to ensure that all relevant costs of maintaining the asset have been included
- Ensure that the cost/income from disposal of the asset at the end of its life has been included
- Review calculation to ensure cash flows from financing activities and income tax have been excluded
- Compare discount rate used to published market rates to ensure that it correctly reflects the return expected by the market

If the asset is impaired and has been written down to recoverable amount, the auditors should review the financial statements to ensure that the write down has been carried out correctly and that the IAS 36 disclosures have been made correctly.

1.7.3 Held for sale non-current assets

In accordance with IFRS 5 *Non-current assets held for sale and discontinued operations* a non-current asset held for sale should be presented separately in the statement of financial position. A non-current asset should be classified as held for sale if its carrying amount will be recovered principally through a sale transaction rather than through continuing use. A number of detailed criteria must be met:

(a) The asset must be available for immediate sale in its present condition.
(b) The sale must be highly probable.

For sale to be highly probable the following must apply:

(a) Management must be committed to a plan to sell the asset.
(b) There must be an active plan to locate a buyer.
(c) The asset must be marketed at a price that is reasonable in relation to its current fair value.
(d) The sale should be expected to take place within one year from the date of classification.
(e) It is unlikely that significant changes to the plan will be made or that the plan will be withdrawn.

A non-current asset held for sale should be measured at the lower of its carrying amount and fair value less costs to sell. An impairment loss should be recognised where fair value less costs to sell is lower than the carrying amount.

Non-current assets held for sale should not be depreciated even if they are still being used by the entity.

The following audit procedures will therefore be relevant:

Confirm that the asset meets the definition of an asset held for sale:

- Discuss with management the availability of asset for sale.
- Assess management commitment, eg recorded in board minutes.
- Evaluate and assess practical steps being taken to sell the asset, eg appropriate real estate agents appointed.
- Determine when the sale is expected to take place by assessing progress to date.
- Determine and assess the basis on which the sale price has been set.
- Discuss with management any significant changes to the plans.

Confirm that the asset has been valued as held for sale in accordance with IFRS 5 and assess how fair value has been determined.

Check that the asset has not been depreciated from the date of reclassification.

Confirm separate disclosure in accordance with IFRS 5.

1.8 Intangible non-current assets

Accounting guidance for intangibles is given in IAS 38 *Intangible assets* and IFRS 3 *Business combinations*. The types of asset we are likely to encounter under this heading include patents, licences, trademarks, development costs and goodwill. All intangibles should be subject to an annual impairment review.

Key term

> An **intangible asset** is an identifiable non-monetary asset without physical substance. It may be held for using in the production and supply of goods or services, or for rental to others, or for administrative purposes. The asset must be:
>
> - Controlled by the enterprise as a result of events in the past; and
> - Something from which the enterprise expects future economic benefits to flow. (IAS 38)

> **IAS 38 *Intangible assets***
>
> Examples of items that might be considered as intangible assets include computer software, patents, copyrights, motion picture films, customer lists, franchises and fishing rights. An item should not be recognised as an intangible asset, however, unless it **fully meets the definition** in the standard. The guidelines go into great detail on this matter.
>
> Internally generated goodwill may **not** be recognised as an **asset**.

The auditor should carry out the following procedures.

Completeness

- **Prepare analysis** of movements on cost and amortisation accounts.

Rights and obligations

- **Obtain confirmation** of all **patents** and **trademarks** held by a patent agent.
- **Verify payment** of **annual renewal fees.**

Valuation

- **Review specialist valuations** of intangible assets, considering:
    - Qualifications of valuer
    - Scope of work
    - Assumptions and methods used
- **Confirm carried down balances** represent **continuing value**, which are proper charges to future operations.

    Additions (rights and obligations, valuation and completeness)

    - **Inspect purchase agreements, assignments** and **supporting documentation** for intangible assets acquired in period.
    - **Confirm purchases** have been **authorised.**
    - **Verify amounts capitalised** of patents developed by the company with supporting costing records.

Amortisation

- **Review amortisation:**
    - Check computation
    - Confirm that rates used are reasonable

Income from intangibles:

- **Review sales returns** and **statistics** to verify the reasonableness of income derived from patents, trademarks, licences etc.
- **Examine audited accounts** of third party sales covered by a patent, licence or trademark owned by the company.

1.8.1 Goodwill

Key tests are as follows.

- **Agree consideration** to a **sales agreement.**
- **Confirm valuation** of assets acquired is reasonable.
- **Check purchased goodwill** is **calculated correctly** (it should reflect the difference between the fair value of the consideration given and the aggregate of the fair values of the separable net assets acquired).
- **Check goodwill** does **not include non-purchased goodwill.**
- **Impairment testing:**
    - Ensure management have carried out annual impairment review.
    - Assess whether their conclusions are reasonable (see Section 1.7.2).
- **Ensure valuation of goodwill is reasonable** by reviewing prior year's accounts and discussion with the directors.

Exam focus point

The May 2022 exam tested candidates knowledge on the audit of goodwill.

1.8.2 Development costs

The accounting treatment for research and development costs is covered by IAS 38 *Intangible assets*.

Key terms

Research is original and planned investigation undertaken with the prospect of gaining new scientific or technical knowledge and understanding.

Development is the application of research findings or other knowledge to a plan or design for the production of new or substantially improved materials, devices, products, processes, systems or services prior to the commencement of commercial production or use. (IAS 38)

IAS 38 *Intangible assets*

- Development costs may be included in the statement of financial position (that is to say, capitalised) only in 'special circumstances' laid out in IAS 38.
- Expenditure on **research** is required to be written off in the year of expenditure.
- IAS 38 states that the **development costs** of a project should be recognised as an asset only when all of the following criteria are met:

    (a) Completion of the asset will be technically feasible.

    (b) The business intends to complete the asset and use or sell it.

    (c) The business will be able to use or sell the asset.

    (d) The business can demonstrate how future economic benefits will be generated, either by demonstrating a market exists or the internal usefulness of the asset.

    (e) Adequate technical, financial and other resources will be available to complete the development and use or sell the intangible asset.

    (f) Expenditure attributable to the development of the asset can be measured reliably. General overhead expenditure, costs of inefficiencies and operating losses, and expenditure on training staff to operate the asset should not be capitalised.

    The development costs of a project recognised as an asset should not exceed the amount that is likely to be recovered from related future economic benefits, after deducting further development costs, related production costs, and selling and administrative costs directly incurred in marketing the product.

- In all other circumstances development costs should be written off in the year of expenditure.

The key audit tests largely reflect the criteria laid down in IAS 38.

- **Check accounting records** to confirm:
    - **Project** is **clearly defined** (separate cost centre or nominal ledger codes)
    - **Related expenditure** can be **separately identified**, and agreed to invoices, timesheets

- **Confirm feasibility and viability**:
    - Examine market research reports, feasibility studies, budgets and forecasts
    - Consult client's technical experts.

- **Review budgeted revenues** and **costs** by examining results to date, production forecasts, advance orders and discussion with directors.

- **Review calculations** of **future cash flows** to ensure resources exist to complete the project.

- **Review previously deferred expenditure** to ensure ISA 38 criteria are still justified.

- **Check amortisation:**
  - Commences with production
  - Charged on a systematic basis

The good news for the auditors in this audit area is that many companies adopt a prudent approach and write off research and development expenditure in the year it is incurred. The auditors' concern in these circumstances is whether the statement of comprehensive income charge for research and development is complete, accurate and valid.

1.8.3 Brands

The key accounting issue with regard to brands is whether the asset is **internally generated** or not. Remember, IAS 38 forbids the capitalisation of internally generated assets.

If a brand has been purchased separately (that is, not as part of goodwill) then auditors should test the value of the brand according to the sales documentation.

1.9 Investments

> **FAST FORWARD**
>
> When auditing investments, the auditors will have to consider both income and the asset.

> **Key term**
>
> An equity instrument of another entity, in other words, a share in another entity, is a **financial asset**.

The accounting requirements for financial assets are found in IAS 32 *Financial instruments: presentation*, IFRS 7 *Financial instruments: disclosures* and IFRS 9 *Financial instruments*. You should be familiar with the examinable parts of most of these standards from your financial accounting studies. IFRS 9 was issued in 2014 and replaces IAS 39.

1.9.1 Valuation of investments

Financial assets are recognised initially at their fair value. Subsequently they are measured at fair value. The cost of shares can be verified by checking the purchase documentation. The fair value of listed shares will generally be the market price, which can be verified by referring to the stock exchange listings or the quotations published in the financial press.

1.9.2 Existence of investments

Again, for listed shares, the auditor can check the company exists by reviewing the stock exchange listings. Unlisted companies can be verified by simple enquiries at the Companies Registry.

1.9.3 Rights and obligations relating to investments

If a company owns shares in another company it should own a share certificate outlining those shares which the auditor can look at. It might be that the company keeps its share certificates in a bank or at a brokers, in which case the auditor will obtain a confirmation from these parties that the share certificate exists (with the client's permission).

1.9.4 Investment income

Investment income is accounted for under IAS 32, which states that interest and dividend income should be recognised in profit and loss.

1.10 Investment property

A key factor to consider when auditing investment property is whether one **exists** according to the **criteria** of IAS 40 *Investment property*.

Key term

> **Investment property** is property (land or a building – or part of a building – or both) held (by the owner or by the lessee) to earn rentals or for capital appreciation or both, rather than for:
>
> - Use in the production or supply of goods or services or for administrative purposes; or
> - Sale in the ordinary course of business

Type of property	Applicable IAS
Property held for sale in the ordinary course of business	IAS 2 *Inventories*
Owner-occupied property	IAS 16 *Property, plant and equipment*
Property being constructed or developed for future use as investment property	IAS 40 *Investment property*
Property being constructed or developed on behalf of third parties	IFRS 15 *Revenue from contracts with customers*

Substantive tests

- Verify **rental agreements**, ensuring that occupier is not a connected company and that the rent has been negotiated at arm's length.
- If the building has recently been built, check **architect's certificates** to ensure that construction work has been completed.

The second important assertion in relation to investment properties is **valuation**. IAS 40 requires that investment properties either be held at **cost** (benchmark treatment) or at fair value. This approximates to open market value. The auditor should be able to verify this by reference to a valuer's certificate, as professional valuation is encouraged under the IAS.

The auditors should seek to verify the cost to appropriate evidence, for example purchase invoice or, if self-constructed, costing records, payroll etc.

The last key issue with regard to investment properties is **disclosure**. The auditor should review the disclosures made in the financial statements in relation to investment properties to ensure that they have been made appropriately, in accordance with IAS 40.

If the benchmark treatment is used, a key disclosure is that of the **fair value** of the asset.

Exam focus point

> The May 2023 exam included a 20 mark question on the audit of investment property.

Question

Non-current assets

You are reviewing the file on the audit of Apollo plc, which is nearing completion. Apollo produces two products; the X and the W. Apollo plc purchased two new pieces of plant in the year. Plant is valued at cost. The X103 was bought to replace the X102, which was scrapped at the start of the year. The W103 was bought to replace the W102. The W102 will no longer be used in producing the W, but will be used to test new products, particularly the V, which Apollo is hoping to be able to market and sell in the next two years.

Required

Describe matters you would consider and the audit evidence you would expect to see on file in respect of the valuation of these pieces of plant.

Answer

Matters to consider

The main matter to consider here is the valuation of the W102. Now it will no longer be used in production, it may be impaired. The asset should be valued in the financial statements at the lower of carrying amount or recoverable amount. Recoverable amount will be fair value, as the W102 no longer has a value in use until the V is marketed. Whether the W102 has a market (fair) value will depend on how specialised a machine it is. The fact that can be transferred to use on a different product to the W suggests that it is not highly specialised and that there may be a second hand market from which a valuation can be taken.

Evidence that should be contained on the audit file

- Indication that the value of the X103 and W103 has been agreed to purchase invoices
- Recalculation of profit/loss on scrapping of X102
- Note of physical inspection to ensure that X102 is no longer on premises
- Minutes of directors' meeting approving the scrapping of the X102 and change in use of the W102 reviewed
- Copy of management's impairment review with regard to the W102
- Fair value of W102 verified by reference to price lists of suppliers of such second hand machines
- Note of observation of operation of machines to ensure W102 no longer used in production

2 Income

> **FAST FORWARD** Revenue recognition is an extremely important issue and completeness is a key assertion to be audited.

2.1 Revenue recognition

Revenue is commonly audited by analytical procedures. This is because revenue should be predictable and there are good bases on which to base analytical procedures, such as:

- Plenty of information, for example, last year's accounts, budget, monthly analyses (companies tend to keep a lot of information about sales)
- Logical relationships with items such as inventory and receivables

Unless complex transactions arise where revenue is not as clear cut as a product being supplied and invoiced for, revenue recognition is generally not an issue. However, in some companies, for example, those that deal primarily in revenue contracts where performance obligations are satisfied over time, revenue recognition can be a **material** issue.

Examples of industries where this might be true:

- Building industry
- Engineering industry

In such industries, auditing revenue recognition will be part of auditing revenue where performance obligations are satisfied over time. The auditor should:

- Obtain a copy of the calculation of revenue recognised in the period and recalculate, including any assets/liabilities recognised
- Assess whether the basis of calculation is comparable with prior years
- Confirm that the method for measuring progress for performance obligations is appropriate and reasonable in line with IFRS 15
- Verify the figures in the calculation, such as:
    - Total contract price to original contract
    - Revenue to amount of performance completed to date
    - Performance completed to date to input methods, such as certification of work completed, cost of work completed (eg to invoices and payroll/clock cards/wage rates)
    - Receivables to sales invoices
    - Payments on account to remittance advices

2.1.1 IFRS 15 *Revenue from Contracts with Customers*

IFRS 15 standard defines revenue as 'income arising in the course of an entity's ordinary activities', and therefore encompasses most income generated by a company, including income such as that arising from the sale of non-current assets.

It establishes a five-step model to apply to revenue earned from a contract to determine when and at what amount revenue should be recognised. It is likely to involve a degree of judgement, as it incorporates factors such as variable consideration and the time value of money, so auditors will have to bear in mind the requirements of ISA 540 *Auditing accounting estimates, including fair value accounting estimates, and related disclosures* when auditing revenue.

The five steps are:

(1) Identify the contract with a customer. These may be written, verbal or implied, but must be enforceable and have commercial substance.

(2) Identify the separate performance obligations in the contract.

(3) Determine the transaction price.

(4) Allocate the transaction price to the separate performance obligations.

(5) Recognise revenue as the entity satisfies a performance obligation (note that a performance obligation may be satisfied at a point in time or over time).

Key term

A **performance obligation** is a promise in a contract with a customer to transfer to the customer either:
- A good or service (or a bundle of goods or services) that is distinct; or
- A series of distinct goods or services that are substantially the same and that have the same pattern of transfer to the customer.

Revenue is recognised as control is passed, either over time or at a point in time.

Control of an asset is defined as the ability to direct the use of and obtain substantially all of the remaining benefits from the asset. This includes the ability to prevent others from directing the use of and obtaining the benefits from the asset. The benefits related to the asset are the potential cash flows that may be obtained directly or indirectly. These include, but are not limited to:

- Using the asset to produce goods or provide services;
- Using the asset to enhance the value of other assets;
- Using the asset to settle liabilities or to reduce expenses;
- Selling or exchanging the asset;
- Pledging the asset to secure a loan; and
- Holding the asset.

An entity recognises revenue over time if one of the following criteria is met:

- The customer simultaneously receives and consumes all of the benefits provided by the entity as the entity performs;
- The entity's performance creates or enhances an asset that the customer controls as the asset is created; or
- The entity's performance does not create an asset with an alternative use to the entity and the entity has an enforceable right to payment for performance completed to date.

Where performance obligations are satisfied over time, they are accounted for at an amount that approximates the selling price of the goods or services transferred to date. The entity must choose an appropriate method for estimating the amount of performance completed to date.

Key terms

Methods include output methods and input methods:

- **Output methods** recognise revenue on the basis of the value to the customer of the goods or services transferred. They include surveys of performance completed and appraisal of units produced or delivered.
- **Input methods** recognise revenue on the basis of the entity's inputs, such as labour hours, resources consumed, costs incurred. If using a cost-based method, the costs incurred must contribute to the entity's progress in satisfying the performance obligation.

If an entity does not satisfy its performance obligation over time, it satisfies it at a point in time. Revenue will therefore be recognised when control is passed at a certain point in time. Factors that may indicate the point in time at which control passes include, but are not limited to:

- The entity has a present right to payment for the asset;
- The customer has legal title to the asset;
- The entity has transferred physical possession of the asset;
- The customer has the significant risks and rewards related to the ownership of the asset; and
- The customer has accepted the asset.

In terms of auditing revenue, the auditor will have to review the assumptions and judgements made by the directors in identifying separate performance obligations and how they determine that the performance obligations are satisfied.

Case Study

Revenue recognition in an e-commerce environment

Companies that engage in e-commerce may have particular revenue recognition issues.

The entity may act as a **principal** or as an **agent**. They must determine whether to disclose their gross sales, or merely their commission. For example, Lastminute.com discloses a figure 'TTV', which does not represent statutory revenue, but represents the price at which goods and services has been sold across the group's platforms. Revenue itself is largely made up of commission on selling those goods and services.

The company may engage in **reciprocal arrangements** with other companies whereby they both advertise on each other's website. Whether such an arrangement results in 'revenue' must be considered. It must then be accounted for.

The company may deal in unusual **discounts** or voucher systems to encourage customers to buy. These must also be accounted for.

Lastly, the company must determine a policy for **cut off**. This may be complex if the company acts as an agent. When is the sale made? When the customer clicks 'accept', when the company emails acknowledgement, when the sale is made known to the principal, when the goods are despatched, when the customer receives the goods, when the customer has taken advantage of the services...? The company must determine a reasonable policy for when the sale has been made.

Question — Revenue recognition and other matters

The senior partner of JLPN, a firm of auditors, has issued as 'Audit Risk Alert' letter to all partners dealing with key areas of concern which should be given due consideration by his firm when auditing public companies. The letter outlines certain trends in audit reporting that, if not scrutinised by the auditors, could lead to a loss of reliability and transparency in the financial statements. The following three key concerns were outlined in the letter.

(a) Audit committees play a very important role together with the financial director and auditor in achieving high quality financial control and auditing. Recently the efforts of certain audit committees have been questioned in the press.

(b) The Stock Exchange had reported cases of inappropriate revenue recognition practises including:

 (i) Accelerating revenue prior to the delivery of the product to the customer's site, or prior to the completion of the terms of the sales arrangement.

 (ii) Recognition of revenue when customers have unilateral cancellation or termination provisions, other than the normal customary product return provisions.

(c) It has been reported that the management of companies had intentionally violated IFRS Accounting Standards by immaterial amounts. The reason for this has been the sensitivity of reported earnings per share in a market place where missing the market's expectation of earnings per share by a small amount could have significant consequences.

Required

(a) Explain the importance if the role of an 'Audit Risk Alert' letter to a firm of auditors.

(b) Discuss the way in which the auditor should deal with each of the key concerns outlined in the letter in order to ensure that audit risk is kept to an acceptable level.

Answer

(a) The '**risk alert letter**' is a memorandum used by the reporting partner to notify fellow partners of concerns emerging from dealings with clients, regulatory authorities or stock exchanges.
It ensures that:

- Key audit risk areas are reviewed
- Significant trends and irregularities are identified
- Quality is maintained
- Litigation risk is reduced
- Investor confidence is maintained as it reduces manipulation

(b) (i) **Audit Committees** are held to secure good a quality of **internal control** and financial reporting in plc's. If the auditor has doubts about the effectiveness of an audit committee then he should **review its structure, independence and membership** to ensure it meets its objectives. Any shortcomings should be reported to the board and/or the members.

(ii) **Revenue acceleration** is a **creative accounting device**. Revenue should **not be recognised until earned and realised** (realisable), so the practices described are not acceptable. Only if the risks of ownership have been fully transferred to the buyer and the seller has not retained any specific performance obligation should revenue be recognised earlier.

Extended audit tests concerning revenue recognition and 'cut off' tests may be appropriate if the auditor suspects anomalies.

(iii) Where **IFRS Accounting Standards violations** have occurred, **materiality judgement** may be affected. The auditor must ensure the audit team is aware that violations of IFRS Accounting Standards **can affect EPS** for certain clients, and that staff are sufficiently experienced and trained in order to detect such violations. It may be that the errors are individually immaterial, but the **aggregate effect** must be considered. Furthermore, the practice of intentional misstatements may indicate that the **management** of the company **lacks integrity** and the auditor should consider whether the client should be retained.

2.2 Government grants and assistance

Government grants and assistance are accounted for under IAS 20 *Accounting for government grants and disclosure of government assistance*. They may be either grants relating to the assets or income.

Key terms

Government assistance is action by government designed to provide an economic benefit specific to an enterprise or range of enterprises qualifying under certain criteria.

Government grants are assistance by government in the form of transfers of resources to an enterprise in return for past or future compliance with certain conditions relating to the operating activities of the enterprise. They exclude those forms of government assistance which cannot reasonably have a value placed upon them and transactions with government which cannot be distinguished from the normal trading transactions of the enterprise.

Grants related to assets are government grants whose primary condition is that an enterprise qualifying for them should purchase, construct or otherwise acquire long-term assets. Subsidiary conditions may also be attached restricting the type or location of the assets or the periods during which then are to be acquired or held.

Grants related to income are government grants other than those related to assets.

Forgivable loans are loans which the lender undertakes to waive repayment of certain prescribed conditions.

IAS 20 *Accounting for government grants and disclosure of government assistance*

Accounting treatment

- **Recognise government grants and forgivable loans** once conditions complied with and receipt/waiver is assured.
- Grants are recognised under the **income approach**: recognise grants as income to match them with related costs that they have been received to compensate.

- Use a **systematic basis** of matching over the relevant periods.
- Grants for **depreciable assets** should be recognised as income on the same basis as the asset is depreciated.
- Grants for **non-depreciable assets** should be recognised as income over the periods in which the cost of meeting the obligation is incurred.
- A grant may be **split into parts** and allocated on different bases where there are a series of conditions attached.
- Where **related costs have already been incurred**, the grant may be recognised as income in full immediately.
- A grant in the form of a **non-monetary asset** may be valued at fair value or a nominal value.
- **Grants related to assets** may be presented in the statement of financial position *either* as a **separate credit** *or* deducted in arriving at the carrying value of the asset.
- **Grants related to income** may be presented in the statement of comprehensive income *either* as a **separate credit** *or* **deducted** from the related expense.
- Repayment of government grants should be accounted for as a **revision of an account estimate**.

Disclosure

- **Accounting policy** note.
- **Nature and extent** of government grants and other forms of assistance received.
- **Unfulfilled conditions** and other contingencies attached to recognised government assistance.

Grants where related costs have already been incurred offer no difficulties to account for or to audit. To audit them, the auditor should:

- Obtain documentation relating to the grant and confirm that it should be classified as revenue.
- The value may be agreed to the documentation (for example, a letter outlining the details of the grant, or a copy of an application form sent by the client).
- The receipt of the grant can be agreed to bank statements.

Capitalised grants can be more difficult to audit, particularly if a non-monetary government grant is being accounted for at fair value.

Audit procedures:

- Consider whether the basis of accounting is comparable to the previous year.
- Discuss the basis of accounting with the directors to ensure that the method used is the best method.
- Ensure that any changes in accounting method are disclosed.

3 Liabilities

FAST FORWARD

The relevant financial statement assertions for liabilities are completeness, rights and obligations and existence. Liabilities must be tested for understatement.

3.1 Fair value

As outlined in Section 1.1, fair value is a key issue when considering certain liabilities. You should bear in mind the issues discussed in Section 1.1 when auditing liabilities.

3.2 Leases

FAST FORWARD

The classification of a lease can have a material effect on the financial statements.

IFRS 16 *Leases* was issued in January 2016 and superseded IAS 17. IFRS 16 aims to bring leases that were previously off-balance sheet back on. It was widely thought that companies were taking advantage of the previous standard, and in particular the distinction between long-term leases (that were on the balance sheet (statement of financial position)) and short-term leases (that were off it). By obtaining an asset on a short-term 'operating lease', a company would still have the benefit of the asset but would be able to keep the liability off its balance sheet (statement of financial position). You could think of IFRS 16 as simply expanding the treatment that used to be reserved for finance leases – bringing them on-balance sheet, with both an asset and a liability – to all leases.

IFRS 16 was the outcome of a joint project between the IASB and the FASB (from the United States), although the two standard-setters did not agree on an approach, with the FASB choosing to retain the distinction between long-term leases (called 'capital leases') and short-term leases ('operating leases').

In a way IFRS 16 does still retain this distinction, by making an exception for very short-term leases and leases of low-value assets. It is expected, though, that most assets that were formerly held on 'operating leases' will now be brought onto the balance sheet (statement of financial position).

Here is a summary of IFRS 16's requirements for lessees.

IFRS 16 *Leases*

Objective

To provide **relevant** information that **faithfully represents** (IFRS 16: para. 1).

Faithful representation is related to the old principle of 'substance over form'.

Exceptions

Some leased assets are exempt from the IFRS 16 treatment (IFRS 16: para. 5):

(a) **Short-term** leases (< 12 months); and
(b) Leases of **low value** assets.

Lessees of these assets can elect to simply **expense the lease payments on a straight line basis** (or another systematic basis).

The same treatment must be applied for all assets within a class, eg all short-term leases must be treated in the same way.

Low value assets

Examples of low value assets would be: tablet and personal computers, small items of office furniture and telephones (IFRS 16: para. B8).

'Low value' is an **absolute** term, ie it is not a relative percentage value, but is the same for all entities. It is not defined by the Standard, but the IASB has indicated that this is up to $5,000 per asset. This is for the value of a new asset – if the asset is acquired second-hand, then it is still assessed on its value when new.

Identifying a lease

This is the closest we get to a definition:

'A contract is [...] a lease if the contract conveys the right to control the use of an identified asset for a period of time in exchange for consideration.' (IFRS 16: para. 9)

Control is conveyed where the customer has both the right to direct the identified asset and to obtain substantially all the economic benefits (IFRS 16: para. B9).

A contract might be for both a lease and something else (such as maintenance). In this case the components are accounted for separately, ie the lease part is still accounted for as a lease. To allocate the consideration between the lease and non-lease parts, the non-lease part is allocated its 'standalone price', and the lease part gets the remainder of the consideration.

Recognition

'At the commencement date, a lessee shall recognise a **right-of-use asset** and a **lease liability**.' (IFRS 16: para. 22)

Both an asset and a matching liability are recognised.

Measurement

Right-of-use asset

'At the commencement date, a lessee shall measure the right-of-use asset at **cost**.' (IFRS 16: para. 23)

IFRS 16 requires a **cost model** for the **asset**. The cost is calculated as follows (IFRS 16: para. 24):

Amount of lease liability (on initial measurement)	X
Add: any lease payments made at or before commencement date (or less incentives received)	X
Add: any **initial direct** costs	X
Add: **dismantling costs** (estimated)	X
Total	X

Although the cost model is required, IFRS 16 does allow entities to deviate from it in order to be consistent with their treatment of other similar assets, eg by using the fair value model of IAS 40 *Investment property*, or IAS 16's revaluation model.

Lease liability

'At the commencement date, a lessee shall measure the lease liability at the **present value of the lease payments** that are not paid at that date.' (IFRS 16: para. 26)

The present value of the liability is measured using the **implicit interest rate**.

The lease liability is therefore initially recognised as follows (IFRS 16: para. 27):

Fixed payments (less incentives receivable)	X
Add: **Variable lease payments** (which depend on an index/rate)	X
Add: Amounts payable under **residual value guarantees**	X
Add: the exercise price of a purchase option (if reasonably certain to exercise)	X
Add: Penalties for **termination payments**, if these will be incurred in line with lease term	X
Total	X

Remeasurement

Right-of-use asset

Depreciation is charged on the asset, in line with IAS 16's cost model.

Depreciation is charged until the earlier of: the end of the useful life, and the end of the lease term. (But if there is an option to buy the asset at the end of the lease, it *must* be depreciated all the way to the end of its useful life.)

Lease liability

In subsequent periods, the liability is remeasured by (IFRS 16: para. 36):

(a) Adding interest to the liability (implicit interest rate)
(b) Reducing the liability by payments made
(c) Remeasuring for any modifications made, or revised lease payments.

Lease term

The lease term is the **non-cancellable period of the lease** (IFRS 16: para. 18).

If there is an option to extend or terminate the lease, then the term will include this if it is **reasonably certain** that they will be exercised.

Presentation

Statement of financial position: the right-of-use asset may be **combined with other assets** (in the same class) on the face of the SoFP, but must be disclosed separately in the notes.

Statement of profit or loss: interest expense included within **finance cost**.

Statement of cash flows: cash payments shown within financing activities.

Disclosures

IFRS 16 gives a long list of disclosures. Here are the most important:

- **Depreciation charge** for right-of-use assets by class of underlying asset;
- **Interest expense** on lease liabilities;
- The expense relating to **short-term leases**;
- The expense relating to leases of **low-value assets**;
- The **expense** relating to **variable lease payments** not included in the measurement of lease liabilities;
- **Income from subleasing** right-of-use assets;
- Total **cash outflow** for leases;
- **Additions** to right-of-use assets;
- Gains or losses arising from **sale and leaseback transactions**; and
- The **carrying amount of right-of-use assets** at the end of the reporting period by class of underlying asset.

Note disclosures are required for when the lease liability will fall due, but these are in line with IFRS 7 (IFRS 16: para. 58). IFRS 7 requires the entity to use its judgement to determine the best time bands, ie these could be the old 1 year / 2–5 years / after 5 years bands, but they could be any other appropriate bands.

Sale and leaseback

The treatment depends on whether the 'sale' qualifies as a sale by satisfying performance obligations in line with IFRS 15. This means that **control** must be transferred to the customer.

If the asset is **not sold under IFRS 15**, then the seller does not 'transfer' the asset and continues to recognise it as before. The 'sales proceeds' are recognised as a financial liability and accounted for by applying and recognising a liability in line with IFRS 9 *Financial instruments*.

If the transaction **does meet IFRS 15 criteria**, then any right-of-use that is retained should continue to be recognised as an asset, as a proportion of the previous carrying amount. A gain or loss is recognised for the proportion that is sold.

If **FV of sale consideration > FV asset**, then this is a **prepayment of lease terms**.

If **FV of sale consideration < FV asset**, then this is **additional financing** (a secured loan).

Exam focus point

Your exam answers in this area could make use of key bits of IFRS 16 terminology, such as:

'A Co should have recognised a **right-of-use asset** and a **lease liability**.'

One of the trickiest parts of IFRS 16 is determining whether or not the contract is a lease at all. Leases may be found in many contracts that until recently were not treated as leases, so there is a risk regarding the **completeness** of leasing transactions – have any been missed out?

The definition of a lease refers to the '**right to control** the use' of an asset. Determining whether there is control involves judgement, which introduces an element of risk for the auditor; likewise the assessment of **lease term** which requires judgement where there are options for either extension or termination.

IFRS 16 requires lease and non-lease components to be separated from one another. For example, a lease might be for just one part of a building, in which case it is necessary to allocate the consideration between the part that is leased and the part that is not leased. Again, this requires judgement and is therefore risky.

Many entities will not want to recognise assets and liabilities for lease transactions, so auditors need to be alert to the risk of distortion in relation to any of these areas of judgement.

The auditor needs to be alert to the possibility of **sale and leaseback** transactions. If there is a sale and leaseback, the auditor needs to check that gains are treated in line with IFRS 16, along with any prepayments or additional financing.

The following audit procedures are relevant:

Classification and rights and obligations

- Obtain a copy of the lease agreement
- Review the lease agreement to ensure that the lease term has been determined correctly in line with IFRS 16

Valuation

- Obtain a copy of the client's workings for their lease liabilities
- Check the additions and calculations of the workings
- Ensure that the implicit interest has been accounted for in accordance with IFRS 16
- Recalculate the interest
- Agree the opening position
- Agree any new assets to lease agreements
- Verify lease payments in the year to the bank statements

Disclosure

- Ensure the leases have been properly disclosed in the financial statements

3.3 Deferred taxation

FAST FORWARD — The auditor needs to audit the movement on the deferred tax liability.

Deferred tax is accounted for under IAS 12 *Income taxes*. This is revised briefly below.

Key terms

Deferred tax is the tax attributable to temporary differences, which are differences between the carrying amount of an asset or liability in the statement of financial position and its tax base.

Deferred tax liabilities are the amounts of income taxes payable in future periods in respect of taxable temporary differences. All taxable temporary differences give rise to a deferred tax liability.

Deferred tax assets are the amounts of income taxes recoverable in future periods in respect of:

- Deductible temporary differences (eg provisions, unrealised profits on intra group trading
- The carry forward of unused tax losses
- The carry forward of unused tax credits

All deductible temporary differences give rise to a deferred tax asset.

Temporary differences are differences between the carrying amount of an asset or liability in the statement of financial position and its tax base. Temporary differences may be either:

- **Taxable temporary differences**, which are temporary differences that will result in taxable amounts in determining taxable profit (tax loss) of future periods when the carrying amount of the asset or liability is recovered or settled.
- **Deductible temporary differences**, which are temporary differences that will result in amounts that are deductible in determining taxable profit (tax loss) of future periods when the carrying amount of the asset or liability is recovered or settled.

The **tax base** of an asset or liability is the amount attributed to that asset or liability for tax purposes.

Deferred tax is the **tax attributable to timing differences**. For example, where a company 'saves tax' in the current period by having accelerated capital allowances, a **provision for the tax charge** is **made in the statement of financial position**.

The provision is made is because over the course of the asset's life, the tax allowances will reduce until the depreciation charged in the accounts is higher than the allowances. This will result in taxable profit being higher than reported profit and the company will be 'suffering higher tax' in this period.

3.3.1 Types of taxable temporary difference

Accelerated capital allowances

The temporary difference is the difference between the carrying value of the asset in the statement of financial position at the end of the reporting period and its tax depreciated value.

Interest revenue (where interest is included in profit or loss on an accruals basis but taxed when received).

The temporary difference is equivalent to the income accrual in the statement of financial position at the end of the reporting period as the tax base of the interest receivable is nil.

Development costs (where development costs are capitalised for accounting purposes but deducted from taxable profit in the period incurred).

The temporary difference is equivalent to the amount capitalised in the statement of financial position at the end of the reporting period. The tax base is nil since they have already been deducted from taxable profits.

Revaluation to fair value (in jurisdictions where the tax base of the asset is not adjusted).

The temporary difference is the difference between the assets carrying value and tax base. A deferred liability is created even if the entity does not intend to dispose of the asset.

Fair value adjustments on consolidation

A temporary difference arises as for the revaluation above but the deferred tax effect is a consolidation adjustment in the same way as the revaluation itself.

Question
Revision: taxable temporary differences

A company, Shelley, purchased an asset costing $3,000. At the end of 20X8 the carrying amount is $2,000. The cumulative depreciation for tax purposes is $1,800 and the current tax rate is 25%.

Required

Calculate the deferred tax liability for the asset.

Answer

Tax base of the asset is $3,000 – $1,800 = $1,200

Deferred tax liability = $800 (2,000 – 1,200) × 25% = $200

3.3.2 Types of deductible temporary differences

Provisions

The provision is recognised for accounting purposes when there is a present obligation, but may not be deductible for tax purposes until the expenditure is incurred.

Losses

Current losses that can be carried forward to be offset against future taxable profits result in a deferred tax asset.

Fair value adjustments

For example, liabilities recognised on business combinations where the expenditure is not deductible for tax purposes until a later period.

Unrealised profits on intra-group trading

The profit is not realised from the group point of view until the items transferred are sold outside the group, but where the tax base is based on the cost to the individual receiving company and no equivalent adjustment for unrealised profit is made for tax purposes a temporary difference arises.

Question
Revision: deductible temporary differences

Ontario recognises a liability of $20,000 for accrued product warranty costs on 31 December 20X8. These product warranty costs will not be deductible for tax purposes until the entity pays the claims. The tax rate is 25%.

Required

Calculate the deferred tax asset.

> **Answer**
>
> Tax base = Nil (carrying amount of $20,000 less the amount that will be deductible for tax purposes in respect of the liability in future periods).
>
> Deferred tax asset = $20,000 (carrying amount) – Nil (tax base) = 20,000 × 25% = $5,000.
>
> This should be recognised in accordance with IAS 12 (see Section 3.3.3 below).

3.3.3 Measurement of deferred tax

The key points to remember are as follows:

- IAS 12 adopts the **full provision** method of providing for deferred tax. This recognises that each timing difference at the period end has an effect on future tax payments.
- Deferred tax assets and liabilities are measured at the tax rates expected to apply to the period when the asset is realised or liability settled, based on the tax rates (and tax laws) that have been **enacted** (or substantively enacted) by the end of the reporting period.
- Deferred assets and liabilities **cannot be discounted**.
- Deferred tax assets are only recognised to the extent that it is **probable** that taxable profit will be available against which the deductible temporary difference can be utilised.

3.3.4 Audit issues and procedures

As part of the **planning process**, if the client receives tax services from the firm, the auditor should consult the tax department as to the company's future tax plans, to ascertain whether they expect a deferred tax liability to arise. This will assist any analytical review they carry out on the deferred tax provision.

Remember that **manipulating the deferred tax figure will not affect the actual tax position**. However, a **deferred tax charge** (the other part of the double entry for the statement of financial position provision) **is recognised in profit or loss before dividends**, even if it is not actually paid to the taxation authorities.

The following procedures will be relevant:

- Obtain a copy of the deferred tax workings and the corporation tax computation.
- Check the arithmetical **accuracy** of the deferred tax working.
- Agree the **figures used** to calculate timing differences to those on the **tax computation** and the **financial statements.**
- Consider the assumptions made in the light of your knowledge of the business and any other evidence gathered during the course of the audit to ensure reasonableness.
- Agree the opening position on the deferred tax account to the prior year financial statements.
- Review the basis of the provision to ensure:
    - It is line with accounting practice under IAS 12.
    - It is suitably comparable to practice in previous years.
    - Any changes in accounting policy have been disclosed.

3.4 Provisions and contingencies

FAST FORWARD

A provision is accounted for as a liability, contingencies are disclosed, so auditors must ensure they have been classified correctly according to IAS 37.

Provisions are accounted for under IAS 37 *Provisions, contingent liabilities, and contingent assets*.

Key terms

A **provision** is a liability of uncertain timing or amount.

A **liability** is a present obligation of the enterprise arising from past events, the settlement of which is expected to result in an outflow from the enterprise of resources embodying economic benefits.

An **obligating event** is an event that creates a legal or constructive obligation that results in an enterprise having no realistic alternative to settling that obligation.

A **legal obligation** is an obligation that derives from:

(a) A contract (through its explicit or implicit terms);
(b) Legislation; or
(c) Other operation of law.

A **constructive obligation** is an obligation that derives from an enterprise's actions where:

(a) By an established pattern of past practice, published policies and sufficiently specific current statement, the enterprise has indicated to other parties that it will accept certain responsibilities; and
(b) As a result, the enterprise has created a valid expectation on the part of those other parties that it will discharge those responsibilities.

A **contingent liability** is:

(a) A possible obligation that arises from past events and whose existence will be confirmed only by the occurrence or non-occurrence of one or more uncertain future events not wholly within the control of the enterprise, or
(b) A present obligation that arises from past events but is not recognised because:
  (i) It is not probable that an outflow of resources embodying economic benefits will be required to settle the obligation, or
  (ii) The amount of the obligation cannot be measured with sufficient reliability.

A **contingent asset** is a possible asset that arises from past events and whose existence will be confirmed only by the occurrence or non-occurrence of one or more uncertain future events not wholly within the control of the enterprise.

(IAS 37)

Under IAS 37, an entity should not recognise a **contingent asset** or a **contingent liability**. However if it becomes probable that an outflow of future economic benefits will be required for a previous contingent liability, a provision should be recognised. A contingent asset should not be accounted for unless its realisation is virtually certain; if an inflow of economic benefits has become probable, the asset should be disclosed.

IAS 37 also gives guidance in regarding a number of specific provisions. These include the following:

Provisions for restructuring

A restructuring is a programme that is planned and is controlled by management and materially changes either:

- The scope of the business undertaken by an entity
- The manner in which that business is conducted

The IAS gives the following example of events that would fall under this definition.

- The **sale or termination** of a line of business
- The **closure of business locations** in a country or region or the **relocation** of business activities from one country region to another
- **Changes in management structure**
- **Fundamental reorganisations** that have a material effect on the **nature and focus** of the entity's operations

In order to make a provision an obligation (legal or constructive) must exist at the period end. In this context, a constructive obligation exists only in the following circumstances:

- An entity must have a **detailed formal plan** for the restructuring.
- It must have raised a **valid expectation** in those affected that it will carry out the restructuring by starting to implement that plan or announcing its main features to those affected by it.

A management or board decision alone would not normally be sufficient.

The IAS states that a restructuring provision should include only the **direct expenditures** arising from the restructuring.

Onerous contracts

Key term

An **onerous contract** is a contract in which the unavoidable costs of meeting the obligations under the contract exceed the economic benefits expected to be received under it. An example might be a vacant leasehold property.

If an entity has a contract that is onerous a provision must be made for the **net loss**.

Decommissioning provisions

A provision is only recognised from the date on which the **obligating event** occurs.

For example when an oil company initially purchases an oil field it is put under a legal obligation to decommission the site at the end of its life. The legal obligation exists therefore on the initial expenditure on the field and therefore the liability exists immediately. The IAS also takes into view that the decommissioning costs may be capitalised as an asset representing future access to oil reserves (ie an asset and a provision are recognised).

3.4.1 Audit procedures

The audit tests that should be carried out on provisions and contingent assets and liabilities are as follows.

- **Obtain details** of all **provisions** which have been included in the **accounts** and all **contingencies** that have been disclosed.
- **Obtain** a **detailed analysis** of all **provisions** showing opening balances, movements and closing balances.
- **Determine** for each material provision **whether** the **company** has a **present obligation** as a result of past events by:
  - **Review** of **correspondence** relating to the item.
  - **Discussion** with the **directors**: have they created a valid expectation in other parties that they will discharge the obligation?
- **Determine** for each material provision **whether** it is **probable** that a **transfer of economic benefits** will be required to settle the obligation by:

- **Checking** whether any **payments** have been **made** after the year-end in respect of the item.
- **Reviewing correspondence** with solicitors, banks, customers, insurance company and suppliers both pre and post year-end.
- **Sending** a **letter** to the **solicitor** to obtain their views (where relevant).
- **Discussing** the **position** of similar **past provisions** with the directors. Were these provisions eventually settled?
- **Considering** the **likelihood** of **reimbursement**.
- **Recalculate** all **provisions** made.
- **Compare** the **amount provided** with any post year-end payments and with any amount paid in the past for similar items.
- In the event that it is not possible to estimate the amount of the **provision**, check that this **contingent liability** is **disclosed** in the accounts.
- **Consider** the **nature** of the **client's business**. Would you expect to see any other provisions, for example, warranties?
- **Consider** whether disclosures of **provisions, contingent liabilities and contingent assets** are correct and sufficient.

3.4.2 Obtaining audit evidence of contingencies

Part of ISA 501 *Audit evidence – specific considerations for selected items* covers contingencies relating to litigation and legal claims, which will represent the major part of audit work on contingencies. Litigation and claims involving the entity may have a material effect on the financial statements, and so will require adjustment to/disclosure in those financial statements.

The auditor must carry out procedures in order to become aware of any litigation and claims involving the entity which may have a material effect on the financial statements. Such procedures would include the following.

- **Make appropriate enquiries of management** including obtaining written representations.
- **Review board minutes** and correspondence with the entity's lawyers.
- **Examine legal expense** account.
- **Use any information** obtained regarding the entity's business including information obtained from discussions with any in-house legal department.

When litigation or claims have been identified or when the auditor believes they may exist, the auditor must seek direct communication with the entity's lawyers. This will help to obtain sufficient appropriate audit evidence as to whether potential material litigation and claims are known and management's estimates of the financial implications, including costs, are reliable.

The letter, which should be prepared by management and sent by the auditor, should request the lawyer to communicate directly with the auditor.

If it is thought unlikely that the lawyer will respond to a general enquiry, the letter should specify the following:

(a) A list of litigation and claims

(b) Management's assessment of the outcome of the litigation or claim and its estimate of the financial implications, including costs involved

(c) A request that the lawyer confirm the reasonableness of management's assessments and provide the auditor with further information if the list is considered by the lawyer to be incomplete or incorrect

The auditors must consider these matters up to the date of their report and so a further, updating letter may be necessary.

A meeting between the auditors and the lawyer may be required, for example where a complex matter arises, or where there is a disagreement between management and the lawyer. Such meetings should take place only with the permission of management, and preferably with a management representative present.

If management refuses to give the auditor permission to communicate with the entity's lawyers, this would result in the auditor not being able to obtain sufficient appropriate audit evidence and should ordinarily lead to a qualified opinion (if material but not pervasive) or a disclaimer of opinion (if material and pervasive).

If the lawyer refuses to respond as required and the auditor can find no alternative sufficient appropriate audit evidence, the auditor's opinion may be qualified or disclaimed (as above).

Other tests that should be carried out on provisions and contingent assets and liabilities are as follows:

- **Obtain details** of all **provisions** which have been included in the **accounts** and all **contingencies** that have been disclosed.
- **Obtain** a **detailed analysis** of all **provisions** showing opening balances, movements and closing balances.
- **Determine** for each material provision **whether** the **company** has a **present obligation** as a result of past events by:
    - **Review** of **correspondence** relating to the item
    - **Discussion** with the **directors**. Have they created a valid expectation in other parties that they will discharge the obligation?
- **Determine** for each material provision **whether** it is **probable** that a **transfer of economic benefits** will be required to settle the obligation by:
    - **Checking** whether any **payments** have been **made** in the period after the reporting date in respect of the item
    - **Reviewing correspondence** with solicitors, banks, customers, insurance company and suppliers both pre- and post-year-end
    - **Sending** a **letter** to the **solicitor** to obtain their views (where relevant)
    - **Discussing** the **position** of similar **past provisions** with the directors. Were these provisions eventually settled?
    - **Considering** the **likelihood** of **reimbursement**.
- **Recalculate** all **provisions** made.
- **Compare** the **amount provided** with any post year-end payments and with any amount paid in the past for similar items.
- In the event that it is not possible to estimate the amount of the **provision**, check that this **contingent liability** is **disclosed** in the accounts.
- **Consider** the **nature** of the **client's business**. Would you expect to see any other provisions eg warranties?
- Consider adequacy of disclosure of **provisions, contingent assets** and **contingent liabilities**.

Question: Provisions

In February 20X7, the directors of Newthorpe Engineering suspended the managing director. At a disciplinary hearing held by the company on 17 March 20X7 the managing director was dismissed for gross misconduct, and it was decided the managing director's salary should stop from that date and no redundancy or compensation payments should be made.

The managing director has claimed unfair dismissal and is taking legal action against the company to obtain compensation for loss of his employment. The managing director says he has a service contract with the company which would entitle him to two years' salary at the date of dismissal.

The financial statements for the year ended 30 April 20X7 record the resignation of the director. However, they do not mention his dismissal and no provision for any damages has been included in the financial statements.

Required

(a) State how contingent losses should be disclosed in financial statements according to IAS 37 *Provisions, contingent liabilities, and contingent assets*.

(b) Describe the audit work you will carry out to determine whether the company will have to pay damages to the director for unfair dismissal, and the amount of damages and costs which should be included in the financial statements.

Note: Assume the amounts you are auditing are material.

Answer

(a) IAS 37 states that a provision should be recognised in the accounts if:
- An entity has a **present obligation** (legal or constructive) as a result of a past event.
- A **transfer** of **economic benefits** will **probably** be **required** to settle the obligation.
- A **reliable estimate** can be **made** of the amount of the obligation.

Under IAS 37 contingent liabilities should not be recognised. They should however be disclosed unless the prospect of settlement is remote. The entity should disclose:
- The **nature** of the liability
- An estimate of its **financial effect**
- The **uncertainties** relating to any possible payments
- The likelihood of any **re-imbursement**.

(b) The following tests should be carried out to determine whether the company will have to pay damages and the amount to be included in the financial statements.

(i) **Review** the director's **service contract** and **ascertain** the **maximum amount** to which he would be entitled and the **provisions** in the service contract that would **prevent** him making a **claim**, in particular those relating to grounds for justifiable dismissal.

(ii) **Review** the results of the **disciplinary hearing. Consider** whether the company has acted in accordance with **employment legislation** and its **internal rules,** the **evidence** presented by the **company** and the defence made by the **director**.

(iii) **Review correspondence** relating to the case and **determine** whether the **company** has **acknowledged** any **liability** to the director that would mean that an amount for compensation should be accrued in accordance with IAS 37.

(iv) **Review correspondence** with the company's **solicitors** and **obtain legal advice**, either from the company's solicitors or another firm, about the likelihood of the claim succeeding.

(v) **Review** correspondence and contact the company's solicitors about the likely **costs** of the case.

(vi) **Consider** the **likelihood** of **costs** and **compensation** being **reimbursed** by **reviewing** the company's **insurance arrangements** and contacting the insurance company.

(vii) **Consider** the **amounts** that should be **accrued** and the **disclosures** that should be made in the accounts. Legal costs should be accrued, but compensation payments should only be accrued if the company has admitted liability or legal advice indicates that the company's chances of success are very poor. However the claim should be disclosed unless legal advice indicates that the director's chance of success appears to be remote.

4 Expenses

> **FAST FORWARD**
>
> The key expense we will look at is borrowing costs, which may sometimes be capitalised as part of an asset.

4.1 Borrowing costs

IAS 23 *Borrowing costs* deals with the treatment of borrowing costs, often associated with the construction of **self-constructed assets**, but which may also be applied to an asset purchased that takes time to get ready for use/sale.

Key terms

> **Borrowing costs** are interest and other costs incurred by an entity in connection with the borrowing of funds.
>
> A **qualifying asset** is an asset that necessarily takes a substantial period of time to get ready for its intended use or sale. (IAS 23)

> **IAS 23 *Borrowing costs***
>
> *Accounting treatment*
>
> - Borrowing costs should be **capitalised** as part of the cost of the asset if they are directly attributable to acquisition/construction/production. Other borrowing costs must be expensed.
> - **Borrowing costs eligible for capitalisation** are those that would have been avoided otherwise. Use judgement where a range of debt instruments is held for general finance.
> - **Amount of borrowing costs available for capitalisation** is actual borrowing costs incurred less any investment income from temporary investment of those borrowings.
> - For borrowings obtained generally, apply the **capitalisation rate** to the expenditure on the asset (weighted average borrowing costs). It must not exceed actual borrowing costs.
> - **Capitalisation is suspended** if active development is interrupted for extended periods. (Temporary delays or technical/administrative work will not cause suspension.)
> - **Capitalisation ceases** (normally) when physical construction of the asset is completed, capitalisation should cease when each stage or part is completed.
> - Where the carrying amount of the asset falls below cost, it must be **written down/off**.
>
> *Disclosure*
>
> - **Accounting policy** note
> - Amount of **borrowing costs capitalised** during the period
> - **Capitalisation rate** used to determine borrowing costs eligible for capitalisation

The **cost of borrowing is interest**, which is disclosed in the statement of comprehensive income.

Interest can often be audited by **analytical procedures**, as it has a predictable relationship with loans (for example, bank loans or debentures).

Alternatively it can be **verified to payment records** (bank statements) **and loan agreement** documents.

However, if borrowing costs are capitalised the auditor should carry out the following procedures:

- Agree figures in respect of interest payments made to statements from lender and/or bank statements.
- Ensure interest is directly attributable to construction.

4.2 Pension costs

IAS 19 *Employee benefits* covers the accounting for post-employment benefits. Pension schemes are the most obvious example, but an employer might provide post-employment death benefits to the dependants of former employees, or post-employment medical care.

Post-employment benefit schemes are often referred to as 'plans'. The 'plan' receives regular contributions from the employer (and sometimes from current employees as well) and the money is invested in assets, such as stocks and shares and other investments. The post-employment benefits are paid out of the income from the plan assets (dividends, interest) or from money from the sale of some plan assets.

There are two types or categories of post-employment benefit plan: defined contribution plans and defined benefit plans.

Key terms

In a **defined contribution plan**, the entity pays fixed contributions into a fund but has no legal or constructive obligation to make further payments if the fund does not have sufficient assets to pay all of the employees' entitlements to post-employment benefits.

A **defined benefit plan** is a post-employment benefit plan other than a defined contribution plan. These would include both formal plans and those informal practices that create a constructive obligation to the entity's employees. (IAS 19)

4.2.1 IAS 19 recap

Accounting for payments into defined contribution plans is straightforward.

(a) The obligation is determined by the amount paid into the plan in each period.

(b) There are no actuarial assumptions to make.

(c) If the obligation is settled in the current period (or at least no later than 12 months after the end of the current period) there is no requirement for discounting.

IAS 19 requires the following.

(a) Contributions to a defined contribution plan should be recognised as an expense in the period they are payable (except to the extent that labour costs may be included within the cost of assets).

(b) Any liability for unpaid contributions that are due as at the end of the period should be recognised as a liability (accrued expense).

(c) Any excess contributions paid should be recognised as an asset (prepaid expense), but only to the extent that the prepayment will lead to, eg a reduction in future payments or a cash refund.

(d) Disclosure is required of a description of the plan and the amount recognised as an expense in the period.

Accounting for defined benefit plans is more complex. The complexity of accounting for defined benefit plans stems largely from the following factors.

(a) The future benefits (arising from employee service in the current or prior years) cannot be estimated exactly, but whatever they are, the employer will have to pay them, and the liability should therefore be recognised now. To estimate these future obligations, it is necessary to use actuarial assumptions.

(b) The obligations payable in future years should be valued, by discounting, on a present value basis using the Projected Unit Credit Method. This is because the obligations may be settled in many years' time.

(c) If actuarial assumptions change, the amount of required contributions to the fund will change, and there may be actuarial gains or losses. A contribution into a fund in any period is not necessarily the total for that period, due to actuarial gains or losses.

An outline of the method used for an employer to account for the expenses and obligation of a defined benefit plan is given below.

Step 1 Actuarial assumptions should be used to make a reliable estimate of the amount of future benefits employees have earned from service in relation to the current and prior years. Assumptions include, for example, assumptions about employee turnover, mortality rates, future increases in salaries (if these will affect the eventual size of future benefits such as pension payments).

Step 2 These future benefits should be attributed to service performed by employees in the current period, and in prior periods, using the Projected Unit Credit Method. This gives a total present value of future benefit obligations arising from past and current periods of service.

Step 3 The fair value of any plan assets should be established.

Step 4 The size of any actuarial gains or losses should be determined, and the amount of these that will be recognised.

Step 5 If the benefits payable under the plan have been improved, the extra cost arising from past service should be determined.

Step 6 If the benefits payable under the plan have been reduced or cancelled, the resulting gain should be determined.

In the statement of financial position, the amount recognised as a defined benefit liability (which may be a negative amount, ie an asset) should be the total of the following.

(a) The present value of the defined obligation at the reporting date, plus

(b) Any actuarial gains or minus any actuarial losses that have not yet been recognised, minus

(c) Any past service cost not yet recognised (if any), minus

(d) The fair value of the assets of the plan as at the reporting date (if there are any) out of which the future obligations to current and past employees will be directly settled

If this total is a negative amount, there is a statement of financial position asset and this should be shown in the statement of financial position as the lower of (a) and (b) below.

(a) The figure as calculated above
(b) The total of the present values of:

   (i) Any unrecognised actuarial losses and past service costs
   (ii) Any refunds expected from the plan
   (iii) Any reductions in future contributions to the plan because of the surplus

The expense that should be recognised in the statement of comprehensive income for post-employment benefits in a defined benefit plan is the total of the following.

(a) The current service cost
(b) Interest
(c) The expected return on any plan assets
(d) The actuarial gains or losses, to the extent that they are recognised
(e) Past service cost to the extent that it is recognised
(f) The effect of any curtailments or settlements

4.2.2 Audit evidence

Scheme assets (including quoted and unquoted securities, debt instruments, properties)	• Ask directors to reconcile the scheme assets valuation at the scheme year-end date with the assets valuation at the reporting entity's date being used for IAS 19 purposes. • Obtain direct confirmation of the scheme assets from the Investment custodian. • Consider requiring scheme auditors to perform procedures.

Scheme liabilities	• Auditors must follow the principles of ISA 620 *Using the work of an auditor's expert* to assess whether it is appropriate to rely on the actuary's work. Specific matters would include:
	   – The source data used
	   – The assumptions and methods used
	   – The results of actuaries' work in the light of auditors' knowledge of the business and results of other audit procedures

	Actuarial source data is likely to include: • Scheme member data (for example, classes of member and contribution details) • Scheme asset information (for example, values and income and expenditure items)
Actuarial assumptions (for example, mortality rates, termination rates, retirement age and changes in salary and benefit levels)	Auditors will not have the same expertise as actuaries and are unlikely to be able to challenge the appropriateness and reasonableness of the assumptions. Auditors can, however, through discussion with directors and actuaries: • Obtain a general understating of the assumptions and review the process used to develop them.
	• Compare the assumptions with those which directors have used in prior years.
	• Consider whether, based on their knowledge of the reporting entity and the scheme, and on the results of other audit procedures, the assumptions appear to be reasonable and compatible with those used elsewhere in the preparation of the entity's financial statements.
	• Obtain written representations from directors confirming that the assumptions are consistent with their knowledge of the business.

Items charged to operating profit (current service cost, past service cost, gains and losses on settlements and curtailments, interest)	• Discuss with directors and actuaries the factors affecting current service cost (for example, a scheme closed to new entrants may see an increase year on year as a percentage of pay with the average age of the workforce increasing).

Where the results of actuaries' work is inconsistent with the directors' auditors', additional procedures, such as requesting directors to obtain evidence from another actuary, may assist in resolving the inconsistency.

4.3 Share-based payment

IFRS 2 *Share-based payment* sets out rules for the measurement of expenses relating to share-based payment schemes. These arise most commonly in relation to payments for employee services and professional services.

4.3.1 IFRS 2 Recap

IFRS 2 requires entities to recognise the goods or services received as a result of share-based payment transactions.

There are three types of share-based payment transactions.

(a) **Equity-settled share-based payment transactions**, in which the entity receives goods or services in exchange for equity instruments of the entity.

(b) **Cash-settled share-based payment transactions**, in which the entity receives goods or services in exchange for amounts of cash that are based on the price (or value) of the entity's shares or other equity instruments of the entity.

(c) Transactions in which the entity receives or acquires goods or services and either the entity or the supplier has a **choice** as to whether the entity settles the transaction in cash (or other assets) or by issuing equity instruments.

An entity should recognise goods or services received or acquired in a share-based payment transaction when it obtains the goods or as the services are received. They should be recognised as expenses unless they qualify for recognition as assets. Transactions are measured at fair value.

- Equity-settled transactions: DR   Assets/Expense
                                   CR   Equity

- Cash-settled transactions: DR   Asset/Expense
                                   CR   Liability

4.3.2 Audit evidence

The auditor will require evidence in respect of all the components of the estimated amounts, as well as reperforming the calculation of the expense for the current year.

Issue	Evidence
Number of employees in scheme/**number of instruments per employee/length of vesting period**	• Revenue scheme details set out in a contractual documentation.
Number of employees estimated to benefit	• Enquire of directors. • Compare to staffing numbers per forecasts and prediction.

Issue	Evidence
Fair value of instruments	• For equity-settled schemes check that fair value is estimated at **measured date.** • For cash-settled schemes check that the fair value is recalculated at the **statement of financial position date** and at the **date of settlement.** • Check that model used to estimate fair value is in line with IFRS 2.

General	• Obtain written representations from management confirming their view that:
	  – The assumptions used in measuring the expense are reasonable, and
	  – There are no share-based payment schemes in existence that have not been disclosed to the auditors.

5 Disclosures

FAST FORWARD The auditor must also ensure disclosures in the financial statements are fairly stated.

5.1 Segment reporting

The disclosure of segmental information is governed by IFRS 8 *Operating segments*.

Key terms

An **operating segment** is a component of an entity:

- That engages in business activities from which it may earn revenues and incur expenses (including revenues and expenses relating to transactions with other components of the same entity);
- Whose operating results are reviewed regularly by the entity's chief operating decision maker to make decisions about resources to be allocated to the segment and assess its performance; and
- For which discrete financial information is available.

Reportable segments are operating segments or aggregations of operating segments that meet specified criteria:

- Its reported revenue, from both external customers and intersegment sales or transfers, is 10% or more of the combined revenue, internal and external, of all operating segments; or
- The absolute measure of its reported profit or loss is 10% or more of the greater, in absolute amount of (i) the combined reported profit of all operating segments that did not report a loss and (ii) of the combined reported loss of all operating segments that reported and loss; or
- Its assets are 10% or more of the combined assets of all operating segments.

> **IFRS 8 *Operating segments***
>
> IFRS 8 requires an entity to report financial and descriptive information about its reportable segments.
>
> If the total external revenue reported by operating segments constitutes less than 75% of the entity's revenue, additional operating segments must be identified as reportable segments (even if they do not meet the quantitative thresholds set out above) until at least 75% of the entity's revenue is included in reportable segments.

The following procedures are relevant.

- Obtain a client schedule of revenue workings.
- Discuss with management the basis for the segmentation.
- Verify a sample of items to backing documentation (invoices) to ensure disclosure is correct.

5.2 Earnings per share

Accounting for earnings per share is governed by IAS 33 *Earnings per share*. It requires that companies of a certain size disclose their earnings per share for the year.

Basic earnings per share should be calculated by dividing the net profit or loss for the period attributable to ordinary equity holders by the weighted average number of ordinary shares outstanding during the period as follows:

$$\frac{\text{Net profit/(loss) attributable to ordinary shareholders}}{\text{Weighted average number of ordinary shares outstanding during the period}}$$

Question
Revision: basic EPS

Fontmell has profit of $1.5 million for the year-ended 31 December 20X8. On 1 January 20X8 the company had 500,000 shares in issue. During 20X8 the company announced a rights issue as follows:

Rights: One new share for every five outstanding (100,000 new shares in total)

Exercise price: $5.00

Last date to exercise rights: 1 March 20X8

Market (fair) value of one share in Fontmell immediately prior to exercise on 1 March 20X8: $11.00

The EPS for 20X7 as originally stated was $2.20.

Answer

Computation of theoretical ex-rights price

$$\frac{\text{Fair value of all outstanding shares} + \text{total received from exercise of rights}}{\text{Number of shares outstanding prior to exercise} + \text{number of shares issued in exercise}} = \frac{(\$11.00 \times 500,000) + (\$5.00 \times 100,000)}{500,000 + 100,000} = \$10.00$$

20X8 EPS

$$\frac{\$1,500,000}{(500,000 \times 2/12 \times 11/10) + (600,000 \times 10/12)} = \$2.54$$

20X7 EPS (restated)

$2.20 \times 10/11 = \$2.00$

Diluted earnings per share is calculated by adjusting the net profit attributable to ordinary shareholders and the weighted average number of shares outstanding for the effects of all dilutive potential ordinary shares.

These include:

- A **separate class of equity shares** which at present is not entitled to any dividend, but will be entitled in future
- **Convertible loan** stock or **convertible preferred shares**
- **Options** or **warrants**

The calculation would be as follows:

$$\frac{\text{Diluted earnings}}{\text{Diluted weighted average number of shares}}$$

		$
Diluted earnings =	Basic earnings	X
	Interest saved on convertible debt (net of tax saving)	X
		X
Diluted shares =	Basic weighted average	X
	Convertible debt: additional shares on conversion	X
	Share options: potential shares less shares purchasable at FV	X
		X

5.2.1 Audit issues

The size of the figure is unlikely to be material in itself, but it is a key investor figure. As it will be of **interest to all the investors** who read it, it is **material by its nature**.

When considering earnings per share, the auditor must consider **two issues**:

- Whether it been disclosed on a comparable basis to the prior year, and whether any changes in accounting policy have been disclosed, and
- Whether it has been calculated correctly

The audit procedures are as follows:

> - Obtain a copy of the client's workings for earnings per share. (If a simple calculation has been used, this can be checked by re-doing the fraction on the face of the income statement.)
> - Compare the calculation with the prior year calculation to ensure that the basis is comparable.
> - Discuss the basis with the directors if it has changed to ascertain if it is the best basis for the accounts this year and whether the change has been adequately disclosed.
> - Recalculate to ensure that it is correct.

5.3 Discontinued operations

Discontinued operations are accounted for under IFRS 5 *Non-current assets held for sale and discontinued operations*. The IFRS Accounting Standards requires that certain disclosures are made for discontinued operations in the statement of comprehensive income or in the notes. This may well be material for the following reasons:

- Potentially material through **size**
- May be **inherently material** if the change in operations is a sign of management policy or a major change in focus of operations

Essentially, the fact that some operations have been discontinued is of interest to shareholders, which is why the IFRS 5 disclosures came about.

IFRS 5 requires that assets which meet the criteria 'held for sale' are shown at the lower of carrying amount and fair value less costs to sell, and that held for sale assets are classified separately on the statement of financial position and the results of discontinued operations are presented separately in the statement of comprehensive income. Held for sale assets have been discussed under assets above.

To require separate classification in the statement of comprehensive income, discontinued operations must be:

- A component (ie separately identifiable)
- Which represents a separate major line of business/geographical area
- In part of a single co-ordinated plan to dispose of a separate major line of business/geographical area
- Or is a subsidiary acquired exclusively with a view to resale

Relevant audit procedures include:

- Obtaining accounting records for component to ensure it is separately identifiable
- Reviewing company documentation (such as annual report) to ensure it is separately identifiable
- Reviewing minutes of meetings/make enquiries of management to ascertain management's intentions

To audit whether the disclosures have been made correctly, the auditor should undertake the following procedures:

- Obtain a copy of the client's workings to disclose the discontinued operations.
- Review the workings to ensure that the figures are reasonable and agree to the financial statements.
- Trace a sample of items disclosed as discontinuing items to backing documentation (invoices) to ensure that they do relate to discontinued operations.

5.4 Statements of cash flows

Cash flows are accounted for under the provisions of IAS 7 *Statement of cash flows*. The statement of cash flows is essentially a reconciliation exercise between items on the statement of comprehensive income (operating profit) and the statement of financial position (cash).

As such, the statement of cash flows is often audited **by the auditor reproducing it from the audited figures in the other financial statements**. This can be done quickly and easily in the modern era by use of computer programs.

However, if the auditor wished to audit it another way, he could check and recalculate each reconciliation with the financial statements. This would involve checking each line of the statement by working through the client's workings and agreeing items to the accounting records and backing documentation (for example, tax paid to the bank statements) and the other financial statements.

Cash flow statements

Why is the statement of cash flows relevant to the auditors?

Answer

Report on the cash flow statement

The statement of cash flows is specified in the audit report. The auditors are reporting on it because financial reports are obliged to include a statement of cash flows under IAS 7 in order to show a true and fair view. The auditors must therefore assess the truth and fairness of the statement of cash flows as required by the revised IAS 7.

Analytical procedures

The information in the statement of cash flows will be used by the auditors as part of their analytical procedures of the accounts, for example, by adding further information on liquidity. This will be particularly helpful when comparing the statement to previous periods.

Going concern

The statement of cash flows may indicate going concern problems due to liquidity failings, overtrading and overgearing. However, the statement is an historical document, prepared well after the year-end, and is therefore unlikely to be the first indicator of such difficulties.

Audit evidence

The auditors will obtain very little direct audit evidence from the statement of cash flows. It has been prepared by the company (not the auditors or an independent third party) from records which are under scrutiny by the auditors in any case. Thus the auditors will already have most of this information, although in different format.

However, the statement of cash flows should provide additional evidence for figures in the accounts, for example, the purchase or sale of tangible non-current assets. Consistency of evidence will be important and complementary evidence is always welcome.

Question — Accounting issues and audit evidence

You work for Pitmans, a firm of accountants. Tinga is a long-standing client of your firm, but this is the first year that Pitmans has carried out the audit. The firm also provides a number of other services to Tinga, including a range of tax planning services and business advisory services. Recently, the firm undertook a review of some forecast financial statements, which Tinga was required to present to the bank.

You have been asked to plan the forthcoming audit of the financial statements for the period ending 31 March 20X7. You have been given the following draft statement of financial position.

	20X7		20X6	
	$'000	$'000	$'000	$'000
Assets				
Non-current assets				
Property, plant and equipment		10,101		12,378
Investments		10,000		2,000
Current assets				
Inventory	196		191	
Receivables	1012		678	
Cash and cash equivalents	–		149	
Prepayments	4		5	
		1,212		1,023
		21,313		15,401

PART C AUDIT STRATEGY, PROCESS AND REPORTING

Liabilities and equity

	20X7		20X6	
	$'000	$'000	$'000	$'000
Current liabilities				
Trade payables	938		900	
Bank overdraft	1,168		–	
Bank loan	3,999		–	
		6,105		900
Non-current liabilities				
Bank loan		12,325		17,002
Deferred tax		5,000		5,000
Equity				
Share capital		100		100
Share premium		1,000		1,000
Revaluation reserve		2,000		–
Retained earnings		(5,262)		(8,601)
		21,268		15,401

Required

Comment on any points arising for your planning of the audit for the year end 31 March 20X7. Your comments should include issues relating to risk and materiality, accounting issues and audit evidence issues and any limitations of the review you have undertaken to date. You should also highlight any further information that you intend to seek.

Approaching the answer

You work for Pitmans, a firm of accountants. Tinga is a long-standing client of your firm, but this is the first year that Pitmans has carried out the audit. The firm also provides a number of other services to Tinga, including a range of tax planning services and business advisory services. Recently, the firm undertook a review of some forecast financial statements, which Tinga was required to present to the bank.

You have been asked to plan the forthcoming audit of the financial statements for the period ending 31 March 20X7. You have been given the following draft statement of financial position.

	20X7		20X6	
	$'000	$'000	$'000	$'000
Assets				
Non-current assets				
Property, plant and equipment		10,101		12,378
Investments		10,000		2,000
Current assets				
Inventory	196		191	
Receivables	1012		678	
Cash and cash equivalents	–		149	
Prepayments	4		5	
		1,212		1,023
		21,313		15,401

Liabilities and equity

	20X7		20X8	
	$'000	$'000	$'000	$'000
Current liabilities				
Trade payables	938		900	
Bank overdraft	1,168		–	
Bank loan	3,999		–	
		6,105		900

18: AUDIT EVIDENCE II

	20X7		20X8	
	$'000	$'000	$'000	$'000
Non-current liabilities				
Bank loan		12,325		17,002
Deferred tax		5,000		5,000
Equity				
Share capital		100		100
Share premium		1,000		1,000
Revaluation reserve		2,000		–
Retained earnings		(5,262)		(8,601)
		21,268		15,401

Required

Comment on any points arising for your planning of the audit for the year end 31 March 20X7. Your comments should include issues relating to risk and materiality, accounting issues and audit evidence issues and any limitations of the review you have undertaken to date. You should also highlight any further information that you intend to seek.

Answer

Matters arising from preliminary review

Going concern

The statements of financial position show a worsening cash position over the year. There are some classic indicators of going concern problems.

- Substantial liabilities
- Excess of current liabilities over current assets
- Bank overdraft
- Substantial increase in receivables
- Bank requiring future profit forecasts, which have been verified by our firm

A profit has been made in the year, but it does not appear that sales are readily being converted into cash.

Sources of audit evidence

- Profit forecasts
- Correspondence with bank
- Any business plans in existence (consult with business advisory department)

Further information required

- We need to confirm for the audit file why the bank required profit forecasts.
- We need to review for audit purposes the results of our work on those forecasts.
- For the purposes of our audit we must satisfy ourselves that Tinga's financial statements should be prepared using the going concern basis of accounting.

Three items within the financial statements stand out as being particularly interesting at a planning stage. These are:

- Deferred tax
- Increase in investments
- Revaluation in the year

Deferred tax

We will need to confirm what the deferred tax balance relates to, particularly as the property, plant and equipment (PPE) in the statement of financial position do not seem particularly high. The deferred tax balance does not appear to have moved, despite an apparent revaluation in the year and other movements on PPE. We will have to check that deferred tax has been accounted for correctly in accordance with IAS 12.

Increase in investments

Investments are usually a straightforward area to audit with good audit evidence existing in terms of share certificates and valuation certificates.

However, as investments have increased, we must ensure that they have been accounted for correctly. We must also ensure that the increase does not represent a holding in another company that would require the results being consolidated into group results.

Revaluation

There appears to have been a revaluation in the year, although PPE have, in fact, decreased. We must discover what the revaluation reserve relates to, and ensure that it has been accounted for correctly.

Materiality

All the accounting issues discussed above are potentially material to the statement of financial position. Non-current assets is the key balance. As the statement of financial position shows high liabilities any as yet unrecorded impairment in either PPE and investments could make the position of the company significantly worse. Conversely, if the liability shown in deferred tax was overstated, this would have the reverse effect.

Limitations of current review

The current review has only taken account of the statement of financial position, so is an incomplete picture. At present, we can only guess at factors on the statement of profit or loss and other comprehensive income which have had implications for the statement of financial position.

As this is a first year audit, and the audit department is not familiar with this client, we have little knowledge of the business to apply to this review.

It is important as part of the planning process that the audit partner and/or manager enter into discussions with the various departments which have dealings with Tinga to increase their knowledge of the business and to obtain audit evidence on issues such as going concern.

However, it is also important for the audit team to bear in mind that, as auditors, they must maintain their independence towards the audit. There is a danger to the audit firm of loss of objectivity in respect of this audit due to the other services offered to the client, which must not be forgotten.

5.5 Changes in accounting policy

Where accounting standards allow alternative treatment of items in the accounts, then the accounting policy note should declare which policy has been chosen. It should then be applied consistently.

The effect of a change in accounting policy is treated as a retrospective adjustment to the opening balance of each affected component of equity as if the accounting policy had always applied.

IAS 8 *Accounting policies, changes in accounting estimates and errors* states that changes in accounting policies are rare, and only allowed if required by statute or if the change results in more reliable and relevant information.

5.6 Transition to International Financial Reporting Accounting Standards (IFRS Accounting Standards)

Additional considerations arise for the auditor in respect of entities adopting IFRS Accounting Standards for the first time. These are covered by IFRS 1 *First-time adoption of international financial reporting standards*.

5.6.1 Recap IFRS 1 First-time adoption of IFRS Accounting Standards

An entity prepares an **opening IFRS statement of financial position** at the date of transition to IFRS Accounting Standards as a starting point for IFRS accounting.

Generally, this will be the beginning of the earliest comparative period shown (ie full retrospective application).

The opening statement of financial position itself need not be presented.

The accounting policies used in the opening IFRS statement of financial position and throughout all periods presented should be those effective **at the reporting date**. The entity does not apply different versions of IFRS Accounting Standards effective at earlier dates.

Preparation of an opening IFRS statement of financial position typically involves adjusting the amounts reported at the same date under previous IFRS Accounting Standards.

All adjustments are recognised directly in retained earnings (or, if appropriate, another category of equity) not in the statement of comprehensive income.

ILLUSTRATION

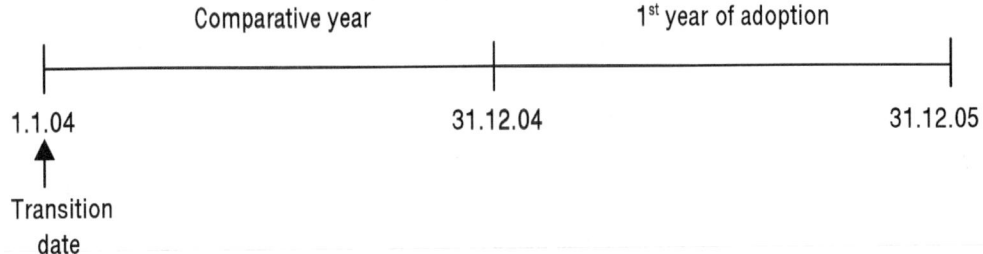

Exemptions from applying IFRS Accounting Standards in the opening IFRS statement of financial position

(a) In general the standard requires full retrospective application of IFRS Accounting Standards.

(b) Specific exemptions to full retrospective applications

　(i)　Property, plant and equipment and investment properties
　　　– Fair value at transition date may be used

　(ii)　Business combinations
　　　– Goodwill on acquisitions pre-transition date as per previous IFRS Accounting Standards

　(iii)　Employee benefits
　　　– At transition date recognise pension assets, liabilities, gains and losses in accordance with previous IFRS Accounting Standards rather than any international equivalent

　(iv)　Cumulative translation differences
　　　– At the transition date recognise the cumulative exchange differences relating to the translation of foreign net investments as calculated under IFRS Accounting Standards rather than any international equivalent

　(v)　Financial instruments
　　　– Transitional arrangements apply to existing hedges under the IFRS 9 model
　　　– Adjustments required at the transition date to reflect existing hedges under the requirements of the IFRS Accounting Standards

(c) Disclosures
   (i) Year-end 31 December 2005 – normal IFRS Accounting Standards disclosures
   (ii) Year-end 31 December 2004 (comparatives)
   - Normal IFRS Accounting Standards disclosures
   - Reconciliation of profit and equity from previous IFRS Accounting Standards to IFRS Accounting Standards
   - Changes to statement of cash flows
   (iii) 1 January 2004 (start of comparative year)
   - Effect on equity of adjustments from previous IFRS Accounting Standards to IFRS Accounting Standards
   - Effect on property, plant and equipment of any deemed cost adjustments
   - Impairment disclosures

5.7 IFRS 14 Regulatory deferral accounts

Many governments regulate the supply and pricing of particular types of activity by private entities, including utilities such as gas, electricity and water. Rate regulation allows suppliers to recover their costs in the prices they charge to customers and is also designed to protect the interests of customers. The recovery of some costs may therefore be deferred in order to keep prices stable and suppliers usually keep track of these deferred amounts in separate regulatory deferral accounts until they are recovered.

The established practice of most entities that already apply IFRS Accounting Standards is not to recognise these regulatory account balances, but to allow the amounts to simply flow through profit or loss as they arise. However, entities reporting under different jurisdictions do recognise these deferred amounts.

IFRS 14 is effective from an entity's first IFRS Accounting Standards financial statements for periods beginning on, or after, 1 January 2016, with early application allowed. It is permitted, but not required, to be applied. An entity which is already reporting under IFRS Accounting Standards cannot apply IFRS 14.

5.7.1 Financial statement presentation

Regulatory deferral account balances and movement in balances will be presented as follows:

Statement of financial position

Two line items:

- Regulatory deferral account debit balances – after total assets
- Regulatory deferral account credit balances – after total liabilities

Statement of profit or loss and other comprehensive income

Two line items:

- Movement in regulatory deferral account balances related to profit or loss
- Movement in regulatory deferral account balances related to other comprehensive income

Chapter Roundup

- Key assertions relating to assets are existence, completeness, valuation and rights and obligations.
- When standard costing is used, the auditor must assess whether the valuation is reasonable.
- Auditors should ensure that both tangible and intangible assets have been subjected to an annual impairment review.
- When auditing investments, the auditors will have to consider both income and the asset.
- Revenue recognition is an extremely important issue and completeness is a key assertion to be audited.
- The relevant financial statement assertions for liabilities are completeness, rights and obligations and existence. Liabilities must be tested for understatement.
- The classification of a lease can have a material effect on the financial statements.
- The auditor needs to audit the movement on the deferred tax liability.
- A provision is accounted for as a liability, contingencies are disclosed, so auditors must ensure they have been classified correctly according to IAS 37.
- The key expense we will look at is borrowing costs, which may sometimes be capitalised as part of an asset.
- The auditor must also ensure disclosures in the financial statements are fairly stated.

PART C AUDIT STRATEGY, PROCESS AND REPORTING

Quick Quiz

1   Match the accounting item with the relevant accounting standard(s).

    (a) Revenue   (i)   IFRS 3
    (b) Intangible non-current assets (ii) IAS 16
    (c) Property, plant and equipment (iii) IFRS 15
                                       (iv) IAS 38

2   Brands may never be capitalised.

    True ☐
    False ☐

3   What key issue related to deferred tax may affect its size and therefore materiality?

4   Name two types of temporary differences which must be provided for under IAS 12 *Income taxes*.

    (1) ....
    (2) ....

5   Name three types of contingency often disclosed by companies.

    (1) ....
    (2) ....
    (3) ....

6   The auditor may request information directly from the client's solicitors.

    True ☐
    False ☐

7   Link the disclosure issue with the accounting guidance.

    (a) Segmental information   (i)   IFRS 15
    (b) EPS   (ii) IFRS 8
    (c) Discontinued operations   (iii) IFRS 5
    (d) Revenue recognition   (iv) IAS 33

8   Why is EPS disclosure likely to be material?

9   Which of the following is not a reason why revenue is often audited by analytical procedures?

    (1) Availability of good, comparable evidence.
    (2) Statement of profit or loss and other comprehensive income is not as important as statement of financial position.
    (3) It is quicker than detailed substantive testing.
    (4) Revenue has logical relationships with other items in the financial statements.

10 Which of the following audit procedures relate to capitalised grants and which to grants put straight to income?

    • Obtain relating documentation and ensure classification is correct.
    • Agree value receipt of grant to:
        – Documentation (above)
        – Bank statements

- Consider reasonableness of transfers to revenue.
- Ensure capitalisation method is comparable.

11 Auditors do not report on the statement of cash flows (only the statement of financial position and statement of profit or loss and other comprehensive income as recorded in the opinion section of the report).

True ☐

False ☐

Answers to Quick Quiz

1. (a) (iv)
   (b) (i) (iv)
   (c) (ii) (i)

2. False. Internally generated brands may not be capitalised. Purchased brands with a separately identifiable value may be capitalised.

3. The future capital expenditure plans of the entity

4. (1) Taxable temporary differences
   (2) Deductible temporary differences

5. From:
   (1) Guarantees
   (2) Discounted bills of exchange
   (3) Uncalled liabilities on shares
   (4) Lawsuits/claims pending
   (5) Options to purchase assets

6. True. However the letter should be written by management and sent by the auditor.

7. (a)(ii), (b)(iv), (c)(iii), (d)(i)

8. It is of interest to the key readers of accounts – the shareholders.

9. (2) The statement of profit or loss and other comprehensive income **is just as important**. However, (3) **is true**, because it is cost-effective to use analytical review as a substantive procedure where good evidence is available.

10.
    - Obtain relating documentation and ensure classification is correct. — C/I
    - Agree value receipt of grant to: — C/I
        - Documentation (above)
        - Bank statements
    - Consider reasonableness of transfers to revenue. — C
    - Ensure capitalisation method is comparable. — C

11. False

End of Chapter Question

Roadking (AIA Nov 2009)

Roadking manufactures a device that can be fitted to cars and other vehicles to warn the driver that the vehicle's speed is being monitored by the police. In the past this product has sold strongly to young drivers who wish to exceed the speed limit without getting caught. Technically, it is illegal to use such devices, but not to manufacture or sell them or to advertise them for sale.

The company has been manufacturing this device for several years. The company's external auditor has relied heavily on analytical review in the audit of sale revenue. Unit sales have been highly correlated with independently verifiable statistics such as new car sales, sales of luxury consumer electronics and the number of drivers who have been fined by the authorities for speeding. The audit partner was, however, disappointed with the results obtained last year. It seemed that there was a weaker relationship between the unit sales figure and the three factors listed. This may have been due to changing consumer attitudes.

Roadking has also received a large number of claims for compensation from people who have been injured by motorists who were speeding while using this device. Roadking's lawyers are analysing the company's legal position. They have advised that it would be prudent to settle these claims before the cases are heard in court. The directors have made a provision in the financial statements for the likely value of this settlement.

Required

(a) Explain why auditors use analytical review in gathering audit evidence. **(4 marks)**

(b) Discuss the advantages and disadvantages of using formal statistical models such as the one used by the external auditor of Roadking. **(8 marks)**

(c) Explain how you would audit the provision for settling the claim for damages. **(8 marks)**

(Total 20 marks)

PART C AUDIT STRATEGY, PROCESS AND REPORTING

Information Technology

19

Topic list	Syllabus reference
1 Audit impact of IT in business	
2 Use of IT by auditors	
3 Data analytics	

Introduction

The use of information technology is growing and constantly developing. The auditor must consider:

- How information technology adopted by audit clients impacts the audit, specifically audit risk
- How information technology can be used by audit firms during audit engagements for an efficient and high-quality audit

There are many efficiencies to be gained by using information technology tools during the audit, as well as considerations when relying on client's computer systems and the information they produce.

PART C   AUDIT STRATEGY, PROCESS AND REPORTING

1 Audit impact of IT in business

FAST FORWARD

> The use of information technology (IT) in business is constantly evolving. Audit firms must have an understanding of IT at their audit clients in order to assess the risk of material misstatement and comply with ISA 315 (Revised 2019) *Identifying and Assessing the Risk of Material Misstatement*. As more and more organisations adopt increasingly complex computerised accounting systems, and use increasingly ingenious IT techniques, auditors have to be aware of the risks that these systems bring to their clients when performing risk assessment.

The adoption of IT by audit clients is rapidly changing the nature of audit work. Auditors will consider IT-related issues in meeting the requirements of many ISAs during the audit. The impact of IT can be seen on the type of work required as well. For example, ISA 315 (Revised 2019) states that the auditor shall obtain an understanding of the entity's information system and communication relevant to the preparation of the financial statements (ISA 315 (Revised 2019: para. 25).

Understanding the implications of IT is likely to be an important aspect of complying with ISA 315 (Revised 2019), and obtaining an understanding of the client's system of internal control and information systems, which are highly likely to be computerised. The company's use of IT and/or business risks it is exposed to as a result of IT will influence the assessment of audit risk, the resultant audit approach and the nature of procedures.

1.1 Adoption of IT by business

Automating the processing of routine accounting transactions was one of the first uses of IT in business. Once wages and salaries calculations, invoice production and other accounting practices were automated, businesses potentially enjoyed:

- Cost savings (fewer accounting staff were needed)
- Greater speed of processing and therefore faster results and more timely information
- Greater accuracy and consistency
- Reduced risk that controls will be circumvented

It is the computerised processing of accounting transactions that has most impact on audits as financial statements are now heavily dependent on the completeness and accuracy of processing. Furthermore, back-up and safeguarding of the computer-held accounting data is of the highest importance as huge amounts of data can be easily lost or stolen. The reliability of the system is also important because, in some businesses, computer malfunctions can mean that business operations have to stop and this could lead to claims from customers (for example, for late deliveries), loss of goodwill, or even place the going concern basis of accounting in jeopardy.

In addition to merely processing accounting information, the IT system can have internal control procedures built in. For example, a sales system can be programmed to reject orders that would take customers over their credit limits. A purchases system can be programmed to prevent staff from placing orders that have values over their authority limits.

If internal controls rely on computer procedures then these will have to be tested as part of a systems-based audit approach and auditors will have to devise ways in which they can test that the controls are operating properly.

1.2 The provision of management information

Once accounting transactions have been computerised then it becomes relatively quick, easy and cheap to examine the data and to produce useful management information. The management information can be used for internal control purposes and for wider management purposes. For example:

- Aged receivables reports help managers to identify and follow up on slow payers.
- Slow moving inventory reports help managers to control inventory.
- Invoices due reports can help managers to decide which supplier invoices need to be paid soon.
- Sales analyses identify key customers and key products.

Management information and control reports form a vital part of internal control systems and auditors might rely on the computer-produced reports for part of their audit work, such as assessing the allowance needed for irrecoverable debts.

1.3 Internal controls in the IT environment

1.3.1 Computer controls

The internal controls in a computerised environment include both manual procedures and procedures designed into computer programs. Such control procedures comprise two types of control, **general IT controls** and **information processing controls**.

Key term

> **General IT controls** are controls over the entity's IT processes that support the continued proper operation of the IT environment, including the continued effective functioning of information processing controls and the integrity of information (ie the completeness, accuracy and validity of information) in the entity's information system.
>
> **Information processing controls** are controls relating to the processing of information in IT applications or manual information processes in the entity's information system that directly address risks to the integrity of information (ie the completeness, accuracy and validity of transactions and other information).
>
> ISA 315 (Revised 2019): para. 12

General IT controls	Examples
Process to manage access	**Authentication:** Controls that ensure a user accessing the IT application or other aspect of the IT environment is using the user's own log-in credentials (ie the user is not using another user's credentials).
	Authorisation: Controls that allow users to access the information necessary for their job responsibilities and nothing further, which facilitates appropriate segregation of duties.
	Provisioning: Controls to authorise new users and modifications to existing users' access privileges.
	Deprovisioning: Controls to remove user access upon termination or transfer.
	Privileged access: Controls over administrative or powerful users' access.
	User access reviews: Controls to recertify or evaluate user access for ongoing authorisation over time.
	Security configuration controls: Each technology generally has key configuration settings that help restrict access to the environment.
	Physical access: Controls over physical access to the data centre and hardware, as such access may be used to override other controls.

General IT controls	Examples
Process to manage program or other changes to the IT environment	**Change management process**: Controls over the process to design, program, test and migrate changes to a production (ie end user) environment. **Segregation of duties over change migration**: Controls that segregate access to make and migrate changes to a production environment. **Systems development or acquisition or implementation**: Controls over initial IT application development or implementation (or in relation to other aspects of the IT environment). **Data conversion**: Controls over the conversion of data during development, implementation or upgrades to the IT environment.
Process to manage IT operations	**Job scheduling**: Controls over access to schedule and initiate jobs or programs that may affect financial reporting. **Job monitoring**: Controls to monitor financial reporting jobs or programs for successful execution. **Backup and recovery**: Controls to ensure backups of financial reporting data occur as planned and that such data is available and able to be accessed for timely recovery in the event of an outage or attack. **Intrusion detection**: Controls to monitor for vulnerabilities and or intrusions in the IT environment.

The auditors will wish to test some or all of the above general IT controls, having considered how they affect the computer applications significant to the audit.

General IT controls that relate to some or all applications are usually interdependent controls, ie their operation is often essential to the effectiveness of information processing controls. As information processing controls may be useless when general IT controls are ineffective, it will be more efficient to review the design of general IT controls first, before reviewing the information processing controls.

The purpose of information processing controls is to establish **specific control procedures** over the accounting applications in order to provide reasonable assurance that all transactions are authorised and recorded, and are processed completely, accurately and on a timely basis.

Information processing controls	Examples
Controls over input: completeness	Manual or programmed agreement of control totals Document counts One-for-one checking of processed output to source documents Programmed matching of input to an expected input control file Procedures over resubmission of rejected documents or transactions
Controls over input: accuracy	Programmes to check data fields (for example value, reference number, date) on input transactions for plausibility: • Digit verification (eg reference numbers are as expected) • Reasonableness test (eg sales tax to total value) • Existence checks (eg customer name) • Character checks (no unexpected characters used in reference) • Necessary information (no transaction passed with gaps) • Permitted range (no transaction processed over a certain value) Manual scrutiny of output and reconciliation to source Agreement of control totals (manual/programmed)

Information processing controls	Examples
Controls over input: authorisation	Manual checks to ensure information input was: • Authorised • Input by authorised personnel
Controls over processing	Similar controls to input must be in place when input is completed, for example, batch reconciliations Screen warnings can prevent people logging out before processing is complete
Controls over master files and standing data	One-to-one checking Cyclical reviews of all master files and standing data Record counts (number of documents processed) and hash totals (for example, the total of all the payroll numbers) used when master files are used to ensure no deletions Controls over the deletion of accounts that have no current balance Access controls

Controls over input, processing, data files and output may be carried out by IT personnel, users of the system, or a separate control group and may be programmed into application software. The auditors may wish to test the following information processing controls.

Testing of information processing controls	
Manual controls exercised by the user	If manual controls exercised by the user of the application system are capable of providing reasonable assurance that the system's output is complete, accurate and authorised, the auditors may decide to limit tests of control to these manual controls.
Controls over system output	If, in addition to manual controls exercised by the user, the controls to be tested use information produced by the computer or are contained within computer programs, such controls may be tested by examining the system's output using either manual procedures or computers. Such output may be in the form of electronic reports (exports to spreadsheets for example) or printouts. Alternatively, the auditor may test the control by performing it with the use of computers.
Programmed control procedures	In the case of certain computer systems, the auditor may find that it is not possible or, in some cases, not practical to test controls by examining only user controls or the system's output. The auditor may consider performing tests of control by using computers, reprocessing transaction data or examining the coding of the application program.

As we have already noted, general IT controls may have a pervasive effect on the processing of transactions in application systems. If these general IT controls are not effective, there may be a risk that misstatements occur and go undetected in the application systems. Although weaknesses in general IT controls may preclude testing certain information processing controls, it is possible that manual procedures exercised by users may provide effective control at the application level.

1.4 Emerging technologies

Audit clients may use emerging technologies because such technologies present opportunities to increase operational efficiency or enhance financial reporting. When emerging technologies are used in the information system relevant for the preparation of financial statements, auditors may need to include them

1.4.1 Cloud computing

Key term

> **Cloud computing** involves the provision of computing as a consumable service instead of a purchased product. It enables system information and software to be accessed by computers remotely as a utility through the internet.

A cloud can be private or public. A public cloud sells services to anyone on the internet. A private cloud is a proprietary network or a data centre that supplies hosted services to a limited number of people or organisations.

When a service provider uses public cloud resources to create their private cloud, the result is called a virtual private cloud. The goal of cloud computing is to provide easy, scalable access to computing resources and IT services.

A cloud computing service has distinct characteristics that differentiate it from traditional hosting:

Characteristic	Explanation
Sold on demand	Users pay for cloud services only when they use them (for example by the day, month or year).
	Cloud computing shifts the bulk of IT costs from capital expenditures (or buying and installing servers, storage, networking and related infrastructure) to an operating expense model, where users pay for the usage of these types of resources.
Elastic	Users can have as much or as little of the service as they want at any given time.
	Cloud computing allows for the expansion and reduction of resources according to specific service requirements.
Fully managed	The service is fully managed by the service provider. The user just needs an internet connection to access it.
On-demand and self-service	The service is available all the time and the user operates the service themselves.

Finance functions use cloud computing in a similar way to other parts of the business. Files and software can be stored in cloud servers so that they can be easily shared by all users and accessed by employees whether they are located in the organisation's offices or not.

Cloud computing is changing the structure and working of the finance function by:

- Allowing flexible working as staff can work in different locations at different times.
- Allowing collaboration as files can be shared and updated by multiple staff in real-time.
- Keeping software continuously up-to-date and improving compliance with data protection regulations.
- Improving the integration of software as, for example, customer relationship management software can be linked to accounting software.
- Improving data security as cloud providers better understand how to protect data.

One application of cloud computing that is specific to finance functions is cloud accounting. Cloud accounting is the provision of accountancy software through the cloud. Users log in to the accountancy software to process financial transactions and produce management reports in the same way as if the software was installed on their own machine. Examples of providers of cloud accounting software include QuickBooks, Xero and Sage.

A key benefit of cloud accounting is that it supports the various finance components to work as a team. Data, such as underlying transactions, is shared and drives the reports and analysis produced by all the teams. Management can quickly and easily pull data from the system to monitor the financial performance of the organisation themselves without having to wait for accounts and reports to be produced. However, this may increase risk of data security and loss of control.

Auditors will be most concerned with the security of the accounting data being held in a cloud accounting system that underlies the financial statements. They will want to see that the cloud provider is competent and proven to be reliable. Access to the audit client's cloud accounting system must be restricted and the auditor will want to see data is encrypted to prevent unauthorised changes.

1.4.2 Big data

Key term

Big data is used to describe the vast volumes of data which is captured from various sources, such as web browsing and the internet of things that can be analysed to reveal patterns or trends, especially relating to human behaviour or interactions.

The main use of big data in organisations is to identify trends that may exist in vast quantities of data in the pursuit of value creation. Historically, organisations have been restricted as to the amount of data that they can process due to the storage limitations of existing computer systems, but with the reduction in storage costs and the availability of cloud computing, even small and medium-sized organisations can collect and store huge amounts of data. Once collected, data analytics is used to identify relationships and patterns in the data in order to assist decision making for improved organisational performance.

1.4.3 Process automation

Key term

Process automation refers to the ability of systems to perform routine activities (such as the processing of data and assembling electronic components) without the input of a human.

Robotic process automation (RPA) is a technology that enables the automation of routine, clerical activities. The main impact on organisations of automation is the increased speed and efficiency of processes and reduced staff costs.

Traditional process automation involves a machine carrying out a simple, repetitive task. Modern process automation has made processes more automated and focusses on complex business areas that were previously thought as beyond the scope of automation.

Auditing a process performed by RPA has the same aim as auditing a process performed by individuals. However instead of asking the client staff what they do in order to understand the process, auditors will need to rely on written process documentation. The auditor will need to understand the controls surrounding the RPA in the same way as they would controls over the client's other processes that directly impact the financial statements.

The auditors will need to be certain they can rely on the data used, stored and processed by the RPA. They will be looking to check that data is encrypted and the RPA is protected against external threats by firewalls and anti-virus software. They will also need to check access to the RPA is restricted to the appropriate individuals and that no unauthorised access has taken place.

The use of RPA in accounting and audit also presents challenges. One of the biggest challenges is the need to ensure that the RPA robots are working correctly, and that the data being used is accurate. Additionally, the use of RPA in accounting can raise **ethical concerns** around the displacement of human workers and the potential for job losses.

1.4.4 Artificial intelligence (AI)

Key term

> **Artificial intelligence (AI)** refers to the ability of a computer system to assist a human operator to make business decisions or help solve problems.

A key impact of automation and AI systems (collectively known as intelligent systems) is that they harness the ability of computers to learn, make decisions and perform actions based on those decisions. This reduces the need for human involvement in a number of business operations, reducing costs and introducing efficient processes that add more value.

Cognitive computing is a collective name for several technologies including AI, machine learning and natural language programming. These technologies enable the automation of more complex tasks such as advanced data analytics and reporting writing.

Machine learning is a subset of AI that involves code being developed and designed to replicate how the human brain works. It uses experience from past events, data, connections and probability and applies it in future situations by detecting patterns and making recommendations of what to do. Such systems are also designed to learn from mistakes and not to repeat them in the future. This way, they adapt and improve their functions over time.

AI enables transactions to be processed without input from humans and for humans to be assisted in making decisions.

Some examples of how AI can support the finance function include:

- Simple processes can be automated.
- Improved fraud detection as systems can better understand 'normal' and 'abnormal' transactions.
- Predictive models can help forecast costs and revenues.
- Enables improved analysis of unstructured data in contacts and emails.

There are some **ethical issues** raised by the use of AI in business. Increasing reliance on algorithms and data in many areas of decision-making risks mirroring and entrenching bias in societies, increasing exclusion from services, delivering unfair outcomes, and reducing social mobility in the process.

Technologies such as machine learning and AI require **training** before they can be effective. The wrong dataset can skew and bias the results. This bias has been seen in many cases, mimicking real world issues. AI systems might continue produce biased results if biased datasets are used to train systems.

1.4.5 Distributed ledger technology and blockchain

Key term

> **Distributed ledger technology** is a technology that allows separate organisations and individuals who are unconnected via ownership to share an agreed record of events, such as ownership of an asset, using networked or cloud based technology.
>
> **Blockchain** is one form of a distributed ledger system.

Distributed ledger technology eliminates the need for data and information to be stored and managed centrally. Furthermore, it allows an accurate, up-to-date, single, trusted and transparent record to be shared between numerous parties.

Blockchain is one form of distributed ledger technology. It is a way of recording transactions in 'blocks' which are linked to one another and secured against being altered using cryptography, based on complex calculations. Any party who has owned the asset can view the previous transaction data, but this information is not necessarily otherwise shared or publicly available.

Key aspects of blockchain

Participants of a blockchain record transactions on an online network that is publicly available and distributed to everyone.

Details of transactions are recorded by all participants. Transactions are only accepted once all participants have updated their ledgers to reflect them.

Network computers verify the transaction to make sure the records have all been updated correctly. Once the validation work is complete, the transaction is authorised and added to the blockchain. This means that a single system cannot itself add new blocks to the chain.

Blocks are connected to a blockchain using a cryptographic hash that is generated from the previous block. This means the chain cannot be broken and each block is preserved permanently. It is only possible to amend previous blocks if the subsequent blocks are altered first.

Stages in a blockchain transaction	Description
Stage 1	A transaction is requested
Stage 2	A digital representation of the transaction is requested (a block)
Stage 3	The block is sent to all nodes in the network (distributed ledger)
Stage 4	The authenticity of the transaction is verified by each node
Stage 5	A reward for the verification is sent to each node (such as a bitcoin)
Stage 6	The completed and authorised block is added to the chain

Case Study

An example of blockchain is the Everledger system used by the diamond industry.

Everledger helps the diamond industry prevent fraud and the transfer of stolen goods. All diamonds have unique characteristics (similar to how humans have individual fingerprints). The Everledger system creates an identity for every diamond by recording these unique characteristics. Every time a diamond is bought or sold, the sale is recorded by the system on the Blockchain so that the diamond's ownership can be traced.

Distributed ledger technology and blockchain can increase the clarity and transparency in the recording of business transactions.

Key uses are in regard to measuring the value of assets and verifying asset ownership and accounting transactions, which are of interest to financial reporting and internal audit. Accurate and transparent records can be created of asset ownership and associated transactions. This helps to reduce the need for internal auditors and financial accountants to check transactions and verify the ownership of assets because they have a source of information about the assets that they can trust.

Blockchain may have the following impacts on the business and finance function:

- The security and traceability of transactions may impact how businesses record their dealings with third parties.
- Smart contracts can be created which are self-executing agreements that utilise cryptography, digital signatures and secure completion. If certain obligations are met, they can be automatically executed on a particular date and time.

- Bitcoin and other cryptocurrencies are not covered by accounting standards and decisions need to be made how to record them (ie are they cash, intangible assets or financial instruments?).
- They allow money to cross borders easily and seamlessly by avoiding traditional intermediaries such as banks.

The 'real time' nature of blockchain technology to record transactions means that it may be possible in the future for the auditor to move towards **continuous transaction monitoring** (CTM) as the distributed nature of the technology means that a copy of the blockchain will be instantly available to the auditor as it is created.

The fact that the information is verified and then cannot be edited has been claimed by some to have the potential to reduce the need for external audit, as the block chain can be guaranteed to be 'correct' as it is immutable.

Whilst the blockchain can provide evidence both of a transaction having occurred and of details about it, there will still be a need for judgement about whether the transaction was authorised, whether it was with a related party or was even fraudulent, and whether it has been accounted for appropriately in accordance with ISAs. The auditor will therefore need to assess the reliability of the information on the blockchain together with its suitability for accounting purposes.

1.4.6 Other trends

Mobile computing: Tablet devices and smart phones are now very common and can affect accounting transactions and records. For example, sales personnel can input new orders whilst visiting customers and these can be transmitted over the internet back to their company for further processing. Unfortunately, tablet computers and smart phones are common targets for theft. Unless properly secured by passwords this might give access to confidential information or they might allow improper transactions to be processed.

Voice recognition: Computers and software are becoming increasingly successful at recognising and responding to spoken information. This can permit transactions to be entered or information obtained by speaking rather than by keyboard input. There can be audit implications arising from this technology. For example, mistakes can be made when people speak with different accents and this can cause incorrect processing.

Biometrics: Passwords have been used for decades to control access to IT systems. However, their use is often abused if the passwords are too easy to guess or are made public. Biometrics, the measurement of a personal quality such as fingerprint or retina recognition, can provide very high levels of access control.

Contactless payment cards: Debit and credit cards with the following symbol

can be used as contactless payment cards. The card is simply waved at or tapped on a reader and funds are transferred without the need for PIN numbers of signatures. Transaction values are kept low to limit losses should a card be lost or stolen. The advantage to the retailers and customers is that transactions are faster to process. It is envisaged that this will increase sales. Transactions are processed over the same networks as traditional chip and pin cards and these devices should pose no greater risk to accounting records and internal control as older card technology.

1.5 Cyber incidents

Key term

A **cyber incident** is an incident that can cause harm to functions and services by impairing the confidentiality, integrity, or availability of electronic information, information systems, services, or networks. Cyber incidents may also be known as 'cyberattacks' or 'computer network attacks'.

Increasing connectivity and the openness of computer networks in the global business environment exposes businesses to system and network failures and to cyberattacks.

Case Study

In December 2013, the US-based retailer Target announced a security breach had resulted in unauthorised access to customer data. Details of up to 40 million customer names, credit or debit card numbers, the expiration date and CVV (Card Verification Value) codes had all been illegally obtained. Target claimed the issue was resolved soon after the announcement but gave advice to all customers to 'remain vigilant for incidents of fraud and identity theft by regularly reviewing bank statements and monitoring free credit reports'.

Source: https://corporate.target.com/news-features/article/2013/12/important-notice-unauthorized-access-to-payment-ca

Cyberattacks can involve:

- Identity theft, fraud, extortion
- Malware (such as viruses), phishing (masquerading as a website), spamming, and spyware,
- Stolen hardware, such as laptops or mobile devices
- Denial-of-service attacks in which internet systems are overwhelmed by messages or access demands.
- Password sniffing
- System infiltration
- Website defacement
- Instant messaging abuse
- Intellectual property (IP) theft or unauthorised access

1.6 Fundamental shifts in business models

New technology can fundamentally change how businesses can operate successfully. Additionally, the internet can provide all businesses with a global stage and this has important effects on the competitive environment in which the business operates. In some cases IT can cause going concern issues if a business is being overtaken by newer commercial approaches. Examples include:

- Music recording and production companies. Not long ago, these companies made profits by making, distributing and selling CDs. Now, most music is distributed by MP3 downloads or is directly streamed and there is little money in CD sales. If a music business had not successfully responded to these changes, its going concern status would be bleak.

- Travel agents. Now many people go directly to airline or hotel websites and brick and mortar travel agents have become rare.

- Book shops. The growing popularity of eBooks and devices such as the Amazon Kindle have caused many book shops to close.

Therefore, when reviewing the going concern basis of accounting that underlies most financial statements, auditors have to assess whether their client's survival is threatened by the rise of IT and the new trading methods that might exist or which are being developed.

2 Use of IT by auditors

> **FAST FORWARD**
>
> In addition to considering the use of IT at their clients, audit firms must consider their own use of IT. The use of automated tools and techniques (ATTs) by audit firms has grown as technology has evolved.

2.1 Automated tools and techniques (ATTs)

Audit procedures can be performed using a number of tools or techniques, which can be manual or automated (and often involving a combination of both). As technology evolves and new approaches to auditing develop, the relevance of a particular ATT and its relative advantages may change. ATTs include:

- Audit software
- Test data
- Embedded audit facilities
- Data analytics
- Robotic process automation (RPA)
- Artificial intelligence (AI) techniques

How IT literate the audit firm is, might affect whether automated tools and techniques are used during the audit, and this may affect timing of procedures in particular.

2.1.1 Audit software

Audit software is software which is owned by the auditor. Most commonly, it is used to read and examine clients' data.

Audit software (auditor's) ⟶ examines ⟶ Client data

It can perform the sort of checks on data that auditors might otherwise have to perform manually. Examples of uses of audit software are:

- Reperforming calculations. For example, adding up the values in the inventory file or adding up receivables and payables ledgers.

- Identification of noteworthy transactions and balances. For example, reporting on negative inventory balances or credit receivables balances.

- Selecting samples for investigation. For example, random samples or stratified samples.

Note that audit software can quickly examine every piece of data and can often reperform every calculation, such as the depreciation charged for each non-current asset. A manual approach can rarely be so thorough or performed so quickly. The use of audit software is therefore particularly appropriate during substantive testing of transactions and balances. By using audit software, the auditors may scrutinise large volumes of data and concentrate skilled manual resources on the investigation of results, rather than on the extraction of information and selection of samples.

Major considerations when deciding whether to use file interrogation software are as follows:

(a) As a minimum auditors will require a basic understanding of data processing and the entity's computer application, together with a detailed knowledge of the audit software and the computer files to be used. For example, the structure of client files must be known and the audit software adapted to read those files accurately.

(b) Depending on the complexity of the application, the auditors may need to have a sound appreciation of systems analysis, operating systems and, where program code is used, experience of the programming language to be utilised.

(c) Often, instead of running the audit software against the client's original data files, a copy of the data is made and transferred to the auditor's computers. Auditors will need to consider how easy it is to transfer a copy of the client's data onto the auditors' PC.

(d) The client may lack full knowledge of the computer system, and hence may not be able to explain fully all the information it produces.

Other less common types of audit software are:

- Comparison programs, which compare versions of a program. This can highlight where programs have been changed. This is important in case the changes are incorrect or unauthorised.

- Interactive software for interrogation of online systems.

- Resident (or embedded) code software to review transactions as they are processed. Resident code software is where an audit program or audit procedures are embedded in a client's accounting system. The software can be set up to carry out various auditing tasks throughout the year.

    For example, in some receivables systems, sales invoices and their related receipts of cash are matched and cancelled from the receivables ledger: there is little to be gained from cluttering up receivables accounts with fully completed sales transactions. However, auditors might then find it difficult to review these matched transactions. Embedded software could be used to record major invoices in a separate memorandum file, where they will not be cancelled, and where they will be available for the auditor to examine at the end of the financial year.

    Similarly, monthly salaries over certain limits could also be recorded for later examination by auditors.

2.1.2 Test data

Test data is auditor's data which is processed by the client's programs.

Auditor's data ⟶ processed by ⟶ Client's programs

An obvious way of seeing whether a system is processing data in the way that it should be is to input some test data and see what happens. The expected results can be calculated in advance and then compared with the results that actually arise. Test data can also be used to check the information processing controls that prevent processing of invalid data by entering data with, say, a non-existent customer code or non-existent product code or with an absurd value (for example, ordering 10,000,000,000 items), or transactions which may, if processed, breach limits such as customer credit limits.

Often test data can be divided into three categories:

- Data which should be processed normally. For example, a sales transaction which should be accepted.

- Data which should be rejected. For example, a sales transaction which fails a credit limit check.

- Data which might 'break' the system. For example, a sales transaction with a negative quantity ordered. This category of test data examines how resilient the system is to rogue input.

 **Case Study** System testing

A mail order company assures its auditors that orders are accepted only after a customer receives a satisfactory result from an automated credit check. Payments are then made for the goods in three instalments. If a customer is late with a payment then a series of follow-up letters is started, eventually threatening legal action. The customer's satisfactory credit rating is removed.

To test that this system is working correctly, the auditor can:

1. Attempt to place an order using the client's system but using a completely false name and address. This should fail the credit check, and the auditor notes if this is the case.

2. Place a legitimate order, ensure that the correct goods are received then stop making payments of the instalments. The series of follow-up letters that are received are audit evidence that the credit control follow-up procedures are as reported.

3. Place a third order after the second stage, as stated above, has been completed. This order should now be refused because the customer's credit rating should now be unsatisfactory.

A significant problem with test data is that it is false data created for test purposes and so it is liable to place false transactions in the client's carefully maintained records. Any resulting corruption of the data files has to be corrected and this is difficult with modern real-time systems, which often have built in (and highly desirable) controls to ensure that data entered cannot easily be removed without leaving a mark. Therefore, it is usual for test data to be run on a specially set up parallel system where errors will not matter. This is known as using 'dead' test data, as opposed to 'live' test data which is processed through to client's real files.

Other problems with test data are that it only tests the operation of the system at a single point of time, and auditors are only testing controls in the programs being run and controls which they know about.

2.1.3 Embedded audit facilities

The results of using test data would be completely distorted if the programs used to process it were not the ones normally used for processing. For example, a fraudulent member of the IT department might substitute a version of the program that gave the correct results, purely for the duration of the test, and then replace it with a version that siphoned off the company's funds into their own bank account.

To allow a continuous review of the data recorded and the manner in which it is treated by the system, it may be possible to use ATTs referred to as 'embedded audit facilities'. An embedded facility consists of audit modules that are incorporated into the computer element of the entity's accounting system.

Two frequently encountered examples are Integrated Test Facility (ITF) and Systems Control and Review File (SCARF). Such systems allow auditors to give frequent and prompt auditor's reports on a wide variety of subject matters, key performance indicators and critical success factors.

For example, in some receivables systems, once payment for an invoice has been received and matched to an invoice, the matched transactions are deleted from the file because the transaction is complete. At period end there might therefore be no trace left of substantial transactions that have gone through the receivables ledger. However, embedded audit facilities can be used to record copies of significant transactions so that the auditor can be presented with a list of transactions for investigation at period end. This is an example of SCARF.

The use of IT to produce such reports means additional risk to auditors. They need to ensure that the reports are filed properly and are protected from interference (hacking) by the client. It also widens the amount of expertise needed from auditors, as they will need IT skills as well as expertise in a number of different areas being reported on.

2.1.4 Data analytics

The IAASB has been actively considering the opportunities and challenges presented by the use of data analytics in the audit of a set of financial statements. The ability of modern computers to process significant amounts of data has opened up the possibility of 100% testing of some populations, allowing greater speed, accuracy and efficiency to be introduced into the audit.

There has been a cautious welcome from regulators, standard-setters, audit firms and other practitioners to the IAASB's proposals for auditors to embrace data analytics further. Issues include the need for enhanced scepticism, training and maintaining quality standards in such a rapidly evolving area. However, this is surely an area where great progress must be expected. The next section of this chapter looks at data analytics in more detail.

2.1.5 Robotic process automation (RPA)

The use of **Robotic Process Automation** (RPA) in audit relates to the execution of repetitive tasks such as testing of specific transactional cycles or payroll and enables much wider testing, sometimes enabling the auditor to test 100% of transactions that have occurred. This means that RPA using data analytics can evaluate **all** transactions with precision. The auditor can then determine whether something has actually gone wrong rather than focus on evaluating the risk of a break-down in the control environment. For example, RPA could identify journal entries that are duplicated or do not balance.

This has the potential to make audit much more accurate through the identification of anomalous transactions, but also to increase the expectation of the client in terms of detection of fraud and error. There is also the potential that the client firm will have access to much better internal control software based on the same software used by the auditor. This may reduce the need for external audit and result in much more reliance on automated internal audit processes.

2.1.6 Artificial intelligence techniques

Artificial intelligence (AI) is currently based on machine learning and continues to reduce the requirement for human input into verification and vouching processes. Machines can also be trained to recognise patterns in vast volumes of data, including unstructured data such as emails or social media. This could be used by auditors in identifying risks of material misstatement for example. It may be that in the future, aspects of judgement may also be adopted by AI software.

One of the biggest challenges is the need for auditors to have a deep understanding of the machine learning algorithms and models being used. Additionally, the use of machine learning in auditing can raise ethical concerns around the use of data and potential biases in the algorithms being used. It is important for auditors to have appropriate controls in place to ensure that the data being used is accurate and unbiased.

Question — RPA and data analytics

You are an audit manager at the firm LS & Co, and are responsible for the audit of Electra Ltd, a manufacturer and distributor of electrical components. The audit is nearing completion. The client has seen exponential growth in sales over the past few years and the number of transactions occurring across all areas of the business has increased substantially. During the audit fieldwork stage, it took the engagement team almost double the time of previous years to sample and test an appropriate number of items across the audit.

Required

Explain how Robotic Process Automation and data analytics might have been used to reduce the time spent on the audit of Electra.

Answer

Robotic Process Automation (RPA) is the use of software to complete rules-based tasks more efficiently than is possible using manual processes. Data analytics is the examination of data to try to identify patterns, trends or correlations. As the quantity of data created by businesses has increased, it has become more and more necessary to evolve ways of processing and making sense of it. The combination of these can enable an auditor to use an automated system to carry out data analytics on an audit client's information.

The automated, digital nature of RPA and data analytics means that the auditor is able to test many more transactions and make a more accurate assessment of controls. In some cases it is possible to test 100% of transactions and look for fraud or error across the entire population rather than undertaking a risk assessment and selecting a sample to test.

In the case of the audit of Electra it would appear that LS & Co had difficulty completing the required testing due to the number of transactions having increased. The use of RPA and data analytics would have automated that process, reducing the time taken to carry out testing, improving the accuracy of the results and potentially enabling the auditor to test more items than would have previously been tested.

This does require the LS & Co to have sufficient technical knowledge to implement RPA software, together with an investment in the software itself. It also requires the integration of the client data into the automation software to enable the testing to take place. However, if these issues can be overcome, then the speed and quality of the audit are likely to increase.

The increased complexity of ATTs will result in a different risk profile in client firms being audited and increased need for assurance services related to these risks. The value in providing such engagements will come from the expertise and skill set of the audit firm.

2.2 Issues encountered in automating the audit process

The main issues that arise in automating the accounting process are:

- Initial set-up costs and difficulties
- Client reservations on sharing confidential financial and other data
- Training staff to use new technology

As mentioned earlier, when audit programs are to be used they have to be amended so that client's files are read accurately. The structure of the file and its records therefore have to be known and this information has then to be embedded in the audit program. This requires both expertise and time. So in the first year of use, audit programs might not appear to be worthwhile financially. However, in subsequent year's audits the audit programs will be capable of generating important information quickly, efficiently and cost-effectively (provided the client's system does not change!)

Similarly setting up a parallel system, getting it to work, and choosing suitable test data takes skill and time in the first year, but this should be rewarded in subsequent years as better and more efficient audits should be possible.

Because the auditors will usually be using parallel systems for their test data investigations, it is extremely important that they can confirm that the test data is being operated upon by the up-to-date version of the client's software. There is little point on operating on test data with a version of the software that the client hasn't used for some years.

Client reservations arise because clients will usually guard their data carefully and are reluctant to place the integrity of their data at risk by allowing auditors to access it with their audit programs or to alter it with their test data. This reluctance is overcome by allowing auditors to examine copies of the accounting system and data so that no damage can be done to the real data. However, this is not quite as satisfactory from the auditor's viewpoint as the actual system that the client is using every day is not being examined.

Emerging technologies are fundamentally reshaping the business landscape, leaving an indelible mark on sectors like accounting and audit. This transformation brings forth a dual narrative of challenges and opportunities, urging businesses to adapt or risk obsolescence. One of the primary challenges lies in upskilling the workforce to meet the demands of the digital age. As automation of audit grows, substantial investments in training and education are necessary to empower employees with the requisite competencies.

2.3 IT specialists

IT related audits are commonly carried out by an IT specialist (within the firm, where available). Therefore there should be proper communication of scope and conclusion between the engagement team and the IT specialists.

3 Data analytics

FAST FORWARD

Data analytics is the science and art of discovering and analysing patterns, deviations and inconsistencies, and extracting other useful information in the data underlying or related to the subject matter.

Auditors can use data analytics to assist in their evaluation of the **risk of material misstatement** in the financial statements and when performing audit procedures.

Organisations and users of financial statements can use data analytics to undertake detailed analysis to gather information on which to base their economic decisions.

3.1 Big data and data analytics

It has been said that there are 3 Vs of big data: there are larger Volumes of data, at faster Velocity, with more Variety.

The general idea is that having so much more data around allows a surprising number of new things to be done. One **example** of this is **Google Maps**, which uses 'big data' to help predict traffic flows. Google is able to process speed data obtained from people's Android smartphones to work out where traffic is moving more slowly than usual. This is then indicated on the Maps app. The whole process, then, is dependent on the collection of enormous quantities of data from smartphones; something that would not have been possible 20 years ago, before the expansion of computing and data collection.

In response to the amount of data, there is a need for **timely data analysis** and interpretation. Data analytics for analysing big data are a range of tools available for the collation and examination of data streams. These include some more **traditional techniques** that emerged historically for use on smaller data sets (such as regression analysis and trend/time series analysis above) but which can be **scaled-up** in a big data context.

3.2 Use of data analytics by auditors

Auditors can use data analytics to help identify risks of material misstatement and also when performing further audit procedures. Advantages of using data analytics to undertake procedures include:

- The extent of testing can be greatly increased.
- Some procedures that are impossible to undertake manually can be automated.
- Previously, the cost of undertaking many of these procedures manually had outweighed the benefits.
- The time taken to undertake repetitive procedures manually can now be spent examining more judgemental areas of the financial statements.

The audit client's nominal ledger will first be extracted and uploaded into the auditor's data analytics software. The reliability of any analysis produced by the data analytics software is dependent on the quality of the raw data uploaded into it. To be reliable, the auditor must be certain that the extract from the nominal ledger is accurate and complete. Engagement teams may lack the required IT knowledge to extract the relevant data in the required format from entities' systems or organise the data extracted by the client's IT personnel into a suitable format for use in data analytics. Where this is the case, specialist staff may be necessary.

The capture, storage and processing of entity data presents firms with challenges in relation to data security and data protection. Audit clients need to have confidence their data is being held and processed securely. Additional clauses might need to be inserted into engagement letters regarding the security and confidentiality of data extracted from the client's accounting system.

Once the extract has been successfully uploaded, the auditor can use the data analytics software to provide analysis. Results are presented using a mixture of visual techniques making it easy for the auditor to spot unusual trends, unexpected results or notable items called 'outliers'. If outliers are identified, further procedures such as inquiry and corroboration should be conducted to obtain an understanding of the outliers.

An example of a data analytics dashboard is shown below:

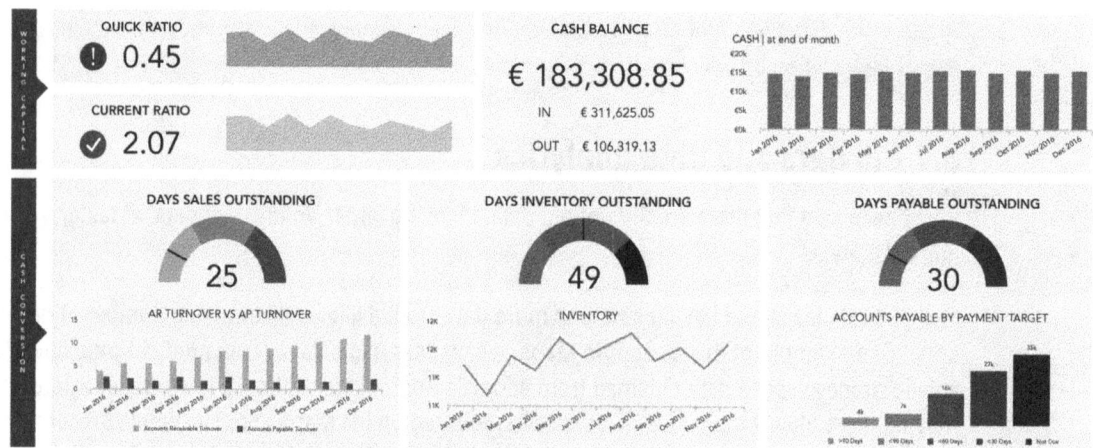

A data analytics dashboard allows the auditor to visualise the data in a dynamic manner. Auditors can use the data analytics software to 'drill down' and look at the data in further detail. For example, the auditor can select the expenses line and then click to see the individual accounts, such as payroll or depreciation, making up the balance. The auditor can then drill down further and see the individual transactions making up each account.

Other parts of a data analytics programme will analyse and illustrate the data in different ways as chosen by the auditor depending on the objective and purpose of the data analytic. For example, the auditor might choose to use the stacked bar chart function to show the number of transactions being posted by each individual in the finance team by day of the week. If one individual is posting regularly over a weekend, this might warrant further investigation (assuming this is not the norm for the organisation).

3.2.1 Outlier Analysis

In the light of the capacity of data analytics to enable the auditor or indeed the internal audit department within the organisation to test close to or even 100% of the transactions, methods have been developed to flag transactions that seem unusual given the normal course of business. One method of identifying such transactions is the use of **outlier analysis** based on the standard deviation of normal transactions within the business.

The standard deviation relates to how transactions are **normally distributed** around the mean, for example, the quantities involved in transactions within a particular nominal code. This means that it could be calculated that, on average, amounts in that particular nominal code would **deviate from the mean by a certain amount** based on historic data. The computer system can therefore be programmed to analyse the data, establish the standard deviation and flag up any transactions that lie a certain amount outside the expected values.

In this way, it becomes possible for the organisation or the auditor to have an initial starting point when looking for material misstatements as such transactions are often **outside of what is expected** in the normal course of business.

This technique becomes much more effective when combined with AI / RPI as described above. Currently, firms are developing software that will mine the data from previous years and analyse it to determine trends and identify deviations with much **more precision**. In this way, auditors will be able to identify with much more precision the outliers that do not conform to expectations.

3.2.3 Use of data analytics in assessing risk of material misstatement

Analytical procedures can be automated to a great extent through the use of data analytics. These **automated techniques** are used to undertake a risk assessment to evaluate the **risk of material misstatement** in the financial statements. Examples of how data analytics can be used to undertake a risk assessment include:

- Analysing 100% of transactions in a population, stratifying the population and then identifying outliers for further examination (revenue analytics).
- Comparing entity data to externally obtained data.
- Semantic or sentiment monitoring of textual information, such as that contained in emails or social media commentary. External commentary could highlight risks such as reputation damage (that may impact the valuation of intangible assets) or fraud.
- Mapping of core processes to check accounting transactions against expected accounting patterns (such as revenue being recorded through the sales ledger) to identify any deviations.
- Monitoring data to assess compliance with 'Benford's Law', which observes that, for much 'real-life' numerical data, low-value leading digits are predominant (significant deviations should be investigated as they may be due to fraudulent manipulation).
- Supporting analytical procedures, for example using visualisation techniques to assist in trend analysis.

Many of these techniques are examples of **predictive analytics** that can be used to undertake various types of analysis that will help in identifying potential areas of mis-statement. Predictive analytics can be used to establish a 'baseline' of everyday transactional performance within an entity that can be used to identify unusual transactions. This version of analytics will cover 100% of the transactions undertaken by the entity and will also involve **journal entry analysis** to ensure coverage of all high-risk areas.

Such analysis can be undertaken in **'real time'** by either enabling the external audit to access the cloud-based system of the entity and run analytical software on the data on a continual basis that can identify the unusual trends or transactions that require investigation. Analysis can also be undertaken by the internal audit function within the entity and will enable any required investigation to be undertaken immediately.

If key ratios and procedures can be calculated continually from the general ledger rather than using historic data, there is a **dynamism** in the identification of mis-statements that was previously not possible. In addition, the understanding that is gained from this analysis is enhanced continually via the addition of new data. The presentation of this data in a dashboard platform enhances the usability, and well-trained members of staff will be able to use this to better identify potential problems.

> **Exam focus point**
>
> The November 2021 exam contained a 13 mark question on how data analytics could enhance the quality of audit work at a client.

3.2.4 Use of data analytics as substantive audit procedures

Data analytics can be used to perform both substantive analytical procedures and tests of details. Regardless of whether data analytics or manual techniques are used for audit testing, there must be compliance with the ISAs.

The use of data analytics enables higher precision and more effective substantive analytical procedures. The auditor can use their data analytics software to identify any unexpected trends or anomalies and investigate to see if these are due to a material misstatement.

Where data analytics are used as a test of detail, these will be designed to test a particular assertion.

Case Study — Test of detail

An auditor is testing the occurrence of payroll in an audit client. During planning, the auditors assessed that there is a high risk of material misstatement from leavers and joiners not being added to or removed from the payroll at the correct time. Payroll is run once per month.

A data analytics test was used which reviewed all payroll transactions in the year. The data analytic was designed to flag any payroll payments made to joiners before their first day of work at the client and any payroll payments made to leavers after their last day of work at the client.

One payroll payment to a new joiner was found to be made prior to that individual starting work with the audit client. Inquiry with management found that the individual was paid in advance as they were moving to the UK from overseas. The client was able to corroborate this explanation with a copy of the company policy on the company intranet. The auditor was also able to agree the explanation to the terms and conditions in the employee's contract. The auditors concluded this was not a misstatement and no further audit work was required.

3.2.5 Real world applications

We should by now have an appreciation that the identification of misstatements within the financial statements is becoming a **data-driven operation** with the ability to analyse very large data sets. The algorithms used to search and analyse them is now able to become more efficient over time through the use of machine learning, but how is this manifesting itself in the real-world application of this technology.

The key functionality required is the ability to conduct the analysis on the data and produce a useable, visually appealing report as a result of the analysis undertaken. It is possible to do this for small audits with data up to a limited number of rows within **Microsoft Excel**. Someone with sufficient capabilities in using the functions within the excel program can conduct a very detailed analysis, for example, the outlier analysis that we mentioned above can easily be undertaken for this size of dataset within excel. Excel also enables the visualisation of this analysis through its internal tools.

For richer detail, Microsoft Excel can be combined with more advanced visualisation software such as **Power BI** which integrates with data sources such as excel and enables live dashboards and reports to be created. This enables 'live time' decision making, collaboration and sharing of easily digestible information much more easily within the organisation. One of the advantages of Power BI is that can be integrated with many existing data sources such as excel and much larger current database solutions that an organisation may already have in place. The richness of the reports and visualisations that can be produced mean that many organisations are using this package to make the vast quantities of data meaningful. From the point of view of **identification of potential material misstatements**, Power BI enables the visualisation of trends and outliers within the data set and in this way makes the identification of anomalous data easier.

Another solution for organisations to consider would be the use of **R**, a language and environment for statistical computing and graphics. This environment enables the analysis and visualisation of data with the added benefit that it is available as **free software**.

If relying on more simple applications such as Microsoft Excel, once the size of the data reaches a certain size, it will require a **more sophisticated application** to undertake the analysis. With sufficient programming knowledge it is possible to use a relatively simple programming language such as **Python** to create a bespoke application to analyse the data in the exact way required by the auditor. With many data **visualisation libraries** available for Python, the results of the analysis can be presented in a visually appealing way.

Other software is available, such as **ACL (Now Galvanize)**, which is a cloud-based solution that uses robotic automation to undertake analytics on data sources for such functions as:

- Risk Management Integration
- Audit Workflow Management
- Fraud Detection and Prevention
- Cybersecurity Management
- Internal Control Management
- Policy Compliance Management

All of these functions rely on **robotic automation** of processes and the use of data analytics to provide useable information to cut costs and improve efficiency, for example in the reduction of fraud risk. Rather than just displaying data, or looking for data that meets set parameters that do not change without human intervention (as with excel or Power BI), the algorithms used in this process are **learning in real time** what constitutes 'business as usual' and adjusting their assessment of what constitutes anomalous data.

In this way there is **adaption to changes** in the business environment and adjustments made quickly to reflect the fact that the data produced currently does not necessarily conform to expectations from previous months/years. Anomalous amounts can still be identified by the system automatically adjusting to the new parameters and changing expectations of what is anomalous in real time.

Such systems are at the forefront of what is now possible in the field of data analytics and it is likely that the identification of material misstatements will become more and **more dependent** on their use by auditors and accountants.

3.3 Use of data analytics by organisations and users of financial statements

Organisation and users of financial statements can use data analytics to quickly undertake detailed analysis to gather more comprehensive information on which to base their economic decisions. This **automation** analytical procedures above enables decisions to be made on a much timelier basis and the analysis to be undertaken in much greater detail incorporating a wider range of data.

The availability and volume of the data mean that there is a requirement for software that is capable of interpreting and presenting the results of the analysis in a user-friendly format. The need for timely **data analysis** and **interpretation** has also created a trend towards a '**dashboard**' approach that presents various analyses summarised on one page, tailored to the needs of decision makers, allowing an 'at a glance' strategic overview.

Other techniques that were previously unavailable to users such as **'sentiment analysis'** using data mined from social media feeds can be used to further enhance the analysis possible. By combining all of these techniques' users can undertake a very detailed analysis of financial and non-financial information that was not possible using traditional methods.

3.3.1 Fraud Analytics using Benford's Law

Benford's Law relates to a discovery by physicist Frank Benford of a phenomenon in the **distribution of numbers in large data sets**. He discovered that in such sets a much larger proportion of numbers (30%) begin with the digit 1 than with the digit 2 (18%). This percentage falls as you work through the digits to the digit 9 (5%). This predominance of numbers beginning with smaller digits is little understood and there have been several theories proposed as to why the distribution of large data sets should conform to this distribution. However it is well established empirically and it can be used to **identify figures that do not lie within the expected distribution**.

One area in which this is useful is in identification of fraud. It is unlikely that an employee conducting a fraud and having to either reconstruct data or make data that has been falsified **appear convincing** will be aware of Benford's Law or be able to create data that conforms to it. As such, the falsified data may well lie **outside the expected distribution** based on Benford's discovery. Analysis of the data can reveal such anomalous figures and can be applied to particular nominal codes to identify the overuse of particular digits. For example, an analysis of accounts receivable may reveal that 10% of the numbers within that nominal code begin with the digit 1 rather than the expected 30%. This would indicate potentially **anomalous data**.

With the advent of data analytics, this analysis can be done on a much greater scale and with much **more precision** than was previously possible leading to a much greater ability by the organisation to identify potential misstatements as a result of fraud.

Chapter Roundup

- The use of information technology (IT) in business is constantly evolving.
- Audit firms must have an understanding of IT at their audit clients in order to assess the risk of material misstatement and comply with ISA 315 (Revised 2019) *Identifying and Assessing the Risk of Material Misstatement*.
- As more and more organisations adopt increasingly complex computerised accounting systems, and use increasingly ingenious IT techniques, auditors have to be aware of the risks that these systems bring to their clients when performing risk assessment.
- In addition to considering the use of IT at their clients, audit firms must consider their own use of IT. The use of automated tools and techniques (ATTs) by audit firms has grown as technology has evolved.
- Data analytics is the science and art of discovering and analysing patterns, deviations and inconsistencies, and extracting other useful information in the data underlying or related to the subject matter.
- Auditors can use data analytics to assist in their evaluation of the risk of material misstatement in the financial statements and when performing audit procedures.
- Organisations and users of financial statements can use data analytics to undertake detailed analysis to gather information on which to base their economic decisions.

PART C AUDIT STRATEGY, PROCESS AND REPORTING

Quick Quiz

1. What advantages arise from the simple automation of accounting transactions and record-keeping?
2. What management information could arise from the computerisation of invoicing and receivables accounting?
3. Name three types of cyberattack or cyber incident.
4. Name two types of automated tools and techniques.
5. An auditor wants to use an ATT to look for slow-moving inventory. Which type of ATT would be used?
6. Identify two advantages of using data analytics to evaluate the risk of material misstatement in the financial statements.

Answers to Quick Quiz

1. Cost savings (fewer accounting staff), increased processing speed, increased reliability and accuracy.

2. The management information available includes: sales analyses by customer, by product and by geographical area; key customer analysis; slow payers; CR balances, customers over credit limit; dormant customers.

3. Any three from the following:

    - Viruses
    - Hackers
    - Theft of hardware
    - Denial of service
    - Phishing
    - Interception of data
    - Destruction of hardware
    - Malware
    - Identity theft

4. Any two from audit software, test data, embedded audit facilities, data analytics, AI applications.

5. Audit software would be used to read the inventory file and to identify slow-moving inventory.

6. Any two of:

    The extent of testing can be greatly increased.

    Some procedures that are impossible to undertake manually can be automated.

    Previously, the cost of undertaking many of these procedures manually had outweighed the benefits.

    The time taken to undertake repetitive procedures manually can now be spent examining more judgemental areas of the financial statements.

End of Chapter Question

IMJ

Kelly & Co has just been appointed as the auditor of IMJ plc, a large insurance company, for the year ending 31 January 20X0. IMJ has purchased an automated investment decision making programme that has enabled IMJ to reduce its team of 160 analysts to 20. The analysts had previously been responsible for instigating the company's investments, managing the overall liquidity position of the company, and recording the company's performance. This software uses machine learning based artificial intelligence on an initial set of parameters around risk levels and liquidity requirements to attempt to maximise investment returns.

The investments that are chosen by the system are enacted and settled using a blockchain ledger. The blockchain was set up by a group of global securities exchanges with the aim of providing a single system to invest in shares, bonds, commodities and other stocks traded on various exchanges around the world. The blockchain ledger also records investment transactions and provides real time investment data.

The blockchain ledger uses 'blocks' of information with a unique encrypted code for each, to store and record information on a digital 'chain' once the transaction is completed. The blockchain transaction is recorded and distributed across a large network of computers but cannot be edited by the exchange or investment companies providing a control around the validity and completeness of transactions.

The blockchain is accessed by many global investment companies who have successfully implemented a rigorous application process which includes minimum liquidity and IT security requirements.

The benefit of accessing the blockchain is that it allows for almost real-time settlement that had previously taken several days and frees up liquidity for the company, allowing much greater agility to alter its investment strategy quickly. In addition, information produced is fully encrypted and cannot be altered before it feeds directly into the company's financial reporting system to track gains and losses on investments, to automatically value investments, and to provide automated liquidity analysis and other investment trading data in real time.

IMJ holds a large amount of its customers' data, including banking details, and is concerned at recent news reports of data breaches at similar companies.

Required

(a) Discuss the potential impact of the following new systems on the external auditor of IMJ plc.

    (i) Automated investment decision making software; and

    (ii) Blockchain ledger.

(b) Explain TWO cybersecurity risks that IMJ plc faces and suggest how they could mitigate against those risks.

Reporting

Topic list	Syllabus reference
1 Forming and critiquing an audit opinion	LO1
2 The communication problem	LO1
3 Special considerations	LO1
4 Reporting to those charged with governance	LO1
5 Other information	LO1
6 Internal audit reports	LO1
7 Non-statutory audit or review reports	LO1

Introduction

As a student at this stage of your studies, you will be familiar with the external audit opinion. If this is not the case, before you read any of this chapter, you must go back to the learning materials from your earlier studies and revise the basic features of the report, the various modifications that can be made, the concept of a true and fair view and the statutory requirements in relation to the audit opinion.

If, however, you took the Professional 1 Level auditing exam some time ago, you may not be familiar with the wording of the **standard auditor's report** as set out in ISA 700. We reproduce it in this chapter.

At Professional 2 Level, students are expected not only to know what the audit opinion is and how it is presented, they are required to draw audit opinions.

In this chapter we shall also consider the form of the auditor's report, the criticism that it receives and whether it enables an auditor to express properly a true and fair view.

We shall also look at the occasions when special considerations apply and we shall also look at the auditors' requirements in relation to reporting to those charged with governance.

1 Forming and critiquing an audit opinion

> **FAST FORWARD**
>
> Auditors express an opinion on financial statements based on the work they have done, the evidence obtained and conclusions drawn in relation to that evidence.

1.1 Forming an audit opinion

When the auditors have gathered all the evidence required, the audit engagement partner will form the audit opinion as to truth and fairness of the financial statements as a whole.

You should already be aware of the various audit opinions and modifications to the report that can be given. The following table summarises these for you. Some examples of the various auditor's reports in each case are given in the appendix to this Learning & Practice Workbook or in the remainder of this chapter.

Type of Report	Explanation	Relevant ISA	Example Auditor's Report
Unmodified auditor's report	The financial statements present fairly, in all material respects (or give a true and fair view).	ISA 700 (Revised)	Section 1.2.2
Qualified opinion	There is a material but not pervasive misstatement in the financial statements.	ISA 705 (Revised)	Example 1, Appendix
Adverse opinion	There is a material and pervasive misstatement in the financial statements.	ISA 705 (Revised)	Example 2, Appendix
Qualified opinion	The auditor was unable to obtain sufficient appropriate audit evidence for a material issue that is not pervasive.	ISA 705 (Revised)	Example 3, Appendix
Disclaimer of opinion	The auditor was unable to obtain sufficient appropriate audit evidence for a material and pervasive issue.	ISA 705 (Revised)	Examples 4 and 5, Appendix
Key audit matter (KAM)	For audits of listed entities. The auditor wants to highlight a matter, which is already included in the financial statements, that has required significant auditor time/attention. KAMs do not constitute a modification.	ISA 701	Section 1.3
Emphasis of matter paragraph	The auditor needs to highlight a matter that has been appropriately disclosed in the financial statements, but that is fundamental to users' understanding of the financial statements.	ISA 706 (Revised)	Example 6, Appendix

Type of Report	Explanation	Relevant ISA	Example Auditor's Report
Other matter paragraph	The auditor needs to highlight a matter that is relevant to users' understanding of the audit, the auditor's responsibilities or the auditor's report.	ISA 706 (Revised)	Example 6, Appendix

When forming their opinion, there are some key matters that the auditor must consider. These can be illustrated in the form of three questions:

Question 1 Have all the procedures necessary to meet auditing standards and to obtain all the information and explanations necessary for the audit been carried out?

Question 2 Have the financial statements been prepared in accordance with the applicable accounting requirements?

Question 3 Do the financial statements present fairly, in all material respects (or give a true and fair view)?

Attention!

> **True**: Information is factual and conforms with reality, not false. In addition the information conforms with required standards and law. The accounts have been correctly extracted from the books and records.
>
> **Fair**: Information is free from discrimination and bias and in compliance with expected standards and rules. The accounts should reflect the commercial substance of the company's underlying transactions.

The process of forming an audit opinion in an exam question can be summarised in a step format, as follows.

Step 1 Read through all the information given in the question carefully.

Step 2 Analyse the requirement.

Step 3 Read through the information given in the question again in the light of the requirement, making notes of any key factors.

Step 4 Ascertain whether all the evidence reasonably expected to be available has been obtained and evaluated.

Step 5 If not, identify whether the effect of not gaining evidence is such that the financial statements could as a whole be misleading (disclaimer of opinion) or in material part could be misleading (qualified opinion).

Step 6 Ascertain whether the financial statements have been prepared in accordance with the applicable financial reporting framework.

Step 7 If not, determine whether departure was required to give a true and fair view and if so, whether it has been properly disclosed.

Step 8 Decide whether any unnecessary departure is material to the financial statements (qualified opinion) or is pervasive to them (adverse opinion).

Step 9 Conclude whether the financial statements as a whole give a true and fair view.

Even if the answers to Steps 4 and 6 are yes, you must still carry out Step 9 and make an overall assessment of the truth and fairness of the financial statements in order to conclude that an unmodified opinion is appropriate.

PART C AUDIT STRATEGY, PROCESS AND REPORTING

1.2 The unmodified auditor's report

1.2.1 Basic elements of the auditor's report

A measure of **consistency** in the form and content of the auditor's report is desirable because it **promotes credibility** in the global marketplace, and also helps to promote the **reader's understanding** of the report and to **identify unusual circumstances** when they occur.

The auditor's report must be **in writing** and includes the following basic elements, usually in the following layout. You should remember these from your earlier studies. Following the table is the standard unmodified auditor's report.

Basic elements of auditor's report	Explanation
Title	The auditor's report must have a title that clearly indicates that it is the report of the independent auditor. This signifies that the auditor has met all the ethical requirements concerning independence and therefore distinguishes the auditor's report from other reports.
Addressee	The addressee will be determined by law or regulation, but is likely to be the shareholders or those charged with governance.
Opinion paragraph	The opinion paragraph must identify the entity being audited, state that the financial statements have been audited, identify the title of each statement that comprises the financial statements being audited, refer to the summary of significant accounting policies and other explanatory notes, and specify the date or period covered by each statement comprising the financial statements. If the auditor expresses an unmodified opinion on financial statements prepared in accordance with a fair presentation framework, the opinion shall use one of the following equivalent phrases: • The financial statements present fairly, in all material respects, …in accordance with [the applicable financial reporting framework]; or • The financial statements give a true and fair view of … in accordance with [the applicable financial reporting framework].
Basis for opinion	The basis for opinion paragraph must state that the audit was conducted in accordance with the ISAs, and refer to the 'Auditor's responsibilities for the audit of the financial statements' section which describes the auditor's responsibilities under the ISAs. The auditor must also state that they are independent of the audited entity, in accordance with the relevant ethical requirements relating to the audit. Finally, the auditor must state that they believe the audit evidence obtained is sufficient and appropriate to provide a basis for the audit opinion.
Material uncertainty relating to going concern	Where the auditor considers a material uncertainty related to going concern exists, this should be described in a separate paragraph headed 'Material uncertainty related to going concern.'
Key audit matters	For the audit of listed entities, or where required by law or regulation, the auditor should include a 'Key audit matters' paragraph. This paragraph describes the matters that, in the auditor's professional judgement, are most significant to the audit. (See section below.)

Basic elements of auditor's report	Explanation
Responsibilities for the financial statements	This part of the report describes the responsibilities of those who are responsible for the preparation of the financial statements. This section should describe management's responsibility including the following: • The preparation of the financial statements in accordance with the applicable financial reporting framework; • The implementation of such internal control as are necessary to enable the preparation of financial statements that are free from material misstatement, whether due to error or fraud. • The assessment of the entity's ability to continue as a going concern, the appropriateness of the going concern basis of accounting and adequacy of related disclosures; Reference shall be made to 'the preparation and fair presentation of these financial statements' (or 'the preparation of financial statements that give a true and fair view') where the financial statements are prepared in accordance with a fair presentation framework.
Auditor's responsibilities for the audit of the financial statements	The report must state that the auditor's objectives are to obtain reasonable assurance whether the financial statements as a whole are free from material misstatement, whether from fraud or error, and to issue an auditor's report that includes the auditor's opinion. The auditor must state that reasonable assurance is a high level of assurance, but is not a guarantee that an audit conducted in accordance with the ISAs will always detect a material misstatement when it exists. Further, the auditor must explain that misstatements can arise from fraud or error, and describe the meaning of materiality. The report must explain that the auditor exercises professional judgement and maintains professional scepticism throughout the audit, and describe the auditor's responsibilities in an audit. The description of the auditor's responsibilities must either be set out in the body of the auditor's report, in an appendix to the auditor's report or by including a specific reference in the body of the auditor's report to such a description on the website of an appropriate authority, where this is permitted by law and regulation.
Other reporting responsibilities	If the auditor is required by law to report on any other matters, this must be done in an additional paragraph below the opinion paragraph which is titled 'Report on other legal and regulatory requirements' or otherwise as appropriate.
Name of the engagement partner	The name of the engagement partner should be identified, unless such a disclosure is reasonably expected to lead to a significant personal security threat.
Auditor's signature	The report must contain the auditor's signature, whether this is the auditor's own name or the audit firm's name or both.
Date of the report	The report must be dated no earlier than the date on which the auditor has obtained sufficient appropriate audit evidence on which to base the auditor's opinion on the financial statements.

1.2.2 The standard unmodified auditor's report

The standard unmodified auditor's report is shown in ISA (Revised) 700 *Forming an opinion and reporting on financial statements* and is reproduced below.

INDEPENDENT AUDITOR'S REPORT

To the Shareholders of ABC Company [or Other Appropriate Addressee]

Report on the Audit of the Financial Statements

Opinion

We have audited the financial statements of ABC Company (the Company), which comprise the statement of financial position as at 31 December 20X1, and the statement of comprehensive income, statement of changes in equity and statement of cash flows for the year then ended, and notes to the financial statements, including a summary of significant accounting policies.

In our opinion, the accompanying financial statements present fairly, in all material respects, (or **give a true and fair view of**) the financial position of the Company as at 31 December 20X1, and (of) its financial performance and its cash flows for the year then ended in accordance with International Financial Reporting Accounting Standards (IFRS Accounting Standards).

Basis for Opinion

We conducted our audit in accordance with International Standards on Auditing (ISAs). Our responsibilities under those standards are further described in the *Auditor's Responsibilities for the Audit of the Financial Statements* section of our report. We are independent of the Company in accordance with the International Ethics Standards Board for Accountants' *Code of Ethics for Professional Accountants* (IESBA Code) together with the ethical requirements that are relevant to our audit of the financial statements in [jurisdiction], and we have fulfilled our other ethical responsibilities in accordance with these requirements and the IESBA Code. We believe that the audit evidence we have obtained is sufficient and appropriate to provide a basis for our opinion.

Key Audit Matters

Key audit matters are those matters that, in our professional judgement, were of most significance in our audit of the financial statements of the current period. These matters were addressed in the context of our audit of the financial statements as a whole, and in forming our opinion thereon, and we do not provide a separate opinion on these matters.

[Description of each key audit matter in accordance with ISA 701.]

Other Information

Management is responsible for the other information. The other information comprises the [information included in the X report, but does not include the financial statements and our auditor's report thereon.]

Our opinion on the financial statements does not cover the other information and we do not express any form of assurance conclusion thereon.

In connection with our audit of the financial statements, our responsibility is to read the other information and, in doing so, consider whether the other information is materially inconsistent with the financial statements or our knowledge obtained in the audit or otherwise appears to be materially misstated. If, based on the work we have performed, we conclude that there is a material misstatement of this other information, we are required to report that fact. We have nothing to report in this regard.

Responsibilities of Management and Those Charged with Governance for the Financial Statements

Management is responsible for the preparation and fair presentation of the financial statements in accordance with IFRS Accounting Standards and for such internal control as management determines is necessary to enable the preparation of financial statements that are free from material misstatement, whether due to fraud or error.

In preparing the financial statements, management is responsible for assessing the Company's ability to continue as a going concern, disclosing, as applicable, matters related to going concern and using the going concern basis of accounting unless management either intends to liquidate the Company or to cease operations, or has no realistic alternative but to do so.

Those charged with governance are responsible for overseeing the Company's financial reporting process.

Auditor's Responsibilities for the Audit of the Financial Statements

Our objectives are to obtain reasonable assurance about whether the financial statements as a whole are free from material misstatement, whether due to fraud or error, and to issue an auditor's report that includes our opinion. Reasonable assurance is a high level of assurance, but is not a guarantee that an audit conducted in accordance with ISAs will always detect a material misstatement when it exists. Misstatements can arise from fraud or error and are considered material if, individually or in the aggregate, they could reasonably be expected to influence the economic decisions of users taken on the basis of these financial statements.

As part of an audit in accordance with ISAs, we exercise professional judgement and maintain professional scepticism throughout the audit. We:

- Identify and assess the risks of material misstatement of the financial statements, whether due to fraud or error, design and perform audit procedures responsive to those risks, and obtain audit evidence that is sufficient and appropriate to provide a basis for our opinion. The risk of not detecting a material misstatement resulting from fraud is higher than for one resulting from error, as fraud may involve collusion, forgery, intentional omissions, misrepresentations, or the override of internal control.

- Obtain an understanding of internal control relevant to the audit in order to design audit procedures that are appropriate in the circumstances, but not for the purpose of expressing an opinion on the effectiveness of the Company's internal control.

- Evaluate the appropriateness of accounting policies used and the reasonableness of accounting estimates and related disclosures made by management.

- Conclude on the appropriateness of management's use of the going concern basis of accounting and, based on the audit evidence obtained, whether a material uncertainty exists related to events or conditions that may cast significant doubt on the Company's ability to continue as a going concern. If we conclude that a material uncertainty exists, we are required to draw attention in our auditor's report to the related disclosures in the financial statements or, if such disclosures are inadequate, to modify our opinion. Our conclusions are based on the audit evidence obtained up to the date of our auditor's report. However, future events or conditions may cause the Company to cease to continue as a going concern.

- Evaluate the overall presentation, structure and content of the financial statements, including the disclosures, and whether the financial statements represent the underlying transactions and events in a manner that achieves fair presentation.

We communicate with those charged with governance regarding, among other matters, the planned scope and timing of the audit and significant audit findings, including any significant deficiencies in internal control that we identify during our audit.

We also provide those charged with governance with a statement that we have complied with relevant ethical requirements regarding independence, and to communicate with them all relationships and other matters that may reasonably be thought to bear on our independence, and where applicable, related safeguards.

From the matters communicated with those charged with governance, we determine those matters that were of most significance in the audit of the financial statements of the current period and are therefore the key audit matters. We describe these matters in our auditor's report unless law or regulation precludes public disclosure about the matter or when, in extremely rare circumstances, we determine that a matter should not be communicated in our report because the adverse consequences of doing so would reasonably be expected to outweigh the public interest benefits of such communication.

Report on Other Legal and Regulatory Requirements

[*The form and content of this section of the auditor's report would vary depending on the nature of the auditor's other reporting responsibilities prescribed by local law, regulation, or national auditing standards. The matters addressed by other law, regulation or national auditing standards (referred to as 'other reporting responsibilities') shall be addressed within this section unless the other reporting responsibilities address the same topics as those presented under the reporting responsibilities required by the ISAs as part of the Report on the Audit of the Financial Statements section. The reporting of other reporting responsibilities that address the same topics as those required by the ISAs may be combined (ie included in the Report on the Audit of the Financial Statements section under the appropriate subheadings) provided that the wording in the auditor's report clearly differentiates the other reporting responsibilities from the reporting that is required by the ISAs where such a difference exists.*]

The engagement partner on the audit resulting in this independent auditor's report is [name].

[Signature in the name of the audit firm, the personal name of the auditor, or both, as appropriate for the particular jurisdiction]

[Auditor Address]

[Date]

1.3 Key Audit Matters (KAMs)

FAST FORWARD — Listed company auditor's reports include a description of the key audit matters.

ISA 701 *Communicating key audit matters in the independent auditor's report* sets out the auditor's responsibility to communicate KAMs. Let's start with the definition:

Key term

Key audit matters. Those matters that, in the auditor's professional judgement, were of most significance in the audit of the financial statements of the current period. Key audit matters are selected from matters communicated with those charged with governance.

KAMs are a relatively new concept introduced by the publication of ISA 701 in 2015. Reporting on KAMs aims to improve **transparency** by helping users to understand the most significant issues the auditor faced. This should enhance the **communicative value** of the auditor's report making it more relevant to investors and other users of the financial statements. In its 2015 publication *Auditor Reporting - Key Audit Matters*, the IAASB states that it believed KAMs would:

- **Increase transparency** about the audit that was performed.

- **Focus investors and other users on areas in the financial statements that are subject to significant management judgement and significant auditor attention**, which may assist investors and other users in better understanding the entity and financial statements, and the outcome of the audit as reflected in the auditor's opinion.

- **Provide users a basis to further engage with management and TCWG** (eg, audit committees) about certain matters related to the entity, the audited financial statements, or the audit that was performed.

- **Enhance communications** between the auditor and audit committee about the most significant matters in the audit, and potentially result in **increased attention to disclosures** about those matters in the financial statements by management and the audit committee.

- **Renew auditor focus** on matters to be communicated, which could indirectly result in an increase in professional skepticism, among other contributors to audit quality.

Overall, it was hoped that the inclusion of KAM in the auditor's report would help restore and enhance the confidence of users in the auditor's report and the audited financial statements, thereby contributing to robust and resilient capital markets. In a post implementation review performed by the IAASB in 2020, almost 80% of respondents stated that they found KAMs 'useful' or 'very useful'. Respondents stated that 'KAMs are most useful when they are specific to the entity'.

KAMs are part of every listed company auditor's report, and can be included by other auditors if needed. **KAMs do not constitute a modification of the report** or of the opinion. They are a part of the standard report which must be tailored to each company's circumstances. KAMs are not a substitute for disclosures, for EoM/OM paragraphs, nor for modified opinions. KAMs must always relate to matters already included within the financial statements.

The auditor's objectives are as follows.

> **ISA 701.7**
>
> The objectives of the auditor are to determine key audit matters and having formed an opinion on the financial statements, communicate those matters by describing them in the auditor's report.

KAMs are communicated **after the opinion**. This is because the reported **KAMs do not include matters which have resulted in a modified opinion** – any explanations in relation to these issues would already have been included in the 'Basis for' modified opinion paragraph.

The auditor must do four main things:

- Determine the matters which should be described as KAMs
- Communicate the KAMs in the auditor's report
- Communicate the KAMs to those charged with governance
- Keep appropriate audit documentation

1.3.1 Determining KAMs

KAMs should be selected from the matters communicated to those charged with governance, and they should represent the issues which have required the most audit attention during the audit. In working out which matters to report as KAMs, the auditor takes into account:

- Areas of **higher risk** of material misstatement, or 'significant risks' identified in line with ISA 315 (Revised 2019) (eg at the planning stage)

- **Significant judgements** in relation to areas where management made judgements

- The effect of **significant events or transactions**

The key part of the definition of KAMs above is that these are the **most significant matters**, and are more significant than the other matters communicated to those charged with governance. In other words, the auditor must edit out the less significant issues, and only include the really important ones in the auditor's report. This involves using the auditor's **professional judgement**.

It should be obvious that KAMs are **audit matters**, not just difficult areas of financial reporting. You could think of these as the areas that have given the auditor the biggest headaches.

The decision-making framework looks like this:

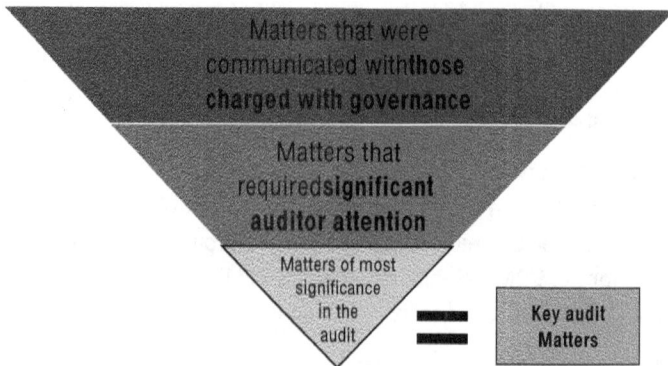

Source: IAASB The New Auditor's Report, slide presentation, March 2015

One approach might therefore be to begin with the audit matters communicated to those charged with governance, and to **pick the key matters** from those.

ISA 701 notes that these 'matters of most significance' may be the ones that there has been most discussion with management about. Other things to consider when determining KAMs include:

- The importance of the matter to intended **users' understanding**, including **materiality**
- The nature of the underlying accounting policy relating to the matter or the **complexity** or **subjectivity** involved
- Any **misstatements** related to the matter, and the nature and materiality of the misstatements
- The nature and extent of **audit effort** needed to address the matter (including the need for specialised knowledge and for consultations outside the audit engagement team)
- The nature and severity of **difficulties** in applying audit procedures, obtaining evidence or forming conclusions, including **more subjective judgements**
- The severity of any **control deficiencies**
- Whether **several separate issues** interacted, eg if a long-term contract had repercussions in several areas (revenue recognition, litigation or contingencies)

How many KAMs should the auditor report? This is a matter of judgement and depends on the circumstances, but the auditor should not just report everything. They are **key** matters, and by definition not everything is 'most significant'.

Exam focus point

> Key audit matters are part of the unmodified auditor's report. You could therefore be asked to assess the content of an unmodified auditor's report which includes KAMs. A key part of this would be assessing whether the auditor in question has determined KAMs appropriately, and whether the KAMs have been presented correctly.

1.3.2 Choosing not to include a KAM

The auditor may choose not to communicate a matter identified as a KAM, but only under specific circumstances:

The description of each KAM says **two main things**:

> **ISA 701.14**
>
> The auditor shall describe each key audit matter in the auditor's report unless:
>
> (a) Law or regulation precludes public disclosure about the matter; or
>
> (b) In extremely rare circumstances, the auditor determines that the matter should not be communicated in the auditor's report because the adverse consequences of doing so would reasonably be expected to outweigh the public interest benefits of such communication. This shall not apply if the entity has publicly disclosed information about the matter.

One example of this is where the auditor suspects **money laundering**. In some jurisdictions (eg the UK), regulations prohibit communications which might prejudice an investigation – so including suspicions of money laundering as a KAM would be **tipping off**.

1.3.3 Communicating KAMs

KAMs are communicated in a separate subsection of the auditor's report. There is a general introduction first, and then each KAM is presented in detail. The general introduction states that:

- These are the 'matters of most significance'; and
- No separate opinion is provided on them because they are covered by the audit opinion.

The description of each KAM then says **two main things**:

> **ISA 701.13**
>
> The description of each key audit matter in the Key Audit Matters section of the auditor's report shall include a reference to the related disclosure(s), if any, in the financial statements and shall address:
>
> (a) Why the matter was considered to be one of most significance in the audit and therefore determined to be a key audit matter; and
>
> (b) How the matter was addressed in the audit.

The example below contains a separate paragraph for each of these, and includes a reference to where the disclosures are for goodwill.

Here is an example of how KAMs could appear, taken from the IAASB's guidance publication *Auditor reporting – illustrative key audit matters*:

> **Key Audit Matters**
>
> Key audit matters are those matters that, in our professional judgement, were of most significance in our audit of the financial statements of the current period. These matters were addressed in the context of our audit of the financial statements as a whole, and in forming our opinion thereon, and we do not provide a separate opinion on these matters.
>
> **Goodwill**
>
> Under IFRS Accounting Standards, the Group is required to annually test the amount of goodwill for impairment. This annual impairment test was significant to our audit because the balance of XX as of 31 December 20X1 is material to the financial statements. In addition, management's assessment process is complex and highly judgemental and is based on assumptions, specifically [describe certain assumptions], which are affected by expected future market or economic conditions, particularly those in [name of country or geographic area].
>
> Our audit procedures included, among others, using a valuation expert to assist us in evaluating the assumptions and methodologies used by the Group, in particular those relating to the forecasted revenue growth and profit margins for [name of business line]. We also focused on the adequacy of the Group's

> disclosures about those assumptions to which the outcome of the impairment test is most sensitive, that is, those that have the most significant effect on the determination of the recoverable amount of goodwill.
>
> The Company's disclosures about goodwill are included in Note 3, which specifically explains that small changes in the key assumptions used could give rise to an impairment of the goodwill balance in the future.
>
> **Revenue Recognition**
>
> The amount of revenue and profit recognized in the year on the sale of [name of product] and aftermarket services is dependent on the appropriate assessment of whether or not each long-term aftermarket contract for services is linked to or separate from the contract for sale of [name of product]. As the commercial arrangements can be complex, significant judgement is applied in selecting the accounting basis in each case. In our view, revenue recognition is significant to our audit as the Group might inappropriately account for sales of [name of product] and long-term service agreements as a single arrangement for accounting purposes and this would usually lead to revenue and profit being recognized too early because the margin in the long-term service agreement is usually higher than the margin in the [name of product] sale agreement.
>
> Our audit procedures to address the risk of material misstatement relating to revenue recognition, which was considered to be a significant risk, included:
>
> - Testing of controls, assisted by our own IT specialists, including, among others, those over: input of individual advertising campaigns' terms and pricing; comparison of those terms and pricing data against the related overarching contracts with advertising agencies; and linkage to viewer data; and
>
> - Detailed analysis of revenue and the timing of its recognition based on expectations derived from our industry knowledge and external market data, following up variances from our expectations.

1.3.4 KAMs should not give original information

The KAMs are **matters that are already disclosed** in the entity's financial statements. They may refer to financial reporting issues, but they describe the matter in the context of the audit.

KAMs should not therefore give original information about the entity, ie information that is not already in the financial statements. If something is not disclosed but the auditor thinks it should be, then the auditor should ask management to disclose it.

1.3.5 No KAMs?

It is possible that there might not be any KAMs to communicate. ISA 701 does allow for this possibility, but **only extremely rare circumstances**, eg for a listed entity which has very limited operations (eg if it has not traded during the period).

In this case the auditor's report still has a section on KAMs, but states that there were none to communicate.

1.3.6 Relationship with the auditor's opinion

The basic relationship is this:

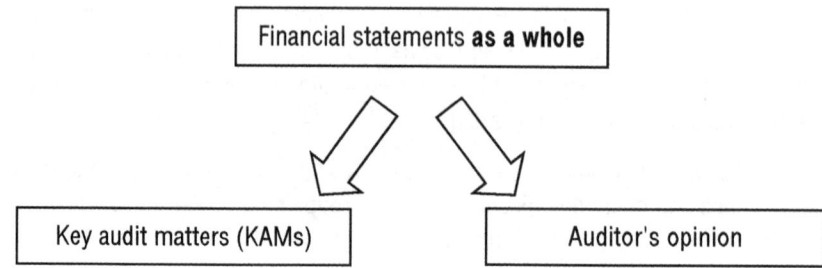

The KAMs are the key matters for the audit of the whole financial statements. They are **not** separate auditor's opinions for each little part of the financial statements, but merely further information on the process that led up to the opinion on the financial statements as a whole. Likewise, the auditor's opinion refers to the financial statements as a whole: as a whole they might give a true and fair view, or as a whole they might be true and fair but 'except for' one area (and so on).

If the auditor is going to express a **modified opinion**, then logically the matter giving rise to the modification is a key audit matter. However, the description of the matter will be given in the 'basis for modified opinion' paragraph, so it is **not included as a KAM** in the report. The auditor should **include a reference to the basis for modified opinion paragraph instead**.

ISA 701 also makes special mention of **going concern** problems. Where there is a material uncertainty in relation to going concern, the matter **should not be described as a KAM**, but should be discussed in the 'Material uncertainty in relation to going concern' paragraph' instead.

1.3.7 Relationship with Emphasis of Matter and Other Matter paragraphs

Key Audit Matters do not overlap with Other Matter paragraphs because KAMs must refer to issues present in the financial statements, whereas Other Matter paragraphs do not by definition.

There is some degree of overlap with Emphasis of Matter (EoM) paragraphs. The difference is that **KAMs do not modify the report**, and are included as standard in every listed company auditor's report. An EoM, on the other hand, does modify the report – although neither modifies the opinion. You could think of the issues giving rise to an EoM as being like KAMs but just more extreme: the EoM is for a 'matter of such importance that it is fundamental for users' understanding', whereas KAMs are merely 'most significant matters', ie less than fundamental. Where a matter has been included in an EoM paragraph, it must not be included as a KAM as well.

Exam focus point

This could be tested easily if you had to assess an auditor's report that included both KAMs and an EoM paragraph – the same issue must not be included in both.

1.3.8 Communication of KAMs with those charged with governance, and documentation

The auditor must communicate the KAMs to those charged with governance.

The audit documentation must include the 'significant audit matters' from which the KAMs were selected, together with the auditor's reasons for selecting the KAMs.

If no KAMs are communicated, then the reasons why must be documented. Likewise if a matter determined to be a KAM is not communicated (eg to avoid 'tipping off' in relation to money laundering), this must be documented.

1.4 Modified opinions in auditor's reports

There are three types of **modified opinion**: a **qualified opinion**, an **adverse opinion**, and a **disclaimer of opinion**.

As you will be aware from your earlier studies, ISA 705 (Revised) *Modifications to the opinion in the independent auditor's report* sets out the different types of modified opinions that can result. We will go over them below.

ISA 705 (Revised) identifies three possible types of modifications:

- A **qualified** opinion
- An **adverse** opinion
- A **disclaimer** of opinion

1.4.1 Types of modifications

Key term

> **Pervasiveness** is a term used to describe the effects or possible effects on the financial statements of misstatements or undetected misstatements (due to an inability to obtain sufficient appropriate audit evidence). There are three types of pervasive effect:
>
> - Those that are not confined to specific elements, accounts or items in the financial statements
> - Those that are confined to specific elements, accounts or items in the financial statements and represent or could represent a substantial portion of the financial statements
> - Those that relate to disclosures which are fundamental to users' understanding of the financial statements

The type of modification issued depends on the following two things:

- The **nature of the matter** giving rise to the modifications (ie whether the financial statements **are materially misstated**, or whether they **may be misstated** when the auditor cannot obtain sufficient appropriate audit evidence); and
- The auditor's judgement about the **pervasiveness** of the effects/possible effects of the matter on the financial statements.

A modified opinion is required when:

- The auditor concludes that the financial statements as a whole are not free from material misstatements; or
- The auditor cannot obtain sufficient appropriate audit evidence to conclude that the financial statements as a whole are free from material misstatement.

1.4.2 Qualified opinions

A qualified opinion must be expressed in the auditor's report in the following two situations:

(1) **The auditor concludes that misstatements are material, but not pervasive, to the financial statements.**

   Material misstatements could arise in respect of:

   - The appropriateness of selected accounting policies;
   - The application of selected accounting policies; or
   - The appropriateness or adequacy of disclosures in the financial statements.

(2) **The auditor cannot obtain sufficient appropriate audit evidence on which to base the opinion but concludes that the possible effects of undetected misstatements, if any, could be material but not pervasive.**

   The auditor's inability to obtain sufficient appropriate audit evidence could arise from:

   - Circumstances beyond the entity's control (eg accounting records destroyed);
   - Circumstances relating to the nature or timing of the auditor's work (eg the timing of the auditor's appointment prevents the observation of the physical inventory count); or
   - Limitations imposed by management (eg management prevents the auditor from requesting external confirmation of specific account balances).

1.4.3 Adverse opinions

An adverse opinion is expressed when the auditor, having obtained sufficient appropriate audit evidence, concludes that misstatements are both **material and pervasive** to the financial statements.

1.4.4 Disclaimers of opinion

An opinion must be disclaimed when the auditor **cannot obtain sufficient appropriate audit evidence** on which to base the opinion and concludes that the **possible effects** on the financial statements of undetected misstatements, if any, **could be both material and pervasive**.

The opinion must also be disclaimed in situations involving **multiple uncertainties** when the auditor concludes that, despite having obtained sufficient appropriate audit evidence for the individual uncertainties, it is not possible to form an opinion on the financial statements due to the **potential interaction of the uncertainties and their possible cumulative effect** on the financial statements.

One example of when a disclaimer of opinion is used was given in Chapter 17 where, in relation to going concern, management is unwilling to make or extend its assessment. Another example might be where the auditor is unable to attend the inventory count and unable to request receivable confirmations, and there is no other realistic means of gathering evidence on these two areas. If these two areas form a significant element of the total assets value, a disclaimer may be appropriate.

1.4.5 Impact on the auditor's report

When the auditor has had to express a modified opinion, the auditor's report must include a paragraph after the opinion paragraph providing a description of the matter giving rise to the modification. This paragraph will be entitled 'Basis for qualified opinion', 'Basis for adverse opinion' or 'Basis for disclaimer of opinion' depending on the type of modification.

The section of the auditor's report containing the opinion will be headed either 'Qualified opinion', 'Adverse opinion' or 'Disclaimer of opinion', again depending on the type of modification.

When the auditor expresses a qualified or adverse opinion, the section of the report on the auditor's responsibilities must be amended to state that the auditor believes that the audit evidence obtained is sufficient and appropriate to provide a basis for the auditor's modified audit opinion.

You can find examples of different types of modified opinion in the Appendix to this Learning & Practice Workbook.

1.4.6 Communication with those charged with governance

ISA 705 (Revised) states that when the auditor expects to express a modified opinion, the auditor must **communicate with those charged with governance** the circumstances leading to the expected modification and the proposed wording of the modification in the auditor's report.

This allows the auditor to give **notice** to those charged with governance of the intended modification and the reasons for it, to **seek agreement or confirm disagreement** with those charged with governance with respect to the modification, and to give those charged with governance an **opportunity to provide further information and explanations** on the matter giving rise to the expected modification. As a result, it is possible that the financial statements will be amended and that a modified opinion will not be expressed in the end.

1.5 Emphasis of matter paragraphs and other matter paragraphs in the auditor's report

> **FAST FORWARD**
>
> **Emphasis of matter paragraphs** and **other matter paragraphs** can be included in the auditor's report under certain circumstances. Their use does not modify the auditor's opinion on the financial statements.

ISA 706 (Revised) *Emphasis of matter paragraphs and other matter paragraphs in the independent auditor's report* provides guidance to auditors on the inclusion of paragraphs in the auditor's report that either draw users' attention to a matter that is of such importance that it is **fundamental** to their understanding (emphasis of matter paragraph) or that is **relevant** to their understanding of the audit, the auditor's responsibilities or the auditor's report (other matter paragraph).

1.5.1 Emphasis of matter paragraphs

Key term

> An **emphasis of matter paragraph** is a paragraph included in the auditor's report that refers to a matter appropriately presented or disclosed in the financial statements that, in the auditor's judgement, is of such importance that it is fundamental to users' understanding of the financial statements. (ISA 706)

Emphasis of matter paragraphs are used to draw readers' attention to a matter **already presented or disclosed** in the financial statements that the auditor feels is **fundamental** to their understanding, provided that the auditor has obtained sufficient appropriate audit evidence that the matter is **not materially misstated**.

When an emphasis of matter paragraph is included in the auditor's report, it comes **immediately after the 'Basis for Opinion' section** and is entitled 'Emphasis of matter' (or appropriate). The paragraph must contain a **clear reference** to the matter being emphasised and to where relevant disclosures that fully describe it can be found in the financial statements. The paragraph must state that **the auditor's opinion is not modified** in respect of the matter emphasised.

The following are examples of situations in which the auditor might include an emphasis of matter paragraph in the auditor's report:

- An uncertainty relating to the future outcome of **exceptional litigation or regulatory action**
- **Early application of a new accounting standard** that has a **pervasive effect** on the financial statements
- A **major catastrophe** that has had, or continues to have, **a significant effect** on the entity's financial position

1.5.2 Other matter paragraphs

Key term

> An **other matter paragraph** is a paragraph included in the auditor's report that refers to a matter other than those presented or disclosed in the financial statements that, in the auditor's judgement, is relevant to users' understanding of the audit, the auditor's responsibilities or the auditor's report. (ISA 706)

Other matter paragraphs are used where the auditor considers it necessary to draw readers' attention to a matter that is **relevant** to their understanding of the audit, the auditor's responsibilities or the auditor's report.

The other matter paragraph must be included **immediately after the 'Basis for Opinion' section** and any emphasis of matter paragraph, or elsewhere in the auditor's report if the content of it is relevant to the other reporting responsibilities section. The content of the other matter paragraph must reflect clearly that the other matter is not required to be presented and disclosed in the financial statements, and does not include information that the auditor is prohibited from providing by law and regulations or other standards, or information that is required to be provided by management.

Here are some specific circumstances when an other matter paragraph must be used, in accordance with ISA 710 *Comparative information – corresponding figures and comparative financial statements*:

- Where prior period financial statements were audited by a predecessor auditor
- Where prior period financial statements were not audited
- When reporting on prior period financial statements in connection with the current period's audit, if the auditor's opinion on such prior period financial statements differs from the opinion the auditor previously expressed

1.5.3 Communication with those charged with governance

Exam focus point

ISA 706 (Revised) states that when the auditor expects to include an Emphasis of Matter paragraph or an Other Matter paragraph in the auditor's report, then the auditor must communicate with those charged with governance the circumstances and the proposed wording of the paragraph in the auditor's report. It is vital for your exam performance that you can analyse a set of facts given to you and draw audit conclusions from them. This is a basic skill at this level. Work through the following question to practise this skill.

Question — Forming an audit opinion

You are an audit senior. You are nearing the end of the audit of Nesta for the year ended 30 June 20X6. Nesta owns a small chain of high-street clothing stores and also has a manufacturing division where it makes it own label brand 'Little Miss'. Own label clothing represents 50% of the inventory and sales of Nesta. The financial statements show a profit before tax of $7 million (20X5: $3 million) and a statement of financial position total of $23 million (20X5: $15 million). The following points have arisen on the audit.

(1) Nesta owns a number of its retail premises, which it revalues annually. This year several of its shops did rise sharply in value due to inflated property prices in their locality. Nesta also capitalises refits of its shops. Two shops were refitted in the year. The total increase in assets due to refits and revaluations is $10 million. Nesta does not revalue its factory premises, which are held in the statement of financial position at $175,000.

(2) Nesta values its inventory at the lower of cost or net realisable value. Cost is determined by deducting a suitable estimated profit margin from selling price. Inventory in the statement of financial position at 30 June 20X6 was $1,265,000.

(3) Nesta has a refunds policy which states that a customer who is not satisfied with their purchase may return their goods within 28 days of purchase and obtain an exchange or a cash refund. Experience has shown that exchanges and refunds are common, as Nesta's shops do not provide fitting rooms, space being at a premium. Nesta does not make any provision in the financial statements for refunds.

Required

Comment on the matters you will consider in relation to the implications of the above points on the auditor's report of Nesta.

Answer

(1) **Non-current assets**

There are two issues here. The first is whether Nesta's policy of revaluations is correct and the second is whether Nesta should capitalise re-fit costs.

The most important thing to consider is materiality as only material items will affect the audit opinion. The revaluations and refit total is material to the statement of financial position. It is possible that any revaluation of the factory premises would also be material.

(i) **Revaluation policy**

Per IAS 16, non-current assets may be held at cost or valuation. Where a company applies a revaluation policy, (an allowable alternative treatment under IAS 16), IAS 16 requires that revaluations are made with sufficient regularity that the carrying amount does not differ materially from that which would be determined using fair value at the reporting date. Nesta revalues annually, so meets that requirement.

Nesta revalues property, so as IAS 16 requires that all items in the same class of assets be revalued, the question arises as to whether it should also revalue the factory. This might have a material effect on the statement of financial position. IAS 16 states that a 'class' of property, plant and equipment is a grouping of assets of a similar nature and use in an enterprise's operations. Although the IAS implies that buildings is one class, in this case, the **nature** and **use** of the two kinds of building are quite distinct. In this case, creating two classes ('retail premises' and 'manufacturing premises') would appear to be reasonable.

(ii) **Refits**

Assets should be held at cost or valuation as discussed above. However, in some cases, IAS 16 allows the cost of refits to be added to the original cost of the asset. This is when it is probable that future economic benefits **in excess** of the **originally assessed** standard of **performance of the existing asset** will flow to the enterprise. A retail shop will be subject to refitting and this refitting may enhance its value. However, it is possible in a shop that such refitting might be better classified as expenditure on fixtures and fittings. This is a matter of judgement. Nesta's policy should be consistent and comparable, so if they have followed a policy of capitalising refits into the cost of the shop in the past, this seems reasonable.

Conclusion

The issues relating to non-current assets were material and could have affected the auditors' report. However, having considered the issues, it appears that there are no disagreements between the auditors and the directors on these issues. As there appears to have been no limitation on the scope of the auditors' work in relation to non-current assets, the audit opinion would be unqualified in relation to these issues.

(2) **Inventory**

IAS 2 requires that inventory be valued at the lower of cost or net realisable value. IAS 2 defines cost as all costs of purchase, costs of conversion and other costs incurred in bringing the inventories to their present location and condition.

The IAS outlines a number of methods at arriving at an approximation of cost in the absence of a satisfactory costing system. One such method is the use of a selling price less an estimated profit margin, called the retail method. This is a costing method commonly used in retail enterprises. However, this is reasonable only if it can be shown that the method gives a reasonable approximation of cost.

Given that 50% of Nesta's inventory is manufactured in house, it appears to be unlikely that they cannot ascertain the cost of the inventory in a better way than the selling price method. The chain of shops is small, and there should be sufficient controls over inventory transfer to enable the company to establish the cost of inventory using a FIFO system.

While the auditors might suggest to the directors that they look into the costing systems and make improvements in future years, it is unlikely that they would modify the auditor's report in the current year over this matter, assuming that the directors have shown that the accounting policy gives a reasonable approximation of cost.

This is because if a reasonable approximation of cost is given, the difference is not going to be material to the financial statements. Also, if Nesta has had the policy for a long period, the policy is at least consistent with itself. If the auditors had made recommendations that the system was reviewed in future years and the directors refused to make any amendments to the system in future, the auditors might want to consider taking further action in future years.

Conclusion

If there are no other audit matters arising in relation to inventory, the auditor's report will be unqualified in this respect.

(3) **Provisions**

Nesta offers refunds and exchanges to unhappy customers and experience shows that this offer is commonly taken up. If a sale is refunded, it is as if the sale never took place. It is therefore not prudent for Nesta to recognise profits on such sales. If items are exchanged, the profit element would still exist, so only the inventory element would be potentially misstated.

As the refund period is 28 days, the issue is isolated to sales made in the last month of the year. In the absence of specific figures, this approximates to 1/12 of annual revenue and profit, and is therefore potentially material. Using these approximations, this would mean that if more than a quarter of Junes sales were refunded, this could be material to revenue, and potentially to profit.

Given that the accounts are unlikely to be finalised before the end of July, the refunds figure for June should be available to both the directors and to the auditors. They should both be able to assess whether the potential provision required is material to the financial statements, and how much the provision should be, if one is required.

Conclusion

The audit opinion would only be modified in respect of this matter if the auditors felt that a material provision was required and the directors refused to include one in the financial statements. In which case, the auditors would issue an 'except for' opinion, on the grounds of disagreement.

Overall conclusion

It appears likely that the auditors will issue an unmodified report for the year ended 30 June 20X6.

1.6 Critiquing an audit opinion

Critiquing an audit opinion is an extension of forming an audit opinion. It is necessary to form an audit opinion yourself in order to ascertain whether someone else's conclusions on the same facts is fair and reasonable.

1.6.1 When will it be necessary to critique an audit opinion?

The obvious answer to this is 'in exam questions'. However, the exams will be based in real-life scenarios and it is important for you to consider the genuine contexts in which audit opinions will be critiqued. Consider the following situations:

- Engagement partner reviewing the audit work and conclusions drawn
- Auditor asked for second opinion about an audit opinion
- Second partner required to review an audit file

Probably the most common example is the engagement partner conducting a file review before drawing an opinion, which will then be given on the auditor's report for which he takes responsibility. The audit team have carried out the work, and in doing so have drawn audit conclusions about each aspect of the audit work. The audit partner must appraise these conclusions and determine whether or not they are correct.

Where a second partner review has been required, most commonly, if the client is listed or public interest, one of the things the second partner is required to do is to review the audit opinion and judge whether it is reasonable.

The issue of second opinions, as you know, is a tricky one. It is rarely advisable for an auditor to give a second opinion on an audit opinion because he is likely not to be in possession of the full facts.

1.6.2 How should an auditor critique an audit opinion?

An auditor should form his own opinion on the basis of the facts and then evaluate the original audit opinion in the light of his own opinion. As this is a matter of judgement, it is possible that two different, yet reasonable conclusions could be drawn. For instance, auditors might disagree on whether a matter was material or not. If this was the case, further judgements and risk assessments would have to be made.

In exam questions, then, you should bear in mind the step process required to form an audit opinion in the first place. If you work through each step, you may be able to see that the person who formed the original opinion has missed out steps or failed to notice something important. This is a skill that you must practise to be able to do well. Try the following question.

Question

Critiquing an audit opinion

You are an audit partner. Your firm carries out the audit of Branch, a listed company. Because the company is listed, you have been asked to perform a second partner review of the audit file for the year ended 30 June 20X6 before the audit opinion is finalised. Reported profit before tax is $1.65 million and the statement of financial position total is $7.6 million.

You have read the following notes from the audit file:

'Earnings per share

As required by IAS 33 *Earning per share*, the company has disclosed both basic and diluted earnings per share. The diluted earnings per share has been incorrectly calculated because the share options held by a director were not included in the calculations. Disclosed diluted earnings per share are 22.9c. Had the share options held by the director been included, this figure would have been 22.4c. This difference is immaterial.

Financial performance statement

The directors have currently not amended certain financial performance ratios in this statement to reflect the changes made to the financial statements as a result of the auditors' work. The difference between the reported ratios and the correct ratios is minimal.

Opinion

We recommend that an unqualified auditor's report be issued.'

You have noted that there is no evidence on the audit file that the corporate governance statement to be issued as part of the annual report has been reviewed by the audit team. You are aware that the company does not have an audit committee.

You are also aware that the director exercised his share options last week.

Required

Comment on the suitability of the proposed audit opinion and other matters arising in the light of your review. Your comments should include an indication of what form the auditor's report should take.

Answer

Earnings per share

The problem in the EPS calculation relates to share options held by a director. As they are held by a director, it is unlikely that they are immaterial, as matters relating to directors are generally considered to be material by their nature. The fact that EPS is a key shareholder ratio which is therefore likely to be material in nature to the shareholders should also be considered.

As the incorrect EPS calculation is therefore material to the financial statements, the auditor's report should be modified in this respect, unless the directors agree to amend the EPS figure. This would be an 'except for' modification, on the grounds of disagreement.

Share options

The share options have not been included in the EPS calculations. The auditors must ensure that the share options have been correctly disclosed in information relating to the director both in the financial statements and the other information, and that these disclosures are consistent with each other. If proper disclosures have not been made, the auditor will have to modify the auditor's report due to lack of disclosure in this area.

Exercise of share options

The fact that the director has exercised his share options after the year end does not require disclosure in the financial statements. However, it is likely that he has exercised them as part of a new share issue by the company and if so, the share issue would be a non-adjusting subsequent event that would require disclosure in the financial statements. We should check if this is the case and, if so, whether it has been disclosed. Non-disclosure would be further grounds for modification.

Financial performance statement

The financial performance statement forms part of the other information that the auditor is required to review under ISA 720 (Revised). The ISA states that the auditors should seek to rectify any apparent misstatements in this information. The ratio figures are misstated, and the auditor should encourage the directors to correct them, regardless of the negligible difference.

The ISA refers to material items. The ratios will be of interest to shareholders, being investor information and this fact may make them material by their nature. However, as the difference is negligible in terms of value, on balance, the difference is probably not sufficiently material for the auditors to make any modifications or explanations in their auditor's report.

Overall conclusion

None of the matters discussed above, either singly or seen together are pervasive to the financial statements. The auditor's report should be qualified on the material matter of the incorrect EPS calculation. We should ensure that all the other disclosures are in order and also review the corporate governance statement. If the corporate governance statement does not adequately address the issue of the company not having an audit committee, we will need to include this in the Other Information section of our report. Our opinion will not be modified in this respect.

2 The communication problem

> **FAST FORWARD**
>
> A standard format is used to promote understandability because the auditor's report is widely available to both accustomed users and users who are not accustomed to audit and audit language.

2.1 The act of communication

In essence, the auditors' job is straightforward: auditors carry out tests and enquiries and evaluate evidence received with the purpose of drawing an audit opinion. They then **communicate** that opinion, in the form of an auditor's report, as we have been discussing. This is where difficulties can arise.

The communication problem is caused by a number of different issues that can be categorised under three headings, although broadly linked. The three problematic areas are:

- Understandability
- Responsibility
- Availability

2.1.1 Understandability

Although the essence of the auditors' role is simple, in practice it is surrounded by auditing standards and guidance, and is highly **technical**. It also involves **relevant language**, or 'jargon' that non-auditors may not understand.

Take a standard definition of an audit. 'An audit is an exercise designed to show whether financial statements are free from **material misstatement** and give a **true and fair view**.' The highlighted words reveal areas of ambiguity.

Communicating the audit opinion in a way that people can understand it is a challenge.

2.1.2 Responsibility

Related to the problem of understanding what the audit is and what the audit opinion means is the issue of what the auditors are **responsible** for. As far as the **law** is concerned, auditors have a restricted number of duties. **Professional standards** and other bodies place other duties on auditors.

Users of financial statements, and the public, may not have a very clear perception of what the auditors are responsible for and what the audit opinion relates to, or what context it is in.

The issue of **auditors' liability** ties in here. Auditor's reports are addressed to shareholders, to whom auditors have their primary and legal responsibility. However, audited accounts are used by significantly more people than that. Should this fact be addressed in the auditor's report? This issue was also considered in Chapter 6.

2.1.3 Key audit matters

In 2015 the IAASB issued ISA 701 *Communicating key audit matters in the independent auditor's report*. This standard requires the auditor to determine which of the matters communicated to those charged with governance are key audit matters. Such matters include areas of significant risk, difficulties encountered during the audit, and significant deficiencies internal control. There is also more emphasis on going concern and transparency regarding the work carried out by the auditor, with the aim of improving the quality of the auditor's report.

2.2 Availability

> The availability of auditor's reports has been increased by the trend to publish financial statements on companies' websites. Auditors should consider the risks of this. When financial information is available electronically, auditors must ensure that their report is not misrepresented.

The fact that a significant number of people use audited accounts has just been mentioned. Auditor's reports are publicly available, as they are often held on **public record**. This fact alone may add to any perception that exists that auditors address their report to more than just shareholders.

The problem of availability is exacerbated by the fact that many companies publish their **financial statements** on their **website**. Listed companies in the UK are required to publish their annual reports and accounts on a website by the *Companies Act* 2006 (Section 430). This means that millions of people around the world have access to the auditor's report.

This issue may add significant misunderstandings.

- **Language** barriers may cause additional understandability problems.
- It may not be clear **which financial information** an auditor's report refers to.
- The auditor's report may be subject to **malicious tampering** by hackers or disgruntled personnel.

If an auditor's report is published electronically, auditors lose control of the **physical positioning** of the report, that is, what it is published with. This might significantly impact on understandability and also perceived responsibility.

2.2.1 Appropriate wording and controls

The auditors should ensure that their report is worded so that it is appropriate for inclusion on a website. This will include reference to specific financial statements rather than the use of page numbers, for example.

Where the auditors' report is to be published electronically, the auditors should carry out a series of checks.

- They should **review the process** for deriving the electronic information from the hard copy financial statements.
- They should **check** that the electronic copy is **identical** to the hard copy.
- They should **check** that the **presentation** has **not** been **distorted** (ie that certain items have not been given greater emphasis in the new presentation).

As the directors are responsible for controls in their business, they are responsible for ensuring that the report is not tampered with once it is on the website.

2.3 The standard report

The auditor's report with which you should be are familiar is the standard auditor's report outlined in ISA 700 (Revised) and reproduced in Section 1.2.2. This standard report was specifically developed to counter problems of lack of understandability inherent in the communication process.

The auditor's report has certain elements designed to eliminate common misconceptions.

- It is clearly addressed to shareholders
- Introductory paragraphs outlining what the report refers to
- Paragraphs outlining the responsibilities of directors and auditors
- An explanation of the basis on which the auditors have come to their conclusion
- An expression of opinion

However, some parties still argue that the auditor's report is a difficult document to understand. It still includes technical terms which require further explanation. It is sometimes argued that the existence of standard report adds complexity to the situation and that users would be better served by having auditor's reports tailored to each specific client.

2.3.1 Advantages of a standard report

The key advantages of having a standard report is that it is **easier for users to understand** an auditor's report that has **elements in common** with all other auditor's reports. It also means that auditor's reports can be more easily compared.

When a standard report is used, there is less chance of isolated misunderstanding caused by the way one firm of auditors chooses to express itself or in relation to the explanation of a particular issue.

3 Special considerations

> **FAST FORWARD**
>
> Auditors may issue special reports on summary financial statements, special purpose financial statements, revised accounts and distributions following an audit qualification.

3.1 Summary financial statements

Summary financial statements contain historical financial information that is derived from financial statements but contains less detail than the financial statements. The audit of summary financial statements is covered by ISA 810 (Revised) *Engagements to report on summary financial statements*.

The auditors can only accept an engagement to report on summary financial statements where **they are also the auditor of the financial statements** from which the summary financial statements are derived.

When the auditor has concluded that an **unmodified opinion** on the summary financial statements is appropriate, the auditor's opinion shall, unless otherwise required by law or regulation, use one of the following phrases:

(a) The accompanying summary financial statements are consistent, in all material respects, with the audited financial statements, in accordance with [the applied criteria]; or

(b) The accompanying summary financial statements are a fair summary of the audited financial statements, in accordance with [the applied criteria].

If the summary financial statements are **not consistent**, in all material respects, with or are **not a fair summary** of the audited financial statements, in accordance with the applied criteria, and management does not agree to make the necessary changes, the auditor shall express an **adverse** opinion on the summary financial statements.

3.1.1 Reference to the auditor's report on the audited financial statements

The auditor's report on the audited financial statements may include one of the following paragraphs.

- A qualified opinion
- An emphasis of matter paragraph or another matter paragraph
- A material uncertainty related to going concern section
- Communication of key audit matters
- A statement that describes an uncorrected material misstatement of the other information

If so, the auditor's report on the summary financial statements must state which of these paragraphs is included in the auditor's report on the audited financial statements. In addition, the auditor's report on the summary financial statements must include the relevant description.

- The basis for the qualified opinion on the audited financial statements and the effect, if any, on the summary financial statements

- The matter referred to in the emphasis of matter paragraph, the other matter paragraph, or the material uncertainty related to going concern section in the auditor's report on the audited financial statements and the effect(s), if any, on the summary financial statements

- The uncorrected material misstatement of the other information and the effect(s), if any, on the information included in a document containing the summary financial statements and the auditor's report

When the auditor's report on the audited financial statements contains an adverse opinion or a disclaimer of opinion, the auditor's report on the summary financial statements shall:

- State that the auditor's report on the audited financial statements contains an adverse opinion or disclaimer of opinion

- Describe the basis for that adverse opinion or disclaimer of opinion

- State that, as a result of the adverse opinion or disclaimer of opinion on the audited financial statements, it is inappropriate to express an opinion on the summary financial statements

3.2 Special purpose financial statements

A special purpose framework is a financial reporting framework designed to meet the financial information needs of specific users, for example:

- A tax basis of accounting for a set of financial statements that accompany an entity's tax return
- The financial reporting provisions established by a regulator to meet the requirements of that regulator
- The financial reporting provisions of a contract, such as a loan agreement

Special purpose financial statements are financial statements prepared in accordance with a special purpose framework.

ISA 800 (Revised) *Special considerations – audits of financial statements prepared in accordance with special purpose frameworks* states that the auditor should report on the special purpose financial statements, applying the requirements of ISA 700 (Revised). They shall make sure that:

- The financial statements refer to the applicable financial reporting framework.
- If the financial statements are prepared in accordance with a contract, the auditor shall evaluate whether the financial statements adequately describe any significant interpretations of the contract on which the financial statements are based.
- The auditor's report must describe the purpose for which the special purpose financial statements are prepared.
- The management responsibility paragraph must state that management is responsible for ensuring the financial reporting framework is suitable in the circumstances.
- The auditor's report on special purpose financial statements shall include an emphasis of matter paragraph alerting users of the auditor's report that the financial statements are prepared in accordance with a special purpose framework and that, as a result, the financial statements may not be suitable for another purpose.

3.3 Distributions following an audit qualification

In some countries it may be the case that companies whose accounts have been qualified by the auditor may make a distribution (pay a dividend) only under certain circumstances.

The question whether a company has profits from which to pay a dividend is determined by reference to local/national company legislation. If the auditors have modified their report on the accounts they may have also stated (in writing) whether, in their opinion, the subject matter of their qualification (if it relates to statutory accounting requirements) is material in determining whether the dividend may be paid.

Question — Distributions

Find out what the rules are on distributions and distributable profits in your country. If possible, find out what happens when a distribution is made after a qualification and what the auditor's duties are, if any.

3.4 Revised accounts

Annual accounts may be found, after their laying or delivering, to be defective. In some countries it may be possible to revise such defective accounts, in some such revision may be compulsory and in others revision may not be permitted.

The use of hindsight is likely to be limited in determining whether accounts failed to comply with IFRS Accounting Standards, local legislation or standards to events that took place **before** the accounts were approved. This means that estimated figures in the accounts need only be corrected if the facts on which the estimates were made are fundamentally wrong (as opposed to a change in the accounting policy chosen to calculate the estimate or changes in the intentions and forecasts of management).

The revision of the accounts may be undertaken by:

- **Revision by replacement**, replacing the original with a new set of accounts or report, or
- **Revision by supplementary note**

In both these cases, it is assumed that accounts should be prepared as if prepared and then approved by management as at the **date of the original annual accounts**, which means that the extent of any revision is limited to that resulting from the **facts** which were **known** or **discoverable** at the **original date of approval**.

Management should include a statement in a prominent place in the revised accounts which gives full details of the revision.

As far as the duties of the auditors are concerned, after the date on which they have signed the auditor's report on the original accounts, the auditors have no duty to search for evidence of further matters which may affect the accounts to which the report relates. However, if such a matter comes to their attention, they should discuss any appropriate revision with management. If management are unwilling to revise the accounts then the auditors should take legal advice.

The following specific procedures should be undertaken.

(a) **Review** the **original audit plan** in the light of the analysis of the matter leading to revision and the extent to which additional audit evidence is required should be considered.

(b) **Reassess** the **various matters of judgement** involved in the preparation of the original accounts would be considered.

(c) **Obtain evidence specific** to the **adjustments** made to the original accounts.

(d) **Review** the **period** after the **date on which the original accounts were approved**.

(e) **Review** the **revised accounts** to a sufficient extent, in conjunction with the conclusions drawn from the other audit evidence obtained, to give the auditors a reasonable basis for their opinion on the accounts.

(f) **Consider** any legal and regulatory consequences of the revision.

Examples of the auditors' report on revised accounts are given here, based on ISA 700 (Revised) (opinion paragraph only).

> In our opinion, the revised financial statements present fairly, in all material respects (or 'give a true and fair view), as at the date the original financial statements were approved, of the financial position of the company as of 31 December 20X1, and of the results of its operations and its cash flows for the year then ended in accordance with [relevant national legislation].
>
> In our opinion the original financial statements for the year to 31 December 20X1, failed to comply with [relevant national standards or legislation].
>
> AUDITOR
>
> Date
> Address

4 Reporting to those charged with governance

FAST FORWARD

Auditors must report relevant audit matters to those charged with governance and will also produce a report to management detailing control weaknesses observed during the audit.

4.1 Report to those charged with governance

ISA 260 (Revised) *Communication with those charged with governance*, gives guidance in this area. The scope of ISA 260 (Revised) is limited to matters that come to the attention of the auditors as a result of the audit – the auditors are not required to design procedures to identify matters of governance interest.

Key term

Those charged with governance is the term used to describe the role of persons or organisations with responsibility for overseeing the strategic direction of the entity and obligations relating to the accountability of the entity. This includes overseeing the financial reporting process.

The objectives of the auditor are to:

- Communicate clearly with those charged with governance the responsibilities of the auditor in relation to the financial statement audit and an overview of the planned scope and timing of the audit.
- Obtain from those charged with governance information relevant to the audit.
- Provide those charged with governance with timely observations arising from the audit that are significant and relevant to their responsibility to oversee the financial reporting process.
- Promote effective two-way communication between the auditor and those charged with governance.

ISA 260.11

The auditor shall determine the appropriate persons within the entity's governance structure with whom to communicate.

The auditors may communicate with the whole board, the supervisory board or the audit committee depending on the governance structure of the organisation. To avoid misunderstandings, the engagement letter should explain that auditors will only **communicate matters** that come to their attention as a **result** of the **performance** of the audit. It should state that the auditors are **not required** to **design procedures** for the purpose of identifying matters of governance interest.

The letter may also:

- **Describe** the **form** which any **communications** on governance matters will take
- **Identify** the **relevant persons** with whom such communications will be made
- **Identify** any **specific matters** of **governance** interest which it has agreed are to be communicated

Matters to communicate include:

- Auditors' responsibility to form and express an opinion on financial statements prepared by management
- Fact that audit does not relieve management of responsibility for financial statements
- An overview of timing and planned scope of the audit

- The auditor's views about **significant** qualitative aspects of the entity's accounting practices including **accounting policies**, accounting estimates and disclosures
- **Significant** difficulties encountered during the audit
- Other **significant matters** such as material deficiencies in internal control, questions regarding management integrity, and fraud involving management
- Other **matters** that are significant to the oversight of the financial reporting process
- The relevant ethical requirements, including those relating to independence

For listed companies, the communication should include:

- A statement that the engagement team, firm and network firm have complied with relevant ethical requirements
- All matters between firm and client that could be thought to bear on independence (including total fees for all services)
- Safeguards that have been applied to reduce risks or eliminate them

4.1.1 Communication methods

Matters may be communicated orally or in writing, but they should be recorded in the audit working papers, however discussed. Auditors should make clear that the audit is not designed to identify all relevant matters connected with governance.

The extent, form and the frequency of reports will be affected by:

- The size and nature of the client;
- The attitude of those charged with governance; and
- The importance of the issues to be raised.

For example, reports of relatively minor matters to a small client may be best handled orally via a meeting or telephone conversation.

4.1.2 Timing of communication

Reports should be made promptly to allow those charged with governance to take appropriate action.

4.1.3 Other communications

You should be familiar with ISA 265 *Communicating deficiencies in internal control* from your earlier studies. It gives more information to auditors about how to report deficiencies and how to define significant deficiencies.

It gives two key definitions for the auditor in making those judgements.

Key terms

A **deficiency in internal control** exists when:

(a) A control is designed, implemented or operated in such a way that it is unable to prevent, or detect and correct, misstatements in the financial statements on a timely basis; or

(b) A control necessary to prevent, or detect and correct, misstatements in the financial statements on a timely basis is missing.

A **significant deficiency in internal control** is a deficiency or combination of deficiencies in internal control that, in the auditor's professional judgement, is of sufficient importance to merit the attention of those charged with governance.

The auditor must determine if he has identified significant deficiencies in internal control while obtaining an understanding of the system and testing it, and if he has done so, he must communicate these with management and those charged with governance **in writing**. The auditor must also communicate less significant deficiencies with management.

The communication must include a **description of the deficiency and its potential effect**.

In addition, the communication must make clear that it relates to deficiencies discovered while carrying out audit work, that it therefore does not necessarily include all existing deficiencies and that the purpose of the work was not to report on deficiencies in the system.

Case Study

Example: Report to management covering letter

Private & Confidential

The Directors [Could be to audit committee]
XYZ Co
1 High Street
Anytown

24 June 20XX [Should be dated soon after completion of audit]

Dear Sirs

XYZ Co

Following our recent audit of your company, we are writing to advise you of various matters which came to our attention.

We set out on the attached schedule the major areas of deficiency which we noted, together with our recommendations. These recommendations have already been discussed with ... and their comments have been included.

As the purpose of the audit is to form an opinion on the company's financial statements, you will appreciate that our examination cannot necessarily be expected to disclose all shortcomings of the system and for this reason, the matters raised may not be the only ones which exist. [Managing expectations]

We should appreciate your comments as to how you propose to deal with the matters raised in this letter. If you require any further information or advice, please contact us. [Requesting feedback]

We have prepared this letter for your use only. It should not be disclosed to a third party and we can assume no responsibility to any person to whom it is disclosed without our written consent. [Disclaiming liability to third parties]

We would like to take this opportunity to thank you and your staff for your help and co-operation during the course of our audit.

Your faithfully

ABC & Co

The detailed recommendations included in the appendix would be structured as per the following example.

Preparation of payroll and maintenance of personnel records

Deficiency — [Sufficient detail to enable directors to follow up]

Under your present system, just two members of staff are entirely and equally responsible for the maintenance of personnel records and preparation of the payroll. Furthermore, the only independent check of any nature on the payroll is that the chief accountant confirms that the amount of the wages cheque presented to him for signature agrees with the total of the net wages column in the payroll. This latter check does not involve any consideration of the reasonableness of the amount of the total net wages cheque or the monies being shown as due to individual employees.

Implications — [Explain potential effect on client business]

It is a serious deficiency of your present system, that so much responsibility is vested in the hands of just two people. This situation is made worse by the fact that there is no clearly defined division of duties between the two of them. In our opinion, it would be far too easy for fraud to take place in this area (eg by inserting the names of 'dummy workmen' into the personnel records and hence on to the payroll) and/or for clerical errors to go undetected.

Recommendations — [Workable recommendations, discussed with management in advance]

(i)   A person other than the two wages clerks should be made responsible for maintaining the personnel records and for periodically (but on a surprise basis) checking them against the details on the payroll.

(ii) The two wages clerks should be allocated specific duties in relation to the preparation of the payroll, with each clerk independently reviewing the work of the other.

(iii) When the payroll is presented in support of the cheque for signature to the chief accountant, he should be responsible for assessing the reasonableness of the overall charge for wages that week.

---

5 Other information

> **FAST FORWARD**
>
> Auditors should always seek to resolve material inconsistencies between financial statements and other information.

5.1 What other information?

ISA 720 (Revised) *The auditor's responsibilities relating to other information* establishes standards and provides guidance on the auditors' consideration of other information, on which the auditors have **no obligation to report**, in documents containing audited financial statements.

Key terms

> **Other information** is financial and non-financial information (other than the financial statements and the auditors' report thereon) included in an entity's annual report.
>
> **Annual report.** A document, or combination of documents, prepared typically on an annual basis by management or those charged with governance in accordance with law, regulation or custom, the purpose of which is to provide owners (or similar stakeholders) with information on the entity's operations and the entity's financial results and financial position as set out in the financial statements. An annual report contains or accompanies the financial statements and the auditor's report thereon and usually includes information about the entity's developments, its future outlook and risks and uncertainties, a statement by the entity's governing body, and reports covering governance matters.

> **Misstatement of the other information.** A misstatement of the other information exists when the other information is incorrectly stated or otherwise misleading (including because it omits or obscures information necessary for a proper understanding of a matter disclosed in the other information).(ISA 720)

Examples of other information are:

- A report by management or the board of directors on operations
- Financial summaries or highlights
- Planned capital expenditures
- Financial ratios
- Explanations of critical accounting estimates and related assumptions
- Overview of strategy
- Descriptions of trends in market prices of key commodities or raw materials

Auditors have no responsibility to report that other information is properly stated because an audit is only an expression of opinion on the truth and fairness of the financial statements. However, they may be **engaged separately**, or **required by statute**, to report on elements of other information. In any case, the auditors should give consideration to other information as inconsistencies with the audited financial statements may undermine their report.

Some countries require the auditors to apply specific procedures to certain other information, for example, required supplementary data and interim financial information. If such other information is omitted or contains deficiencies, the auditors may be required to refer to the matter in their report.

When there is an obligation to report specifically on other information, the auditors' responsibilities are determined by the **nature of the engagement** and by **local legislation** and professional standards. When such responsibilities involve the review of other information, the auditors will need to follow the guidance on **review engagements** in the appropriate ISAs.

5.2 Access to other information

Timely access to other information will be required. The auditors therefore must make arrangements with the client to obtain such information prior to the date of their report.

In circumstances where all the other information may not be available prior to that date, the auditors should follow the guidance in Section 5.6.

5.3 Reading and considering the other information

The auditor must read the other information, looking for:

- Material inconsistencies between the other information and the financial statements.
- Material inconsistencies between the other information and the auditor's knowledge obtained in the audit.

The auditor must then 'remain alert' for indications of material misstatements in the other information that is not related to the audit.

5.4 Material misstatements

> **ISA 720.16**
>
> If the auditor identifies that a material inconsistency appears to exist (or becomes aware that the other information appears to be materially misstated), the auditor shall discuss the matter with management and, if necessary, perform other procedures to conclude whether:
>
> (a) A material misstatement of the other information exists;
> (b) A material misstatement of the financial statements exists; or
> (c) The auditor's understanding of the entity and its environment needs to be updated.

If a material misstatement is discovered, then the auditor's duties may be summarised as follows.

Material misstatement of other information	
Revision needed to	**Action**
Financial statements	Respond in line with other ISAs, ie further procedures if necessary. Consider effect on the auditor's report.
Other information	Ask management to revise other information. If management refuses, ask those charged with governance. If still not corrected, then consider effect on auditor's report or withdraw from engagement.
Auditor's understanding	Respond in line with other ISAs (ISA 315 (Revised 2019)).

5.4.1 Revision needed to financial statements

If it appears to be the financial statements which are misstated, then the auditor must obtain evidence about the misstatement by performing further procedures. This may involve obtaining a better understanding of the entity in line with ISA 315 (Revised 2019). The misstatement would then be evaluated in line with ISA 450 *Evaluation of misstatements identified during the audit*.

If the financial statements are materially misstated then this is treated in the same way as any other material misstatement. If the financial statements are not amended, then the auditor's opinion would be modified as appropriate in line with ISA 700 (Revised) *Forming an opinion and reporting on financial statements*.

The situation is slightly different if the material inconsistency is only identified after the auditor's report has already been issued. If the financial statements need to be revised, then the guidance given in ISA 560 *Subsequent events* applies.

5.4.2 Revision needed to other information

Some misstatements do not give rise to an inconsistency with the audited financial statements, or with evidence obtained by the auditor. There is no duty to look for these misstatements (the auditor 'remains alert' for them), but if the auditor does find one then the effect is the same as if there were an inconsistency with the financial statements, ie the table above applies.

Further explanation may be needed before a conclusion can be reached: it is possible that it really is a misstatement of fact, but it is also possible that the auditor will not be able to evaluate its validity, eg because the auditor does not have specialist knowledge of it. There could be a valid difference of opinion between the auditor and management on the matter. However the auditor should also consider whether management's rationale implies a lack of management integrity. The auditor may wish to obtain legal advice.

5.5 Auditor's report

The **auditor's report will always include a separate Other Information section** when the auditor has obtained some or all of the other information as of the date of the auditor's report. For listed entities, the section is also included if other information is expected to be received after the date of the auditor's report.

Where the other information is **not materially misstated**, the standard unmodified section is placed after the key audit matters, and looks like this. (The 'X report' means the annual report.)

> **Other Information**
>
> Management is responsible for the other information. The other information comprises the [information included in the X report, but does not include the financial statements and our auditor's report thereon.]
>
> Our opinion on the financial statements does not cover the other information and we do not express any form of assurance conclusion thereon.
>
> In connection with our audit of the financial statements, our responsibility is to read the other information and, in doing so, consider whether the other information is materially inconsistent with the financial statements or our knowledge obtained in the audit or otherwise appears to be materially misstated. If, based on the work we have performed, we conclude that there is a material misstatement of this other information, we are required to report that fact. We have nothing to report in this regard.

The auditor may only have obtained part of the other information, and ISA 720 (Revised) covers various possible scenarios here. This is the effect on the auditor's report if **no other information has been received**:

> **Other Information**
>
> Management is responsible for the other information. The other information comprises the [information included in the X report, but does not include the financial statements and our auditor's report thereon]. The X report is expected to be made available to us after the date of this auditor's report.
>
> Our opinion on the financial statements does not cover the other information and we will not express any form of assurance conclusion thereon.
>
> In connection with our audit of the financial statements, our responsibility is to read the other information identified above when it becomes available and, in doing so, consider whether the other information is materially inconsistent with the financial statements or our knowledge obtained in the audit, or otherwise appears to be materially misstated.

The following example is for an unmodified opinion, but where there is a **material misstatement of the other information**. In this case, the other information section is placed immediately after the opinion paragraph, ie it moves up above the key audit matters:

> **Other Information**
>
> Management is responsible for the other information. The other information comprises the [information included in the X report, but does not include the financial statements and our auditor's report thereon.]
>
> Our opinion on the financial statements does not cover the other information and we do not express any form of assurance conclusion thereon.
>
> In connection with our audit of the financial statements, our responsibility is to read the other information and, in doing so, consider whether the other information is materially inconsistent with the financial statements or our knowledge obtained in the audit or otherwise appears to be materially misstated.
>
> If, based on the work we have performed, we conclude that there is a material misstatement of this other information, we are required to report that fact. As described below, we have concluded that such a material misstatement of the other information exists.
>
> [Description of material misstatement of the other information]

5.6 Availability of other information after the date of the auditor's report

All 'other information' should be obtained as early as possible. If the other information is received after the date of the auditor's report and, on reading the other information, the auditors identify a material inconsistency or become aware of an apparent material misstatement, they should decide whether the audited financial statements or the other information need revision.

(a) When revision of the audited financial statements is appropriate, the guidance in ISA 560 *Subsequent events* would be followed.

(b) When revision of the other information is necessary and the entity agrees to make the revision, the auditors should carry out any **necessary procedures**, including a review of the steps taken by management to ensure that individuals in receipt of the previously issued financial statements, the auditors' report thereon and the other information are informed of the revision.

The above procedures will apply if management refuse to revise other information as the auditors consider necessary.

6 Internal audit reports

> **FAST FORWARD**
>
> The internal auditors' report may take any form as there are no formal reporting requirements for internal review reports.

6.1 Reporting on internal review assignments

Internal audit make reports to directors and management as a result of work performed. These reports are internal to the business and are unlikely to be shared with third parties other than the external auditors.

We looked in detail at the types of assignment internal audit will carry out in your earlier studies. These may be summarised as '**risk-based**', where the internal auditors consider internal and external risks and discuss company operations and systems in place in respect of them or '**performance enhancement**' where internal audit consider risk and strategy on a higher level.

For the most part, work is likely to be **risk-based**. Regardless of the nature of the assignment, however, all internal audits are likely to result in a formal report.

There are **no formal requirements** for such reports as there are for the statutory audit. The statutory auditor's report is a highly stylised document which is substantially the same for any audit. A report from the internal auditors in relation to an assignment can take essentially any form. However, some points should be borne in mind.

There is a generally accepted format for reports in business, which is laid out below. This format makes reports useful to readers as it highlights the conclusions drawn and gives easy reference to the user.

Standard report format
TERMS OF REFERENCE
EXECUTIVE SUMMARY – summarising conclusions drawn from assignment
BODY OF THE REPORT
APPENDICES FOR ANY ADDITIONAL INFORMATION

The report is likely also to be dated, designated as to whether it is draft or final and have a 'distribution list' of directors and management who should read it attached.

Some internal audit reports will be modified as responses are made to it may various members of staff. If this is the case, the report should clearly state which version it is. The distribution list may also be annotated to show who has commented on the report at any time.

6.2 Contents of the report

The **executive summary** of an internal audit report should give the following information.

- Background to the assignment
- Objectives of the assignment
- Major outcomes of the work
- Key risks identified
- Key action points
- Summary of the work left to do

The **main body** of the report will contain the detail; for example the audit tests carried out and their findings, full lists of action points, including details of who has responsibility for carrying them out, the future time-scale and costs.

7 Non-statutory audit or review reports

FAST FORWARD There are no legal requirements for non-statutory audit or review reports.

Where an audit has been carried out for a reason other than legal requirement, there will be no formal requirements on the nature and format of the report. This is most likely to be set by the terms of agreement between the auditor and the users or management of the entity being audited. Auditors are likely to find it useful to keep to the best practice set out by auditing standards, particularly in specifying the extent of their responsibility and the scope of the engagement they have performed.

Bear in mind that they could have liability to third parties if the report is publicised, so they might wish to make appropriate disclaimers of liability in a non-statutory report to protect themselves.

Chapter Roundup

- Auditors express an opinion on financial statements based on the work they have done, the evidence obtained and conclusions drawn in relation to that evidence.

- Listed company auditor's reports include a description of the key audit matters.

- There are three types of **modified opinion**: a **qualified opinion**, an **adverse opinion**, and a **disclaimer of opinion**.

- **Emphasis of matter paragraphs** and **other matter paragraphs** can be included in the auditor's report under certain circumstances. Their use does not modify the auditor's opinion on the financial statements.

- A standard format is used to promote understandability because the auditor's report is widely available to both accustomed users and users who are not accustomed to audit and audit language.

- The availability of auditor's reports has been increased by the trend to publish financial statements on companies' websites. Auditors should consider the risks of this. When financial information is available electronically, auditors must ensure that their report is not misrepresented.

- Auditors may issue special reports on summary financial statements, special purpose financial statements, revised accounts and distributions following an audit qualification.

- Auditors must report relevant audit matters to those charged with governance and will also produce a report to management detailing control weaknesses observed during the audit.

- Auditors should always seek to resolve material inconsistencies between financial statements and other information.

- The internal auditors' report may take any form as there are no formal reporting requirements for internal review reports.

- There are no legal requirements for non-statutory audit or review reports.

Quick Quiz

1 Name the different opinions auditors may issue in their auditors' report.

   (1) ....

   (2) ....

   (3) ....

2 Complete the definitions.

   (a) ....: information is free from .... and .... and in compliance with the expected standards and rules.

   (b) .... is an expression of the relative .... or importance of a particular matter in the .... as a whole.

   (c) ....: information is .... and conforms with ...., not .... Information conforms with required standards and law.

3 List the main contents of the ISA 700 (Revised) standard, unmodified report.

4 State five matters which might be covered in a letter to those charged with governance.

   (1) ....

   (2) ....

   (3) ....

   (4) ....

   (5) ....

5 Which of the following could be reported as key audit matters?

   (a) Material uncertainties over going concern.

   (b) Explanations of the auditor's view on other information included in the annual report, and which is consistent with the financial statements.

   (c) Explanations of judgements made by the auditor in material areas.

   (d) Explanations of judgements made by the auditor on matters that are of such importance that they are fundamental to users' understanding of the financial statements.

6 Explain what is meant by an 'emphasis of matter' paragraph.

Answers to Quick Quiz

1. (1) Unmodified
   (2) Modified due to material misstatement (qualified or adverse)
   (3) Modified due to lack of sufficient appropriate audit evidence (qualified or disclaimer of opinion)

2. (a) Fair, discrimination, bias
   (b) Materiality, significance, financial statements
   (c) True, factual, reality, false

3. Title, addressee, opinion paragraph, basis for opinion, key audit matters, other information, responsibilities of management and those charged with governance, auditor's responsibilities, report on other legal and regulatory requirements, auditor's signature, auditor's address, date.

4. From:
   - Auditors' responsibility to form and express an opinion on financial statements prepared by management
   - Fact that audit does not relive management of responsibility for financial statements
   - An overview of timing and planned scope of the audit
   - The auditor's views about **significant** qualitative aspects of the entity's accounting practices including **accounting policies**, accounting estimates and disclosures
   - **Significant** difficulties encountered during the audit
   - Other **significant matters** such as material deficiencies in internal control, questions regarding management integrity, and fraud involving management
   - Other **matters** mentioned in **terms** of **engagement**
   - Relevant **ethical requirements**, including **independence** requirements

5. Explanations of judgements made by the auditor in material areas are KAMs. All of the other answers are incorrect. Why? Let's see:
   - Material uncertainties over going concern would be explained in a separate section of the report.
   - Explanations of the auditor's view on other information included in the annual report is not a key audit matter as it does not relate to the financial statements.
   - Explanations of judgements made by the auditor on matters that are fundamental to users' understanding may be key audit matters, but since they may require an emphasis of matter paragraph they would not be reported in the key audit matters section of the auditor's report.

6. An **emphasis of matter paragraph** is a paragraph included in the auditor's report that refers to a matter appropriately presented or disclosed in the financial statements that, in the auditor's judgement, is of such importance that it is fundamental to users' understanding of the financial statements. It is placed after the Basis of Opinion paragraph and clearly states that the auditor's opinion is not modified in respect of the matter emphasised.

End of Chapter Question

Bigoil (AIA November 2004)

Bigoil is a multinational oil producer. The company's annual report contains an unaudited section of disclosures about its oil reserves. This section describes the quantities of oil in each of the company's major oil fields throughout the world. It is regarded as an important measure of the company's long-term prosperity and also of the competence of its management team.

The information in the oil reserve figures is compiled by an independent consulting firm which has a number of major clients in the oil industry. Its geologists make a number of measurements and estimate the size of the oil reserves based on a host of assumptions. This is a complicated calculation and it is not an exact science.

Just prior to the finalisation of the financial statements for the year ended 30 September 20X4, the consulting firm revised its estimates for Bigoil's Indonesian oil field. Recent production activities have uncovered unforeseen problems with the extraction of oil and the exploitable reserves have now been reduced by 25%. This information was published immediately and led to a massive decrease in Bigoil's share price.

Bigoil's external auditor does not have to express an opinion on the oil reserve figures. The auditor did, however, make a point of reviewing the consultant's findings because of the importance and sensitivity of this information. The audit firm is, therefore, embarrassed because it can now be seen that the oil reserves stated in the 20X3 annual report were overstated. The auditor has announced that the auditor's report for the year ended 30 September 20X4 will be delayed indefinitely.

Required

(a) Explain whether it is realistic to hold an external auditor responsible for expressing an opinion on a technical matter such as the size of an oil field. **(10 marks)**

(b) Press speculation suggests that the external auditor has delayed the publication of the auditor's report because of fears about becoming implicated in compensation claims by shareholders whose investments have declined in value.

Explain whether it would be justifiable for the auditor to delay or suspend the auditor's report for this reason. **(10 marks)**

(Total 20 marks)

PART C AUDIT STRATEGY, PROCESS AND REPORTING

Appendix

APPENDIX

Client Acceptance Form - Audit clients   Form A1.1

We perform our client acceptance procedures, and in particular the investigation procedures, as early in the proposal process as possible to avoid incurring significant time and effort on a prospective client that we might later decide not to accept.

Background Information

Prospective client _____ Accounting period _____

Address _____

Nature of business (eg industry, products or services, major customers, major suppliers) _____

_____

_____

If the business was started within the past 5 years, indicate the year: 20 ___   Company reg. no. _____

Type of service(s) to be rendered _____

Does the prospective client meet the definition of a "Stock Exchange engagement"? Yes _____ No _____

Is the prospective client considering "going public" in the next year? Yes _____ No _____ N/A _____

Anticipated person in charge _____

Anticipated independent reviewer, if identified _____

Total estimated fee (if available):

Year 1   £ _____ recurring   £ _____ non-recurring

Year 2   £ _____ recurring   £ _____ non-recurring

Billing and payment agreement and any special fee arrangements _____

_____

Financial information (for last two years):

Year end	Total assets	Total debt	Shareholders' funds	Total revenue	Profit/(loss)
_____	_____	_____	_____	_____	_____
_____	_____	_____	_____	_____	_____

Has the prospectice client been investigated? Yes _____ No _____ If not, document in an attached memorandum the reasons for not requesting an investigation.

Was there any information in the investigative agency's (oral or attached written) report that indicates we should question whether to accept the prospective client? Yes _____ No _____ If yes, discuss in an attached memorandum along with any mitigating factors.

Key officers, directors, and major shareholders	Officer	Director	Own%	Other businesses/comments
_____	_____	_____	_____	_____
_____	_____	_____	_____	_____
_____	_____	_____	_____	_____
_____	_____	_____	_____	_____

APPENDIX

Client Acceptance Form - Audit clients   Form A1.2

List the principal solicitors, commercial bankers, and investment bankers with whom the prospective client has a relationship (indicate with an asterisk those individuals who are contacted as part of our client acceptance procedures) and other individuals contacted:

Individual	Firm or Bank
_____	_____
_____	_____
_____	_____
_____	_____

Did any matters arise in our contacts with the solicitors, commercial bankers, investment bankers, or others that need further consideration in deciding whether to accept the prospective client?   Yes _____   No _____

If yes, describe the matters in an attached memorandum.

Predecessor Auditors/Accountants

Enquiries of prospective client regarding predecessor auditors/accountants:

Firm name and office _____

Length of firm's relationship with the prospective client _____

Services rendered to the prospective client _____

_____

Type of opinion issued last year _____

Prospective client's reason(s) for changing auditors/accountants _____

_____

Were there any disagreements with the predecessor auditors/accountants over accounting principles, audit, review, or compilation procedures, or other significant matters during the entity's two most recent fiscal years and any other subsequent interim period? Yes _____ No _____ If yes, describe the disagreements in an attached memorandum.

Any reportable conditions/material weaknesses in the internal control structure?   Yes _____   No _____

If yes, describe the conditions/weaknesses in an attached memorandum.

Enquiries of predecessor auditors/accountants:

Date of inquiries _____

Names and titles of individuals who responded to our enquiries (should include the partner in charge) _____

_____

Predecessor's understanding of the reason(s) for changing auditors/accountants _____

_____

Any facts that might bear on the integrity of management _____

_____

_____

Have the predecessor's fees been paid in full? Yes _____ No _____ If not, indicate the reasons _____

_____

Were there any disparities between the prospective client's replies and the preceding auditor's replies?

Yes _____ No _____ If yes, describe the differences in an attached memorandum.

APPENDIX

Client Acceptance Form - Audit clients   Form A1.3

Other significant considerations (Explain answers with an asterisk in an attached memorandum)

	Yes	No			Yes	No
1 Are there possible conflicts of interest with concerns of existing clients (eg conflicts with litigation services engagements)?	*		6	Will we be auditing all entities under common control?	—	—
2 Are there any independence issues, including family relationships, that need to be considered before we could accept the prospective client?	*		7	Are there significant related party transactions with consolidated or other entities that we will not be auditing?	*	
3 Will the engagement require specialised (eg industry specific) knowledge and experience not now available in the local or area office?	—	—	8	Does management have a proven track record in this or other businesses?	—	—
If yes describe in an attached memorandum the plan to obtain the neccessary expertise from other offices and/or to develop it within the office and obtain the concurrence of the national regional director of industry services.			9	Does the prospective client have a high likelihood of (continued) business success?	—	—
			10	Are there any conditions or events that indicate there could be substantial doubt about the prospective client's ability to continue as a going concern?	*	
Will the addition of the client adversely affect the ability of the office to staff any of its other engagements requiring similar expertise?	*		11	For non-public entities, are there third parties (eg lenders or investors) whom we know would be receiving copies of our reports on the client's financial statements?	*	
4 Have any significant accounting or auditing issues been identified?	*		12	Will the firm be assuming more than a low level of risk if this prospective client is accepted?	*	
5 Does the prospective client expect the firm to accept an accounting policy the predecessor auditors did not accept?	*		13	Are there any other factors that should be considered in evaluating the prospective client?	*	

Other procedures

1. Seek information and advice from others in the firm who are likely to have significant information bearing on a decision to accept the prospective client, including other partners in the office, in other offices in the area, and where applicable, in other offices in cities where the entity has significant operations or where we have performed other services.

2. For a prospective client in a specialised industry, consult with the partner of industry services with regard to industry specific factors that should be addressed in considering the prospective client for acceptance.

3. For public and significant non-public prospective audit clients, contact the partner in charge of litigation services to determine if there are any conflicts or potential conflicts that need to be evaluated.

4. In the space below, list any head office personnel consulted when performing the client acceptance proceedures. If there are any unresolved issues remaining from those consultations, describe them in an attached memorandum.

APPENDIX

Client Acceptance Form - Audit clients   Form A1.4

Attachments (attach the following, where applicable, to this form)

- Memoranda, as required, to document considerations described elsewhere on this form
- Investigation report or memorandum documenting the reasons for not requesting an investigation

Accompanying information

- Public companies - the most recent annual shareholders' report, the form reporting the change in auditors and the predecessor auditors' letter. Any recent placing or other documents.

- Private companies - the most recent annual financial statements, and if available, the latest interim financial statements.

Conclusions

I have considered the professional, business, and economic factors regarding this engagement and recommend the acceptance of this prospective client.

Client will be ___ /will not be ___ designated for close-monitoring.

Evaluating Person_____ Date _____

Approvals

I am satisfied that this recommendation is in compliance with our policy on client acceptance of this prospective client. Acceptance of this client does ___ /does not ___ require the concurrence of the National Managing Partner.

Office Managing Partner _____ Date _____

I concur with the acceptance of this prospective client.

National Managing Partner_____ Date _____

APPENDIX

Example 1: An auditor's report with a qualified opinion due to a material misstatement

Inventories are misstated. The misstatement is deemed to be material but not pervasive to the financial statements.

INDEPENDENT AUDITOR'S REPORT

[Appropriate Addressee]

Report on the Audit of the Financial Statements

Qualified Opinion

We have audited the financial statements of ABC Company (the Company), which comprise the statement of financial position as at 31 December 20X1, and the statement of comprehensive income, statement of changes in equity and statement of cash flows for the year then ended, and notes to the financial statements, including material accounting policy information.

In our opinion, except for the effects of the matter described in the Basis for Qualified Opinion section of our report, the accompanying financial statements present fairly, in all material respects, (or give a true and fair view of) the financial position of the Company as at 31 December 20X1, and (of) its financial performance and its cash flows for the year then ended in accordance with International Financial Reporting Accounting Standards (IFRS Accounting Standards).

Basis for Qualified Opinion

The Company's inventories are carried in the statement of financial position at xxx. Management has not stated the inventories at the lower of cost and net realizable value but has stated them solely at cost, which constitutes a departure from IFRS Accounting Standards. The Company's records indicate that, had management stated the inventories at the lower of cost and net realizable value, an amount of xxx would have been required to write the inventories down to their net realizable value. Accordingly, cost of sales would have been increased by xxx, and income tax, net income and shareholders' equity would have been reduced by xxx, xxx and xxx, respectively.

We conducted our audit in accordance with International Standards on Auditing (ISAs). Our responsibilities under those standards are further described in the Auditor's Responsibilities for the Audit of the Financial Statements section of our report. We are independent of the Company in accordance with the ethical requirements that are relevant to our audit of the financial statements in [jurisdiction], and we have fulfilled our other ethical responsibilities in accordance with these requirements. We believe that the audit evidence we have obtained is sufficient and appropriate to provide a basis for our qualified opinion.

Key Audit Matters

Key audit matters are those matters that, in our professional judgement, were of most significance in our audit of the financial statements of the current period. These matters were addressed in the context of our audit of the financial statements as a whole, and in forming our opinion thereon, and we do not provide a separate opinion on these matters. In addition to the matter described in the Basis for Qualified Opinion section we have determined the matters described below to be the key audit matters to be communicated in our report.

[Description of each key audit matter in accordance with ISA 701.]

Responsibilities of management and those charged with governance for the financial statements

[Reporting in accordance with ISA 700 (Revised) – see Illustration 1 in ISA 700 (Revised).]

Auditor's responsibilities for the audit of the financial statements

[Reporting in accordance with ISA 700 (Revised) – see Illustration 1 in ISA 700 (Revised).]

Report on Other Legal and Regulatory Requirements

APPENDIX

[Reporting in accordance with ISA 700 (Revised) – see Illustration 1 in ISA 700 (Revised).]

The engagement partner on the audit resulting in this independent auditor's report is [name].

[Signature in the name of the audit firm, the personal name of the auditor, or both, as appropriate for the particular jurisdiction]

[Auditor Address]

[Date]

APPENDIX

Example 2: An auditor's report with an adverse opinion due to a material misstatement that is deemed to be pervasive

The financial statements are materially misstated due to the non-consolidation of a subsidiary. The material misstatement is deemed to be pervasive to the consolidated financial statements. The effects of the misstatement on the consolidated financial statements have not been determined because it was not practicable to do so.

INDEPENDENT AUDITOR'S REPORT

[Appropriate Addressee]

Report on the Audit of the Consolidated Financial Statements

Adverse Opinion

We have audited the consolidated financial statements of ABC Company and its subsidiaries (the Group), which comprise the consolidated statement of financial position as at 31 December 20X1, and the consolidated statement of comprehensive income, consolidated statement of changes in equity and consolidated statement of cash flows for the year then ended, and notes to the consolidated financial statements, including a summary of significant accounting policies.

In our opinion, because of the significance of the matter discussed in the Basis for Adverse Opinion section of our report, the accompanying consolidated financial statements do not present fairly (or do not give a true and fair view of) the consolidated financial position of the Group as at 31 December 20X1, and (of) its consolidated financial performance and its consolidated cash flows for the year then ended in accordance with International Financial Reporting Accounting Standards (IFRS Accounting Standards).

Basis for Adverse Opinion

As explained in Note X, the Group has not consolidated subsidiary XYZ Company that the Group acquired during 20X1 because it has not yet been able to determine the fair values of certain of the subsidiary's material assets and liabilities at the acquisition date. This investment is therefore accounted for on a cost basis. Under IFRS Accounting Standards, the Company should have consolidated this subsidiary and accounted for the acquisition based on provisional amounts. Had XYZ Company been consolidated, many elements in the accompanying consolidated financial statements would have been materially affected. The effects on the consolidated financial statements of the failure to consolidate have not been determined.

We conducted our audit in accordance with International Standards on Auditing (ISAs). Our responsibilities under those standards are further described in the Auditor's Responsibilities for the Audit of the Consolidated Financial Statements section of our report. We are independent of the Group in accordance with the ethical requirements that are relevant to our audit of the consolidated financial statements in [jurisdiction], and we have fulfilled our other ethical responsibilities in accordance with these requirements. We believe that the audit evidence we have obtained is sufficient and appropriate to provide a basis for our adverse opinion.

Key Audit Matters

Except for the matter described in the Basis for Adverse Opinion section, we have determined that there are no other key audit matters to communicate in our report.

Responsibilities of management and those charged with governance for the consolidated financial statements

[Reporting in accordance with ISA 700 (Revised) – see Illustration 2 in ISA 700 (Revised).]

Auditor's responsibilities for the audit of the consolidated financial statements

[Reporting in accordance with ISA 700 (Revised) – see Illustration 2 in ISA 700 (Revised).]

APPENDIX

Report on Other Legal and Regulatory Requirements

[Reporting in accordance with ISA 700 (Revised) – see Illustration 2 in ISA 700 (Revised).]

The engagement partner on the audit resulting in this independent auditor's report is [name].

[Signature in the name of the audit firm, the personal name of the auditor, or both, as appropriate for the particular jurisdiction]

[Auditor Address]

[Date]

APPENDIX

Example 3: An auditor's report with a qualified opinion due to the auditor being unable to obtain sufficient appropriate audit evidence, having a material effect on the financial statements

The auditor was unable to obtain sufficient appropriate audit evidence regarding an investment in a foreign affiliate, resulting in a material but not pervasive effect on the consolidated financial statements.

INDEPENDENT AUDITOR'S REPORT

[Appropriate Addressee]

Report on the Audit of the Consolidated Financial Statements

Qualified Opinion

We have audited the consolidated financial statements of ABC Company and its subsidiaries (the Group), which comprise the consolidated statement of financial position as at 31 December 20X1, and the consolidated statement of comprehensive income, consolidated statement of changes in equity and consolidated statement of cash flows for the year then ended, and notes to the consolidated financial statements, including a summary of significant accounting policies.

In our opinion, except for the possible effects of the matter described in the Basis for Qualified Opinion section of our report, the accompanying consolidated financial statements present fairly, in all material respects, (or give a true and fair view of) the financial position of the Group as at 31 December 20X1, and (of) its consolidated financial performance and its consolidated cash flows for the year then ended in accordance with International Financial Reporting Accounting Standards (IFRS Accounting Standards).

Basis for Qualified Opinion

The Group's investment in XYZ Company, a foreign associate acquired during the year and accounted for by the equity method, is carried at xxx on the consolidated statement of financial position as at 31 December 20X1, and ABC's share of XYZ's net income of xxx is included in ABC's income for the year then ended. We were unable to obtain sufficient appropriate audit evidence about the carrying amount of ABC's investment in XYZ as at 31 December 20X1 and ABC's share of XYZ's net income for the year because we were denied access to the financial information, management, and the auditors of XYZ. Consequently, we were unable to determine whether any adjustments to these amounts were necessary.

We conducted our audit in accordance with International Standards on Auditing (ISAs). Our responsibilities under those standards are further described in the Auditor's Responsibilities for the Audit of the Consolidated Financial Statements section of our report. We are independent of the Group in accordance with the ethical requirements that are relevant to our audit of the consolidated financial statements in [jurisdiction], and we have fulfilled our other ethical responsibilities in accordance with these requirements. We believe that the audit evidence we have obtained is sufficient and appropriate to provide a basis for our qualified opinion.

Key Audit Matters

Key audit matters are those matters that, in our professional judgement, were of most significance in our audit of the consolidated financial statements of the current period. These matters were addressed in the context of our audit of the consolidated financial statements as a whole, and in forming our opinion thereon, and we do not provide a separate opinion on these matters. In addition to the matter described in the Basis for Qualified Opinion section, we have determined the matters described below to be the key audit matters to be communicated in our report.

[Description of each key audit matter in accordance with ISA 701.]

Responsibilities of management and those charged with governance for the consolidated financial statements

[Reporting in accordance with ISA 700 (Revised) – see Illustration 2 in ISA 700 (Revised).]

Auditor's responsibilities for the audit of the consolidated financial statements

[Reporting in accordance with ISA 700 (Revised) – see Illustration 2 in ISA 700 (Revised).]

Report on Other Legal and Regulatory Requirements

[Reporting in accordance with ISA 700 (Revised) – see Illustration 2 in ISA 700 (Revised).]

The engagement partner on the audit resulting in this independent auditor's report is [name].

[Signature in the name of the audit firm, the personal name of the auditor, or both, as appropriate for the particular jurisdiction]

[Auditor Address]

[Date]

Example 4: An auditor's report with a disclaimer of opinion due to the auditor being unable to obtain sufficient appropriate audit evidence, having a material and pervasive effect on the financial statements

The auditor was unable to obtain sufficient appropriate audit evidence about a single element of the financial statements. That is, the auditor was also unable to obtain audit evidence about the financial information of a joint venture investment that represents over 90% of the company's net assets. The possible effects of this inability to obtain sufficient appropriate audit evidence are deemed to be both material and pervasive to the financial statements.

INDEPENDENT AUDITOR'S REPORT

[Appropriate Addressee]

Report on the Audit of the Consolidated Financial Statements

Disclaimer of Opinion

We were engaged to audit the consolidated financial statements of ABC Company and its subsidiaries (the Group), which comprise the consolidated statement of financial position as at 31 December 20X1, and the consolidated statement of comprehensive income, consolidated statement of changes in equity and consolidated statement of cash flows for the year then ended, and notes to the consolidated financial statements, including a summary of significant accounting policies.

We do not express an opinion on the accompanying consolidated financial statements of the Group. Because of the significance of the matter described in the Basis for Disclaimer of Opinion section of our report, we have not been able to obtain sufficient appropriate audit evidence to provide a basis for an audit opinion on these consolidated financial statements.

Basis for Disclaimer of Opinion

The Group's investment in its joint venture XYZ Company is carried at xxx on the Group's consolidated statement of financial position, which represents over 90% of the Group's net assets as at 31 December 20X1. We were not allowed access to the management and the auditors of XYZ Company, including XYZ Company's auditors' audit documentation. As a result, we were unable to determine whether any adjustments were necessary in respect of the Group's proportional share of XYZ Company's assets that it controls jointly, its proportional share of XYZ Company's liabilities for which it is jointly responsible, its proportional share of XYZ's income and expenses for the year, and the elements making up the consolidated statement of changes in equity and the consolidated cash flow statement.

Responsibilities of management and those charged with governance for the consolidated financial statements

[Reporting in accordance with ISA 700 (Revised) – see Illustration 2 in ISA 700 (Revised).]

Auditor's responsibilities for the audit of the consolidated financial statements

Our responsibility is to conduct an audit of the Group's consolidated financial statements in accordance with International Standards on Auditing and to issue an auditor's report. However, because of the matter described in the Basis for Disclaimer of Opinion section of our report, we were not able to obtain sufficient appropriate audit evidence to provide a basis for an audit opinion on these consolidated financial statements. We are independent of the Group in accordance with the ethical requirements that are relevant to our audit of the financial statements in [jurisdiction], and we have fulfilled our other ethical responsibilities in accordance with these requirements.

Report on Other Legal and Regulatory Requirements

[Reporting in accordance with ISA 700 (Revised) – see Illustration 2 in ISA 700 (Revised).]

[Signature in the name of the audit firm, the personal name of the auditor, or both, as appropriate for the particular jurisdiction]

[Auditor Address]

[Date]

APPENDIX

Example 5: An auditor's report with a disclaimer of opinion due to the auditor being unable to obtain sufficient appropriate audit evidence, having a material and pervasive effect on the financial statements

The auditor was unable to obtain sufficient appropriate audit evidence about multiple elements of the financial statements. That is, the auditor was unable to obtain audit evidence about the entity's inventories and accounts receivable. The possible effects of this inability to obtain sufficient appropriate audit evidence are deemed to be both material and pervasive to the financial statements.

INDEPENDENT AUDITOR'S REPORT

[Appropriate Addressee]

Report on the Audit of the Financial Statements

Disclaimer of Opinion

We were engaged to audit the financial statements of ABC Company (the Company), which comprise the statement of financial position as at 31 December 20X1, and the statement of comprehensive income, statement of changes in equity and statement of cash flows for the year then ended, and notes to the financial statements, including a summary of significant accounting policies.

We do not express an opinion on the accompanying financial statements of the Company. Because of the significance of the matters described in the Basis for Disclaimer of Opinion section of our report, we have not been able to obtain sufficient appropriate audit evidence to provide a basis for an audit opinion on these financial statements.

Basis for Disclaimer of Opinion

We were not appointed as auditors of the Company until after 31 December 20X1 and thus did not observe the counting of physical inventories at the beginning and end of the year. We were unable to satisfy ourselves by alternative means concerning the inventory quantities held at 31 December 20X0 and 20X1, which are stated in the statements of financial position at xxx and xxx, respectively. In addition, the introduction of a new computerized accounts receivable system in September 20X1 resulted in numerous errors in accounts receivable. As of the date of our report, management was still in the process of rectifying the system deficiencies and correcting the errors. We were unable to confirm or verify by alternative means accounts receivable included in the statement of financial position at a total amount of xxx as at 31 December 20X1. As a result of these matters, we were unable to determine whether any adjustments might have been found necessary in respect of recorded or unrecorded inventories and accounts receivable, and the elements making up the statement of comprehensive income, statement of changes in equity and statement of cash flows.

Responsibilities of management and those charged with governance for the financial statements

[Reporting in accordance with ISA 700 (Revised) – see Illustration 1 in ISA 700 (Revised).]

Auditor's responsibilities for the audit of the financial statements

Our responsibility is to conduct an audit of the Company's financial statements in accordance with International Standards on Auditing and to issue an auditor's report. However, because of the matters described in the Basis for Disclaimer of Opinion section of our report, we were not able to obtain sufficient appropriate audit evidence to provide a basis for an audit opinion on these financial statements. We are independent of the Company in accordance with the ethical requirements that are relevant to our audit of the financial statements in [jurisdiction], and we have fulfilled our other ethical responsibilities in accordance with these requirements.

APPENDIX

Report on Other Legal and Regulatory Requirements

[Reporting in accordance with ISA 700 (Revised) – see Illustration 1 in ISA 700 (Revised).]

[Signature in the name of the audit firm, the personal name of the auditor, or both, as appropriate for the particular jurisdiction]

[Auditor Address]

[Date]

Example 6: An auditor's report with a key audit matters section, an emphasis of matter paragraph and an other matter paragraph

INDEPENDENT AUDITOR'S REPORT

To the Shareholders of ABC Company [or Other Appropriate Addressee]

Report on the Audit of the Financial Statements

Opinion

We have audited the financial statements of ABC Company (the Company), which comprise the statement of financial position as at 31 December 20X1, and the statement of comprehensive income, statement of changes in equity and statement of cash flows for the year then ended, and notes to the financial statements, including a summary of significant accounting policies.

In our opinion, the accompanying financial statements present fairly, in all material respects, (or give a true and fair view of) the financial position of the Company as at 31 December 20X1, and (of) its financial performance and its cash flows for the year then ended in accordance with International Financial Reporting Accounting Standards (IFRS Accounting Standards).

Basis for Opinion

We conducted our audit in accordance with International Standards on Auditing (ISAs). Our responsibilities under those standards are further described in the Auditor's Responsibilities for the Audit of the Financial Statements section of our report. We are independent of the Company in accordance with the ethical requirements that are relevant to our audit of the financial statements in [jurisdiction], and we have fulfilled our other ethical responsibilities in accordance with these requirements. We believe that the audit evidence we have obtained is sufficient and appropriate to provide a basis for our opinion.

Emphasis of Matter

We draw attention to Note X of the financial statements, which describes the effects of a fire in the Company's production facilities. Our opinion is not modified in respect of this matter.

Key Audit Matters

Key audit matters are those matters that, in our professional judgement, were of most significance in our audit of the financial statements of the current period. These matters were addressed in the context of our audit of the financial statements as a whole, and in forming our opinion thereon, and we do not provide a separate opinion on these matters.

[Description of each key audit matter in accordance with ISA 701.]

Other Matter

The financial statements of ABC Company for the year ended 31 December 20X0, were audited by another auditor who expressed an unmodified opinion on those statements on 31 March 20X1.

Responsibilities of Management and Those Charged with Governance for the Financial Statements

[Reporting in accordance with ISA 700 (Revised) – see Illustration 1 in ISA 700 (Revised).]

Auditor's Responsibilities for the Audit of the Financial Statements

[Reporting in accordance with ISA 700 (Revised) – see Illustration 1 in ISA 700 (Revised).]

Report on Other Legal and Regulatory Requirements

[Reporting in accordance with ISA 700 (Revised) – see Illustration 1 in ISA 700 (Revised).]

The engagement partner on the audit resulting in this independent auditor's report is [name].

[Signature in the name of the audit firm, the personal name of the auditor, or both, as appropriate for the particular jurisdiction]

[Auditor Address]

[Date]

APPENDIX

Answers to end of chapter questions

Chapter 2 Megafirm (AIA November 04 amended)

(a) The Corporate Governance Statement is intended to ensure that shareholders and other users are confident in the structures and systems in place to manage the company. If these structures and systems are in place then the auditor will have greater assurance that there is less likely to be a forced accounting irregularity.

The fact that the company has a dominant chief executive who is not really accountable to the non-executive directors is worrying from an audit point of view because this person might feel inclined to bully the board and senior management into unsound business decisions. That could lead to problems with the financial statements because any decisions that go wrong might then be concealed through manipulation of the accounts. This is a surprisingly common cause of accounting scandals and is one of the reasons for the current fashion for non-executive directors.

Another common finding in companies with this type of board arrangement is that there is often a weak control environment. This is due to the chief executive ignoring rules and undermining confidence in the system of internal control. That can lead to problems further down the hierarchy in terms of the working of the system. Also, the fact that the directors are willing to create the impression of sound control at the very highest level, without consideration of the system actually working, might undermine attitudes towards control at lower levels in the company.

The fact that the audit committee is weak will also make it more difficult for the auditor to have an effective dialogue with the board about audit findings or the suitability of accounting policies. The main benefit of such a committee is that it ensures a wider representation from the board in settling any difficult issues or discussing any other audit findings. If the committee is effectively controlled by the chief executive then he or she will have absolute control over all accounting matters.

If this problem comes to light, the auditor is likely to be criticised by the shareholders and other commentators. The auditor will be regarded as guilty by association even if the problems are not accounting matters. Anyone who suffers because of the chief executive's management style will look for a scapegoat and the auditor will normally fit the bill.

(b) The disagreement has not lead to any disagreement over accounting figures or lack of sufficient appropriate audit evidence on the audit. The accounts give a true and fair view and so the auditor can give an unmodified opinion in the auditor's report. There is no material misstatement and so it can be argued that the auditor has had no place to disclose these disagreements.

Generally speaking, the auditor has no particular mandate for commenting on the relationship between the chief executive and the rest of the board. The scenario does not actually disclose any instances in which the chief executive has behaved dishonestly or recklessly. In the UK, the auditor is required to report on whether a listed company has reported appropriately on meeting UK Corporate Governance Code requirements but this is a fairly narrow remit.

The auditor's opinion about the effectiveness of the committees is easy to challenge. It is a fact that the company has employed non-executive directors and has established an audit committee. That makes it difficult to argue that the Corporate Governance Statement is inaccurate. If the auditor were to make a statement that accused the chief executive of bullying then there could be serious consequences, not least because the auditor would have breached an ethical duty of confidence to the company. The auditor could also be open to accusations of defamation.

The *Companies Act* 2006 requires the auditor to report 'by exception' if there is a material inconsistency between information published with the audited financial statements and the auditor's understanding of the entity and its environment as obtained during the course of the audit.

In addition ISA 720 (UK) *The Auditor's responsibilities relating to other information* requires the auditor to identify any material consistencies between the Corporate Governance Statement, and the auditor's knowledge obtained in the audit. The auditor's opinion does not cover the information in the Corporate Governance Statement, but the auditor's report will need to contain an 'other information' section which amongst other things will describe any uncorrected misstatements in the Corporate Governance Statement. As there are no misstatements to be corrected, the other information section will not require this disclosure.

(c) The recent reforms of corporate governance have been motivated, at least in part, by legitimate concerns about the manner in which companies are managed. This has led to the introduction of reforms that are observable and measurable, otherwise shareholders would have no reason to believe that any real change had taken place.

Changing the reality of corporate governance will always be difficult. Those seeking promotion to the very highest levels are likely to be ambitious and even aggressive. These traits will be difficult to constrain once they reach the very top. Arguably, shareholders are looking for strong leadership from their chief executives and will not want too much 'management by consensus'.

The pressures that have led to the establishment of corporate governance mechanisms (agency, etc) have not disappeared because of new mechanisms. It will be difficult to ensure that every board of directors does make nothing but prudent decisions that are motivated by the best interests of the shareholders.

In general, control mechanisms reward whatever is measured and disclosed. If the creation of an audit committee is valued by the market then audit committees are likely to become commonplace. If the effectiveness of such committees cannot be observed then there are no external controls to ensure that the committee's establishment is more than a box-ticking exercise.

Chapter 3 Integrated reporting

> **Tutorial note.** This question is drawn from Section 4 of the syllabus: towards a wider accountability and assurance. It tests candidates' understanding of the issues associated with integrated reporting. This question is excellent practice for you to consider the benefits of having an assurance report reviewed (remember to do this from the perspective of the entity creating the integrated report).
>
> When answering the second part of this question, think about the contents of an auditor's report and any other reports that you have seen so far and then consider what might be most appropriate to use in the context of an integrated report.

(a) Perceived benefits of assurance work on integrated reports include:

- The assurance report adds credibility to the data reported.
- It reassures investors by promoting transparency (and may improve the chances of securing fresh capital).
- There is added prestige of having the information audited.
- It gives a competitive advantage over those whose reports are not audited.
- It identifies areas of weakness which can be addressed.
- It may be a requirement for trading with some companies/countries or governments.
- ESG performance is taken more seriously, which in turn will improve performance and (hopefully) reduce costs.

In some jurisdictions, some or all of this type of reporting may now be mandatory (eg GHG emissions, compliance with other carbon reporting frameworks) which suggests that investing in systems that support the creation of this information is also of benefit to the reporting entity. However, for smaller entities who are not yet obliged to report this kind of information, it offers an opportunity to prepare for a time when this might be necessary

(b) Contents of the practitioner's reported conclusions

- Note of the objectives of the review
- Opinion (if the engagement was agreed-upon procedures rather than assurance, there will be no opinion given)
- Basis on which the opinion (if any) has been reached
- Work performed
- Limitations (if any) to the work performed
- Limitations (if any) to the opinion given

There is no specific guidance on the contents of a practitioner's conclusion on an integrated report on social and environmental issues; the above points represent the minimum you should expect to see included. The International Integrated Reporting Framework (denoted by the term <IR>) is a voluntary scheme that suggests the areas where companies might wish to report on their social and environmental credentials in a combined format with other financial and non-financial performance

Should a different reporting methodology be considered (such as ISAE 3000) there will be a recommended format for the practitioner's report. For ED-5000, the order of the practitioner's report on a sustainability assurance engagement will follow the structure of the auditor's report

Chapter 4 Flatbuilder plc (AIA November 2006 amended)

Tutorial note. This question is drawn from Section 3 of the syllabus: audit independence, ethics, and the public interest. It tests candidates' ability to explain the independence issues associated with members of an audit firm accepting gifts and discounts from client companies. This can be a complex area because of the difficulties in measuring independence.

(a) This transaction is completely unacceptable for the following reasons.

The engagement partner is involved. The engagement partner has such a significant responsibility for the audit that his/her personal relationship with a client company has to be even more honest and open to scrutiny than anyone else working for the firm.

The fact that the partner has been dealing with the company's finance director creates the possible impression that he was seeking special treatment from the company. It is certainly more difficult to claim that the 'extras' thrown into the deal were given in the normal course of business, as could have been the case if they had been granted by a member of the sales staff.

The company has demonstrated that it is capable of influencing the partner's mortgage provider, thereby providing an on-going source of influence over the partner himself.

It is unlikely that any third party who was aware of these facts would be prepared to accept that the engagement partner was independent of the company.

(b) The first step would be to appoint a replacement engagement partner with immediate effect. The present engagement partner should not have any further involvement in the active management of the audit, although he might be asked to support the management team in terms of providing background information about the company.

The firm should review any and all matters of audit judgement for at least the previous year and possibly further back. All matters of professional judgement for the present year should be revisited by the replacement engagement partner and the results of those deliberations recorded in the audit working papers.

The original audit partner should, perhaps, be disciplined – perhaps by making him meet the additional costs incurred by the firm on the review of professional judgement. He should also be asked to provide assurances concerning his relationship with other clients. Perhaps another partner should review these other relationships.

The engagement partner has not complied with the requirements of ISA 220 (Revised) which requires them to 'identify, evaluate and address threats to compliance with relevant ethical requirements, including those related to independence' (ISA 220 (Revised) para. 17). The engagement partner might need additional training to remind them of their responsibilities with regards to audit quality and ethics.

The situation should never has arisen and indicates a deficiency in the firm's system of quality management. The firm should determine the root cause of the deficiency and whether remedial action is necessary to address it.

A senior partner from the firm should arrange a meeting with Flatbuilder plc's audit committee and explain the reasons for the changes of personnel and also to provide assurances (and possibly a warning) that all matters of judgement that were previously compromised will now be reviewed. It is important that the client understands the reasons for independence and does not attempt to compromise that independence.

The audit firm should consider its ability to continue as external auditors of Flatbuilder plc. It is probably acceptable to continue to act given the other steps described above, although much depends on the results of the review of previous audits. If those have been impaired in any way by the outgoing engagement partner then it would be impossible for the firm to continue in good faith.

(c) Independence is an attitude of mind. It might be difficult for an individual to fully appreciate the extent to which his or her judgement might be affected by a gift, a relationship, or some other matter. Other members of the firm will be able to take a more detached view of things.

The appearance of independence is as important as its fact. An individual might be quite convinced of the fact of independence without realising that outside observers would take a different attitude entirely. Colleagues will be more objective about external perceptions.

All members of the partnership are likely to be affected by the adverse publicity associated with any concerns about independence. The firm is entitled to be consulted about potential threats to its reputation and to offer advice or even impose decisions on partners and staff.

Independence can be a complex issue, one that is often difficult to understand in practical terms. Professional guidance provides quite detailed suggestions, but interpreting the spirit behind those rules can require discussion with relatively impartial colleagues.

ANSWERS TO END OF CHAPTER QUESTIONS

Chapter 5 Horrow (AIA May 2015 Amended)

Tutorial note. This question deals with the auditors providing more specific information to the shareholders. This question tests understanding of the role of the external auditor and the nature of the material that the auditor gathers and records.

(a) Shareholders pay a significant amount for an external audit investigation, and they benefit from the assurance that the financial statements have been checked and they give a true and fair view. Audit used to provide very little specific information, over and above the general assurance. For example, the audit working papers will contain valuable insights drafted by the audit partner and other members of the audit team and those were never shared with the shareholders.

For example, giving shareholders some insights into audit risks and the materiality decisions might enable them to have a better understanding of the quality of the assurance that they should draw from the auditor's report. The shareholders might be better equipped to ask questions of the board and of the auditor during the general meetings. The expectations gap may be reduced as a result.

The shareholders might also benefit from having some insight into the auditor's opinions on the business itself. The auditor has access that is unique and that could be extremely valuable to the shareholders. That insight could also extend to governance issues and so could encourage sound management practices.

(b) The biggest danger is that these insights could undermine confidence in the audit. Shareholders could, for example, believe that materiality thresholds are too high and that more work is necessary. That could lead to the cost of audit being driven up by concerns that the shareholders misunderstand the audit approach that is being described.

The publication of Key Audit Matters that required some judgement could cloud the question of whether the auditor's report was qualified. An unmodified report that indicated that the auditor was concerned about a particular figure might undermine confidence in that figure and so in the financial statements as a whole. Also, directors might try to persuade the auditor to accept a misleading figure on the grounds that it can be highlighted as a matter of significant audit judgement in the commentary.

In some respects, auditor could be discouraged from maintaining full and accurate records in their working papers because some of the concerns that are raised during the audit may have to be reported to the shareholders. That could discourage the retention of detailed working papers so that those disclosures do not have to be made.

ISA 701 could also raise the profile of the auditor's report. At present, an unmodified auditor's report can be dismissed very quickly because it does not contain any specific information. The inclusion of Key Audit Matters will require much more attention to be paid to the auditor's report.

Chapter 6 Suspect (AIA May 2009)

Tutorial note. This question is drawn from Section 4 of the syllabus: towards a wider accountability and assurance. It tests candidates' understanding of the issues associated with money laundering.

(a) Money laundering enables criminals to enjoy some benefit from their activities. There is very little point in owning large quantities of cash, in the form of currency which is vulnerable to theft or loss and cannot be spent conveniently.

If money is passed through an apparently legitimate business then it can be banked without fear of the bank informing the authorities and thereby risking confiscation.

It might be preferable to pay tax on the proceeds of criminal activity. The alternative might be that the tax authorities will investigate the criminal for non-declaration of income if he or she appears to be enjoying a lifestyle that is beyond his or her reported income.

(b) Money laundering is difficult to detect because those perpetrating it have an obvious incentive to cover their tracks very carefully. The nature of money laundering means that the owners or senior management of the business would have to be implicated and they can normally distort and manipulate records so that the auditor will struggle to detect any problems.

Money laundering is a form of fraud, but it would be more difficult to detect than a typical fraud because it involves cash flowing into the business. Normally fraud involves attempts to conceal an outflow of assets. It would be difficult to design audit procedures to detect the recording of fictitious revenue that was backed up by cash in the bank.

The fact that money laundering is associated with criminal activity might give all of those involved a significant incentive to co-operate or at least to deny any knowledge. Even members of the audit team might be reluctant to voice any suspicions that money laundering may have occurred.

(c) The fact that the company has a high gross profit percentage is consistent with the possibility that the company is banking cash that did not come from legitimate trading activities and recording it as revenue from normal business sales.

The auditor should check that all of the company's shops actually exist and that all are stocked and open for trading. There would not necessarily be a reason for the auditor to visit every location of a business like this and the easiest way to organise a money laundering scheme would be to create a fictitious shop and record all of the laundered cash as sales for that shop.

Sales records should be investigated to establish whether cash appears to have been recorded for a series of individual sales. It would, for example, be suspicious if there were no till records showing a series of 'typical' sales occurring steadily from day to day.

Closed-circuit television tapes could be reviewed to establish whether there were actually customers in the shops to corroborate the till records. It would be suspicious if, for example, the company had logged large numbers of sales on a day on which the shop had been almost empty.

Inventory records should be checked to establish whether the company was, in fact, buying sufficient quantities of inventory to match the sales that are being made. If not, then there is a clear basis to suspect that money laundering has occurred.

The purchase invoices should be checked to establish whether the sales director's claims that the company bought at keen prices were substantiated.

If the inventory records and invoices agree to the company's recorded sales then the auditor should contact the suppliers directly as a further check that the records are, in fact, accurate. Otherwise there is a risk that the company has forged documents to create the impression that it was buying inventory for resale.

Chapter 7 Partner (AIA November 2006)

Tutorial note. Part (a) of this question is drawn from Section 3 of the syllabus: audit independence, ethics, and the public interest and part (b) from Section 4: towards a wider accountability and assurance. It tests candidates' ability to discuss the need to maintain the credibility of audit and to consider the factors that might have undermined that credibility in the light of audit scandals. This is an important issue for accountants, particularly auditors. An understanding of the manner in which audit is perceived can have major implications for the manner in which it is practised.

ANSWERS TO END OF CHAPTER QUESTIONS

(a) The IESBA *Code of Ethics* makes it clear that publicity by individual professional accountants in public practice is acceptable provided the object of the publicity is to notify the public of matters of fact in a manner that is not false, misleading or deceptive. The partner's first comment was a statement of opinion. It would be difficult, if not impossible, for any member of the profession to substantiate such a statement because very few practitioners are in a position to observe the quality of work being done by another firm. The partner does not know, and cannot prove, that other firms are managed in an incompetent or unprofessional manner.

The guidance also requires that any such publicity should be in good taste and be professionally dignified. Both of the comments breach these requirements.

The closing remark comes very close to constituting advertising, which among other things should not consist of self-laudatory statements that are not based on verifiable facts or make comparisons with other professional accountants in public practice.

Even ignoring professional guidance, the tone and content of the comments were unprofessional and defamatory. It is unacceptable for a member of any professional body to behave in this way. Professional firms should seek work by promoting their own effectiveness, not by defaming their competitors. Such unprofessional behaviour undermines the credibility of the profession as a whole.

It is also foolish and unprofessional for an auditor to offer to take on an appointment without first establishing that there are no ethical or professional reasons for turning the offer of work down. Some potential clients could be too large or require specialist skills that the firm did not have. Others could involve conflicts of interest. In any case, no accounting firm is free to accept an appointment without first discussing the matter with the existing accountant.

(b) Auditors are the only independent professionals who have access to the inner workings of a company and who have the opportunity to report to the public. Even though the auditor's duties are far more limited than the public appreciates, auditors provide those who deal with companies with a great deal of comfort as to the safety and security of those dealings.

Alleged audit failures can have significant effects on the investors, lenders, employees and pension holders of the business. This means that the press and government agencies with a responsibility for audit must pay close attention to the matter, thereby adding to the publicity for the issue.

There is a tendency to treat auditors as scapegoats because of the so-called 'deep pockets' theory. Anyone who feels as if they have suffered a loss may try to blame the auditor, regardless of who is to blame. The auditor may well settle out of court and is also likely to be able to pay any compensation that is awarded by the courts. Other parties may be more to blame, but less lucrative targets.

The growth of business enterprises and the drive towards globalisation means that any apparent distortion in the financial statements is likely to affect a larger number of stakeholders than would have been possible in the past, when business was generally smaller and more fragmented.

There is a general 'blame culture' in society as a whole. People are becoming more litigious, with increasing use of class actions and contingency fee damages claims becoming the norm throughout the world. That is placing all professionals, including auditors, under greater scrutiny than ever before.

… ANSWERS TO END OF CHAPTER QUESTIONS

Chapter 8 Audit firm approach (AIA May 2009 amended)

> **Tutorial note.** This question is drawn from Section 1 of the syllabus: audit independence, ethics, and the public interest. It tests candidates' ability to discuss the quality management aspects associated with the evaluation of inherent risk. It does so from a variety of perspectives associated with documenting audit work and also the provision of training and other materials to enable professional staff to make decisions in a consistent manner.

(a) One approach would be to gather statistics concerning the inherent risk evaluations for a large number of audits, ideally for every audit completed by the firm in the past year. That would be a relatively simple clerical task and could be delegated to someone from the firm's administrative staff. That would then make it possible to compare averages by audit group and by partner. Any discrepancies between audit groups or between partners should be investigated in case a partner with an unusually high average is unduly pessimistic whereas another with a low average is unduly optimistic.

This investigation could be supported by considering any differences that might arise between the types of audits assigned to different people. If, for example, different audit groups dealt with different industries or some partners specialised in smaller clients then that could lead to legitimate differences in averages.

The firms should be rotating engagement partners over time. A sample of audit files should be obtained for the years before and after a change in audit partner in order to check whether there has been consistency from one year to the next. If there has tended to be a significant change then the files should be reviewed in greater depth to establish whether that was due to changing circumstances or a different interpretation of what were broadly the same facts.

Finally, a small-scale simulation exercise could be conducted. Detailed extracts could be taken from the planning sections of a small number of audit files and a panel of audit partners could be asked to decide what the inherent risk evaluations should be. If they find that there is insufficient information to make a decision then that would tend to suggest that the files are not sufficiently detailed and that should be addressed as a separate but related matter. If they reach wildly different conclusions then the firm does have a problem in achieving consistency.

(b) The evaluation of inherent risk is an important factor in determining the amount of evidence to be gathered from detailed substantive testing. If the partners and managers responsible for evaluating inherent risk are inconsistent then the firm might be gathering insufficient evidence on some audits.

Each partner is affected by the decisions made by his or her colleagues. An audit opinion that is not supported by sufficient evidence could lead to a massive loss of reputation or a major claim for compensation.

If the firm's own partners cannot agree on the correct evaluation of inherent risk, then the firm may struggle to convince any external observer, such as an expert witness commenting on an allegation of negligence or a reviewer conducting a professional oversight investigation, that its standards of assurance are acceptable.

(c) The starting point is to document clear processes for evaluating inherent risk. This will always be a complex area of professional judgement, but any support that can be provided in the form of checklists or indicators of high, medium or low risk can only help.

Documenting inherent risk factors that indicate higher risks can only be the start. It is generally understood that checklists can only offer partial support for such decisions. There should be a programme of ongoing training and professional development for senior staff up to and including audit partners. This training should provide an opportunity for managers and partners to interact and share their views on matters of judgement. Such a dialogue should encourage a collective opinion on the approach to particular problems.

ANSWERS TO END OF CHAPTER QUESTIONS

There should be a formal process to ensure that all senior parties involved in evaluating inherent risk work together and agree on a figure. The results of discussions between the engagement and review partners and the audit manager should be recorded in the audit working papers. Any dissenting views should be recorded and the reasoning behind the final decision noted. As far as possible, each audit team should have a unique combination of partners and managers so that individuals did not become over familiar with one another and complacent.

Chapter 9 Startfund (AIA November 2009 amended)

Tutorial note. This question is drawn from Section 1 of the syllabus: audit independence, ethics, and the public interest. It tests candidates' ability to discuss the auditor's responsibilities with regard to group financial statements.

(a) IFRS 10 *Consolidated financial statements* defines a subsidiary as 'an entity that is controlled by another entity' (known as the parent). The auditor must decide which of the companies that Startfund has invested in, if any, are controlled by Startfund. It would appear that many of them are. The fact that Startfund's interest is intended to be short-lived and motivated by the desire to provide start-up funding is not relevant to this classification and IFRS 10 would not permit the subsidiaries to be excluded for this reason.

In determining control, it is important to consider whether Startfund has power over the other companies, the right to returns, and whether Startfund uses its power.

Therefore an important issue is whether Startfund holds more than 50% of the voting shares. Those companies will almost certainly be subsidiaries. Another important issue is the fact that Startfund appoints directors with the intention of exercising control over board decisions.

The status of the other companies depends on the extent to which the two directors appointed by Startfund can actually exercise control. For the first two years, if they do have total control, then the company must be considered a subsidiary. If, under normal circumstances, the directors can do no more than influence then the company might no longer be a subsidiary. It will be important to check further. For example, reading the minutes of Startfund's board or management meetings might indicate that Startfund can do more than influence these companies. Alternatively, management might be asked whether they ever do exercise effective control.

The impact of the clause that gives control when a company is in difficulty should also be considered. If this provision comes into effect frequently then there might be grounds to treat all investment companies as subsidiaries. Again, this might be determined from board minutes or management assurances.

When reviewing these matters it is also important to consider the possibility that Startfund can exert significant influence. In that case it may be necessary to treat the company as an associate.

(b) It would never be acceptable to accept an appointment that was conditional in this way. The auditor must always be free to arrive at an independent opinion on the financial statements. It would be difficult to reach final agreement on the correct treatment before taking office because the auditor will be unable to gather evidence before taking office.

It is legitimate to discuss potential problems that might arise before accepting an appointment, but the auditor must make it clear during those discussions that the final decision would not be reached until the review stage just prior to expressing an audit opinion and that the auditor's views could easily change at that stage or before.

If the auditor did agree to such terms then it might create further difficulties with the firm's relationship with the directors. If the auditor is willing to accept such extraordinary conditions before being appointed then it will be difficult to exercise a great deal of authority during the appointment. The directors will feel that they have the upper hand even if that is little more than a psychological advantage.

(c) The component auditors will be responsible for expressing an opinion on the truth and fairness of their own client company financial statements. If they do so in accordance with auditing standards then the financial statements that are to be consolidated should give a true and fair view of the group as a whole.

The component auditors will have no direct responsibility for the group financial statements. Startfund's auditors will be responsible for the opinion on the group financial statements and their signature will appear on the parent company's auditor's report.

Auditing the group financial statements will require the cooperation of the component auditors. The directors of Startfund will be able to arrange that and the component auditors will be required to furnish the group auditor with all information and assurances that are required under ISA 600 (Revised). That will not necessarily give them any responsibility for the consolidated financial statements. It will remain the responsibility of the group auditor to request the information that should be passed on.

Chapter 10 Tap!

(a) **Audit risks**

There is a higher audit risk associated with a charity as in the event of problems arising and litigation taking place, the audit firm could experience a significant amount of bad publicity.

Inherent risks

(i) **Cash**. The charity operates with a high number of cash and cheque transactions. A substantial part of their **income** comes from cash donations. Put another way, it is likely that very little of their income comes from direct bank transfers. Also, it is likely that many of the **expenses** which 'Tap!' incurs are also cash expenses. Cash is **risky for audit purposes** because it is **susceptible to loss, miscounting or misappropriation**.

(ii) **Charity**. The theatre company is a charity, and is therefore subject to a high degree of **regulation**. This raises the risk for our audit.

(iii) **Accounting specialist**. The charity employs an administrator, but there is no mention of an accountant. It is **unclear who is going to draft the charity accounts** (which must comply with specialist requirements) but it does not appear that a specialist exists to undertake this job. This increases the risk of errors existing in the accounts.

(iv) **Completeness of income**. As the charity appears to have **no control** over the primary collection of income from box office receipts, there is a significant **risk that income is understated** and that the theatres have not accounted properly to the theatre.

(v) **Disclosure of income**. The disclosure of income must be considered. It is unlikely to be appropriate to show the 'net income from theatres' figure. Rather, the gross income less commission should probably be disclosed.

(vi) **Expenditure**. The charity expenses may be well-recorded, or they may be **difficult to substantiate** – this is not clear. It may also be difficult to substantiate payments made to build wells in Africa. We currently have no knowledge about how that aspect of the charity operates. It will be important to check that expenditure is made in accordance with the trust deed. Some necessary administrative expense will not necessarily be conducive to the aims of the charity. We must ensure that it is all analysed correctly.

Control

There currently appear to be **no controls over cash** in the charity.

ANSWERS TO END OF CHAPTER QUESTIONS

Detection

This is a **first year audit**, so there is little knowledge of the business at present. It is also the **first ever audit** of the charity, so the comparatives are unaudited. We must make this clear in our report, and we will need to undertake more detailed work on the **opening balances**. As the charity is to a large degree **peripatetic**, we may find audit evidence difficult to obtain, if it has not been properly returned to the administrative offices.

Conclusion

This appears to be a high risk first year audit. It is likely to result in a modified audit opinion.

(b) **Audit procedures**

Income from box office takings

Income from box office can be **verified to the statement from the theatre** and the **bank statements** to ensure that it is complete. The **commission** can be agreed by **recalculation**.

It might be necessary to request **external confirmation of the seats sold** for each performance to ensure that income is completely stated on the return from the theatre. [However, if theatres have been defrauding the charity, they are unlikely to confirm this to the auditors. This may have to be an area which is aided by stronger controls over income.]

Income from buckets (theatres and streets)

We must discover whether the charity fill out 'counting sheets' when the buckets of money are originally counted. If so, the **money in buckets can be verified from the original sheet to the banking documentation**.

However, in the **absence of strong controls** over the counting, it will be **impossible to conclude that this income is complete.**

Income from other donations

Donations made over the phone should have been noted on documents then retained at the administrative offices. Donations made by post should have **original documents**. A sample of these should be **traced to banking documentation** and bank statements.

Again, in the **absence of originating documentation**, it will be **difficult to conclude that income is fairly stated.**

(c) **Controls over cash**

> **Tutorial note.** Three good suggestions should be sufficient to gain you six marks. We have included others as there are a large number of suggestions that can be made.

Income from box office takings

It would be a good control over completeness of income to request a **schedule of seats sold** from the theatres for every night a performance is given. This is likely to be information that theatres can print off their systems with no trouble. This will lead to the theatre company having more assurance as to the completeness of income.

Income from buckets

As this income is highly susceptible to loss or misappropriation, strong controls should be put in place:

(i) **Number of people**. If possible, the charity should assign **two people** to each bucket during the collection phase and two people should count the money in the bucket at the end of the day. These people will act as a **check on each other** to ensure that cash is kept more secure.

(ii) **Security**. The security arrangements for buckets should be strong. The charity could invest in a **transportable safe** in which to store the money between collection and banking. It might also be wise to use **collecting tins** rather than buckets, as this simple measure would ensure that the cash was less open to the public. The cash should also be **banked frequently**. It should not be kept not banked for 24 hours after collection.

(iii) **Recording**. A record should be made of cash counts and it should be signed by both the people that undertook the count. These can provide an initial record of the cash takings.

Other income

The controls over other income will be restricted by the number of staff at the Leicester office. It appears that only the administrator may work there regularly. If this is the case, it is going to be difficult to introduce supervision into the cash operations.

All phone donations should be **recorded on pre-numbered documentation** so as to give evidence of completeness.

As the administrator largely works alone, it would be a good idea for the board of trustees to carry out a cyclical review of the work of the administrator. This would provide a useful protection from problems for both the charity and the administrator.

Chapter 11 City Trading (AIA November 2007)

> **Tutorial note.** This question is drawn from Section 2 of the syllabus: advanced aspects of quality management. It tests the ability to conduct a risk assessment and the development of a system for measuring and reporting performance.

(a) The risks associated with each type of accident should be dealt with in turn. For example, the risk of a customer slipping or tripping while on the company's premises should be considered by examining all public entrances and all of the public areas within the store to ensure that all surfaces are suitably skid resistant, that there are no likely tripping hazards and so on. The logs prepared by the shop's cleaning staff should be reviewed to ensure that all surfaces are kept clean and safe.

The types of accident that should be assessed and managed should be listed from as many relevant sources as possible. The accident logs maintained by other shops, checklists prepared by the shop's insurers and advice prepared by government departments should be considered. Also, different types of customer should be considered, such as the visually impaired or those with mobility problems.

The company's insurance policies should be reviewed to ensure that the company is not exposed to undue levels of risk. The internal auditor should take care to ensure that the company is insured for all relevant risks and that it is fully in compliance with any terms and conditions of the policy. This will not prevent accidents, but it will mitigate the risks associated with serving members of the public.

The company should have a formal system for recording all incidents that could indicate the presence of a risk. For example, the first aid staff should be required to log each and every occasion that they have to treat anybody. Departmental managers should be required to complete incident logs whenever there are accidents. This will reduce the risk of accidents repeating themselves and will also demonstrate that the company is taking steps to ensure that problems are dealt with as soon as they come to light.

(b) Information about the mix in other shops may be helpful. This could be based on both the company's experience in its other shops and the layout of any competing shops in the same city. If the new shop has a different mix from these comparatives then it might be worth reconsidering.

The sales per square metre should be calculated for each department. This statistic is usually one of the most informative in the retail industry. This analysis could also take margins into account in case space is reallocated to products which have high sales values, but low mark-ups on cost.

The auditor should also calculate profit per square metre of sales space, although care should be taken to avoid confusing the issue by potentially misleading allocations of fixed costs.

The management of costs should be considered in terms of cost drivers rather than traditional management accounting practices. It may be, for example, that one department is particularly expensive to run because it attracts a disproportionate proportion of certain costs. This could happen if, say, store security tended to be concentrated in a particular department that had lots of portable and high value inventory. Closing that department might make the shop less vulnerable to theft and so security costs could be reduced.

The buying behaviour of individual customers might be worth considering. It might be possible to gather information about the buying habits during a 'typical' visit by tracking the credit card numbers of shoppers or even by issuing customers with loyalty cards. It might be discovered, for example, that customers tend to shop in more than one department. If that is the case then changes to the sales mix could discourage customers from coming into the shop because they are attracted by the range of goods on offer.

Chapter 12 Kilo plc (AIA May 2004) (amended)

(a) ISA 315 (Revised) *Identifying and assessing the risks of material misstatement* requires auditors to understand the system of internal control and to identify and assess the risks of material misstatement at both the financial statement level and the assertion level. These factors should be taken into account in developing a plan for the audit.

There is a lack of internal control over the payroll system. The fact that the payroll and personnel departments have been merged means that it would be easier for bogus members of staff to be created and for those responsible to share the resulting salary payments.

The fact that management is prepared to create this arrangement also casts doubt on the quality of the control environment. If management is prepared to skimp on important control procedures then other controls might be dispensed with.

The auditor will have to review the risk created by this control deficiency. The payroll should be reviewed in detail and a sample of new starts should be selected. The auditor should then ensure that each and every one of the selected staff have been formally appointed and that each one actually exists and works for the company. If necessary, the auditor should arrange to meet each one.

The auditor should also discuss the control issues created by this merger with management. If the directors are aware that this impaired the system of internal control then the auditor should discuss the longer-term implications of this attitude for the audit. Ultimately, it could require an increased emphasis on detailed substantive testing.

The fact that the company is losing sales could affect management's motivation. For example, if the profit is unacceptably low the directors might be tempted to overstate profits by adopting manipulative accounting policies or by some other distortion. The auditor will, therefore, have to pay greater attention to any judgemental areas of the financial statements such as estimates and provisions.

The directors might also be tempted to overstate sales in order to conceal any decrease in revenue from the previous year. The auditor should consider matters such as the year-end cut-off to ensure that sales from the beginning of the new financial year have not been booked early.

If the lost sales are really significant then the company might not be able to continue as a going concern. The auditor should seek evidence from the directors that they have plans and budgets in place to ensure that the company's future is secure.

Advising the company on ways to make it more efficient and profitable will put the auditor under some pressure to collude with any overstatement of profit in order to further the impression that the advice provided was sound.

(b) *Wages system*

The IESBA *Code of Ethics for Professional Accountants* states that taking responsibility for designing, implementing, monitoring or maintaining internal control is a management responsibility. Providing advice on remedying deficiencies in the wages system might, therefore, create the risk of the audit firm assuming a management responsibility. When a firm or a network firm assumes a management responsibility for an audit client, self-review, self-interest and familiarity threats are created.

Offering specific advice about remedying deficiencies in the wages system might create a self-review threat where, in future years, the auditors might be reluctant to point out deficiencies in controls surrounding the wages system that they themselves have designed.

Website

Having one of the audit firm's IT consultant's redesign Kilo's website may create a risk of the audit firm assuming a management responsibility. The IESBA *Code of Ethics for Professional Accountants* only permits auditors to provide IT services to an audit client that is not a public interest entity where the auditor:

- Designs or implements IT systems that are unrelated to internal control over financial reporting;
- Designs or implements IT systems that do not generate information forming part of the accounting records or financial statements;
- Implements "off-the-shelf" accounting or financial information reporting software that was not developed by the firm or network firm, if the customization required to meet the client's needs is not significant.

There is also a risk of a self-review threat to independence if the information generated by the company website form part of the financial statements on which the auditor's report. If designing the website is permitted, separate staff must perform the audit and website redesign work to safeguard the self-review threat.

In addition, if the fees from the IT services offered to Kilo represent a very large proportion of the total fees of the firm, this can create an self-interest threat and an intimidation threat to independence. The firm might be tempted to overlook issues that arise during the audit as they are concerned about the potential loss of fees from the IT work if the client is unhappy with the audit and threatens to cancel the other work.

(c) This approach will save time and disruption, saving costs both in terms of fees and the need to brief and assist junior audit staff.

Well designed, computerised accounting systems are unlikely to generate material misstatements. The greatest threat to the truth and fairness of the financial statements is the attitude of management. The senior members of the audit team will be better equipped to deal with this threat.

The detailed notes and minutes generated by this process will provide better quality evidence that matters of opinion and judgement have been considered by the audit firm.

Audit partners will have greater confidence in the quality of the audit opinion because of their greater involvement in the process.

ANSWERS TO END OF CHAPTER QUESTIONS

Chapter 13 Netseller (AIA May 2009)

Tutorial note. This question is drawn from Section 2 of the syllabus: advanced aspects of quality management. It tests understanding of the controls that ought to exist over a computerised system.

(a) First of all, customers have to trust that the system is secure, otherwise they will not entrust their bank details to the company. This means that the company cannot afford to risk any publicity concerning security breaches or actual leakage of data.

The system automatically collects customer payments. Any system breakdown could lead to a loss of revenue.

The system keeps track of all disks that are in customers' hands. If the system breaks down then there will be no way to recover disks from customers.

The computer files all disks that are on hand. Any breakdown means that the disks are effectively lost to the company because holdings will have to be substantial to make any real income from this venture.

If the system breaks down then there will be delays in sending DVDs to customers, which might lead to a large number cancelling their subscriptions.

The system handles bank transfers and issues valuable inventory and yet it has to be accessible over the internet. That makes it both a tempting target to hackers and also quite vulnerable to an expert.

(b) The system itself will have to be kept secure. Physical security will have to be of paramount importance, with adequate consideration given to factors such as fire prevention and similar physical safeguards. This will have to extend to associated systems, such as the power supply to the system, to reduce the risk of temporary disruption.

All records will have to be backed up frequently, with the backups kept at a secure and remote site. Ideally, this should be done by means of a networked facility that would permit data to be mirrored at another location.

Customer access means that the system must be connected to the internet at all times. The system should be designed to deter unauthorised access. Each customer should have both a user name and a password. The password should have basic criteria in its design, such as a minimum length and the requirement for it to contain both letters and numbers. That should reduce the risk of unauthorised access to customer accounts. There should be a second 'security word' so that a customer who wishes to access a more sensitive part of his or her records (eg postal address or banking details) has to input two digits from the security word (eg 'input the second and fourth letters of your favourite pet's name').

Banking details should not be stored on the system that is accessible from the internet. Whenever a customer creates an account the necessary details to collect payment should be transferred electronically to an independent system. That system can handle the collection of funds from customer accounts and can send a list of current, paid-up customers to the primary system on a daily basis.

All attempts to gain unauthorised access should be logged carefully and analysed from time to time. The company should ensure that security software is kept up to date to deal with threats as they emerge.

Chapter 14 Working papers and review (AIA November 2007 amended)

(a) ISA 230 *Audit documentation* states that the auditor should document matters which are important in providing audit evidence to support the auditor's opinion and evidence that the audit was carried out in accordance with ISAs.

If work is not properly documented then the audit firm cannot conduct adequate supervision and review. The working papers enable the audit manager and partner to check that sufficient work has been done in order to support the audit opinion.

The working papers are also necessary in the event of an external review by a government department or professional body. External reviewers have no other source of insight into the conduct of particular audits. Assurances sought from the audit staff themselves will be of little value because their knowledge and understanding of ISAs and similar documents will give them an idea of the answers that the reviewers are looking for.

The working papers are an important source of comfort in the event that the auditor has to defend an audit opinion. If there is an allegation of audit failure then the auditor must be able to show that the work done was sufficient to form a valid opinion.

The working papers contain a wealth of useful information that might inform and simplify future audits of the same company. The previous year's file contains details of the audit approach taken, problems encountered and so on. This will avoid spending time discovering and resolving the same issues as before.

The process of preparing orderly and efficient working papers encourages audit staff to conduct their work in an orderly and efficient way.

(b) The working papers will be prepared with a view to defending the opinion expressed. It may be deliberately partial and biased in terms of what is recorded.

Ideally, the working papers should record everything that was known at the time each and every matter of professional judgement was dealt with. That might not be practical and the auditor might be inclined to excise certain facts that could be used to undermine the audit opinion.

Audit staff have been known to engage in the premature sign-off of work done in order to keep pace with tight time budgets and deadlines. The working papers could, therefore, contain falsified evidence.

Each audit firm will have its own culture. This will result in different attitudes towards work, risk-taking and so on. Such cultural differences might be impossible to read from audit working papers.

A great deal of the process of forming an audit opinion relies on the expertise and the experience of the staff making professional judgements. Such factors will not necessarily be readily reflected in the working papers.

The working papers will not necessarily record much of the debate and discussion between senior members of the team, such as the engagement and review partners.

Chapter 15 Bulldoze (AIA November 2007)

(a) The fact that the cost of the equipment was overstated does not, in itself, prove that the auditor was negligent. Negligence involves a failure to act with reasonable skill and care. Bulldoze would have to prove that the auditor had failed to do so before it would be possible to seek compensation.

ISA 500 *Audit evidence* requires that the auditor obtain sufficient appropriate audit evidence to be able to draw reasonable conclusions on which to base the audit opinion. Sufficiency and appropriateness are matters requiring professional judgement and so the auditor would have had some discretion in deciding what to examine and what to accept.

This purchase was material and so it was automatically selected for investigation by the audit team. The transaction was supported by third party, documentary evidence. The auditor would have regarded such documents as highly persuasive. The invoice itself is not a forgery, nor is there anything in the company's records to suggest that it was suspect.

The transaction was authorised by a member of the board. That does not provide conclusive evidence, but auditors would normally regard assurances from directors as having greater validity than those from more junior members of staff, particularly when they are supported by evidence from other sources.

In this case, the only way that the auditor could have detected the fraud would have been to have read the production director's emails. Even that might not have been successful because the production director might have deleted the emails or could have emailed from outside the office using a personal email account.

ISA 240 *The Auditor's responsibilities relating to fraud in an audit of financial statements* states that an auditor cannot obtain absolute assurance that material misstatements in the financial statements will be detected because of the limitations of the audit, such as the use of judgement, the use of testing, the inherent limitations of internal control and the fact that much of the audit evidence available to the auditor is persuasive rather than conclusive in nature.

The ISA goes on to say that the primary responsibility for the prevention and detection of fraud rests with both those charged with governance of the entity and with management. The board should have supervised the purchase of the equipment more carefully.

(b) Major investments in non-current assets should be managed as part of the project appraisal system. There should be a project team in charge of implementation. This will provide for discussion and interaction and this will reduce the risk of dishonesty as well as errors of judgement.

Tenders should be sought from at least two suppliers. These should be specific as to the nature of the item to be supplied. Tenders should be submitted in sealed envelopes and opened in the presence of at least two members of the project team.

The winning tender should normally be the cheapest, provided it meets the criteria of quality and service. There should be a written justification for the selection of any bidder other than the cheapest.

The internal audit department should review all paperwork and should make direct contact with the supplier's finance department before the contracts are finally signed and the asset paid for. This review should focus on the authenticity of the facts and figures underlying the acquisition.

Any and all corporate hospitality, gifts and other perks from suppliers should be declined unless they have only a token value (eg a diary or a calendar). This should be a matter for the terms and conditions of employment of all employees.

Chapter 16 Powerplant (AIA May 2009 amended)

> **Tutorial note.** Parts (a) and (b) of this question are drawn from Section 2 of the syllabus: advanced aspects of quality management. These parts deal with the use of an auditor's expert to support the audit work to be done on a complex area of the audit requiring considerable technical support for the audit team. Part (b) tests candidates' ability to decide the correct form of auditor's report in a situation of material misstatement due to disagreement over the disclosures that are being made in the financial statements.

(a) There are three aspects to this: the expert has to be appointed, then briefed and, finally, the auditor has to decide on the implications of the expert's report.

The auditor will have to identify an expert with the necessary technical qualifications and experience to advise on this problem in a credible way. This particular case requires some very specific expertise and it may be difficult to tell whether any given individual is a suitable person to approach. It may be possible to seek advice from, say, a professor of nuclear physics at a local university for suggestions as to who might be able to help.

The auditor will have to ensure that any expert appointed to assist is either independent of the company or that any economic relationship between the expert and the company is taken into account in evaluating the results.

The company's support will have to be sought beforehand. This is normally the case, but this particular investigation raises very real concerns about health and safety and the possibility of a nuclear accident. The responsibilities of all those involved for the various contingencies should be discussed and recorded in writing.

The expert will have to be briefed on the accounting issues arising from the investigation. Essentially, the auditor wishes to know the broad probabilities of the forthcoming government investigation either demanding replacement of the component or concluding that it will be safe for a further five years' operations. If the inspector states that there is only a remote possibility of the component being deemed unsafe then there will be little need to treat it as having been impaired.

The briefing should, perhaps, cover differences in terminology. A nuclear scientist dealing with a potentially lethal reactor might regard any possibility as serious, no matter how low the likelihood of it occurring. An auditor might be of the opinion that a probability of, say, 5% is an acceptable risk whereas a nuclear scientist would not.

The expert's report will have to be read thoroughly and any concerns or qualifications discussed and clarified. The report should indicate the work undertaken in support of the opinion. The auditor would prefer to have a categorical assurance that the component is either totally reliable or defective. It is unlikely that the expert will give such a clear statement.

(b) The auditor must always accept full responsibility for the opinion on the financial statements. If a third party furnishes the auditor with assurances in support of the audit opinion then the auditor should come to a conclusion as to whether these give sufficient evidence when combined with the work done by the audit team.

The auditor must accept full responsibility because experts might not have the necessary accounting knowledge to appreciate the implications of their findings for the financial statements.

If the auditor's report refers to evidence obtained from a third party then readers of the report might be confused as to whether the report has been qualified. This confusion can be avoided only by the auditor making a realistic assessment of the evidence and accepting full responsibility for the opinion on the accounts.

(c) This is a material misstatement due to a disagreement over the disclosures associated with an inherent uncertainty. The auditor will have to issue a modified report expressing a qualified opinion as the matter is material but not pervasive.

The report should include a paragraph stating the uncertainties that have not been disclosed in the financial statements. This statement will indicate the possibility that an asset with a value of $40 million on the statement of financial position may have to be written down to zero because of impairment.

There is no need for the auditor to refer to the possibility that replacement of the component will lead to an additional $100 million cost. The circumstances that would lead to such an outlay have not occurred. The company's ability to continue as a going concern has not been called into question.

This is a material matter, but it is not pervasive. The auditor should issue a qualified opinion ('except for') rather than an adverse opinion. This would state that the financial statements give a true and fair view except for the possibility that the accounts should have included disclosure of the inherent uncertainties raised by the potential impairment of this asset.

Chapter 17 Sink plc (AIA May 2007)

> **Tutorial note.** Parts (a) to (c) of this question come from Section 2 of the syllabus: advanced aspects of quality management.
>
> Overall, the question tests candidates' ability to deal with the problems and responsibilities created by going concern issues. It does so by describing a scenario where the auditor must express an opinion prior to the resolution of the circumstances that are creating the doubts about going concern. This could well reflect the reality of an audit where interested parties might delay finalising decisions until they have had an opportunity to read the latest audited financial statements.

(a) ISA 570 *Going concern* states that the auditor's responsibility is to consider the appropriateness of management's use of the going concern assumption in the preparation of the financial statements, and consider whether there are material uncertainties about the entity's ability to continue as a going concern that need to be disclosed in the financial statements.

The auditor should review the board's basis for believing that the company will be a going concern if the company is successful in winning the order and obtaining the bank loan. The audit partner should request detailed budgets and forecasts based on the assumption that the negotiations are successful. These should be reviewed carefully and the basis on which they have been prepared should be subjected to a sceptical appraisal.

The board should be asked to minute their confidence in the recovery plan in writing. If necessary, this minute should make clear any reservations or qualifications. The minute should be signed on behalf of the board by the chairman of the audit committee and at least one member of the executive board.

The auditor must then review all correspondence, reports and memos relating to both the loan application and the potential order. These documents cannot provide conclusive evidence that either will succeed, but the auditor should ensure that there is nothing to indicate that there is significant doubt about the outcome of either.

The auditor should ensure that the documentation supports any factual claims made by the directors. For example, did the bid for the contract meet the buyer's tender conditions? Is the information supporting the loan application accurate and does the application provide all of the information requested?

ANSWERS TO END OF CHAPTER QUESTIONS

The auditor should ask to meet with the members of sales and finance staff responsible for the negotiations and should form an opinion of their confidence of the outcome. Again, the auditor should approach this discussion with a healthy degree of scepticism.

(b) Provided the auditor believes that the company stands a reasonable chance of winning the additional business and raising the finance, it would be legitimate to express an unqualified opinion on the financial statements, provided the uncertainties were properly explained in the notes to the financial statements. In that case, the auditor would add 'Material Uncertainty Related to Going Concern' section, to highlight the importance of the disclosures concerning the risks to users of the financial statements.

This assumes that the notes to the financial statements make adequate disclosure of the uncertainties that might affect the truth and fairness of the accounts. These should give sufficient detail for readers to appreciate the nature and extent of the risks.

If there is inadequate disclosure of the uncertainties then ISA 570 (Revised) requires that the auditor should issue a modified opinion which makes specific reference to the going concern issues.

(c) IAS 1 *Presentation of financial statements* requires the board to make an assessment of the company's ability to continue as a going concern. The audit committee does not have a specific duty to undertake this activity, beyond that of the board as a whole, but it is normally part of the audit committee's remit to consider any significant matters of accounting judgement.

A large part of the purpose of an audit committee is to facilitate communication between the company and the auditor. That means that it is very appropriate for the committee to request a meeting such as this. The non-executive directors who make up the audit committee have a legitimate right to seek the advice of the external auditor and also a duty to satisfy themselves that the external auditor is fully aware of any concerns about the truth and fairness of the financial statements.

The involvement of the chief executive and finance director might be slightly unorthodox because the audit committee is meant to be a sub-committee composed of non-executive directors to ensure independence of the executive board. It would, however, be somewhat artificial and probably counterproductive to exclude the executive directors from every meeting. In this case, the convener of the audit committee could chair the meeting. The chief executive and finance director might be involved largely in order to provide information when asked and could be regarded as observers rather than full participants.

Chapter 18 Roadking (AIA Nov 2009)

Tutorial note. This question is drawn from Section 2 of the syllabus: advanced aspects of quality management. Parts (a) and (b) deal with analytical review and the problems associated with obtaining evidence from analytical review techniques. Part (c) deals with the audit of a claim for damages.

(a) Analytical review can be a very cost-effective source of audit evidence. The auditor team will always look at the figures for credibility in any case. If making this a formal part of audit fieldwork means that the results can be documented and evaluated then the auditor will obtain some assurance for very little cost.

It might also be argued that failure to use analytical review could leave the firm open to accusations of negligence. If the auditor overlooks some matter where the figures can be seen to be out of line with expectations then any subsequent dispute over those figures will be very difficult to defend. The plaintiff will ask why the auditor did not investigate the apparent anomaly and will not be satisfied that the auditor's detailed testing was completed without incident.

(b) Formal statistical methods give a result that can be justified in terms of statistical theory. That means that the auditor can then use more sophisticated models and methods of analysis than a straightforward review or comparison. For example, the auditor might use correlation techniques to demonstrate that there is a link between reported results and some external data, such as sales versus economic indicators such as interest rates. The auditor can then use this model to measure the most recent figures according to the draft accounts with updated figures obtained from independent sources dealing with those indicators. If the results match then the auditor can claim to have gathered some useful evidence.

The fact that the results can be evaluated statistically might be an advantage in terms of credibility. The auditor will be able to express the probability that the model is valid as a percentage and thereby have a more formal acceptance criterion. Anyone challenging the decision will not be able to do so on the basis of the results obtained, although they can still do so on the basis of the formal criteria used in developing and assessing the model.

The greatest strength of these techniques is that they are more scientific and potentially more reliable than simply judging relationships by thinking about the figures.

The biggest disadvantage is that the models themselves may become outdated without the auditor realising. For example, the relationship between sales and interest rates might not apply if the product's market changes and consumers are prepared to carry on buying it even if interest rates rise. There is also the risk that the model is badly specified and that the results are misleading. For example, the auditor could correlate an accounting figure against an external factor without realising that both are simply increasing over time and that the apparent relationship is purely coincidental. The comfort gained from the model would then be illusory.

(c) The first thing would be to review all correspondence. The auditor should tabulate the number of claims and the amounts, if any, stated on each.

The auditor should seek confirmation from the board of its understanding of the claim. The matter should be discussed with the chief executive and the finance director. Their verbal assurances should be compared to the comments recorded in the board minutes.

The basis of the provision should be considered from an accounting perspective. The auditor should ensure that the amounts being recorded should be in accordance with IAS 37 *Provisions, contingent liabilities and contingent assets*. The provision should be a realistic estimate of the amount that is actually payable.

The auditor should seek confirmation of the facts and their interpretation from the company's legal adviser. It is unlikely that a lawyer will give a clear confirmation of the likely outcome, but the auditor could at least ask for an indication of whether the lawyer has anything to add to this information.

The auditor should seek confirmation from the board in the letter of representation. This will give some assurance that the auditor has not been misled in any way by the directors in the course of seeking verbal assurances.

Chapter 19 IMJ

(a) (i) Automated Investment Software

The automated investment decision making software is an example of robotic process automation (RPA) where software uses pre-determined parameters and rules to complete investment trading decisions more efficiently and quickly than is possible using manual processes.

This software will certainly have an impact on the audit to the extent that it interacts with the blockchain ledger which feeds into IMJ's financial reporting system and in relation to the assessment of going concern. The treatment of the investments in the financial statements will be based upon the information that is produced by the automated software, so transactional integrity will carry greater audit risk. Kelly & Co will need to plan a greater level of audit work to confirm effectiveness of general IT controls and authorisation and system access controls to gain sufficient assurance.

Kelly & Co will need to increase reliance on IT security controls to confirm only transactions are processed within pre-authorised investment policy trading limits decided by the directors of IMJ. The audit of investment trading parameters and confirmation of who can access and change investment trading parameters, in line with authorised personnel, will be critical. Furthermore, Kelly & Co will need to incorporate the audit of IT controls designed to prevent and detect hacking and fraud as audit risk in these areas will be higher with introduction of new systems.

Kelly & Co will need to consider how automated tools and techniques (ATTs) can test the system transactional data and other information that is automatically produced by the system to ensure all transactions lie within authorised investment parameters and are processed completely and accurately.

Data analytics are also likely to lead to an improvement in audit quality, although this is of course dependant on data analytics processes being implemented intelligently. The use of automated data analytics can analyse overall investment activity to confirm activity lies with accepted parameters and trends. Automated data analytics can also report specific groups of transactions which lie outside expected parameters, in terms of:

- High value
- Material profit or loss
- Unexpected trading patterns of investment profit or loss which is exceptional or is unusual given the market trends at the time of the transaction.

Automated data analytics may also help Kelly & Co in the following ways:

- Analyses of revenue trends into investment products, region or by timeframe
- Matches of investment orders to cash settlement and report exceptions
- Testing of user codes for evidence any inappropriate combinations of users have been involved in processing transactions

Furthermore, the use of test data through the system could be used to test investment parameters on the system and observe whether it performs in the way expected by Kelly & Co. It would be essential that Kelly & Co can ensure that the introduction of test data does not affect actual transaction data and all test data can be removed.

In addition, Kelly & Co should consider whether the risks associated with important new systems have been adequately taken into account in the director's assessment of effective internal controls operating throughout the year and ongoing going concern.

Kelly & Co will also need to consider how to acquire, access and store IMJ's data in order to carry out any ATTs, and consider if the audit of data creates any data security or data protection concerns.

(ii) **Blockchain transaction recording**

Kelly & Co will also need to gain an understanding of the interaction between IMJ's financial reporting system and the automation software. By tracing a number of transactions from purchase of investments by the system, investment valuation changes due to market changes, sale and cash settlement and the recording of gains and losses, Kelly & Co will be able to test whether the system is correctly recording the investment performance. Where there is a large number of investment transactions, it may be more efficient for Kelly & Co to use audit software to automate this testing.

The use of block-chain technology theoretically reduces the risk of misstatement related to the new system as the ledger is unalterable and cannot be manipulated. Again, it is crucial that Kelly & Co obtain a thorough understanding of exactly how this system works and has full access to the ledger.

The 'real time' nature of using blockchain technology to record transactions means that Kelly & Co will need to consider incorporating continuous transaction monitoring (CTM) into the audit strategy. The distributed nature of the technology means that a copy of the blockchain will be instantly available to Kelly & Co as it is created allowing for real time audit of transactions, which could be audited against investment policy and supporting documentation, with checks that investment gains or losses are accurately recorded.

Kelly & Co will need to consider the need to rely on the work of an expert if it does not have the technical knowledge to satisfactorily audit IT controls around the blockchain. *ISA 620 Using the work of an auditor's expert* may be relevant. The blockchain is likely to be audited by an audit firm on behalf of the exchanges who operate it. Kelly & Co will need to consider the requirements of ISA 402 *Audit considerations relating to an entity using a service organisation* in its reliance on IT controls related to the blockchain ledger.

Ultimately the impact on the audit will be in the risk of misunderstanding the system or not picking up a problem that exists, leading to Kelly & Co not detecting a misstatement.

Kelly & Co will need to consider its overall audit approach, reliance on IT controls and any training needs for its audit staff in order to perform and evaluate the results of IT based audit techniques.

However, the automated nature of the investment system and the use of blockchain may well make it easier to identify errors and misstatement than the previous manual system as there is less room for intentional manipulation or human error, which may have a positive effect on overall audit risk.

(b) Given both the nature of the business and the data held on behalf of customers, the main cybersecurity risks to IMJ and ways to mitigate those risks will be as follows:

Cybersecurity Risk	Control to Mitigate
Hacking Hackers gaining access to IT systems from outside the organisation to steal data	• All networks protected by firewalls • All user accounts protected by passwords and usernames • Sensitive documents password protected • Access restrictions amongst employees • Detailed audit trail of all access to each area of the system
Insider Threat Mistaken or malicious leaking of data by employees	• Provision of mandatory training on the risk of leaks due to mistakes • Limiting staff access to the system to the minimum required to undertake their roles • Restricted use of portable storage devices • Immediate removal of access for employees who leave the company

Cybersecurity Risk	Control to Mitigate
External Disks and Drives Loss of data or introduction of threats via external data storage devices	• Restrict all such devices to those owned and purchased by the company • Restrict the use of company devices with third party computers • Track who is using all company owned devices via a logging system and erase after use • Scan all devices with anti-malware software each time they are connected to a company computer

Chapter 20 Bigoil (AIA November 2004)

(a) External auditors must express considered opinions on the truth and fairness of financial statements. That means that they must make a host of judgements about 'technical' matters, even some that are of the complexity of the example of oil reserves. Auditors should have sufficient understanding of the business to be able to understand major events and issues, such as the process of valuing oil reserves.

The auditor's task is not to attach a value to the amount itself, but to form an opinion on the figures provided by management. The auditor can start by questioning the assumptions behind the recorded figure and by ensuring that they are consistent with accepted accounting practice. That does not necessarily require any specific technical expertise. The auditor can enhance the quality of such evidence by comparing findings from different sources. ISA 500 *Audit evidence* talks about the effects of corroboration. The auditor can ask different people engaged in the measurement or estimate to explain their reasoning and understanding. If each confirms the others' explanation then the auditor can have greater confidence that they are both being truthful and that they have an underlying basis for their figure.

The auditor can consider the extent to which assurances have been provided by management and can ask for written confirmation that these assurances have been given honestly and openly. ISA 580 *Written representations* makes it clear that obtaining such representations is not sufficient for gathering evidence in itself, but it does have the effect of focusing management's attention on the representations that they have made to the auditor. It would be a criminal offence to make such representations dishonestly or recklessly. That should be enough in itself to enhance the quality of the evidence obtained.

The auditor may be able to draw upon evidence provided by an external consultant. That should provide evidence of a nature that can be evaluated by a non-expert. For example, the auditor can consider the consultant's qualifications and experience, the consultant's independence and the relevance of the consultant's findings to the financial statements. In some cases, the auditor can consider obtaining an independent expert's opinion purely for audit purposes. This would only be necessary if the auditor cannot reach a satisfactory conclusion in other ways, but it is always an option if the auditor is faced with an issue that really does require technical expertise that he/she does not have. ISA 620 *Using the work of an auditor's expert* provides an indication of the work that can be done to rely on an expert's opinion.

(b) The auditor has a statutory duty to report on the truth and fairness of the financial statements. The shareholders also have a contractual right that the auditor will express an opinion. The auditor is not obliged to support the statements provided by management. It is perfectly acceptable to express a qualified opinion, or even to disclaim opinion altogether. This means that the auditor should not be deterred from making an honest report in uncertain circumstances.

The auditor has a moral duty to express an opinion. That is implied by the statutory protection given to the role of auditor and also by the fact that the auditor is the only independent professional who makes public assurances concerning most companies. If the auditor does not discharge this duty then it will affect shareholder confidence and could make a difficult situation such as the one described in the scenario even more difficult. Forcing the delay of the annual report will only make the uncertainty faced by the company even greater.

The revelations could have accounting implications though. Even though the oil reserves are not directly part of the financial statements, the fact that their quantity has been downgraded could have implications for the valuation of extraction rights according to the statement of financial position. This problem should lead to an impairment review, even though the asset may not actually be impaired in terms of IAS 36 *Impairment of assets*. The auditor would be justified in seeking a delay in order to ensure that such a review had been conducted and its findings taken into account in the financial statements.

The auditor also has a problem because of 'deep pockets'. Historically, events that have affected share prices have tended to be blamed on auditors. One reason for this is that the auditor might be the only person associated with the event who has sufficient wealth to make it worthwhile seeking damages. While this is not necessarily a valid reason to withhold the auditor's report, the auditor cannot really be criticised for taking reasonable steps to protect his reputation and reduce exposure to litigation. A short delay might enable the problems with the oil reserves to be both resolved by the company and assimilated by the shareholders so that the publication of the financial statements does not become associated with this controversy.

Finally, if the auditor really does not wish to express an opinion on the financial statements then it is possible to resign and leave the company free to appoint a replacement. It would possibly be rather irresponsible to do so at this stage of the financial year, but it would be more honest to resign and to make the various declarations associated with resignations than it would be to merely delay reporting indefinitely.

ANSWERS TO END OF CHAPTER QUESTIONS

Practice question bank

1 Zapp

You are the partner in charge of the external audit of Zapp, a company that manufactures textiles for the garment industry. Zapp specialises in weaving and dying cotton for companies who manufacture T-shirts and similar items for major retailers.

The audit manager in charge of Zapp's audit has left the following voicemail on your mobile phone:

'I need to speak with you urgently concerning the Zapp audit.

The final audit work is almost complete. We have four members of staff working at the company's head office, Terry Jones and three assistants.

The audit staff are all using their laptop computers to record the audit working papers using the firm's standard filing system. The files on all four machines are synchronised at 5.00pm every evening and Terry backs his copy of the working papers up to our office server using an encrypted internet link.

Yesterday morning, one of the audit assistants left her laptop in the office that had been set aside for the use of the audit team while she spoke to the chief accountant. The laptop was secured to the desk with a reinforced cable that was looped round a metal water pipe and attached to the laptop's security slot. When she returned the laptop was gone. Somebody had cut through the reinforced cable with a pair of bolt cutters and had taken the laptop. Zapp's management have denied that their employees would have stolen the laptop and claim that it must have been taken by an intruder. The audit assistant had locked the door when she left and there was no sign of damage to the door or the lock when she returned.

The laptop had a complete set of the current audit working papers both for this year and for last year's audit.

I had a telephone call from Zapp's finance director this afternoon. He wished to discuss a change of accounting policy for the recognition of revenue. Judging from some of the things that he said, I wondered whether he had read the copy of last year's audit working papers on the missing laptop. Basically, he was keen to reopen the discussion that we had last year concerning the recognition of revenue from sales to large customers.

Could you please read through item 47 in last year's points for partner's attention and then call me back as soon as you are free?'

The audit manager was referring to the following note that was contained in last year's audit file:

Accounting policy

I had a very long and difficult meeting with the finance director concerning the recognition of sales revenue. He believes that sales can be booked in advance of the despatch of goods to customers. He has prepared the following table using the recognition criteria set out in IFRS 15 *Revenue from contracts with customers*:

(a)	The entity has a present right to payment for the asset;	Zapp buys cotton yarn on a just in time basis to meet its production requirements. All goods are made to meet very specific customer orders. There is no significant risk of ownership to Zapp because the goods are manufactured immediately after receipt of the yarn and are then shipped immediately.
(b)	The customer has legal title to the asset;	Zapp's finance director does not believe that the company ever has any involvement with the goods. They are quickly made to order and despatched immediately.

(c)	The entity has transferred physical possession of the asset;	Zapp's largest customers place orders once every three months for the forthcoming three months' deliveries. These orders specify delivery dates that are phased throughout the period and Zapp invoices for goods once they have been despatched. These orders are very specific about the quantity, quality and price of the goods and so Zapp can predict the revenue from each of these orders very reliably.
(d)	The customer has the significant risks and rewards related to ownership of the asset; and	The customers placing these large orders rarely request changes after the order has been placed.
(e)	The customer has accepted the asset.	Zapp has expert buyers who study the commodity markets for cotton yarn on a constant basis. There are futures markets that enable Zapp to fix prices for cotton yarn in advance in order to reduce the risks associated with price increases.

The finance director believes that Zapp should be permitted to recognise revenues and profits immediately on receipt of a three month order from a large customer. That is a change from the current policy of recognising sales and costs as and when the goods are despatched and invoiced.

I have to say, that I found it difficult to disagree with the finance director's interpretation of IFRS 15.

Partner's response

I agree that we should resist this proposal to recognise profits as soon as an order has been received, although I would find it difficult to argue against the finance director's logic. He has clearly read IFRS 15 very carefully.

Your firm has a policy of issuing all audit staff with laptops. The firm's staff procedures manual contains the following section on laptop security:

Laptop security

Each member of the audit department is issued with a laptop computer, for which he or she is personally responsible.

- The firm's Information Services department sets up the power management settings on each laptop before it is issued. All laptops are set to go into sleep mode after two minutes' inactivity. Audit staff are not permitted to interfere with the setting that puts their laptops into sleep mode.

- When a laptop is in sleep mode it can only be reactivated by the input of a user password. Each member of staff is to set a secure password for awakening a laptop from sleep mode. Passwords must be at least eight characters long and must include at least two numbers.

- Laptops are to be backed up to the office server on a daily basis, both to prevent the loss of files and to enable prompt and efficient review.

- It is recognised that it would be impractical for staff to have physical custody of laptops at all times during the working day. It is permissible to leave a laptop in a locked office provided only members of the audit team have access to that office and provided the laptop is secured to a solid object or fitting using an approved security cable.

Required

(a) Draft a memo to your firm's managing partner that:

  (i) Evaluates the difficulties that could arise for the audit firm if Zapp's directors have had access to the audit assistant's laptop and recommend responses to those difficulties.

  (8 marks)

  (ii) Recommends, stating reasons, the steps that the audit firm should take if the audit manager's ongoing investigations suggest that Zapp's directors are likely to have stolen the audit assistant's laptop. **(6 marks)**

(b) Evaluate the arguments set out by Zapp's finance director in the table which purports to show that Zapp can recognise revenues and profits whenever an order is received. **(11 marks)**

(c) Advise the audit partner of the potential quality management implications of having the audit staff upload their working papers to the firm's server on a daily basis. **(9 marks)**

(d) Evaluate the potential strengths and weaknesses associated with the audit firm's laptop security procedures. **(8 marks)**

(e) Zapp's management has indicated that this year it intends to include performance information, including KPIs, in this year's strategic report. Advise the audit partner of the likely impact of this on this year's audit. **(8 marks)**

(Total 50 marks)

2 Beetown office

An audit firm has several offices in its home country. The firm has recently been involved in a major scandal involving the partner in charge of its Beetown office.

The partner in question has been studying the audit working papers of the office's publicly traded clients. He has been looking for information that might affect the company's share price. For example, the draft financial statements of one major client showed a much higher profit than had been expected. He told his brother about this and his brother bought shares in the company before the financial statements were published. The share price rose when the profits were announced and the brother sold the shares immediately at a large profit, which he shared with the audit partner.

This behaviour was only uncovered when the stock exchange's investigations department identified the unusual patterns of the brother's trades.

The audit partner has been charged with the criminal offence of insider trading. The case has not yet gone to trial, but it has attracted a great deal of publicity because of the fact that it involves a qualified accountant in a senior position within the accountancy profession.

The audit firm itself has not yet taken any action, but the partners plan to hold a meeting in order to decide how best to proceed.

Required

(a) Advise the partners on the importance of professional confidentiality. **(10 marks)**

(b) Recommend, stating reasons, the actions that the firm should take in order to protect its reputation in response to the charges that have been made against the partner. **(11 marks)**

(c) Identify the situations in which an accountant's duty of confidentiality may be breached. **(4 marks)**

(Total 25 marks)

3 Radletts (AIA November 2015)

Helen Majors is the engagement partner for the professional firm Radletts in charge of the external audit of Plover. Plover operates ten restaurants in Capital City and its surrounding towns.

The Audit Manager in charge of the audit team conducting the external audit fieldwork at Plover has emailed Helen to seek her advice:

From: Charles Denton (C.Denton@Radletts.com)
To: Helen Majors (H.Majors@Radletts.com)
Subject: Plover audit

I have been reviewing the minutes of Plover's monthly board meetings. I am quite concerned about the following extract, from a meeting dated 16 April 2015:

'The board noted that the Capital City planning department has reversed its previous opposition to the expansion of the Grove Street restaurant. The submission of a report commissioned from Torvil Architects was sufficient to persuade the planning department that all relevant planning regulations had been complied with.'

I have two big concerns about this minute. Firstly, Torvil Architects is owned by Mr Vega, who is also a very senior member of the Capital City Council. Secondly, the fee paid for this report was $200,000. I have examined a copy of it and it consists of an eight page memo signed by Mr Vega which explains why he believes that the Planning Department should withdraw its objections. The report shows no evidence of any significant work on the part of Torvil Architects' professional staff. I believe that Plover has bribed Mr Vega to support its application.

Please advise on whether you require any further work to be done on this and, if so, what I should do.

Capital City is located in a country that has legislation that is based on the UK's Bribery Act 2010, with identical provisions.

Required

Draft a response from Helen to Charles that:

(a) Identifies the auditor's responsibilities in relation to non-compliance with laws and regulations.

(5 marks)

(b) Advises on the audit significance of Charles' concerns. **(8 marks)**

(c) Advises on the work that the audit team should undertake on this payment, stating reasons.

(8 marks)

Professional points for clarity of this report **(4 marks)**

(Total 25 marks)

4 Forgewood (AIA May 2016)

The Forgewood charity provides medical aid to areas in developing countries that have been affected by disasters. It has 25 full-time employees, who receive salaries that are in line with their qualifications and experience. The charity owns a building that has both office space and space for storage of equipment and relief supplies.

The charity aims to respond quickly to events. For example, an earthquake could leave a large number of people without food or medical care. Forgewood would charter a plane and would load it with basic supplies such as bottled water, rice, medical supplies and so on and would fly those out immediately. The hope would be to offer immediate assistance while larger charities and governments are working on organising longer-term support.

Forgewood raises funding by making public appeals. The charity's website has a link that can be used to make payments using credit cards and some donors make regular monthly payments using bank transfers. Forgewood also has a small number of corporate sponsors who tend to make annual gifts.

Forgewood is based in a country that does not require charities of Forgewood's size to have an audit. Instead, charities such as Forgewood are required to have an 'independent examination' which requires an independent examiner to review the bookkeeping records to ensure that the charity's financial statements are consistent with them. The independent examiner is asked to provide only a 'negative assurance' that no evidence of fraud or malpractice has been found. The independent examiner is not expected to vouch for or check any transactions unless there is reason to believe that an irregularity may exist, in which case the examiner would be required to investigate further.

Forgewood's independent examination is carried out by a firm of accountants, who undertake the work on a voluntary basis, charging no fees. They have never suspected fraud or malpractice and so they have rarely conducted any detailed testing of the bookkeeping records.

Forgewood's board believes that the charity's financial statements would be more credible if the charity commissioned a full external audit. The charity prepares accruals-based financial statements and complies with all relevant International Financial Reporting Standards. They have approached the partner responsible for their independent examination to undertake the external audit. In preparation for the audit, the board has undertaken a thorough review of Forgewood's control systems.

Required

(a) Advise the partner in charge of the independent examination of the matters that should be considered in deciding whether it would be appropriate to accept appointment as Forgewood's external auditor. **(12 marks)**

(b) Critically evaluate the difficulties faced by Forgewood's board in designing an efficient and effective system of internal control over revenues and expenses. You should indicate how those difficulties would be overcome. **(13 marks)**

(Total 25 marks)

5 Lamara (AIA May 2016 Amended)

Lamara is an accountancy firm that provides audit and other accountancy services. The firm is presently involved in a legal case in which it has been threatened with legal action concerning an audit investigation.

In November 2015, Lamara was asked to prepare a report on interim financial statements for the ten months to 31 December 2015 for Glora Enterprises ('Glora'). Glora manufactures gearboxes for wind turbines. Lamara was appointed by Jedfry, a manufacturer of wind turbines. Jedfry had negotiated terms for the purchase of 100% of Glora's issued shares on that date, subject to a satisfactory due diligence audit of the financial statements that were being prepared for the ten months ended 31 December 2015.

Lamara issued an engagement letter to Jedfry, the terms of which stated the following:

- Lamara would audit the figures in the statement of profit or loss for the ten months ended 31 December 2015 and the statement of financial position as at that date.

- Lamara would issue a non-statutory report, addressed to Jedfry on those financial statements.

- Lamara's standard terms and conditions would apply in the interpretation of the contract between Lamara and Jedfry. A copy of those terms and conditions was attached.

The agreed reporting date for this assignment was 16 January 2016. On that date, Lamara delivered an unmodified audit report in a non-statutory format. The report stated that it was prepared in order to assist Jedfry in its negotiation with Glora's shareholders. It also stated that Lamara's liability with respect to this assignment would be restricted to the first $250,000 of any claim.

Lamara's terms and conditions state that the firm is not liable for losses arising from reliance on its reports, unless a specific agreement has been reached to the contrary. The terms and conditions document is 8 pages long and contains 42 numbered paragraphs, including the paragraph denying liability.

The acquisition of Glora was completed on 30 January 2016 and Jedfry's accountants have subsequently studied the company's books closely. They have discovered that there was a serious problem with cut-off as at 31 December 2015. Several large sales that occurred in January 2016 had been recorded as December sales. This went undiscovered because Lamara did not conduct a direct confirmation of trade receivables because of the limited amount of time before the reporting date. Instead, Lamara vouched a sample of trade receivables to the invoices making up the total receivable and agreeing those details to Glora's despatch records and customer orders. It is now clear that Glora's staff had been ordered to predate the despatch records for several major sales.

Jedfry's accountants believe that they would have paid $1 million less for Glora if the financial statements had not contained this irregularity.

The applicable laws on auditor liability, including case law, are similar to those applying in the UK.

Required

Jedfry's chief executive has asked you, the company's chief accountant, to draft a report that:

(a) Identifies the components of a system of quality management that an audit firm is required to put in place. **(4 marks)**

(b) Advises on the quality of work undertaken by Lamara on trade receivables and revenue. **(8 marks)**

(c) Advises on the likelihood of damages being awarded against Lamara in the event that a court agrees that the firm was negligent. **(9 marks)**

Professional points for clarity of this report **(4 marks)**

(Total 25 marks)

6 Lion Manufacturing

Assume it is 2016. Lion Manufacturing ('Lion') is a large publicly traded company. The company's directors are firm believers in transparency and in honest and accurate financial reporting. Lion has won several awards for publishing clear and informative financial statements.

The convener of Lion's audit committee has scheduled a meeting to discuss the European Union rules on audit reform.

Lion's directors are interested in the rules to introduce mandatory rotation of audit firms. The new rules force public interest entities to put their audit out to tender every ten years and to rotate the audit firm at least every 20 years.

The convener has drafted the following briefing paper as a basis for discussion by the members of the audit committee:

- Lion's present external auditor is a major audit firm whose first appointment was in 2012. We have reappointed the same firm annually ever since. We have always had very good service from this firm and feedback from our stakeholders suggests that the firm is considered to be credible and so our financial statements appear to be regarded as reliable.

- The audit firm rotates audit partners every four or five years. We always have the opportunity to meet with the replacement partner before he or she takes over the audit. In theory, we could request that someone else be assigned, but we have never felt it necessary to do so.

- Rotation of audit firms will involve a number of costs. I have also read some research reports which suggest that 'audit failures' frequently occur in the first few years of an audit firm's appointment, so there could be concerns that we will receive a poorer service.
- It is anticipated that big data, and data analytics in particular, are likely to change the audit profession in the future. It would be helpful if the committee were informed of developments in this area.

I look forward to discussing these matters further at our next meeting.

Required

(a) Critically analyse the implications of mandatory rotation of audit firms for the independence of Lion's external auditor. **(10 marks)**

(b) Critically analyse the implications of mandatory rotation of audit firms for the quality of audit work. **(10 marks)**

(c) Explain what the term 'data analytics' means, and discuss current thinking about their anticipated impact on the auditing profession. **(5 marks)**

(Total 25 marks)

7 Zando (AIA November 2014 amended)

Zando is one of the largest accountancy firms in its home country. Zando has several hundred partners and has offices in every major city in its home country.

In April 2006 the firm completed the audit of Paper for the year ended 31 March 2006. Paper was a parent company that had several lines of retail business. One of Paper's biggest subsidiaries was Vowcher, a company that helped customers who had low incomes to save for family holidays. Customers used to deposit monthly cash instalments with Vowcher. Every 12 months, each customer would receive a holiday voucher that could be used to pay for a holiday with a large chain of travel agents that was independent of the Paper Group. Vowcher did not pay any interest on the monthly deposits, but the company had negotiated a discount for its customers from the travel agent. Customers were generally happy with this arrangement because they found it a convenient means of saving.

Most of Vowchers' customers redeemed their vouchers in July and August every year. The travel agency then invoiced Vowcher for the redemption of the vouchers and so Vowcher's cash flows were generally positive throughout the year from customers' monthly instalments, with substantial outflows in the months of July, August and September.

Paper had several other subsidiaries, all of which operated on a more traditional retailing model than Vowcher. The subsidiaries were growing rapidly and needed substantial cash injections to maintain their solvency. Paper drew upon Vowcher's bank balance to fund the other group members. In return, the group companies all guaranteed Vowcher's liabilities.

In May 2006 the directors of Paper realised that the Paper Group had insufficient cash at its disposal to meet the cost of the holiday vouchers that were due to be issued to Vowcher's customers. Paper's chief executive had been in poor health for much of the previous twelve months and the company's strategic management had suffered. Paper Group members had been permitted to grow too rapidly. Attempts to negotiate a bank loan and to seek a postponement of the payments to the travel agent were unsuccessful. Vowcher went into liquidation in May 2006 before the issue of that year's holiday vouchers. The remainder of the group was also wound up shortly afterwards. None of Vowcher's customers received any of the funds that had been deposited with the company.

This case attracted substantial criticism in the press and from government. Vowcher's customers generally had very little money and most were unable to have a holiday that year.

Zando's regulatory body conducted a thorough investigation of the audit of the Paper Group. This investigation resulted in a report that was published in March 2014. The regulator criticised the engagement partner, who retired from public practice in 2008, for failing to recognise the going concern problems faced by the Paper Group in general and Vowcher in particular. Zando was also criticised for failing to supervise the engagement partner correctly. The engagement partner was fined $50,000 and Zando was fined $500,000.

Required

(a) Critically evaluate the implications of these fines for the credibility of Zando and also for the credibility of the accountancy profession. **(12 marks)**

(b) Critically evaluate the fact that the report was not published until March 2014, despite the events occurring in 2006. **(8 marks)**

(c) Explain the impact that a company being in going concern difficulties will have on its auditor's report. **(5 marks)**

(Total 25 marks)

8 Ethics committee (AIA November 2014 amended)

An audit firm has 15 partners and a single office. The firm employs almost 200 staff. None of the firm's clients are publicly traded companies.

The firm has an ethics committee that reviews matters relating to professional standards. The committee discusses both specific cases and is responsible for the maintenance of the firm's own policies and procedures that operate in parallel with the IESBA *Code of Ethics for Professional Accountants*.

Two cases have been placed on the agenda for the next meeting of the ethics committee, the first involves a retiring partner's acceptance of an appointment with an audit client and the second relates to complaints by a continuing partner following her most recent annual appraisal.

The first case arose when Frank retired recently at the age of 55. It is firm policy that partners should retire at that age in order to maintain a healthy progression of new partners into the firm. Partners retire with a generous pension and are free to carry on working for somebody else if they wish to do so, or to relax and enjoy their retirement.

Frank had been the engagement partner on the audit of Hoss, one of the audit firm's largest clients. Shortly after Frank's retirement, Hoss announced that he would be joining the company as their new finance director. Frank had completed the audit of Hoss for the year ended 31 March 2014 in June of that year. Barry had taken over as engagement partner at that point, with a view to avoid a change of engagement partner during the year ended 31 March 2015.

This is the first time that the audit firm has had an outgoing partner join an audit client and the ethics committee has been asked to consider the implications of this event.

The second matter arises from a complaint from Hannah, who was admitted to partnership just over two years ago. The firm has a policy of annual appraisals for all professional staff, including partners. Hannah's appraisal was conducted by a senior partner. Hannah received positive feedback on all areas of her performance apart from 'practice development'. The partner conducting her evaluation complained that she had not persuaded any of the audit clients for which she is responsible to offer the firm any non-audit appointments, such as tax planning. Hannah's response was that she objected to being evaluated on this criterion and she has written to the ethics committee to ask that it be removed from the evaluation of audit partners.

Required

(a) Advise the ethics committee on the implications of Frank's appointment to the board of Hoss.

(15 marks)

(b) Advise the ethics committee on an appropriate response to the points raised by Hannah.

(10 marks)

(Total 25 marks)

9 Rocco

Rocco is a partner in GHY, an audit firm. GHY has four offices, each of which is located in a major city in the firm's home country. GHY is one of the six largest accounting firms in each of the cities in which it has offices.

Rocco has been a partner in GHY's Southtown office for two years. He has been with the firm for a total of ten years, having trained with GHY after graduating from university. He has specialised in audit throughout his time with GHY.

GHY has provided Viper PLC ('Viper') with external audit and other services for seven years. The firm is about to accept nomination for an eighth year, having recently completed the audit for the year ended 31 January 2014. Sarah, the engagement partner, has just completed her second year as partner in charge of Viper's external audit. Alan has just completed his fifth year as engagement quality review partner. Alan will now step down from the Viper audit because GHY has a policy that no audit partner should be associated with any client's audit for more than five consecutive years. GHY has appointed Rocco to replace Alan for the audit of the financial statements for the year ended 31 January 2015.

Rocco has studied the audit files from the previous year's audit of Viper and has met with Sarah and Alan. He has expressed the following concerns about GHY's ability to continue with this audit:

- The Viper audit generates 4% of GHY's total fee income, but that equals 14% of the Southtown office's fee income.

- Reviewing the time budgets for the year ended 31 January 2014, the audit staff were required to work significant amounts of overtime in order to complete the audit. Ideally, an additional member of staff would have been added to the audit team, but none was available because of other client commitments.

- GHY audit staff spend so much time at Viper's head office that a room has been set aside at Viper's head office for the exclusive use of the audit team. This room has four desks and members of the audit team joke that they spend more time there than at GHY's office.

- Viper's finance director is becoming increasingly interested in 'financial engineering', with the firm issuing increasingly complicated financial instruments in order to raise finance. During the year ended 31 January 2014 it was necessary for Sarah and Alan to meet with a panel of GHY's partners to discuss the suitability of Viper's proposed accounting treatment of preference shares that had been issued in order to raise long term finance. The bank who had advised on the issue of these shares had assured Viper's finance director that they should be accounted for as equity, but GHY's partners had agreed, after considerable discussion, that the preference shares should be classified as debt.

- Viper's finance director has asked Sarah to set some time aside in the next few weeks for a meeting to discuss GHY's views on a new financial instrument that the firm is developing in conjunction with its bank.

- Rocco's concerns have been passed to GHY's managing partner, who is based in the firm's Capital City branch. She has commended Rocco for his courage in raising these concerns. She has asked him to produce a briefing paper that discusses the issues associated with the decision to continue with Viper or to stand down, both positive and negative. She believes that the briefing paper should cover both GHY's independence and the audit risks associated with Viper's use of complicated financial instruments.

Required

Draft a briefing paper for Rocco's attention which:

(a) Advises GHY's partners of the factors that should be taken into account in determining GHY's independence of Viper **(10 marks)**

(b) Advises GHY's partners of the audit risks associated with continuing to audit Viper **(11 marks)**

Professional marks to be awarded for the clarity of the briefing note and its relevance to the managing partner's requirements. **(4 marks)**

(Total 25 marks)

10 Farr Hume

Farr Hume is an audit firm with 15 partners. It is the largest independent firm in the city in which it is based. The managing partner of Farr Hume has been approached by the trustees of Hunger Relief, an international charity that is based in Farr Hume's home city. Hunger Relief raises money using television and newspaper advertising to seek donations from the general public. The cash that is raised is used to purchase food and medicine for distribution to poor people in developing countries.

Hunger Relief has been growing steadily and is now too large for its present external audit firm to provide an adequate service. The trustees have approached three much larger firms, including Farr Hume, to invite them to tender for the audit.

The financial statements contained in Hunger Relief's annual report are prepared in accordance with IFRS Accounting Standards and the external auditor's report complies with the requirements of ISA 700. The annual report also includes a description of the charitable activities undertaken by Hunger Relief and the external auditor reports on the financial aspects of that report. For example, the external auditor confirms that funds reported as having been applied to the charity's works have actually been spent on those activities.

The trustees of Hunger Relief have indicated that they need to pay a normal commercial rate for the charity's external audit, otherwise it will have very little credibility to stakeholders. They have reached an agreement with their previous auditor that the firm will pay a very substantial donation to Hunger Relief after receiving payment for the external audit. That donation is generally for most of the audit fee, with a small amount being retained to cover for out of pocket expenses. This arrangement is not made public, although all of the trustees are aware of it.

The trustees have indicated that they would particularly welcome a tender from Farr Hume because the firm's junior staff organise an annual fundraising event for the charity.

Required

(a) Advise the partners of Farr Hume on the factors that they will have to take into account in deciding whether to tender for the Hunger Relief audit. Your advice should not take account of the fact that the trustees have asked for a substantial annual donation. **(15 marks)**

(b) Advise the partners of Farr Hume on whether it is acceptable for them to agree to repay most of the external audit fee to Hunger Relief as an annual donation. **(10 marks)**

(Total 25 marks)

11 Journal

You are the partner in charge of the external audit of Journal, a major multinational media group. Your firm has audited the company's financial statements for the past 20 years and this is your third year as partner in charge of the audit.

Journal's chairman, Mr Ed Blanc, is a French national. Journal's chief executive is Mr James Blanc, Ed Blanc's nephew. The group's holding company is registered in the capital city of your home country and its financial statements are prepared in accordance with International Financial Reporting Standards. The company was established in the distant past by Ed Blanc and has since been floated on the stock exchange. Ed Blanc retains a significant shareholding in the company and he uses that to ensure that James Blanc retains his place as chief executive.

Journal has two main operating divisions: newspapers and internet communications. The newspaper division publishes major newspapers in 17 different countries. The newspaper division contributes 60% of Journal's revenues and 45% of profit before tax and interest. The internet communications division provides subscriber-based information to readers across the world. Content is drawn from the newspapers and from other sources. The internet division contributes 40% of Journal's revenues and 55% of profit before tax and interest.

Journal has recently been involved in a major scandal surrounding one of its European newspapers. The editor of that newspaper has been found guilty of bribing police officers to provide information about ongoing criminal investigations and also private details of individuals such as the home addresses of entertainers and television actors. This information has been used to enable the newspaper to publish stories that would otherwise have been impossible to print. Many of those stories were intrusive and there has been a very negative reaction to the editor's conviction.

James Blanc attempted to minimise the impact of this scandal by pointing out that much of the information gathered was used to publish stories that were in the public interest. For example, one of the newspaper's most important stories concerned a corrupt politician who might not have been brought to trial if it had not been for a Journal's newspaper applying pressure on the police by publishing details of the allegations. That argument did not restore confidence in the newspaper and many of the large companies who purchased advertising space in it cancelled their contracts, although they continued to advertise in other newspapers published by Journal.

Ed Blanc announced that the newspaper would cease publication, even though it was very profitable and had sold well for many years. He pointed out that this would have very little impact of Journal's profits because it provided only 2% of group revenues and less than 1% of group profits.

Ed Blanc also announced the appointment of a former senior politician as an additional non-executive director. This new director will take direct responsibility for reviewing the moral and ethical issues arising from Journal's editorial policies.

These events occurred during the final stages of the external audit for the year ended 30 April 2012. The draft financial statements are being finalised. The head of the audit committee has already indicated that your firm will be asked to continue to audit Journal.

You have received an email from your firm's managing partner:

managingpartner@firm.com

Re: Journal audit

23 May 2012

To: auditpartner@firm.com

I note that we have been asked whether we wish to be nominated for a further term of office on the Journal audit. This is a difficult question because it is clearly one of our largest clients. I can see that almost 10% of your office's chargeable hours in the past year were charged to the Journal audit. I can also see that Journal's directors have generally been happy with our work and have been prepared to pay for all of the time that has been charged to this account. My difficulty is in deciding whether those matters are sufficient to justify the retention of this audit when considered from the perspective of the firm as a whole.

PRACTICE QUESTION BANK

Could you please address both the ethical and the commercial implications of our continued involvement with this client. These should take account of the recent publicity attaching to the company. I would appreciate your thoughts on whether we should continue to act for Journal. I plan to raise this matter with the firm's managing committee and I will include your views in our deliberations.

Required

Draft a response to the managing partner's email. Your response should:

(a) Evaluate the implications of Journal's governance arrangements for the external audit of the group's financial statements. **(12 marks)**

(b) Critically analyse the arguments for and against continuing as external auditor of Journal. **(13 marks)**

(Total 25 marks)

12 Openness principle

An audit firm's partners have met in order to discuss the governance of their firm. In order to prompt discussion, the partners have obtained a copy of a document that is intended to offer guidance on governance for the largest audit firms in a particular country. The firm is not subject to the requirements of that code, but the partners believe that the guidance offered by the code is of interest to a wider range of firms than the defined readership.

The document offers the following guidance under the heading 'openness principle':

A firm should maintain a culture of openness which encourages people to consult and share problems, knowledge and experience in order to achieve quality work in a way that properly takes the public interest into consideration.

The firm's managing partner has had a long and distinguished career with the firm. She believes that the openness principle should be implemented across the firm in any and every possible way. Unfortunately, her experience suggests that it is extremely difficult to ensure that staff and partners are motivated to behave in the manner indicated by the principle.

As an example, the managing partner made a rather worrying discovery when reviewing the working papers of a major client that was the direct responsibility of a junior partner within the firm. The audit team had been supervised by one of the firm's most senior audit managers in order to compensate for the partner's relative lack of experience at this level. The audit manager had uncovered two issues for the partner's attention:

- The first was that the audit team had tended to describe any problems associated with the evaluation of inherent risk in very positive and optimistic terms. For example, a board minute concerning a loan application being made by the company had been summarised in the audit working papers and all of the stress in this summary had been on the fact that the directors were confident that the loan would be granted. The member of the audit staff who had prepared this summary then recommended that no specific action should be taken as a result of this application.

- The second issue was an email from the audit manager to the audit partner in charge of the audit concerning a complex accounting judgement that appeared to have been biased. The audit partner had replied immediately to state that the matter was under review, but no further correspondence took place and the audit manager simply accepted the company's figures without any further discussion.

The managing partner is not so much concerned about these specific observations or about this particular audit. She is worried that there may be a lack of openness generally in the workings of the audit firm.

Required

(a) Evaluate the difficulties associated with implementing the openness principle within an audit firm. **(12 marks)**

(b) Evaluate the problems that will arise from any failure to implement the principle. **(13 marks)**

(Total 25 marks)

13 Garrity (AIA November 2015)

Garrity is a small airline that provides local flights within its home country. In common with other airlines, Garrity's biggest operating expense is aviation fuel. Garrity has been growing steadily and it purchases one or two new aircraft every year.

Susanna, Garrity's Finance Director, has always been responsible for the day to day financial management of the company, but she believes that it would be better to employ a corporate treasurer, supported by a treasury department. The treasurer's role will include the management of cash flows and also the management of the financial risks arising from volatility in the price of aviation fuel.

At present, Susanna spends a great deal of time managing financial risks faced by Garrity. She does this mainly by buying and selling financial instruments that can manage Garrity's exposure to factors such as the price of settling a US Dollar or Euro payment for a new plane or to volatility in the price of aviation fuel. Susanna has developed a deep understanding of these risks and their implications for Garrity, which is important because it is not always desirable to eliminate every risk. Leaving Garrity exposed to risk can mean that a new aeroplane is cheaper if the Dollar or Euro weakens or that its operating costs are reduced if the price of fuel falls.

Susanna has proposed creating a new treasury department that will free her to focus more on strategic management, as is appropriate for a board member. This department will comprise an experienced treasurer, who will be recruited from outside, supported by an administrative team. In order to make this new department a success, the board will have to grant the treasurer a great deal of flexibility in terms of buying and selling financial instruments.

Garrity's board agrees with the idea of establishing a corporate treasury in the manner suggested by Susanna, but they are concerned that the new treasurer will be liable to expose the company to undue risk. They are particularly concerned about the 'rogue trader' scenario in which a senior manager speculates with his or her employer's resources and leaves the employer exposed to undue risks. For example, the treasurer could take a position that would generate significant profits for Garrity if, say, the Euro falls in value. Such a position could leave the company exposed to major risks in the event that the Euro rises. Companies have been forced out of business by such unauthorised speculation.

Required

(a) Advise Garrity's board as to how best to communicate the company's 'appetite' for risk to the new treasurer, so that the treasurer knows which risk exposures to eliminate and which to accept.
(10 marks)

(b) Advise Garrity's board as to the manner in which the board might control the activities of the treasury department in order to address the 'rogue trader' threat. **(15 marks)**

(Total 25 marks)

14 Trent

Trent is an audit firm that has three offices. The firm has a total of 18 partners, 10 of whom are based at the firm's main office, with another 5 at the Eastown office and the remaining 3 at Westown.

Trent has a policy of conducting regular reviews of audit quality. All three offices are relatively quiet during the summer months and so it is possible to set aside time for audit partners and audit managers to conduct cold reviews of samples of audit files for assignments that have been completed during the previous year.

A review team comprising a partner and manager has been sent from the main office to the Westown office. The team members selected a small number of audits, including the audit of Spare, a small company that carries out repairs on office equipment. Spare was chosen partly because it is one of the smallest audits undertaken by the Westown office and by Trent as a whole.

The review team are concerned with the audit file on Spare for two reasons:

- Frank, the partner in charge of the audit of Spare, has insisted that the audit team undertake an audit that relies very heavily upon detailed substantive testing. Frank's view is that Spare is too small to justify a heavy investment in the review of inherent risk. The fact that it is a small company also means that the systems of internal control are not particularly good.

- The audit working papers indicate that most of the planned detailed testing was completed, but that some of the tests associated with the existence of non-current assets were not completed. Spare's engineers all have company vans and they are equipped with specialised tools that are extremely expensive. The engineers work at clients' premises and their vans and other equipment are rarely available for a physical inspection during normal working hours. Frank authorised the audit team to cut short its detailed testing on property, plant and equipment and stated that the fact that inherent risk would have been classified as low if it had been evaluated meant that there was little need to conduct full substantive tests on every balance.

The review team is dissatisfied with Frank's decisions concerning the approach to the audit of Spare. Frank disagrees with their concerns and has asked them to put their arguments in writing so that he can prepare a formal response.

Required

Draft a memo from the partner in charge of the review team to Frank that:

(a) Critically evaluates the decision to undertake the audit of Spare on a substantive test basis.

(12 marks)

(b) Critically evaluates the decision to reduce the detailed testing carried out on Spare's company vans and engineers' equipment. **(13 marks)**

(Total 25 marks)

15 Payne Engineering (AIA May 2015 amended)

Payne Engineering is a major multinational corporation. The company's internal audit function is located at head office, although there are regional offices in each of the countries in which Payne Engineering operates.

Graham, a university student, spent last summer as an intern working in Payne Engineering's internal audit department. As part of his university course, he has written a report on the cultural issues affecting internal audit. The head of internal audit has requested a copy of the report and is concerned with some of Graham's findings.

Payne Engineering's internal audit investigations focus on compliance. Each investigation focuses on a specific range of procedures at a designated location. At the conclusion of the investigation, the audit team compiles a detailed report, with an executive summary that includes a checklist of the major procedures investigated. Each procedure is classified as 'green', 'amber' or 'red'.

- Green means that no material compliance errors were discovered. Immaterial errors will be recorded in the audit working papers and reported to the head of the department being audited, but will not be reflected in the auditor's report itself.

- Amber means that one or more material compliance failures was discovered in that procedure. The results will be reported to the head of the auditee department and will be described in the auditor's report, with a view to a follow-up visit to ensure that steps have been taken to ensure compliance in the future.

- Red means that a critical compliance failure has been discovered. A critical failure would mean that the company was exposed to the risk of fraud or major accounting error. These failures require the head of the auditee department to submit a separate report to Payne Engineering's senior management, explaining how the breach occurred and what steps have been taken to rectify matters.

Graham's report described his experience of participating in two investigations during his internship. Each was in a different auditee department and each was with a different team of internal auditors. Both auditor's reports were discussed with the head of the auditee department before being submitted and both were changed. In the first case, the audit team had listed four reds, six ambers and eleven greens. Three of the reds were reclassified as ambers and four of the ambers as greens. In the second audit three reds were downgraded to amber and two ambers to green.

Graham's report indicated that both internal audit teams regarded such behaviour as acceptable because it was not in the interests of the internal audit function to alienate auditees and that internal audit was intended to be a constructive service.

Required

(a) Critically evaluate Payne Engineering's policy of classifying compliance errors using this three point scale. **(12 marks)**

(b) Critically evaluate the argument that the internal audit team should be permitted to downgrade the scoring of compliance errors in order to avoid conflict. **(13 marks)**

(Total 25 marks)

16 Rasp

You are the partner in charge of the external audit of Rasp, an engineering company that is not publicly traded. You have just received the following email from the manager in charge of the audit:

From: Adam Lin <adam.lin@auditor.com>
To: Sally Lee <sally.lee@auditor.com>
Subject: Rasp – financial instruments

Hi Sally,

I am sorry to bother you this late on a Friday evening, but I have just had a meeting with Rasp's finance director and I am concerned about some of the issues that were raised. The agreed deadline for the finalisation of the financial statements and the completion of the audit is only one week away and the directors have only just decided to make a substantial change to the draft financial statements. It might be necessary for you to come out on Monday morning to discuss these changes. I am reluctant to suggest a delay in the completion of the auditor's report, but that is beginning to look like a possibility.

I have attached a copy of the financial instruments note to this email.

Problems have arisen with the accounting treatment of each of the two types of financial instruments held by Rasp.

Rasp's directors believe that the bonds, which have a current market value of $31 million, have been impaired. Rasp has held these bonds since they were issued at a discount 5 years ago. They carry a 5% coupon rate and have a further 10 years until they mature. On maturity they will be redeemed at their par value of $60 million.

The bonds were issued by one of Rasp's largest customers. The customer has recently cut back on its orders from Rasp and Rasp's sales director believes that the customer is experiencing some financial difficulties and has had to downsize its activities. Rasp's finance director is concerned that there may be a risk of default on the bond and has recommended that the bond be carried at an impairment value of $30 million. That figure is based on the current market value of the bond, with a slight adjustment to reflect Rasp's detailed knowledge of the bond issuer's business.

I do not believe that Rasp can justify an impairment adjustment on this basis unless the directors can demonstrate that there is objective evidence that future cash flows have been affected by some event. IFRS 9 does not permit an impairment adjustment on the basis of suspicions on the part of the bondholder.

The derivative financial instruments held by Rasp are bespoke derivatives that were created by negotiation between Rasp and the derivative counterparties. There are, therefore, no observable market values for these assets. The fair values have been determined by Rasp's accounting staff, using a recognised valuation model. The problem is that the results are significantly different from the market values for broadly similar derivatives that are traded on the exchanges. I have discussed this with both our own specialist consulting staff and with Rasp's finance director. Our consultants believe that Rasp's valuation model may have been mis-specified and that a more suitable model may be appropriate. Rasp's finance director is willing to have the derivatives independently valued, but has stressed that the timing is a potential issue. It would not be possible to brief a suitable valuer and receive a report in time to finalise the statements.

Our specialist consulting staff have confirmed that they could conduct a satisfactory valuation within 48 hours of being briefed. Rasp's finance director is aware of this and has no objection in principle to appointing our consultants. It is now up to you to decide how best to proceed with this.

I hope that this email does not ruin your weekend! I will check for any replies on Saturday and Sunday and will telephone you first thing on Monday morning in order to keep things moving.

Adam

The email had the following draft note attached (This note was drafted before the issue discussed above came to light):

Note 27 – Financial instruments

Carrying value and fair value of financial assets

	Amortised cost $m	Fair value $m	Carrying value $m
Bonds	39		39
Derivative financial instruments	—	90	90
	39	90	129

Fair value calculation methodology

Derivative financial instruments are forward contracts that are valued based on market rates and market-accepted models. Fair value for financial instruments held at amortised cost has been estimated by discounting cash flows at prevailing interest rates and by applying year end exchange rates.

All derivative financial instruments are in level 2 of the IFRS 7 fair value hierarchy.

The derivatives are designated as cash flow hedges.

	$m
Euro	30
Commodities – raw materials	60
	90

Changes in fair value are recognised directly in other comprehensive income, to the extent that they are effective, with the ineffective portion being recognised in the statement of profit or loss.

Rasp uses forward contracts to hedge Euro transaction currency risk (comprising revenues from sales denominated in the Euro) and commodity costs (comprising imports of raw materials and other costs associated with the acquisition and maintenance of equipment). Where these hedges are assessed as highly effective, gains and losses are deferred in other comprehensive income and transferred to the statement of profit or loss or cost of property, plant and equipment when the related cash flow occurs.

The cumulative net gains deferred in shareholders' equity are as follows:

	$m
Euro	8
Commodities – raw materials	17
	25

These gains are expected to mature within 12 months.

You have accessed the audit working papers electronically. The audit work on financial assets was undertaken by Paula, a qualified accountant who was in charge of the supervision of the audit work at Rasp.

Paula checked the calculations relating to the bonds and reviewed the bonds for impairment shortly after the year end. The calculations were correct and there was nothing to suggest that an impairment adjustment was necessary. There was a subsequent file note from Adam to indicate that the directors propose the impairment adjustment as an adjusting event after the reporting period. The file note expanded upon Adam's concern that an impairment adjustment is not justified.

Paula's working papers also indicated that a great deal of work had been undertaken on the valuation of the derivatives. Paula had raised this area as a matter for Adam's attention and there were several review points, each of which Paula had addressed. Paula had listed several valuation models that could have been used for this valuation exercise and had also listed the acceptable ranges for each of the assumptions that had to be made in order to obtain inputs for these models. Her conclusion was that Rasp's valuation could possibly be justified, but that their proposed figures were at the top end of an acceptable valuation. The working papers indicated that she had discussed her concerns with Adam and that Adam had discussed them with Rasp's finance director. You are satisfied that Paula and Adam have communicated properly with one another, but are dissatisfied with the responses that Adam has received from Rasp's finance director. Generally, the finance director has refused to make any changes and has failed to produce any evidence to support Rasp's proposed treatment of the financial assets. Adam has pressed for replies, but has received nothing of any value.

None of the proposed adjustments are reflected in the draft note shown above. All of the adjustments will be material.

Rasp's chief executive has contacted you recently to advise you that the directors have agreed to reappoint your firm as external auditor and has asked you to confirm that you will accept reappointment.

Required

(a) Prepare a briefing note for your firm's managing partner that evaluates the professional implications of using the audit firm's specialist consulting staff to advise on the valuation of the derivatives in the circumstances described by the audit manager. **(15 marks)**

(b) Advise the audit manager on the work that should have been undertaken on the valuation of the bonds held by Rasp and on the further work that should be undertaken on their possible impairment. **(15 marks)**

(c) Recommend, stating reasons, an appropriate form of auditor's report for Rasp, assuming that the issues that have been identified as problems by the audit manager are not addressed by Rasp. **(10 marks)**

(d) Evaluate the arguments for and against continuing to conduct Rasp's external audit. **(10 marks)**

(Total 50 marks)

17 Voltage group

Voltage Group arrangements for inter-company sales:

You are the partner in charge of the external audit of Volt, a company that supplies and fits car exhausts through a chain of 210 exhaust centres in Homeland, where both you and Volt are located.

Volt is a member of the Voltage Group, a multinational group of companies. All of the exhausts that Volt sells have been manufactured by Tubes, the Voltage Group's wholly owned manufacturing subsidiary. The arrangements for Volt's purchases are as follows:

- Tubes is located in the country of Sealand. Tubes manufactures all of the exhausts sold by the members of the Voltage Group.

- Tubes sells all of its output to Logistic, the Voltage Group's wholly owned distribution subsidiary, which is located in Pondland, a small island state in the Caribbean. Pondland has a very low rate of corporation tax.

- Logistic employs only six people, who operate a computer system that organises the logistics for the Voltage Group's worldwide operations. Whenever a retailing subsidiary, such as Volt, requires inventory it places an order with Logistic. Logistic then places an order with Tubes and Tubes delivers the exhausts directly to the retailing subsidiary. Legally, Tubes sells the exhausts to Logistic, who then resells them to the retailing subsidiary.

- Logistic pays Tubes only a little more than the manufacturing cost of the exhausts. It resells the exhausts to the retailing subsidiaries at only a little less than their retail selling prices. The overall effect is that Logistic is the only member of the Voltage Group to report a significant profit. That is to the group's advantage because those profits are taxed at Pondland's low rate.

Volt is a major company in your country, with very substantial revenues. The national press in Homeland has obtained Volt's annual reports and has discovered that Volt has not paid any tax in Homeland for at least five years. The company has not earned any taxable profits throughout that period. That has led to a consumer backlash, with many motorists choosing to buy their exhausts from Volt's competitors.

Your national government has tax law similar to that of the UK which means that transactions that have no commercial justification other than the avoidance of tax can be set aside. Volt does not believe that this legislation applies to its arrangements because the distribution company provides logistical support.

Volt has agreed to make a payment of $20 million of tax to Homeland as a 'goodwill gesture'. Homeland's tax authorities have announced that they will investigate Volt carefully with the intention of pressing for a much larger payment. Volt's draft financial statements show this $20 million as the only provision for corporation tax.

The tax authorities will not have completed their investigation before the deadline for the completion of the external audit that is under way.

Volt's directors have asked your firm's tax partner to assist them in their dealings with Homeland's tax authorities. That will be a separate appointment from the external audit and will be billed separately. The tax partner has been asked to advise on a strategy to avoid making any payment apart from the $20 million 'goodwill gesture'.

Required

(a) Recommend the audit work that should be undertaken on the provision for corporation tax in Volt's financial statements. **(12 marks)**

(b) Advise the tax partner on the ethical implications of agreeing to minimise Volt's tax liability. **(13 marks)**

(Total 25 marks)

18 Paloma (AIA November 2015 amended)

June is the partner in charge of the external audit of Paloma. Howard is the manager in charge of the external audit. At the initial planning stage of the audit, June instructed Howard to seek the support of Ken, the manager in charge of the audit firm's computer audit department. June has just placed the following review point on the audit file:

> 'I am concerned that there has been a lack of coordination over the audit of Paloma's IT systems. Ken's team appears to have done a good job of testing the operation of general IT controls, but have left the operation of information processing controls to Howard's auditors. A lot of Paloma's information processing controls depend on system generated information. For example, the payroll system prints out a list of all new members of staff added to the payroll during the latest processing cycle and that is signed by a supervisor in the Human Resources department in order to confirm that no invalid names have been added to the payroll. The audit team's only compliance test of this control has been to review the file of signed printouts. I don't feel that Howard's staff members have the necessary skills to test the operation of such controls effectively.'

Ken's response is as follows:

> 'I agree with June's concern that the compliance tests on the information processing controls were inadequate. Unfortunately, my department's brief was restricted to the general IT controls.'

Howard's response is as follows:

> 'All auditors are effectively IT auditors nowadays. Ken's computer audit specialists have very high hourly charge out rates and I decided that it was unnecessary for them to test the operation of the information processing controls. Paloma's control environment is strong and so I disagree that we needed to involve the computer audit specialists.'

Required

(a) Critically evaluate Ken's response that the compliance tests on Paloma's information processing controls were inadequate, using June's example of the payroll system to explain your answer. **(12 marks)**

(b) Critically evaluate Howard's arguments for restricting the amount spent on the compliance testing of Paloma's information processing controls. **(13 marks)**

(Total 25 marks)

19 Crank

Crank manufactures electronic components. The company's year-end is 31 May and the audit for the year ended 31 May 2012 is well under way.

The present audit was planned in June 2011. At that stage the audit partner and manager had assumed that the revenue for the year ended 31 May 2012 would be approximately $500 million and profits would be $40 million. The materiality threshold for testing purposes was determined in relation to those two figures and set at $4 million.

There were two interim audit visits and transactions recorded during the period from 1 June 2011 until 31 March 2012 were tested and no material irregularities were discovered. The external auditor used statistical testing techniques wherever it was possible to do so.

Throughout the year Crank's management accounts indicated that the company's performance was barely keeping up with the budgets that had been set at the start of the year by management. The budgets were updated and flexed during the year and the targets were progressively revised to a total revenue of $480 million and profit of $35 million.

In April 2012 the external audit team discovered that there were significant problems with cut-off. Most of Crank's sales are for goods made to specific order. The company's stated accounting policy is to invoice and record sales at the time the associated goods are despatched to customers. Throughout the second half of the year ended 31 May 2012 Crank's sales manager has been recording sales before the goods have been despatched in order to achieve budgeted sales targets. All of the sales recorded in this way were for goods that had been ordered by customers. The sales manager has argued that there is nothing wrong with recording revenue in this manner because the company has a contract with the customer and the order would not have been accepted unless the customer was expected to complete the transaction.

The audit team estimates that total sales recorded for the year will be $470 million and reported profit will be $32 million if the figures are left unadjusted. If the pre-booking of sales is adjusted then sales will be $430 million and profit will be $29 million.

At the planning stage of the audit, the engagement partner had evaluated risks for sales as follows:

- Inherent risk 70%
- Control risk 50%
- Analytical review risk 80%
- Detailed testing risk 17%

The engagement partner is concerned that the correction of this cut-off problem will have an impact on the validity of the findings reported by the audit staff on the individual account balances in the financial statements. The engagement partner has asked the review partner to offer some advice on whether the audit testing is satisfactory.

Required

(a) Advise the audit engagement partner on the acceptability of Crank's policy of recording revenue in respect of goods that have been ordered but not yet delivered. **(7 marks)**

(b) Advise the audit engagement partner on the validity of the $4 million materiality threshold used throughout the audit work. **(8 marks)**

(c) Advise the audit engagement partner on the extent to which the work undertaken on Crank's bookkeeping records provides an adequate basis for forming an audit opinion. **(10 marks)**

(Total 25 marks)

PRACTICE QUESTION BANK

20 Mable (AIA May 2016 amended)

Harold is the engagement partner in charge of the external audit of Mable Contractors ('Mable'), a company which is not publicly traded.

Mable has always conducted very small-scale projects that have tended to be completed within a few weeks from start to finish. The company has, however, employed an experienced project manager to enable the company to bid for bigger contracts. Mable signed its first large-scale contract in June 2015. The intention is that the company will build a residential tower block on a new site. The terms of the contract are outlined below:

- Likely duration – 36 months
- Contract value – $42 million
- Mable's estimate of total cost – $34 million
- Payment terms – an independent civil engineering company will visit the site every three months to assess the quality of the work and the contract performance completed. The engineer's report will provide the basis for Mable to invoice the contract client for the value of the work done to date. The contract client will pay 90% of the invoice value within 30 days and the remaining 10% 6 months after the contract has been completed and the tower block accepted by the contract client.

Most large contracts use subcontracted labour and leased equipment, so Mable's small size is not necessarily a major drawback.

Mable will have to pay for subcontracted labour, materials and equipment hire throughout the contract. Most suppliers will invoice on a monthly basis and will expect to be paid within 30 days of invoice. Mable took out a $4 million bank loan, repayable in December 2018, to cover the working capital requirements imposed by this project.

The contract commenced on 1 September 2015 and the civil engineer submitted reports in respect of the three months ended 30 November 2015 and 29 February 2016. These reports stated that work to the value of $3.1 million had been completed by 30 November 2015 and $6.7 million had been completed by 29 February 2016. These figures are cumulative.

Mable's year end is 30 April 2016. By that date, the contract account had costs totalling $5.7 million. The company had invoiced a total of $6.7 million, of which $0.67 million was outstanding as a retention.

Mable's directors had estimated the remaining cost of completing the contract at $31 million when they prepared the forecast as at 30 April 2016.

Mable's directors have approached Harold and asked for a report on the company's systems with respect to the recording of contract revenues and expenses and on the approach taken to the application of IFRS 15 *Revenue from contracts with customers*.

Required

(a) Advise Harold on the inherent risks arising from Mable's contract. **(12 marks)**

(b) Advise Harold on the work that should be done with respect to the civil engineer's reports that form the basis of the recognition of profit on this contract. **(13 marks)**

(c) Advise Harold on whether it is acceptable to advise Mable's directors on the recording and accounting treatment of this contract. **(13 marks)**

(d) Advise Harold on the specific matters that will have to be considered before signing an unmodified audit report on the financial statements of Mable. **(12 marks)**

(Total 50 marks)

21 Silver and Bronze

Silver and Bronze ('S and B') is a firm of external auditors. The firm has 3 offices and a total of 18 partners. Each partner is supported by two or three audit managers and several other professional staff, including both qualified accountants and trainees.

S and B's largest client is a manufacturing company called White. Sarah is the audit partner in charge of this audit. This is the third year of her association with this company. Michael is the audit manager on the White audit. This is his first year of involvement with White. The previous audit manager left S and B just before the planning of the White audit commenced. Michael requested that he be appointed as audit manager because he felt that being given such a responsibility for the firm's largest client would significantly enhance his career prospects.

Sarah and Michael met several times during the planning stage of the audit. They agreed the approach that was to be taken and they set out the initial evaluation of inherent risk and control risk. They mapped out the overall audit strategy in some detail. They agreed that Sarah would maintain contact with White's chief executive and finance director throughout the course of the audit and that Michael would focus on managing the audit itself. They agreed that Michael should consult Sarah over any problems arising with the audit and that Sarah would keep Michael informed of any matters arising from her meetings with White's directors.

Sarah met the finance director and chief executive regularly throughout the period since the initial planning stage of the audit. These meetings did not provide any information that had any significant implications for the audit. The finance director did comment on two occasions that Michael was a very pleasant person to work with and that the audit fieldwork appeared to be progressing very smoothly.

White's year end is 31 October 2012. The audit fieldwork was completed by the middle of November 2012 and Sarah reviewed the working papers in some detail. She was concerned about the manner in which the audit had been conducted and asked Michael to prepare a detailed report covering a number of specific matters. Michael's report is set out below. Each of the headings, apart from the introduction and concluding remarks, relates to a specific matter raised by Sarah.

To:	Sarah, audit partner
From:	Michael, audit manager
Concerning:	Audit of White for the year ended 31 October 2012
Date:	16 November 2012

Introduction

This report addresses the specific matters raised during the partner's review of the audit working papers for the audit of White for the year ended 31 October 2012.

As requested, I have addressed the specific matters raised by the partner during her review of the audit working papers.

Staffing

The audit fieldwork was conducted by Colin, who is a recently qualified accountant. Colin was assisted by Louise and Martin, two trainee accountants.

Ideally, this audit would have been assigned to Steven, who qualified as an accountant three years ago and has been in charge of the White audit fieldwork for the past two years. Unfortunately, a more senior manager requested Steven for another audit and so it was impossible to have a member of staff with prior experience on the audit of White.

Colin is as experienced as Steven was when Steven first took charge of this audit and so there was every reason to believe that he would be a suitable person to lead the audit team.

Colin received a detailed briefing on the audit approach to White before the first of the two interim audit visits.

I would have preferred to have used more experienced staff on this assignment, but that was not possible because of other commitments.

Inherent risk and analytical review

At the planning stage of the audit it was agreed that the inherent risk was classified as moderate and was quantified at 70% at the global level.

We were unable to obtain any assurance from analytical review, although extensive use was made of analytical review throughout the audit in order to support the planning and execution of other audit tests. Nothing of any great significance was revealed by our analytical review.

Colin conducted a thorough analysis of the figures according to the latest draft of the financial statements and concluded that they did not contain any significant anomalies that required further investigation. I reviewed his analysis and confirmed his conclusion.

The draft financial statements are attached as appendix 1 to this report.

Lives of intangible assets

White's only intangible asset is the right to use the 'Whitebar' trademark. That right was purchased in 2001, although the trademark has been in use since long before then.

White has always regarded the trademark as having an indefinite useful life.

The work undertaken on this figure was based on the audit approach taken during the audit of the year ended 31 October 2011 (as obtained from my study of the previous year's working papers). As in previous years, I discussed the decision to treat the asset's life as indefinite with both the chief executive and the finance director. In my opinion, the directors are fully aware of the requirements with respect to the review of the useful life as required by IAS 38 *Intangible assets*. I have included minutes of those discussions in the audit working papers.

When Louise reviewed the minutes of the board meetings she did not uncover any evidence that the directors were concerned about the value of this asset.

Furthermore, the draft letter of representation includes the following paragraph:

'Significant assumptions used by us in making accounting estimates, including those measured at fair value, are reasonable.'

This will cover us in the event that the decision to treat the asset life as indefinite is ever challenged by a user of the financial statements.

Conclusion

I believe that this covers all of the points raised in your memo regarding the audit of White. I will be happy to expand on any of the above matters if you so wish.

I have enjoyed the challenge of managing this audit and I hope that I will be able to continue with it into the foreseeable future.

Appendix 1 – draft financial statements with comparatives

White
Statements of profit or loss

	Draft for the year ended 31 October 2012 $'000	Year ended 31 October 2011 $'000
Revenue	227,000	331,000
Cost of sales	(187,000)	(198,000)
Gross profit	40,000	133,000
Distribution costs	(1,140)	(1,280)
Administrative expenses	(1,260)	(1,090)
Operating profit	37,600	130,630
Interest received	10	9
Interest paid	(1,200)	(660)
Profit before tax	36,410	129,979
Tax	(14,000)	(16,000)
Profit for the financial year	22,410	113,979

White
Draft statement of changes in equity
for the year ended 31 October 2012

	Share capital $'000	Share premium $'000	Retained earnings $'000	Revaluation reserve $'000	Total $'000
Opening balance	1,720,000	415,000	42,779	3,823	2,181,602
Gain on revaluation				714	714
Profit after tax			22,410		22,410
Dividend			(30,000)		(30,000)
	1,720,000	415,000	35,189	4,537	2,174,726

White
Statements of financial position

	Draft as at 31 October 2012 $'000	As at 31 October 2011 $'000
Non-current assets		
Property, plant and equipment	2,084,000	2,088,000
Trademarks	100,000	100,000
	2,184,000	2,188,000
Current assets		
Inventory	12,000	11,000
Trade receivables	19,000	17,000
Bank	31	127
	31,031	28,127
Total assets	2,215,031	2,216,127

Equity		
Share capital	1,720,000	1,720,000
Share premium	415,000	415,000
Revaluation reserve	4,537	3,823
Retained earnings	35,189	42,779
	2,174,726	2,181,602
Non-current liabilities		
Loans	15,000	11,000
Deferred tax	1,005	825
	16,005	11,825
Current liabilities		
Trade payables	10,500	7,800
Tax	13,800	14,900
	24,300	22,700
	2,215,031	2,216,127

Sarah was extremely unhappy with the content of Michael's report. She has scheduled a meeting with him in the very near future to discuss a number of the matters that he has raised. As things stand, Sarah is unwilling to sign the auditor's report.

Required

(a) Prepare an analytical review of the figures shown in the draft financial statements and advise the audit partner about the matters arising that could have an impact on the inherent risks associated with the audit of White. **(15 marks)**

(b) Critically analyse the quality of the supervision provided by both Michael and Sarah of the audit of White. **(15 marks)**

(c) (i) Recommend work that should be undertaken on the evaluation of the useful life of White's trademark. **(10 marks)**

(ii) Advise Sarah of the implications for the auditor's report if the work undertaken on the trademark is not conclusive. **(10 marks)**

(Total 50 marks)

22 Harvey

Harvey is an audit firm's largest client. The firm obtains 5% of its gross recurring fee income from the Harvey audit.

Harvey owns and operates a small fleet of deep sea trawlers. The directors of Harvey have decided to expand their fleet by having the Lucky Mascot shipyard build a new trawler to Harvey's specifications. Harvey has agreed to pay for this transaction by an exchange of shares. The Lucky Mascot shipyard has agreed to accept a block of shares that will give the company a 15% stake in Harvey.

Lucky Mascot has no other relationship with Harvey. It is a well-established company that builds ships to order for a range of customers. Each ship is costed on the basis of materials and labour and the selling price is determined by negotiation. Typically, it will take several months of planning and negotiation to agree a price with a customer. Lucky Mascot does not generally disclose the selling prices of individual ships because that information is commercially sensitive.

The directors of Harvey have approached their audit firm to ask for professional support for the forthcoming acquisition of the new trawler. Harvey's accountant has been studying the requirements of IFRS 2 *Share-based payment* and has determined that the trawler should be accounted for on the basis of the fair value of either the trawler itself or the fair value of the shares that are issued. The chief accountant is unsure how to arrive at either of these figures and Harvey's directors have asked the partner in charge of their external audit to arrange some accountancy support to assist with this exercise.

This request has posed a dilemma for the audit firm's managing partner because the firm has always had a policy of providing its audit clients with little or nothing in the way of non-audit services.

Harvey's proposal would generate substantial consultancy fees, which could be as high as the audit fee. Harvey's directors have stated that they are keen to have the work done by their external auditor because they wish to deal with an accountancy firm that is familiar with their circumstances. If the firm does not agree to undertake the consultancy then Harvey will consider appointing a new auditor, who will also provide such professional services.

The managing partner has called a meeting of the audit firm's partners to discuss this proposal. Harvey is not a publicly traded company. The audit firm has a single office, with 7 partners and 40 professional staff.

Required

(a) Advise the partners of the independence issues arising from Harvey's proposal. **(12 marks)**

(b) Recommend, stating reasons, the work that should be undertaken by the audit firm to assist Harvey with the application of IFRS 2 to this transaction. **(13 marks)**

(Total 25 marks)

23 Gamble

You are the partner in charge of the external audit of Gamble, a new client to your firm. Gamble was previously audited by a smaller firm of accountants.

Your firm agreed to undertake the audit in July 2012. At that time you met with the chief executive, Mr Vincent, and the finance director, Mr Costello. You made the following notes of the meeting on your laptop:

'Gamble is an internet-based gaming company. It was founded in 2008 by a small group of US investors who invested $8 million in equity. The company borrowed a further $60 million which was used to fund the initial investment in non-current assets. These included a $50 million payment for the right to use the 'Gamble' trademark and associated internet domain name, both of which had been registered by a third party, the acquisition of an IT facility in South America and a corporate headquarters in the UK. None of the company's activities are based in the US because the company's business practices do not comply with US law.

The two executive directors, Mr Vincent and Mr Costello, were appointed to the board when the company was founded. They each received $1 million of the company's equity as fully-paid shares and a contract that specified a profit-related bonus.

Mr Vincent and Mr Costello have agreed to appoint a non-executive director as a condition of our accepting the audit appointment (file note amendment: Mr Harris was appointed to Gamble's board as a non-executive on 1 October 2012. He is retired from full-time employment, but has been on the board of two major publicly traded companies during his career).

Gamble appears to be a highly successful business that is capable of expanding rapidly. It allows customers to set up an account that enables them to play poker over the internet. The company's activities are within the law in the UK and so there are no legal issues associated with our acting for them. The two executive directors have many years of management experience in casinos in Nevada, USA.

The company's revenues comprise a percentage of every bet made through its website. Customers deposit funds with Gamble and use those to place bets against other customers. 5% of every bet placed is transferred to Gamble as a commission. Losing bets are then deducted from account balances and winning bets are credited. Customers can make additional payments into their accounts or make withdrawals at any time.'

The audit of the financial statements for the year ended 30 April 2013 is presently under way. You have just received the following email from the audit manager:

Gamble audit – review of inherent risk

Mike Smith – Audit manager m.smith@audit-firm.com
Sent: Wednesday 22 May 2013
To: Lee-partner@audit-firm.com

I have just completed a detailed review of the audit working papers to date and have uncovered some concerns about the governance and risk issues associated with Gamble.

Firstly, our analysis of revenues for the segmental reporting has identified some major anomalies. There has been a surge in revenue that is difficult to explain. The company has a number of customers who each appear to be spending tens of thousands of dollars every day through Gamble's website. All customers must deposit their gambling stakes with the company by either credit card payment or electronic bank transfer and it is possible to identify approximately twenty customers who have deposited at least $10 million each in the course of the year ended 30 April 2013. These spending patterns lack credibility, although Mr Vincent has assured me that many of Gamble's biggest customers are professional card players who regard playing on the site as their full-time occupation. My most obvious concern is that Gamble is being used for money laundering purposes.

Secondly, Mr Harris has warned us that he plans to resign as soon as he has taken legal advice on the matter. Mr Vincent and Mr Costello wish to buy the 80% of the company that is held by the founding shareholders. They have warned the shareholders that the company faces a difficult future because of changing social attitudes towards gambling and growing competition in that sector. For that reason they have written off $48 million of the cost of the Gamble trade name as an impairment adjustment. Mr Vincent and Mr Costello told Mr Harris that they planned to offer the existing shareholders $24 million for their shares, which was determined as three times their initial investment in the company. Mr Harris has been asked to support the other two directors in their negotiations with the shareholders. Mr Harris is unwilling to assist the two executive directors in this way.

I am keen to meet with you as a matter of some urgency to discuss these developments. I attach the draft financial statements as they currently stand.

Gamble
Statements of profit or loss

	Draft for the year ended 30 April 2013 $'000	Year ended 30 April 2012 $'000
Revenue	347,000	268,000
Cost of sales	(50,890)	(2,231)
Gross profit	296,110	265,769
Distribution costs	(1,480)	(896)
Administrative expenses	(11,400)	(5,300)
Operating profit	283,230	259,573
Interest paid	(1,200)	(660)
Profit before tax	282,030	258,913
Tax	(3,000)	(4,500)
Profit for the financial year	279,030	254,413

Gamble
Draft statement of changes in equity
for the year ended 30 April 2013

	Share capital $'000	Retained earnings $'000	Total $'000
Opening balance	10,000	41,958	51,958
Profit after tax		279,030	279,030
Dividend		(313,346)	(313,346)
	10,000	7,642	17,642

Gamble
Statements of financial position

	Draft as at 30 April 2013 $'000	Year ended 30 April 2012 $'000
Non-current assets		
Property, plant and equipment	24,900	25,100
Intangibles	2,000	50,000
	26,900	75,100
Current assets		
Trade receivables	6,000	4,800
Bank	42	158
	6,042	4,958
Total assets	32,942	80,058
Equity		
Share capital	10,000	10,000
Retained earnings	7,642	41,958
	17,642	51,958

	Draft as at 30 April 2013 $'000	Year ended 30 April 2012 $'000
Non-current liabilities		
Loans	2,000	16,000
Current liabilities		
Trade payables	10,500	7,800
Tax	2,800	4,300
	13,300	12,100
	32,942	80,058

Required

(a) Prepare a briefing note for your firm's managing partner that critically analyses the concerns expressed by the audit manager on the possibility of money laundering by Gamble. Your analysis should take account of the figures in the draft financial statements. **(18 marks)**

(b) Advise the audit manager on the possibility that the executive directors' desire to purchase the remainder of the company's equity has led to them acting against the best interests of the other shareholders. **(12 marks)**

(c) (i) Recommend audit tests that the audit manager should undertake concerning the impairment adjustment on intangibles. **(10 marks)**

(ii) Assess the difficulties associated with determining the materiality of the impairment adjustment on intangibles. **(10 marks)**

(Total 50 marks)

24 Pension audit

One of your audit clients, a small company with total assets according to the draft statement of financial position of $9.7 million, has a defined benefit pension plan. The following figures have been provided by the company's finance director as the basis for the figures that will appear in the financial statements for the year ended 30 April 2013:

Present value of obligations at 1 May 2012	$2.2m
Fair value of plan assets at 1 May 2012	$2.1m
Discount rate on corporate bonds	9.0%
Expected rate of return on plan assets	11.0%
Current service cost	$0.46m
Benefits paid	$0.32m
Contributions received	$0.2m
Present value of obligations at 30 April 2013	$2.4m
Fair value of plan assets at 30 April 2013	$2.5m

The finance director has obtained most of these figures from the plan actuary, who is an independent consultant. The finance director has indicated that the directors rely totally on the actuary's report when it comes to the pension calculations and so there is no need for you to undertake any additional work on the pension figures, beyond checking that the necessary disclosures have been made under IAS 19 *Employee benefits*.

At your request, the plan actuary has provided a duplicate copy of the report that was posted directly to your office. That report was identical to the copy that was provided by the company's finance director.

The pension note in the draft financial statements has been prepared using the above figures. You have had a member of the audit team check that the figures in the note agree to the actuary's report and check that the calculations are arithmetically correct.

Required

(a) Evaluate the audit implications of the fact that the directors are relying totally on the work undertaken by the independent actuary. **(8 marks)**

(b) Recommend, stating reasons for your recommendations, a programme of work that should be undertaken on the pension figures. **(17 marks)**

(Total 25 marks)

25 Madbox (AIA November 2015) (Amended)

Jacob is a partner in the Barneytown office of JAND, an audit firm that has six offices spread across the major cities of its home country. Jacob is the partner in charge of the external audit of Madbox, a publicly traded company that designs and sells computer games. Madbox is the Barneytown office's only publicly traded client.

The following extracts have been drawn from the planning section of the audit working papers for the current year's audit:

Timetable

The client's year end is 31 October 2015.

The directors aim to have the first draft of the financial statements completed by the middle of November 2015.

We have been asked to have our audit fieldwork completed shortly afterwards, with a view to finalising the audit report before the end of November 2015.

If the audit is not completed by 30 November 2015 then the client's reporting timetable will be disrupted.

Fieldwork

The audit will be conducted by Alison (manager), Derek (recently qualified in-charge), Kate (final year trainee) and Bob (first year trainee).

There will be two interim audit visits. The first will take place in February 2015, to update systems files and to conduct compliance and substantive tests on transactions for the period 1 November 2014 to 31 December 2014. The second will be in September 2015 and will cover compliance and substantive tests on transactions for the period 1 January 2015 to 31 August 2015.

The final audit visit is scheduled to commence in the middle of October 2015 and will conclude by the third week in November.

Materiality

Reported revenue for the year ended 31 October 2014 was $1.2 billion and reported profit was $0.3 billion. These figures reflect steady growth over the years ended 31 October 2011, 2012, and 2013.

Planning materiality was set at $15 million for the year ended 31 October 2014 and reporting materiality was set at $20 million.

Based on discussions with Madbox's board, it is proposed to set planning materiality at $17 million for the year ended 31 October 2015.

Risk evaluation

Our past experience of working with Madbox is that the directors have always demonstrated considerable personal integrity in their dealings with us. We have always regarded inherent risk as moderate at the global level and I propose that we continue to do so for the year ended 31 October 2015.

The company designs its own computer games and manufactures DVDs for distribution through retailers. The games can also be downloaded, for a fee, from Madbox's website. This is a fast moving industry, with many sales of boxed games occurring during the months of August and September while retailers prepare for the Christmas rush. The company launches a number of new games every year, with each selling heavily while the games are new and continuing to generate revenues for three to five years. Development costs are capitalised and amortised over three years.

We regard inventory of games as high risk because of the threat of obsolescence. Intangible assets are also high risk because the development costs of new games are high and the same risk of obsolescence applies.

It is now mid-November 2015 and Jacob is conducting his partner's review of the audit working papers. This is his third detailed review because he reviewed the files as they stood at the conclusion of each of the interim audits.

Jacob has noted the following review points:

Revenue

I am shocked to see that revenue for the year ended 31 October 2015 is expected to be only $0.9 billion. The company was meeting its budgeted targets for the first half of the financial year, but sales in the second half of the year have been bitterly disappointing because Madbox was depending on the successful launch of several new games in July, with a view to capturing the Christmas market.

I am not convinced that our detailed testing has been adequate and I am considering conducting an additional substantive testing exercise.

Unbeknown to us, Madbox lost its chief games designer to a major competitor in March 2014 and he took several of Madbox's designers and programmers with him. At that point, the company was still developing the games that were due for release in May 2015. The games that have been developed by the replacement staff are not nearly as good as earlier releases.

Risk evaluation

Madbox's directors have already warned the stock market that this year's profits will be poorer than expected, but they have not been as clear about the full extent of the decline as they should have been. In particular, the development costs of Madbox's older games have not been reviewed for impairment.

Derek's responses to these points are as follows:

I accept that the figures are disappointing. We do not have sufficient time to extend the detailed tests if we are to meet the deadline. We have our prior experience of auditing this company to rely on and we can also ask the directors to highlight any uncertainties over the figures in the financial statements.

I was unaware that the design team had left. I would have had to have followed the games industry news in some detail to have realised that because Madbox's senior management did not bring that to our attention. There was no discussion of the departure in the board minutes.

I disagree that we should insist that management should review the existing games titles for impairment. They were designed by the original team.

The capital markets are very well aware of Madbox's problems. There is very little danger of any criticism being directed at us regardless of any additional work that we may or may not do or how we report our opinion.

Required

(a) Critically evaluate Derek's argument that sufficient evidence has been obtained from detailed substantive testing. **(12 marks)**

(b) Critically evaluate Derek's failure to note the fact that Madbox had lost its chief games designer and members of the programming department. **(13 marks)**

(c) Advise Jacob on the most appropriate form of auditor's report for the year ended 31 October 2015, assuming that there is insufficient time to complete additional testing. **(12 marks)**

(d) Critically evaluate Derek's suggestion that the audit firm need not respond to Jacob's concerns because the capital markets are already well aware of Madbox's problems. **(13 marks)**

(Total 50 marks)

26 Link (AIA May 2015)

DF is an audit firm. The firm's largest client is Link, a publicly traded company that offers social media content.

In July 2014, Link paid $88 million in the form of a share for share exchange for 100% of the equity of Webtok. Webtok's main asset was in the form of the rights to a recently developed computer application that enables individuals to gather together information about all of their friends' texts, emails, posts to social media and blog entries in one convenient report. Webtok's application had suddenly become extremely popular and was attracting considerable interest from both individuals and businesses, who could use Webtok's application to send targeted advertising in a form that would appeal to young people.

Link's year end is 30 June 2015. The directors intend to consolidate Webtok on the basis that the amount paid for the company included $80 million for the application. That sum will, therefore, be capitalised in Link's consolidated financial statements and goodwill on the acquisition of Webtok will be calculated accordingly.

Link's draft financial statements, based on projected figures, show revenue of $1,950 million and profit of $703 million.

Assuming that the treatment of the acquisition of Webtok is permitted, the Link Group's total intangible assets arising from intellectual property such as computer applications will be valued at $1,850 million, based on the acquisition cost less amortisation of seven major websites over the past ten years.

The partner in charge of the external audit of Link is concerned about the valuation of these intangible assets. Each has been the subject of an annual impairment review and no single site has ever been shown to be impaired, but DF believes that Link's directors have always taken an unduly optimistic view of the future of the social media industry.

Required

(a) Advise DF's audit partner of the approach that should be taken to determining the fair value of the intangible assets acquired through the acquisition of Webtok. **(12 marks)**

(b) Recommend, stating reasons, the work that DF should undertake on intangible assets before issuing an unmodified auditor's report on Link. **(13 marks)**

(Total 25 marks)

27 Grean (AIA November 2014)

Grean is an online retailer that sells DVDs and books.

Grean's chief buyer queried a purchase requisition that had been raised by the company's sales manager for an Android tablet computer. The staff in the purchasing department queried the validity of this requisition. The sales manager replied that one of the sales department staff had been using an Android tablet, which was his own personal property, to compile reports. The staff member had left the company and had emailed the sales manager copies of the work-related files that he had on his machine. The computers in the sales department could not run the software app that the staff member had used to prepare these files and so the sales manager was keen to purchase a compatible tablet so that the files could be accessed and, hopefully, converted to a format that could be updated on Grean's own systems.

An app is a piece of software that is typically designed to fulfil a very specific purpose. Apps are generally small programs that can be downloaded from the internet or even written by users themselves. They are typically run on portable devices such as mobile phones and tablets.

The chief buyer reported this matter to Grean's head of IT, who decided to investigate. The head of IT spent a morning walking around Grean's offices and found several instances of staff who were working on a variety of systems, including smartphones, iPads and other forms of tablet. There was at least one instance in every major department, including the IT department. Indeed, a network administrator had written an app for his smartphone that enabled him to monitor Grean's network performance from anywhere that had an internet connection. His phone could connect to the server over the internet and gather key management information to enable the network administrator to identify problems.

The head of IT submitted a report to Grean's directors. The board was unsure how to respond to this issue. Some of the directors took the view that the company was benefitting from the evaluation and even the introduction of new technology at little or no cost because staff were equipping themselves. Others felt that the company was being exposed to potential threats, although they were unsure what those threats might be. The business press had reported this phenomenon in very general terms and had called it BYOD, which stands for 'bring your own device'.

Required

(a) Advise Grean's directors on the potential risks associated with the BYOD phenomenon. **(12 marks)**

(b) Recommend, stating reasons, policies for managing the use of personal devices and software apps by Grean's staff. **(13 marks)**

(Total 25 marks)

28 Fastrun (AIA November 2014)

Fastrun is a courier company that collects and delivers packages within a 50 mile radius of its depot. The company has a reputation for offering a fast and reliable service and it is used by many business customers.

Fastrun's internal auditor has been called in to investigate the possibility that one of its staff is stealing. Fastrun has had a significant increase in the number of complaints concerning lost items, most of which have been relatively valuable.

The company employs 40 drivers. Packages for delivery are logged on Fastrun's computer system. At the start of every shift, each driver is issued with a picking list that includes all of the items to be delivered within a specific area. Drivers load their vans with the items listed for delivery. Each driver also receives a list of collections that have to be made during the run. Once these deliveries and collections have been completed the driver returns to the depot and logs the collected packages into the system.

Over the past six weeks there has been a steady increase in the number of complaints of incomplete deliveries. For example, one complaint concerned a package that should have contained six wristwatches, but there were only five in the package when it was opened by the addressee. In another case, a laptop computer appeared to have been replaced with a book. In each case, the package appears to have been opened and the contents either removed or replaced before being reclosed carefully so that the interference is difficult to detect.

Fastrun's management is keen to investigate this, but they cannot risk accusing the drivers without proper cause. The drivers could easily claim that the customers are making false declarations when they send packages or that the addressees are taking items from their deliveries and making false claims that they were incomplete. Furthermore, any interference by Fastrun's staff could be by the driver making the collection or the driver making the delivery. Fortunately, the security at the depot is tight and so there is very little risk of anything being taken from there.

Fastrun is not large enough to require more than one internal auditor. Management has asked her to suspend work on the current round of audit investigations and to investigate the possibility that one or more of the drivers is stealing from the company. The auditor was reluctant to do so because she does not believe that this is a valid assignment for internal audit, but had no choice when management insisted.

Required

(a) Advise Fastrun's internal auditor on the work that should be undertaken to investigate management's suspicions of theft by drivers. **(15 marks)**

(b) Critically evaluate the internal auditor's assertion that this investigation is not an appropriate assignment for internal audit. **(10 marks)**

(Total 25 marks)

29 Gold

Gold manufactures processors for the computer industry. The process requires a special factory building that has a number of 'clean rooms' that have very precise regulation of temperature, a very low humidity and filters that eliminate almost all dust and other contaminants from the air. The equipment in these clean rooms is very sensitive and must be protected from anything that could damage their very fragile circuitry.

Gold's most popular product is the processor that is used in many modern mobile phones. Gold used to manufacture processors for many major manufacturers, but four years ago the company signed an exclusive contract to manufacture processors for Lane, the market leader in this industry. Lane provided Gold with the necessary information required to manufacture the very powerful processors that were used in Lane's products. Lane was keen to prevent rivals from obtaining any information about the manufacture of its products and so Gold had to sign an exclusive contract that prevented it from working for anybody else. In return, Lane agreed that it would order all of its processors from Gold for a five-year period, with the possibility of further contracts at the end of that period.

Lane has been very successful and its requirements have grown every year for the past four years. Gold has been able to expand its operations and its production capacity has doubled since the start of the contract.

The partner in charge of the external audit of Gold is concerned about the figures that will appear in the company's financial statements for the year ended 30 April 2012. The contract with Lane has just one year left to run. Gold's directors have reassured the audit partner that the renewal is virtually certain, but it will not occur until after the financial statements have been published, partly because Lane is keen to see audited accounts before granting an extension.

The audit partner has asked Gold's finance director for an indication of the implications of a problem with the contract for Lane. The finance director has said that there are no implications because Gold will have no difficulty in finding alternative customers. The fact that the company has supplied Lane, the market leader, will reassure potential buyers. Furthermore, the company's assets are all relatively new and current and so there should be no difficulty in selling them for more than their present book values in the event that the contract is lost. If the going concern basis has to be abandoned then there would be no effect upon valuations in the statement of financial position.

The audit partner is concerned because Gold is the only company of its type in its home country. The other businesses in the industry moved offshore over the past few years because of cheaper skilled labour and the availability of government subsidies from the countries who attracted this inward investment. At the time Gold chose to stay because its location was ideal for servicing the Lane contract and also because it would have been very expensive to dismantle its factory and relocate its equipment. Gold's competitors are generally much smaller and have smaller production facilities that made it easier to recreate the necessary buildings and transport the equipment to another country.

Gold's sales director has indicated that negotiations with Lane are proceeding smoothly, but the audit partner has reviewed correspondence which suggests that Lane has voiced some concerns about Gold's quality control in the past few months and also that Lane would wish any continuation of the contract to be at a slightly lower unit price to reflect the substantial volumes of business being given to Gold. Gold's draft financial statements are as follows:

Draft statement of profit or loss for the year ended 30 April 2012

	$m
Revenue	1,700
Cost of sales	(900)
Gross profit	800
Distribution costs	(50)
Administrative expenses	(120)
Operating profit	630
Interest received	80
Interest paid	(65)
Profit before tax	645
Tax	(28)
Profit for the financial year	617

Draft statement of changes in equity for the year ended 30 April 2012

	Share capital $m	Share premium $m	Retained earnings $m	Revaluation reserve $m	Total $m
Opening balance	100	49	877	130	1,156
Shares issued for cash	20	39			59
Gain on revaluation				73	73
Profit after tax			617		617
Dividend			(45)		(45)
	120	88	1,449	203	1,860

Statements of financial position as at 30 April

	2012 (draft) $m	2011 $m
Non-current assets		
Property, plant and equipment	2,080	1,542
Current assets		
Inventory	250	130
Trade receivables	450	360
Prepaid expenses	4	2
Bank	262	144
	966	636
Total assets	3,046	2,178
Equity		
Share capital	120	100
Share premium	88	49
Revaluation reserve	203	130
Retained earnings	1,449	877
	1,860	1,156
Non-current liabilities		
Loans	800	700
Deferred tax	10	7
	810	707
Current liabilities		
Trade payables	344	290
Accrued expenses	6	3
Tax	26	22
	376	315
	3,046	2,178

Draft statement of cash flows for the year ended 30 April 2012

	$m	$m
Cash flows from operating activities		
Cash receipts from customers	1,610	
Cash paid to suppliers and employees	(1,083)	
Cash generated from operations	527	
Income taxes paid	(21)	
Net cash from operating activities		506
Cash flows from investing activities		
Purchase of property, plant and equipment	(707)	
Proceeds from disposal of property, plant and equipment	190	
Net cash used in investing activities		(517)

	$m	$m
Cash flows from financing activities		
Proceeds from issue of share capital	59	
Proceeds of loan	100	
Interest paid	(65)	
Interest received	80	
Dividend paid	(45)	
Net cash from financing activities		129
Net decrease in cash and cash equivalents		118
Cash and cash equivalents at beginning of period		144
Cash and cash equivalents at end of period		262

Required

(a) Critically analyse the finance director's assertions concerning the going concern issues associated with Gold's draft financial statements. **(10 marks)**

(b) (i) Advise the audit partner on the specific matters that will have to be taken into account in deciding whether Gold is a going concern. Your advice should reflect the information contained in the draft financial statements. **(13 marks)**

    (ii) Advise the audit partner on the specific ways in which advice from an independent expert might be used in order to determine the nature and extent of any adjustments that will have to be made in the event that Gold's status as a going concern is called into doubt. **(7 marks)**

(c) Advise the audit partner on the implications for the audit firm of the fact that Lane will not decide on the renewal of its contract until it has had the opportunity to study Gold's audited financial statements for the year ended 30 April 2012. **(10 marks)**

(d) Advise the audit partner on the factors that will have to be taken into account in deciding whether to issue a qualified auditor's report on Gold's financial statements and state the most likely form that a qualified auditor's report should take. **(10 marks)**

(Total 50 marks)

Practice answer bank

1 Zapp

> **Tutorial note.** Overall, the question deals with the relationships between the audit firm and the board of an audit client and also that between the audit firm and its staff. There is a suspicion that a laptop belonging to a member of the audit team has been stolen and hacked by the company's management. That raises questions about the use to which the information on the audit working papers might be put by the directors. There are further questions about the integrity of the directors. The question also deals with the behavioural issues associated with electronic working papers and the potential for constant review of files. The final part of the question deals with the controls over computer security. The fact that it is pitched at the security of machines used by the audit staff does not alter the fact that the question is about the core matter of internal control in a computerised environment.

(a) Memo
   To: Managing partner
   From: Audit partner
   Re: Zapp – stolen laptop

   (i) You may be aware that a laptop was stolen from the team involved in the Zapp audit. The laptop contained a full set of working papers for last year's audit and a full set of working papers for the year to date.

   We must work on the assumption that the directors have accessed the content of this laptop. Assuming that they have, this puts us in a highly embarrassing position.

   Firstly, the directors know the approach that we plan to take to the audit. They know which figures we plan to test in detail and which we plan to test lightly. That will make it far easier for them to manipulate figures without us detecting them. We will have to exercise extreme caution over any large adjustments to low-risk figures in the finalisation of the financial statements. We will need to conduct very careful analytical procedures of the figures during the final review.

   There is a controversial accounting choice in this audit. The directors now know that we found it difficult to reject their plans to recognise revenue in an aggressive manner and they are now pushing for that same policy. Knowing that we found it difficult to reject their arguments in the past will undermine our bargaining position in any future negotiations on this matter. We should pre-empt this by having a meeting of partners and senior managers to establish a clear policy, with justification, so that we can resolve the debate in a manner that protects our firm's interests.

   The directors have details concerning time budgets and other information that we use for pricing the audit. That may make it more difficult for us to negotiate an acceptable margin on top of our costs. We will have to decide whether to accept a reduced fee for this year's audit.

   (ii) We do know that the laptop was stolen, but we do not know who took it. If we continue to suspect that the board has the laptop then we should really consider resigning.

   If the laptop came into the directors' possession then they should have returned it immediately. The fact that they did not do so indicates a major lack of integrity, which would make it difficult for us to sign an unmodified auditor's report. If the directors are prepared to steal property and invade our privacy then they are clearly highly dishonest and we cannot continue to work for them.

   Our resignation would have to be with immediate effect. We would, however, have to be careful not to make defamatory statements in our letter of resignation unless we have outright proof of theft.

In any communication with our replacement, we should indicate that we had concerns about the board's integrity. We should inform our replacement of our suspicions without making an outright accusation.

(b) The most effective response is to work through the criteria listed in IFRS 15 and to respond to each of the points made by Zapp's board in turn:

(i) The entity has a present right to payment for the asset

The significant risks and rewards in this situation arise from the fact that Zapp has to buy the yarn in order to meet its commitments. The cost of that yarn has yet to be determined and so Zapp is totally exposed to the risks. The buyer bears no risk until such time as the goods have been delivered because a fixed-price order has been placed with Zapp.

(ii) The customer has legal title to the asset

The fact that the yarn is converted quickly is not relevant. Zapp's production management must organise the just-in-time manufacturing so that labour and other resources are scheduled to meet delivery requirements. There will be considerable management involvement before the yarn arrives and while it is being converted.

(iii) The entity has transferred physical possession of the asset

That is true, provided Zapp's contracts are binding. Given the size of these customers, it may still be possible for them to withdraw from a contract before taking delivery. Zapp may also find it difficult to enforce a contract if a customer runs into difficulty and cancels.

(iv) The customer has the significant risks and rewards related to ownership of the asset

This is the one assertion that is undoubtedly true. Zapp's records will indicate that there is a strong probability that benefits will flow once an order has been placed.

(v) The customer has accepted the asset

Zapp cannot hold back the market forces that could raise or lower yarn prices over a three-month period. The fact that the company has analysts who can predict likely price movements does not mean that future prices can be measured reliably. The only possible exception would be if Zapp used commodity futures to fix prices in advance.

To sum up, the proposed recognition criteria are not consistent with IFRS 15. Revenues will be recognised before it is permissible to do so.

(c) There are two conflicting quality management implications.

On the positive side, the manager and partner will be able to review the working papers far more frequently than if they had to travel to the client's premises to review the working papers on site. They will not have to rely on verbal assurances made during telephone calls that the work is progressing well. The manager and partner may be able to identify problems at an early stage and offer feedback and support to resolve them quickly.

The manager and partner may be able to interpret problem signs more effectively than the junior members of the audit team. Reading through the working papers on a regular basis will make it easier to identify such problems and to revise the audit plan in response while there is time for additional work to be undertaken.

The filing system will log access by the manager and partner and will provide evidence that their reviews have taken place. That could be useful evidence to offer to any quality reviewers who review the firm's audit files.

The danger is that this system will encourage irregular auditing. Junior staff will be concerned that any adverse time variance will be noted and held against them. That may lead to the fabrication of audit evidence in order to keep up with the work. It will be far harder to offset favourable and adverse variances if supervision could potentially occur on a daily basis.

(d) First of all, the procedures appear to offer a realistic acceptance of the fact that a laptop cannot be totally secure. Audit staff must be free to speak to client staff and to fetch documents without carrying their laptops with them at all times.

The sleep mode is a sensible precaution because it means that any stolen laptop will have to be activated with a password. The problem is that this will prove inconvenient to audit staff because they will have to enter a password many times in the course of a day. They may be tempted to disable the sleep mode or to increase the time before the laptop enters this mode, which may mean that an intruder can access a live machine.

Complicated passwords may be written down or even taped to laptops. Most users should be able to remember an eight character password, so this is a realistic compromise.

It is common practice for audit staff to have the exclusive use of an office for the duration of the audit, but it is unrealistic to view that space as secure. Staff should recognise that they do not know how many people have keys. Furthermore, there may be limits to the protection offered by a typical office door. The procedures should, at the very least, require that laptops be removed from the office if it is to be unoccupied for an extended period – and certainly overnight.

(e) The inclusion of performance information in the strategic report does not affect the audit directly. The auditor's responsibility is to audit the financial statements, and to report to Zapp's members. The auditor is not required to audit information included within the strategic report as such.

The matter is complicated, however, by the potential inclusion of the strategic report in the same document as the auditor's report. In this case the strategic report will be 'other information' for audit purposes, and the auditor will have certain responsibilities in relation to it under ISA 720 *The auditor's responsibilities relating to other information in documents containing audited financial statements*. These responsibilities are:

(a) To consider whether there is a material inconsistency between the other information and the financial statements;

(b) To consider whether there is a material inconsistency between the other information and the auditor's knowledge obtained in the audit; and

(c) To respond appropriately when the auditor identifies that such material inconsistencies appear to exist, or when the auditor otherwise becomes aware that other information appears to be materially misstated.

The auditor is required to read the strategic report in order to consider whether there is a material inconsistency. The key point here is that the auditor is not just looking for an inconsistency with the financial statements, but with their understanding of the entity, and it is likely that in order for them to perform a good quality audit, their understanding would include the issues being measured by Zapp's KPIs.

If there is an inconsistency then the auditor must first consider whether the other information is correct. If the other information is correct and the auditor's understanding and/or the financial statements is incorrect, then more audit work is required.

If the other information is misstated then the auditor would need to ask Zapp to correct it. If they refused then they would need to report on the matter in the auditor's report, where they would include within the 'other information' section a statement that the other information is materially misstated.

In general terms, providing an opinion on the other information should not cost the audit firm too much in the sense of it requiring additional work to be done. It should help the firm to provide a better service to its clients, and may act as a incentive for the firm to ensure that it is providing a high quality audit to them.

2 Beetown office

> **Tutorial note.** This question tests candidates' understanding of the issues associated with professional confidence. It reflects a recent case involving a US audit partner who was charged with similar offences.

(a) Auditors are required by the IESBA *Code of Ethics for Professional Accountants* to apply professional confidentiality. Specifically, accountants should not disclose information outside the firm and they should not use confidential information to their personal advantage. The partner in charge of the Beetown office is clearly in breach of both of those specific restrictions. The accountancy profession's credibility will always be undermined whenever its members do not live up to the standards set out in formal professional regulations.

Confidentiality is a key factor in enabling auditors to gather audit evidence effectively. Auditors must be free to examine books and records in order to gather evidence and much of that information is commercially sensitive. If there is a perceived risk that auditors will pass that information on to third parties then companies will wish to restrict the auditor's access and that may make the audit less effective or, at the very least, less efficient. Clients may, for example, insist that only senior members of the audit team review sensitive matters. The client may also request that certain aspects of the audit findings be kept confidential from junior members of the audit team and that may lead to a less effective audit if knowledge cannot be shared.

If an auditor is removed from office because of a breach of confidence then there is likely to be a great deal of adverse publicity. That will affect the audit firm itself because other clients may feel that their confidence may be compromised and they may seek to replace that firm in order to reassure the shareholders.

(b) The partner should be asked to resign from the firm with immediate effect. While nothing has been proven, it would take too long for the case to be resolved through the criminal courts and the risk of losing further credibility is too high. Even if the partner is cleared of any criminal charges, there will be a lingering suspicion. The firm could buy the partner's equity at a generous price in order to encourage his departure.

ISQM 1 requires the firm is to have quality objectives, policies and procedures addressing the relevant ethical requirements as part of its system of quality management. Clearly, something is amiss and the system of quality management is not working as it should. The matter should be investigated and remedial action to address the matter be designed and implemented so that the firm can ensure its system of quality management is functioning effectively.

The firm should announce that all staff will receive training on confidentiality. Staff should also be asked to formally acknowledge that they have been made aware of their responsibilities to protect client confidence. These steps will be largely symbolic because they will not introduce any additional safeguards, but they will make it easier for the firm to justify the removal of any partner or employee who breaches confidence.

The firm should review safeguards for access to client files. Information is likely to be stored electronically and staff will have their own logins. Staff and partners should only be able to access files for clients that they have actually worked on. Any partner or member of staff who wishes to have a wider access should be required to make a formal request for access and that request should only be granted in case of need.

The firm's managing partner should contact the management of client companies to offer reassurance of the firm's intention to enforce confidentiality. Again, that is a symbolic act, but it should provide some reassurance that the firm takes this matter seriously.

(c) An accountant's duty of confidentiality is not absolute, but may be breached in certain limited circumstances. These include:

- Where the accountant has evidence of non-compliance with laws and regulations (NOCLAR); and
- Where the accountant has reasonable suspicions of money laundering.

In the case of NOCLAR, the accountant must first ask the client to rectify the situation and to inform the relevant authorities. If the client's response is not satisfactory, and the accountant is confident in their understanding of the situation, then the accountant may choose to inform the relevant authorities in the public interest.

In the case of money laundering, where an accountant has reasonable suspicions that a money laundering offence has been committed, then they are required to report this matter to their firm's Money Laundering Reporting Officer (MLRO), who will decide whether to make a report to the National Crime Agency. The accountant must then also take care not to 'tip off' the suspected money launderer.

3 Radletts

Tutorial note. This question deals with the topical area of bribery. It requires an explanation of the external auditor's role with respect to the discovery of factors that raise suspicions concerning bribery. It also requires the development of an audit programme to indicate the work that should be undertaken.

From: Helen Majors H.Majors@Radletts.com
To: Charles Denton C.Denton@Radletts.com
Re: Plover audit

(a) Management is responsible for ensuring that the business complies with laws and regulations, and to address any non-compliance. However, if the auditor discovers non-compliance, they first obtain an understanding of the matter. The issue should be discussed with management or those charged with governance.

The auditor should advise management/TCWG to:

- Rectify the situation
- Deter further non-compliance
- Disclose the non-compliance to the appropriate authority

Then the auditor must assess whether management's response is appropriate, taking into account whether:

- The response is timely
- The non-compliance has already been investigated
- Action has been taken to remedy it
- Action has been taken to deter it
- Steps have been taken to prevent re-occurrence
- The non-compliance has been disclosed

The auditor then decides whether further action is needed in the public interest. This essentially depends on the urgency and seriousness of the matter, and how likely it is to re-occur.

Further action might include:

- Disclosing the matter to the relevant authorities
- Withdrawing from the engagement

Disclosure should be made if the matter is serious; examples include: if the entity is engaged in bribery, as it may be here.

(b) The principal regulation here is ISA 250 (Revised) *Consideration of laws and regulations in an audit of financial statements*. This is important because the IESBA *Code of Ethics for Professional Accountants* imposes a specific duty of confidentiality. This discovery is relevant because it could have an impact on the financial statements due to there being an unlimited fine for acts of corporate bribery.

As auditors, we have no specific responsibility to detect acts of bribery.

There could be an argument that the misclassification of a bribe as a professional fee (for architectural services) is a material misstatement. Plover's shareholders may regard such a treatment as a sign of weak governance or as evidence of mismanagement.

Quite apart from the ISA, we may have to consider the implications of this discovery for our understanding of the integrity of management. If the directors are prepared to break the law in order to bypass planning regulations then they may be willing to act in other dishonest ways, including the manipulation of the financial statements. This could affect our understanding of the inherent risk at the global level and could affect our willingness to accept reappointment.

(c) Firstly, review all correspondence relating to the planning application. Identify the problems that were holding back the application. If they were matters of interpretation then Mr Vega's report could have been an honest response to the objections and could have required time and effort to write. If the objections were matters of fact then the provision of a report as described was not a particularly convincing reason that Mr Vega's intervention was honest and that Plover had behaved honestly.

The correspondence between the board and Torvil Architects should also be reviewed. What is the basis for the fee for this work? Does it appear that a realistic engagement has been commissioned and that Torvil is receiving an economic fee for a consultancy service? If not then there is further evidence of bribery.

The whole appointment should be discussed with the board. The directors should be asked to explain why they appointed this particular firm and why they agreed to pay so much for what appears to be such a brief report. Arguably, Mr Vega should not involve his firm in appeals against the city Planning Department, but that is really a matter for him and not that of his clients.

4 Forgewood

Tutorial note. This question deals with the non-statutory audit of a charity, raising questions of the role of audit and also the auditor's client acceptance decision.

(a) The most immediate question would be that of independence. If the auditor has a long association with the charity then it may be inappropriate for the firm to continue to conduct the audit. There are other independence issues, because the first audit will require work that could uncover shortcomings in the opening figures. In other words, there is a self-review threat in relation to the audit possibly revealing issues concerning the examiner's role that has been undertaken in the past.

Secondly, the firm should consider whether it has the capacity to undertake the additional work. The charity may not be willing or able to pay for a full audit and the work will be far more demanding than the examinations that have been conducted in the past. It may be necessary to tell the board that it will not be possible to offer a greater commitment.

The firm will also have to consider the exposure to litigation risk or loss of reputation. When conducting an independent examination, the examiner is not really expected to conduct a thorough investigation and need only respond to particular risks if they are uncovered. If an irregularity emerges then it would be sufficient for the examiner to argue that there had been no reason to suspect that the problem existed. If an audit is undertaken then the expectations concerning the standard of care will be very much higher and the audit firm may be exposed to claims if, say, the charity is ever involved in an accounting scandal.

The firm should also consider whether a full audit is a practical proposition. Given that work is undertaken around the world and that the auditor will not be able to observe much of the distribution of relief, it may be impossible to gather sufficient, appropriate evidence.

(b) The most immediate problem is that the charity is a small entity. There are only 25 full-time staff, many of whom will be engaged in relief work and will not be available for ensuring that administration and controls are operating effectively. It may be difficult to ensure that an adequate system is in place to prevent fraud or abuse of the charity's finances, but it may be possible for the board to deal with that to some extent by paying close attention to the charity's activities. That oversight will assist them to make the best possible use of the charity's resources and may also highlight serious discrepancies.

The nature of the relief work will also tend to make controls more difficult. There is a clear need to move quickly with respect to chartering aircraft and despatching supplies, which may make traditional authorisation more difficult to fit in. It may be possible to overcome this by having very clear procedures in place that give staff sufficient guidance as to when it would be appropriate to respond. Those procedures could include a formal review of the cases where a manager or supervisor uses this initiative so that there is a clear understanding that decision makers will be held accountable for their actions.

Aid is distributed on the ground with no direct supervision and it may be abused. Forgewood's workers may not be able to ensure that the resources are being applied to the intended use because there could be theft or corruption. The only way to address this would be to ensure that relief is only despatched to areas where there is reasonable confidence that work can be conducted in a safe and secure environment; for example, by checking that there is a police or military presence to protect aid workers. Aid workers should also be asked to make video records of their activities, partly to enable review by the board and partly to assist in fundraising by showing donors how their money is being spent.

The board is likely to be held responsible for any abuses because stewardship is a major issue facing all charities.

5 Lamara

> **Tutorial note.** This question deals with the topical area of audit quality and the associated area of auditor liability in respect of any shortcomings in the auditor's work. As with any question involving recent developments, it is not anticipated that candidates will have read any specific articles or materials. Those who have kept abreast of this development may be at an advantage, but it should be sufficient to approach this question with a clear understanding of the syllabus.

(a) Audit firms are required to apply ISQM 1 *Quality Management for Firms that Perform Audits or Reviews of Financial Statements, or Other Assurance or Related Services Engagements*.

ISQM 1 states that a firm's system of quality management shall include address each of the following components:

- The firm's risk assessment process
- Governance and leadership
- Relevant ethical requirements
- Acceptance and continuance of client relationships and specific engagements
- Engagement performance
- Resources
- Information and communication
- The monitoring and remediation process

(b) Direct confirmation of trade receivables is regarded as offering better evidence because it provides third party, documentary evidence of the customer's acknowledgement of the debt. Vouching balances in the manner stated forces the auditor to rely on documents that have been prepared by the company's staff in some cases, such as despatch records, and even third party documents, such as customer orders, have been handled by staff.

A direct confirmation would have highlighted the differences due to the cut-off problem. Customer responses would have led to the auditor checking that differences were due to legitimate timing differences. Unfortunately, the audit team might not have detected the problem. They would have vouched reconciling items to customer orders, which would have agreed. They would then have vouched them to despatch records, which would also have agreed because Glora's staff were predating despatch records.

It is debatable whether the auditor could have detected the predating. Normally, the auditor is forced to rely on segregation of duties within client companies to enable them to rely upon internally generated documents. The segregation appears to be present, but the control has been overridden by management.

The only realistic argument that the auditor has been negligent is that this was a high risk audit because it supports the selling price of the company. Perhaps the auditor should have insisted on more time or should have conducted a more thorough approach, such as a very detailed review of transactions posted towards the end of the reporting period.

(c) The auditor's liability depends on three factors: negligence, duty of care and consequential loss. The court has decided that the auditor was negligent, so that leaves consequential loss and duty of care.

Consequential loss is difficult because it is unclear whether Jedfry has overpaid for assets. The receivables did not exist at 31 December 2015, but they came into existence soon afterwards. Glora would almost certainly have had to pass the rights and benefits associated with them on to Jedfry and so no loss would have been incurred.

Jedfry could argue that it paid a multiple of reported earnings as its consideration. Overstating cash flows and profits of the ten months ended 31 December 2015 could have led to an overpayment for goodwill.

The auditor is reporting to a specific addressee, who has communicated that the audit report will be used for the purpose of negotiating the sale of this company. That would generally create the basis of a duty of care.

The terms and conditions paragraph is of dubious value. The courts might regard it as unacceptable for the auditor to take a fee in return for a report addressed to a known reader who has a specific and known interest in the accounts and then to refuse to accept any responsibility. It is unlikely that the auditor will be able to deny any liability on the basis of that paragraph.

The Bannerman case may enable the auditor to rely on the provisions in the clause in the report itself. That makes an implicit offer to accept a liability of up to $250,000, so the auditor is offering some recompense in the event of failure. The limitation is realistic in relation to the amount being claimed and so the courts might be persuaded to accept that the liability be pegged at $250,000, subject to the loss of up to $1 million being agreed.

6 Lion Manufacturing

Tutorial note. This question tests candidates' understanding of the issues associated with auditor independence and audit quality that arise from the r mandatory rotation of audit firms that was made mandatory following EU audit reforms in 2016.

(a) One of the biggest threats to auditor independence is the fact that the audit fee grants the directors a degree of influence over the auditor. The fact that auditor appointments are generally renewed year after year means that the auditor will be keen to avoid upsetting the board and thereby threatening the possibility of a further appointment. The mandatory rotation of audit firms will mean that the auditor's economic incentives would change. There will no longer be any possibility of an indefinite stream of income from any given audit client. Auditors may be more willing to risk confronting the board if they have only, say, a maximum of three further appointments before they have to stand down anyway.

Auditor independence may also be compromised by the fact that audit scandals rarely come to light unless there is either a failure or a second look at the accounts. If auditors face mandatory replacement within a few years then they will; be aware that their replacement will study the accounting processes and policies and any irregularities that have been deliberately overlooked may come to light.

In the case of the Lion audit it would appear that the directors are generally honest and open in their approach to financial reporting and so they would not wish to compromise their auditor's independence. Lion's directors would not necessarily behave any differently if the auditor's independence was enhanced and so the company's financial reporting would not be improved. The auditors themselves may feel a little more free to speak openly, because they may not wish to disagree with Lion's board too forcefully just in case they lose a continuing appointment. Also, the perception of independence is just as important as the fact of independence. If mandatory rotation improved the shareholders' confidence in the auditor's independence then they may be less inclined to question the figures.

The fact that a new audit firm will be coming into Lion from time to time and taking a fresh look will enhance independence. Familiarity can lead to auditors taking a relaxed attitude and basing the audit opinion on perceptions rather than applying professional scepticism.

(b) Audit failure could be defined as the expression of an invalid audit opinion. In practice, there is very little risk that an auditor will express a modified auditor's report when an unmodified report would be more appropriate. In that event, the directors would investigate the reasons for qualifying the report and would quickly reassure the auditor that a mistake had been made. Audit failures are generally audits in which an unmodified auditor's report is published in circumstances where a modified report would have been more appropriate.

Audit quality depends heavily upon the auditor understanding the business and its systems. Any incoming auditor will be able to take a fresh look at the figures, but will not necessarily be able to make the best use of the information obtained. A longer association with the company will enable the auditor to consider the implications of changes, such as the appointment of a new person to the board or changes in the business environment. Making an informed response to control risks or inherent risks requires more than just the ability to spot the threat. Experience of the client's past behaviour will enable the auditor to put this information into a context.

One explanation for the statistics concerning audit failure is that incoming auditors are not well equipped to identify risks. For example, there may be peculiarities of a business that mean that a pattern of cash flows that would be perfectly acceptable in most companies would indicate a threat to going concern. Mandatory rotation could mean that auditors will not have sufficient understanding during the first year or two and will then have to stand down once they have some experience.

There will be a financial cost associated with processing these risks in the first year or two because auditors will have to invest more in planning and the review of audit files. It is almost inevitable that audit fees will increase.

Some of the arguments that are put forward may be misleading. The fact that audit failures are relatively common during new audits could simply suggest that auditors are standing down from high risk audits. That would bias the distribution of audit failures because the replacement auditors would be faced with the risks that their predecessors had avoided by refusing reappointment. This factor would remain under mandatory rotation, but it would not necessarily become any worse because of it.

(c) Data analytics is the examination of data to try to identify patterns, trends or correlations. As the quantity of data has increased, it has become more necessary to evolve ways of processing and making sense of it. Data analytics is thus part of the 'Big data' movement, namely the qualitative shift in the amount of data that can be held and analysed by modern computers.

Recent advances in IT make it increasingly possible for auditors to examine and to manipulate a complete data set, ie 100% of the transactions. This has the potential to change the way audit testing works; rather than eg performing controls testing on a sample of items, it is possible to perform risk analysis on a whole population. In an audit environment so saturated with data about a client, one of the key challenges for auditors is knowing how to make the best use of the data. To help avoid the phenomenon of 'drowning in data', audit data analytics tools allow auditors to visualise trends graphically, and to develop new ways of interrogating data to find trends and relationships.

Current auditing standards, such as ISAs, are based on the technique of risk-based auditing which first became the norm in the 1970s, when it replaced the fully substantive approaches that had preceded it. It has been claimed in some quarters that these techniques will bring about changes of this magnitude to the profession. The sheer scale of the work that can be performed using data analytics techniques makes such a difference to auditors that modifications to existing auditing standards have been required and are ongoing. ATTs (including data analytics) have been woven into ISA 315 (revised 2019) and examples have been built into the application material in an attempt to bring the use of technology by auditors into the ISAs. The IAASB's technology consultation group has also published a number of guidance documents, for example on using automated tools and techniques (ATTs) including data analytics in planning and performing audit procedures.

PRACTICE ANSWER BANK

7 Zando

Tutorial note: This question deals with the implications for the profession of a major audit firm being fined for allegedly negligent audit work. The scenario mirrors recent examples of broadly similar cases reaching their conclusion, with the questions arising from the damage being done to the firms themselves and also to the profession's reputation because the investigations and reports can be somewhat protracted.

(a) Users of audited financial statements expect a very high standard of assurance and so they often feel let down by allegations of audit failure. In this case, the apparent negligence has led to significant losses borne by apparently vulnerable members of society.

The fact that a major audit firm was fined is a concern because it suggests that there was, indeed, a case to answer. It is relatively common for professional people to be accused of negligence, but that does not mean that they have actually done anything wrong. The fine confirms that an error occurred.

This was one of the very largest audit firms, whom one would expect to set the standard for the profession as a whole. If such a large firm could be criticised and fined then there could be doubts about less prestigious firms.

There is nothing to suggest that the firm has compensated the injured parties, who are almost certainly unable to pursue a case against a major firm. There is no obvious act of contrition, with the firm making an *ex gratia* compensation payment to the customers who lost their deposits.

The fact that the individual partner was fined also suggests that the firm was incapable of exercising adequate supervision over its partners.

It could be argued that the significant fines are evidence that the profession takes its responsibility as a regulator seriously. It would have been relatively straightforward for the regulators to have conducted a superficial enquiry and concluded that the auditor had been innocent of all charges.

(b) The delay in completing the report might be interpreted cynically as a failure on the part of the profession to deal with problems swiftly and efficiently. Any lessons to be learned from this case and the regulator's report would not have been available for several years. That message would have been diluted by the passage of time, for example the partner responsible has since left the profession and the firm may claim that it has changed since the events that led to this criticism.

The delay also increases the adverse publicity because the publication of the report after all these years rekindles the press' interest. Thus, the report may attract almost as much attention as a fresh news story in itself as Vowcher's original failure.

These delays could be viewed as a necessary implication of conducting a full and uninhibited investigation. The investigation could not necessarily commence until the situation had settled down. For example, Paper and its subsidiaries would have to be wound up in order to determine the full extent of any losses.

The regulators would have to avoid interfering with any criminal or civil lawsuits against either Paper or Zando. That would lead to a delay in commencing a full investigation.

The investigation itself would not have taken years to complete, but it would have been time-consuming in its own right. The various people involved would have had to be interviewed and documentary evidence gathered and sifted. It would have been necessary to corroborate findings and so clarify any conflicting arguments or explanations.

(c) Where a company is experiencing going concern (GC) difficulties, this means that there are significant doubts relating to going concern. From the auditor's point of view there are therefore material uncertainties relating to those doubts.

There are several possible situations, each of which should have a different effect on the auditor's report. There are two main ways things can go wrong here: either the GC basis of accounting is appropriate but there is a material uncertainty, or the GC basis of accounting is inappropriate.

Where the GC basis of accounting is appropriate but there is a material uncertainty, then:

- If disclosure in the financial statements is adequate, then the auditor expresses an unmodified opinion and includes a section headed 'Material Uncertainty Related to Going Concern'
- If disclosure is inadequate, then the opinion is qualified or adverse

Where the GC basis of accounting is inappropriate, then:

- If the treatment in the financial statements is adequate, then the auditor expresses an unmodified opinion. The auditor may also include an emphasis of matter paragraph to draw attention to alternative basis of preparation
- If the treatment in the financial statements is inadequate, then the auditor expresses an adverse opinion.

8 Ethics committee

Tutorial note: This question deals with the independence issues arising from an audit partner accepting a seat on the board of a client company. This is a topical concern that has been discussed due to cases involving publicly traded companies. This case is a little more subtle because the client concerned was not a public interest entity. The question also deals with the independence issues associated with evaluating the performance of audit partners on the basis of their ability to persuade audit clients to purchase non-audit services. Again, this has become a topical issue.

(a) The ethics committee has to address two matters. The first is whether the firm was in any way compromised in terms of Frank's past behaviour as the engagement partner on the audit of Hoss. The second question is whether the firm can continue to audit Hoss without allegations of compromise.

The audit firm should investigate the relationship between Frank and Hoss during the last audit. It is important to establish when Frank was made aware of the possibility of joining the company's board. The previous incumbent's departure was almost certainly known long before he or she actually left and so the date that Frank applied and was interviewed is really quite irrelevant. It would be ideal if a meeting could be arranged with Frank in order to discuss the timings of the various steps.

The working papers from the audit should be reviewed by an appropriate reviewer in order to ensure that any matters requiring professional judgement were handled carefully and without any bias. Any concerns should be investigated carefully so that the firm can be confident in its report on the financial statements.

The IESBA *Code of Ethics* also requires the firm to consider its present position. Frank's past experience of acting as engagement partner creates a number of threats to independence. For example, a familiarity threat might be created where the audit team are too familiar with Frank and are too trusting of what he says leading them to be less sceptical or not challenge him enough. An intimidation threat might also be created where a member of the audit team who was previously more junior than Frank might feel unable to challenge or question him.

It may be expedient to replace the audit team, so that there is a complete change of staff in charge of this audit. Frank's replacement as engagement partner and the new manager can then reconsider the overall audit strategy and plan with a view to changing the approach as far as possible. That will make it more difficult for Frank to anticipate the firm's audit approach. The new audit partner should have sufficient experience relative to Frank.

The firm must also ensure it follows the requirements of the IESBA Code that:

- Frank is not entitled to any benefits or payments from the firm that are not made in accordance with fixed pre-determined arrangements;
- Any amount owed to Frank is not material to the firm; and
- Frank does not continue to participate or appear to participate in the firm's business or professional activities.

If the firm manages its relationship with Hoss carefully then it should be possible to continue to audit the company, otherwise it would be prudent to resign.

(b) The first issue that has to be addressed is that a recently-appointed partner feels that she has been asked to behave in an unprofessional manner. The ethics committee should act immediately to address those concerns, otherwise this may undermine that partner's professionalism.

Hannah has only been a partner for two years and so she has had very little opportunity to use her position as engagement partner to bring in fresh business. If the pressures are excessive then she may behave in a rash manner that undermines the firm's independence and its credibility in the eyes of client management.

Partners should be encouraged to bring in business because audit firms are commercial entities that exist to sell professional services. Indeed, broadening the client base makes the firm more independent of individual clients.

However, the IESBA *Code of Ethics for Professional Accountants* states that partners selling non-audit services to audit clients might create a self-interest threat whereby the partner is less likely to issue an unmodified auditor's report for fear of losing the lucrative non-audit work. The Code states that 'a firm shall not evaluate or compensate a key audit partner based on that partner's success in selling non-assurance services to the partner's audit client. (IESBA Code: para. R411.4)'. If Hannah's compensation is based on her appraisal then Hannah's objection is valid and also raises a concern that the firm's compensation policies breach this rule in the IESBA Code.

The ethics committee should consider the manner in which practice development is discussed during appraisal interviews. If there is, for example, a section in the form or document used to record the feedback then the wording should be considered carefully in case it is open to misinterpretation. All senior partners should be briefed on what should be communicated to junior partners with respect to the firm's policies in this area. The policy needs to be amended so that it is compliant with the IESBA Code.

ISQM 1 requires the firm is to have quality objectives, policies and procedures addressing the relevant ethical requirements as part of its system of quality management. If the partner compensation policy breaches the IESBA Code, then the system of quality management is not working as it should. The matter should be investigated and remedial action to address the matter be designed and implemented so that the firm can ensure its system of quality management is functioning effectively.

9 Rocco

> **Tutorial note.** This question deals with the decision to accept reappointment with a long standing audit client.

Briefing notes
To: Managing partner
From: Rocco
Re: Client acceptance decision – Viper PLC
Date: XX May 2014

I am writing in my capacity as the recently appointed engagement quality review partner on the audit of Viper PLC. The purpose of this memo is to identify the independence and audit risk issues arising from our continuation with this client.

In my opinion, it may not be in GHY's best interests to accept further appointment. It may be better for us to decline rather than running the risk of harming our reputation.

(a) Viper provides a significant percentage of the Southtown office's recurring fee income. In the event of any criticism, this statistic may make it difficult to argue that we behaved in an independent manner. Having said that, we could reduce that risk by appointing a partner from Capital City to advise on all major issues of professional judgement.

Independence requires that we are free to gather sufficient audit evidence. Staffing issues seem to be in danger of constraining the audit fieldwork. It may not be cost-effective to appoint additional staff in Southtown, but we could possibly second some staff from other offices to ensure that adequate resources were available for an independent investigation.

Staff familiarity is becoming an issue. In the Enron case, the fact that the external auditor had a permanent room at the client's head office was criticised on the grounds that it implied a lack of independence. This threat can be addressed in part by reinforcing the need for all of GHY's staff to conduct themselves in a professional manner at all times.

(b) Viper's directors appear to be taking an increasingly aggressive line over the use of complex financial instruments in order to enhance the appearance of the statement of financial position. That is an attitude that should concern GHY because they are not committed to fair presentation in the financial statements. The fact that they are prepared to pay the fees that will be charged by a bank for the design of such a scheme indicates that they are committed to manipulate the financial statements.

The fact that a bank is being used in this way suggests that the schemes will be very carefully designed to abuse any loopholes that can be found in IAS 32 *Financial instruments: presentation*. It may be difficult to dissuade Viper's board from insisting on the classification that best suits their purpose because they will have the recommendation from the bank who designed the instrument that it is equity. GHY's credibility may be threatened if we accept the board's treatment, even if the instrument does meet the definition of equity because this is likely to be a controversial matter. The desire to manage the appearance of the financial statements may not be restricted to the area of financial instruments. The directors may become increasingly aggressive in the question for more acceptable ratios.

While creative accounting will always be a matter of some concern, we always have the right to modify our auditor's report. The damage that the directors might inflict is self-limiting because we will never agree to extreme cases.

10 Farr Hume

> **Tutorial note.** This question deals with the auditor's duties with respect to the tendering for the audit of a major charity. The question raises issues concerning the auditor's independence and professionalism.

(a) The first matter is whether Farr Hume can provide a satisfactory service. The fact that this charity is a major undertaking could mean that the audit firm's resources will be stretched. The fact that the charity operates internationally may affect the firm's ability to conduct a satisfactory audit unless it has corresponding offices through an international network.

Farr Hume will have to consider the technical expertise required. The charity will require some understanding of the relevant legislation, which may differ from that affecting company audits. It may be necessary to budget time for the engagement and review partners to attend external courses or otherwise equip themselves for this role.

There could be considerable exposure from this audit. That could be positive if it means that Farr Hume is associated with a high-profile client. It could be bad if there are ever any allegations about mismanagement or malpractice on the part of the charity. Major charities have to be accountable to donors and other stakeholders. There are major risks associated with activities that involve distribution of wealth in developing countries. Farr Hume could easily become involved in a major audit scandal.

The fund raising activities undertaken by the junior staff could compromise the appearance of independence. It may be necessary to adopt a different charity in the future if the audit tender is accepted.

(b) This proposal raises a number of major ethical problems.

The audit fee is an important factor in determining whether the auditor has applied appropriate professional competence and due care. If the auditor is seen to be claiming a fee then that will reassure stakeholders that a satisfactory audit is being carried out. The fact that the audit fee is being overstated in this way seems somewhat dishonest.

From a purely technical point of view, this appears to be a connected transaction. The concept of substance over form or that of fair presentation would require the fact that the payment of a fee will also trigger the connected payment of a donation to be accounted for more clearly.

The fact that the auditor has effectively agreed to work for nothing raises a self-interest threat to the professional competence and due care. To what extent can the audit firm sustain this major expenditure in terms of chargeable hours for which no recovery can be made? To what extent might this affect the firm's willingness to undertake additional testing that becomes necessary?

The auditor should either charge a realistic audit fee and keep that, on the basis that the audit will still enhance the charity's ability to generate income and support its activities, or it should apply safeguards including:

- Making Hunger Relief aware of the terms of the engagement, including the basis on which fees are charged and which services are covered by the quoted fee.

- Maintaining records such that Farr Hume is able to demonstrate that appropriate staff and time are spent on the engagement.

- Complying with all applicable assurance standards, guidelines and quality management policies and procedures.

11 Journal

> **Tutorial note.** This question deals with the governance and audit issues associated with an entity's reputation being brought into disrepute because of actions taken by a senior manager.

(a) The fact that the group operates on a multinational basis creates potential problems for the audit. It is more difficult for a parent to exercise effective governance when operating on a global basis. To an extent that may explain how the editor of a newspaper can engage is such unacceptable behaviour. Local newspaper editors will be operating in accordance with their own cultural norms and those may be unacceptable to the group's shareholders and senior management. This has implications for the auditor's evaluation of the overall control environment, including the possibility of major unrecorded liabilities and contingent liabilities arising from slack management of the editorial process.

The fact that the founder remains on the board as chairman is a potential concern. Ed Blanc has more than just a financial stake. There will be a great deal of pride and reputation at stake when managing Journal and so he may be prepared to stretch any governance matters. Ed Blanc is still a major shareholder and that may be enough in itself to call his ability to provide useful and impartial oversight of the board into question. He may be tempted to abuse his chairmanship in order to protect his personal financial stake. The external auditor will be concerned that Ed Blanc's involvement will lead to distortion and manipulation of the financial statements. The global risk will be increased by these arrangements.

The fact that the chairman is associated with the decision to close down the newspaper title is a matter of some concern. The chairman should not be involved in making executive decisions and should not be holding himself out as a representative of the company in this way. His responsibility should be more private and should focus on the management of the board. This is a further concern for the evaluation of inherent risk at the global level.

It is debatable whether the new non-executive will have a significant impact on the editorial problems. This looks like a high-profile token appointment. It is also debatable whether a non-executive should have such a specific role in the management process.

The fact that the founder's nephew is the chief executive of such a major part of the business is a matter of some concern. Clearly, there appears to be some confusion about whether Journal is an independent, publicly traded company (which is what it ought to be) or a family business that was founded and is managed by the Blanc family. Ed Blanc should not be voting on James' reappointment and certainly should not be using his shareholding as a lever to ensure that. Any public criticism of this relationship will reflect badly on Journal's external auditor.

Answers should be formatted and written as an emailed response to the managing partner.

(b) The most obvious argument in favour of continuing with this appointment is that the audit will be profitable for the firm. There is no compelling reason to throw away the revenue that can be generated from continuing. The scandal itself did not involve any obvious accounting matters and so the auditor's responsibility is not really open to question.

Journal will clearly remain a going concern despite the closure of the offending title. That suggests that there is a further case for retaining the audit. The scandal will pass and everything will get back to normal, apart from the loss of a very small percentage of revenue (which could be recouped if some of Journal's other newspapers are positioned properly in this market).

The fact that the editor could get away with bribing police officers in return for access may suggest that the control environment is weak. A weak control environment can create a serious risk that the financial statements will contain material irregularities. That may be a matter for investigation before making a final decision about accepting the appointment. The auditor's reputation will be affected if the company is ever implicated in an accounting scandal in the future because the users of the financial statements will wonder why the audit investigation was not more thorough in the light of the apparently unprofessional behaviour of the company's management. This threat would not increase the probability of overlooking an accounting irregularity, but it would mean that any allegation that the auditor had missed anything would prove even more serious than it would normally be.

There is a possibility that this scandal will undermine confidence in anything that Journal says or does and so the financial statements may not be regarded as credible even if there are no specific concerns about particular figures. If that is the case then the auditor's reputation may be undermined by association with an allegedly dishonest newspaper and so it may be worth considering withdrawing from the engagement.

12 Openness principle

Tutorial note. This question tests aspects of the control environment within an audit firm. The question contains a quote from a document published in order to strengthen governance within accounting firms, but there is no particular need to have read that document in order to attempt this question.

(a) The structure of a typical audit firm has a tendency to create rivalry between members of staff at any given level. Typically, firms have a hierarchy that refreshes itself by staff being promoted as they gain experience. Those who do not get promoted to the next level tend to be 'counselled out' so that there is a steady flow of people through the firm. That means that staff may be very reluctant to consult and to share. Arguably, admitting to a problem or providing a colleague with a solution may reduce one's standing in the competition for promotion.

Passing information down to subordinates may also be discouraged by this structure. Typically, junior staff will be in a pool of staff available to assist in audit work. If a manager invests time and energy in training and educating junior staff then those individuals may not work in any further audits conducted by the manager and the benefit will be enjoyed by the firm as a whole but not by the individual who made the effort.

As with any agency-based analysis, it is potentially misleading to focus exclusively on self-interest. Most audit staff will take a personal pride in their work and will wish to conduct themselves properly. The problem may be exaggerated, although the firm will have to consider the possibility of audit quality being affected by selfish behaviour by staff.

The public interest is difficult to understand, partly because public interest considerations can be inconsistent with professional ethics. For example, the public interest may require whistleblowing, which would be inconsistent with the concept of client confidence. Furthermore, the public interest is not a single unitary concept. There may be a host of stakeholders whose interests are in conflict and so the public interest may not be easily observable. There may be disagreements between staff as to how the public interest should best be considered and that could lead to crises of conscience on the part of the staff who believe that insufficient attention is being paid to the public's right to know about information that is being suppressed because senior audit staff have decided that the need to maintain confidence is paramount in a particular case.

(b) A lack of openness may be potentially disastrous because it implies that audit quality may be impaired. For example, a member of the audit team may be concerned that reporting a problem will lead to the substantive testing risk being reduced with no additional time being made available to conduct the extra testing. That could lead to irregular auditing in the form of the deliberate omission of information from the audit working papers. The risk of such behaviour is linked to the degree of trust that junior staff have in the integrity of more senior staff.

A lack of openness will encourage a culture where members of staff focus on their own career progression rather than the interests of the firm. For example, problems such as budget overruns and failure to meet deadlines may not be shared with colleagues and so these difficulties may not be addressed and managed effectively.

In the event of an audit scandal, the injured party will have the benefit of hindsight and may be able to show that insufficient attention was drawn to serious concerns. The audit firm's position will be further weakened by the fact that junior members of staff were unwilling to pass on information because the firm's culture discouraged such behaviour. If an audit firm is faced with a claim then there may be very little scope for mounting an effective defence if staff will be forced to admit under oath that they suppressed findings.

The fact that the public interest may be overlooked will be bad for the firm concerned and may be bad for the profession as a whole. All auditors, including junior trainees, have a responsibility to tell the truth, regardless of the consequences, arising from their professional status.

13 Garrity

> **Tutorial note:** This question deals with the role of the board in establishing the risk appetite (and control environment) for a new treasury department and in controlling and monitoring the treasury, either directly or through the use of internal audit.

(a) The risk appetite will not really lend itself to explicit quantification. The most realistic course of action would be to give the treasurer the opportunity to study Garrity's past results and transactions. That would enable the treasurer to fully understand the types of risks that Susanna has identified as worth controlling when she was responsible. Talking through these decisions will give the new treasurer a better understanding of the board's attitudes.

Next, the treasurer could discuss some 'what if' scenarios with Susanna. The objective of this would be to articulate the risks in a realistic scenario and the costs and benefits of managing those risks. For example, if it was known that Garrity's competitors were not buying futures to fix fuel prices then the treasurer might consider the advantages and disadvantages of copying that strategy or taking a different direction. If Garrity buys futures and the fuel price rises then Garrity will have a cost advantage and can undercut competitors' fares. Buying futures could leave Garrity at a disadvantage if the price falls after buying futures.

Susanna could 'shadow' the treasurer for a while after appointment. She could offer advice and seek clarification on any transactions that she disagreed with.

Finally, the board could communicate its expectations concerning risk appetite by setting a budget for the running of the treasury department. The budget might indicate the maximum amount that should be spent on buying futures and other financial instruments so that the treasurer has a targeted level of activity. That would not prevent the treasurer from seeking permission to exceed that limit in the event that there was unexpected volatility in the markets.

(b) The board should start by taking care in the appointment of competent and professional treasury professionals. Qualified treasurers will be able to ensure that any transactions are for acceptable purposes as defined by the department's standing instructions. They will also have reputations that must be maintained for the sake of their long-term careers.

There should be sufficient administrative staff in the department to permit adequate internal check and segregation of duties. Adequate segregation requires that the professional treasury staff can decide upon an appropriate position to take in order to offset a risk and then pass an instruction to clerical staff to record the transactions. If the clerical staff are required to maintain detailed records and to reconcile the bookkeeping records to ensure that all open positions are recorded then it will be very difficult for the 'rogue trader' phenomenon to remain undetected.

Garrity's board should ensure that there are clear operating procedures for the treasury department and should set out the limits of the treasurer's authority. In general, the treasury department should never instigate a net position in any currency or other investment, so every transaction should be to counter a specific and known financial risk. For example, futures contracts should reflect the quantities of fuel that would be purchased at the maturity date.

Every transaction undertaken by the treasury department should be supported by a report that indicates the purpose of the purchase or the sale. There should be a clear, commercial purpose for every position taken by the treasury department, with a specific statement of when that position will be closed out in response to the end of the exposure, such as the purchase price of a specific aircraft.

The treasurer should be required to provide the finance director with a detailed statement of all material outstanding treasury positions at the close of business every day. That would deter any positions being entered into recklessly or left in place after the need for them ceased.

Garrity's internal audit department could conduct a regular investigation of the treasury department. The focus of the investigations should be on ensuring that the positions held by the treasury department are supported by the documentation prepared to ensure that there is no speculation using Garrity's resources. The investigation could, therefore, focus on the completeness and accuracy of reports.

14 Trent

Tutorial note. This question tests candidates' understanding of the merits of the risk-based approach to gathering audit evidence. Candidates should be aware that the risk-based approach is more than simply a less expensive alternative to vouching. The question also raises questions about the need for formal documentation of audit evidence.

(a) Historically, auditors have relied heavily upon substantive testing techniques in the past. In principle, it is possible to gather sufficient evidence from substantive testing alone.

ISA 315 (Revised 2019) *Identifying and assessing the risks of material misstatement* requires the auditor to identify and assess the risks of material misstatement. Substantive testing does not really discharge that responsibility. At best, if the tests are sufficiently comprehensive and are appropriate, the auditor can be satisfied that there are no material irregularities in the bookkeeping records. In the absence of an audit plan that refers to inherent and control risks the auditor could overlook serious threats to the fair presentation of the financial statements.

Auditors are expected to form a view on the governance of their clients and to assist with the improvement of that governance. Stakeholders may feel let down if Trent simply conducts a heavy substantive approach to the audit of Spare.

There could be an argument that Frank has left Trent exposed to criticism by agreeing to work for Spare. If Spare's systems and governance are weak then it may be almost impossible to compensate by extending substantive testing samples. Even the abandonment of sampling and resorting to 100% vouching may not uncover every threat to the financial statements. For example, the ready availability of scanners and colour printers means that documentary evidence may have little value unless the auditor is satisfied that it has gone through a sound control system in order to establish its validity.

The fact that Spare is a very small company may also mean that Trent has been exposed to this reputational risk for the sake of a correspondingly small audit fee. Frank's decision may make very little commercial sense.

(b) Frank's position appears to be that an implicit and informal evaluation of inherent risk and control risk is acceptable. There is a sense in which it could be argued that Frank would have been able to justify some reliance on the evaluation of these risks if a formal review had been conducted. For example, even with a small staff complement, there is likely to be some proprietorial control being exercised by Spare's managers and directors. Frank appears to be taking some comfort from the fact that such a review would have been fruitful without having actually undertaken the work. Frank's position may be supported by the fact that his dealings with the company will provide some insight into the extent to which the directors are aware of the routine operations and whether, for example, they are capable of identifying cases where property, plant and equipment has been misappropriated.

At the very least, Frank is in breach of ISA 230 *Audit documentation* because the audit working papers do not indicate that this informal reliance has been placed on controls. That has left Trent's other partners unable to evaluate the quality of the work undertaken in order to conduct quality management procedures. It has also left Trent exposed in the event that the firm is ever required to substantiate the quality of its work.

The vans themselves are unlikely to be overstated because Spare would not be able to generate revenue if its vans did not exist, so there is very little risk of Frank's approach leading to an audit failure relating to their existence. There could be issues relating to the condition of the vans and their associated expected useful lives.

The equipment is a more difficult issue. It is, by definition, portable and valuable. If an engineer had, say, fraudulently sold some of this kit then it may not render the engineer incapable of repairing customers' machines and so the fraud would not have easily come to light. If the engineers were based locally and the vans were parked at Spare's premises overnight then it might have been possible for a member of the audit team to have conducted a surprise audit visit at the beginning or end of the working day in order to inspect the equipment. Alternatively, one or more of the engineers could have been asked to visit Spare's office at very short notice so that the audit team could conduct a physical inspection.

15 Payne Engineering

> **Tutorial note.** This question deals with the role of internal audit and also the independence of the internal audit function.

(a) The classification of errors is helpful to all parties. Auditee departments will not be subject to criticism because of minor errors that could otherwise become major issues if senior managers exaggerate their importance. Senior managers receiving auditor's reports will find it easier to deal with documents that classify reported errors on a very simple two-point scale. If, for any reason, senior management wishes to know what was included in the green category then it will always be possible to obtain the list from the internal audit function. Auditors may also find it helpful to be permitted to demonstrate their understanding of the system by offering this classification.

It could be argued that the control environment may be undermined by the suggestion that compliance errors can be excluded from the auditor's report. Managers may believe that errors classed as green do not matter because no further action is taken. Even amber failures have a relaxed response because there is no great urgency attached to their resolution. Senior management may regard amber failures as matters that will be automatically dealt with by internal audit and so feel that they can be overlooked.

Scoring errors may distract attention from the fact that errors occurred at all. Senior management should be considering whether amber errors have an underlying implication that local supervision is deficient and that it is simply good luck that more serious failures have not occurred.

The fact that there are only three points on the scale could mean that there could be some inconsistency between auditors in terms of classification. There is quite a significant step in severity going from green to amber to red and some auditors may be more conservative than others.

(b) In an ideal world, the internal audit function will be regarded as offering auditee departments a constructive and supportive service. The internal audit function should assist managers in motivating their staff to comply with procedures and so make it easier to discharge their responsibilities. The fact that the internal audit team can classify some failures as 'red' and that department heads are then subject to a process that appears to be almost disciplinary in nature could undermine that spirit of cooperation and partnership.

If auditee departments are afraid of having reports of critical failures lodged against them then they may be uncooperative and may hamper internal audit investigations. The ability to negotiate grades could, to some extent, assist the audit team in building a spirit of trust in the process so that they receive the support that they need from auditee departments.

The process of negotiation is, potentially, a useful means of communicating the severity of the matters that have been discovered during the audit. If the auditor classifies a problem as red, knowing that there could be scope for changing it to amber during the process of drafting the final report, then it will be clear to the head of the auditee department that the matter is serious. If the auditor agrees to classify a failure as amber or green after a serious debate then the auditee department will pay greater attention to it in future than if it had simply been classed as amber or green in the initial draft.

The fact that changes can occur could leave managers with the impression that the internal auditor is indecisive or lacks independence. Managers may feel that they can be rewarded for aggressively resisting the work of the internal auditor. The classification scheme will have far less impact if it is widely known that the scores can be negotiated down.

16 Rasp (amended)

Tutorial note. Overall, the question deals with the audit issues associated with the need to show financial assets at their fair values. The scenario is complicated by the fact that the company directors do not appear to have taken adequate steps to ensure the correct valuation of the assets and are now using the reporting timetable as an excuse to pressure the auditor into dealing with the issues quickly.

(a) **Briefing note**

First of all, the fact that the deadline is pressing does not reduce the need to gather sufficient audit evidence. We must also ensure that we meet all of our professional responsibilities with respect to independence. The fact that the valuation is to appear in the financial statements means that there is a danger that we will be auditing our own work.

The International Ethics Standards Board for Accountants (IESBA) *Code of Ethics for Professional Accountants* states that the performance of valuation services for an audit client may create a self-review threat. The extent of that threat depends upon the circumstances. The following issues apply to the work done for Rasp:

- The value attributed to these assets will almost certainly be material. Indeed, the point of the valuation is that it may reveal the need for an adjustment that will, in itself, be material.

- There is a choice of models that may be used. The fact that the directors have already chosen a model that shows a high value and recognises a gain may mean that the staff conducting the valuation will come under some pressure.

- There is considerable subjectivity in the inputs put into this model. The draft note states that the assets are valued using techniques appropriate to level 2 of the hierarchy put in place by IFRS 7, which means that inputs have had to be based on assumptions. (**Note.** It would have been acceptable to refer to IFRS 13 with respect to valuation.) That means that there is no objectively correct solution to this process because the valuer must decide, for example, on an appropriate quoted security to use as a basis for comparison.

The materiality of the adjustment is also an issue in deciding whether it is acceptable for Rasp to apply hedge accounting. It may be that the adoption of an alternative valuation method will undermine the assumption that the hedge is highly effective and that could have a further impact on the financial statements.

If Rasp had been a publicly traded company (or another public interest entity) then the IESBA Code would not have permitted the audit firm to provide a valuation service in addition to performing the audit.

The IESBA Code does not permit audit firms to provide valuation services to companies that are not public interest entities where the valuation involves a significant degree of subjectivity and the valuation will have a material effect on the financial statements on which the firm will express an opinion. Given that it is a material matter, we need to decide whether there is so much subjectivity associated with the valuation that it would be impossible for us to have sufficient safeguards in place. I will discuss this matter with the partner in charge of consulting in order to establish just how significantly the valuation exercise is affected by subjective decisions. If there is a relatively narrow band of acceptable valuations that would lead to figures that are broadly in line with values attributed to similar publicly traded securities then there should be very little problem with their involvement in the exercise.

If permitted, the valuation service will need to be provided by a separate team to that performing the audit. In addition, the auditors should arrange for an independent review of the audit or valuation work by an appropriate reviewer.

(b) The fact that the bonds are valued at amortised cost means that the interest rate implicit in the bonds should have been verified. The first step is to ascertain the cost of the bonds, the cash flows and the redemption value. The internal rate of return function on a spreadsheet should have been used to determine the effective rate of interest on the bond.

The motive for holding the asset should have been discussed with management and also the nature of the asset itself. This has to be an asset that will give rise to cash flows that are essentially principal and interest.

The bonds should have been reviewed for impairment at every period end. The fact that management considers the bonds to be impaired requires investigation because IFRS 9 *Financial instrument* sets out the conditions that must be met before an impairment can be recognised.

A financial asset measured at amortised cost can only be written down because of impairment if there is objective evidence of impairment. That does not seem to have occurred in the case of these bonds. The sales director's concerns are prompted by the fact that the bond issuer has been placing smaller purchase orders with Rasp. That alone is hardly evidence that the issuer is in financial difficulties that could cause the collectability of the bonds to be threatened. It would require something far more persuasive, such as a default on an interest payment, to indicate that the issuer was in distress. At the very least, the auditor should obtain independent evidence that the bonds are impaired.

In the event that we agreed that there had been an impairment, we would require management to justify its estimates of future cash flows in order to establish the recoverable amount. This would then have to be studied carefully to ensure that the estimates and assumptions were acceptable.

(c) These matters both amount to disagreement over the facts. Rasp is making an unjustified impairment adjustment to the bond and appears to be overstating the value of the derivatives.

This disagreement is material and so the auditor's report will have to be modified as the financial statements are materially misstated. The fact that the adjustments will tend to offset one another, both in terms of reported earnings and total assets, does not affect the need for a qualification.

The auditor's report will have to state the facts concerning the bond. The asset itself does not appear to be impaired in terms of the requirements of IFRS 9. That has led to the understatement of both profit and net assets.

The fact that an over-optimistic valuation model has been used for the derivatives will also have to be stated. The auditor's report should indicate the range within which a realistic valuation should have fallen. The effect on the figures should be indicated, and the possibility that hedge accounting is not appropriate should also be disclosed.

This misstatement is material, but not pervasive. ISA 705 (Revised) *Modifications to the opinion in the independent auditor's report* requires a qualified opinion in these circumstances. The auditor's report should state that the financial statements give a true and fair view except for the matters indicated in the report.

(d) The information in the scenario suggests that this is a fairly high-risk audit. The directors are reluctant to accept our position concerning the financial assets, which could lead to a public dispute or a qualified auditor's report. If we are able to justify the acceptance of Rasp's treatment then we will have pushed the accounting rules to their limit and so we will be exposed to the threat of being implicated in an accounting scandal.

The fact that the directors have permitted these concerns to continue until the very end of the reporting timetable suggests that they are not above pressuring the auditor. The Rasp audit could prove to be a significant drain on partner and manager time within the firm. In the event that the publication of the statements is delayed because of a failure to reach agreement then the firm may be made to look inefficient if the directors blame the delay on the audit.

On the other hand, the directors do not appear to be misstating the figures by any means other than creative accounting and so there is no reason to suspect outright falsification of the numbers. They have not threatened to remove us from office because of our concerns and so there are no major independence issues. Being independent auditors, we can charge for the time and effort associated with dealing with these accounting issues. Provided we refuse to permit ourselves to be compromised we can earn a realistic fee from this audit and so it is not in our commercial interests to turn down a reappointment.

If we stand down then we will be replaced by a competing firm, who may not be as well equipped to deal with Rasp's problems and so there may be a greater risk of an audit failure by our replacement.

17 Voltage group (amended)

Tutorial note. This question deals with the audit of the provision for tax by a multinational company that appears to have been using a fairly transparent scheme for tax avoidance. This question will require the ability to address the audit risks arising from the need to provide for figures that could turn out to be highly volatile.

(a) The first step is to check that the tax computation has been prepared properly. Volt should have prepared a schedule that restates accounting profit to show taxable profit and that must be checked to ensure that all disallowed expenses have been added back and all non-accounting deductions have been made. The tax rates should be checked and the computations recast.

The correspondence with the tax authorities will have to be reviewed in some detail. The tax authorities will almost certainly have made their concerns clear before commencing their investigation. The substance of those concerns will have to be considered in order to form a view as to whether the tax authorities have a strong case. This may be a speculative attempt by the tax authorities to make Volt pay more tax or it may be that Volt has very little chance of defending this claim.

Volt will almost certainly have consulted tax experts and lawyers. All correspondence will have to be checked in order to ensure that Volt's advisers are confident. The logic behind those views will have to be reviewed and the auditor will have to consider whether that confidence is justified. Case law should be studied for precedents that might indicate whether Volt has a realistic chance of defending this tax avoidance scheme.

Volt's directors should be asked to confirm their intentions in writing. It will be embarrassing if the financial statements are published with a clean auditor's report and then Volt agrees to settle its tax assessment for a large amount that had not been provided for.

(b) Providing a service to advise Volt on tax strategy might result in a self-review threat where the audit firm audits tax figures it has calculated itself and is therefore less likely to point out any errors in the calculation. The IESBA Code has stricter rules for public interest entities (PIEs) such as Volt in this respect. It does not permit auditors to provide advisory and tax planning services to audit clients that are PIEs if the provision of such a service will create a self-review threat.

Assisting Volt in the resolution of a dispute with the tax authority might result in an advocacy threat whereby the auditor is seen to be advocating for or representing their audit client. It can also result in a self-review threat when there is a risk that the results of the service will affect the accounting records or the financial statements on which the firm will express an opinion. The IESBA Code states that the auditors shall not provide assistance in the resolution of tax disputes to an audit client that is a PIE if the provision of that assistance might create a self-review threat.

The other issue is whether it is morally acceptable for any accountant to provide such advice, regardless of auditor independence. Tax accountants have a duty to serve their clients' interests by working within the law to arrange tax affairs in an efficient manner. That advice should remain within the law.

Volt's tax avoidance scheme is technically lawful, but it overrides the spirit of the law. The arrangements hinge on a series of wholly artificial arrangements that have no commercial substance. There is no reason for the distribution company to buy the exhausts simply to resell them immediately at a higher price to a fellow group member without adding any value. Volt is clearly exploiting the opportunities that are often available to large multinationals to step around the law in the jurisdictions where they operate.

Overall, it seems unlikely that no self-review threat will be created from accepting the additional tax work and so by accepting the work the auditors will be breaching the IESBA Code. The tax partner should be advised to decline the separate tax engagement (or if they wish to accept it, resign as auditor).

18 Paloma (amended)

Tutorial note. This question deals with concerns that audit firms do not always employ staff who have sufficient IT skills to adequately conduct compliance tests on information processing controls.

(a) The only realistic way to check that an information processing control that depends on system-generated information is to use an automated tool or technique (ATT). ISA 315 (Revised 2019) *Identifying and assessing the risks of material misstatement* requires that the auditor shall evaluate whether the control has been designed effectively and 'determine whether the control has been implemented'. If the control depends on system generated information then the results of any compliance tests could be misleading.

In the case of payroll, the objective is to ensure that all new appointments are listed on the printout. A computer audit specialist could have tested that by introducing test data, specifically new starts, into the system to ensure that they were listed. Alternatively, the auditor could have run audit software to replicate the control by looking for new starts who have joined during the period and checking that all of those names are on the printout.

All that the audit team has done is check that the manager has signed the schedule produced by the system, which is not the key issue arising from the control. If the manager has been signing a false incomplete printout every month then the audit team has relied upon a false assurance. Indeed, the system could have broken down completely either because the software has been reprogrammed to omit some additions, or because of a simpler fraud involving retyping the printout with key names omitted before it is shown to the manager.

(b) It is highly unlikely that auditors will encounter many systems that are wholly manual and so all auditors will have to audit IT-based systems. That does not automatically mean that all auditors have the necessary skills to implement ATTs or otherwise test the operation of systems.

ISA 315 (Revised 2019) highlights the importance of the control environment. The control environment is, arguably, the most important element of the system of internal control because it reflects the entity's attitude towards internal control. If the control environment is strong then it is more likely that the system is well designed and that the controls will be operating correctly. That does not absolve the auditor of the responsibility to highlight key controls and to check their operation.

The control environment is difficult to evaluate without some study of the controls themselves. Testing the proper operation of controls indicates whether management's oversight of the system has been effective. The senior management could create the impression that they are interested in the system without that actually leading to effective implementation in practice.

Howard's argument is essentially self-serving and potentially misleading. ISA 300 *Planning an audit of financial statements* requires that the engagement team has the appropriate competence and capabilities to perform the work assigned. It may be that audit staff should be trained more thoroughly in computer audit skills than has been the case in the past in order to keep pace with the prevalence of IT systems.

19 Crank (amended)

Tutorial note. This question tests the ability to discuss planning and reporting materiality and also to consider the impact of creative accounting practices.

(a) IFRS 15 *Revenue from contracts with customers* recognises revenue according to a five step model. Step five of this process allows revenue to be recognised only when an individual performance obligation is satisfied. A performance obligation is satisfied when control of the asset is passed to the customer which can be over time or at a point in time.

Crank is arguing that a sale has taken place because an order has been received and work on fulfilling that order is under way. That is not sufficient for Crank to argue that it has transferred control to the customer because Crank still has the ability to prevent the customer from directing the use of and obtaining the benefit of the asset.

Clearly, Crank retains a considerable degree of managerial involvement in any work in progress. The company can certainly schedule the rate at which any given order is processed and it may be

decided that a batch of goods that is in process is to be set aside in order to make way for a more urgent order.

Provided the customer's order constitutes a binding contract and it is possible to be certain that the goods have been manufactured to the customer's requirements then it may be possible to book sales once the goods have been completed and while they are awaiting despatch. Given the urgency with which Crank is pushing to complete orders it seems unlikely that this will permit the booking of many sales.

(b) There is no clear and universally accepted materiality threshold, although 1% of revenue and 10% of profit are usually regarded as upper limits for the quantification of the materiality decision. The planning and testing materiality figure set at the start of the audit was within 1% of revenue but slightly exceeded 10% of forecast profit. The audit testing was effectively cut to the bare minimum (and possibly just less than the bare minimum) during the year.

Now that we have draft accounts it would appear that a realistic materiality threshold may be closer to $3 million than $4 million. That means that the auditor's test results are insufficient to establish that the financial statements present fairly.

The auditor will require further information before reaching a final conclusion on this. Materiality is really about the decisions that will be reached by users of the financial statements and so it may be that users will be happy to accept that the maximum misstatement could be as high as $4 million depending on the figures in the statement of financial position and also on the manner in which the entity's performance is judged.

ISA 320 *Materiality in planning and performing an audit* requires that the materiality figure should have been reviewed and revised as necessary while the audit progressed. At the reporting stage the auditor must be able to express an opinion on the basis that no material irregularities have been overlooked during fieldwork. The threshold applied during testing has been too high to support a valid opinion.

(c) The audit of revenue appears to have been conducted badly. The audit staff responsible should have followed a sample of transactions through the system and they should have noticed the disparity in the dates when it came to posting sales. Arguably, sales have been overstated by $470m – 430m = $40m, which is approximately 8.5% of reported sales. That implies that the pre-booking has averaged almost 8.5% × 365 = 31 days. Audit staff should have spotted that the pre-booking has occurred consistently throughout the year.

There is further doubt associated with the corollary testing conducted on trade receivables. Crank has apparently pre-booked almost a whole month's worth of sales, which implies that there should have been significant timing differences between the responses to receivable circularisation requests and Crank's receivables ledger. The audit team has clearly failed to link related findings in the working papers.

The fact that Crank has been struggling to keep pace with budgets suggests that the company should have been audited with greater scepticism. In particular, the auditor should have focussed on any risks that could have led to the overstatement of revenue and profit. There should have been specific tests carried out to investigate the possibility of the aggressive pre-booking of sales.

The planned risk factors appear to be relatively optimistic. The audit team should have picked up the performance issues and timing errors during the first of the two interim audits and those findings should have been drawn to the engagement partner's attention. It is unacceptable that the work has been completed to a standard that now appears to be inadequate without the engagement partner having had the opportunity to request a change of direction. Even a basic analytical review should have highlighted the very slow receivables turnover that would have arisen from the pre-booking. The fact that an assurance of 20% was taken from analytical review risk indicates that a formal analytical review was planned but this does not appear to have been followed through.

(**Note.** It is not necessarily expected that candidates will interpret the risk probabilities in any particular way, although it is clear that the auditor is assuming that relatively little emphasis be placed on detailed testing, which suggests that great care should be taken with the evidence that is gathered.)

20 Mable (amended)

Tutorial note. Overall, the question deals with the issues arising from a client's activities with respect to revenue contracts where performance obligations are satisfied over time. This is a new direction for the company and so the auditor must plan an audit approach that addresses the risks that are arising.

(a) IFRS 15 *Revenue from contracts with customers* requires a forecast figure for the profit that will be earned from this contract. That leaves scope for forecasting errors or even aggressive accounting. Mable also has to determine the basis on which it will measure the performance completed and therefore recognise profits and revenues during the course of the contract, which creates further risk because the directors have no prior experience and they may distort the results through this decision.

There could be going concern issues because Mable has to find the cash to work on the contract for the periods between quarterly reports. There will be further delays in collecting cash because of the need to wait for the engineer's report and then the client has 30 days to pay. Mable's average spend is approximately $1 million per month and so substantial outflows could occur between progress payments. The bank loan that has been taken out to fund working capital looks as if it may be insufficient because it covers only four months' expenses and the directors may be reluctant to go back for more finance in case they appear to be out of their depth.

Mable has taken out a bank loan to cover the working capital requirements. The bank may have imposed covenants based on accounting numbers, which may impose further pressures on Mable's financial statements, if the directors come under pressure to meet the covenant targets.

Mable will be under pressure when seeking further contracts. Potential clients will wish to see a strong company that will be capable of completing the contract and so the board may feel pressured to manipulate the financial statements in order to win further contracts.

(b) Firstly, Harold needs to be certain of the civil engineer's independence and expertise. Any shortcomings could lead to misleading figures being reported in the financial statements. The first step would be to discuss the selection and appointment with Mable's management. Harold may be able to rely heavily upon the investigations undertaken by Mable's management when they were negotiating the contract with the client. Harold should obtain independent evidence of the engineer's qualifications and standing. There may, for example, be a professional body and Harold could confirm that the engineer is listed on its website as having the necessary licence to practise.

Harold should contact the engineer and seek confirmation that the firm is independent of Mable. Any lack of independence would enable Mable to manipulate the recognition of revenues and profits from year to year. Independence of the client has a less immediate audit impact, although it could disrupt Mable's cash flows if the client can influence the reports.

Harold should study the reports for any indication of problems with the work to date. Any qualifications in the report or mention of problems could lead to Mable having to incur additional expense without necessarily being able to recover those costs. That could lead to changes to the predicted outcome of the contract. In extreme cases, it could have an impact on Mable's going concern status.

Harold should check the 'bottom line' concerning the stage of completion against Mable's calculations of revenue and profit.

(c) The request raises some immediate concerns about auditor independence. If Harold is assisting the board in setting policies and developing systems then there will be a self-review threat where the results of the service provided will form part of the internal controls over financial reporting on which the firm will express an opinion; It will be difficult to argue that there are any shortcomings in the approach being taken to the valuation of the contracts if Harold was associated with the development of the system. There is also the risk of Harold assuming a management responsibility which is prohibited by the IESBA Code.

Mable is not publicly traded, and so there is a little more latitude with respect to assisting with accounting exercises. Having said that, the contract has the potential to be a material aspect of the company's financial reporting and so that may mean that any compromise in auditor independence is unacceptable. The IESBA Code states that a firm can only provide accounting services to an audit client where the services are of a routine and mechanical nature and the firm addresses any threats that are not at an acceptable level.

It could be argued that the business risk assessment approach would require Harold to study the contract and the associated accounting issues carefully. Any concerns would have to be discussed fully with the board and resolutions negotiated. In other words, it may be that the directors could obtain most of the benefit of a separate review by simply allowing Harold to conduct the audit and to identify any issues as part of the audit approach.

It would probably be inappropriate to accept a separate fee for feeding back on the system, unless the board wished Harold to comment on issues that were not directly relevant to the audit, such as improvements to the management reports or greater efficiency in managing costs.

Harold may benefit from an independent review of the system to be conducted by a third party because that fresh insight could help identify shortcomings and weaknesses. Also, Harold may not be particularly expert with respect to such contracts if Mable is the only client involved in such activities.

(d) Harold will need to conduct a detailed review of the audit working papers to ensure that there is sufficient evidence on all aspects of the contract. The audit team may not have a great deal of experience of auditing such figures and so there may be a temptation to cut corners. The audit team may also do insufficient work simply because they do not know enough about the tests that are appropriate.

Harold will need to ensure that the basis that has been selected to measure the performance completed and therefore for the recognition of profits and revenues is consistent with IFRS 15. The calculations used by Mable will have to be consistent with the company's stated policy.

The financial statements will have to reflect any material uncertainties that remain after audit testing is complete. Harold must study the work undertaken by management and the associated audit work and he must decide whether there is sufficient evidence that the figures in the financial statements are satisfactory. In particular, Harold must consider the validity of the forecasts of costs to completion. The fact that the board has asked Harold to offer advice on the systems relating to the contract suggest that this should be a particular area of concern during the final review stage of the audit. Harold should review the concerns expressed by management and should have already requested specific tests to be conducted on those aspects of the recording of the contract.

21 Silver and Bronze

> **Tutorial note.** This question deals with the quality issues associated with the management of the audit process. It raises issues about the gathering of evidence, review of audit working papers and the roles of senior members of the audit team.

(a) The fact that revenue has declined by more than 30% is a serious cause for concern. It could imply that there are going concern problems. Alternatively, the directors may be put under greater pressure to manipulate the financial statements in order to make the downturn appear less severe.

The declining revenue casts doubt on the decision to leave the carrying amount of trademarks unimpaired.

The gross profit % has declined from 133/331 = 40% to 40/227 = 18%. Apart from adding weight to the concerns about declining profitability, this could indicate errors in the recording of revenue or closing inventory.

The company has paid a dividend that is far greater than the profit for the year. Again, that implies that the directors are attempting to signal strength and stability to the shareholders.

The company has a very low gearing and yet the rate of interest charged on borrowings has increased from 660/11,000 = 6% to 1,200/15,000 = 8%. That suggests that the lenders are concerned about White's credit worthiness and casts further doubt on the company's going concern.

When the tax rate is expressed as a percentage of profit before tax it increases from 16,000/129,979 = 12% to 14,000/36,410 = 38%. That is a worrying shift because it implies that White may have understated its accounting profit but been unable to manipulate its tax charge in the same manner.

There are some signs that liquidity could be an issue. The current ratio of 31,031/24,300 = 1.3:1 is not out of line with the previous year's 28,127/22,700 = 1.2:1. However, trade receivables turnover is slowing down from 17,000/331,000 × 365 = 18 days in 2011 to 19,000/227,000 × 365 = 31 days in 2012. Trade payables turnover has also slowed down from 7,800/198,000 × 365 = 14 days to 10,500/187,000 × 365 = 20 days. Combining those figures with the fact that the company's cash balance has fallen to a very low level suggests that the problems with the business could be affecting cash flow and liquidity too.

Note. The nature of an analytical review is that there is not necessarily a correct approach and so different points could have been raised or a different interpretation attached to the same points.

(b) Sarah does not appear to have had a great deal of contact with Michael during the course of the audit. The explanations that are provided in his report refer to matters that she should have been aware of, such as the downturn in business. Michael is new to this audit and should have had much greater support from the audit partner.

In any case, the audit manager and partner should work together on a more or less continuous basis because each has a distinct, but complementary, role within the audit team. They are jointly responsible for the audit strategy, but the manager should be supervising progress on a regular basis and the partner should make a point of checking that matters are well under review.

Michael has not made a good job of supervising this audit.

He should have insisted on a more senior and experienced audit team. If more senior managers have refused to release alternatives then Michael should have raised this with Sarah so that she could either review the situation or use her influence to obtain a more experienced team.

Michael has not kept the quantification of inherent risk under review. Clearly, an initial estimate was required for planning purposes, but that figure should have been reviewed and revised as more information became available. There is a strong possibility that insufficient evidence has been gathered from detailed substantive testing because of this oversight.

The work undertaken on the trademark is clearly inadequate and Michael appears to be negligent. It is unacceptable to base the audit approach so directly on the work done in the previous year because that will lead to mistakes being repeated. Also, circumstances may have changed since last year. Michael should also have had the matter referred to as a specific issue in the letter of representation.

The review of board minutes was conducted by a trainee accountant. This is an important task that requires some understanding and experience. Colin should have read the board minutes. If he has left that to his junior then there may be other aspects of his conduct that were lacking and Michael should have been aware of that.

(c) (i) The fact that this is an old and well-established brand supports the possibility that the trademark has an indefinite life, but the auditor must obtain evidence to support that.

The arguments that have been used in the past to justify this treatment should be reviewed. The auditor must consider whether those arguments remain valid in the face of declining sales and other changes that have taken place in White's industry.

The nature of the product should be reconsidered on an annual basis. Its life is only truly indefinite if there is no foreseeable limit to the period over which this product will be sold under the Whitebar trademark. The directors should be asked to justify that belief on an annual basis. Amongst other things, they should present evidence from their marketing activities and market research that demonstrates that the trademark remains popular. They should demonstrate that they intend to maintain the trademark's position by budgeting for advertising and brand support.

The auditor should review secondary sources, such as the business press, for any comments about the trademark and any analysis that could inform this evaluation. This review should also examine the industry in general to determine whether there are any competitors who are gaining ground and who may undermine the claim that the trademark will continue to generate revenue.

The directors should be asked to make a specific reference to the life of the trademark in the letter of representation. If they are unwilling to give such an assurance then they should be asked to withdraw the assertion that the trademark has an indefinite life.

(ii) The first point is that the carrying amount of the trademark is large relative to reported profit. Amortising the trademark over, say, ten years would impose a material cost on the statement of profit or loss.

This is a classic example of inherent uncertainty, which should be dealt with by disclosure in the financial statements rather than by a modification of the auditor's report. The fact that the amount is shown separately in the statement of financial position helps users to see that this major asset is in the books and that its value is unchanged. The auditor should check that the note is clear and that the fact that the life has been taken as indefinite is indicated.

If there are any specific doubts about the indefinite lifespan then they should be stated in the notes to the accounts. If such disclosures are adequate then it would be acceptable for the auditor to refer to that note in an emphasis of matter statement in the auditor's report, which would remain unqualified.

In the event that there are undisclosed and material uncertainties then the auditor will be forced to issue a modified opinion. This problem is very unlikely to be pervasive and so the auditor will issue an 'except for' qualified report that describes the uncertainties.

22 Harvey (amended)

> **Tutorial note.** This question tests candidates' understanding of the independence issues associated with providing non-audit services to audit clients. This is a topical area that has been revisited recently in an update to the IESBA *Code of Ethics for Professional Accountants* on such work. It also addresses the audit implications of fair value accounting, which is itself a topical area.

(a) Harvey provides a substantial proportion of the firm's fee income. The additional fees will make it an even more important client. A self-interest threat might be created where a large proportion of fees charged by the firm to Harvey is generated by providing services other than audit, due to concerns about the potential loss of either the audit engagement or other services. Such circumstances might also create an intimidation threat. Safeguards that could address the threat include:

- Having an appropriate reviewer who was not involved in the audit or the service other than audit review the relevant audit work.
- Reducing the extent of services other than audit provided to Harvey

In addition, there is a risk that the extra engagement results in the total fees from Harvey being a large proportion of the total fees of the firm. The dependence on, and concern about the potential loss of, fees from audit and other services from Harvey impacts the level of the self-interest threat and creates an intimidation threat. Safeguards to address these threats include:

- Having an appropriate reviewer who is not a member of the firm review the audit work.
- Reducing the extent of services other than audit provided to Harvey.
- Increasing the client base of the firm to reduce dependence on Harvey.
- Increasing the extent of services provided to other clients.

However, if the appointment is refused then the loss of Harvey's fee income will put the auditor under greater pressure to retain the other audit clients and so that could undermine independence on those clients.

The nature of the work could create problems because the results will provide the basis for the recognition of a transaction that Harvey has agreed is worth 15% of the company's equity. This will have a material impact upon Harvey's statement of financial position. On the other hand, there is nothing in the scenario to imply that Harvey's directors wish to distort the accounting treatment of this acquisition. The tone of their request implies that the accounting exercise involves some work that is beyond the expertise of the company's own accounting staff. They seem keen to ensure that the transaction is presented fairly.

The fact that the audit firm will be so heavily involved in this major transaction will ensure that the audit team is better informed. Harvey have asked for accountancy support in ensuring a transaction is accounted for in accordance with IFRS 2. This might create a self-review threat whereby the firm later provides an audit opinion on the financial statements which contain the transaction on which they have advised. There is also the risk of the firm assuming a management responsibility.

According to the IESBA Code, the firm shall not provide Harvey accounting and bookkeeping services unless the services are of a routine or mechanical nature and the firm addresses any threats that are not at an acceptable level. Accounting and bookkeeping services that are routine or mechanical involve information, data or material in relation to which Harvey has made any judgements or decisions that might be necessary and require little or no professional judgement. Harvey's request would involve the auditor passing judgement on whether the trawler should be accounted for on the basis of the fair value of either the trawler itself or the fair value of the shares that are issued and how to arrive at those figures. Therefore, the audit firm must decline the request for a non-audit service from Harvey or they will be breaching the IESBA Code.

(b) Ideally, the fair value of the trawler should be determined. If that can be done then that amount will be debited to property, plant and equipment and the same total will be credited to share capital (split between equity shares and share premium as appropriate).

The starting point for determining the fair value of the trawler would be a review of any correspondence between Henry and Lucky Mascot. It is unlikely that there was not a stage at which the question of the normal cash selling price of the trawler was discussed and that is likely to be a realistic fair value for the asset.

Alternatively, the auditor could simply contact Lucky Mascot and ask for written confirmation of the normal cash selling price of a similar trawler.

The fact that Lucky Mascot intends to become a major shareholder means that the company cannot be considered independent of Harvey and so any valuations obtained directly or indirectly from the company have to be confirmed by the auditor.

The audit firm could study the financial statements of other companies in the same industry as Harvey in order to establish the typical costs and fair values of ocean-going trawlers. These are likely to vary substantially depending on the size and level of equipment, but they should at least provide the auditor with some assurance that the fair value determined for Harvey's trawler is in the correct range of prices.

The auditor should also consider the fair value of the shares that have been issued by Harvey. It may be possible to find a publicly traded company in the same industry that offers some relevant statistics that can be used for valuation purposes. The auditor could, for example, take a publicly traded company's P/E ratio and apply that to Harvey's earnings in order to obtain an estimate of the company's (hypothetical) market capitalisation.

Ideally, the fair value of the issued shares will be reasonably similar to the fair value determined for the trawler. If they are then there is a degree of mutual confirmation of the auditor's calculations. If the results differ and the auditor believes that both are credible then the auditor should ensure that the fair value for the trawler is the figure that is taken because IFRS 2 requires that the fair value of the asset be used, with the fair value of the equity being taken only as a surrogate for that of the asset in the event that the asset does not lend itself to the determination of a fair value.

23 Gamble

> **Tutorial note.** This question deals with the audit risks associated with the possibility that the directors are dishonest and are abusing their positions in the company. Specifically, there appears to be evidence that the company is being used for money laundering purposes and that the directors are keen to buy the company from the main body of the shareholders at an understated price.

(a) **Briefing note**

The concerns expressed in your email appear to be well founded. We need to gather evidence with a view to determining whether Gamble really has a case to answer.

Is money laundering occurring?

The nature of the business would lend itself to money laundering. Customers deposit cash from wherever they happen to be in the world. There are no real costs that could be used to track the credibility of the scale of business being reported by the company.

Revenues of $347 million imply that customers have deposited $347m/5% = $6,940m into their accounts during the year. If we assume that trade payables comprise the customers' account balances then payables account for $10.5m/$6,940m × 365 = 0.8 days' worth of business. It seems unlikely that customers would not leave more of their deposits online with which to play.

Trade receivables may be the cash owed from credit card companies, arising from customers adding to their accounts. Again, the ratio of $6m/$6,940m × 365 = 0.3 days seems rather rapid.

These ratios imply that it is possible that Gamble's directors have been paying the proceeds of some criminal activity into the company's bank balances so that they can claim that these funds have been deposited by customers.

The fact that there are customers whose accounts are worth millions of dollars is a major concern because the large receipts and payments of cash through these accounts would be particularly well-suited to concealing the laundering of criminal proceeds.

Our responsibilities

Under UK law, the Proceeds of Crime Act 2002 obliges us to report our suspicions if we believe that money laundering may be occurring. The Money Laundering Regulations require that we make this report to the Serious Organised Crime Agency (SOCA).

Our responsibilities are fairly clear, but we should ensure that we are actually suspicious before we make such a report because doing so will constitute a breach of client confidence and we have a responsibility to avoid making spurious reports. We should investigate the manner in which a sample of customers manage their account balances to determine whether the rapid average turnover is suspicious. We should also track cash receipts backwards to establish whether they are actually coming from credit card companies and also whether the payments are as rapid as the turnover ratio implies. Finally, we should request details of the procedures applied for checking the identities of the major customers who hold significant accounts with the company. Gamble is, itself, responsible for monitoring its customers for indications of money laundering and there should be detailed records that establish the existence and identity of such large players.

We have further responsibilities under ISA 250 (Revised) *Consideration of laws and regulations in an audit of financial statements* to investigate the implications of our suspicions for Gamble's financial statements. Apart from the possibility of fines and other criminal penalties, money laundering would involve the deliberate misclassification of transactions. In the first instance, we ought to discuss our suspicions with Mr Harris rather than Mr Vincent or Mr Costello because these two gentlemen are suspected of being involved in this criminal activity.

(b) The fact that Mr Vincent and Mr Costello wish to purchase the company suggests that they may have an interest in manipulating the financial statements. The warning given to the founding shareholders would suggest that the directors are prepared to use dishonesty in order to achieve their objectives.

Gamble is clearly very profitable with an operating profit that is many times greater than total assets. The company was started with a large loan that has been almost completely paid off. The company paid a dividend last year that, in itself, massively exceeded the shareholders' investment.

The very large dividend payment, which exceeds reported profits for the year, suggests that Mr Vincent and Mr Costello may be willing to take significant risks with the financial management of the company in order to make it look weaker. An alternative explanation is that the directors paid the dividend with the intention of enjoying the 10% of the total payment that each is entitled to as a shareholder. The dividend payment is not, in itself, an audit matter but it does indicate that the two executive directors may be willing to pursue their own self-interest at the company's expense.

The impairment adjustment on the brand name is further evidence of poor corporate governance. It seems unlikely that the brand's value itself could be impaired given the phenomenal financial performance according to the draft financial statements. One explanation for this is that the reported earnings do not reflect the underlying economic and business reality and so the brand's impairment suggests that the reported revenue and profit have been overstated. An alternative

explanation is that the directors are keen to overstate expenses in order to minimise reported profits as much as possible in order to reduce the asking price for the 80% of the shares held by the founding shareholders. Either explanation implies that there is a threat to the fair presentation in the financial statements arising from the governance of the board.

(c) (i) The starting point is the fact that two conditions have to be met before any impairment can be justified: the carrying amount of the asset must exceed the market value of the brand and also its net present value. Even a quick look at the figures suggests that neither condition is likely to have been met and so the directors should be asked to justify the adjustment.

The brand name was purchased by Gamble a few years ago and, presumably, that involved a revaluation exercise that can be repeated. The auditor would be looking for evidence that the valuation basis that was used when the rights were purchased will yield a substantially poorer value despite the fact that the brand name is clearly well established. If the directors argue that bad publicity or some other factor has undermined the brand's value then the auditor should seek confirmation of that explanation, including an analysis of the effects that any such explanation has had on sales.

The present value of the brand name will be difficult to determine, but it does appear very likely that it exceeds the earlier carrying amount. At the very least, the directors should be asked to provide evidence that future sales are likely to be depressed, otherwise the adjustment will lack all credibility. The auditor should examine sales forecasts and budgets as part of this exercise and should take a sceptical view of anything that does not follow on from the recent dramatic increase in sales.

(ii) Materiality has to be determined in terms of the impact of a disclosure in terms of the behaviour of users of the financial statements. The fact that Gamble's brand name is a reflection of the company's ability to generate sales revenue is an important factor to be taken into account when considering the materiality of any adjustments. The impairment of the asset will send a signal that future sales are in doubt.

In monetary terms the adjustment is clearly material. The brand name was worth almost twice the value of all of Gamble's other assets combined. On the basis of any asset-based measure of materiality the impairment adjustment is highly material.

When comparing the adjustment to the figures in the statement of profit or loss, the $48 million loss is almost 14% of revenue and 17% of pre-tax profit.

There is a counter argument to the above points. The carrying amount of an intangible asset is likely to be regarded as a fairly 'soft' figure in the financial statements. Any adjustment or write-off may be regarded as an attempt by the directors to eliminate a relatively meaningless balance from the financial statements. The shareholders could regard the impairment as a reflection of the difficulty associated with valuing the figure rather than a genuine concern about the company's future. On balance, the impairment is almost certainly material. As is often the case with auditing, there could be a counter-argument to the effect that it is not.

24 Pension audit

Tutorial note. This question deals with the audit of a defined benefit pension plan, which raises a host of implications for the audit team. This question will require the ability to relate the objectives of a risk-based audit to the specific figures that comprise the expenses and balances associated with pension plans.

(a) Nothing can absolve the directors of their responsibility for the fair presentation of the financial statements. The fact that they have relied upon an independent actuary may well imply that the figures have been calculated correctly, but even that is not guaranteed because the actuary will have been forced to rely on the information and data provided by the directors. The directors are responsible for ensuring that the actuary has used appropriate information and that the actuary's calculations are based on the correct method and are accurate.

The auditor may find it difficult to determine exactly how the figures were arrived at. The actuary may claim to have relied on the information provided by the directors and the directors may claim that many of the figures were obtained by the actuary. Thus, the auditor must ensure that the directors understand their responsibility for the figures and that they have reviewed, and accept full responsibility for the work done by the actuary. This is clearly a matter that will have to be clarified in the letter of representation.

The auditor will have to ensure that the actuary is competent and independent and will have to apply the usual tests as laid down by ISA 620 *Using the work of an auditor's expert* – even though the actuary will have been appointed by management. The fact that the actuary has been appointed and briefed by the directors means that the actuary will not be totally independent, but that may not be too serious an issue if the actuary is professionally qualified and is subject to formal ethical guidance. The actuary's expertise can also be established on the basis of appropriate academic and professional qualifications.

(b) The opening balances for both assets and liabilities can be agreed back to last year's closing balances, which should have been audited satisfactorily. The auditor should be able to check that against last year's audit working papers.

The discount rate used to predict plan liabilities should be a matter of fact. The actuary should be asked to provide written evidence to support the 9.0% used. That should be based on a credible source, such as an official market listing.

The expected rate on plan assets is a matter of opinion on the part of the actuary. The auditor should discuss the logic underlying that estimate and should ensure that there is a realistic justification for it. This is an area where the actuary's judgement will be crucial. The auditor will have to document and logic underlying the actuary's valuation and that should be supported by an evaluation of that logic, so that the auditor has a formal working paper that demonstrates that the validity of the expected rate figure has been considered in some detail.

The calculations underlying the current service cost should be reviewed and checked for accuracy. Their basis will have to be checked for consistency with the requirements of IAS 19.

Benefits paid will be checked on a sample basis to ensure that these amounts have been paid to pensioners and that they should be offset against plan liabilities. The eligibility of the recipients can be checked against the formal list of pensioners. Each selected pensioner's file can be reviewed as a further check for existence.

Contributions received should be checked for completeness. The audit team should investigate any employee contribution during the audit of payroll. The employer's contribution should be checked for completeness also, perhaps by analytical review to ensure that the amounts set aside are a reasonable approximation to the total gross salary multiplied by the contribution rate. The completeness of these credits could be considered as a matter for inclusion in the audit of payroll. The auditor could ensure that the appropriate amount has been set aside from each selected salary payment.

The auditor will have to discuss the assumptions relating to the calculation of the plan liability in some detail. This is unlikely to be within the auditor's direct expertise, but it should be possible to check that the assumptions are, at the very least, credible. There may be externally verifiable sources that feed into this process and the auditor should check the actuary's assumptions against such documents.

The value of plan assets will, hopefully, be open to checking against market values. If any assets do not have a verifiable market price then the auditor should review the models being used for credibility. The auditor may have sufficient expertise within the firm to check the validity of these valuations, or it may be necessary to seek third party experts to advise.

25 Madbox (amended)

> **Tutorial note.** Overall, the question deals with the issues arising from a badly supervised audit. The audit manager has not revised the parameters that affect the materiality decision and the values attached to risk and detailed testing. The audit partner is now faced with the stark choice between delaying the auditor's report and basing an opinion on an inadequate level of detailed testing.

(a) ISA 500 *Audit evidence* requires the auditor to obtain sufficient appropriate audit evidence to be able to draw reasonable conclusions on which to base the auditor's opinion.

The audit work has been conducted on the basis of a materiality threshold of $17 million. Actual sales of $0.9 billion suggest that the materiality threshold should have been $9 million (1% of revenue) when designing audit tests. The materiality levels used in testing mean that an error of between $9 and $17 million could have been overlooked, despite being material. This means that the audit work was not designed to detect all material misstatements and so the auditor cannot claim to have discharged the responsibilities set out in the ISA.

There is a further concern arising from the evaluation of inherent risk. The audit work has been designed on the basis of a thriving and profitable company. In fact, the company is under pressure because of poor performance. The level of detailed testing was based on an estimate of inherent risk that has since turned out to be optimistic. It is highly likely that revisiting the audit risk model will reduce the acceptable level of substantive testing risk, which would lead to the auditor having to undertake more detailed testing. This would further stress the need to conduct additional detailed testing.

There are further specific concerns about the audit of closing inventory and amortisation of intangibles. These items clearly have a high specific risk attached to them and should have been audited more fully.

(b) ISA 315 (Revised 2019) *Identifying and assessing the risks of material misstatement* requires auditors to have an understanding of the factors that affect the business and its risk profile. Part of that requires an understanding of the industry. It is clear that the company's designers and programmers had very specific skills and were effectively difficult to replace, if not irreplaceable. The audit manager should have been aware of the importance of the designer to Madbox's performance and should have been able to appreciate the significance of the departure of the design and programming team. Identifying such threats falls within the criterion of 'reasonable skill and care'.

It could be argued that Derek could not be expected to keep track of the departure of every member of staff, however, it seems likely that the press would have publicised the fact that a key designer had been recruited by another company. The audit firm should make regular checks for press stories about their clients and the industry. The recruitment of a rival's designer is likely to be publicised as major industry news.

The audit manager should have regular meetings with senior members of the client's management team in order to evaluate performance and progress. Those meetings should cover matters such as the progress of the company towards meeting its budgets. Management should have been asked to indicate progress towards completing important projects, such as the launch of new computer games. There is nothing to indicate that Madbox's management has concealed anything. It appears that the manager has failed to ask some very basic questions. At the very least, the audit managers should have asked whether the design and programming team is intact and expected to meet all targets.

(c) This is a complicated matter because the company does not appear to have done anything wrong. The fact remains that the auditor has a very specific duty to form an opinion on whether the financial statements present fairly. The fact that insufficient evidence has been collected means that the auditor cannot express an unmodified opinion.

If Jacob can negotiate an extension to the reporting deadline then it would be possible to extend the audit testing. That would make it possible to express an unmodified opinion provided the financial statements are found to be free of material irregularities.

The basic concern here is uncertainty. The auditor has gathered some evidence and has not uncovered any specific irregularity, so the uncertainty is not pervasive. There is no particular reason to believe that management lacks integrity and so it would be unnecessary to disclaim opinion.

The uncertainty arises from a limitation in the scope of the audit. ISA 705 (Revised) *Modifications to the opinion in the independent auditor's report* indicates that a qualified opinion should be expressed. The auditor's report would have to indicate that there was insufficient time to complete all of the audit testing that was required to express an unmodified opinion and so the financial statements express fairly, except for the adjustments that may have been necessary in the event that fuller tests had uncovered material irregularities.

(d) The auditor's only responsibility is to express an opinion on the fair presentation of the financial statements. Fair presentation can only be judged in terms of the disclosures themselves and the audit evidence gathered in support of the auditor's opinion on those disclosures.

Even if the capital markets are fully aware of any concerns about the financial statements, the auditor's report is intended to confirm the reported facts so that the users can confirm their understanding. The shareholders may well have concerns about Madbox, but could be unwilling to act upon those concerns without having had sight of the audited financial statements.

Management would be able to undermine the auditor's independence if the market's understanding could be used to determine whether an uncertainty was material. If the directors could argue that the auditor's concerns were already known to the market then there could be an argument for expressing an unmodified opinion even if there are serious shortcomings.

It may be difficult to be certain of the market's knowledge because the auditor cannot establish exactly what is known and understood by the market as a whole. Even if problems are clearly described in the financial press, there may be individual shareholders who have not read the information and so they will be at a disadvantage to more sophisticated investors in the absence of a clear set of financial statements and an appropriate audit opinion.

Derek's argument would undoubtedly undermine the credibility of both the firm and the audit profession. If the markets are aware of the concerns then they will be waiting to see how they are reflected in the financial statements. If there is nothing to indicate the uncertainties over intangibles and inventory then the market may feel that the auditor has behaved unprofessionally.

PRACTICE ANSWER BANK

26 Link

> **Tutorial note.** This question deals with the topical area of valuations of intangible assets following on from a number of very substantial acquisitions of companies for the sake of obtaining control over intellectual property. As with any question involving recent developments, it is not anticipated that candidates will have read any specific articles or materials. Those who have kept abreast of this development may be at an advantage, but it should be sufficient to approach this question with a clear understanding of the accounting issues associated with the recognition and valuation of intellectual property.

(a) The most obvious starting place is to discuss this with Link's management. It is the responsibility of Link's board to identify an appropriate valuation for the sake of the company's consolidated financial statements.

Link should be able to provide significant support for their valuation because there should have been substantial due diligence on the acquisition of Webtok. The fact that this was such a significant purchase should mean that the work has been done to a high standard by Link's management and is well supported by evidence. The auditor should follow up on some of these sources to corroborate the valuation. The auditor cannot rely totally on these materials because Link has a very clear incentive to overstate the value of its investment in Webtok in order to reassure the shareholders.

The auditor should check that the recognition criteria set out in IAS 38 *Intangible assets* are met. The asset is almost certainly separately identifiable, but it may be difficult to determine its cost because here will be other reasons for buying Webtok. For example, Link may have wished to obtain Webtok's management team or simply remove the company from the market. The purchase consideration was in the form of Link's own shares and their fair value will have to be determined.

(b) Intangible assets are clearly a very material issue for Link. Their total carrying amount is more than double the value of profit and comes close to annual revenue. It would not take a very significant shift in value to cause a substantial adjustment to Link's financial statements.

One of the biggest problems is that these assets could easily become impaired and could lose their value almost without warning. A competitor could launch alternative software that captures much of Link's market. Fashion and trends have a lot of influence over the use of social networking sites.

ISA 700 (Revised) *The independent auditor's report on financial statements* requires that the auditor has to be careful of estimates. It is not sufficient just to look at each separate website owned by Link and to ensure that each is not necessarily impaired. The auditor also has to ensure that cumulative concerns are addressed, such as a sense that problems with specific assets that are immaterial in themselves may be material when looked at together.

The audit staff should conduct desk research into Link's industry and establish what respected industry commentators are saying about the company. Any reservations in the business press should be discussed with the board and that discussion should be both in the context of the potential impairment of each separate asset and of the assets as a whole.

27 Grean

> **Tutorial note.** This question deals with the control implications of the phenomenon of BYOD (bring your own device), which is a topical matter in terms of the evolution of IT and IS systems. As with any question involving recent developments, it is not anticipated that candidates will have read any specific articles or materials. Those who have kept abreast of this development may be at an advantage, but it should be sufficient to approach this question with a clear understanding of internal control in an IT environment.

(a) The most immediate risk is that these devices may circumvent some of the basic environmental controls in the company's IT system. Many of these devices will be connected to the internet and may be susceptible to viruses and other problems. Those viruses may corrupt files that are uploaded to Grean's systems.

For example, the network manager's smartphone may not have the ability to run commercial-grade antivirus software. The manager's app links the smartphone into the server and the app itself is a simple program that could be easily hacked. Even if it does not transmit malware, the app may corrupt Grean's systems because it has not been checked and tested to the same standard that would be applied to a program written under traditional operating systems.

There are more direct risks, such as the security of software. Grean's staff are carrying data around on portable electronic devices that are tempting targets for thieves. If a phone or tablet is lost or stolen then sensitive customer information may be exposed. Grean could lose revenue if customers lose confidence in the company's security arrangements.

Grean may also lose information because of compatibility issues. That has already occurred with the sales reports. If a member of staff leaves the company or switches to a new device with a different operating system then Grean may be unable to access important files that require the original platform. Staff may also delete files if they leave Grean rather than submitting copies and the information will be lost forever.

(b) Grean should start by developing a clear code of practice for all staff. That code should make it a disciplinary matter if an unauthorised device is used. That could be enforced by making it clear that any member of staff who is found responsible for introducing a virus or losing a file through breach of the code will be dismissed.

Grean should then evaluate the more popular platforms in order to understand their security and reliability. IT staff should identify systems that can be safely integrated with Grean's, subject to safeguards. Staff should agree not to use these platforms unless they also adhere to the specific precautions advised by Grean's IT staff, such as loading anti-malware packages or encrypting work-related files.

Grean should provide access to all necessary software for these systems to ensure their security. Otherwise, staff may cut corners and imposing disciplinary action against them will do little to protect Grean.

All personal systems should be backed up before leaving the office every evening, so that copies are available if the device is lost or stolen.

The logic of any apps used by staff should be reviewed by a colleague or a member of the IT department. This is to prevent errors due to mistakes in the programming, particularly if the app has been written by the staff member rather than purchased commercially.

Grean should consider negating the BYOD phenomenon by investing in some of these devices for itself. If staff work more efficiently because of the design or interface of these devices then Grean should take control and buy its own.

28 Fastrun

Tutorial note. The question deals with the design of an audit investigation into suspected staff fraud. This is a novel situation and so it should test candidates' ability to design assurance tests. The question also considers the implications of asking the internal audit function to conduct fraud investigations.

(a) The first step would be to tabulate the complaints in order to look for any patterns. For example, if the complaints come from a particular customer, which would suggest that the customers are responsible for the losses. Similarly, if the complaints started shortly after a new driver started then that would indicate a potential culprit.

Each contested package has potentially had two drivers handle it: the driver making the collection and the driver making the delivery. The tabulation might indicate whether losses tend to be associated with any given driver or drivers.

If a particular driver is a suspect then Fastrun could set a trap by packaging valuable goods and listing them on the shipping documentation. Those packages could be sent to an address that has been allocated to the suspect and the goods inspected on delivery. This will have to be repeated because it is unlikely that a fraudulent driver would steal every valuable consignment. The auditor should ensure that there is a witness to the packing and receipt of the packages to prevent the driver from blaming any shortage on the staff who conducted the test.

The test packages should be opened immediately and any shortage notified to the internal auditor. The van could be followed and searched in the hope that the missing item will be in the van, which would provide clear evidence of the driver's dishonesty.

If any of these test packages are opened then the driver should be formally interviewed and asked to explain the shortage. The interview should be conducted by two managers so that there is a witness and it may be prudent to make an audio recording, with the driver's permission.

(b) It might be argued that the internal auditor's role is to check compliance. If so, it would be important to maintain a friendly and constructive relationship with the company's staff so that internal audit investigations are not hindered. If the auditor is known to be conducting fraud investigations then staff may be a little more wary of interacting with the auditor and so the quality of internal audit may decline.

It could also be argued that the interruption of normal internal audit investigations to conduct fraud investigations is a distraction from normal activities. It could be more cost-effective for the company to bring in an external auditor to investigate any concerns relating to staff dishonesty.

Both of these concerns are particularly acute because Fastrun is a small company with only one internal auditor. Personal relationships will be all the more important and there are fewer audit resources to allocate.

Having said that, it is not for the internal audit function to decide its own role. The auditor should respond to management's wishes.

It could be argued that the internal auditor is well qualified to conduct a fraud investigation. Firstly because of knowledge of the business, which means that the auditor may be better qualified to identify any shortcomings. Secondly, because of expertise in designing and conducting audit tests.

29 Gold (amended)

> **Tutorial note.** This question deals with the going concern implications that can be identified from the information provided in the scenario.

(a) ISA 570 (Revised) *Going concern* states that makes the auditor's responsibility is to obtain sufficient appropriate audit evidence about the appropriateness of management's use of the going concern assumption. The auditor should also conclude whether there is a material uncertainty about the entity's ability to continue as a going concern. To a very large extent it is the finance director's responsibility to convince the audit partner that Gold is definitely a going concern despite the possibility that the contract from Lane will not be renewed.

The finance director's arguments seem rather unrealistic. The argument that Gold has worked with the market leader, which will impress other potential customers ignores the fact that Gold will be seeking contracts after appearing to have failed to meet Lane's standards. Presumably, Lane would not have gone to the effort of replacing a major supplier without good reason and so it will be difficult for Gold to convince potential customers to award contracts to Gold (presumably in place of existing and trusted suppliers) without having an argument to deal with that concern. From an audit point of view, the finance director will have to be able to substantiate this claim. Presumably, the sales director will have only a very small staff whose primary role will be to liaise with Lane. Ideally, the finance director will be able to offer some evidence that the sales managers have sufficient contact with the industry to have the ability to create and pursue sales leads effectively. The fact that Gold's competitors are located overseas where labour costs are low will have to be taken into account in the plans that the finance director provides.

The other argument is that the abandonment of going concern would have very little effect on the financial statements because the assets are all new and highly sellable. That is extremely naïve because the company's property, plant and equipment is all very specialised. It was purchased to service the market leader's requirements for very powerful chips. The equipment may not be particularly attractive to other manufacturers because it would be expensive to move it to another site and so Gold would have to sell the entire factory. The finance director has also ignored the fact that Gold has $250 million of inventory, much of which will be computer chips that have a proprietary design that can only be sold to Lane.

(b) (i) Matters that provide some reassurance:

Gold is profitable. The company has enjoyed a return on capital employed of 710/(1,860 + 810) = 27%. That provides a sound basis for any discussions with lenders or potential stakeholders because the company could not have generated such significant returns without it being efficient.

Gold's substantial cash surplus of $262 million, provides a degree of assurance on going concern because, in the worst possible case, it would be sufficient to maintain operations for a reasonable period while the company is searching for new business. That balance represents approximately one quarter of the cash paid to suppliers and employees during the year ended 30 April 2012, which suggests that the company could maintain that level of activity for three months without requiring any further funding. That may not be sufficient on its own, but it is also the worst possible case and there should be scope for reducing cash outflows in the event of the cancellation of the Lane contract.

Matters that cause concern:

The financial statements indicate that Gold is gearing up to meet Lane's needs. The cash flow statement indicates that large quantities of property, plant and equipment have been sold and replaced. That equipment will almost certainly have lost a great deal of its value simply because it is now used. The equipment may be specialised and may be designed to meet the requirements associated with the Lane contract. If that is true then there would be a very substantial write-down in the event that the contract is not renewed.

The financial statements also indicate that Gold is building up inventory in response to demand from Lane. Presumably, that inventory cannot be sold to any other customer because of Lane's patents and contractual terms and so it will have to be scrapped if it is not taken as an ongoing part of the contract. The nature of the inventory means that it will have virtually no scrap value and so most of the inventory will have to be written off in full unless it can be established that Lane will buy it in the course of winding up the remainder of the current contract.

The figures also indicate that Gold is expanding rapidly. Total assets have increased by almost 50% and so the company would be in danger of overtrading if it lost the steady cash inflow from this major customer. Even if the contract is renewed, it is important that Gold has plans in place to manage the cash flows. The present surplus has been created largely through borrowing and also a share issue. The directors must be able to demonstrate that there will be sufficient cash from ongoing operations and from the surplus to meet any peaks in demand while any extension to the contract is working through.

(ii) Gold has recognised a major revaluation during the year. It would be desirable for an expert on this industry to evaluate the basis upon which that revaluation was carried out. Given the concerns about the specialist nature of the assets and the fact that they may not be economically viable when located in Gold's home country, it would be desirable for the auditor to have the board's assumptions reviewed. As part of this evaluation, it would also be useful to seek expert advice on whether the PPE has the potential to be used for other business in this industry and whether its value to Gold will have to be reduced to reflect any impairment in the event of this change of use.

Given the possibility of a going concern problem, expert advice ought to be sought on what the resale value, if any, of the equipment might be. That will be difficult to determine, given the volatility of market conditions in the prevailing economic climate, but it is important to know just how much will be lost in the event that Gold loses the contract.

An expert will also have to advise on the net realisable value of the inventory that has built up. If it is in the form of patented chips that cannot be sold to anybody but Lane then the expert will have to advise on whether the chips can be melted down and the materials recycled.

(c) The audit firm may be exposed to claims for compensation if Lane renews the contract and Gold fails. The draft financial statements indicate a healthy, thriving business that is capable of providing Lane with a steady supply of microprocessors. If Gold fails then Lane may claim that it has been misled into relying on this source of supply and may choose to seek compensation from the audit firm.

Legally, the case law in the UK (and in other countries) indicates that damages will only be payable if there is a duty of care, which normally requires a close, direct relationship. Such a duty may be created by the fact that Lane's interest was known to the auditor at the time the audit was conducted and that the auditor was aware that the audited financial statements would be a factor in deciding whether to renew the contract. This is consistent with case law such as the Bannerman case, in which the auditor was found to have a duty of care to a specific third party whose interest in the financial statements was known and understood.

The auditor's liability would be restricted to the extent to which it is reasonable for Lane to base this important decision on published financial statements. It is debatable whether Lane will base any major decisions relating to Gold on the published financial statements and so there is unlikely to be an attributable loss. Lane has the ability to guarantee Gold's future and any loss that it suffers as a consequence of it failing to renew the contract will be of Lane's own making.

(d) ISA 570 (Revised) *Going concern* makes it clear that the directors are responsible for determining whether the going concern basis is appropriate. The auditor should conduct a risk assessment that may be based on management's assurances and the result should be discussed with management.

The assurances provided by management should not be taken at face value. There is a clear incentive to play down the threat and so the auditor should pay particular attention to the extent to which management has taken account of the information that was known to the auditor already. Ideally, management's review should be more thorough than the auditor's.

The auditor should examine the usual documentation, such as budgets and forecasts, but this is a case where the budgets and forecasts really have to be prepared on two bases: one where the contract is secured and the other where it is lost. Ideally, management will be able to show that the company will continue even if the Lane contract is lost. If that is the case then the auditor will have to study the assumptions with some care because that will be the most difficult case to substantiate.

The most likely analysis is that the auditor will regard the company as a going concern if the contract is won and as not a going concern if it is lost. In that case the directors should disclose the fact that going concern depends on the contract negotiations and the auditor may be able to express an unmodified opinion with Material Uncertainty Related to Going Concern paragraph.

In the absence of appropriate disclosure, the auditor will have to express an adverse opinion under these circumstances.

Exam question bank

1 November 2021

ALL questions on the paper relate to the work of RTX Corporate LLP in relation to their client Homebuilder plc. The information given in the Homebuilder Scenario therefore is relevant to ALL questions on the paper.

Homebuilder plc – Scenario

Homebuilder plc is a large, international construction company focusing on both traditional building techniques and factory-made wooden kit framed homes. Its operations are focused in Europe and Asia. The demand for the kit homes has grown significantly over the last five years. The kit homes have the advantage of being very quick to construct (assembly on site takes between 6 days and one month), able to be assembled on brown field sites and on stilts with a minimal groundwork requirement and therefore ideal as part of infrastructure rebuilding after natural disasters. The initial surge in demand came from Asia, and the company has had success in winning significant contracts from Asian governments to reconstruct disaster damaged communities. The kits are also proving to be popular in Europe, where the impacts of climate change have increased flood risks, and as a result, the company is anticipating continued growth in this area of their business. The kit homes have an outstanding rating for sustainability, limiting as they do the generation of carbon emissions. They also comply with the highest safety standards and have received an award from the ICC International Fire Safety Standards for the development of their fire-retardant system.

During the year ended 30 September 2020, the company suffered a downturn in activity due to the impact of the global COVID-19 pandemic. This affected both the ability of the company to manufacture kit homes, and to work in traditional construction due to restrictions on activity caused by a series of devastating lockdowns around Europe and in China. This pattern of disruption to working continued through 2020/21, although the Asia division was not affected by second and third wave lockdowns, unlike Europe. However, all aspects of the company's business were affected by significant issues with the supply chain across both years.

One response to the problems was to continue the manufacture of the kit housing and to hold them in stock ready for an upturn in construction once trading conditions improve.

Your firm, RTX Corporate LLP, was appointed auditor to the company in March 2021 after the resignation of the previous firm. You have assessed materiality based on the assumption of similar levels of risk and activity to the 2019/20 period – as the impacts of the Covid-19 pandemic were anticipated to be felt to a similar degree. You are aware that much of the audit for 2020/21 will also need to be conducted remotely due to ongoing issues with restrictions on national and international travel. As your firm has made the move to remote working successfully throughout the last reporting season, this is anticipated to be an ongoing working model.

During the acceptance procedures, you became aware of an accounting irregularity in the treatment of construction revenue for the kit housing. This accelerated the recognition of profits, as the profits anticipated from each kit house were recognised during the manufacturing process, rather than awaiting on site delivery and assembly. As the level of production of kit houses over 2020/21 was for stock rather than to meet specific orders, it has increased to around 40% of current activity. This had inflated profit in the management accounts by £240,000. It also inflated profit recorded for 2019/20 by £130,000 in the financial statements and this been corrected through the expenses recorded in the current year. The audit committee believe that, as the amount is trivial, there is no reason to record the adjustment as a prior year adjustment, and they are seeking to minimise the publicity around the departure of Ms Zhang – the executive director of the kit housing division – who resigned once the irregularity was exposed. The employment contract for Ms Zhang had included a bonus linked to overall profit recorded in the year for this division. During 2020/21 she received a bonus of £100,000.

After her departure, other irregularities in her division were uncovered by an in-depth internal audit. In addition to incorrectly recognising profits on the kit houses, there is evidence that a stringent cost-cutting exercise by Ms Zhang resulted in a change in key suppliers. The review discovered that the contract for the fire-retardant treatment used on the wood for the kit housing was awarded to a company run by a relative of Ms Zhang, which was not on the approved supplier list for either Homebuilder plc or the approved manufacturing regulator. Internal audit has identified that the manufacture of 8,000 of the 16,000 kit homes made in 2021 were affected by this change. As a result, the contract has been cancelled and the fire-retardant chemical is now provided by a recognised and approved supplier. Although the company does not believe that the cheaper supplier compromised fire safety, remedial works have been planned for affected homes.

Extracts from the draft financial statements for Homebuilder plc 30th September 2021
Income Statement

£'million	BEI 2021	EI 2021	Total 2021	BEI 2020	EI 2020	Total 2020
Continuing operations						
Revenue	2,790.2	–	2,790.2	4,341.3	–	4,341.3
Cost of sales	(2,293.5)	–	(2,293.5)	(3,297.2)	–	(3,297.2)
Gross profit	496.7	–	496.7	1,044.1	–	1,044.1
Net operating expenses	(204.3)	(10.0)	(214.3)	(187.3)	–	(214.9)
PBIT	292.4	(10.0)	282.4	856.8	–	856.8
Profit before taxation			264.4			835.9

BEI = Before Exceptional Item; EI = Exceptional Item

Extracts from Accounting Policy Note:

Revenue

Revenue is recognised when the performance obligation associated with the sale is completed. The transaction price comprises the fair value of the consideration received or receivable, net of value added tax, rebates and discounts and after eliminating sales within the Group. Revenue and profit are recognised as follows:

Long term contracts

Revenue arising on contracts which give the customer control over properties as they are constructed, and for which the Group has a right to payments for work performed, is recognised over time. Revenue and costs are recognised over time with reference to the stage of completion of the contract activity at the balance sheet date where the outcome of a long-term contract can be estimated reliably. This is normally measured by surveys of work performed to date. Variations in contract work, claims and incentive payments are included to the extent that it is probable that they will result in revenue and they are capable of being reliably measured. When land is transferred at the start of a long-term contract, revenue is not recognised until control has been transferred to the customer, which includes legal title being passed to them. Where the outcome of a long-term contract cannot be estimated reliably, contract revenue where recoverability is probable is recognised to the extent of contract costs incurred. The costs associated with fulfilling a contract are recognised as expenses in the period in which they are incurred. When it is probable that total contract costs will exceed total contract revenue, the expected loss is recognised as an expense immediately.

Revenue

An analysis of the Group's continuing revenue is as follows:

£'million	2021	2020
Traditional Construction Housing Sales	1,507.9	2,798.3
Kit Housing Sales (including on-site assembly)	1,269.3	1,490.6
Construction Consultancy	13.0	52.4
	2,790.2	**4,341.3**

The Group's revenue includes revenue from construction contracts that are recognised over time by reference to the stage of completion of the contract with the customer.

All other revenue is recognised at a point in time once control of the property is transferred to the customer.

£'million	2021	2020
Recognised at a point in time	2,073.7	2,013.7
Recognised over time	716.5	2,327.6
	2,790.2	**4,341.3**

At 30 September 2021, the aggregate amount of the transaction price allocated to unsatisfied performance obligations on construction contracts was £572.3 million (2020: £692.7 million), of which approximately 46% is expected to be recognised as revenue during 2022.

Fire Retardant Safety Recall

Following the internal audit review of manufacturing changes, the company conducted a detailed review into all current kit homes and worked with building owners and the Fire Services to implement mitigation measures, where applicable. Whilst there is no evidence that the fire retardant used by the company fails to meet applicable fire safety standards, the company accepts that the manufacturing processes affecting a small number of homes did not use the award-winning process expected by our customers. Even though the buildings concerned meet the requirements of building regulations at the time construction was formally approved, the company is undertaking to meet the costs of treating the homes with the fire-retardant system specified in our promotions materials. This decision was taken for buildings recently constructed by the Group because management believe that it is morally right, not because it is legally required. The provision was £10 million to reflect the latest cost estimates of the work to be performed.

1 **Homebuilder plc Audit Issues**

   Required

   (a) Critically appraise the key audit risks arising from the issues according to the kit homes division of Homebuilder plc and outline in brief their impact on your audit approach. You do not need to articulate a detailed audit testing plan. **(25 marks)**

   (b) Your audit tender to Homebuilder plc anticipated that activity levels for 2020/21 would be maintained at those of the previous year and materiality was set at £42 million which equated to 5% of pre-tax profits. Justify and explain any adjustments you intend to make in the materiality level set for the 2021 audit to the audit committee and assess its impact on your audit documentation. **(15 marks)**

   (c) Evaluate the impact that the issues arising in your preliminary assessment of Homebuilder plc may have on your obligation to report irregularities in the revised ISA 700 *Forming an Opinion and Reporting on Financial Statements*. **(10 marks)**

   (Total 50 marks)

2   **Assurance of Task Force for Climate Related Disclosures**

As discussed, Homebuilder plc is a large international housebuilder, specialising in the manufacture and on-site erection of timber frame and clad homes as well as using traditional building techniques. The company has been marketing itself on its sustainability credentials, reducing as it has, the use of concrete and cement and instead using soft woods treated to ensure fire safety and durability. The following is extracted from the sustainability report produced by Homebuilder plc for 2020.

> "Reducing our impact on the environment is very important to us, so we consider it at every stage of our operations.
>
> We work with our partners in the supply chain to source sustainable materials, and with our contractors to minimise the impact of our construction sites. We also design homes to be energy and resource efficient to live in."
>
> Our Sustainability Champions
>
> We have a Sustainability Champion in each of our regional businesses. They help us engage colleagues on resource efficiency and monitor progress at the local level. They use our resource portal to track performance, assess the costs of resource use and waste disposal, and compare progress with other parts of the business. Each Champion has agreed a resource management action plan for their regional business. We held regular webinars for the Champions in 2020 on a range of topics. Champions were able to present their work, hear from others and share experiences.
>
> *Extracted from the Sustainability Report Homebuilder plc 2020*

The finance director is aware that, from 1 January 2021, Homebuilder plc will be required to report upon whether its disclosures are consistent with those required by Taskforce for Climate Related Financial Disclosures (TCFD), and if not, to explain any reasons for lack of compliance. An extract from the 2017 report regarding these disclosures is given below:

> Core Elements of Recommended Climate Related Financial Disclosures
>
> - Governance: The organisation's governance around climate-related risks and opportunities.
>
> - Strategy: The actual and potential impacts of climate-related risks and opportunities on the organization's businesses, strategy, and financial planning.
>
> - Risk Management: The processes used by the organization to identify, assess, and manage climate-related risks.
>
> - Metrics and Targets: The metrics and targets used to assess and manage relevant climate-related risks and opportunities.
>
> *Extracted from the Task Force for Climate Related Financial Disclosures Final Report 2017*

> The UK Financial Conduct Authority (FCA) listing rule 1 requires boards to include a statement in the Annual Report setting out:
>
> - whether disclosures are consistent with the TCFD's recommendations;
> - where any disclosures are not consistent with some or all of the TCFD's recommendations, provide an explanation as to why, and a description of any steps the board are taking to rectify this;
> - where any disclosures have been included in a document other than the Annual Report, an explanation of why; and
> - where in the Annual Report (or other relevant document) the various disclosures can be found.

A recent report by EY (one of the Big Four international professional services firms) has highlighted that, although the quality of such reporting in the construction sector continues to improve, in 2019 over one third of companies in this sector scored less than 5% for their reporting quality. Although the company has been reporting around sustainability issues for a number of years, the finance director is very concerned that the current reports may not be of an adequate standard. The extensive sustainability report currently produced runs to some 35 pages and includes such areas as partnership with nature, building communities, minimising waste, ensuring safety, and reducing the carbon footprint. There is extensive discussion of the range of projects ongoing in each area, with metrics reporting successes in each area. However, each year the format and design alter, as the projects develop, and there is little continuity in the data discussed. There have been accusations that the company is more focused on the idea of solving the issues of home shortages and the role in building communities at the expense of its commitments to the wider environment. The sustainability reporting was initially set up by Dr Constanza Fabio, as operations director, and was supported by an active committee. Dr Fabio left the company three years ago and the sustainability reporting has ceded to the finance director by default, although the main driving force of the projects sits with regional sustainability champions.

You are the audit engagement partner for Homebuilder plc and the finance director has raised his concerns around this issue with you.

Required

(a) Recommend the key issues that the finance director, in association with the audit committee, should review to ensure that taskforce for climate disclosure reporting is embedded within the reporting approach. **(10 marks)**

(b) Appraise the benefits that assurance of reporting of climate disclosure could yield for Homebuilder plc. **(8 marks)**

(c) Justify whether you would be able to provide such assurance for an audit client.

(7 marks)

(Total 25 marks)

3 **RTX Corporate LLP Practice Management Issues**

The issues raised in planning for the audit of Homebuilder plc has raised concerns with the quality partner at your firm. She is aware that the area of fraud is one of much current debate, with the IAASB currently exploring a more root and branch review of ISA 240 *The Auditor's Responsibilities Relating to Fraud in an Audit of Financial Statements*, and she considers that the audit of Homebuilder is exposing the firm to risk. To ensure that the audit quality on this engagement is safeguarded, you have been asked to present your quality assurance review strategy for this client to a meeting of the partners in your firm.

As a mid-tier firm, RTX Corporate LLP has adopted the data analytics solution first developed for one of the Big Four firms. This has enabled the firm to move into the public listed company audit market, and Homebuilder plc is the third such listed company that the firm audits.

There has been resistance from some of the older partners to the adoption of an off-the-peg data analytics solution, although they do concede it has enabled the firm to develop its data analytical capacity more quickly and efficiently than perhaps the development of a bespoke system may have done. The data analytics capability of the firm is underemployed, and you believe that there is a role that it could play in enhancing your audit work for Homebuilder plc.

Required

(a) Evaluate whether you accept that the audit of Homebuilder plc exposes the firm to elevated risk and discuss the benefits you believe would be offered by a hot review of the Homebuilder plc audit files. **(12 marks)**

(b) Critically appraise the potential role that data analytics could play in enhancing the quality of the audit work for this client. **(13 marks)**

(Total 25 marks)

2 May 2022

Scenario

Lovely Nights Group plc

Year Ended 30th April 2022

Company Background

Lovely Nights plc (henceforth Lovely Nights) is a well-established chain of high quality but reasonably priced hotels which was founded in the UK. Initially it was part of a chain of pubs and casual dining restaurants, but the pub element of the business was sold fifteen years ago, and the casual dining element has been incorporated physically and operationally into the hotels, which means that the only operating segment in Lovely Nights is the hotel business.

The chain has expanded rapidly and is now the largest chain of budget hotels in the UK, with approximately 850 premises throughout the country. In 2013 the group expanded into the Netherlands through the acquisition of Zeelander Hotels, which it has re-branded as Lovely Nights. Initially the group acquired 27 hotels, mainly based around Rotterdam. Since 2014 it has grown organically in the Netherlands, building or leasing a further 96 hotels around all of the major cities.

In May 2021, despite the ravages of the COVID-19 pandemic, the group completed the acquisition of Peony Hotels which comprises 14 trading hotels located in mainland China (Peoples Republic of China).

According to the draft accounts for 2021/22, revenue for the year totalled £1,011 million, with around 50% of the turnover achieved prior to the pandemic. Operating losses of £35 million were recorded for the year, showing a considerable improvement when compared with 2020/21.

The company employs 28,200 staff members in three countries and is responsible for supporting a further 50,000 in the wider supply chain. The company engages with a significant number of smaller suppliers internationally as part of its "keeping produce local" initiative and is a core part of the economic life of each community in which it works.

Statement from the CEO of Lovely Nights plc

Despite the significant impact of COVID-19 on markets, our confidence in the market, based on a long-term assessment, remains high and we are excited about the future potential.

Unusually in this sector, we operate a vertically integrated model; by owning all of the value chain, from developing and building the hotels right through to managing the brand, the operations and the direct distribution, we are best positioned to access the structural growth opportunities and continue to create value for our shareholders over the longer term. In the UK, we are focused on continuing to grow and innovate with growth delivered through our existing expansion plans. We have worked hard to nurture our strong brand and our operational model has proven very popular with our customers. As we recover from the turbulence of the last years, we expect to see a significant demand for travel, and we are confident that our high quality, but affordable offering will continue to gain market share. The budget market in which we operate is currently experiencing higher growth than other hotel sectors and will outperform those other sectors in downturns.

Budget branded hotels have outperformed the market in every year since 2008, including a material outperformance during and after the financial crisis, and we are seeing evidence of that once again both during and in the immediate aftermath of the COVID-19 pandemic. We have expanded our operations into the Netherlands, and this year, into China, through strategic acquisitions.

In both the Netherlands and China, we aim to replicate our UK success, and aspire to be the number one budget hotel chain in every national market in which we operate. Whilst the Netherlands presents a safe opportunity, given it has remarkably similar characteristics to the UK with both markets being characterised by long-term migration from independents to budget branded hotels. The recent

COVID-19 crisis has accelerated the pressures on these independents through demand weakness and increased cost pressures, which may worsen as inflationary pressures rise. This decline in independent hotel numbers will allow us to further consolidate our market share and take advantage of the growth in that market.

In China we see a new opportunity to provide excellent budget hotels to meet the demand as travel for both pleasure and work increases. Although the Chinese travel and tourism market has some core differences to that in Europe, we believe that the next decade will see a significant growth in leisure tourism within and into China. The team at Peony Hotels have impressed us with their commitment to excellence in the business and we have every confidence that, with our expertise in this market internationally, we will be able to harness power of the Lovely Nights brand and take advantage of the potential in this region.

Review of Corporate Governance

In May 2021 the CFO, Sachin Guthra, stepped down after 7 years in the position and 17 years with the company. He was replaced by Sara Yin who has extensive experience in the hospitality industry especially in the Far East.

In September of 2021, the chair of the audit committee retired due to ill health. The board decided to appoint Sachin Guthra as a non-executive director and new chair of the audit committee. This decision was unanimously agreed as Sachin Guthra intimately understands the Group, has extensive relevant financial experience and was able to take over at short notice.

It was noted that, as a result of the remuneration package received as an executive director, Sachin Guthra retains a 3% interest in the equity of the company. Although this compromises his independent status, the board believe that, at this time of material uncertainty, the commitment and experience with the company, and the integrity Sachin Guthra has embodied as an AIA member and practitioner, outweighs any potential conflict of interest.

The other two members of the audit committee are Conran Peters, who has previously worked as operations director for a rival hotel chain and Yuxin Gao who is a retired chartered surveyor.

Lovely Nights plc

Year ended 30th April 2022

Extracts from DRAFT notes to the financial statements

14 IMPAIRMENT

During the year, impairment losses of £258.6 million (2020/21: £164.3m) were recognised within operating costs. These impairments are primarily driven by a reduction in anticipated cash flows, particularly over the next 12–24 months within the Chinese market, and an increase in the discount rate reflecting increased market risk and volatility.

The losses were recognised on the following classes of assets:

	2021/22 £m	2020/21 £m
IMPAIRMENT LOSSES		
Property, plant and equipment – impairment review	–	164.3
Property, plant and equipment – site fire	11.2	–
Property, plant and equipment – assets for held for sale	4.9	
Intangible assets – goodwill	238.8	–
Intangible assets – software and IT	3.7	

The Group recognised impairment reversals during the year of £101.7 million (2020/21: £nil).

As a result of the COVID-19 pandemic, the Group identified indicators of impairment and performed an impairment assessment of all trading sites. In 2020/21 this resulted in an impairment of £164.3 million being recorded in relation to property, plant and equipment in the UK and the Netherlands. The Group considers each trading site to be a CGU.

Where indicators of impairment are identified, an impairment assessment is undertaken. In assessing whether an asset has been impaired, the carrying amount of the site is compared to its recoverable amount. The recoverable amount is the higher of its value in use and its fair value less costs of disposal. The Group calculates a value in use (VIU) for each site. Where the VIU is lower than the carrying value of the CGU, the Group uses a range of methods for estimating the fair value less costs of disposal (FVLCD). These include applying a market multiple to the CGU EBITDAR and, for leasehold sites, present value techniques using a discounted cash flow method. Both FVLCD methods rely on inputs not normally observable by market participants and are therefore level 3 measurements in the fair value hierarchy. The key assumptions used by management in estimating value in use were:

Goodwill

Goodwill acquired through business combinations is allocated to groups of CGUs at an operating segment level, being the level at which management monitors goodwill.

An analysis of goodwill by operating segment is:

	Europe £m	China £m	Total £m
As at May 2021	110.5		110.5
Recognised on acquisition of a subsidiary		238.8	238.8
Impairment		(238.8)	(238.8)
As at April 2022	110.5	–	110.5

An impairment of £238.8 million was recorded in relation to goodwill arising on the acquisition of Peony Hotels (see Note 35) reflecting the impact of the COVID-19 pandemic on current and future growth rates.

The recoverable amount is the higher of fair value less costs of disposal and value in use using the same assumptions as those used in the site level impairment reviews. The recoverable amount has been determined from value in use calculations. The future cash flows are based on assumptions from the approved budget and cover a five-year period. These forecasts include management's most recent view of medium-term trading prospects. Cash flows beyond this period are extrapolated using a 2.0% (2021 – 2.0%) growth rate. The pre-tax discount rate applied to cash flow projections is 9.5% for the UK and the Netherlands and 6.3% for China (2021: 9.4% Europe).

As a result of the Chinese goodwill being impaired in the period and the level of headroom within the European segment, there is no reasonably possible change that could result in a further material impairment of goodwill.

Property, plant and equipment – assets held for sale

As a result of the impact of the COVID-19 pandemic and the focused application of investment cash flows, the company decided not to proceed with certain sites resulting in a cost write off of £7.9 million that had been incurred and capitalised. During the period, seven hotels were transferred to assets held for sale, resulting in an impairment charge of £4.2 million. In addition, an impairment charge of £0.7 million was recorded in relation to assets which had previously been classified as held for sale as a result of a reduction in expected sales proceeds.

Property Plant and Equipment – Software and IT assets

An impairment review of IT intangible and tangible assets was carried out as a result of the COVID-19 pandemic which identified a total of £3.7 million of assets which are not expected to generate future economic benefits for the Group.

35 BUSINESS COMBINATIONS

Acquisition in 2021/22 – Peony Hotels

On 31st May 2021, the Group acquired 100% of the share capital of Peony Hotels for consideration of £225.8 million. The acquisition consists of 13 trading hotels which have been rebranded to Lovely Nights as well as the leasehold for a further six future sites. The transaction forms part of the Group's strategic priority of international growth.

	£m
CONSIDERATION TRANSFERRED	
Cash	175.8
Contingent consideration	50.0
TOTAL CONSIDERATION	**225.8**
FAIR VALUE OF NET ASSETS ACQUIRED	
Property, plant and equipment	6.0
Investment property	51.9
Right-of-use assets	193.3
Trade and other receivables	0.5
Cash and cash equivalents	1.4
TOTAL ASSETS ACQUIRED	**253.1**
Trade and other payables	(2.8)
Deferred tax liabilities	(3.5)
Lease liabilities	(245.2)
TOTAL LIABILITIES ACQUIRED	**(251.5)**
NET IDENTIFIABLE ASSETS ACQUIRED AT FAIR VALUE	1.6
Goodwill arising on acquisition	224.2
PURCHASE CONSIDERATION TRANSFERRED	225.8

The goodwill acquired in the above transactions comprises certain intangible assets that cannot be separately identified. This includes the skills and experience of the assembled workforce and the future growth opportunities the business provides to the Group's operations. None of the goodwill recognised is expected to be deductible for income tax purposes. Subsequent to the acquisition, an impairment of the goodwill arising on acquisition has been recorded (see Note 14).

From the date of acquisition, the acquiree has contributed £26.3m of revenue and £6.8m of loss before tax.

Relevant Industry Context

> The UK hotel industry could take four years to return to 2019 levels of business, even if an effective vaccine helps the sector to recover from the deep financial hit caused by COVID-19.
>
> The daily revenue per hotel room – a key indicator for the sector – is not expected to revive to 2019 levels until 2024 in London, and 2023 across the rest of the UK, according to forecasts published on Tuesday by the accounting firm PricewaterhouseCoopers (PwC).
>
> Renewed lockdowns, the decline in foreign tourist numbers and the near disappearance of business travel have left hotels struggling to attract customers, with a dramatic effect on their earnings.
>
> The fall in corporate demand as well as the absence of big live sport or music events meant big city hotels were suffering the most, while missing out on the increase in Britons staying in the UK for their holidays.
>
> Hotel rooms are expected to be occupied for an average of 45% of the time during 2021. While that would represent an improvement on the rate of between a third and two-fifths in 2020, PwC said the industry was still facing an unprecedentedly bleak outlook.
>
> London hotels will be particularly badly hit. Daily revenues per room in the capital have slumped to only £29 in 2020, less than a quarter of the £129 achieved in 2019, PwC said – by far the biggest hit the industry has seen in comparable data dating to the 1970s.
>
> Extracted from Guardian Business October 2020
>
> https://www.theguardian.com/business/2020/oct/27/covid-hit-uk-hotels-unlikely-to-recover-for-four-years-says-pwc accessed 8 November 2024

> Lovely Nights Group plc, the owner of the Lovely Nights hotel chain, says it expects cost inflation for the hospitality sector to reach 7–8% in the coming months.
>
> Higher labour costs, rising energy bills and increased construction costs for its new hotels are putting pressure on the FTSE 350 listed company, says Lovely Nights chief executive.
>
> The group said it expected to offset these increased costs through charging higher rates for rooms in its 850 Lovely Night hotels, as well as through cost efficiencies and by growing its estate. The group is however concerned that the cost of living pressures in the UK will further depress demand and that the fundamental change in business travel will further exacerbate this reduction in occupancy. The CEO expressed her hope that demand will be higher than 2021 as lockdowns become a thing of the past, but is very aware that recovery to 2019 activity will not materialise until 2024. She noted that the group is estimating that occupancy will only recover to around 60% of 2019 levels during 2022.
>
> *Extracted from an interview in Hotel Today Business periodical January 2022*

Regulatory Developments around Public Interest and Audit – a UK perspective

Below are extracts from the Brydon Report of the Independent Review into the Quality and Effectiveness of Audit

> 2.3.6
>
> Create continuity between successive audit reports.
>
> Provide greater transparency over differing estimations, perhaps disclosing graduated findings. Call out inconsistencies in information made public.
>
> Reference external negative signals and how they have informed the audit.
>
> 6.4.2
>
> Auditors are appropriately qualified and exercise professional judgement and appropriate scepticism or suspicion throughout their work;
>
> Auditors act in the public interest and have regard to the interests of the users of their report beyond solely those of shareholders;
>
> 2.4.7
>
> The directors present an annual Public Interest Statement, which explains the company's view of its obligations to the public interest, whether arising from statutory, self-determined or other obligations, and how the company has acted to meet this public interest over the previous year.
>
> *Extracts from Brydon Report of the Independent Review into the Quality and Effectiveness of Audit 2019*

ALL QUESTIONS ARE COMPULSORY

1 Audit Issues arising in Lovely Nights plc

You are the audit manager for BHZ LLP which is an international audit firm with a significant presence in all major financial centres in the world. Although the firm has been auditing Lovely Nights for the last five years, the engagement partner has recently retired, and the audit has been moved from the main London office to the Newcastle office. The files are all fully available to the team electronically, but none of the prior year team will be available to work on the audit this year. For all intents and purposes, this feels like the first year that the client has been audited by the Newcastle office, although much more reliance can be placed on the prior year work.

You have recently attended a meeting with the audit committee of Lovely Nights where there was a somewhat ill-tempered discussion regarding the proposed fees for the engagement. The audit committee are unclear why the audit fee should be increased due to the acquisition of Peony Hotels. The chair of the committee, Sachin Guthra, (who is the former CFO of the Group) stated that "as the acquisition was subject to a due diligence assurance from a firm of auditors familiar with the Chinese hospitality market that therefore they perceived little risk in the numbers and as the balances are hardly material, a limited approach to assurance should be required and a remote approach should suffice."

Following this meeting, you reviewed the audit file from last year and note that there is no mention of issues arising in connection with the audit committee. From the evidence in the file, it seems that the relationship with the previous audit committee chair was very productive and cordial. The previous engagement partner was able to challenge the judgements around the valuation of the impairment of the property, plant and equipment, which was duly increased.

Required

(a) Critically appraise the key audit issues arising from the acquisition of Peony Hotels and in connection with intangible and tangible non-current assets detailed in notes 14 and 35 above and explain where management bias may manifest itself in these issues. **(15 marks)**

(b) Explain and justify your assessment of the risk in connection with the reversal of impairment of £101.7 million in the UK CGU – see note 14 above. **(10 marks)**

(c) Explain and justify your audit work in connection with the fair value of goodwill and property plant and equipment in Lovely Nights plc. **(15 marks)**

(d) Assess the importance of public interest in determining your approach to Lovely Nights plc and evaluate whether the suggestions in the Brydon Report 2019 (see extract given at the end of the Lovely Nights plc case study) might be supportive in improving the ability of BHZ LLP to perform a high-quality audit. **(10 marks)**

(Total 50 marks)

2 Corporate Governance Reporting

"The board confirms that it fully complied with the Code as at 30 April 2022, with the exception of the independence of the chair of the audit committee upon appointment which was fully explained and justified at the time of appointment. The board does not consider that the lack of independence of the chair of the audit committee compromises the independence of the committee nor its ability to discharge its duties under the Code of Governance.

The committee met four times in 2021/22. Meetings were attended by all members of the committee and, by invitation, the chair of the board, the Chief Executive, the Finance Director, the Head of Internal Audit, the Director of Financial Reporting & Control and other relevant people from the business when appropriate.

The external auditor, BHZ LLP, is also invited to meetings except where discussion includes matters relating to its own independence, performance, reappointment, fees or audit tendering.

The audit committee was pleased to welcome Conran Peters as a new member in May 2021.

The Composition of the committee

In accordance with the UK Corporate Governance Code 2018 (the 'Code'), the board has confirmed that all members of the committee, with the exception of the chair of the committee, are independent non-executive directors. The board has also confirmed that I, as chair of the committee, have recent and relevant financial experience through my prior work as Chief Financial Officer of Lovely Nights plc and FTD Holdings plc.

As part of the company's annual compliance with the Code, an evaluation was undertaken of the skills and experience of the committee. In accordance with the Code, the board has agreed that the committee as a whole has the competencies relevant to the sector in which the company operates and the recent evaluation report confirmed that the committee operates effectively.

Audit effectiveness

The effectiveness of the external audit process is dependent on appropriate audit risk identification at the start of the audit cycle. We receive from BHZ LLP a detailed audit plan, identifying its assessment of these key risks. These risks were reviewed and they, together with the work done by the auditor, were challenged to test management's assumptions and estimates around these areas, as well as other areas reported upon.

> Overall, it was noted that the audit team had adapted well to the challenges of remote working and that the audit was effective, executed to a high standard. However, it was noted that there was still room for improvement in respect of the planning and timeliness of audit requests and the overall efficiency of the audit work performed."
>
> *Extracted from the Lovely Nights plc Audit Committee Report – draft accounts for year ended 30th April 2022.*

Required

(a) Critically appraise the quality of the governance **reporting** detailed by Lovely Nights plc in the extract above. **(12 marks)**

(b) Explore the reporting responsibility for BHZ LLP in respect of the corporate governance statement. **(13 marks)**

(Total 25 marks)

3 **Practice Management and Ethics**

Following the latest heated exchange with the audit committee chair, you have returned to the audit file from last year to see whether there is any indication of these issues in the prior audit. As already noted there seems to be no mentions of issues arising in connection with the audit committee. The relationship with the previous audit committee chair was noted to be good and the previous engagement partner had recorded robust challenges to the management judgements around impairments of property, plant and equipment, leading to an increase in the charge for that year.

You are now coming to the conclusion that the issue may reside in the alteration of staff involved in the audit committee and the audit firm. The chemistry is not only awkward between the audit committee, but you have experienced some problems with the CFO Sara Yin.

Required

(a) Critically appraise the ethical issues in Lovely Nights' audit engagement arising from the ongoing difficulties with the audit committee and other staff. **(15 marks)**

(b) Critically explore how the audit committee may fail to meet its responsibilities in respect of the external audit of Lovely Nights and recommend the appropriate responses that BHZ LLP could take to mitigate these issues. **(10 marks)**

(Total 25 marks)

3 November 2022

Polyfine Industries plc

Audit in respect of the Year Ended 30 September 2022

Corporate Background

Polyfine Industries plc is a multinational chemical company which specializes in the development and production of light-weight foams and other polymer-based products. The main product is uniformly dense foam sheets with a consistent cell structure. These foam sheets and blocks are manufactured from common polymers using a unique nitrogen-expansion process and serve the following markets:

	2022	2021
Revenue by market (%)		
Sports and leisure	40	29
Product protection (Packaging)	29	21
Building and construction	11	12
Transportation (Aviation and Automotive)	4	12
Industrial	7	7
Medical	5	16
Other	4	3

The company has been operating for over 100 years and constantly innovates to meet market need. It is developing pioneering products to reduce the waste from the plastics industry and to be a key part of the circular economy through recycling product and reducing waste.

The main production sites are in the US, UK, Poland and China and the geographical markets are:

	2022	2021
Revenue by Geographical Area (%)		
North America	20	22
United Kingdom	11	23
Europe	28	22
China	27	22
Rest of World	14	11

Although the company is highly innovative, two significant competitors, Plasti-Co and EcoPlasma, both based in China, have developed similar products for building insulation and for high-tech sportswear. Both products are priced at around 25% less than Polyfine for similar but inferior performance. Polyfine Industries is focusing on increasing the innovations in its sustainable products, although there has been some discussion that the green credentials of these are being over-claimed and, they may not reduce plastic shed into the environment and may also not be 100% recycled.

Notes from the meeting with the Operations Director of Polyfine Industries plc

In 2022, sales in the Polyfine business expanded to a record £156.2m (2021: £150.9m). As expected, there was no repeat of the 2021 sales for personal protective equipment (PPE) for the UK National Health Service contract.

Overall, Polyfine enjoyed a broad-based recovery in most markets by geography and by application segment. However, as anticipated in 2020 neither the aviation nor the automotive sectors have recovered to their pre-pandemic levels.

Input costs for Polyfine are primarily raw materials derived from the oil industry and, to a lesser extent, energy and operational costs such as labour. Freight costs, whether paid by Polyfine or by customers, can also be a significant factor.

Prices for the main raw material, low-density polyethylene (LDPE), increased rapidly and significantly from the relative lows experienced in 2020. The average price paid during 2021 was around 80% higher than the previous year and 50% higher than the long-run, pre-pandemic average. These costs have further increased during 2022.

The operations director stated: *"Our pricing policy for 2022 reflected our assessment from 2021. We predicted that the inflationary pressures from oil would peak in 2021 and then would correct towards the long-run average relatively quickly and that relatively modest increases in pricing would recover general inflationary pressures plus the catch-up from the relative lows of polymer pricing in the previous period."*

By the final quarter of 2022, ethylene, the main feedstock for LDPE which normally accounts for 70–80% of the LDPE price, was priced around at 175% of its long-run average and LDPE premium pricing was driven by a capacity shortage of polymer processing in Europe. This demand for polymer is expected to remain high leading to unprecedented levels of LDPE pricing.

Input costs for other materials and services also increased markedly, particularly later in the year with respect to energy and products which are energy intensive. As a result, input costs during 2022 were only partially recovered through pricing adjustments, impacting margins in Polyfine significantly.

In setting prices historically, Polyfine have typically absorbed the short-term variability in polymer and freight prices and only act on inflationary pressures when they appear to be more "permanent". In the past this has included changes in employment costs or commodity costs which have undergone a structural change in pricing. Cost increases in polymer, freight, energy and other raw materials were substantially more impactful than expected and Polyfine's 2022 price increases have consequently reflected this.

Polyfine's profit declined to £0.8m (2021: £6.4m), representing a margin of 0.5% (2021: 4.3%), with the variance being accounted for almost entirely by the timing and level of pricing not reflecting increases in raw material and other input costs in the period.

Polyfine Industries plc

DRAFT Income Statement for year ended 30 September 2022

	2022 £'000	2021 £'000
Revenue	156,200	150,900
Cost of Sales	129,646	119,211
Gross Profit	26,554	31,689
Distribution Costs	11,859	10,678
Administrative Expenses	11,467	11,256
Operating Profit	3,228	9,755
Finance Costs	1,116	1,875
Profit before Income Tax	2,112	7,880
Income Tax Expense	1,342	1,435
Profit for the Year	770	6,445

Notes from discussion with the CFO

Although overall performance is disappointing, the board have confidence that the new developments in eco-plastics will prove popular in the market and should be priced at a level to increase gross profit despite increasing raw material fluctuations.

The debt covenant agreement with Industrial and Commercial Bank requires an interest cover of 2.5 and an operating profit percentage of 5% based on a rolling three-year average. Operating profit percentage for 2020 was 16% and this is the level that the company has historically recorded. The current figures reflect the issues arising due to the unprecedented rise in oil costs, which are expected to drop back towards the end of 2022.

Notes from discussion with the chair

There has been some upheaval in the board during 2021/22 with the departure of the CEO, due to ill health and the Operations Director who is now working for a competitor, EcoPlasma. The new CEO and Operations Director have joined the Polyfine Industries from the retail sector, and while both have extensive multinational corporate experience and bring a wealth of new ideas around e-commerce to the company, neither have a background in the plastics industry.

Research and Development Accounting Policy

Expenditure on research activities undertaken with the prospect of gaining new scientific or technical knowledge and understanding is recognised in the income statement as an expense as incurred.

Development costs that are directly attributable to the design and testing of identifiable and unique products controlled by the company are recognised as intangible assets where the following criteria are met:

- It is technically feasible to complete the asset so that it will be available for use;
- Management intends to complete the asset and use or sell it;
- There is an ability to use or sell the asset and it can be demonstrated how the asset will generate probable future economic benefits;
- Adequate technical, financial, and other resources to complete the development and to use or sell the asset are available; and
- The expenditure attributable to the asset during its development can be reliably measured.

Directly attributable costs that are capitalised as part of the asset include the product development employee costs and an appropriate portion of relevant overheads. Other development expenditures that do not meet these criteria are recognised as an expense as incurred. Development costs previously recognised as an expense are not recognised as an asset in a subsequent period.

Extracted from Note 17 in the Draft Financial Statements

Research and Development	2022	2021
	£'000	£'000
Opening Cost	5,026	4,969
Additions	277	234
Currency Movement Adjustment	63	(177)
Closing Cost	**5,366**	**5,026**
Opening Accumulated Amortisation	2,912	2,752
Charge for the Year	194	266
Currency Movement Adjustment	37	(106)
Closing Accumulated Amortisation	**3,143**	**2,912**
Net Book Value	**2,223**	**2,114**

The additions relate to the ongoing development of AirFlow Foam which has the potential to reduce the weight of the product used in construction insulation and sports products (especially trainers). This is manufactured from 100% recycled plastics, is 100% recyclable and reduces micro-plastic shedding into the environment.

The estimated useful life for the company's intangible development assets is assessed as between 5–20 years and these are reviewed by the board at the reporting date.

	£'000
Development Projects:	
Airflow Foam (under development for high tech trainers)	1,023
Polyinsulate (used in construction)	750
Postufoam (used in automotive and aviation)	450

Why are oil prices so high?

In spring 2020, as Covid spread around the world and countries went into lockdown, the price of crude oil crashed because of a lack of buyers.

"Producers were paying people to take the oil off their hands, because they didn't have enough space to store it all," says Ms Dourian After this, Opec+ members agreed to slash production by 10m barrels a day, to help drive the price back up.

In June 2021, with demand for crude beginning to recover, Opec+ started gradually increasing supply, putting an extra 400,000 barrels a day onto world markets. In July and August, it will supply an extra 600,000.

However, it is still supplying some two and a half million barrels a day less than in spring 2020.

When Russia invaded Ukraine, the price of crude soared to well over $100 a barrel, because of panic on the markets. This has caused significant rises in the price of petrol at the pumps.

"When Opec+ cut supplies by 10 million barrels a day in May 2020, they cut too deep," says David Fyfe, chief economist at Argus Media.

"Now they're increasing supply at a slow rate that does not take into account the effects of the Russia-Ukraine crisis."

Extracted from BBC News https://www.bbc.co.uk/news/business-61188579 accessed 7th June 2022.

Economic Forecast

Compounding the damage from the COVID-19 pandemic, the Russian invasion of Ukraine has magnified the slowdown in the global economy, which is entering what could become a protracted period of feeble growth and elevated inflation, according to the World Bank's latest *Global Economic Prospects* report. This raises the risk of stagflation, with potentially harmful consequences for middle- and low-income economies alike.

Global growth is expected to slump from 5.7 percent in 2021 to 2.9 percent in 2022–significantly lower than 4.1 percent that was anticipated in January. It is expected to hover around that pace over 2023-24, as the war in Ukraine disrupts activity, investment, and trade in the near term, pent-up demand fades, and fiscal and monetary policy accommodation is withdrawn. As a result of the damage from the pandemic and the war, the level of per capita income in developing economies this year will be nearly 5 percent below its pre-pandemic trend.

Growth in advanced economies is projected to sharply decelerate from 5.1 percent in 2021 to 2.6 percent in 2022–1.2 percentage points below projections in January. Growth is expected to further moderate to 2.2 percent in 2023, largely reflecting the further unwinding of the fiscal and monetary policy support provided during the pandemic. Among emerging market and developing economies, growth is also projected to fall from 6.6 percent in 2021 to 3.4 percent in 2022–well below the annual average of 4.8 percent over 2011-2019. The negative spill overs from the war will more than offset any near-term boost to some commodity exporters from higher energy prices. Forecasts for 2022 growth have been revised down in nearly 70 percent of EMDEs, including most commodity importing countries as well as four-fifths of low-income countries.

Extracted from World Bank Press Release 7th June 2022.

https://www.worldbank.org/en/news/press-release/2022/06/07/stagflation-risk-rises-amid-sharp-slowdown-in-growth Accessed 7th June 2022

ALL QUESTIONS ARE COMPULSORY

1 Audit of Polyfine Industries plc

You are a newly promoted partner for RYG LLP, a large international professional services firm with offices in all of the major financial centres of the world. You are based in the Hong Kong office, having recently returned from a three-year secondment in the London office.

You have been appointed as the engagement partner for Polyfine Industries plc, which is jointly listed on the UK and the Shanghai stock exchanges.

Required

(a) Critically appraise **three key inherent** audit risks which require detailed consideration in the planning of the 2022 audit of Polyfine Industries plc. **(20 marks)**

(b) Justify your assessment of materiality for this audit explaining why you should set a different balance for performance materiality. **(5 marks)**

(c) Explain and justify the work you intend to perform in respect of the Research and Development balance detailed in note 17 above. **(20 marks)**

(d) Critically appraise the role of management representation in respect of providing audit evidence in support of the Research and Development balance and explain who you would expect such representation to be provided by. **(5 marks)**

(Total 50 marks)

2 Information issued with Polyfine Industries plc Corporate Reports

Polyfine Industries plc Viability Statement

The viability period

In accordance with provision 30 of the 2018 UK Corporate Governance Code, the Directors have assessed the prospects of the Group over a longer period than the twelve months required by the going concern provision. The Directors consider the timeline of five years to be appropriate, as this is the period upon which the Group actively focuses and has reasonable visibility over its opportunity portfolio. This also reflects the nature of capital investment needed to support the Group's anticipated rate of growth, covering investment that in some cases requires long lead times as a result of the unique nature and capital intensity of its technology. A longer period of assessment introduces greater uncertainty since the variability of potential outcomes increases as the period considered extends. A shorter period of assessment impacts the Group's ability to put the right capacity in the right place on time.

> **Assessing viability**
>
> The company is considered to be viable if it maintains interest cover and net borrowings to EBITDA ratios, as prescribed by its existing financial covenants and presented in the CFO Review under 'Debt facility', and if there is available debt headroom to fund operations.
>
> The bottom-up five-year plan is reviewed at least twice annually by the directors. In assessing the future prospects of the company and achievability of this plan, the company has considered the potential effect of risks that could have a significant financial impact under severe but plausible scenarios. The risks considered were identified from the company's principal risks and uncertainties assessment. While testing against each individual scenario, the board has also considered the impact of a combination of the scenarios over the assessment period. This was in order to stress-test an aggregation of severe but plausible risks occurring that should represent the greatest potential financial impact both in the short-term and longer-term viability period.
>
> **Scenarios Tested**
>
> The following downside scenarios have been evaluated:
>
> **Scenario 1: Pandemic disruption.**
>
> We applied our experiences of the 2020 pandemic and the cost and cash saving activities we successfully implemented, to stress-test for company revenue levels that breach banking covenants.
>
> **Scenario 2: Significant operational disruption over a long period.**
>
> This risk focuses on the extreme scenario of a fire at the Shanghai factory, requiring a significant rebuild over a period in excess of a year.
>
> **Scenario 3: Business performance risks.**
>
> Polyfine Industries growth is at rates significantly below those included within the five-year plan.
>
> **Scenario 4: Loss of a key customer.**
>
> This scenario reflects losing the Footwear business.
>
> **Scenario 5 Sterling returning to 20-year highs of two US dollars to one pound sterling.**
>
> This scenario evaluates the cash impact on the Group as a result of forecast growth coming increasingly from US-denominated sales. The euro impact is not considered material given the natural hedge of euro sales against raw materials and the operating costs of the Poland plant.
>
> **Confirmation of longer-term viability**
>
> Based on the assessment explained above, the Directors confirm that they have a reasonable expectation that the Group will continue to operate and meet its liabilities, as they fall due, over the next five years

The CFO has prepared the Viability Statement detailed above for presentation to the audit committee prior to inclusion in the corporate reports. She has emailed a copy of this to your audit manager, for information. You have read the statement in detail and are concerned at the implications this could have for the audit.

Required

(a) Draft a detailed email for your audit manager, Jiang Cui, which critically assesses this viability assessment and explains your concerns regarding the potential impact this could have upon your assessment of audit risk and materiality. **(15 marks)**

(b) Draft notes for your meeting with the chair of the audit committee which:

(i) Recommends possible actions they [the audit committee] should take in light of this statement; and **(5 marks)**

(ii) Justifies the type of report which the audit firm will issue if it is not altered.

(5 marks)

(Total 25 marks)

3 **Practice Management and Ethics**

> "Audit firm culture is a critical component of an audit firm's ability to deliver high quality audits in the public interest. One key attribute of a good, healthy audit culture is auditors being able to challenge effectively and exercise professional scepticism when performing audits. The need for a culture of scepticism and challenge in the audit profession was also highlighted by Sir Donald Brydon in his Review of the Quality and Effectiveness of Audit."
>
> **Audit Firm Culture: Challenge, Trust, Transformation 2021 FRC.**
>
> https://www.frc.org.uk/getattachment/dba4544f-6d28-4185-b987-14e4a1122354/Culture-Conference-Event-Summary_August-2021.pdf accessed 8 November 2024

As a new partner in the Hong Kong firm, you are aware of differences in the culture and practices of this branch of RYG LLP and have made a few observations around this issue in a recent partnership meeting. You are concerned that there is a deferential relationship between the partners, managers and audit seniors which seems to constrain the amount of discussion and questions between the members of the audit team. You believe that there is also a tendency for members of the audit team to under-report the time that they are taking to perform their tasks. After one audit clearance meeting, it was obvious that the team had been unable to complete all of their audit testing to their satisfaction prior to completion and yet had not raised the issue with you, as audit partner. You feel that there is a general culture of fear in the more junior members of staff. This is not the culture that you have been used to in London. You also noted that the audit team are evidencing their professional judgement through a formulaic series of comments that relate back to audit guidance forms rather than reflecting on the specific issues raised in the audit.

Your senior ethics partner has invited you to present your thoughts to an informal lunchtime symposium of partners.

Required

(a) Critically appraise the relationship between audit firm culture and high-quality auditing and explore how your observations regarding the current culture in RYG LLP in Hong Kong may indicate issues with audit quality. **(13 marks)**

(b) Explain why the culture of challenge is regarded as so critical for the development of high-quality audit and explore what practical steps RYG LLP could adopt to improve this aspect of the firm's culture. **(12 marks)**

(Total 25 marks)

4 May 2023

Elite Rentals Group plc

Examination Case Study applies to all questions

Audit in respect of Year Ended 31 March 2023.

Corporate Background.

Elite Rentals Group plc (Elite Rentals) is a commercial property company which manages two very large property portfolios in commercial warehousing and professional furnished housing for short and medium term lettings. The company was formed from the merger of two companies, Elite Properties Ltd and Northern Warehousing Ltd, in 2012. It has grown significantly across both portfolios.

Elite Rentals Group plc is managed as two discrete segments, and each retains a distinct cultural identity reflecting the different business focus. These segments retain their legacy names and trade under these brands.

Although the company is very responsive to the market and well respected for the quality of its estate, two significant competitors, Green Housing and International Logistics are both aggressively expanding and have eroded some of Elite Rentals' market position.

Extracts of Information in the Permanent Audit File.

> Background to Northern Warehousing Ltd
>
> For over 30 years Northern Warehousing Ltd. has provided high-quality industrial and commercial spaces for our clients. Our expertise and reputation for integrity, has built a strong portfolio of well-regarded commercial property. We have the flexibility to support our tenants in growing their businesses and positioning them for success.
>
> We are one of the North's leading commercial and industrial property experts. We specialise in renovating out-of-date properties to create modern fit for purpose spaces close to vital transport links. Our locations close to the city centres and major road networks allow our tenants to forge important and lasting relationships with suppliers and customers. We place our tenants in the right place, at the right time, and in front of the right people.
>
> Northern Warehousing are excited to be developing brand new industrial property both in Newcastle and Darlington to support our clients in taking advantage of the developments in the North East as part of the UK Government's investment programme in this area of the country.

> Background to Elite Properties
>
> Elite Properties are the UK's largest listed residential landlord. We provide high quality homes in excellent locations across the UK.
>
> Our success is attributable to our direct management of properties which ensures excellent service delivery and a good relationship with our tenants.
>
> Elite Properties own and manage over 8,000 rental homes across the UK in most major cities from Newcastle to London.
>
> We provide thousands of modern private rental homes, and we also have a portfolio of homes on historic regulated tenancies.

Elite Rentals Group plc

DRAFT Income Statement for the year ended 31 March 2023

	2023 £m	2022 £m
Revenue	279.2	248.9
Administrative Expenses	31.8	30.2
Operating Profit	**247.4**	**218.7**
Net Finance Costs	33.3	35.2
Profit before Income Tax	**214.1**	**183.5**
Income Tax Expense	69.2	42.6
Profit for the Year	**144.9**	**140.9**

Segmental Reporting

	2023 £m	2022 £m
Gross Rental Income – Northern Warehousing	121.4	97.4
Gross Rental Income – Elite Properties	153.4	146.4
Gross Proceeds from disposal of properties	4.4	5.1
	279.2	248.9

Notes from discussion with CFO

These are extracts from the meeting with the CFO where he stated that he is, once again, pleased with the success of the company. The following is a transcription of relevant parts of the conversation.

"In 2023, we delivered a record increase in income, occupancy, lease up of our new schemes and rental growth. In addition, I believe that we have secured and de-risked our medium-term growth. All of this puts Elite Rentals in an excellent position as the UK emerges from the Covid-19 pandemic. The bounce back from the pandemic stimulated demand internationally which could not be supported by supply – the consequence of which is inflation. This has had the knock-on effect of raising interest rates and creating a squeeze on household incomes and the affordability of rents.

Northern Warehousing

Occupational demand for warehousing remains strong despite adverse economic pressures. There is some evidence that older properties with reduced energy efficiency are proving less attractive to tenants. This strengthens the case for our refurbishment programmes as key drivers of added value. The other critical pattern in the market is around logistical consolidation. This is affecting us in two ways. We have seen thriving companies join together in their warehousing and distributions to benefit from the economies of scale that larger enterprises enjoy. We have also lost tenants as a consequence of corporate distress. In the clothing sector some brands seem to be purchased by online retailers and moved to an online basis. As a preferred warehousing provider to one of these clothing companies, thus far this trend has benefited us.

Elite Properties

Demand for renting over the first half of last year accelerated significantly, while our high-quality homes and scalable operating platform supported the exceptional growth rate in our income and our portfolio. We have delivered record levels of occupancy, rental growth and high levels of customer retention. However, there is evidence of increasing stress on household incomes and the second half of the year started to show a slowdown in demand and some reduction in rental payments.

The estimates and associated assumptions of key balances in the accounts are based on historical experience and various other factors that are believed to be reasonable under the circumstances, the results of which form the basis of making judgements about carrying values of assets and liabilities that are not readily apparent from other sources. Actual results may differ from these estimates. Estimates and assumptions are reviewed on an on-going basis with revisions recognised in the period in which the estimates are revised and in any future periods affected.

A key issue for the company is the importance of maintaining the asset value and interest cover within bank covenant parameters. As the company holds most of its assets as investment property the debt to asset levels assessed by the bank are based on this fixed asset value rather than total assets. Interest cover is required to be 7 or more to ensure that any depression in performance does not threaten liquidity."

Notes from discussion with the chair

The meeting with the chair noted that there has been some upheaval with the board during 2022/23 with the departure of the Operations Director and the CFO. Below are extracts from the discussion:

"The new Operations Director, Colin Hope, has joined Elite Rental from the property development sector, although this is his first experience of board membership in a listed company. He has resigned from his position as CEO of Hope Developments Ltd, although he remains the primary shareholder. Hope Developments Ltd has been a very successful company and a new CEO has been appointed. The other shareholders of Hope Developments are Charlotte and Ben Hope. They have also resigned from their positions in Hope Developments to take up new opportunities in Elite Rentals.

As a consequence of this appointment, the project management team has been expanded. The team is headed up by Charlotte Hope, the wife of the new operations director. This team are responsible for overseeing development contracts for new commercial and residential properties and, as the company extends its activities, additional staff have been recruited. The organisation of the team allocates a project to a specific staff member, but the work is done by the team under the direction of the responsible manager.

The new CFO is a former auditor who has been acting as CFO for a smaller warehouse rental company. Although this company had to refile their accounts in 2022 due to applying the small business exemption to their accounts in error, the interview panel were impressed with his industry experience and his passion for helping the company to succeed.

To attract these new directors the remuneration policy for all board members was reviewed. The new remuneration package was approved by shareholders and relates to the remuneration for the year ended March 2023. This new package links a bonus to the delivery of two key performance indicators – namely profit before taxation of £210 million and an interest cover of 7 to ensure bank covenants are not breached.

Classification of investment property

The Group considers the intention at the outset when each property is acquired in order to classify the property as either an investment or a trading property. Where the intention is either to trade the property or where the property is held for immediate sale upon receiving vacant possession within the ordinary course of business, the property is classified as trading property. Where the intention is to hold the property for its long-term rental yield and/or capital appreciation, the property is classified as an investment property.

Elite Rentals continually reviews properties for changes in use that could subsequently change the classification of properties. A change of use occurs if property meets, or ceases to meet, the definition of investment property which is more than a change in management's intentions. Any changes in the way in which properties are utilised are considered on a case by case basis and to the extent that a change in use is established, property reclassifications are reflected appropriately."

Extracted from Note 14 Investment Property

Investment Property	2023 £m	2022 £m
Opening Cost	2,179.2	1,778.9
Acquisitions	14.4	78.0
Capital Expenditure – Under construction	265.6	261.5
Capital Expenditure – Completed assets	9.2	22.8
Transfer from Inventories	116.5	
Disposals	(19.2)	(38.8)
Net Valuation Gains	210.2	76.8
Closing Balance	**2,775.9**	**2,179.2**

The acquisitions relate to the purchase of retail warehousing on the edge of Darlington.

The reclassification relates to the Old Bond House warehouse site on the canal side in Leeds. This was significantly damaged by fire in April 2022 and the tenant re-located and decided not to renew the lease. Although a sale was negotiated, this failed to complete, and in October 2022 the board took the decision to reclassify this as an investment property as there is the opportunity to re-develop the site as housing and add considerable value as this area of Leeds is re-developed from commercial and industrial into housing. At the date of transfer, the value of the Old Bond House Warehouse was £116.5 million.

The methodology for the year end valuation process for capitalised yield-based valuations is consistent with the prior year. This is considered to be the most appropriate method for valuing assets that are likely to be held as long-term investments and represents 65% of our property.

Investment property is measured initially at its cost, including related transaction costs.

The remaining 35% of properties are valued at market value. The Company's own in-house qualified team provided a vacant possession value for these Company's residential properties as at 31 March 2023. A small, structured sample of these in-house valuations was reviewed by Survey LLP, an external independent valuer. Valuing the large number of properties in this portfolio is a significant task. For this reason, it is undertaken on an external inspection basis only. Invariably, when the in-house valuations are compared with those of the external valuer, around 75% of the valuations are within a small acceptable tolerance. Where the difference is more significant, this is discussed with the valuer to determine the reasons for the difference. Typically, the reasons vary, but it could be, for example, that further or better information about internal condition is available or that respective valuers have placed a different interpretation on comparable sales. Once such reasons have been identified, the Group and the valuer agree the appropriate valuation that should be adopted as the Directors' Valuation.

After initial recognition, investment property is carried at fair value. Fair value is based on active market prices, adjusted, if necessary, for any difference in the nature, location or condition of the specified asset. If this information is not available, the Group uses alternative valuation methods such as recent prices on less active markets or discounted cash flow projections. Investment property falls within Level 3 of the fair value hierarchy as defined by IFRS 13 *Fair Value Measurement*.

Subsequent expenditure is included in the carrying amount of the property when it is probable that the future economic benefits associated with the item will flow to the company and the cost of the item can be measured reliably. All other repair and maintenance costs are charged to the consolidated income statement during the financial period in which they are incurred. Gains or losses arising from changes in the fair value of the Group's investment properties are included in the consolidated income statement of the period in which they arise. When the Group begins to redevelop an existing trading property for continued future use as an investment property, the property is transferred to investment property and held as a non-current asset. The property is remeasured to fair value as at the date of the transfer with any gain or loss being taken to the income statement. Where specific investment properties are expected to sell within the next 12 months, their fair value is shown under assets classified as held-for-sale within current assets. Any loss on the reclassification of these assets from investment properties to assets held-for-sale is charged to the consolidated income statement of the period in which this occurs.

Elite Rental's assessed the fair value of the direct development schemes in the course of construction. These schemes are valued on an income capitalisation basis, with gross yields adopted in the valuations ranging from 4.9% to 6.4%. As the assets are under construction, the valuation takes into account estimated costs required to reach completion.

Extracted from Note 18 Inventories – trading property.

Inventories	2023	2022
	£m	£m
Opening Balance	595.2	657.4
Additions	58.6	12.6
Transfers to Investment Property	(116.5)	–
Disposals	(85.0)	(74.7)
Reversal of / Impairment	1.5	(0.1)
Closing Balance	453.8	595.2

Property held in the residential portfolio was valued as at 31 March 2023 by Elite Properties in-house surveyors. These valuations were reviewed and approved by the Directors.

Investors prepare for slowing global interest rate rises.

George Steer for FT 10 December 2022.

"Three of the world's biggest central banks are expected to raise interest rates this week, but investors wary of economic recessions are turning their attention to where borrowing costs might peak in 2023.

Investors expect the Federal Reserve, the Bank of England and the European Central Bank will increase interest rates at meetings this week but at a slower pace than in recent months. Central banks on either side of the Atlantic have rapidly raised borrowing costs from historic lows this year in an attempt to cool racing inflation that has been exacerbated by Russia's botched invasion of Ukraine.

Interest rates have risen from close to zero to between 3.75 per cent and 4 per cent in the US, 1.5 per cent in the eurozone and to 3 per cent in the UK, hammering global financial markets in the process. However, investors have been encouraged by signs of easing inflation in the US and the eurozone in recent weeks and are shifting their focus from the size of policy moves to the level at which rates will eventually plateau next year."

Extracted from: https://www.ft.com/content/dbc66b48-8b2f-481e-91fc-e818297f0913 accessed 27th January 2023.

Interest Rates – United Kingdom.

BoE Raises Rates, Hints at Further Tightening.

The Bank of England voted by a majority of 6-3 to raise interest rates by 50 basis points to 3.5 percent during its December meeting, pushing the cost of borrowing to the highest level since late-2008, as policymakers try to contain inflation amid fears of a looming economic recession.

Two MPC members preferred to maintain rates unchanged, and one member preferred to increase them by 75 bps, to 3.75 percent.

Officials noted that the labour market remained tight, and inflation and wage growth were still high, which justified a forceful policy response. Looking forward, the MPC agreed that, if the outlook suggested more persistent inflationary pressures, it would continue to tighten policy as necessary.

The central bank's projections suggested the CPI inflation has reached its peak, and it is expected to remain "very high" in coming months. Data earlier this week showed UK inflation easing to 10.7% in November from a 41-year high, remaining well above the central bank's target at 2%.

News Stream 15th December 2022.

https://tradingeconomics.com/united-kingdom/interest-rate accessed 27th January 2023.

Economic Forecast.

Global Economic Prospects.

World Bank Press Release January 10th 2023.

Global growth is slowing sharply in the face of elevated inflation, higher interest rates, reduced investment, and disruptions caused by Russia's invasion of Ukraine, according to the World Bank's latest *Global Economic Prospects* report.

Given fragile economic conditions, any new adverse development—such as higher-than-expected inflation, abrupt rises in interest rates to contain it, a resurgence of the COVID-19 pandemic, or escalating geopolitical tensions—could push the global economy into recession. This would mark the first time in more than 80 years that two global recessions have occurred within the same decade.

The global economy is projected to grow by 1.7% in 2023 and 2.7% in 2024. The sharp downturn in growth is expected to be widespread, with forecasts in 2023 revised down for 95% of advanced economies and nearly 70% of emerging market and developing economies.

Over the next two years, per-capita income growth in emerging market and developing economies is projected to average 2.8%—a full percentage point lower than the 2010-2019 average. In Sub-Saharan Africa—which accounts for about 60% of the world's extreme poor—growth in per capital income over 2023-24 is expected to average just 1.2%, a rate that could cause poverty rates to rise, not fall.

"The crisis facing development is intensifying as the global growth outlook deteriorates," said **World Bank Group President David Malpass**. *"Emerging and developing countries are facing a multi-year period of slow growth driven by heavy debt burdens and weak investment as global capital is absorbed by advanced economies faced with extremely high government debt levels and rising interest rates. Weakness in growth and business investment will compound the already-devastating reversals in education, health, poverty, and infrastructure and the increasing demands from climate change."* Growth in advanced economies is projected to slow from 2.5% in 2022 to 0.5% in 2023.

Extracted from World Bank Press Release 10th January 2023.

https://www.worldbank.org/en/news/press-release/2023/01/10/global-economic-prospects accessed 27th January 2023.

EXAM QUESTION BANK

ALL QUESTIONS ARE COMPULSORY

1 **Detailed Audit of Elite Rentals Group plc**

You are a newly promoted partner for Conan and Zhang LLP, a large professional services firm with offices in all of the major cities in the UK. You are based in the Newcastle office, having recently returned from a three-year secondment in the London office.

You have been appointed the engagement partner for Elite Rental Group plc which is listed on the UK stock exchange.

In order to get to know the client, and to start gathering evidence in support of the "Know your Client" assessment, you decide to invite the CEO and CFO of Elite Rentals to dinner at a local prestigious restaurant. At this dinner you are intending to explore the role of the CFO in establishing an ethical culture at Elite Rentals, in line with IFAC Code of Ethics 2022.

You also ask to include the CEO, CFO and other board members of Elite Rentals as guests of the firm at a charity dinner and event to be held at Newcastle United Football Club – the local premiership football club.

Required

(a) Critically appraise the inherent audit risks which require detailed consideration in the planning of the 2023 audit of Elite Rentals Group plc. **(15 marks)**

(b) Explain and justify the work you intend to perform in respect of the Investment Property detailed in note 14 above. **(20 marks)**

(c) (i) Critically discuss the indications that there may be issues with the ethical behaviour standards of the CFO and identify the ethical responsibility you would expect the CFO to take within Elite Rentals.

(ii) Critique the ethical issues arising through the hospitality planned for the directors of Elite Rentals. **(15 marks)**

(Total 50 marks)

2 **Information issued with Corporate Reports.**

Students are reminded that information issued in the case study is also relevant to this question.

Extracts from Elite Rentals Group plc Risk Report.

MARKET AND TRANSACTIONAL.

Risk description

A significant short to medium economic contraction/recession leading to flat or negative valuation movements pursuant to an external factor including the coronavirus pandemic.

Impact on strategy.

An economic downturn leads to either a lack of appetite for individual assets that the company is disposing of, or a lack of appetite from investors for assets being disposed of as part of our asset recycling strategy. Pressure on rental levels; falling asset values; unable to provide Shareholders with sustainable returns in the long term.

> REGULATORY.
>
> **Failure to meet current or increased regulatory obligations or anticipate and respond to changes in regulation that increase cost**
>
> These include the introduction of rent controls or similar limitations plus reform of building regulations. The operating framework facing UK businesses following its departure from the EU and the uncertainty surrounding the future relationship and changes to the regulatory environment arising in response to the Covid-19 pandemic is currently unclear.
>
> **Impact on strategy**
>
> Fines, penalties, and sanctions; damage to reputation; loss of operational efficiency and competitiveness; increased costs; reduction in market opportunities; impact on ability to finance opportunities; reduced ability to generate rents.

The risk committee has prepared the risk statement, extracts of which are detailed above, for presentation to the audit committee prior to inclusion in the corporate reports.

Colin Hope, head of the committee, has emailed a copy of this to you and your audit manager, for information. You have read the statement in detail and note with concern that this has not been updated since the 2020 report.

During the audit Lucas Suen, a junior member of the team, interviewed the Buildings Quality Manager. He was informed that a member of staff, Ben Hope, had recently been suspended pending an investigation into allegations that bribes had been paid to the Fire Inspector to sign off the fire safety in properties in London relating to three historic buildings developments. These appear to total £25,000 and their source is unclear – although they haven't been paid from Elite Rentals' funds. This investigation indicates that a number of sites were not fire compliant as they had used unsuitable paints and floorings in the recent refurbishments. Fire detectors and sprinkler systems were also not up to building standards and codes and a number of premises had failed to install fire doors.

Lucas followed up the discussion by exploring the purchasing system for evidence of transactions relating to these historic developments. He discovered:

(i) Charlotte Hope had awarded the refurbishment contracts to Hope Developments.

(ii) The value of the refurbishment contract awarded to Hope Developments was £1,142,000, which is below the materiality threshold for the audit.

(iii) Hope Developments is not on the list of approved contractors for Elite Rentals Group plc.

(iv) Hope Developments is owned by Charlotte Hope and her husband, the new Operations Director, Colin Hope and their son Ben Hope.

(v) At the year end, Hope Developments did not appear as a creditor.

From this work, Lucas concluded that the existence of the related parties and the possible conflicts of interest would not have been identified in the normal course of the audit work.

Required

(a) Critically appraise the impact that the issues regarding building materials and fire safety compliance will have upon the audit. **(15 marks)**

(b) Draft notes for your meeting with the chair of the audit committee which critically explores the quality of the current risk report and explains the action you would expect from the committee regarding the issues raised above. **(10 marks)**

(Total 25 marks)

3 **Practice Management and Ethics.**

> "The effective exercise of professional judgement is a critical feature of any audit, and a fundamental requirement of the auditing standards. ISA 200 defines professional judgement as:
>
> The application of relevant training, knowledge and experience, within the context provided by auditing, accounting and ethical standards, in making informed decisions about the courses of action that are appropriate in the circumstances of the audit engagement."
>
> Professional Judgement Guidance (2022) Financial Reporting Council
> https://www.frc.org.uk/library/standards-codes-policy/audit-assurance-and-ethics/guidance/professional-judgement/ Accessed 11 November 2024

You have recently been appointed as the Partner in Charge of Practice Quality for Conan and Zhang LLP. This has been a significant elevation of your profile in the firm, and you are anxious to ensure that you perform the role effectively. You understand that your firm will be reviewed by your regulator in the next few months, and this has focused attention on the process for implementing the Quality Management Standards (ISQM (UK) 1 *International Standard on Quality Management 1*, ISQM (UK) 2 *Engagement Quality Reviews* and ISA 220 *Quality Management for the Audit of Financial Statements*.) This represents a significant opportunity for the firm to ensure that any professional judgement framework that is being applied helps address risks to audit quality and to consider more widely how to train for professional judgement and incorporate it into intellectual resources.

During your supervision of the audit of Elite Rentals Group plc you observed some behaviour within the audit team that caused you some concerns.

As the audit team were under some pressure to complete the work within two weeks, you noted that the audit approach taken in the previous year was used as a baseline and then updated where the team felt appropriate. The audit manager had been the auditor-in-charge for the previous two years and the current auditor-in-charge did not seem to be comfortable questioning the prior work or considering alternative methods of gathering evidence. This resulted in a limited approach to using the new Auditing Software to support the audit – although a significant increase in sample sizes for revenue, calculated by the new Auditing Software, was accepted and the rationale documented, despite there being no evidence of increased risk around this area in the audit plan.

Your senior ethics partner has invited you to present your thoughts regarding the development of professional judgement in Conan and Zhang to an informal lunchtime symposium of the partners.

Given the recent issues regarding the assessment of fraud in the audit of Elite Rentals Group Plc, you decide to illustrate this discussion with reference to your audit experience.

Required

Draft notes to brief your fellow partners which explores how the audit firm can promote the development of high-quality professional judgement which explores:

(a) The role of mindset in professional judgement, and the evidence from the audit of Elite Rentals that this may require development at the firm. What actions could be taken in the management of a specific audit assignment to improve this? **(15 marks)**

(b) How the firm may develop and enhance professional judgement through its culture, policies and practices. **(10 marks)**

(Total 25 marks)

5 November 2023

Kind Chocolate Group plc

Scenario

Please note the scenario applies to ALL questions

You are an AIA qualified accountant of 10 years' experience and are working as Audit Partner for a large UK based firm – Craster and Zhang LLP(CZ). The fee income for the practice is £11 million which the firm aspires to grow over the next few years to £20 million.

You were appointed as engagement partner for Kind Chocolate Group plc (KC) six months ago, taking over from Cath Martinez who is now working as the Ethics and Quality Review partner for the firm.

Kind Chocolate Group plc is a complex client. It has cacao growing estates in West Africa and El Salvador, and has manufacturing, development, distribution and retailing in the UK and distribution and retailing in Europe and the US. It is the only listed company audit that the firm currently serves and the audit fee for the year is set at £ 1,045,000.

The following information summarises meetings that you have had with the Chief Executive Officer (CEO) and Chief Financial Officer (CFO) together with other information from your "Know your Client" investigations.

The structure of Kind Chocolate Group plc is as follows:

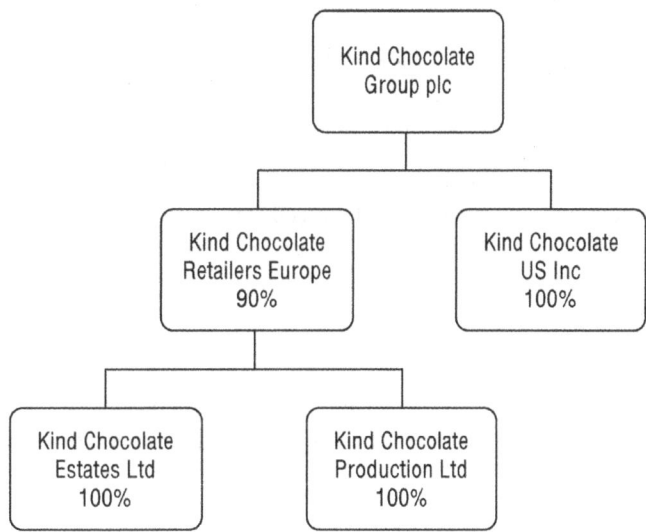

CZ is the sole auditor for the subsidiary companies in the group, with the exception of Kind Chocolate US Inc.

The audit approach taken by CZ is to regard Kind Chocolate Estates Ltd as a high risk element of the audit and to send an audit team of three to west Africa and then to El Salvador for two weeks.

The US subsidiary is not regarded as significant or high risk and a local auditor in New York currently does the work and remits the required analytical information to the CZ team for review. The remainder of the audit is focused at the Oxford, UK site, with information remitted from Europe as required.

The group has been rapidly expanding but 2023 has been a tumultuous year operationally. Due to the economic instability globally, the takeover of JapanChoc in 2018 has been re-evaluated and the board have decided to cease trade in Japan. The business was bought for £7.2 million in 2018 and was sold for £3.2 million in June 2023. The goodwill of £1.1 million was impaired in the 2022 accounts when the decision to sell was made.

The board has also decided to review its activities in the US where it had 25 stores and a very large distribution hub in New York. During the year it has closed 24 stores, retaining the flagship New York 5th Avenue premises and the distribution hub, and has decided to focus its US operations on online sales for the medium term.

This decision has not been unanimously approved by the board and relations between the directors, especially the CEO and chair, have been difficult. The chair feels that the investors are blaming him for poor strategic decision-making and is finding justifying the sale of the Japanese business and partial withdrawal from the US embarrassing. The CFO also feels that the CEO and Chief Operating Officer (COO) have ignored his financial advice but are now seeking to attribute the strategic failure to poor management information.

The CFO has prepared the accounts and his treatment of the US businesses as an exceptional item has been challenged by the CEO. He would prefer to see the costs included in the discontinued business figure to emphasise the non-recurrent nature of this event and the fundamental refocus of the US business. The draft statements given to the auditors have reflected the CEO's preferred treatment and have included the costs in the discontinued operations.

Although there is an audit committee, they have not challenged the CEO in his treatment of the US retail restructuring.

During the financial year, economic conditions in the UK and internationally have been uncertain and often difficult. Currency markets have fluctuated as fiscal policy internationally has tightened and this has resulted in some significant losses on currency hedges by KC.

Power and oil costs have increased causing inflationary pressures in many economies. This, and issues with cocoa supply, are putting pressures on costs.

Group Background extracted from Kind Chocolate Website.

Kind Chocolate is a UK based cocoa grower, chocolate manufacturer and multi-channel retailer with outlets in the UK and Ireland, a flagship store and online distribution hub in New York and cacao estates in West Africa and El Salvador. The group trading revenue is £226m.

Kind Chocolate works with >200 suppliers, employs over 2,200 colleagues and serves an estimated 5 million customers. We grow 40% of our cacao on our own estates which allows us to pioneer ethical and sustainable chocolate production and we insist that our other partner farmers who supply us through West African Cooperatives mirror these standards. We are focused on agroforestry to remove deforestation from our environmental impacts, and we focus on all the little ways we can make our environmental footprint kinder.

We now have 102 stores, as well as cafés and a thriving online business. We have over 30 stores in Europe, and two working cacao estates – one in El Salvador and one in West Africa.

Innovation

We're constantly striving to be fresh, creative, and innovative, and always one surprising step ahead. We take inspiration from everything we love- from our cacao farms' natural beauty to delicious European desserts.

Truth

Chocolate starts at the roots of the cacao tree. As growers ourselves, with direct links to cacao farmers across the globe, we have an intricate understanding of how to turn quality cacao beans into irresistible chocolate.

Ethics

We have a deep sense of fairness that extends to our farmers, our customers and future generations.

We believe cocoa farmers deserve respect and a fair deal. Our Engaged Ethics programme has already transformed the lives of many in West Africa and El Salvador. In 2020, we launched Kind Farming- A pioneering initiative that will further enhance the lives of our farmers in West Africa, where over 60% of our cacao is now grown. We will guarantee our farming partners a certified fair income, in return for working with them to ensure sustainability goals are met including our robust commitments to ethical labour practices are met. We also work with cooperatives and grower schemes in other parts of the world that adhere to our ethical principles.

Extract from draft Kind Chocolate Group plc Corporate Governance Statement 2023

The Kind Chocolate board is fully committed to strong governance of the business within a culture that recognises and delivers on our responsibilities to all the Group's stakeholders, including shareholders, customers, suppliers, colleagues, and the wider community. We have set out our approach to governance and provided further information on how the board and its Committees operates in notes 1–21 below.

The board has adopted, and believes that it complies with, the principles of The QCA Corporate Governance Code (Quoted Companies Alliance code which applies to companies in the Alternative Investment Market listed on the London Stock Exchange). The corporate governance framework within which the Group operates, including board leadership and effectiveness, board remuneration, and internal control, is based upon practices which the board believes are proportional to the size, risks, complexity and operations of the business and reflective of the Group's values. Our governance framework continues to evolve as the business and its operations and ambitions develop.

Note 19:

Promote a corporate culture that is based on ethical values and behaviours.

The Kind Chocolate values of authenticity, originality, and ethics have always underpinned, and are evident in, everything we do. Examples include our Kind Farming Programme, Kind Ethics Programme sustainability commitments, workforce engagement and community activities.

Our sustainability report on pages 31 to 39 (not provided) of the 2023 Report and Accounts shows how our culture impacts positively on our world.

Ethical Business – Modern Slavery – extracted from draft Strategic Review 2023.

- As a UK Group, we adhere to the UK anti-bribery and modern slavery acts and apply a supplier code of conduct which is enhanced by annual risk assessment and audit.

- During the year, we have further developed our enhanced programme - the Kind Farming Charter, which aims to achieve increased farm incomes from funded best practice initiatives aimed to increase yields, price premiums and improved sustainability of land use, with a goal of zero child or forced labour.

- In return for receiving increased payments for cacao along with yield improving resource "on farm", farmers sign up to the charter, which outlines sustainable farming practices and prohibits modern slavery and illegal child labour. Independent third-party visits are undertaken to each farm annually.

- In addition to our existing risk assessments and internal audits of supply-chain partners, we have committed to add a third-party assessment provider against additional ESG metrics, with the aim of all key suppliers being independently assessed by December end 2024.

- Safecall have been our ongoing partner since 2016 providing our whistleblowing hotline and internal media which is communicated and visible at all physical locations.

- Finally, we are working with agencies in West Africa to tackle child and forced labour in the cocoa industry with farm-level audits ongoing and annual review of progress and target setting to achieve our aim of zero child and forced labour incidents across our entire farming community.

Key performance indicators – Modern Slavery – Extracted from Kind Chocolate Group plc draft Key Metrics 2023

- Annual compliance audits for all new suppliers subject to a pre-engagement audit.
- Procurement and HR teams trained on Modern Slavery regulations and guidance.
- Cocoa in West Africa and El Salvador is purchased from a registered audited group of cocoa farmers.
- Child labour and forced labour are illegal in the countries where we source our beans and our Technical Officers and Support teams are engaged with farmers daily to educate, advise and report issues.
- A formal Child Labour Monitoring and Remediation Scheme is funded by us and is running within our West Africa cocoa districts with 100% farmer participation.

Extracts from Modern Slavery Act 2015.

Securing services etc by force, threats or deception.

(5) The person is subjected to force, threats or deception designed to induce him or her—

    (a) to provide services of any kind,

    (b) to provide another person with benefits of any kind, or

    (c) to enable another person to acquire benefits of any kind.

Securing services etc from children and vulnerable persons.

(6) Another person uses or attempts to use the person for a purpose within paragraph (a), (b) or (c) of subsection (5), having chosen him or her for that purpose on the grounds that:

    (a) he or she is a child, is mentally or physically ill or disabled, or has a family relationship with a particular person, and

    (b) an adult, or a person without the illness, disability, or family relationship, would be likely to refuse to be used for that purpose.

Transparency in supply chains etc.

(1) A commercial organisation must prepare a slavery and human trafficking statement for each financial year of the organisation.

A slavery and human trafficking statement for a financial year is—

    (a) a statement of the steps the organisation has taken during the financial year to ensure that slavery and human trafficking is not taking place—

        (i) in any of its supply chains, and

        (ii) in any part of its own business, or

    (b) a statement that the organisation has taken no such steps.

An organisation's slavery and human trafficking statement may include information about:

    (a) the organisation's structure, its business and its supply chains;

    (b) its policies in relation to slavery and human trafficking;

    (c) its due diligence processes in relation to slavery and human trafficking in its business and supply chains;

(d)	the parts of its business and supply chains where there is a risk of slavery and human trafficking taking place, and the steps it has taken to assess and manage that risk;	
(e)	its effectiveness in ensuring that slavery and human trafficking is not taking place in its business or supply chains, measured against such performance indicators as it considers appropriate;	
(f)	the training about slavery and human trafficking available to its staff.	

Corporate Liability for breaches of Modern Slavery Act 2015 (MSA 2015)

Certain large companies must produce a modern slavery statement under section 54 MSA 2015 outlining the steps they have taken to verify that their businesses and supply chains are slavery free (or otherwise, produce a statement confirming they have taken no such steps). At present, although businesses could face commercial and reputational consequences for non-compliance with section 54 MSA 2015, there is no provision for monetary penalties to be imposed in the event of a breach.

Although there are no financial penalties currently provided for in the event of a breach of section 54 (to which, see further information below), an organisation which publishes a modern slavery statement must ensure that its content is both accurate and consistent, to mitigate the risk of civil action from parties who have acted in reliance on the information within the statement, including consumers, investors or commercial partners.

Corporate liability for breaches of the Modern Slavery Act 2015 I Simmons & Simmons (simmons-simmons.com) accessed 25 June 2023

Kind Chocolate Group plc
Consolidated Statement of Comprehensive Income Year Ended September 30 2023

	2023 £'000	2022 £'000
Continuing Operations		
Revenue	226,133	164,551
Costs of Sales	(93,810)	(62,877)
Costs of Sales – Exceptional	(5,501)	
Gross Profit	126,822	101,674
Operating Expenses	(110,140)	(89,873)
Operating Expenses – Exceptional	(11,849)	(2,119)
Operating Profit	4,833	9,682
Finance Expenses	(1,910)	(1,650)
Net Profit before tax	2,923	8,032
Taxation Expense	(720)	(1,857)
Profit after tax	2,203	6,175
Discontinued Operations		
Loss for the period from discontinued operations	(5,600)	
Total loss/profit for the period from operations	(3,397)	6,175
Other comprehensive loss		
Currency translation differences on consolidation	(1,890)	(1,450)
Losses on cashflow hedges	(1,451)	(724)
Loss/ Profit for the Period	(6,738)	4,001
Attributable to:		
Group Shareholders	(5,390)	3,201
Minority Interests	(1,348)	800

Loss on Discontinued Operations:

	£'000
Sales Revenue for JapanChoc	3,200
Closure Costs for JapanChoc	(4,925)
Lease Penalty Costs – US Retail	(1,200)
US Redundancy Costs	(973)
Legal and Advisory Costs	(1,702)
Total	**(5,600)**

Cocoa Commodity Information as at 30 June 2023.

Cocoa futures hovered above $3,300 per tonne, remaining near the 7-1/2-year high of $3,324 touched on June 30th amid persistent concerns of low supply from the world's top producers. Above-average rain in the Ivory Coast flooded plantations and threatened the start of the main crop in October. Poor weather conditions also hurt crop prospects in Ghana. The dent in supply from the globe's top two producers drove the International Cocoa Organization to forecast a global supply deficit of 142,000 tonnes, more than twice that of previous estimates of a 60,000 shortfall.

Cocoa is traded on New York Mercantile Exchange (NYMEX) and the Intercontinental Exchange (ICE) in London. The prices in New York are based on the South-Asian market and prices in London are based on cocoa from Africa. The size of each cocoa contract on the NYMEX is 10 metric tons. The biggest producers of cocoa are Ivory Coast and Ghana which together account for more than 60% of the world's output. Other major producers include: Indonesia, Nigeria, Cameroon, Ecuador and Brazil. Although cocoa is one of the world's smallest soft commodity markets, it has global implications on food and candy producers, and the retail industry. Cocoa prices displayed in Trading Economics are based on over-the-counter (OTC) and contract for difference (CFD) financial instruments.

Actual	Previous	Highest	Lowest	Dates	Unit
3,290.00	3,277.00	5,379.00	211.00	1959 – 2023	USD/MetricTonne

Current Prices of Cocoa Futures as at 30th June 2023

1 Audit Issues for Kind Chocolate Group plc

As engagement partner for Kind Chocolate Group plc, you are overseeing the ongoing audit work at the Oxford UK site and from your team currently at the Cacao Estates in West Africa and El Salvador.

Your audit team have alerted you to an internal email regarding purchases from a new supplier, Boxtree Cacao Cooperative.

Suppliers are audited by Ethics in Cacao (EiC) – an independent sustainability organisation committed to sustainable cacao production and ethical treatment of employees. Boxtree Cacao Cooperative was certified as compliant in all aspects of its business practice with the exception of its monitoring of child labour. The EiC Team were unable to verify that all staff were over the age of 18 and were concerned with the culture around child labour at a number of the farms in the Cooperative.

A whistleblower has contacted Safecall and alleged that a number of children employed on three Boxtree farms have been trafficked from Ghana as part of a system of recovering loans made to their families by Boxtree Cooperative managers. This information was forwarded to the CFO of KC three weeks before the Boxtree Cooperative contract was awarded, and your team have seen an email from the CFO to the purchasing team regarding these allegations.

These reports were not included in the Boxtree Cacao Cooperative suppliers' file and the supplier was approved as ethically compliant by the Cacao Production Manager and the COO. It was, unusually, not reviewed by the accounts department when placed on the approved supplier list.

During 2023, £9.124 million was paid to Boxtree Cacao Cooperative. This equated to around $2,200 per tonne which is considerably lower than the $2,750 per tonne average that the remainder of the cacao has been costing.

Required

(a) Critically evaluate and justify the key inherent risks for Kind Chocolate Group plc for the audit of the 2023 financial statements. **(15 marks)**

(b) Develop and justify your audit approach for the discontinued business. **(20 marks)**

(c) Critically evaluate your response to the recent revelations regarding the importation of cacao through the Boxtree Cacao Cooperative and assess how the concept of public interest impacts on your decisions. **(15 marks)**

(Total 50 marks)

2   Your team have been at the KC Oxford site for the last three days and have been unable to contact the CFO. They have heard a rumour that he and the chair have resigned with immediate effect following a very acrimonious board meeting.

At your request, you have received a copy of the board meeting minutes by email. You suspect that this has been heavily redacted and edited as it merely states that the board accepted the resignations of the chair and CFO and thanked them for their years of service and contribution to KC.

The minutes do record that the disagreement over the future of the US business has continued and the CEO appeared to blame the chair and CFO for the previous failure in this venture. The CEO has stated that he believes passionately in the US future for the company and would be keen to revisit a greater US presence in the near future.

You have also received a copy of a report by the internal auditors of KC into the failure of the Japanese venture. This noted that the decision to purchase the 25 retail shops in the US and the takeover of JapanChoc, failed to adequately explore the assumptions around the sales market, growth potential and trajectory. It also significantly under-estimated the costs of developing both the distribution infrastructure in these countries. The report concluded that adequate planning had not taken place and that the board had failed to ask for sufficient detailed information to support the decision.

The KC CEO has contacted you by phone to let you know of the problems with the board, but you were in another meeting. He left a message with your secretary and has asked for your advice regarding the KC strategy and also if you could help with the recruitment of the new CFO. He is hoping that you will return the call as soon as possible as he is very concerned about the impact of the recent board problems on investor confidence.

Required

(a) Critically appraise the implications of the resignations for your audit work and reporting on the corporate governance statements and justify your response to the CEO's requests.

(15 marks)

(b) You have been at a CPD event which has highlighted that the corporate governance code in the UK is being updated and strengthened in response to recent government and regulatory reviews following the Carillion plc scandal in 2016.

The following three areas in particular were discussed in some depth at the session.

Extract of New UK Corporate Governance Reporting Requirements from 2024.

---

1   Audit and Assurance policy: Companies will need to explain their approach to assurance over the information reported in the front half of annual report and accounts, including disclosing their internal auditing and assurance process.

2   Fraud statement: Companies will need to prepare a Directors' fraud statement setting out the actions they have taken to prevent and detect fraud.

3   Statement on internal controls: The UK Corporate Governance Code will be updated to require an explicit Directors' statement on the effectiveness of internal controls.

Required

Evaluate how these requirements may impact on the reporting and assurance for Kind Chocolate Group plc for the next financial period and conclude how this may affect the audit relationship between your firm and KC going forwards. You should assume that Kind Chocolate Group plc corporate governance requirements will be affected by these changes. **(10 marks)**

(Total 25 marks)

3   **Practice Management and Ethics.**

Your fellow partners have recently been approached by Drummond Associates – one of the challenger audit firms in the global market. They have 175 offices in 30 countries and are a highly influential voice in the network of firms. They produce excellent professional materials which are widely used in the profession and have an extensive online and in-person training provision.

In addition to their 175 Drummond Associates LLP offices, the firm is affiliated with a further 300 offices in another 100 countries. This gives an extensive global coverage and significant market share internationally.

Drummond Associates is aware that CZ audits a listed company client in Kind Chocolate Group plc and believes that they can offer a great support to any international growth aspirations that CZ may have through becoming affiliated with Drummond Associates and becoming DA Craster and Zhang LLP.

The majority of the partners are broadly in favour of the affiliation but Callum Zhang (the founding partner) fears that such a move would dilute the brand that CZ is building for itself and might expose the firm to risks from poor practice by other affiliates or by Drummond Associates themselves. One of the key advantages that the Drummond Associates team highlighted was the ability to use affiliate firms internationally to provide the audit work of foreign subsidiaries or divisions of CZ clients and thus to reduce overall audit costs – but Callum Zhang is not persuaded by this argument.

Required

(a) Critically appraise the advantages to CZ of becoming an affiliate firm to Drummond Associates, with specific focus on any benefits it may offer to the audit of Kind Chocolate Group plc. **(9 marks)**

(b) Critically evaluate whether Callum Zhang is correct in his assessment that the use of affiliates may not be of financial beneficial to the firm. **(8 marks)**

ISQM 2 *Engagement Quality Reviews* requires audit firms to extend the scope of their engagement quality reviews and to provide a more robust approach to this within the firm. Cath Martinez is leading CZ's response to this and is proposing to act as the Engagement Quality Reviewer for KC. This new guidance requires the following:

Enhanced Eligibility Criteria for Engagement Quality Reviewer (EQR)

- a cooling-off period of at least two years before the engagement partner can become the EQ Reviewer (and comply with other relevant provisions of law/regulation/ethical requirements); and
- the EQ Reviewer should have appropriate competence, capabilities, time and authority.

Areas which the EQR may document considerations:

- where the audit team exercises judgement on the relative weight of different sources of audit evidence in support of a material judgement;
- where audit team and management views differ on a material estimate;
- planning for difficult-to-audit areas;
- audit work on a material area that significantly differs to the planned approach; and
- demonstrating professional scepticism where material judgements tend to side with views of management.

Extracted from ISQM 2 Engagement Quality Reviews *ISQM 2 First-Time Implementation Guide I IAASB* accessed 25 June 2023

(c) Justify the approach that an Engagement Quality Review should take for Kind Chocolate Group plc and critique the role that Cath Martinez should take in this process. Assess what advantages becoming an affiliate of Drummond Associates may have for the development of Engagement Quality Reviews. **(8 marks)**

(Total 25 marks)

Exam answer bank

1 November 2021

1 **Rationale**

As the first sitting of the new syllabus, the main audit question is positioned in an area which should not pose too many difficulties to a prepared candidate. It considers the issues arising as a result of potential director fraud in an international house building company, looking at the impact on audit planning, the assessment of materiality and the impact on the audit report. The figures and aspects of the disclosures have been adapted from the last set of corporate reports by Taylor Wimpey – but the scenario around mis-accounting is fictitious. The issues around the audit of fraud are broad and should test understanding of the relevant accounting requirements and the issues of control environments and internal controls. The materiality assessment should again be a familiar issue but reflects the impact of accounting in a time of material uncertainty due to the pandemic, on this assessment. The final part of the question is touching on a relatively new aspect of reporting around the audit work in connection with NOCLAR (Non-compliance with laws and regulations).

Part a: LO 2; Chapter Reference 15; 17; 18
Part b; LO 2; Chapter Reference 12
Part c: LO 2: Chapter Reference 15 and 19

(a) In ISA 240 *The Auditor's Responsibilities Relating to Fraud in an Audit of Financial Statements* states that "when identifying and assessing the risks of material misstatements due to fraud, the auditor shall, based on the presumption that there are risks of fraud in revenue recognition, evaluate which types of revenue, revenue transactions or assertions give rise to such risks." The usual approach to rebutting the presumption of fraud in revenue is on the basis of internal controls working well. However, the recent exposure of the incorrect recognition of contract income in the 2020 financial statements and consequent resignation of the executive director of the kit housing division, indicates that there have been problems within the accounting for these accounting estimates which were not mitigated by existing controls.

There are also wider issues with the reliability of the control system within the company highlighted by the ability of Ms Zhang to change from an approved supplier to an unapproved supplier for such a critical component of the process.

The key revenue stream therefore which creates a risk of fraud is the recognition of contract income from the construction of kit houses and their assembly on the site of the client. This represents some 45% of revenue (34% in 2020) and is therefore material. IFRS 15 *Revenue Recognition contains* specific and precise guidance to be applied in determining whether revenue is recognised over time subject to the compliance with the following criteria:

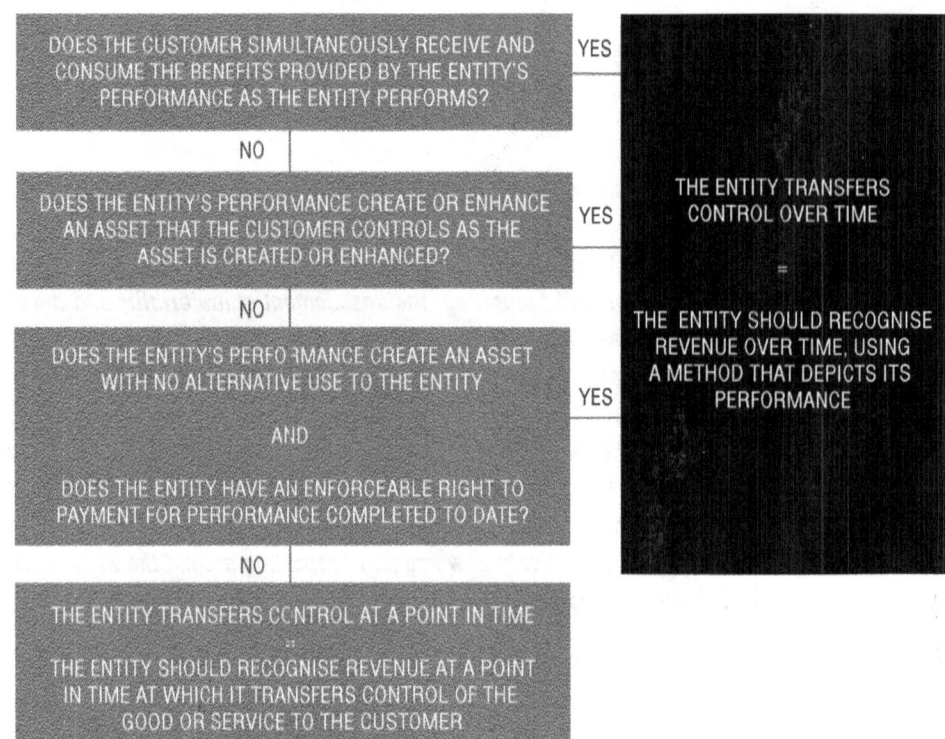

Extracted from IFRS 15 Revenue Recognition

The kit home may be constructed either to a specific customer order or may be constructed for stock. Given that there are a limited number of defined designs and specifications that the company makes, Homebuilder is not making an asset controlled by the customer and the kit home can be sold to an alternate customer once it is completed – therefore the profit from the manufacturing of the kit home cannot be recognised until the kit is despatched to site for assembly. Although assembly can be complex, it rarely takes more than one week and so should not result in profit being recognised at a point in time. The audit team must ensure that the changes required to the recognition of revenue from kit homes has been actioned within the accounting system and that the adjustment in light of the error are calculated and accounted for appropriately.

The second key issue arising from the kit homes division relates to the potential breach of contract conditions in the change to the manufacturing specifications around the fire-retardant system employed, or potential breach of fire safety standards. Under ISA 250 *Consideration of laws and regulations in financial statement audit* non-compliance may involve conduct designed to conceal it, such as collusion, forgery, deliberate failure to record transactions, management override of controls or intentional misrepresentations being made to a regulator or the auditor. There is some indication that the audit committee may be attempting to conceal the change in fire-retardant process which may breach regulations and fire safety.

Key issues in this for us will be determining whether an act constitutes non-compliance but this is ultimately a matter for legal determination to be determined by a court of law or other appropriate adjudicative body. Although the company has stated that the revision to the process did not compromise fire safety or breach any regulations, there is a significant risk to the reputation of the company and confidence in the kit home safety which may impact on future growth. We must ensure that the statement made by the company in the draft accounts around the exceptional item is correct, and that fire safety was not compromised and we should review correspondence with relevant regulators to ensure that the change was not concealed. The provision of £10 million to amend the error must be critically appraised to ensure that it is sufficient to correct the issue. The audit team should also ensure that no further legal action has been taken by any customers affected by the breach in the contract terms. The audit team must also ensure that the current manufacturing specification is in line with the claims made by the company in respect of its award-winning fire-retardant technology.

The final significant issue relates to the potential that Ms Zhang awarded the contract for the fire-retardant supply fraudulently, and that this and her accounting treatment was intended to deliberately inflate her bonus. This would indicate the existence of fraud – defined as an intentional manipulation of accounting to maximise personal bonuses – and effectively obtaining those bonuses under false pretences. The response of the audit committee to this is worrying. Although there is no requirement for an immaterial error to be treated as a prior year adjustment the concealment of a related party transaction is a serious omission. The situation indicates that there has been significant opportunity for management override of controls and that the current internal control regime including internal audit has not been robust. There is also the possibility that further issues in connection with this director's conduct will come to light and further embarrass or damage the company. The audit team must therefore focus work on an assessment of the control environment, which may be compromised by the audit committee attitude and other issues with board culture. They must also ensure that the internal controls are robustly assessed for susceptibility to management override and for weaknesses caused by at home working of staff during the pandemic. If found lacking this will also have a significant impact on the substantive audit work required as the control system cannot be relied upon. This would result in additional audit costs as more experienced staff will be required to undertake the substantive audit work needed.

(b) Auditing during the COVID-19 pandemic must recognise the profound impact that this has had on Homebuilder plc. This has increased the risk inherent within the financial statements as the business adapts to the ongoing disruption and resulted in the considerable downturn to operating profits which have reduced from 19.7% to 10.1%. There are clearly increased risks evidenced by the override of controls by Ms Zhang which may be due to fraud. There may also be a weakening of the control environment caused by the administrative staff working from home and a reduction in the numbers of onsite workers. Working from home may have been a key factor which enabled the change in supplier to be actioned unchallenged and unnoticed.

From this analysis, performance materiality is likely to be lowered and we must consider whether an alternative benchmark upon which to base materiality should be considered. The significant drop in profit before exceptional items and the shift in income stream towards the kit homes do indicate that business may have changed and that perhaps is a reason to reconsider the approach to setting materiality. If a consistent benchmark is used for 2020/21 audit then materiality will reduce from £42 million to £13.2 million. Additionally, should knowledge regarding the potential fraudulent conduct of Ms Zhang be disclosed, users may be more interested in the revenue recognition and related party disclosures in the accounts.

This reduction in materiality will require more audit work and this will have an impact on audit fees. It is therefore critical that this is discussed with the audit committee to ensure that the audit approach and increased duration and fees are expected and understood.

It is vital that the judgements made – the thought processes, assumptions and factors taken into account in determining materiality are documented in detail. If we retain the benchmark as profit before tax and set it at 5% again, we must justify this. We could alter the approach and look at a % of net assets as an alternative, and this will alleviate the issues created by the volatility in profit currently, although this may not resolve the lack of consistency in the figures caused by the change in the inventory profile of the company as a result of the stockpiling of the kit homes However, given the changes in the risk profile it may be more prudent to retain a similar approach to prior years and perhaps reduce the % to give a materiality of nearer to £10 million.

(c) All audit reports must include an explanation of the extent to which the audit was capable of detecting irregularities, including fraud. The circumstances created by the COVID-19 pandemic have increased fraud risk in Homebuilder plc as evidenced by the irregularity in the change of supplier showing that management override went undetected. It is also possible that auditing remotely, especially with the impossibility of visiting overseas sites in person, may compromise our ability to address this risk. However, from the work above, our audit approach is designed to focus on the issues around the internal controls within the company, whether the issues have been corrected and the extent to which further management override could have occurred and around related party transactions and the change to suppliers and manufacturing specifications.

We should therefore disclose the following:

Our approach to assessing the risks of material misstatements.

Our audit procedures that are designed to respond to the risks of non-compliance with laws and regulations around the use of non-approved suppliers which may compromise fire safety and contract law.

Our procedures designed to respond to the risk of management override.

The transactions (related parties, recognition of contract income, provisions for correction of the contract breach) which display these risk criteria.

Considerations around detection.

As we are required to make specific disclosure of how our audit addresses NOCLAR, we must ensure that our audit work is consistent with the approach we describe – especially in the area of ensuring that fire safety and contract specifications are complied with as these are areas where our audit work may not ordinarily take us.

Additional areas where credit might be given, note this is not an exhaustive list:

- The suggested answers are not exhaustive. Credit will be given for other relevant points presented
- Credit will be given for answers which consider the auditors responsibilities for fraud in this scenario in more depth
- Credit will be given for answers which focus more exclusively on the challenges of the audit of revenue recognition

2 **Rationale**

This question specifically explores the development of assurance for ESG (Environmental, Social and Governance) and requires the evaluation of the issues around extending accountability for climate disclosure into the corporate report through the adoption of the Task Force for Climate Related Financial Disclosures. This is very topical, coming in the year of COP 26 and the renewed vigour by the International Financial Reporting Standards Foundation in establishing a global framework for sustainability reporting. The question is applying what should be familiar ideas around the benefits of assurance and the role of the auditor in providing such assurance to what may be an unfamiliar set of reporting standards. The initial part of the question requires students to consider their approach to the implementation of new reporting standards and should be within their common sense understanding of any change project.

Reconciliation of Questions:
(2a) LO 1; LO 4 Textbook Chapter 1–1.2 Chapter 3–1.3
(2b) LO 4; Textbook Chapter 1; Chapter 2 3.3
(2c) LO 1; LO 4 Textbook Chapter 3–4.3; 4.2

(a) There are a number of key areas that the audit committee, and the finance director, who will be implementing these requirements, should consider in preparing for mandatory climate related disclosures.

Gap Analysis – the initial stage of the review would entail understanding where the current reporting of sustainability issues sits against the requirements of the TCFD. From the information given, it appears that there may be issues with all aspects of the disclosure around the role of governance and responsibility for climate related risks, the risk management and internal controls as a minimum. Given that the company has not been formally addressing their sustainability reporting in this framework, there may be differences in emphasis between current reporting and the new requirements – and the KPI metrics used may not be entirely compliant.

Internal Control and Risk Management for Climate – the review would explore the system whereby climate related risks are identified by the company and how they are assessed when determining the strategy, business plans and financial performance, to ensure that these are robust and embedded within all aspects of the company's operations – and not an issue left to the sustainability champions and their teams (effectively being decoupled from the organisation and exposing Homebuilder to potential criticisms of greenwashing).

Identification of Climate Related Risks – are all material climate related risks defined and considered in the disclosures made by Homebuilder's latest corporate reports?

Quality of the Information supporting Climate Related Risk Disclosure – how is the information / data which supports climate related risk disclosure produced and analysed? Is there a robust system to ensure that the information is accurate, consistent, comparable, transparent, relevant and reliable?

Role of Assurance – Should assurance be sought around this new disclosure regime – would this be helpful and if so who should provide it?

(b) Following on from the review into TCFD reporting, there are a number of advantages which arise from a robust and credible assurance of this disclosure:

Future Proofing Reporting – as sustainability becomes an ever more pressing issue, and in light of COP26 and the work of the IFRS® Foundation with SASB on sustainability standards, the reporting of these issues will be a mandatory requirement and be considered to be as critical to investors as the financials. It is therefore inevitable that assurance for these disclosures will also become mandatory – there are some indications that investors will require high quality assurance on these issues as part of their need for comprehensive and high quality information around risk in this area.

Creating Strategic Advantage – TCFD assurance will ensure that Homebuilder's reputation as a sustainable company in this industry will have credibility. Given the level of poor information in this sector, this should differentiate the company in the eyes of investors who are seeking assurance on the levels of climate related risk in the company potentially giving access to wider finance options.

Supporting the Audit Committee – assurance supports the audit committee in the development of high-quality reporting around a key risk area and ensures they are able to ensure that risk management and reporting standards are improved within the company.

Building Stakeholder Confidence – assurance of TCFD sends a clear signal to stakeholders that Homebuilder is taking its responsibilities in this area seriously and where investment or engagement decisions are being taken with consideration of the climate impacts in mind, enables confidence around Homebuilder.

(c) Although there is a prohibition on the provision of non-audit services, we would be able to provide such assurance as this is a permitted service. There are a number of persuasive points in favour of the audit firm acting in this area for Homebuilder plc. The TCFD disclosures at the front of the corporate report are required to link into the impact of climate change on measurement and recognition in the financial statements. As we audit these statements, we are in a unique position to have the required insight into these implications and will be able to assess the quality of the overall reporting in this area. The skills required to perform this assurance are similar to the skills required to perform financial audit – and in this area the vital skills of challenging management judgements, estimates and disclosures will be critical – an area where our professional scepticism and independence will enable us to act in a robust way. We are already familiar with your business and industry, and as independent qualified professionals our insights should be valuable. Although non-audit services are generally prohibited, this reporting is an extension of the corporate report and therefore is not considered to pose a challenge to independence, as it will not create either an advocacy threat nor a self-interest threat as the uplift in fee income will not be material.

Additional areas where credit might be given, note this is not an exhaustive list:

- The suggested answers are not exhaustive. Credit can be given for other relevant points presented.

- Credit will also be given for any discussion around the importance of our existing skills of challenging management judgement and discussion around the ideas of ISA 540 *Auditing Accounting Estimates and related disclosures* and any critical appraisal of weaknesses of these.

- Credit will be given for any in depth discussion of what is meant by professional scepticism and independence and its importance for providing a robust opinion in this subjective area of reporting.

3 Rationale

This question is exploring two key aspects of practice management – the role of quality reviews in risky audits and the role of data analytics/ technology in promoting high quality audit. Both issues are subject of much current debate but should be familiar to a well prepared student. Part a asks students to recognise the risk of a Homebuilder plc company audit to the audit firm and to explore the benefits of a hot review to mitigate this. Part b explores the specific ways in which data analytics/ technology could help the audit of Homebuilder and the challenges which may face the audit firm.

(3a) LO 3; Textbook Chapters 8 and 14;
(3b) LO 3; LO 1 Textbook Chapter 3 Section 5

(a) The audit of Homebuilder plc is exposed to considerable risks of non-detection of both fraud and non-compliance of laws and regulations, exacerbated by the move to remote working compromising the ability to engage in more traditional in-house audit work. Much of the risk around these issues relates to the potential for concealment – which may be more difficult to detect without the ability to make face to face enquiries of staff perhaps not normally connected with the audited systems. Additionally, remote working may prevent the auditor from gaining a feel for whether the actual culture and control environment is, consistent with that reported to or by the audit committee and other directors. As a public limited company, Homebuilder is a public interest entity and the public interest in the results and the quality of the reporting is increased – supporting the elevated risk to RTX Corporate LLP.

EXAM ANSWER BANK

The hot review could reduce our exposure to reputation risk or to audit failure by ensuring that our audit work has complied with the extensive range of applicable auditing standards, the level of objectivity, and professional scepticism maintained during the audit, and the relevance and sufficiency of audit evidence supporting the audit opinion. Key within the auditing standards is the requirement to ensure that adequate documentation is maintained so that an experienced auditor, unconnected with the audit, can understand what was done, what was found, what matters were considered to be significant and what judgements were made. A key factor in driving audit quality is the ability to take a step back and consider the evidence – this may be compromised by remote working disconnecting the team, and time pressure resulting from the additional work caused by remote working. A hot review will enable any issues missed by the audit team, or poor documentation of work by the team, to be addressed in real time and ensure that high quality audit is carried out and recorded.

(b) Data analytics has been developed with a view to improving audit quality. Audit quality is not a function of the tools themselves – although it depends on tools that are fit for purpose – rather, it lies in the quality of analyses and judgements thereby facilitated. The value is not in the transformation of the data but in the audit evidence which results from the in-depth discussions generated from an analysis of that data. During a remote audit, having such primers for conversations may prove invaluable in enabling the auditor to ask probing questions, and to prevent Homebuilder's directors from avoiding difficult discussions.

The following features of data analytics have the capacity to enhance audit quality in this engagement significantly:

- the ability to graphically visualise results - this would enable findings from complex interrogation of the contracts internationally and the costs associated with them and the patterns of revenue recognition arising to be communicated more effectively to the audit team – and perhaps to the audit committee, which may expose other irregularities in the treatment of contracts;
- sophistication, and the breadth of interrogation options – this may enable the auditor to more effectively track the contracts for kit homes which used the non-standard fire-retardant materials by tracing the invoices whose costs are attributed to their code – this would enable the auditor to establish the true nature and extent of the issue, and be able to satisfy themselves that the provision of £10 million against this issue is sufficient;
- ease of use by non-specialists; and
- scale and speed.

The ability to navigate much bigger external data sets quickly and to obtain analysis at a more granular level will enable us to have more confidence in our understanding of the company and the make-up of revenue and costs, which will be especially helpful for a new audit client.

Key limitations to the effective use of data analytics tools in the firm are their sensitivity to inaccurate set up – we will need to be very clear in the purpose of the tools as we set them up and this may require additional time of more senior and expert staff. It may also limit the work that more junior team members can usefully do which may compromise their training and could result in a more expensive initial audit fee.

Additional areas where credit might be given, note this is not an exhaustive list:
- The suggested answers are not exhaustive. Credit can be given for other relevant points presented.
- Credit will also be given for more in depth discussion relating to ISA 230 *Audit Documentation*
- Credit will also be given for more in depth discussion relating to ISQC 1 *International Standard on Quality Control*

2 May 2022

1 **Audit issues arising from the audit of Lovely Nights plc**

This question is applying audit knowledge to an emerging problem in accounting practice – the recognition of goodwill and the application of impairment. This has been placed in the context of a hotel group based on Whitbread plc whose hotel chain is Premier Inn – with some fictionalisation of poor accounting practice although the write off of the acquisition goodwill for their German subsidiary and the subsequent justification for the lack of need to impair the rest of the UK goodwill is real but rephrased and relocated!

The question is assessing LO 1 2 and 4

The material is covered in the textbook

(a) Chapter 12
(b) Chapter 12
(c) Chapter 18
(d) Chapter 5

(a) The acquisition of Peony Hotels should be accounted for in accordance with IFRS 3 *Business Combinations*. This will require accounting judgements around the fair value assessments of the assets and liabilities acquired, judgements around the valuation of separable intangible assets acquired and adequate disclosure to ensure that the users of the corporate reports are able to understand the impact of the acquisition on the group, including a recognition of the performance of the acquisition. Although conceptually these values seem straightforward, there is a challenge in assessing the fair value of assets during a time of material uncertainty and therefore the auditor must apply ISA 540 *Auditing Accounting Estimates and Related Disclosures* diligently in this assignment.

One of the key risks associated with the audit of the acquisition is that it comprises a new element to the group and the auditor has no prior experience of this – compounded with its distant location. It may prove very difficult for the audit team to travel to China to perform the audit work in person.

Often this can be resolved through the use of a component auditor, either from BHZ LLP or from another firm in China. However, there is some argument from the audit committee, that, having incurred costs to perform due diligence on the purchase, having the audit team request the assistance of a local branch of your audit firm or another local audit firm, will incur additional costs for an immaterial element of the business. There are therefore potential audit risks caused by the difficulty in obtaining auditor generated evidence from the inspection of assets to verify the fair value of the assets and acquired. Although the valuation of the consideration and the value of the liabilities incurred, two key aspects of the balance, can be verified remotely, understanding the investment property and the right to use assets, where their condition and locations may be critical, could be challenging.

Other significant risks with the acquisition relate to the immediate impairment of the goodwill. The rationale justifying this given in the draft disclosure states:

"An impairment of £224.2m was recorded in relation to goodwill arising on the acquisition of Peony Hotels (see Note 35) reflecting the impact of the COVID-19 pandemic on current and future growth rates. These impairments are primarily driven by a reduction in anticipated cash flows, particularly over the next 12-24 months within the Chinese market, and an increase in the discount rate reflecting increased market risk and volatility."

This seems to be inconsistent with the economic conditions prevailing by May 2021, where China seemed to be recovering more rapidly from the effects of the pandemic. It also creates doubt over the negotiation of the consideration paid for the business and the due diligence performed at that time. The goodwill is described as relating to "the skills and experience of the assembled workforce and the future growth opportunities the business provides to the Group's operations." It would seem that the future growth opportunities have reduced the anticipated discounted cashflows due to an increase in the discount rate caused by risk and volatility. It seems unlikely that the risk and volatility in the market between May 2021 at purchase and April 2022 at revaluation have altered significantly despite the increase in energy costs and other geopolitical instability as the impact of the pandemic is surely abating.

This casts doubt over the rationale behind the impairment – or the strategic competence of the board. The rationale which has impaired the goodwill in Peony Hotels would seem to also apply to the goodwill arising on the European operations generated from the acquisition of the former Zeelander Hotels company. Goodwill should be assessed on its cash generating units and the claim that there is headroom in the European sector would require diligent and sceptical investigation.

Given the concern that appears over the immediate write off of the goodwill balance in this acquisition, it is possible that there is some creativity being applied to the accounting of the acquisition. By reducing the fair value assessments for the separately identifiable assets in Peony Hotels, the ongoing depreciation impact on the income statement and therefore dividend is reduced. By writing the goodwill off in the year of acquisition and ascribing this to the impact of the pandemic, this may be considered to disguise the bad news of a poorly considered strategic move or could be a method of accelerating the costs of the business through the income statement in a year when performance is expected to be poor. This would enable the directors to appear very competent once the post pandemic recovery is underway. This is a form of income smoothing or big bath accounting. The auditor should be alert to this potential management bias as it is not providing information that is fair and balanced.

(b) As stated in IAS 36 *Impairment*:

"An impairment loss for goodwill is never reversed. For other assets, when the circumstances that caused the impairment loss are favourably resolved, the impairment loss is reversed immediately in profit or loss (or in comprehensive income if the asset is revalued. On reversal, the asset's carrying amount is increased, but not above the amount that it would have been without the prior impairment loss. Depreciation (amortisation) is adjusted in future periods".

The relevant issues for the audit relate to an assessment of whether the circumstances that caused the impairment loss have been favourably resolved. This is a matter of judgement by the directors and should be based upon a fair and balanced evidential assessment of the economic conditions facing the group.

The initial impairment in 2020/21 reflected the impact that the COVID-19 pandemic had inflicted on the hospitality industry both in the UK and internationally. The assumptions of the directors that the conditions for impairment – assets being idle as a result of lockdown and ongoing issues with the economic conditions in the hospitality market – are confirmed in the media article and would support this recognition. It is less certain whether the conditions that caused this recognition have been resolved – the recent interview with the CEO in Hotel Today would indicate that the recovery in 2022 does not reverse the conditions fully as occupancy for the hotels in the UK will remain significantly depressed and there will also be cost pressures on the profit margin from energy and food price increases. This reversal of the impairment does not appear to be supported by the opinions expressed by the CEO and therefore the audit team must review the factors used to justify this accounting reversal with scepticism. The auditors should ensure that they obtain detailed evidence in support of the assumptions used to justify the impairment reversal and agree this to external third party evidence from industry sources.

(c) The audit of the fair value of assets is a significant accounting estimate and in accordance with ISA 540 *Audit of Accounting Estimates (revised)* the auditor should assess the potential for management bias with the balance. This indicates that the fair value for both goodwill and property plant and equipment in the European businesses may be overstated, whereas the fair value of the property plant and equipment in the Chinese subsidiary may be understated.

The detailed audit work should include:

Obtaining an understanding of both the methods, assumptions and source data used to calculate the fair values and the obtaining a detailed understanding of the rationale employed by the management team to develop these.

Obtain an understanding of the level of uncertainty and subjectivity within these estimations. As the fair values are developed by comparing the carrying value of the asset with the value of the asset in use, there is a considerable degree of estimation around the estimated cashflow and the discounted rate applied to these. The management team have disclosed discount rates for Europe as a whole and for China. The auditor needs to compare these rates to current industry practice to ensure that these are reasonable. They should obtain some third party or expert verification of the appropriateness of these figures.

Assess the prior record of the management team in developing fair value assessments. This will require the team to review the methods employed by the team for prior years and come to an assessment regarding the reliability that these assessments proved to have. From the level of bias and the extraordinary context in which the estimates are being calculated, it may not be possible to place any reliability on past conduct as an indicator of current competence.

In assessing fair value the audit team must obtain evidence regarding the following:

The length of time assumptions cover.

The number and complexity of assumptions around the assessment of discounted cashflow. Given that the material uncertainty regarding the economic trading conditions have not resolved, the degree of estimation here is likely to be high.

The lack of objective data around the certainty of future cashflows and the appropriateness of the discount rates applied.

The potential for subsequent events, such as the ramifications of the geopolitical unrest in Europe and the impact of energy costs, may have on these figures.

The competence, knowledge and skills of the audit team should be reviewed to ensure that they have sufficient professional expertise to assess the fair value evidence.

(d) It is a core responsibility of a professional accountant to ensure that their work is discharged with due regard to the public interest. The public interest is not defined in the code of ethics but, for the auditor, can be considered to be the collective well-being of the community that is served by the corporate reports upon which the auditor reports.

For Lovely Nights plc, the company is a public interest entity by nature of its public trading, but it also employs a significant number of staff internationally and is part of a large supply chain further supporting employment. As some of the supply chain seems to involve small companies, there are issues at play in terms of the difference in economic influence between the supplier and the Group. Therefore, whilst the audit is primarily focused at the shareholders of the Group, there is a significant dependence on the future success of the Group by a large number of employees, and there would be considerable harm if the Group were to collapse or behave unethically in its treatment of these stakeholders.

The Brydon Report has identified a number of ways in which the public interest could be better safeguarded through the corporate governance, reporting and auditing.

This includes suggestions that auditing be extended beyond the financial reports and include disclosure around public interest, that the auditor be obliged to acknowledge external signals of concern, and to introduce the concept of suspicion into the audit. For the audit of Lovely Nights plc, there are a number of indications that the treatment of significant accounting balances may not be fair and balanced and there are issues in the independence of the audit committee chair and therefore the effective discharge of governance. Although the auditor will employ professional scepticism in the assessment of the evidence provided by the Group, strengthening this to suspicion around the limitations being placed on their ability to obtain audit evidence from Peony Hotels, this might improve the robustness of the actions of the auditor in this area.

The Brydon Report also looks at the idea of a public interest statement from the directors in depth. It is suggested that "the directors present an annual Public Interest Statement, which explains the company's view of its obligations to the public interest, whether arising from statutory, self-determined or other obligations, and how the company has acted to meet this public interest over the previous year. This statement would provide an opportunity for directors to articulate in a holistic way how the company they govern serves the wider public interest.....Again, the Report discusses the role auditors would be obliged to play in providing assurance in relation to this statement, and recommends that an opinion be provided as to whether the statement has been presented fairly". This would require disclosures around the treatment of wider stakeholders beyond that currently required by s172 of the Companies Act in the UK and would enable the impact of corporate behaviour to be reported upon by the auditor, allowing a more robust relationship with the public interest.

Additional areas where credit might be given, note this is not an exhaustive list:
- marks will be given for any relevant additional points

2 **Corporate Governance Reporting**

This question is exploring the issues of the functioning of the audit committee and the reporting of corporate governance and the responsibilities of the auditor in respect of this.

This is assessing the following learning outcomes: LO 1, 2 and 4.

The discussions are supported by Chapter 2 Corporate Governance Sections 3 and 5

(a)

> (1) a statement of how the company has applied the principles set out in the UK Corporate Governance Code, in a manner that would enable shareholders to evaluate how the principles have been applied.
>
> (2) a statement as to whether the listed company has:
>
> (a) complied throughout the accounting period with all relevant provisions set out in the UK Corporate Governance Code; or

> (b) not complied throughout the accounting period with all relevant provisions set out in the UK Corporate Governance Code and if so, setting out:
>
> (i) those provisions, if any, it has not complied with;
>
> (ii) in the case of provisions whose requirements are of a continuing nature, the period within which, if any, it did not comply with some or all of those provisions; and
>
> (iii) the company's reasons for non-compliance.
>
> https://media.frc.org.uk/documents/Improving_the_Quality_of_Comply_or_Explain_Reporting.pdf Accessed 11 November 2024

The code requires a lack of compliance to be disclosed clearly and transparently and to identify:

The context and background to the non-compliance. This has not been detailed by the company. It is not disclosed that the appointment of Sachin Guthra was made to resolve an emergency vacancy and there is no detail given of the nature of the lack of independence or the likely duration of the non-compliance.

A rationale (which is convincing) justifying the approach taken. This is not given – there is a rationale that having an experienced former member of the board on the audit committee during a time of material uncertainty might enable robust challenge to be made to management around their judgements. However, some of the issues being reviewed, such as the way in which goodwill was not impaired last year, and the calculation of impairment on property plant and equipment which are being reversed this year, may relate to legacy decisions from his time as CFO and the ability to be independent around such a challenge – or the appropriateness of such from BHZ – may be compromised.

Consider the risk from the non-compliance and how this has been mitigated. The code identifies that the loss of independent directors could reduce challenge to board decision-making and leave effective control of the company with a small number of individuals. Within the audit committee of Lovely Nights, in addition to the issues around independence of the chair of the audit committee above, there is also an issue of familiarity between the board and the chair of the audit committee which could make it difficult for the chair to challenge the decisions and also difficult for the chair to perceive issues due to sub conscious bias. The risk from the non-compliance is not sufficiently considered and mitigation is not discussed within the disclosure.

Explanations should be understandable and persuasive – the explanations regarding the breach of the code are limited and not persuasive.

(b) The auditor has a responsibility to review the Corporate Governance Statement in connection with the audit committee to verify that the audit committee comprises of two or three independent non-executive directors, and at least one of whom has relevant financial experience.

From the information disclosed by the company, there is a failure to comply with this key aspect of the audit committee composition as the key member with the relevant financial experience is not independent as he has a small but not insignificant shareholding in the company. Although this is disclosed, as discussed above, the auditor would be required to bring this to the shareholders' attention in the "other matters upon which we are required to report by exception."

Under ISA 720 *Auditors responsibilities relating to other information*, BHX LLP must perform procedures sufficient in their professional opinion to identify whether the corporate governance statement is materially misstated in the context of the auditor's understanding of the legal and regulatory requirements applicable to that information.

The audit procedures in connection with this aspect of assurance is usually obtained through inspection of audit committee and board minutes, inspection of relevant audit committee policies and procedures and attendance at relevant meetings.

A key issue being raised within this aspect of governance is the difficulty in developing a working relationship with the audit committee and some evidence that the focus of the committees work is not on ensuring the effectiveness of the audit. Within the current statement, there is mention that this lack of compliance is not affecting the independence of the chair and it would be difficult for BHZ to make a statement that this is untrue as there is no concrete evidence of that currently.

> **Additional areas where credit might be given, note this is not an exhaustive list:**
> - marks will be given for any relevant additional points

3   **Practice Management and Ethics**

This is twist a on the usual issues around ethics and is exploring the idea that sometimes the audit committee isn't as independent as it looks – and can therefore have its own reasons for thwarting a high quality audit. In this scenario this is caused by a combination of a very competent but not independent chair and two not competent other members. It is a slightly open question and is assessing the student's ability to think around the practical issues arising and relate this to their application of the auditors' professional ethics and their understanding of what the audit committee is supposed to be doing.

This is assessing LO 1 and LO 3.

Part a is covered in Chapters 2, 5 and 8
Part b is covered in Chapters 2, 5, 8 and 14

(a) The audit committee, in its relationship with the external auditor should:

"Review and monitor the external auditor's independence and objectivity and the effectiveness of the audit process, taking into consideration relevant UK professional and regulatory requirements".

It seems that the financial difficulties of the Group may be causing a resistance to incurring additional audit fee costs, despite the increased complexity of the Group audit in 2022. The acquisition of a new overseas subsidiary plus the difficulties in assessing subjective estimates affected by the ongoing economic uncertainty in impairment and fair value in use recognition would be factors that BHZ LLP might wish to explore the time implication of in assessing the likely fee required. Fee pressure creates a conflict of interest for the auditor which may impact on their objectivity and professional competence. If the fees agreed with the audit committee fail to cover the anticipated costs, the audit team may feel pressurised into attempting to reduce the time taken with the audit work which may lead to a lack of professional scepticism being brought to an audit where there may be issues with the quality of management judgements and estimates.

Although the advent of data analytics and sophisticated virtual communication does enable much audit work to be carried out remotely, this creates challenges for maintaining client confidentiality, which should be part of normal internal controls within the systems used by BHZ LLP.

Working remotely also creates difficulties in developing a good working relationship with staff at Lovely Nights and additionally makes obtaining and challenging information difficult. One of the key limitations from remote working relates to the difficulty in understanding the culture and working practices at the Group. Reports and documents may be able to create an impression of the working environment, controls and practices that are inconsistent with the reality. This may be part of the reason for the problems being experienced at present – although the change in staffing with the CFO and the audit committee may also be an issue.

There are a number of potential ethical pressures compromising the judgement of both the chair of the audit committee and the CFO as they try to present a favourable picture of a competent board, and a Group with a bright future and return the Group to profit and dividend distribution.

The pressure from the audit committee to keep the auditors away from the real business may be a desire to reduce costs – but may also be a desire to minimise the opportunity for the auditor to detect inconsistencies between what is reported and what is happening operationally. Given the lack of independence of the chair of the audit committee – who is a significant shareholder in the Group, this latter motivation may be caused by a conflict of interest and lack of independence here.

The knowledge that the audit committee chair is not independent is a breach of corporate governance best practice and may indicate wider issues with governance and control in the Group.

However, the difficult relationships in the audit may also lead to a more robust and sceptical approach to the audit as there will be minimal sub conscious bias in the assessment of the judgements by the management team – and in turn this may lead to a more independent and therefore higher quality audit.

(b) The audit committee has responsibility for overseeing the company's relationship with the external auditor and reviewing the effectiveness of the external audit process. In assessing the effectiveness of the audit, there are a number of actions that are expected which could be compromised by the conflict of interest in the chair of the committee and not resolved by the actions of the other members, due to their lack of relevant knowledge and experience.

The audit committee is responsible for considering whether the auditor has contributed to enhancing the quality of the company's financial reporting (including whether they have exercised professional scepticism, made appropriate challenges of management and discussed issues with the audit committee). If the audit committee is not independent, they may not wish the auditor to make these appropriate challenges and may not be available to discuss issues thus compromising the ability of the auditor to act effectively.

The audit committee is also responsible for ensuring how well the 'key audit matters' are addressed in the auditor's external report (including the auditor's risk assessment; the consistency with matters communicated to the audit committee; and with the audit committee's own views). Here an audit committee which is not independent could misdirect the auditor in their risk assessment, and create difficulties in the discussion of the key audit matters as perceived by the auditor.

As the audit committee is responsible for ensuring the quality of the external audit and on that basis makes recommendations the board on the approach taken to the appointment or reappointment of the external auditor, information on the length of tenure of the current audit firm, when a tender was last conducted and advance notice of any retendering plans. This enables the audit committee to influence whether the audit firm should be replaced and whether, in a retender process, they are included. Potentially, this creates a self-interest threat for BHZ LLP. If they robustly stand up to the audit committee and perform a high-quality audit which reduces the dividend payable or the value of the shares, they may find themselves removed from the audit next year. This could be a considerable embarrassment to the Newcastle engagement partner.

The safeguards against this threat which the engagement partner could employ would be to request that the audit work is subject to a review by another independent partner and to alert the ethical partner in the practice of the potential pressures to compromise audit quality being brought to the audit team.

Additional areas where credit might be given, note this is not an exhaustive list:
- marks will be given for any relevant additional points

EXAM ANSWER BANK

3 November 2022

Polyfine Industries plc

1 Audit in respect of the Year Ended 30 September 2022

(a) **This is a normal audit planning and audit testing question but placed into the scenario of an inflationary cost base – which may be a new issue for today's auditors. The audit risk assessment is addressing the development of revised ISA 315 Risk Assessment which has emphasised the move away from Business Risk assessment into inherent risk and has reclassified the consideration into Complexity, Subjectivity, Change, Uncertainty and Susceptibility to Misstatement. The second part of the question is exploring the audit of research and development which is the application of ISA 540 Audit of Accounting Estimates and the final part of the question is exploring the need for written representations. LO 1 and 2 Syllabus 1 and 2; Chapters 17; 18**

Question requires THREE key risks and marks are capped to 8 marks per risk

Polyfine is exposed to a number of risk factors, but answers must focus on INHERENT risks rather than business or control risks and credit will be given for key risks rather than more minor factors. This reflects the new requirement from ISA 315 Risk Assessment to assess inherent risk separately from control risks. The textbook uses an older model of inherent risk which I have used to base this answer around, but credit will be given for other approaches including the revised ISA 315 of Complexity, Subjectivity, Change, Uncertainty and Susceptibility to Misstatement.

Nature of the Business

Polyfine Industries manufactures highly complex polymer foams required as a key component in a number of different industries. These products are highly innovative and could become obsolete if other competitors develop newer, cheaper approaches. The company is dependent upon the availability and the price of ethylene which is a product from the oil industry. As observed by the Operations Director and CFO, oil price rises have been unprecedented and are squeezing margins and may compromise the availability of the raw material in the future. This could critically compromise the future for the company.

The chemical industry is subject to complex regulation around product specification, safety and environmental impact which may create pressures on the management team in terms of cost management and may also expose the company to the risk of non-compliance with laws and regulations. As an international company with manufacturing capacity in a number of different jurisdictions, this may be especially problematic.

Industry Factors

As Polyfine is manufacturing highly advanced products which are priced at a premium, there is a risk that customers may opt to move their business to the cheaper competitors. The move of the previous Operations Director to EcoPlastic may increase the likelihood of such customer loss as they may be able to exploit their industry contacts and knowledge of Polyfine's customer database to entice customers.

There are also significant risks with industry sectors and geographical locations of the customers. Although the demand from China and Europe seems to be increasing and these markets are becoming more important to the company, there is a significant drop in the revenue from the UK and a stagnation in the US. The UK economy appears to be in some trouble with high inflation and stagnant recovery both adversely affecting the currency. This may be adding to cost pressures throughout the company as this is a key manufacturing base for the company. The drop in demand in a key market may also increase pressure on the overall profitability of the company.

The reduction of demand in aviation and automotive sectors, which is dramatic, is focusing the company into the sports and leisure and product protection sectors. As both of these sectors relate into retail they are also susceptible to global recessionary forces. This could further compromise the outlook for the company and confidence in the performance from key capital providers.

The industry appears to be exposed to serious uncertainty and change from environmental and economic forces and, as discussed, these changes in the validity of the business model due to issues with raw material costs, will create issues for the management team in maintaining profitability.

Management Experience

The loss of experienced CEO and operations director mean that the competence of the board may be compromised. This could affect both the quality of the strategic decision making of the board, as evidenced in the pricing difficulties reported by the operations director, and the quality of the accounting estimates and judgements made in the corporate reporting.

Management Pressures

Overall, there are significant pressures on the management team at present. The reduction in profitability caused by the ongoing inflation in raw material costs has eroded the business model against which the Industrial and Commercial Bank has provided its loan. Although the debt covenant agreement has not yet been breached, the reduction of interest cover to 2.89 is now getting very close to the limit of 2.5%. Of more concern is the reduction in operating profit margin from 16% in 2020 down to 2.1%. This has been driven by this steep rise in raw material costs and if these continue unabated, the covenant will be breached in the future. From the BBC article, there is little evidence that oil prices will drop back and, as they are dependent on geo-political factors, it would be very difficult for the directors to have any confidence in the future of these prices.

This pressure on the management team to comply with the bank covenant creates management bias in the calculation of operating profit and may lead to a lack of objectivity and balance in the recognition of costs and the desire to aggressively recognise income. This increases the susceptibility of subjective account balances to misstatement.

(b) Materiality is the assessment of the level of misstatement which is considered by the auditor to influence the economic decisions of users taken on the basis of the financial statements as a whole. For Polyfine Industries the key performance indicator influencing viability assessments for the company is the operating profit percentage and interest cover. Given the reduction in profitability of the company, it would seem likely that the key balance influencing shareholders will be profit before tax. The usual benchmark for materiality is 5% of this figure – so for 2022 this would be £105,600. Performance materiality is set lower than this figure to ensure that constituent misstatements which would combine to cause a material error are not overlooked. Conventionally, this is set between 50% and 70% of overall materiality, although may be set differentially for different account balances. Given the level of risk in the audit, which is high, the performance materiality is set at £52,800 representing 50% of materiality.

(c) The audit of research and development balance requires the application of ISA 540 *Audit of an Accounting Estimate*. Under IAS 38 *Intangible Assets*, an asset may be recognised as an intangible asset where:

- It is technically feasible to complete the asset so that it will be available for use,
- Management intends to complete the asset and use or sell it,
- There is an ability to use or sell the asset. It can be demonstrated how the asset will generate probable future economic benefits,

- Adequate technical, financial, and other resources to complete the development and to use or sell the asset are available; and
- The expenditure attributable to the asset during its development can be reliably measured.

Risk Assessment – for Development balance

The development asset is at risk of being over-valued either through the inclusion of costs which do not relate to the specific project which meets the standard, the inclusion of a project which no longer meets the criteria for recognition, or through under-amortisation of development now generating revenue. As the costs of research not recognised as development and the subsequent amortisation of development both reduce the operating profit, they therefore affect the key performance indicator which ensures that the bank covenant is not breached. The balance must therefore be considered to be highly susceptible to management bias and as the recognition of the cost may be complex and subjective, this balance must be considered high risk.

We must ensure that we obtain an understanding of how management identifies relevant methods, assumptions and data for assessing the costs applicable to the development of a specific project and for ensuring that such developments meet the criteria for recognition as an asset.

Method

The audit approach will need to obtain sufficient relevant and reliable evidence regarding the appropriateness of the method supporting the identification and valuation of development.

Is the method correct?

Are judgements applied by management fair and balanced or subject to management bias?

Are calculations accurate?

For each project we will need to ensure that the carrying value for the development recognises any impairment as a consequence of changes in economic conditions.

Assumptions

The audit testing will need to ensure that the development meets the critical criteria for recognition as a capital asset.

Is the development in relation to a specific discrete project whose future sales will generate future economic benefit to the company?

Is the development technically feasible?

Does the company have sufficient technical and financial resources to complete the project?

Data

Is the cost data utilised to generate the overall development value accurate and relevant?

Airflow Foam

As this is a current project, amortisation will not be attributed to this balance and the costs increasing the balance will relate to this project.

The audit work will need to review the method by which costs of research and development are allocated to this specific project, with specific attention being paid to the attribution of semi-fixed, fixed and indirect costs. The assumptions supporting the allocation of indirect costs to the project will require a challenge from the auditor to ensure that these costs are not overstated in the year. This could be done through comparison with previous year's approaches for consistency and then through tracing of the costs into the detailed invoices to ensure that they relate to items relevant to the project. This should include staff costs.

The evidence that Airflow Foam is technically feasible will need to be reviewed. We should consult with the project team to understand the most recent evidence that they have supporting the viability of the product. We could consider contacting an independent expert in the field and commissioning a review of the data to ensure that the feasibility is reasonably certain.

The evidence that the Airflow Foam will be financially feasible should be reviewed. The calculations of the production costs for the product and the estimated price that the market will support should be obtained. These should be flexed to reflect increases in the costs of the raw materials to identify at what oil costs the product fails to make a profit. We should then review economic predictors of oil pricing to ascertain the likelihood that Airflow fails to be profitable.

Postufoam

For the £450,000 relating to Postufoam, there is a risk that the downturn in aviation and automotive manufacturing means that the reduction in future cashflow may mean that the Value in Use (VIU) of this asset has eroded and the balance should be either impaired or the rate of amortisation increased. We will need to enquire of the management to obtain details of the revenue streams in respect of Postufoam for the past two years and review the management's assumptions in support of the increases in this activity. We will review the order book after the year end in respect of this product and see whether there are indications of increase or decrease in demand. We will need to challenge these assumptions by review of external economic indicators and predictions for activity.

Polyinsulate

For Polyinsulate, there is no evidence that the product is likely to suffer a downturn in demand due to economic conditions. Therefore, we can ensure that the carrying value is lower than the VIU through reviewing the sales pattern for the product over the year and reviewing the order book for future sales to ensure that there is evidence of consistent demand.

We should ensure that the opening balance of the cost is carried forward correctly through a comparison with the closing balance in the lead schedules from previous year's audit files.

We should review the remaining useful economic life of the product and reperform the amortisation calculation to ensure this is accurate. We should review any correspondence from customers regarding product satisfaction and enquire of the sales team regarding indications that the product is likely to become obsolete from competitors' products.

(d) Written representations are a critical component of audit evidence as they confirm the auditor's understanding of information provided to the auditor in the course of their work from management and provide a written record that such understanding is shared by the auditor and the management team.

For the research and development balance there are a number of areas where the validity of the accounting treatment depends upon the assessment of future trading conditions – either costs of raw materials or product demand – or the assessment of the technical feasibility of the product. Since the management team are responsible for the preparation of the financial statements, they would be expected to have sufficient understanding of any assumptions behind the figures, although in the case of the technical feasibility of AirFlow Foam, management may seek to rely on the assessment of the chief scientist in charge of the project. As the sensitivity of the compliance with the debt covenant is critical and could be affected by the accounting treatment of this balance, it would be appropriate to obtain such written representation from those charged with Polyfine Industries governance.

> **Additional areas where credit might be given, note this is not an exhaustive list:**
> - marks will be given for any relevant additional points.
> - Given the volatility of oil prices and the issues with inflation and other geopolitical recessive forces any reflection of additional relevant factors as at the date of the examination recognised by students will be credited.

2 **Information issued with Corporate Reports.**

Question Rationale – Learning Outcomes 2 and 4; Syllabus Topic 1 and 4; Chapter 2 and 3.

The debate regarding the importance of viability statements continues and they are now routinely required in all listed companies. Much of the recent debate has been around the consequences of the Covid-19 Pandemic on business operations. However, since the end of the pandemic, the challenges to business have continued and, after decades of global low inflation and interest rates, the Russian invasion of Ukraine and the low production of oil has caused exponential rises in energy costs. As explored in question one, Polyfine Industries manufactures polymers from a key product of oil and is therefore very badly affected by these cost inflationary pressures.

The current viability statement fails to adequately reflect the risks that are actually emerging and therefore casts a doubt over the management assessment of this viability. It considers the auditors and audit committee responsibility for this information issued with the corporate reports.

(a) Email from: Engagement Partner Polyfine Industries
To: Jiang Cui – Audit Manager Polyfine Industries
Subject – Polyfine Audit – Issues arising from Viability Statement
Date – x/11/22

Dear Jiang,

Thank you for forwarding the viability statement to me – you were correct to raise concerns and my advice regarding our response is as follows:

The timeframe that the directors are considering appears to be appropriate and is consistent with their previous practice and practice more widely used through the industry. However, given the level of inflationary pressures currently experienced by Polyfine, I would be concerned that assessing over five years may not be reliable. There are pressures coming from both the uncertainty around the post-pandemic recovery and the international consequences of the war in Ukraine. It is difficult to have any confidence in anyone's ability to predict how long these factors will continue to influence world oil prices. It is also very likely that major economies may now be faced with the challenges of stagflation which may have a serious impact on consumer demand around the sports and leisure and transportation industries.

The key consideration of viability reflects financial solvency and the risks that interest rates may rise have not been factored into the assessments.

However, my major concern around this statement relates to the five key scenarios used to stress test the company. From current economic projections, I would not consider that there is any possibility that UK Sterling will increase in value – indeed based on current information, it seems much more likely that Sterling will continue to devalue against all major currencies.

Although scenarios one, three and four are all considering a reduction in demand, I think that the most pressing risk is the increase in cost base – which has gone from 79% of income in 2021 to 83% of income in 2022 – continuing and squeezing gross margins to the extent that the rises can not be passed onto customers. As Polyfine is a premium approach to foam manufacture, if prices rise too high, customers may then move to lower quality competitors – none of which is considered in this discussion.

The audit implication of the current phraseology of the viability statement are two-fold.

Either the viability statement reflects the CFO's genuine assessment of key risks facing the company which casts doubt over her competence and the level of objectivity with which the financial statements are being compiled. This could affect the reliability of any management confirmations or assertions around future prospects and mean that the financial statements are overly optimistic.

Alternatively, the CFO is only too aware of the real factors impacting on the viability of Polyfine, but is choosing to conceal this in the public discussions. This means that the objectivity and transparency of reporting is compromised and creates the risk that the corporate reports are not providing a balanced assessment of future prospects. This again will affect the reliance that we can place on any management confirmations and assessments.

Overall, the impact of this statement on our audit is to increase our assessment of the audit risk as there is evidence of management bias and poor management estimates. It therefore means that materiality should be decreased and we should increase the scepticism with which we audit any management estimates.

If you have any further concerns I will be in the office tomorrow morning from seven thirty and we can have a chat over a coffee before my first meeting.

Regards
Engagement Partner

(b) (i) It is the responsibility of the audit committee to monitor the integrity of the corporate reports of Polyfine Industries plc and this would include the integrity of the Viability Statement. In the UK, under which jurisdiction the company is reporting, the following responsibilities are articulated in the Corporate Governance Code.

"The audit committee should review, and report to the board on, significant financial reporting issues and judgements made in connection with the preparation of the company's financial statements (having regard to matters communicated to it by the auditor) interim reports, preliminary announcements and related formal statements."

"The audit committee should review the clarity and completeness of disclosures in the financial statements and consider whether the disclosures made are set properly in context." In this situation, the audit committee should raise their concerns regarding the Viability Statement to the board and should support the auditor in challenging the management team around the key risks appropriate for inclusion in the scenarios used to stress test this viability.

(ii) The auditor's responsibility for the Viability Statement is covered by ISA 720 *The Auditor's Responsibilities Relating to Other Information*. Therefore, RYG will review the Viability Statement for consistency with other knowledge gained through the audit and assess whether the disclosure is fair, balanced and understandable.

We are also required to report in the audit report, whether there is anything material to draw shareholder's attention to regarding the directors' confirmation that they have carried out a robust assessment of the key risks facing Polyfine Industries and how these are disclosed in the viability statement. If this viability statement is not altered then we will need to report the inconsistency regarding the risks used to assess future viability of the company and also to make a statement in the Corporate Governance report that disclosures around the going concern of the company as reported in the viability statement are not consistent with our knowledge of the business gained from our audit.

This will NOT result in a modification of the audit opinion.

EXAM ANSWER BANK

> **Additional areas where credit might be given, note this is not an exhaustive list:**
> - marks will be given for any relevant additional points.

3   **Practice Management and Ethics**

Question Rationale – this question is exploring the emerging discussion regarding the fundamental importance that audit culture has in supporting the delivery of high quality audits. This is specifically building on the work of the UK regulator, the FRC, during summer 2021 but is reflecting the work of the IFAC around factors to support the development of professional scepticism.

This is examining LO 3 and Syllabus Topic 2 Chapter 8.

(a) A key aspect of an effective audit is the ability of the auditor to consider evidence with professional scepticism and to effectively challenge management – indeed the Brydon Report has identified that the notion of management challenge should be reflected in the key aspects of corporate auditing.

Audit firm culture is accepted as a critical component in enabling RYG to deliver high quality audit. A good audit firm culture develops and supports the ability of its staff to exercise professional scepticism and challenge management and nurtures and retains these staff. Independence is a key attribute which must be developed – this being a mindset embedded in the culture rather than a compliance exercise of form filling. The use of audit guidance to underpin formulaic comments to provide evidence of scepticism rather implies that this is scepticism in appearance rather than in practice. It is not providing evidence that the audit guidance is being applied with scepticism to the specific issues within the client audit and is not providing insight into the considerations made by the audit team.

There is also evidence that professional scepticism will be compromised if the staff feel they are under undue time pressure, as this stops the mulling over of audit evidence and the overall consideration of findings. Staff must feel that the audit reporting deadline can be slipped if additional work is required to gather adequate evidence to support their professional opinions, and having a culture where the client deadlines are more important than the quality of audit evidence must be avoided.

Having a culture of fear within the audit team also means that problematic issues or concerns will not be raised in a timely manner with audit manager or partners. This creates the risk that key audit evidence or risks are not raised with the audit partner and hence not reflected in the audit opinion – leading to the risk that audit opinions may be incorrect.

Another key attribute which is required within the audit culture is professional expertise. Although this is developed through professional examinations, it is also more critically developed through practical experience and learning from other professionals in the firm. A culture of fear and a resistance to raise issues and ask questions will prevent this learning environment from developing – and certainly fails to nurture and retain the talented staff.

(b) A culture of challenge empowers auditors to use their professional expertise and skills to verify the reporting practices of the client and therefore to formulate robust and rigorous audit opinions.

There are a number of ways in which this culture of challenge could be developed within RYG.

On-the-job training of staff

Audit scepticism and the ability to challenge management are developed through practical experience and building up the confidence and interpersonal skills of staff. It is therefore important for practical training to encompass more complex aspects of audit work rather than focusing the work of junior staff on routine compliance tasks. We must build such training time into our audit schedules, allowing additional time for review of junior work on complex tasks and real time observation, teaching and discussions. Within the audit team we must ensure that junior staff are allowed to make errors of judgement which are then explored and discussed in a supportive and collegiate manner.

Leadership and Tone at the Top

The audit partners and managers must ensure that they show that a key aspect of our work is the in-depth probing and verification of evidence and that finding issues is not to be avoided or resisted. This will empower other staff in their work and will develop staff confidence that this is the correct way to conduct their work. We must ensure that we encourage staff to call out clients for potential misreporting.

Reward Systems

We must review our reward systems to ensure that they reflect the importance of robust audit practice through management challenge and scepticism rather than looking at client retention, client satisfaction, revenue generation or profit.

Additional areas where credit might be given, note this is not an exhaustive list:
- marks will be given for any relevant additional points.

4 May 2023

Elite Rentals Group plc

The paper considers the audit issues around the audit of a commercial and domestic property company and allows the exploration of the impact of emerging economic challenges on this sector. Once again, the new issues in ISA315 *Identifying and Assessing the Risks of Material Misstatements* are examined and the accounting issues around investment property are explored.

The paper then goes onto to look at the issue of fraud and the auditing implications and links this into the wider public interest in building safety and the role of the audit committee where fraud, management override and poor risk reporting are identified.

The final question explores the issues of professional judgement currently under review by the FRC and the role of practice quality management in supporting this.

The case study information is developed through an amalgamation of Towngate plc (where the issue of incorrect filing was identified) and Grainger plc (where the issues in the investment property valuation approach is raised).

1 **Detailed Audit of Elite Rentals Group plc**

This is a normal audit planning and audit testing question but placed into the scenario of a property rental company exposed to risks in interest rate rises. The audit risk assessment is once again addressing the development of revised ISA 315 *Identifying and Assessing the Risks of Material Misstatement* which has emphasised the move away from Business Risk assessment into inherent risk and has reclassified the consideration into Complexity, Subjectivity, Change, Uncertainty and Susceptibility to Misstatement. The second part of the question is exploring the audit of property around the issue of classification and treatment as well as conventional ideas of valuation which is the application of ISA 540 *Audit of Accounting Estimates* and the final part of the question is exploring ethics, both from the perspective of an accountant in business and the ethical expectations that the auditors have of the CFO and within the firm around the issue of GIVING hospitality. Students will be very familiar with the requirements around acceptance of hospitality but this question is exploring their understanding of the limitations of giving hospitality. These issues are all highlighted in the revised *IFAC Code of Ethics for Accountants (2022)*.

LO 1 and 2 Syllabus 1,2 and 3; Chapters 17; 18.

(a) **Inherent Audit Risk assessment**

Inherent risk is the susceptibility of an assertion about transactions, balances or disclosures to a potentially material misstatement, either individually or in aggregate, before consideration of related controls. Inherent risk factors help determine where a risk sits on the inherent risk spectrum. They include complexity; subjectivity; change; uncertainty; management bias; other fraud risk factors; and other events or conditions, such as the entity's past history of misstatements and control deficiencies, or lack of personnel with appropriate financial reporting skills. (*ISA 315 Identifying and Assessing the Risks of Material Misstatement revised 2019*).

One of the key issues creating high risk for the audit relates to the new directors. Neither director has experience of the governance requirements for a listed entity and there is limited evidence that the new CFO will have the financial skills required for such a complex company.

Management Bias

The directors are all remunerated through a bonus scheme whose critical driver is the level of profit before taxation Additionally, debt covenants require that interest cover is maintained at 7. This will create a conflict of interest for the reporting of performance for the directors.

There is evidence of a slow-down in demand in the second half of the year, and there are significant inflationary pressures. Although this is more likely to impact on the costs of the company through rising interest rates and therefore finance charges, the cost of living crisis may lead to tenant defaults. This may be more likely to impact the warehousing division as commercial tenants come under financial stress and may cease to trade, leaving bad debts. The assessment of the business by the CFO seems to recognise some of these issues, but is very confident and may indicate an over optimistic assessment of investment property valuations.

Subjectivity

The investment property portfolio classification between investment property and trading property is inherently subjective. The classification depends upon the intentions of the directors regarding future sale. By classifying property as investment there is no charge to the income statement unless impairment occurs. Annually the property is revalued, which reflects property valuations which depend on anticipated future market performance.

Trading property is held at the lower of cost and net realisable value and therefore may not reflect rising property valuations in the asset value.

There is some doubt over the likely performance of the UK property market over the next few years and this may require recognition as impairment, which will depress results and may be resisted by the directors. As the assessment of valuation is subjective this may be very difficult for the auditor to challenge.

(b) **Audit of Investment Property and Investment Inventory Balances**

Real estate that meets the definition of 'investment property' is accounted for in accordance with IAS 40 *Investment Properties* even during the period when it is under construction. Further, an investment property under redevelopment for continued future use as investment property also continues to be recognised as investment property.

The property assets are at risk of being over valued either through incorrect classification as investment properties carried at fair value rather than cost, the over statement of fair value which fails to recognise market conditions or through failure to recognise impairment of the valuations.

As the costs of investment properties do not impact on profit unless they are impaired, they therefore affect the key performance indicator which ensures that the bank covenant is not breached. Unusually the bank assesses the level of safe debt against the value of the fixed assets rather than the total asset base. The classification and valuation of this property must therefore be considered to be highly susceptible to management bias and as the assessment of fair value for the property portfolio may be complex and subjective, this balance must be considered high risk.

We must ensure that we obtain an understanding of how management identifies relevant methods, assumptions and data for assessing the fair value applicable to the property and for ensuring how they meet the criteria for recognition as either investment or inventory.

The audit approach will need to obtain sufficient relevant and reliable evidence regarding the appropriateness of the method supporting the identification and valuation of development.

There are key points in this process that require a detailed understanding of the approach taken by management.

Identification of the asset as an investment rather than a trading asset.

Classification of the asset

IAS 40 *Investment Properties* defines investment property as property that is held to earn rentals or capital appreciation or both. [IAS 40 *Investment Properties* para 5]. This excludes:

- Property intended for sale in the ordinary course of business or for development and resale.
- Owner-occupied property, including property held for such use or for redevelopment prior to such use.
- Property occupied by employees.
- Owner-occupied property awaiting disposal.
- Property that is leased to another entity under a finance lease.

The statement of the accounting policy in the accounts is consistent with the standard and so, for a sample of the investment portfolio, evidence that rentals are flowing from its use through the existence of letting or lease agreements and payments from tenants would be required. This should be done for all acquisitions and reclassifications from trading property and for a sample of other property.

The team will need to understand how the reclassification of the asset when it is intended for sale/ or now kept for investment occurs and then inspect the related documentation for all of the reclassifications. It is likely that this evidence may come from notes of discussions and perhaps evidence that rental agreements have ceased. This may require management representation to provide documentary assurance of the management's intentions.

For this year, the process of reclassification of The Old Bond Warehouse would need to be reviewed in detail ensuring that the carrying valuation of the property in inventory at cost is consistent with the transfer into investment property.

Valuation of the assets

For the valuation of investment property IAS 40 *Investment Properties* gives the following choices:

- The income approach: under this approach, future amounts are converted into a single current amount using discounted cash flows;
- The market approach: under this approach, prices and other information generated by market transactions of similar assets are used to determine fair value; and
- The cost approach: this approach reflects the amount that would be required to replace the asset.

The accounting policy disclosed indicates that Elite Rentals uses the first and second approach for its assets – it is unclear what drives this selection from the accounting policy and the auditor would need to ensure that the rationale behind this is appropriate and consistently applied to each asset year on year.

For valuation using the income approach we would need to obtain detailed schedules of the calculations in support of these valuations for a sample of property. This will include the key information from rental agreements regarding current income flows to be agreed to these lease agreements. The assumptions regarding occupancy of the property would need to be identified and agreed to historic patterns adjusted in light of any rising risk of falling demand. The discounted cashflow rate applied will need to be identified and justified by the directors and assessed for consistency in the sector by the auditor.

The judgements applied by management should be critically appraised to ensure they are fair and balanced. Through sensitivity analysis, the auditor should alter these key assumptions to assess how robust the valuations are to changing scenarios and assess whether the assumptions selected are subject to management bias.

These calculations should be reperformed to ensure they are accurate.

For valuations using the market approach, there are clearly assumptions and approximations in the use of a valuation from external inspection which can be upgraded. The current valuations are created by internal staff, who are experts in valuation but are not independent and are not using an accurate technique. This valuation may be depressed and may leave the opportunity to window-dress increases in property valuations at a later date, smoothing performance.

Assessing the market valuation could be done using an independent chartered surveyor to reperform the valuation. Here, the credentials of the surveyor would need to be assessed to ensure that they are professionally competent. The approach taken by the expert will need to be reviewed to ensure it is consistent with industry standards.

Assets Under Construction

Assets under construction represent a significantly material balance and is a highly complex and subjective valuation. Under IAS 40 *Investment Property* under construction is initially measured at cost. Cost is usually the price paid to the developer to construct the property, together with any directly attributable costs of bringing the asset to the condition necessary for it to be capable of operating in the manner intended by management.

Costs that are eligible for capitalisation include, but are not limited to:

- contract costs with the developer;
- architecture fees;
- civil engineer fees; and
- staff costs for employees employed specifically for the construction process.

Costs that are not eligible for capitalisation include but are not limited to:

- feasibility studies in identifying development opportunities; and
- staff costs for project management if these would be incurred irrespective of any development.

The audit must obtain schedules of the costs attributed to a sample of the projects under construction and verify that the costs exclude feasibility studies and project management departmental costs as Elite Rentals has a full time project management staff team and therefore they are not costs which can be specifically allocated to individual projects.

Under the standard IAS 23 *Borrowing costs*, borrowing costs should be capitalised while construction is actively underway. These costs include the costs of: 1. specific funds borrowed for the purpose of financing the construction of the asset; and 2. general borrowings, being all borrowings that are not specific borrowings for the purpose of obtaining a qualifying asset.

The general borrowing costs attributable to an asset's construction should be calculated by reference to the entity's weighted average cost of general borrowings. Capitalisation starts when all three of the following conditions are met:

1. expenditures for the asset are incurred;
2. borrowing costs are incurred, and
3. the activities necessary to prepare the asset for its intended use are in progress.

Capitalisation of borrowing costs in respect of real estate developments can commence before the physical construction of the property (for example, when obtaining permits, completing architectural drawings, or other activities necessary to prepare the property for its intended use).

The audit of this aspect of the accounting estimate must track the timing of borrowing cost capitalisation to evidence that the project is actively underway – this could include evidence of obtaining permits, receiving architectural drawings etc. and to evidence that borrowing has been taken out and that costs on the asset have been incurred against which such borrowing is needed.

The weighted costs of capital should be assessed for reasonableness through review of Elite Rentals' loan agreements and the calculation should be re-performed. There is a risk that the changes in interest rates as fiscal policy in the UK tightens is translated into fluctuations in this figure, which may make its calculation more subjective than in previous years.

(c) **Ethical Issues – Client and Firm**

Under the *IFAC Code of Ethics – Professional Accountants in Business* articulates the expectations of accountants in business regarding ethical leadership within the organisation. Section 200.5 of the Code expects accountants to encourage and promote an ethics-based culture.

As CFO there is a greater ability and opportunity to access information, and to influence policies, decisions made, and actions taken by others involved with Elite Rentals Group plc and therefore the commitment to ethical behaviour needs to be high.

The concern that we may have regarding the ethics of the CFO is around the professional judgement and competence in the preparation of corporate reports given the failure to comply with legal requirements in the previous position.

Examples of actions that we would expect the CFO to be responsible for would include the introduction, implementation and oversight of:

- Ethics education and training programs.
- Management processes and performance evaluation and reward criteria that promote an ethical culture.
- Ethics and whistle-blowing policies.
- Policies and procedures designed to prevent non-compliance with law and regulations.

The ethics guidance regarding hospitality applies to accountants in business as well as to accountants in practice. The revised ethical standards now explicitly refer to both hospitality accepted and received and is a two-way street for independence purposes.

There are two key issues at play here. One is regarding the impact on independence in appearance – whereby a reasonably informed third party may infer that independence is compromised through the provision if the value of the hospitality is not trivial or inconsequential. Therefore, a modest working lunch may be acceptable whereas an evening at an expensive restaurant would not be – and the charity dinner at the local football ground may not be acceptable.

The second issue is the creation of a familiarity threat. Through getting to know the client in an informal setting there is a danger that a friendship could develop, and a subconscious bias be created due to the trust and comfort in the relationship. This could compromise independence.

The final issue that is created is around the ability of the audit partner to adequately document the issues discussed which inform the "know your client" assessment. As assessing ethical culture is a matter of professional judgement, this requires detailed documentation of the discussions and the gathering of supporting evidence regarding policies and procedures around ethics. Although an informal setting may allow the auditor to see a more unguarded version of the CEO and CFO which could allow for a more robust assessment of their ethics, the advantage of this would not outweigh the difficulty in using such discussions as reliable evidence.

Additional areas where credit might be given, note this is not an exhaustive list:

- Any sensible discussions around inherent risk in Elite Rentals which may recognise potential economic issues in either the commercial or domestic rental markets in more depth.
- The marks guidance for part b is very extensive but students may focus on the use of expert valuations to support the assessment of fair value judgements in more depth.
- Students may split the answer in b between justification of the approach through identification of areas of subjectivity and then tests to provide evidence on these.
- In part b, marks for statement of generic tests which are not explained or justified will be limited to 5.
- The marks guidance in part c is very extensive although students may identify additional relevant points not already given.
- Marks will be given for any relevant additional points.

2 **Information issued with Corporate Reports**

This question is considering the issues of fraud where the amount of financial loss is currently not material although the potential costs may be. It is asking student to consider the wider issues around management override of controls and poor management integrity and the serious public interest that such a breach of safety would incur. This is then linked into the quality of risk reporting by Elite Rentals and the responsibilities of the audit committee around all of these issues.

LO 1 and 4.

(a) **Impact of Fraud on the Audit**

The lack of fire doors plus the use of non-fire compliant paint and flooring means that the rental properties are not complying with relevant law and regulations and therefore, from ISA 250 *Non-compliance with Laws and Regulations,* the firm will need to consider whether they are required to report this to authorities outside the organisation. However, in the first instance, the issue should be raised with the audit committee, of which Colin Hope is not a member, and Elite Rentals should report themselves, arrange a new fire inspection and then organise to have the work done to standard. If this is not enacted then Conan and Zhang should take advice regarding reporting this breach of fire safety to the relevant authorities from the firm's solicitors. It is likely that, as this is a matter of public safety, and that the auditor is acting in good faith, that the breaching of the duty of confidentiality to report would be required.

The potential impact on Elite Rentals is very significant. Housing tenants in unsafe conditions will breach the licensing conditions and may then require that the tenants are rehoused at Elite Rentals' expense. This, together with the refurbishment costs and potential fines, may amount to a significant cost to the company. This will be an adjusting subsequent event and will require recognition in the financial statements.

This will also damage Elite Rentals' reputation for quality housing and may further depress demand in a difficult market. We should therefore review the potential impact this could have on the future viability of the company.

There is evidence that this is fraudulent activity as it appears that the purchasing controls regarding approved suppliers has been overridden to the benefit of the new director, Colin Hope and his family, and that a bribe was paid by Ben Hope to hide the poor quality work in the historic developments which was performed by Hope Developments on behalf of Elite Rentals. The audit work around suppliers, and the disclosure of related parties, did not highlight the existence of this possible conflict of interest and incentive for fraud at an earlier stage of the audit. It isn't clear that the bribe was financed by Elite Rentals and appears it may have been paid by Hope Developments, but this casts significant doubt over the integrity of the new director and the reliability of any evidence provided by his representations or those of his wife.

ISA 240 *Auditors responsibilities relating to fraud in an audit of financial statements* guides the firm's response to this situation. Despite the immaterial amount represented by the contract and the bribe, the nature of the fraud should be disclosed in the audit report as this casts significant doubt on integrity of one of the directors and the safety of the residential estate. Additionally, further work should be undertaken by our team to review any other unusual suppliers in the purchasing system. Any issues where the audit has relied on the representations or evidence supplied by Colin or Charlotte Hope should also be revisited to obtain corroboration from other sources. The auditor will also need to ascertain the relationship between Ben Hope, Colin and Charlotte Hope and Hope Developments.

(b) **Risk Reporting and Audit Committee Responsibilities**

Research by the FRC Financial Reporting Lab identifies that "Investors consider the reporting of principal risks to be an important factor in their decision-making process. Having an understanding of the principal risks faced by a company is important, both before making an investment and during the holding of that investment. Changes in risks faced by a company are one factor which may cause an investor to change the size of their shareholding or bondholding." There is inherent tension between the desire to provide succinct and useful information to investors, and the pressure to disclose a list of principal risks which does not give away any competitive advantage, and which may result in unspecific and excessive disclosure.

The risk report example given does articulate the potential impact of the risks upon the business but this is very generic and doesn't articulate the magnitude of these potential consequences. It also omits the mitigation/risk management actions undertaken by Elite Rentals and therefore doesn't allow investors to understand whether these risks are managed or not.

The critical weakness with the reporting is that it has been rolled over from previous years and is not reflecting current economic challenges facing the company from inflationary impacts on refurbishment costs or challenges to demand caused by cost of living pressures.

The regulatory risk has not reflected the issues with building and fire safety regulation currently under review – and an issue where the company is exposed due to lack of compliance.

As the discovery of the lack of compliance with laws and regulations, the override of management controls and the payment of alleged bribes illustrate, the internal control environment of Elite Rentals is weak. The impact of the new staff seem to have adversely affected this crucial aspect of the business and the audit committee should initiate an urgent internal audit review of supplier approval and ensure that fire safety and building safety standards are appropriately safeguarded with robust systems.

The audit committee should review the revisions to the draft accounts to ensure correct disclosure of the related party transactions with Hope Developments and the provision of refurbishment costs and any other associated financial consequences of the fraud.

Additional areas where credit might be given, note this is not an exhaustive list:

- In part a, additional credit may be given for a discussion around the conflict between confidentiality and public interest.

- Students may link the ideas in part a to specific cases of lack of building regulation compliance in practice to illustrate the potential impact on Elite Rentals' reputation – they could also consider whether criminal legal proceedings against the company and the directors may be appropriate.

- In part b students may consider quality of risk reporting using alternative frameworks and criteria and assess the example given against this.

- Students may consider the existence of the bribe in more depth and link this into the illegal conduct in the company.

- Marks will be given for any relevant additional points.

3   **Practice Management and Ethics.**

This question is exploring a key area of audit practice under discussion at present – namely the need to improve the development of professional judgement and the role of the audit firm in promoting a culture which supports this. Part a is exploring professional judgement in depth with an exploration of the factors influencing bias This links into the ideas of robust practice quality management as articulated in the ISQM 1 Quality Management for Firms (2020). This also requires a working knowledge of IFAC Code of Ethics (2019).

LO 1 and 3

Professional Judgement requires the consideration and interaction of:

(i)   Mindset – An appropriate mindset for auditors exercising professional judgement.

There are a range of biases that can hinder logical and objective reasoning. These can subconsciously affect the judgement processes of everyone, including highly skilled and experienced auditors. Such biases may include:

- Availability bias: a tendency to place more weight on events or experiences that immediately come to mind or are readily available than on those that are not.

- Confirmation bias: a tendency to place more weight on information that corroborates an existing belief than information that contradicts or casts doubt on that belief.

- Groupthink: a tendency to think or make decisions as a group that discourages creativity or individual responsibility.

- Overconfidence: a tendency to overestimate one's own ability to make accurate assessments of risk or other judgements or decisions.

- Anchoring bias: a tendency to use an initial piece of information as an anchor against which subsequent information is inadequately assessed.

- Automation bias: a tendency to favour output generated from automated systems, even when human reasoning or contradictory information raises questions as to whether such output is reliable or fit for purpose.

Within Elite Rentals there is evidence that the audit team suffered from anchoring bias around the past audits when designing the approach which may lead to risks being overlooked and developments in the client's business not being reflected in the audit work overtime.

There is also evidence of automation bias whereby the information generated by the Audit Software system is accepted regardless of the auditor's evidence.

Other relevant psychological factors may impact on judgement too. For example, certain personality traits may be detrimental to the exercise of good judgement, such as an undue fear of conflict, unwillingness to challenge figures of authority where appropriate, impatience or stubbornness. Conversely, some are likely to support an effective judgement process, such as perceptiveness and a willingness to consult and listen.

These personality factors should be considered in our recruitment specifications and screening – although some may be more difficult to screen for. We should perhaps consider some case study or role play training exercises where willingness to challenge, consult and listen are explored.

These factors are all affected by our firm's culture and the training we offer to our staff. Staff must be encouraged to question the decisions and approaches taken by clients and others in the firm – this challenge should not be perceived as threatening but rather as an opportunity for junior staff to learn or for senior staff to avoid bias. A key issue within the audit of Elite Rentals was the time pressure which made using existing approaches more attractive and stopped staff from taking a step back to consider whether the approach was sufficiently robust.

In addition to the other aspects of mindset discussed here, it is important that the auditor is committed to making quality judgements, or else the other factors may not be brought to bear in an appropriate way. The motivation behind such a commitment can stem from many sources, including the ethical values required of professional and trainee accountants, an understanding of the public interest role of audit and appropriately aligned incentives from the audit firm.

Our training must emphasise the compliance with the IFAC Code of Ethics and the importance of professional competence, integrity and applying key auditing standards including the need to apply professional judgement.

(ii) Environmental Factors

Environmental factors may be present in the environment of those making a judgement and can impact on how challenging it is to exercise professional judgement in an appropriate manner.

Improving judgement isn't just about training and recruitment though – it is also critically about having the correct culture in the audit firm. This can be actioned by looking at the following areas of our management:

(1) The leadership of the firm especially around the way in which we as partners are seen to prioritise the interest of the public in enacting the highest audit standards and challenging clients without placing the need to retain the client and the business interests of the firm first.

(2) The way in which audit teams are staffed to ensure the correct mix of experience and expertise – and the rotation of staff around clients to avoid legacy practices and bias.

(3) Clarity over the additional resources available to staff and clear guidance regarding when they should be accessed.

(4) Detailed guidance around the process of recording professional judgement Effective documentation allows individuals in the engagement team, and relevant third parties (file reviewers for example) to understand how judgements in the audit were made and the rationale and quality of evidence for the decision reached. Documentation can help an auditor to identify flaws in their reasoning, or gaps in evidence. Documentation is unlikely to take place at a single point in the audit but will iterate over time.

(5) The incorporation of professional judgement into the appraisal system to reward the development of judgement as a key aspect of the auditor skill set – as well as client satisfaction and budget performance.

Additional areas where credit might be given, note this is not an exhaustive list:

- In part a, the model answer uses a framework developed from a report by FRC to assess mindset – credit will be given for any sensible discussion around the factors in the audit which indicate that there may be bias. Students may explore the impact of technology on audit quality in more depth or may explore the impact of legacy staff on the audit more extensively.

- In part b, students may specifically focus on culture in the firm in more depth or may explore the factors identified in ISQM 1 *Quality Management for Firms* 2020 and apply these more widely.

- Marks will be given for any relevant additional points.

5 November 2023

1 **Audit Issues relating to Kind Chocolate plc**

(a) **Inherent Risks AIA 14 Chapter 12 ISA 315** *Identifying and Assessing the Risks of Material Misstatement Through Understanding of the Entity and Its Environment.*

LO 1; LO 2

The inherent control assessment is structured around the framework articulated under the revisions to ISA 315 *Identifying and Assessing the Risks of Material Misstatement Through Understanding of the Entity and Its Environment.*

Underpinning the assessment is the importance of recognising the susceptibility of misstatement due to management bias or fraud. The recent difficulties facing KC expansions internationally which have resulted in a refocus of US operations and cessation of activities in Japan have created tensions in the board and some dissatisfaction with investors. This will have increased the pressure on the management to re-establish their credentials as competent stewards of the company and may create bias to be overly optimistic around future performances and to attempt to show that the core business activities are performing well This bias will therefore be towards under-recognition of costs or over-recognition of income.

Against this background bias, all items subject to management estimation and subjectivity may be considered to be high risk. For KC this would include impairment of intangible and tangible assets, especially relating to valuations of the overseas Estates, capitalisation of research and development costs, and any recognition of brands.

Balances which are complex also attract higher risk assessment and for a complex group such as KC, this would consider the consolidation calculations and the recognition of relevant constituents. For this year, some of the activities of the group have changed which may increase the issues facing the reporting accountants as items subject to change also raise the risk profile.

Foreign currency year end balances and losses recorded in the year and on consolidation are also high risk. Under IAS 21 *The effects of changes in foreign exchange rates,* the impact of foreign currency on the accounting treatment relates to both the translation of KC's overseas subsidiaries in the US, West Africa and El Salvador in consolidation and the translation of currency in sales to and purchases from overseas. KC has a complicated international trading operation and the volatility in exchange rates against pound sterling, due to the economic uncertainty in the UK, may create challenges in accuracy and the opportunity to misstate for the benefit of the reported results.

The valuation of losses from discontinued operations is a complex accounting issue where the decision to recognise an operation as discontinued has caused disagreement. Currently the treatment recorded is not in accordance with the recognised accounting treatment and shows that the professional authority of the CFO has been weakened in the company. This may increase the likelihood of management override of accounting controls around subjective accounting estimates.

Compliance with Modern Slavery Laws may also present a risk to the audit – and other critical regulations around food production etc. could also be at risk of poor compliance.

It appears that the internal controls around the approval of the suppliers were not complied with, and this raises the risk of management override of internal controls being an issue on this audit – an issue exacerbated by the current turmoil on the board. The use of Boxtree could indicate the prioritisation of costs over ethics to improve the performance of the company. This could create further risks of reputation damage.

Auditor's duty under ISA 250 *Consideration of Laws and Regulations in the Audit of Financial Statements,* is to consider all regulations where non-compliance could cause a material misstatement, including those which cause impact either on operational capability or due to impact of fines or reputation damage. Therefore, the risk that the COO has overridden controls over the approval of suppliers alerts us to risks of management override on controls around product quality, through compliance with food safety regulations.

There is also a risk of the loss of key personnel especially the CFO which could increase the inherent risk of misstatement of all aspects of the reports and could make the conduct of the audit problematic if access to the CFO was no longer possible – or if the group lost core accounting competence across the audit timeframe.

(b) **Audit Issues and Approach relating to Discontinued Operations AIA 14 chapter 18 pp 406–407**

IFRS 5 Non-current assets held for sale and discontinued operations; ISA 500 Audit Evidence; ISA 540 Auditing accounting estimates and related disclosures.

LO 2

Although the discontinuation of the majority of retail stores in the US and cessation of trade in Japan are not of themselves material, they represent a significant refocus of the KC business and therefore are materially interesting to the investors, as they indicate a change in management policy – and a potential failure of a previous strategic direction. Therefore, under *IFRS 5 Non-current assets held for sale and discontinued operations,* disclosure is required in the income statement and in the notes.

The audit issue for KC relates to the financial accuracy with which the discontinuation is described in the income statement and the consistency with which it is explored in the CEO and other narrative statements. From the assessment of management bias, it is possible that KC may attempt to overstate the costs and therefore the losses associated with the discontinuation or attribute income to the continuing business to increase shareholders confidence in the recovery of the results.

Clearly the initial intention of the board involving the cessation of all retail business in the US and Japan would represent both a line of operations and two geographical areas, which are separately identifiable components which are being disposed of as part of a single coordinated plan. However, it appears from the information in the recent board meeting, that there is some doubt over the future of the US business. The COO and CFO both seem to express an intention to retain the New York flagship store and the warehousing operations on the East Coast of the US to enable the direct online selling capability to be retained – this would mean that the losses incurred in the sale of the other US stores and the costs of redundancy etc. would not meet the classification of a discontinuation.

The valuation of the discontinued assets held for resale should be at the lower of cost or fair value less the costs of sale and should be classified separately on the statement of financial position. The profit or loss of the discontinuation of the Japanese and possibly US business should be shown as discontinued operations on the income statement.

The audit work required is as follows:

- Reviewing management accounting and other financial records within the company including the organisational and reporting charts and budgeting processes to ensure that both the Japanese and US retail enterprises were run as separately identifiable components within KC. Japanese retail had resulted from the takeover of Japan Choc as a discrete subsidiary which means that this is a separately identifiable component which can therefore be classified as a discontinued operation.

- Review all board minutes and obtain management representation regarding the intention to discontinue activities in Japan and in the US. The management intentions regarding the US will require scrutiny of events after the year end to confirm whether the New York store and the East Coast Warehouse have been included in a future sales listing or are subject to any sales contracts or are being retained as a US foothold.

- From the information in the discussion, it appears that the CFO does not believe that the US retail store reduction should be classified as a discontinuation and therefore any costs attributable to this (£2,173 million) and any element of the legal and advisory costs related to the US restructure should be reclassified as exceptional.

- For each business which meets the criteria as a discontinuation (JapanChoc) we must obtain a detailed schedule of the costs and income which have been recognised. The additions must be reperformed and the total agreed to the income statement.

- For a sample of each cost centre allocated into the discontinuation (namely JapanChoc) we must trace the items back into the financial records to ensure that they relate to the geographical area and the time frame after the decision to discontinue had been made. This will ensure that items included are not overstated.

- To test that discontinuations are not omitted, especially around income received, testing must originate from the financial records NOT included in the classification – for sales proceeds for stores, auditors must review any significant unusual income receipts in the bank or large items in receivables and ensure that the underlying records are consistent with the classification of the credit entry.

(c) **ISA 240 The auditor's responsibilities in relation to a fraud in an audit; ISA 250 Consideration of Laws and Regulations in the audit of financial statements AIA 14 Ch 4, 5; 15 18 ; LO 1; LO 2**

As we are aware of information concerning an instance of non-compliance or suspected non-compliance with modern slavery laws and regulations our audit response is:

(a) To obtain an in depth understanding of whether the contract with Boxtree breaches the laws on modern slavery and whether the COO was aware of this when the supplier was awarded the contract.

(b) To consider the impact of the lack of compliance on the financial statements through further discussion with the CFO and COO and those charged with governance. We should also obtain further information to evaluate the possible effect on the financial statements.

If the COO (who is implicated in the lack of compliance) or the management do not provide sufficient information that supports that the entity is in compliance with laws and regulations and, our judgement, and as the effect of the suspected non-compliance may be material to the financial statements, we shall consider the need to obtain legal advice.

If sufficient information about suspected non-compliance cannot be obtained, we should evaluate the effect of the lack of sufficient appropriate audit evidence on the auditor's opinion. We also need to evaluate the implications of the non-compliance with Modern Slavery laws on our duty to report on the information issued with the financial statements around this area of regulation. We also need to consider the impact on our assessment of the risk of management override and the reliability of written representations and therefore consider the impact on our ability to formulate opinions around issues reliant on internal controls or management representation.

Communicating and Reporting Identified or Suspected Non-Compliance

As the KC Group plc has a team of non-executive directors who are not involved in the of management of the entity, and therefore are not aware of matters around breaches in modern slavery compliance due to Boxtree, we should communicate our findings to the audit committee. The issue is not inconsequential as it affects the reputation and ethical integrity of the group which is a critical aspect of its brand and identity. In addition, it indicates issues with management override.

As KC is a public interest entity, we must inform the KC board and audit committee and invite it to investigate the matter and take appropriate measures to deal with such irregularities and to prevent any recurrence of such irregularities in the future. If, we come to the conclusion that the breaching of modern slavery law was intentional and material, we must communicate with the audit committee as soon as possible.

Our requirement to report on the lack of compliance with modern slavery law is limited to whether the disclosure statements in the corporate governance statement is inconsistent with our understanding of the reality within the company.

The only statement regarding modern slavery which is specifically made in the disclosures is "we adhere to the UK anti-bribery and modern slavery acts and apply a supplier code of conduct which is enhanced by annual risk assessment and audit."

We should consider whether we could report that the supplier code of conduct was not applied in respect of Boxtree Cooperative and that therefore KC did not take appropriate steps to ensure that modern slavery was not happening in its supply chain. However, there are no financial penalties as a consequence of this breach unless a civil case is brought and there is an argument that the requirement of KC to produce a statement regarding its systems to ensure modern slavery is not applicable in its supply chain, is accurate and complies with the Act.

This limitation in our ability to make the breach of the systems around modern slavery public and to show that the chocolate is not free from child labour relates to the boundary on our duty to report on items in the financial statements. As the KC auditor, we are bound by a duty of confidentiality to the client which we cannot breach unless legally required so to do – which we aren't in this case – or there is a public interest duty. This is unclear and we would have to take legal advice to ensure that any reporting of the breach did not compromise our contractual and ethical duty of confidentiality with KC.

> **Additional areas where credit might be given, note this is not an exhaustive list:**
>
> - Any sensible discussions around inherent risk in Kind Chocolate which may recognise potential economic issues on the sales of chocolates due to their discretionary nature and susceptibility to cost of living crisis, or further issues around the cacao supply limitations.
> - Students could explore issues with going concern in depth as this group has been loss making and any adjustment to the discontinued operations figures will show that the underlying profit of the group may not be as strong as the current figure reflects. Students may structure the response around specific account balances or issues rather than following the framework from ISA 315 revised.
> - The marks guidance for part b is very extensive but students may focus on the need for additional audit work on the costs incurred in the US.
> - The marks guidance in part c is very extensive although students may identify additional relevant points not already given.
> - Marks will be given for any relevant additional points.

2   **Resignation of chair and CFO Chapter 2, 18 ISA 720 The auditor's responsibilities in relation to other information; LO2; LO4**

(a) The key objectives of the reporting of corporate governance relates to the need to enforce good practice in directors and to communicate adherence to this with the investors and wider stakeholders. The recent resignations of the chair and the CFO appear to relate to the recent discontinuation of the Japanese and US retailing aspects of the business and some deeper disagreements around the strategic and sustainable direction of the company. This creates risk in the company due to a loss of key personnel alongside their knowledge and competence and also means that there may be limited access to key players to obtain audit evidence.

The chair is responsible for the overall leadership of the board and its effectiveness in directing the company, and this resignation may indicate a personal responsibility for the failure of recent strategic decisions or of a profound schism in the working relations between the board, rendering his position untenable. Part of their role is to ensure objective judgement and a culture of openness and debate which appears to have been lacking if the assessment by the internal auditors is accurate. By changing the board leadership, this should assuage some of the concerns of the investors regarding the future direction of the company which may reduce the pressure on the management team from investors and hence management bias. However, the retention of the CEO and other senior board figures who did not support the change in direction may mean that the strategic naivety which caused the ill-fated expansion into the US and Japan will continue and the ongoing risk to the future of the company may continue – which may mean that the discussions in the strategic report remain overly optimistic and that we need to be vigilant around the need for professional scepticism around management judgements.

From ISA 720 *The auditor's responsibilities for other information* the auditors role in corporate governance reporting is to perform such procedures to identify whether there are any material inconsistencies between the corporate governance report and the financial statements; whether there are any material inconsistencies between the corporate governance statement and the auditor's knowledge obtained during the audit and whether the corporate governance statement appears to be materially misstated in the context of the relevant legislation applicable to the statutory other information. The auditor should report that the information in the Strategic Report and the Director's Report is consistent with that contained in the audited financial statements and complies with the relevant legislation for such disclosure.

The review should encompass the following areas:

- The responsibility of the directors in preparing statements supported by a statement from the auditor around their reporting responsibilities.

- That the board has conducted a review of the internal controls – this should cover all material controls including financial, operational and compliance controls and risk management systems.

- That an audit committee has been established which complies with the code of corporate governance and that it has met at least three times, has at least three independent members, one of whom has recent financial experience.

As auditors we must ensure that we do not create an advocacy threat where we act as directors and become too intimately involved in the management of the company and lose independence and objectivity. It is therefore inappropriate for us to advise on the recruitment of a new CFO or on the strategic wisdom of the CEO's stated intention to return to the US market in the near future.

(b) **AIA 14 Chapter 4. LO 1; LO 3; LO 4**

As a consequence of the recent government review of audit and assurance in the UK, next year the following statements will be required by KC:

Audit and Assurance policy: KC will need to explain their approach to assurance over the information reported in the front half of the annual report and accounts, including disclosing their internal auditing and assurance process. This could potentially be quite onerous as much of the information at the start of the accounts relates to the extensive sustainability agenda of KC. This could create an impetus to either create a separate sustainability report which could be referred to and contain the disclosures in the financial statements to those required by law. Potentially, this will increase the work of internal audit or could create an opportunity for our audit to be extended into these areas.

Fraud statement: Companies will need to prepare a directors' fraud statement setting out the actions they have taken to prevent and detect fraud. As external auditors we will need to review this statement to ensure that it is consistent with our understanding of the systems in KC.

Statement on internal controls: The UK Corporate Governance Code will be updated to require an explicit directors' statement on the effectiveness of internal controls. The impact on our audit work will be to extend our work to review how the directors have established the effectiveness of the internal controls.

This would serve to potentially increase the scope of our audit work and would require a renegotiation of the audit fee. The increase in this fee may cause an issue for our independence through a self-interest threat if the audit fees overall exceed 10% of the practice income for CZ. As KC currently contributes 9.5% of our fee income, we will have to ensure that any loss of audit fees from other clients is carefully monitored and that we pursue new audit opportunities within the practice capacity.

> **Additional areas where credit might be given, note this is not an exhaustive list:**
>
> - Any sensible discussions around the impact of the resignation of the chair and the CFO. Students may chose to explore the impact on the practicality of the audit without a CFO in more depth and discuss the impact on reporting where access to audit evidence is limited.
>
> - The marks guidance for part b is very extensive but any additional observations around the potential impact of the new guidance on the audit of KC will be credited. Students may focus more extensively on the issues of a growing client and the breach of independence rules.
>
> - Marks will be given for any relevant additional points.

3 **Practice Management and Ethics.**

AIA 14 Chapter 9 LO 3

(a) There are a number of advantages to CZ firm in joining a cooperation of international firms.

This would give us access to an international network of so-called sister firms. We would be able to rely on the audit quality of these sister organisations as they would be working to the same audit quality standards. Potentially, this would enable us to use DA affiliated firms to support our audit of KC and reduce some of the costs and our carbon footprint travelling out to West Africa, and reduce the impact on our staffing availability in the UK when the KC audit work is ongoing.

Additionally, attaching Drummond Accounting (DA) into our name to become DA Craster and Zhang LLP would signal our international credentials and quality into the UK market and would enable us to tender for transnational audits and build on our expertise with KC.

It would also give us access to developments in best practice as DA is part of the international firms who have significant influence over regulation and standard setting globally. It will allow us to access training and education materials and potentially audit technology that will enhance the quality of our work. It will also allow us to access global best practice materials supporting audit documentation, audit procedures and quality assurance. With the implementation ISQM 2 *Engagement Quality Reviews* increasing the focus on audit quality systems this could be particularly beneficial.

It could also increase our areas of competence and further expand our potential markets.

Another advantage is the option to retain our own audit approach which could give us increased flexibility but the adoption of the DA affiliate systems, whilst removing that advantage, would potentially reduce the costs of developing and updating our audit approaches.

(b) **AIA 14 Chapter 9 ISA 600 Audits of Group Financial Statements. ISA 330 The auditors responses to assessed risks. LO 3**

However, Callum Zhang is quite correct that there would be different costs incurred using a secondary auditor, as we would still have a duty to evaluate the audit work and conclusions of the component auditor and the audit work on the consolidation to draw a conclusion on the Group's accounts.

It is clear that the Kind Estates should be considered a component in the business of KC for audit purposes as there is a significant risk of material misstatement around and work is required in these areas. Thus any work carried out by a component auditor, affiliated or otherwise, would require a detailed consideration of the audit evidence around any material issues for the Group.

The challenges of working with a component auditor relate to the reliance that we can place on the quality of the work. This should be mitigated in part by the affiliation of the local firm to DA. Under ISA 330 *The auditor's response to assessed risk* we would need to determine the type of work required for the Estate audit by the component auditor and establish whether this is a full audit or focused at specific high risk areas in order to provide sufficient evidence for us to express an opinion of the financial statements of the Group. As a minimum, we will need to discuss the business activities of the Estates with the component auditor, explore the susceptibility of the Estates to fraud or non-compliance with law and regulation and the susceptibility of the Estate's financial statements to misstatement as a consequence of these, and review the resulting documentation around areas of risk of material misstatement for the Group.

The use of the local affiliated firm could overcome the language difficulties and cultural differences encountered at the Estates and the local firm would be familiar with any local accounting or other regulations – this could avoid us missing issues of non-compliance with law and regulation due to lack of familiarity with issues in West Africa and El Salvador.

However, Callum is correct in that the use of the affiliate, whilst offering some improved confidence in quality of the audit work, will not remove the time in the evaluation of that work and therefore the costs.

ISQM 2 *Engagement Quality Reviews* AIA 14 Chapter 8. LO 3

(c) ISQM 2 *Engagement Quality Reviews* require CZ to extend the scope of audits requiring engagement quality reviews to those where there is a quality risk, those of listed entities and any required by local law or regulation. As KC is a listed entity it would fall under these requirements.

The new standard requires a focus on the objective evaluation of the significant judgements made by the engagement team and the conclusions reached thereon. The key areas requiring EQR are identified in the standard as:

- In the planning of difficult to audit areas. For KC this would encompass the valuation of the Estates, impairment reviews, and the assessment of goodwill amongst others.

- Where the audit team have to consider the weight of different conflicting evidence sources in assessing the validity of subjective judgements. For KC this would consider the decision by management to include the costs of the closure of the US stores as a discontinuation where the CFO has disagreed with board.

- Where the audit team views differ from management's on a material estimate. Again this would encompass the treatment of the discontinued businesses.

- Where the audit team views support that of managements on a material estimate to ensure that sufficient management challenge and professional scepticism has been applied.

Robust documentation of the reviewer's opinions regarding the work of the audit team will be required and this must demonstrate that the reviewer has exercised professional scepticism and stood back from the audit to consider what a reasonably informed third party would consider to be sufficient and appropriate evidence and conclusions.

As the engagement review is conducted at an appropriate time, it is vital that CZ LLP has identified the relevant staff able to act as reviewer and that these are allocated time to the KC audit stages – this includes at planning, review and formulation of conclusions and at the reporting stage.

The allocation of Cath Martinez to the role of EQ Reviewer for KC would not be appropriate as she was the engagement partner six months ago and therefore has not served out the two year cooling off period. We therefore need to appoint additional EQ Reviewers who have sufficient expertise, competence and authority – these can be from outside the firm and the affiliation with DA would enable us to access additional competence in this area.

Additional areas where credit might be given, note this is not an exhaustive list:

- The marks guidance for part a is very extensive but the impact on the credibility of the firm or its identity could be explored in more depth.
- The marks guidance for part b is very extensive but students may focus on the detailed work required to assess the competence of a component auditor in more depth.
- The marks guidance in part c is very extensive although students may explore the role of Cath Martinez in more depth.
- Marks will be given for any relevant additional points.

Mock exam questions and answers

AIA PROFESSIONAL QUALIFICATION

PROFESSIONAL 2

DEVELOPMENTS IN ASSURANCE AND ACCOUNTABILTY

Question Paper

Time Allowed: 3 hours

Answer ALL questions

You are allowed an additional 15 minutes reading time before the exam begins.

Specimen questions are published to provide candidates with an indication of the style of question and the nature of requirements they can expect to encounter in examinations, together with the related allocation of marks. They are not intended to indicate the precise coverage of topics or mark allocation for the examinations in any specific session and should not be read as such.

CREATING WORLD CLASS ACCOUNTANTS

MOCK EXAM QUESTIONS

1 Retail

GH is an accounting firm that has twelve partners and a total of 150 professional staff. The firm's largest client is Retail Ltd (Retail), a large business that sells canned and bottled food. Retail has branches spread across the country. Gillian is the partner in charge of the audit of Retail. She has been responsible for the audit for the past three years. Retail has a year end of 31 March 2015.

The audit file contains the following planning information, updated at the initial planning stage of the audit in February 2015, with respect to the audit of inventory:

> Retail has 37 branches, one in almost every major town or city in the country. Each branch will have its inventory counted on 31 March 2015.
>
> Retail pays a professional inventory counting company to attend every branch so that the inventory can be counted quickly and efficiently. The company will send a count team to every branch to commence the count at the close of business on 31 March. The count teams will prepare a detailed set of count records which will then be valued by Retail's accounts staff.
>
> We have always attended four branch inventory counts. The branches are chosen at random every year, but we have always restricted our visits to the branches that are within a two hour travelling time from our office. There are nine GH branches within that area. This year I have decided that we will attend the branch that is furthest from our office plus three others that are within normal travelling distance. The member of staff who attends the most distant branch will have to travel up during the day of the 31st, attend the inventory count in the evening and stay overnight in a hotel before travelling back next day. I have budgeted for the costs of doing so.

Gillian found the following file note marked for partner's attention in the GH working papers on 2 April 2015:

> I attended the inventory count at Retail's Longtown branch.
>
> The count was conducted by four inventory counters from a company called Count. These counters worked as two pairs and took approximately three hours to complete the count.
>
> Count's employees were assisted by the branch manager, who acted as an overall supervisor and by two shop assistants who assisted with the location and identification of items.
>
> I was not entirely satisfied with the count procedures employed by Count's staff. They did not open any cartons, even on a sample basis. All of the bulk inventory in the shop's storage area was boxed in cartons and remained unchecked apart from confirming the numbers of cartons. Also, the count staff did not check the best before dates on any of the inventory on the shop's shelves, apart from items at the very front. The branch manager assured them that the shop staff refilled all shelves by placing fresher goods at the back and so older inventory was always closest to the front.
>
> I queried these matters with Count's staff and pointed out that they were in breach of the count instructions and were also failing to do their work in the manner that GH has used at other counts that I have attended in previous years. The response was that it would take too long for two pairs of counters to complete the count in the manner that I had suggested.
>
> Matthew
>
> Audit senior

Gillian asked Retail's finance director to investigate these concerns. The finance director replied ten days later in the following email:

Dale Holmes Dale.Holmes@retail.com

Sent: Mon 14 April 2014

To: <Gillian.Partner@GH.com>

Dear Gillian,

Apologies for the delay in responding to you, but it has taken some time to investigate these concerns fully.

I have contacted all of our branch managers and have requested a detailed report on the inventory counting arrangements. It would appear that the events at Longtown were an isolated incident.

At all of our stores, apart from Longtown, Count's employees opened a sample of cardboard cartons. They also removed samples of inventory from shop shelves for inspection.

There was a problem at Longtown because Count's local office was short-staffed at the time of the count and could provide only four counters instead of the six who had been booked. We have received an apology from Count and they have sent a full team to repeat the count, the result of which has reduced our valuation of inventory at that store by 3%. We do not believe that this is a material sum in the context of inventory at all branches or in the context of the financial statements as a whole. I have, nevertheless, instructed that the closing inventory figure be corrected for the miscount at Longtown.

I apologise for this, although we are not directly responsible for the error, having relied on the services of a respected inventory counter.

Best wishes

Dale

Gillian was not satisfied with this response and spoke to GH's managing partner. She recommended that GH should resign from the Retail audit on the grounds that the directors were reckless with respect to the preparation of the financial statements and that she was unwilling to trust the reported inventory figure. Given that lack of trust, she did not feel it appropriate to continue to audit Retail.

The managing partner's response was that Gillian had not planned the audit of inventory properly in the first place and that the concerns created by these events could be rectified by additional audit testing. He did not believe that it would be appropriate to resign at this stage, partly because it would reflect on GH's credibility. He requested that Gillian conduct additional work on inventory, at GH's expense, before reporting back for a further discussion on the need to resign.

Expansion plans

Management is planning to expand the group's operations into a new market, opening a series of wine bars and cafes. This is considered to represent a fruitful avenue for the company's future because the same products can be sold in the shops and in the new outlets. It is likely that expansion would be through the acquisition of an existing company which operates outlets of this kind. A potential target, Doug's Wine Cafe Ltd, has been identified and preliminary discussions have taken place between the management of the two companies. The company's managing director has asked for our firm's advice about the potential acquisition, and specifically regarding the financing of the transaction. Doug's Wine Cafe Ltd is an audit client of our firm, so we have considerable knowledge of its business.

Required

(a) Critically evaluate the approach that GH has taken to the audit of inventory at Retail. **(10 marks)**

(b) Critically evaluate Gillian's decision to recommend resigning from this audit. **(10 marks)**

(c) Advise Gillian on the additional work that she should have undertaken on the inventory figure. **(10 marks)**

MOCK EXAM QUESTIONS

(d) Critically evaluate the decision by GH's managing partner to undertake this additional testing at the firm's own expense. **(10 marks)**

(e) Discuss any ethical issues arising in relation to the group's expansion plans, and recommend the relevant actions to be taken by our firm. **(10 marks)**

(Total 50 marks)

2 Public interest and IR Reporting

IFAC's mission is to serve the public interest by:

- Contributing to the development, adoption and implementation of high-quality international standards and guidance;
- Contributing to the development of strong professional accountancy organisations and accounting firms, and to high quality practices by professional accountants;
- Promoting the value of professional accountants worldwide; and
- Speaking out on public interest issues where the accountancy profession's expertise is most relevant.

IFAC defines the public interest as:

'The net benefits derived for, and procedural rigor employed on behalf of, all society in relation to any action, decision or policy.'

Extracted from IFAC Policy Position 5 *A definition of the public interest*

Required

(a) Critically explore the IFAC definition of the public interest and discuss how consideration of the public interest may present challenges to the audit firm when developing its business. **(18 marks)**

The International Integrated Reporting (IR) Framework was issued in 2013, and provides a set of principles to help a business to report on how it creates value.

Required

(b) Briefly discuss the types of capital given in the International IR Framework, commenting on each type of capital. **(7 marks)**

(Total 25 marks)

3 BNM

BNM is an audit firm that has 14 partners and is one of the largest firms in the city in which it is based. BNM's partners meet every month to discuss routine business matters.

Jessica, BNM's managing partner raised two concerns for discussion during the most recent meeting:

- A competing audit firm has been criticised for failing to pay sufficient attention to year-end journal entries. Jessica decided to raise this during the regular partners' meeting because she believes that all year-end journals should be reviewed by the partner in charge of the audit. She has had one of the audit partners review a sample of audit files and has discovered that, in many cases, BNM's partners were requesting little or no evidence to support last-minute journal entries.

- The partners responsible for the work undertaken by BNM for Gotan, a large client, had attended the April meeting of Gotan's audit committee. Frank attended as the partner in charge of the external audit and Kevin attended as the tax partner who advises Gotan. Frank and Kevin had attended in order to discuss arrangements for the work that would be undertaken for Gotan by BNM in respect of the financial year ended 31 December 2015. Frank and Kevin had collaborated on a PowerPoint presentation to the audit committee. Jessica believes that it was inappropriate for the two partners to have attended jointly and to have made a joint presentation.

Jessica's concerns were discussed at length. There was no clear agreement on either of Jessica's concerns and so she imposed the following rules:

- All audit files will contain a separate section that deals with year-end journal entries and that section will be supported with a detailed commentary on each journal by the partner in charge of the audit engagement.

- When BNM provides the same client with both audit and non-audit services, the partners responsible for the audit and non-audit services will not meet jointly with senior management. Each partner will meet the company's management separately, even if there is an overlap such as an audit problem associated with the tax provision in the financial statements.

Frank stated that the partners would implement Jessica's new rules, but he was concerned that they would do so in a very literal manner, without any regard for Jessica's underlying intention to improve audit quality.

Required

(a) Critically evaluate the advantages and disadvantages of Jessica's requirement concerning the audit of journal entries. **(8 marks)**

(b) Critically evaluate the advantages and disadvantages of Jessica's requirement concerning joint meetings with client management. **(6 marks)**

(c) Critically evaluate Frank's statement that the firm's partners will comply with these rules in a very literal manner without addressing Jessica's concerns. **(6 marks)**

The audit profession has seen significant change in recent years, particularly in relation to the increasing prevalence of audit data analytics. Jessica has stated that this is an area in which the firm is lagging behind its competitors. She has recently begun to advocate for significant investment in these new technologies in order to prevent the firm from losing any further market share.

(d) Explain what the term 'data analytics' means, and discuss current thinking about their anticipated impact on the auditing profession. **(5 marks)**

(Total 25 marks)

[End of question paper]

AIA PROFESSIONAL QUALIFICATION

PROFESSIONAL 2

DEVELOPMENTS IN ASSURANCE AND ACCOUNTABILITY

MODEL ANSWERS

> Valid alternative points, whether or not they are shown in the Model Answers, will be given credit where appropriate.

CREATING WORLD CLASS ACCOUNTANTS

MOCK EXAM ANSWERS

1 (a) ISA 501 *Audit evidence – specific considerations for selected items* requires that the auditor evaluate the count instructions and observe to ensure that the instructions are being complied with. The audit firm has failed to comply with this very basic requirement in two ways.

Firstly, the firm has become very predictable in its visits to inventory locations. There are nine branches, out of which management knows that the auditor is likely to attend four, and no others. That could mean that the inventory is counted more carefully at the locations closest to head office and that management is less careful with more distant branches. Essentially, the auditor has been relying on what is effectively a potentially biased sample.

Following on from that concern, when the firm attended a more distant count on a truly surprise basis the problems that were discovered now have a greater significance. The audit partner is unsure whether the lower standard of care discovered was restricted to that branch or whether the other branches other than those close to head office were similar.

The other issue that has arisen is that the member of the audit team who attended that stock count did not raise the matter at the time of the count. The fact that the count instructions were not being complied with should have been reported back to the audit partner as a matter of some urgency. The audit partner could then have asked Retail's finance director to intervene with a view to conducting a proper count at Longtown and ensuring that no other shops were similarly affected.

(b) It could be argued that the partners of an audit firm are required to demonstrate their commitment to audit quality and to professionalism. Resignation from Retail would send a strong message to staff, consistent to ISQM 1, that the firm is unwilling to compromise its integrity. Having said that, resignation is a rather extreme response under the circumstances.

At worst, GH has been a little complacent in its audit of inventory counts. It has done so in order to offer the shareholders a cost-effective service because it is expensive in terms of time and travelling costs to attend more distant stores. It is debatable whether this constitutes a grave breach of professional standards. Indeed, ISA 200 *Overall objectives of the independent auditor and the conduct of an audit in accordance with International Standards on Auditing* requires the costs and benefits of gathering evidence to be taken into account.

The audit risks here are relatively low. The inventory is canned food, which means that it is bulky and has a relatively low value. It would be difficult for employees to steal a material quantity of canned food and conceal that theft. Also, the year-end inventory is counted by independent inventory counters. If inventory has been distorted during the year then the counters will be unaware of that and will have no motive to misstate their count figures in any case. Thus, it is debatable whether GH has been negligent.

Resignation would be costly to both GH and retail. Resigning seems to be a rather needless and empty gesture under those circumstances and so GH should not resign.

(c) The additional work should be planned in order to establish the risks that are being addressed. Gillian is unsure whether inventory has been overstated by counting empty cardboard boxes as full and also whether inventory on store shelves could have lain unsold and gone beyond its sale date. These concerns relate to inventory at the Longtown branch and, by implication, to other branches that lie beyond the two-hour radius from Retail's head office.

The first step would be to gather as much evidence as possible from other sources. For example, Retail's inventory management system should be capable of generating useful analytical review information so that Gillian can target specific stores. She should identify stores that have slow inventory turnover ratios, which generally implies that closing inventory may be overstated.

The reports from the various count teams should be reviewed to establish whether Longtown was the only branch at which there were too few staff to conduct an adequate investigation.

There should be follow up visits to the Longtown branch and also a sample of other branches out with the usual selection area. These visits should target the specific matters of concern. Are empty containers being used to conceal the theft of inventory and are old items of inventory being held? The visits should be organised as quickly as possible and store managers should not be notified in advance. All visits should be conducted simultaneously so that stores are not warned that a visit may be imminent.

During the visits, the count teams should check that a large sample of cartons is full. A sample should be opened to check that the contents correspond to the inventory records. The focus should be on relatively high-value items in case shop staff have emptied cartons of expensive items and replaced them with cheaper items before sealing them up again.

The audit staff should also conduct spot checks on the inventory rotation by checking that shelves are filled with the older inventory to the front. These checks should be supplemented by inquiry of store staff to gather evidence that staff rotate inventory as a matter of routine.

(d) The biggest concern about GH bearing the cost is independence. It could be argued that GH cannot be independent unless it is being compensated for all of the work that it does. The uncharged time could be viewed as an investment in the relationship with Retail and, as such, might undermine GH's independence. External reviewers might be concerned that GH has an incentive to conduct insufficient evidence because it is incapable of recovering all of its costs.

A counter-argument could be that GH has been a little deficient in its collection of audit evidence and so should be liable for the costs of putting matters right. The concerns arising from the past sample bias are largely down to GH's failure to attend a representative sample of stores. The concerns arising from the work done during the Longtown inventory count should have been dealt with more effectively at the time. That would suggest that GH should bear the cost of the additional work because it is unfair to charge Retail for additional tests that were only required because of GH's failings.

Retail's shareholders could also be a little concerned if the additional tests require a significant increase in this year's audit fee. They may be concerned that GH is overcharging, in which case it could cost the firm a lucrative appointment. The shareholders may also ask why GH had to charge more and be rather unimpressed by the shortcomings of the inventory audit. It could be a commercially sound decision for GH to bear the cost of the additional testing, although it may also be regarded as a little unprofessional if they do so in order to conceal the facts from the shareholders.

(e) **Ethical issues**

Potential acquisition

There is a potential conflict of interest here, as the audit firm may effectively be advising both sides of a potential acquisition negotiation. The IESBA *Code of ethics* requires safeguards to be applied here. Crucially, both parties should be informed of the potential conflict, and should be asked for their consent to the arrangement. If either party declines, then the engagement should not be accepted.

If both say yes, then safeguards could include:

- Separate engagement teams, separated by information barriers
- Confidentiality agreements signed by employees and partners of the audit firm

There is also a self-review threat in relation to the due diligence, as we will be performing procedures on financial statements which we have already audited. Safeguards here would include:

- Separate engagement teams
- Pre-issuance review of the non-audit service report by an independent professional accountant
- Independent review of the audit work

Financing

Providing advice on financing raises an advocacy threat if the audit firm is asked to represent Retail's interests, for example to any potential lenders. Such a role should therefore be avoided.

There is a risk that we could be seen as playing (or could actually play) a management role. This would be the case if eg we recommended a particular form of finance to Retail. The threat can be mitigated by making it clear that any decisions rest with Retail's management, and that we are providing them with advice only.

There may be a self-review threat here if the financial statements come to include amounts in relation to any financing obtained using our advice. Possible safeguards include:

- Using a separate corporate finance team from the audit team
- Pre-issuance review of the corporate finance service, and of the relevant area of the financial statements, by an independent professional accountant

If safeguards would not reduce the threat to an acceptable level, the engagement should not be accepted.

Conclusion

From the above it can be concluded that the audit of Retail is of relatively high risk overall, with particular risks in relation to overstatement of assets, understatement of expenses, and the company's ongoing solvency and liquidity problems.

Several important ethical issues are raised by Retail's request, and these must be considered carefully before any engagements are accepted.

Additional areas where credit might be given, note this is not an exhaustive list:

- **The solution considers a wide range of possible issues that candidates could consider and the answer given is more exhaustive than would be expected from a candidate within the time. Additional credit will be given for other valid issues raised.**

MOCK EXAM ANSWERS

2 (a) Within the audit function, the mission of IFAC and the wider accounting profession to serve the public interest comes from its contribution to the development and implementation of auditing standards and the establishment of a relevant and robust reporting framework coupled with the development of high quality auditing practices by accountants and their firms.

The definition of who the public considers to be interested in or in some way affected by the accounting world is extensive and varies between professional bodies and international jurisdictions. On the broadest level, IFAC and many of the accounting professional bodies consider that the 'public' includes the widest possible scope of society.

From IFAC's Policy Position 5 on A definition of the Public Interest, the examples recognised refer to individuals and groups sharing a marketplace for goods and services (including those provided by government), as well as those seeking sustainable living standards and environmental quality, for themselves and future generations. This includes:

- Investors, shareholders, and business owners of public and private institutions – This encompasses all parties whose resources and well-being depend upon the performance of such institutions

    These parties rely upon sound financial information to make decisions about the allocation of their resources. This not only includes investors but also employees and those who have pensions and other vested interests tied to the performance of such institutions.

- Consumers and suppliers – this encompasses all parties who are affected by the costs, quality, and availability of goods and services

    Consumers and suppliers ultimately bear the impact of financial decision makers (and those who advise them). The quality of financial information and decision making impacts the efficiency of resource management, which in turn impacts goods and services produced.

- Taxpayers, electorates, and citizens – this encompasses all parties who are impacted by the work of public sector accounting professionals, who facilitate financial information, make financial decisions, and advise policymakers and elected officials. These include immediate short-term impacts, as well as medium and longer-term considerations and matters of sustainability.

The efficient management of public resources (eg tax revenues, public properties, governmental organisations, infrastructure, and other resources) affects their costs, quality, and availability and, through these, society as a whole.

Although IFAC acknowledge that the impact of the work of the accountancy profession differs among these groups, they believe that there is a fundamental obligation for the profession to act in the public interest regardless of its proximity to these different groups. This potentially creates issues for the accounting firm when considering the focus of their work in practice as the interests that are required may not always be clear.

The wide scope of stakeholders with a potential interest in the audit can expose the audit team to a wide range of conflicting pressures especially in the arena of auditing public interest entities. The primary focus of the audit should be at the public interest, but the day to day consideration of issues will tend to focus at the needs of the investors, shareholders and business owners. The duty of confidentiality to the client, coupled with the direct impact on the wealth of these interest groups may compromise the attention and priority that the auditor gives to other groups affected. However, whistle blowing guidance and other national regulations around criminal acts, for example money laundering, does give additional guidance to the auditor where the duty of confidentiality and the public interest seem to clash.

IFAC identify that, in the broadest respect, 'interests' are all things valued by individuals and by society. IFAC note that this includes rights and entitlements (including property rights), access to government, economic freedoms, and political power. Interests are things we seek to acquire and control; they may also be ideals we aspire to, and protections from things that are harmful or disadvantageous to us. The accountancy profession helps realise certain interests of society, many of which are economic in nature and related to the efficient management of resources. However through audit these interests are somewhat limited to:

- Increased economic certainty in the marketplace and throughout the financial infrastructure (eg banking, insurance, investment firms, etc.);

- Sound, decision-useful financial and non-financial reporting for stakeholders, investors, and all parties in the marketplace (directly or indirectly) impacted by such reporting;

- Sound and transparent financial and non-financial information and decision making on the part of governments public interest entities and public sector organisations to their constituents; sound corporate governance and performance management in private and public sector organisations;

IFAC notes that, as auditors and the accountancy profession play a central role in realising the public interests. Individual professional accountants within the firm should:

- Provide sound financial, non-financial, and government reporting to stakeholders, investors, taxpayers, and all parties in the marketplace directly and indirectly impacted by financial and non-financial reporting from all organisations, across all sectors, and spanning all sizes, including public sector institutions; and

- Provide truthful, effective communication with parties (eg boards, stakeholders, management, and others) directly and indirectly related to the corporate governance processes for which they are accountable.

These are both recognised as key ethical principles by all accounting bodies and auditors enshrined in the ideas of professional competence and integrity and objectivity.

In order to serve the public interest, individual auditors and the firm should:

- Apply high standards of ethical behaviour and professional judgement

- Achieve and maintain appropriate educational requirements and qualifications to ensure their professional competence in all aspects of their work;

- Comply with disciplinary arrangements in place (eg the respective committee, regulatory mechanism, or oversight group responsible for imposing sanctions or disciplinary measures) to ensure that they address unethical matters, violations of law, or non-compliance with professional regulations

It is the guidance above that helps individual firms to ensure that they develop their business in line with the public interest. It is clear that this may impose a significant overhead on the firm's business requiring robust and considered policies and procedures to comply with appropriate regulations and standards and extensive CPD arrangements to keep up to date.

(b) The International IR Framework describes six types of capital, as follows.

Financial

This is the pool of funds that is:

- Available for use in the production of goods/the provision of services
- Obtained through financing, or generated through operations/investments

Manufactured

These are manufactured physical objects, including:

- Buildings
- Equipment
- Infrastructure (eg roads, ports, bridges and waste and water treatment plants)

Manufactured capital is often created by other organisations, but includes assets manufactured by the reporting organisation for sale or when they are retained for its own use.

Intellectual

Organisational knowledge-based intangibles, including:

- Intellectual property, eg patents, copyrights, software, rights and licences
- 'Organisational capital', eg tacit knowledge, systems, procedures and protocols

Human

People's competencies, capabilities and experience, and their motivations to innovate, including their:

- Alignment with and support for an organisation's governance framework, risk management approach and ethical values
- Ability to understand, develop and implement an organisation's strategy
- Loyalties and motivations for improving processes, goods and services, including their ability to lead, manage and collaborate

Natural

All environmental resources and processes that support the prosperity of an organisation, including:

- Water, land, minerals and forests
- Biodiversity and ecosystem health

Social and relationship

The institutions and the relationships within and between communities, groups of stakeholders and other networks, and the ability to share information to enhance individual and collective wellbeing.

Social and relationship capital includes:

- Shared norms and common values and behaviours
- Key stakeholder relationships and the trust and willingness to engage that an organisation has developed and strives to build and protect with external stakeholders
- Intangibles associated with the brand and reputation that an organisation has developed
- An organisation's social licence to operate

MOCK EXAM ANSWERS

> **Additional areas where credit might be given, note this is not an exhaustive list:**
>
> - The solution considers a wide range of possible issues that candidates could consider and the answer given is more exhaustive than would be expected from a candidate within the time. Additional credit will be given for other valid issues raised.

3 (a) The proposal is sound because of the nature of journal entries. Most staff time during the audit is devoted to the audit of routine transactions. The journals during the closing stage of the audit are likely to be either corrections in respect of errors that have been discovered with the figures or adjustments to accounting policies.

The audit firm should be very concerned about errors that management has been forced to correct at the closing stage of the audit because they suggest that the routine audit work has not been undertaken to a high enough standard. The reasons for problems having been missed should be considered in case there has been a problem with the audit approach. The fact that a correction is being made does not necessarily mean that sufficient change has been made and the audit team may have to undertake additional work on the journal before it is accepted.

The journals that have significant accounting implications also have to be considered. For example, the audit team may not have undertaken any work on a provision that is being recorded. Or a journal could have the effect of making a significant change to the accounting policies in use.

The partner must also be fully aware of the extent of the changes. Many small journals could have a substantial cumulative effect on the financial statements.

(b) The basic question is about how the directors perceive their relationship with the firm. If the firm provides both audit and non-audit services then it is important to ensure that the directors view those as two separate appointments.

If both partners attend a joint meeting then it will create the impression that the partner in charge of, say, tax can also have a role to play in the management of the annual audit. Even if that is untrue, it would send a clearer message if the two partners met with the board separately and with two clearly separate agendas.

This proposal may, however, be unrealistic. Firstly, it would be inefficient to refuse to hold joint meetings over matters where the non-audit service affects the audit. For example, valuing a tax provision for audit purposes will always be a matter for management but they will require advice from experts in both tax and audit. It would also be very artificial because it would clearly be necessary for the audit partner to consult the tax partner at some stage in this process. The board needs to be reassured that the audit partner can count on the support and assistance of the tax partner when the need arises.

The two partners may also find it useful to hold occasional joint meetings with the audit committee. The audit committee has a responsibility to ensure that the auditor is committed and independent and so a regular meeting with all engagement partners would help the committee to explore the ways in which independence was being maintained. Refusing to meet jointly would probably indicate that there was a problem and that the audit committee should recommend a change of auditor.

(c) Any audit procedure could be implemented in a legalistic manner without necessarily providing any meaningful assurance.

For example, requiring the audit partner to write a commentary on journal entries could result in some very superficial analyses. The partner could write a 'standard' paragraph about each journal entry without investigating the reasons for the adjustment and a superficial review of the working papers would suggest that the rule had been complied with.

In the same way, the partners in charge of audit and non-audit services could avoid joint meeting with company boards, but could make it very clear to the directors that they were working in partnership to add value. The partners could do so easily by expressing familiarity with their colleagues' views during meetings with the board or they could offer to discuss any matters of overlap when they return to the office.

It is debatable whether any partner would be foolish enough to behave in such a childish and deceitful manner. The partners are aware that their behaviour sets the tone with respect to quality and that they act as role models for the rest of the firm. If the partners were to behave in this manner then the employees who report to them would swiftly become demotivated and the firm's credibility could suffer. Furthermore, the firm's quality management procedures should pick up such behaviour. It is unlikely that a partner who submitted weak evidence of a review or who undermined confidence in the firm's independence would remain in post.

(d) Data analytics is the examination of data to try to identify patterns, trends or correlations. As the quantity of data has increased, it has become increasingly necessary to evolve ways of processing and making sense of it. Data analytics is a part of the shift that is known as 'big data', which refers to the larger, more complex datasets that can be held by modern computers. The term refers to a qualitative shift in the amount of data that is available in comparison with the past.

Recent advances in IT make it increasingly possible for auditors to examine a complete data set – 100% of the transactions – and to represent trends graphically, almost instantly. Some have claimed that these techniques may bring about a long-term revolution in audit approaches, since they enable auditors to focus on 100% of the transactions, rather than just a sample (as auditing standards assume).

This raises a question not only about sampling, but about the whole approach of placing reliance on an entity's internal controls. It is a basic assumption of the concept of an audit contained in ISAs that it is impractical to test 100% of transactions. It is because of this that the audit is conceived as a risk management exercise, in which the auditor obtains evidence of the effectiveness of the entity's own internal controls, as a way of assessing the risk of there being a material misstatement.

It appears likely that, even if they do not eliminate controls testing entirely, data analytics will lead to a reconsideration of how controls are tested, particularly controls in an IT environment. Data analytics are also likely to lead to an improvement in audit quality, although this is, of course, dependent on data analytics processes being implemented intelligently.

Additional areas where credit might be given, note this is not an exhaustive list:

- **The solution considers a wide range of possible issues that candidates could consider and the answer given is more exhaustive than would be expected from a candidate within the time. Additional credit will be given for other valid issues raised.**

MOCK EXAM ANSWERS

Index

Note. Key Terms and their page references are given in **bold**.

Absolute assurance, 5
Accelerated capital allowances, 396
Accepting nomination, 156
Access to other information, 481
Accounting and bookkeeping services, 74
Accounting estimate, 374
Action for negligence, 110
Actual and threatened litigation, 80
Actuarial assumptions, 406
Adverse opinion, 463, 464
Advertising, 141
Advocacy threat, 64, 77
Affiliation, 183
Aggregation risk, 174
Aggressive earnings management, 306
Analytical procedures, 270
Annual General Meeting (AGM), 15
Annual report, 480
Appropriateness, 340
Artificial intelligence, 432, 439
Assets, 374
Assurance engagement, 4, 95
Assurance services, growth in, 5
Attestation Engagement, 4
ATTs, 249
Audit, 6, 15
Audit agreement, 143
Audit approach, 8
Audit committee, 94
Audit committees, 19, 21
Audit engagement letter, 143
Audit evidence, 340
Audit fee, 137
Audit of group financial statements, 170
Audit plan, 235
Audit proposal, 163
Audit report, 9, 456, 486
Audit risk, 256
Audit risk model, 258
Audit rotation, 139
Audit sampling, 340
Audit software, 436
Audit staff, 247
Audit strategy, 8, 235
Audit working papers, 295
Auditing components located abroad, 183
Auditing standards, 111, 156
Auditors, 14
Auditor's expert, 332
Auditor's point estimate, 375
Auditor's range, 375

Automated tools and techniques (ATTs), 51, 436
Availability, 472

Bad publicity, 154
Banks and other major lenders, 114
Basic earnings per share, 410
Basic elements of the auditor's report, 454
Being bribed, 125
Benefits of an audit, 7
Benford's Law, 446
Big data, 51, 431, 441
Blockchain, 432
Books and documents, 144
Borrowing costs, 404
Brands, 384
Bribery, 125
Bribery Act 2010, 125
Bribery offences, 125
Business relationships, 69
Business risk, 154, 263

Cadbury Report, 14, 16, 22, 112
Caparo Industries plc v Dickman and Others 1990, 112
Capping liability, 122
Carrying amount, 379
Cash-generating unit, 379
Cash-settled share-based payment transactions, 408
Change, 257
Change in auditors, 136
Changes in accounting policy, 416
Charities, 193, 246
Chronology of an audit, 8
Client acceptance procedures, 119
Client care procedures, 156
Client loss, 154
Client management, 248
Client rights to information, 144
Client screening, 161
Climate change, 265
Climate-related physical risks, 41
Climate-related risks, 40
Climate-related transition risks, 41
Close family, 70
Cloud based audit working papers, 295
Cloud computing, 430
Cold review, 73
Combined Code, 16, 21
Commissions, 142

INDEX

Common controls, 176
Communication, 471
Communication methods, 478
Communication problem, 471
Communication with those charged with governance, 465, 467
Comparative financial statements, 352, 353
Comparative information, 352
Competition, 155
Complexity, 256
Compliance audits, 213
Compliance based audit approach, 214
Compliance risk, 265
Comply or explain, 17
Component, 170
Component auditor, 170
Component performance materiality, 174
Confidentiality, 62, 84, 144
Conflicts of interest, 86
Consolidation, 179
Consolidation adjustments, 180
Construction contract, 378
Constructive obligation, 399
Contingencies, 399
Contingent asset, 399
Contingent fees, 71
Contingent liability, 399
Contracting-out, 216
Control activities, 238
Control environment, 25, 237
Control risk, 256, 258
Controls, 8
Co-operation, 183
Corporate finance, 76
Corporate governance, 14, 212
Corporate governance statement, 20
Corporate Sustainability Reporting Directive (CSRD), 41
Corresponding figures, 352, 353
Critiquing an audit opinion, 469
Cyber incident, 435

Data analytics, 51, 438, 441
Data processing, 220
Deadlines, 249
Decommissioning provisions, 400
Deductible temporary differences, 396
Deferred tax, 396
Deferred tax assets, 396
Deferred tax liabilities, 396
Deficiency in internal control, 478
Defined benefit plan, 405

Defined contribution plan, 405
Depreciation, 379
Detection risk, 256, 258
Development, 383
Development costs, 381, 383
Diluted earnings per share, 411
Direct assistance, 330
Direct controls, 258
Direct Engagement, 4
Directors, 14
Disciplinary action, 154
Disciplinary action by AIA, 155
Disclaimer of opinion, 463
Disclaimers, 119, 121
Disclosures, 40, 245
Discontinued operations, 411
Distributed ledger, 432
Distributions following an audit qualification, 475
Documentation, 294, 311
Drawing an audit opinion, 471
Due diligence, 221
Duty of care, 110

Earnings per share, 410
E-commerce, 248, 266, 267, 388
ED ISSA 5000 General Requirements for Sustainability Assurance Engagements, 43
Embedded audit facilities, 438
Emphasis of matter paragraph, 357, 466, 488
Employment with an audit client, 69
Engagement letter, 143
Engagement quality review, 291
Engagement quality reviewer, 291
Equity instrument, 384
Equity-settled share-based payment transactions, 408
Estimation uncertainty, 374
Ethical framework, 63
European Sustainability Reporting Standards (ESRS), 41
Expectations gap, 6, 99
Extended External Reporting (EER), 50
External confirmations, 341

Fair, 453
Fair value, 374, 376, 379, 392
Familiarity threat, 64, 78
Family and personal relationships, 70
Fee dependency, 72
Fees, 141, 162
Fidelity guarantee insurance, 120

INDEX

Financial Action Task Force on Money Laundering, 123
Financial asset, 384
Financial indications, 359
Financial interest, 67, 69
Financial risks, 264
Financial statement assertions, 4, **340**
Five forces model, 263
Fomento (Sterling Area) Ltd v Selsdon Fountain Pen Co Ltd 1958, 111
Forgivable loans, 390
Forming an audit opinion, 453
Forming and critiquing an audit opinion, 452
Forum of Firms, the, 184
Framework, 475
Fraud, 7, 15, 25, **306**
Fraud Analytics, 446
Fraud risk factors, 309
Fraudulent financial reporting, 306
FRC *Risk management, internal control and related financial and business reporting*, 38
Full provision method, 398
Fundamental principles, 62

General IT controls, 239, **427**
General planning matters, 247
Gifts and hospitality, 71
Global Reporting Initiative (GR), 48
Globalisation, 183
Going concern, 359
Going concern basis of accounting, 359
Goodwill, 381, 382
Governance, 477
Government assistance, 390
Government grants, 390
Grants related to assets, 390
Grants related to income, 390
Group, 170
Group audit, 170
Group audit plan, 174
Group audit strategy, 174
Group auditor, 170
Group engagement partner, 170
Group financial statements, 170

Held for sale non-current assets, 380
Hospital, 192
Hot review, 73, 295
Housing association, 193
Human resources, 218

IAS 1 *Presentation of Financial Statements*, 359
IAS 12 *Income taxes*, 396
IAS 16 *Property, Plant and Equipment*, 374, 378
IAS 19 *Employee Benefits*, 405
IAS 2 *Inventories*, 377
IAS 20 *Accounting for Government Grants and Disclosure of Government Assistance*, 390
IAS 23 *Borrowing costs*, 404
IAS 24 *Related Party Disclosures*, 342
IAS 32 *Financial Instruments: Presentation*, 384
IAS 33 *Earnings Per Share*, 410
IAS 36 *Impairment of Assets*, 379
IAS 37 *Provisions, Contingent Liabilities, and Contingent Assets*, 399
IAS 38 *Intangible Assets*, 381, 383
IAS 40 *Investment property*, 385
IAS 7 *Statement of Cash Flows*, 412
IAS 8 *Accounting Policies, Changes in Accounting Estimates and Errors*, 416
IESBA Code of Ethics, 62, 65, 66, 126
IFRS 1 *First-Time Adoption of International Financial Reporting Standards*, 416, 417, 418
IFRS 14 *Regulatory deferral accounts*, 418
IFRS 15 *Revenue from Contracts with Customers*, 378
IFRS 16 *Leases*, 392
IFRS 2 *Share-Based Payment*, 408
IFRS 3 *Business Combinations*, 381
IFRS 5 *Non-Current Assets Held for Sale and Discontinued Operations*, 374, 380, 411
IFRS 7 *Financial Instruments: Disclosures*, 384
IFRS 8 *Operating Segments*, 409
IFRS 9 *Financial Instruments*, 384
IFRS S2 Climate-related, 40
Immediate family, 70
Impairment, 379
Impairment of non-current assets, 379
Impairment review, 379
Income, 386
Incorporation, 120
Independence, 63, 139
Independence in appearance, 64
Independence of mind, 64, 98
Independent opinion, 7
Indirect controls, 258
Information processing controls, 427, 428
Information system and communication, 238
Information technology, 218, 220
Inherent risk, 256
Inherent risk factors, 256
Initial audit engagement, 351
Input methods, 388
Insider dealing, 85, 109
Insourcing, 216

INDEX

Institutional investors, 15
Intangible asset, 381
Intangible non-current assets, 381
Integrated reporting, 45
Integrated Test Facility (ITF), 438
Integrity, 62, 87
Internal audit, 22, 25, 76, 162, 210, 212, 213, 328
Internal audit reports, 484
Internal control, 24, 210
Internal control effectiveness, 19, 24
Internal review assignment, 484
Internally generated goodwill, 381
International Auditing and Assurance Standards Board (IAASB), 156
International Framework for Assurance Engagements, 4
International IR Framework, 45
International network, 183
Intimidation threat, 64, 79
Inventories, 377
Investigations, Disciplinary and Appeals Committees, 108
Investment property, 385
Investments, 384
ISA (UK) 250B The auditor's statutory right and duty to report to regulators of public interest entities and regulators of other entities in the financial sector., 320
ISA (UK) 320 *Materiality in Planning and Performing an Audit*, 243
ISA 200 *Overall Objectives of the Independent Auditor and the Conduct of an Audit in Accordance with International Standards on Auditing*, 7, 234
ISA 210 *Agreeing the Terms of Audit Engagements*, 144
ISA 220 (Revised) *Quality Management for an Audit of Financial Statements*, 157, 285
ISA 230 *Audit Documentation*, 294
ISA 240 *The Auditor's Responsibilities Relating to Fraud in an Audit of Financial Statements*, 307
ISA 250 (Revised) *Consideration of Laws and Regulations in an Audit of Financial Statements*, 126, 314
ISA 250A *Consideration of Laws and Regulations in an Audit of Financial Statements*, 85
ISA 260 *Communication with Those Charged with Governance*, 477
ISA 265 *Communicating Deficiencies in Internal Control*, 478
ISA 300 *Planning an Audit of Financial Statements*, 235
ISA 315 (Revised 2019) *Identifying and assessing the risks of material misstatement*, 236
ISA 330 *The Auditor's Responses to Assessed Risks*, 273
ISA 402 *Audit Considerations Relating to an Entity using a Service Organisation*, 221
ISA 450 (Revised) *Evaluation of misstatements identified during the audit*, 365
ISA 500 *Audit Evidence*, 332, 340
ISA 501 *Audit Evidence – Specific Considerations for Selected Items*, 401
ISA 505 *External confirmations*, 341
ISA 510 *Initial Audit Engagements – Opening Balances*, 351
ISA 520 *Analytical procedures.*, 270
ISA 530 *Audit Sampling*, 340
ISA 540 *Auditing Accounting Estimates and Related Disclosures*, 374
ISA 550 *Related Parties*, 342
ISA 560 *Subsequent Events*, 355, 484
ISA 570 (Revised) *Going Concern*, 359
ISA 580 *Written Representations*, 348
ISA 600 (Revised) *Special Considerations – Audits of Group Financial Statements (Including the Work of Component Auditors)*, 171, 187
ISA 610 (Revised) *Using the Work of Internal Auditors*, 212, 328
ISA 620 *Using the Work of an Auditor's Expert*, 332
ISA 700 (Revised) *Forming an Opinion and Reporting on Financial Statements*, 200, 456
ISA 700 *Forming an Opinion and Reporting on Financial Statements*, 101
ISA 701 *Communicating key audit matters in the independent auditor's report*, 458
ISA 705 (Revised) *Modifications to the Opinion in the Independent Auditor's Report*, 463
ISA 706 (Revised) *Emphasis of Matter Paragraphs and Other Matter Paragraphs in the Independent Auditor's Report*, 465
ISA 710 *Comparative Information – Corresponding Figures and Comparative Financial Statements*, 352, 466
ISA 720 (Revised) *The Auditor's Responsibilities Relating to Other Information*, 27
ISA 720 *The Auditor's Responsibilities Relating to Other Information*, 480
ISA 800 (Revised) *Special Considerations – Audits of Financial Statements Prepared in Accordance with Special Purpose Frameworks*, 475
ISA 810 (Revised) *Engagements to Report on Summary Financial Statements*, 474

ISQM 1 *Quality Management for Firms that Perform Audits or Reviews of Financial Statements, or Other Assurance or Related Services Engagements*, 83, 157, 280
ISQM 2 *Engagement Quality Reviews*, 291

James McNaughton Paper Group Ltd v Hicks Anderson & Co 1990, 113
Joint audit, 186

Key audit matter (KAM), **458**, 462
Key audit partner, 79
Key man insurance, 156
Know your client, 124, 160
Knowledge gap, 15

Laws and regulations, 314
Leases, 392
Legal action, 143
Legal obligation, 399
Liability, 391, **399**, 472
Liability limitation agreement, 122
Licences, 381
Lien, 144
Limitation of liability, 119
Limited Liability Partnership Act 2000, 121
Limited liability partnerships, 121
Litigation, 120, 154, 156
Litigation and claims, 401
Litigation avoidance, 119
Loans and guarantees, 71
Local councils, 193
Long association of senior personnel with audit clients, 78
Loss of key personnel, 154
Lowballing, 73, 162

Management, 348
Management bias, 374
Management bias or fraud, 257
Management responsibility, 74
Management's expert, 332
Management's point estimate, 374
Material uncertainties, 360
Materiality, 243
Misappropriation of assets, 306
Misconduct, 94, 98, 100, 108, 155
Misstatement of the other information, 481
Modified opinions in auditor's reports, 463
Money laundering, **122**, 160
Money Laundering Compliance Principal, 123

Money Laundering Regulations 2017, 123
Money Laundering Reporting Officer, 123
Monitoring, 284
Monitoring of controls, 237
Multi-site operations, 214

National Crime Agency, 123
Negligence, 110, 120
Non statutory audit reports, 485
Non-executive directors, 19
Non-statutory audits, 7
Not-for-profit organisations, 192

Objectivity, 62, 87
Obligating event, 399
Omega Trust Co Ltd v Wright Son & Pepper 1997, 114
Onerous contract, **400**
Opening balances, **351**
Opening IFRS Statement of Financial Position, 417
Operating indications, 360
Operating segment, **409**
Operational audits, **213**
Operational risks, **265**
Other information, **480**
Other matter paragraph, 27, **466**
Other public interest entities, **184**
Other services, 77
Outlier, 442
Output methods, **388**
Outsourcing, **216**
Outsourcing finance and accounting functions, 220
Outsourcing internal audit, 219
Overall review of the financial statements, 365
Overdue fees, 71
Owner managed businesses, 15, 246

Partnerships, 120
Patents, 381
Peach Publishing Ltd v Slater & Co 1997, 113
Peer review, 295
Penalties for misconduct, 108
Pension costs, 405
Pensions, 220
Performance materiality, 244
Performance obligation, **387**
Pervasiveness, **464**
PEST analysis, 263
Politically exposed persons, 160
Porter's value chain, 263

Post-issuance review, 73
Practice management, 136
Pre-issuance review, 73
Principles-based, 34
Proceeds of Crime Act 2002, 123
Process automation, 431
Process based audit approach, 214
Professional behaviour, 62
Professional competence and due care, 62, 87
Professional indemnity insurance, 120
Professional judgement, **98**, 235
Professional liability, 109
Professional scepticism, 6, 87, **98**, 234
Professional standards, 156
Projected Unit Credit Method, 406
Proportionate liability, **122**
Provision, **399**
Provisions for restructuring, 399
Public interest, 34, 36, 38, 62
Public interest entity, 65
Public sector, 203
Publicity, 154
Purpose, 475

Qualification requirements, 155
Qualified opinion, 463, 464
Qualifying asset, **404**
Quality management, 83, 119
Quality management at a firm level, 280
Quality management on an individual audit, 285
Quality objective, 281
Quality risk, 281

Ratios, 270
Re Kingston Cotton Mill, 111
Re Thomas Gerrard & Son Ltd 1967, 111
Recent service with an audit client, 79
Recoverable amount, **379**
Recruitment, 73
Registered Auditors, 142
Related parties, 181, 342
Related party, **343**
Related party transaction, **343**
Remediation, 284
Report to management, 9, 479
Reportable segments, **409**
Reputation risks, 160
Research, **383**
Responses (in relation to a system of quality management), 281
Revenue recognition, 386
Review, 9

Review engagements, 481
Review reports, 485
Revised accounts, 475
Revision by replacement, 476
Revision by supplementary note, 476
Right of lien, 144
Rights to information, 144
Risk, 154
Risk management, 19, 24, 156, 212, 213
Risk of material misstatement, 256
Robotic process automation, 439
Robotic process automation (RPA), **431**
Royal Bank of Scotland v Bannerman Johnstone Maclay and Others 2002, 115

S1 *General Requirements for Disclosure of Sustainability-related Financial Information*, 40
Sale and leaseback, 395
Schools, 193
Second opinion, 80, 469
Second partner review, 469
Section 172 statements, 37
Segment reporting, 409
Segregation of duties, 197
Self-interest threat, 64, 67
Self-review threat, 64, 74
Service auditor, **221**
Service organisation, **221**
Serving as a director or officer of an audit client, 70
Settlements out of court, 115
Share-based payment, 408
Shareholders, 14
Significant deficiency in internal control, **478**
Significant risks, 242, 257
Significant transactions across national borders, **184**
Singapore Code of Corporate Governance, 34
Single company audit, 170
Smith Report, 21
Spectrum of inherent risk, 257
Staff disclosure procedures, 86
Standard audit report, 473
Standard costing system, 377
Standard unmodified auditor's report, 456
Statements, 474
Statements of cash flows, 412
Statements of recommended accounting practice, 193
Statutory audit, 4
Stranded assets, 265
Subjectivity, 256
Subsequent events, **355**

Subsidiary objectives of the assignment, 250
Substantive procedures, 9
Sufficiency, 340
Sufficient and appropriate audit evidence, 340
Suspicion, 160
Sustainability, 39
Sustainability information, 44, 45
Sustainability matters, 44
SWOT analysis, 263
System, 8
System of internal control, 237
System of quality management, 280
Systems Control and Review File (SCARF), 438

Tangible non-current assets, 378
Tax base, 396
Taxable temporary differences, 396
Taxation services, 75
Taxes, 221
Temporary differences, 396
Temporary personnel assignments, 77
Tender, 138, 162, 163
Test data, 437
Tests of controls, 9
The entity's risk assessment process, 237
Third parties, 112
Those charged with governance, 95, 477
Threats to independence, 64, 65
Time budgets, 249
Tort of negligence, 110
Trade marks, 381

Transition to International Financial Reporting Standards, 416
Transnational audit, 184
Transnational Auditors Committee, 184
True, 453
Truth and fairness, 7
Type 1 report, 223
Type 2 report, 223

UK Corporate Governance Code, 16, 17, 20, 114, 210
Ultra vires, 204
Uncertainty, 257
Understandability, 472
Unmodified auditor's report, 454
Use of IT, 249
Useful life of the asset, 379
User auditor, 221
User entity, 221

Valuation, 75
Valuation of non-current assets, 378
Value in use, 379, 380
Virtual organisation, 218
Voluntary code, 20

Why outsource?, 216
Working papers, 144, 147, 294
Written representation, 345, **348**, 353

INDEX